Microsoft Windows 7 Administrator's Reference

Microsoft Windows 7 Administrator's Reference

Upgrading, Deploying, Managing, and Securing Windows 7

Jorge Orchilles

Contributors
Denny Cherry
Carlos Leal
Kenneth Majors
Derrick Rountree

Technical Editor
Rodney Buike

AMSTERDAM • BOSTON • HEIDELBERG • LONDON
NEW YORK • OXFORD • PARIS • SAN DIEGO
SAN FRANCISCO • SINGAPORE • SYDNEY • TOKYO

SYNGRESS.

Syngress is an Imprint of Elsevier

ELSEVIER

Syngress is an imprint of Elsevier
30 Corporate Drive, Suite 400, Burlington, MA 01803, USA
The Boulevard, Langford Lane, Kidlington, Oxford, OX5 1GB, UK

Microsoft Windows 7 Administrator's Reference

Notices

Knowledge and best practice in this field are constantly changing. As new research and experience broaden our understanding, changes in research methods, professional practices, or medical treatment may become necessary.

Practitioners and researchers must always rely on their own experience and knowledge in evaluating and using any information, methods, compounds, or experiments described herein. In using such information or methods they should be mindful of their own safety and the safety of others, including parties for whom they have a professional responsibility.

To the fullest extent of the law, neither the Publisher nor the authors, contributors, or editors, assume any liability for any injury and/or damage to persons or property as a matter of products liability, negligence or otherwise, or from any use or operation of any methods, products, instructions, or ideas contained in the material herein.

Library of Congress Cataloging-in-Publication Data
Microsoft Windows 7 administrator's reference : upgrading, deploying, managing, and securing Windows 7 / Jorge Orchilles . . . [et al.].
    p. m.
Includes index.
ISBN 978-1-59749-561-5
1. Microsoft Windows (Computer file) 2. Operating systems (Computers) I. Orchilles, Jorge.
QA76.76.O63M5241174 2010
005.4'46–dc22   2010008746

BritishL ibraryC ataloguing-in-PublicationD ata
A catalogue record for this book is available from the British Library.

ISBN:978-1-5974 9-561-5

Printed and bound by CPI Group (UK) Ltd, Croydon, CR0 4YY

Transferred to digital print 2012

Elsevier Inc., the author(s), and any person or firm involved in the writing, editing, or production (collectively "Makers") of this book ("the Work") do not guarantee or warrant the results to be obtained from the Work.

For information on rights, translations, and bulk sales, contact Matt Pedersen, Commercial Sales Director and Rights; e-mail: *m.pedersen@elsevier.com*.

For information on all Syngress publications visit our
Web site at *www.syngress.com*.

Dedicated to my wife, Danielle. I love you

Contents

Aboutt heA uthor

Jorge Orchilles has been involved in the information technology field since 2001. He began his career as a network and system administrator for a small private high school that he attended. Realizing his passion for IT, he opened up a branch of a small business in 2002, The Business Strategy Partners – IT Consultants. Here, he began serving residential and small business clients in the South Florida area as an IT consultant. While gaining work experience, he was a very involved full-time student at Florida International University (FIU). He founded the FIU MIS Club and continues to be a contributor to the club. While at FIU he was contracted to work on the university's Active Directory Migration Project. After completing the project, he decided to move to a corporate environment to continue gaining knowledge and experience in the IT field. After two years of working in corporate IT, he developed a large interest in IT security and has chosen to move in that direction. He currently holds a position as a security operating center analyst while continuing to be a full-time student. He also is involved in various IT, security, and business organizations in the South Florida area. He is currently vice president of the South Florida ISSA chapter.

Jorge recently completed a master's of science program in management information systems at FIU. He also holds a BBA in MIS from FIU. Jorge is a Cisco Certified Design Associate (CCDA), Cisco Security Solutions and Design Specialist (SSSE), CompTIA Security+ (2008), Microsoft Certified Professional (70-228, 70-282, 70-284), and Microsoft Certified Technology Specialist(70-620).

Preface

Welcome to *Microsoft Windows 7 Administrator's Reference*, the only Windows 7 book for system administrators written by system administrators. As you might have seen among the other books on the shelves or e-commerce sites, most books on Windows 7 are either for the end user or for administrators, but not for both. This is because most books are written by technical writers, who are not real-world system administrators and lack the understanding of a system administrator. As experienced system administrators, we know that you need to master not only how to use Windows 7 from an end-user perspective but also how to manage and eventually share your knowledge with your users. This book will cover everything you need to know to successfully plan, deploy, configure, manage, administer, and troubleshoot Windows 7 systems. We have deployed thousands of end-user machines and know what administrators are really looking for. Additionally, we offer multiple methods of accomplishing certain tasks, not just the way Microsoft dictates.

With that said, congratulations, by picking up this book, you have begun your journey of mastering Windows 7. As opposed to Vista, most reviews for Microsoft's latest operating system are very positive. In reality, and as you will soon see, Windows 7 is awesome! Not only will it be easier, quicker, and better to use for you, but it will also make business users more productive and efficient. Windows 7 is more reliable, compatible, and secure.

On that note, security has become one of the biggest issues with end-user operating systems. Unlike other books that are dedicated to securing the operating system after the fact, this book considers security very seriously, showing you how to securely deploy and configure the operating system from the start. Since starting its security initiative, Microsoft has done an incredibly good job securing its latest products.

Windows users currently make up almost 90 percent of the desktop market; this means that more likely than not, you and your users will be migrating to this new and improved operating system soon. Some surveys also suggest that between 75 and 90 percent of corporations skipped migrating to Windows Vista in their enterprise environment. Taking this into consideration, we note that this book does not require Windows Vista experience, although it is recommended.

HOW TO USE THIS BOOK

This book can be your guide through the journey of Windows 7 administration from start to finish. You can begin reading from Chapter 1, "Introduction to Windows 7," and go through the book chronologically to cover all of the topics a typical administrator would typically encounter. Remember, this book is written by real administrators; we know what you need to know to support these systems.

Additionally, this book is a reference; you will be able to look for certain topics, flip right to them, and get on with your day.

Acknowledgments

I would like to acknowledge and thank everyone who has been close to me while I worked day and night to finish this book. As we all learned, writing a book is not as simple as it may sound. My beautiful wife, thank you so much for the support all these months! My parents, thanks for raising me perfectly; I love you! Brother, you're the best; keep up the hard work! Tio Marco, I know I can always count on you for advice; thanks for everything. Frank, keep working hard, man; you are a great person with a great heart that will get what you deserve. Thanks to all my friends and family who supported on this project.

I would like to thank everyone from my current company who supported my work from the beginning. In particular, Pete Nicoletti, Albert Caballero, Robert Rounsavall, Jimmy Martinez, Omar Garcia, Michael Rose, Sanders Diaz, Felipe Medina, Diego Vargas, Juan Bonilla, and the rest of the SIS crew. Thanks for giving me a chance to prove myself!

Thanks to all the professors at Florida International University who supported me through FIU's Master of Science in Management Information System program as I worked on this book, particularly Dr. Monica Temblay, Dr. Kaushik Dutta, Dr. Debra Vandermeer, Dr. Dinesh Batra, and Professor Faisal Kaleem. The Black Team – Adrian Marrero, Elvis Veliz, Pablo Santos, Paul Lowman, and Josh Vetere, thanks for being the best team in MSMIS history! Thanks to everyone from Cohort 19 and a special shout out to the FIU MIS Club!

I would also like to thank everyone from Syngress and Elsevier. Angelina Ward, thanks for contacting me and making all this possible. Thanks to Gary Byrne for working patiently with me and the other contributors to get this great work out. Thanks to all the contributors; without you this book would not be complete. Thanks to the entire team!

Contributors

Denny Cherry (MCSA, MCDBA, MCTS, MCITP) is a database administrator and architect for Awareness Technologies in Marina del Rey, CA. In this role, he manages not only the production databases but also the entire production environment, including the VMware environment, SAN Storage Array, Windows Domain, and all production virtual servers. Denny has been working with Microsoft technology for more than 15 years, starting with Windows 3.51, and he was an official Windows 7 beta tester.

In 2009, Denny was named a Microsoft MVP for the Microsoft SQL Server product. Denny has written dozens of articles for a variety of Web sites, as well as print magazines on a variety of subjects, including SQL Server, clustering, storage configuration, and SharePoint.

Kenneth Majors (MCSE, MCITP, ITIL v3, Project+, VMware VCP, Citrix CCEA, CCA) is the vice president of systems architecture for Choice Solutions LLC, a systems integrator headquartered in Overland Park, KS. Choice Solutions provides IT design, project management. and support for enterprise computing systems. Kenneth is a key contributor to defining best practices and developing documentation standards for Microsoft technologies, including Windows Server, Hyper-V, and Systems Center; and other technologies such as Citrix XenApp, XenServer, and XenDesktop, and VMware vSphere and View. He develops technology solutions and methodologies focused on improving client business processes. These technology solutions touch every part of a system's life cycle – from assessment, blueprint, construct, and deployment on projects to operational management and strategic planning for the business process.

Kenneth holds a bachelor's degree from Colorado Technical University. He currently resides in Olathe, KS, with his loving and supportive wife, Sandy, and near their daughter, Tabitha, and their grandsons, Wesley ("Peanut") and Austin. Their son, Keith, is currently on active duty with the US Navy.

Derrick Rountree (MSCE, MCT, CCEA) is a part of the Enterprise Architecture team for a large software company. He is responsible for determining the future architectural landscape for the company. He specializes in infrastructure technologies. Throughout his career, Derrick has worked as an administrator, an integrator, and a QA engineer. Derrick has contributed to other publications in the areas of networking and Citrix technologies.

TECHNICAL EDITOR

Rodney Buike (MCSE) is an IT pro advisor with Microsoft Canada. As an IT pro advisor, Rodney spends his day helping IT professionals in Canada with issues and challenges they face in their environment and careers. He also advocates for a stronger community presence and shares knowledge through blogging, podcasts, and in-person events.

Rodney's specialties include Exchange Server, virtualization, and core infrastructure technologies on the Windows platform. Rodney worked as a LAN administrator, system engineer, and consultant and has acted as a reviewer on many popular technical books. Rodney is also the founder and principal content provider for www.thelazyadmin.com and a former author for www.msexchange.org.

Rodney enjoys all his personal and professional activities and is up-front about the support he gets from his family and especially his wife, Lisa. Without her support, what he does would not bepos sible.

TRADEMARKS

Microsoft, Windows 7, Windows Vista, Windows XP, Windows NT, Windows 2000, Windows ME, Windows 98, Windows 95, MS-DOS, Active Directory, ActiveX, Aero, BitLocker, DirectX, Internet Explorer, Windows Server, Windows Powershell, Windows Media, ReadyBoost, and Windows are either registered trademarks or trademarks of Microsoft Corporation in the United States of America and/or other countries. Other products and company names mentioned herein may be the trademarks of their respective owners.

The examples in this book related to companies, organizations, products, domains, e-mails, logos, persons, places, and events depicted herein are fictitious. No association with any should be inferred.

This book expresses the author's view and opinions. The information contained herein is provided without any warranties. The author may not be held liable for any damages caused or alleged to be caused either directly or indirectly by this book.

Introduction

This book is for Windows end users and system administrators alike. We understand that to be a great system administrator, you also need to know how to use the operating system. Therefore, this book is tailored to a range of Windows users. Whether you administer a few computers in a home, home office, or small to medium-sized business or hundreds or thousands of desktops in a large organization or public institution, this book is for you. With this book, you will learn everything you need to know about Windows 7 from the start, so that you may use and administer it for its life cycle.

HOW THIS BOOK IS ORGANIZED

This book will follow the flow an administrator generally takes with a new operating system. First, you will find out what is new with the operating system. Then, you will install and/ or upgrade to it and begin using the new features – this phase generally involves navigating the desktop environment and networking/mobility. Following your experimentation with and acceptance of the new operating system, you will begin the planning and deploying phase of the new operating system in your environment. You will then need to be able to manage all the new deployments, implement security features, and troubleshoot the environment. All of these skills, when mastered, will make you an excellent administrator. Remember to share the knowledge with your users because it will help them help you!

CHAPTER1 : INTRODUCTION TO WINDOWS7

The first chapter begins by introducing the new Microsoft operating system that was built on many of the new features of Windows Vista. Because Windows Vista was not the biggest success in Microsoft's history, many lessons were learned and improvements were made to make Windows 7 the great operating system that it is. This chapter will introduce the hardware requirements and the difference between 32-bit and 64-bit computing. Next, the newest and best features of Windows 7 will be highlighted with quick *how-to* for referencing in the future.

CHAPTER2 : INSTALLING AND UPGRADING TO WINDOWS7

The second chapter in this book will walk the end user and administrator through the task of getting Windows 7 on their systems. There are many different tasks and methods to reach this goal, and they depend heavily on the individual deployment scenario – whether it is a new system, upgrade, refresh, or replace, this chapter will describe the process to go about it. It is critical for an administrator to learn and understand the deployment process for Windows 7 because it has been changed from earlier versions of Windows. Furthermore, understanding a single system deployment will assist in an enterprise-wide deployment.

CHAPTER3 : DEPLOYING WINDOWS7 IN AN ENTERPRISE ENVIRONMENT

Deploying Windows 7 across an entire organization or environment does not have to be so daunting. This chapter will provide the knowledge and references required to make deploying Windows 7 easier and quicker for both the administrator and end users. Every environment is different, making it tricky to provide a step-by-step guide. Instead, this chapter will introduce you to tools and methodology for deploying Windows 7 in an enterprise environment. In case we do not mention a specific task, there are many references to online documentation to assistyou.

CHAPTER4 : THE NEW WINDOWS7 DESKTOP ENVIRONMENT

The new Windows 7 desktop environment is the biggest difference the end user will see when using Windows 7. This chapter focuses on all those changes, and introduces the end user and administrator to new features and how to use them. Many of the new features, including the new user interface, Windows Aero, Internet Explorer 8, and Windows Explorer, are core features of what makes Windows 7. The administrator must master these features in order to properly configure the user desktop environment, and end users also need to master them to be efficient and productive when using the Windows 7 system. Applications make Windows the operating system it is today by allowing a range of productivity software to be used on Windows 7. User Account Control is one of the biggest features related to Windows 7, and it is explained in depth in this chapter to allow an administrator to deploy applications without issues. Many of the items in this chapter will need to be passed on to your users, and mastering them will make thate asier.

CHAPTER5 : MANAGING THE WINDOWS7 DESKTOP ENVIRONMENT

This chapter focuses on managing the Windows 7 environment from the system itself. Microsoft provides many tools for local system administration, and these are introduced and referenced in this chapter. More administrative tasks such as managing devices and drivers and managing disks and file systems are the core of this chapter because they are tasks performed to manage the Windows 7 desktop environment. This chapter will serve as a great reference when trouble-shooting and working with drivers, devices, printers, and file systems.

CHAPTER6 : NETWORKING AND MOBILITY

Chapter 6 will first introduce the administrator to Transmission Control Protocol/Internet Protocol (TCP/IP) in Windows 7 and Microsoft's next-generation TCP/IP stack, which uses both IPv4 and IPv6. Other new features in Windows 7 networking include network location and network discovery that allow easier networking for end users. The Network and Sharing Center provides a centralized location to perform almost all network-related tasks. The same is true for mobile users with the Mobility Center and wireless networking. HomeGroup will be referenced as well for users and administrators working in home networks. Power management is also covered in this chapter because it plays a large role when dealing with mobile systems. Finally, Windows 7 enhancements with Windows Server 2008 R2, including DirectAccess, Branch Cache, and VPN Reconnect, will be introduced.

CHAPTER7 : MANAGING WINDOWS 7 IN AN ENTERPRISE ENVIRONMENT

Most administrators will be working with Windows 7 in an enterprise environment. Microsoft has improved a multitude of tools for easily and quickly performing these tasks. This chapter will look at Group Policy and PowerShell, two of the most powerful tools for managing Windows 7 systems in an enterprise environment. Like Chapter 3, "Deploying Windows 7 in an Enterprise Environment," not every scenario or environment is the same, so managing many computers will not be exactly the same for each administrator. Therefore, this chapter will present the tools and methodologies for using the most common tools.

CHAPTER8 : SECURING WINDOWS7

Microsoft and security have never been closely associated. Windows Vista showed huge improvements on Microsoft's side to improve security in the desktop. Windows 7 has improved on those steps and proves to be the most secure desktop operating system released by Microsoft. This chapter begins with user accounts and access rights in Windows 7 and then moves to protecting the system. The Action Center will be used to manage antivirus, antispyware, Windows Updates, and User Account Control. Biometric devices will be referenced. Internet Explorer 8 has many security features that will need to be relayed to your users, and AppLocker keeps great control of installed applications. BitLocker and BitLocker to Go offer drive encryption, while Encrypted Files System protects the file system. Other new features such as DNSSec, Windows Filtering Platform, and Certificates will also be reviewed in this chapter.

CHAPTER9 : VIRTUALIZATION AND WINDOWS7

Virtualization is one of the newest and favorite technologies for system administrators. Windows 7 allows both running the system in a virtualized environment and running a virtual machine within the Windows 7 system. This chapter will look at running Windows 7 as a virtualized desktop with technology like Virtual Desktop Infrastructure. It will also focus on Windows Virtual PC and XP Mode, which allows a virtual instance of Windows XP to run within Windows 7 fors oftwarec ompatibility.

CHAPTER10 : WINDOWS7 TROUBLESHOOTING AND PERFORMANCE TOOLS

Troubleshooting has traditionally been one of the main tasks of administrators. Microsoft attempts to change that by making Windows 7 easier than ever to troubleshoot. This chapter will introduce troubleshooting and performance tools. Using these tools correctly will reduce the time it takes to troubleshoot issues within Windows 7. Some of the features in this chapter, such as the Problem Step Recorder, need to be relayed to your users to help them help you troubleshooti ssues.

Introduction to Windows 7

INFORMATION IN THIS CHAPTER

- Builton Vista
- DifferentE ditions
- 32-Bit and 64-Bit Computing
- HardwareR equirements
- Choosing the Right Windows 7 Version
- Major Changes in Windows 7
- New Features
- Summary

Less than three years after the release of Windows Vista, Microsoft released their latest operating system, Windows 7. Built on top of Vista technology, Windows 7 offers a wealth of versatility and security for system administrators. This chapter serves as an introduction to Windows 7, the six different editions, and the system requirements to get the planning phase underway as to what version you will be installing and working with in your environment. Next, a brief introduction to what has changed in Windows 7 will be highlighted for quick reference. Then the chapter will introduce new and improved features in Windows 7 over Windows Vista and Windows XP. While most of the new features were built and first introduced in Vista, Microsoft has greatly improved most of them. For those that skipped Vista, do not worry as Vista's failure to capture the market has been taken into account. Most of the features will be elaborated on in other chapters and references to other chapters will be included for each feature. Some of the features introduced in this chapter require Microsoft Windows Server 2008 R2; Microsoft has strategically released these two operating systems at the same time and some features of Windows 7 will only work with those

DOI: 10.1016/B978-1-59749-561-5.00001-2

servers. Windows Server 2008 R2 will be referenced and elaborated on as much as possible.

BUILT ON VISTA

Most importantly, it is critical to know that Windows 7 was built on top of Vista. Given the amount of time between releases this may be assumed, but to be clear, Windows 7 is built on the architecture introduced with Vista. If you have used Vista, many of the features will seem more like improvements instead of new features. However, if you skipped Vista, many of the features will seem brand new and welcoming especially when coming from Windows XP or prior operating systems. Furthermore, many of the changes between Windows Vista and Windows 7 are below the surface so identifying them takes a bit more work than with prior releases.

DIFFERENT EDITIONS

Some administrators believe Microsoft has gone crazy with their different editions. This section defines the current editions of Windows that might be running in your environment and the Windows 7 editions that were released. This information will be useful to decide what version of Windows 7 to purchase, install, and/or deploy in your environment. This will also serve to clear the doubt between the editions, so you are educated when asked by your users as to what your environment runs as opposed to their home environment and/or personal machines.

Often Windows editions are referred to as *stock keeping unit* or *SKUs*; we will use the terms edition, version, and SKU interchangeably in this book and specifically in the next sections.

WindowsX PE ditions

In 2001, Microsoft released Windows XP in two editions: Windows XP Home and Windows XP Professional. Deciding what version to use was very simple. As time passed, Microsoft released a few other editions of Windows XP:

- Windows XP Starter Edition – for underdeveloped countries
- Windows XP Embedded – installed in embedded devices
- Windows XP Home N – for the European Union antitrust ruling
- Windows XP Media Center – for media center computers
- Windows XP Tablet – for Tablet PCs
- Windows XP Professional N – for the European Union antitrust ruling
- Windows XP Professional K – for the South Korean market

- Windows XP Professional x64 – for 64-bit computers
- Windows XP for Itanium-based systems – for 64-bit Itanium systems

As you can see, there are a total of 11 different versions of Windows XP. The N and K editions were due to antitrust rulings in the European Union and South Korea, respectively. These versions removed certain features of Windows XP such as Internet Explorer (IE) and Windows Media Player. Such editions still exist today in Windows 7 but should not be an issue as they do not cost less and there is not much sense in paying the same while losing features that you might require later on down the road.

To determine what version of Windows XP is running on a system, you must pull up the System Properties. As shown in Figure 1.1, the **General** tab will

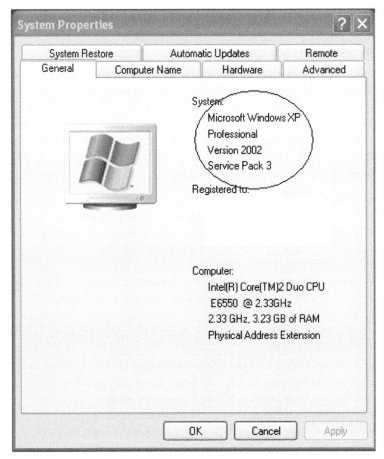

■ **FIGURE 1.1** Windows XP System Properties

inform you of what version of Windows XP is running on the system. There are several to open System Properties in Windows XP:

- **Start | Control Panel** (Classic View) | **System**
- **Start | Control Panel** (Category View) | **Performance and Maintenance | System**
- Right-click **My Computer** on the desktop or Start menu and choose **Properties**

Some editions such as the Tablet PC and Media Center Editions were released with added features from the original Windows XP release. The market accepted these different editions because of their tailoring to specific systems and Microsoft liked the capability to charge premium pricing for more features. The premium pricing of more features evolved into the different versions of Windows Vista and Windows 7 currently available.

Windows VistaE ditions

Windows Vista was released in even more editions than Windows XP. Unlike Windows XP, 32-bit and 64-bit versions were available for all editions. The next section will discuss 32-bit and 64-bit computing in detail. Depending on how Windows Vista was obtained, the same media could include the 32-bit and 64-bit versions. However, for this section, we will consider each 32-bit and 64-bit version as a different release. There were a total of 18 different editions released for Windows Vista:

- WindowsV istaS tarter
- Windows Vista Home Basic – standard home user version
- Windows Vista Home Basic 64-bit – same as Basic but for 64-bit
- Windows Vista Home Premium – premium home user version with addedf eatures
- Windows Vista Home Premium N – for European Union antitrust ruling
- Windows Vista Home Premium 64-bit – same as Home Premium but for64 -bit
- Windows Vista Home Premium N 64-bit – EU edition of Home Premium for 64-bit
- Windows Vista Business – standard release for business/professional
- Windows Vista Business K – for South Korea antitrust ruling
- Windows Vista Business N – for EU antitrust ruling
- Windows Vista Business 64-bit – for 64-bit computing
- Windows Vista Business K 64-bit – South Korea version for 64-bit computing
- Windows Vista Business N 64-bit – EU version for 64-bit computing
- Windows Vista Enterprise – for volume licensing customers/businesses
- Windows Vista Enterprise 64-bit – same as above for 64-bit computing

- Windows Vista Ultimate – all features in Enterprise and Home Premium
- Windows Vista Ultimate 64-bit – same as above for 64-bit computing
- Windows Vista Ultimate Product (RED) – special edition of Vista

The 32-bit and 64-bit versions had the same features but made for the respective processing architecture. Additionally, Windows Vista versions were sold as retail or OEM versions. OEM stands for original equipment manufacturer, which means that they came with a new PC. However, it was possible to buy OEM versions standalone or with a piece of hardware, say an audio cable.

To determine what version of Windows Vista is running on a system, you must pull up the System console. As shown in Figure 1.2, the main System console screen will inform you of what version of Windows Vista is running

■ **FIGURE 1.2** Windows Vista System Console

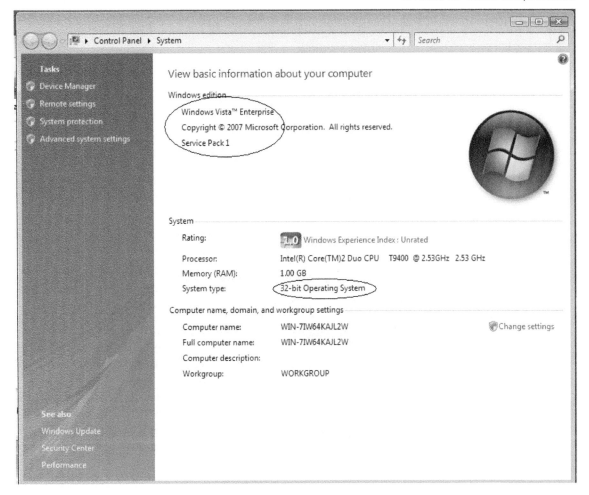

on the system. There are several to open the System console in Windows Vista:

- **Start** | **Control Panel** (Classic View) | **System**
- **Start** | **Control Panel** (Category View) | **System and Maintenance** | **System**
- Right-click **Computer** on the desktop or Start menu and choose **Properties**

Windows7 E ditions

After seeing the different versions of Windows that may be running in your environment, you will be pleased to know that Windows 7 editions are not as complex. Microsoft released 11 different Windows 7 editions, counting the different 32-bit and 64-bit versions as separate versions. Some versions you might never see as most administrators will be working with the Professional and/or Enterprise/Ultimate editions. Below is a listing of the 11 different versions:

- Windows7H omeB asic
- Windows7S tarter
- Windows7H omeP remium
- Windows 7 Home Premium 64-bit
- Windows 7 Home Premium N
- Windows7P rofessional
- Windows7P rofessional64- bit
- Windows7E nterprise
- Windows7E nterprise64- bit
- Windows7U ltimate
- Windows7U ltimate64- bit

As you can see, this is less confusing than previous releases. As an administrator, your decision is further clarified because the method of obtaining some versions likely excludes them. First, a brief introduction to each version:

- Windows 7 Starter – the most basic version of Windows 7, also known as the budget version. This version can only be obtained preinstalled through a manufacturer and is expected to be popular on netbooks. Not all features will be included in this version, including Windows Aero.
- Windows 7 Home Basic – the home edition for emerging markets. This version will not be available for sale in developed countries such as the United States, United Kingdom, and Australia. Not all features will be included in this version, including some Windows Aero features.

- Windows 7 Home Premium – the home edition for developed nations. This edition is aimed at the home market segment. Most computers sold at retail stores will include this version with all home features including Windows Media Center, Windows Aero, and touchscreen.
- Windows 7 Professional – the preferred edition for small business and enthusiasts. This edition includes everything the Home Premium edition includes as well as the capability to join Windows Server domains. Other features such as Remote Desktop, location aware printing, Encrypting File System (EFS), Presentation Mode, and Windows XP Mode will be included in this version.
- Windows 7 Enterprise – the corporate edition of the operating system. This version is for the enterprise and is only available through volume licensing. This version supports Multilingual User Interface, BitLocker Drive Encryption, and UNIX application support. This version is not available from manufactures or retail.
- Windows 7 Ultimate – the Enterprise version for home or enthusiast users. This version includes everything from the Enterprise edition through retail and some manufacturers.

The above explanation should be enough to give you an idea as to what version you will be working with at home or in your environment. Windows Starter will most likely be seen only on netbooks in the future. Windows Home Basic will not be seen in developed markets meaning Home Premium will be the choice for home users while Professional and Enterprise will be the choice for corporate and business environments. The Ultimate Edition will most likely be used by power home users and in some businesses that require the features that come with the Enterprise edition but do not have the licensing for it.

Table 1.1 includes more detailed tables as to what features are included with each version.

32-BIT AND 64 -BIT COMPUTING

Microsoft introduced 64-bit computing with Windows XP in 2001. Thankfully, 64-bit computing has changed substantially in terms of hardware support since then. In Windows 7, 64-bit versions run faster and more secure than their equivalent 32-bit edition. All editions except for Windows 7 Starter are available in both 32-bit and 64-bit versions. To run the 64-bit version of Windows 7, 64-bit capable hardware is required. If the hardware is present, then 64-bit is the better choice. The quick reason for this is that 32-bit processors and operating system versions do not know how to manage more

Table 1.1 Edition Comparisons

Features/Licensing	Starter OEM	Home Basic *Emerging Markets*	Home Premium	Professional *Retail and OEM*	Enterprise *Volume*	Ultimate *Retail and OEM*
32-bit version	Yes	Yes	Yes	Yes	Yes	Yes
64-bit version	No	Yes	Yes	Yes	Yes	Yes
Aero over RDP	No	No	No	No	Yes	Yes
AppLocker	No	No	No	No	Yes	Yes
Backup and Restore Center	Local only	Local Only	Local Only	Yes	Yes	Yes
BitLocker Drive Encryption	No	No	No	No	Yes	Yes
BranchCache Distributed Cache	No	No	No	No	Yes	Yes
Desktop Wallpaper Changeable	No	Yes	Yes	Yes	Yes	Yes
Desktop Window Manager	No	Yes	Yes	Yes	Yes	Yes
DirectAccess	No	No	No	No	Yes	Yes
Encrypting File System	No	No	No	Yes	Yes	Yes
Fast user switching	No	Yes	Yes	Yes	Yes	Yes
Home Group (create and join)	Join	Join	Both	Both	Both	Both
Location Aware Printing	No	No	No	Yes	Yes	Yes
Maximum physical CPU supported	1	1	1	2	2	2
Maximum memory (64-bit mode)	N/A	8GB	16GB	192GB	192GB	192GB
Multilingual User Interface Pack	No	No	No	No	Yes	Yes
Multiple monitors	No	Yes	Yes	Yes	Yes	Yes
Multi-Touch	No	No	Yes	Yes	Yes	Yes
Premium Games Included	No	No	Yes	Yes	No	Yes
Presentation Mode	No	No	No	Yes	Yes	Yes
Remote Desktop Host	No	No	No	Yes	Yes	Yes
Remote Media Experience	No	No	Yes	Yes	Yes	Yes
Subsystem for Unix-based Applications	No	No	No	No	Yes	Yes
Virtual Hard Disk Booting	No	No	No	No	Yes	Yes
Windows Aero	No	Basic	Yes	Yes	Yes	Yes
Windows Media Center	No	No	Yes	Yes	Yes	Yes
Windows Mobility Center	No	Yes	Yes	Yes	Yes	Yes
Windows Server domain joining	No	No	No	Yes	Yes	Yes
Windows XP Mode	No	No	No	Yes	Yes	Yes

than 4 gigabytes (GB) of RAM. The latest computers include 4 GB or more of memory and therefore should run 64-bit versions of Windows 7.

Even if there is less than 4 GB of memory, a 64-bit architecture and operating system have many advantages including more security. However, there are also limitations to be considered:

- 16-bit applications will not run on 64-bit Windows versions. These include MS-DOS and Windows 3.x and 9x applications. Windows XP Mode can be used to run these applications, however. Chapter 9, "Virtualization and Windows 7," is dedicated to explaining how.
- Hardware drivers must be 64-bit. This means that you need to pay extra attention to the planning and preparing stage of the deployment to ensure all hardware components have 64-bit drivers.

64-bitExp lained

The terms 32-bit and 64-bit refer to the way a computer's processor handles information. The amount of bits stands for integers, memory addresses, registers, address buses, or data buses of the respective size. Therefore, a 64-bit processor, or CPU, can handle much more memory than a 32-bit CPU does. A 32-bit processor and operating system cannot handle more than 4 GB of memory and therefore does not know how to manage it correctly. A 64-bit processor and Windows 7 Professional and Ultimate can handle up to 192 GB of memory efficiently.

> **NOTE**
> To compare the 32-bit and 64-bit difference in bytes, the math is simple:
>
> For3 2-bit:
>
> 2^{32} = 4,294,967,296 bytes
>
> 4,294,967,296 / (1,024 × 1,024) = 4,096 MB = 4 GB
>
> For6 4-bit:
>
> 2^{64} = 18,446,744,073,709,551,616
>
> 18,446,744,073,709,551,616/ (1,024 × 1,024) = 16 EB (exabytes)

The operating system is the first layer that needs to understand what to do with the 64-bit architecture, then the software. Even if the software is not designed for 64-bit, it will still work on a 64-bit version of Windows 7. It is worth noting that some 32-bit software might run quicker on a 32-bit version. Windows 7 64-bit editions support 32-bit applications using the Windows on Windows 64 (WOW64) x86 emulation layer. This layer isolates the 32-bit application from 64-bit applications to prevent issues with the file system and/or registry. There is interoperability across this boundary with the Component Object Model (COM) for basic operations such as cut, copy, and paste using the Clipboard. However, 64-bit processes cannot load 32-bit DLLs and vice-versa.

64-bitA rchitectures

There are two different types of 64-bit architectures an administrator might encounter: x64 and IA64. The most used is x64. This is an extension of the x86 instruction set designed by AMD and licensed to Intel. It is the most common as most new CPUs in the home and business use this architecture. The IA64 or Intel Itanium architecture as it is now known was developed by Intel and HP and marketed for use in enterprise servers and high-performance systems. This book assumes that x86 and x64 architectures are being used in the environment.

Tests for 64-bit Hardware

There are a few ways to test if your system is compatible with 64-bit versions of Windows 7. The first and easiest method is with a freeware program developed by Steve Gibson from Gibson Research Corporation called Securable (Figure 1.3). Securable not only tells you if your computer is 64-bit capable but also tells you if it has hardware Data Execution Prevention (DEP) and Hardware Virtualization enabled. Hardware DEP is a hardware capability in modern processors that marks all memory regions not containing executable code as nonexecutable. This protects the system's heaps, stacks, data, and communications buffers from running any executable code. In other words, it protects against the buffer overrun attacks that are very common today. Hardware Virtualization allows for Windows XP Mode to run and will be elaborated on in Chapter 8, "Securing Windows 7." Securable can be obtained from the GRC.com Web site at www.grc.com/securable.htm along with more information about how it works and how these three components make systems more secure. Figure 1.3 displays the Securable screen, as you can see it is a simple but informative application.

■ **FIGURE 1.3** Securable

The issue with the Securable method of checking hardware compatibility is that only one machine can be checked at a time. This can be a huge issue for administrators with many machines.

A second method that may be scripted uses PowerShell. PowerShell is further explained in Chapter 6, "Networking and Mobility." Below is the code to determine 64-bit compatibility on your current system without a third-partypr ogram.

- To determine what architecture is being used by an operating system you may use the OSArchitecture property of the Win32_OperatingSystem object: `get-wmiobject -class win32_operatingsystem | format-list osarchitecture`
- To determine where a system supports x64 architecture you may use the Name and Description properties of the Win32_Processor object: `get-wmiobject -class win32_processor | format-list name, description`

Another method of determining if the systems in your environment are 64-bit compatible is by using an asset management application that determines CPU type, name, and/or description. Such applications are common in larger networks and examples of these include Microsoft SMS or SCCM, ManageEngine's Asset Explorer, etc.

HARDWARE REQUIREMENTS

Like any software, Microsoft has published their minimum requirements for systems running Windows 7. As a general guideline, any 32-bit Vista machine should be able to run Windows 7 32-bit as well; the same is true for 64-bit versions. The requirements were elevated for the 64-bit versions of Windows 7 to 2 GB of memory; however, systems with 1 GB have been known to run Winows 7 64-bit without issues. Table 1.2 outlines Microsoft'sh ardwarer equirements.

Table1. 2 Minimum Hardware Requirements for Windows 7

Architecture	32-bit	64-bit
Processor Speed	1 GHz 32-bit CPU	1 GHz 64-bit CPU
Memory (RAM)	1 GB	2 GB
Graphics Card	For Aero – DirectX with 128 MB and WDDM 1.0 support	
HDD free space	16 GB	16 GB

Additionally, some features of Windows 7 have more specific hardware requirements. Windows XP Mode requires an additional 1 GB of RAM, 15 GB of free hard disk space, and a processor that is capable of hardware virtualization (Intel VT or AMD-V for example). The Windows Aero feature requires a graphics card with 128 MB of memory or more and support for DirectX 9 and Windows Display Driver Model 1.1 or higher. These requirements are highlighted in the New Features section of this chapter.

Windows 7 Upgrade Advisor

Microsoft released an upgrade advisor to test your current systems prior to deploying Windows 7 to ensure compatibility and minimum requirements. Windows 7 Upgrade Advisor not only checks your hardware but also your entire system for compatibility. The Windows 7 Upgrade Advisor will be discussed further with step-by-step instructions on how to use it in Chapter 2, "Installing and Upgrading to Windows 7."

CHOOSING THE RIGHT WINDOWS7 VERSION

Hopefully after going through the chart, you have a better idea as to what version of Windows 7 you will be using. To assist with your decision, here are some recommendations:

- 64-bit if possible: If the hardware allows it, go with the 64-bit versions, remember that these versions do not cost more. Take into account applications and driver requirements to ensure they are 64-bit compatible. 16-bit applications will not work on 64-bit and will either need a 32-bit version or Windows XP Mode.
- For home users: Go with Windows 7 Home Premium, the Windows 7 Ultimate features will rarely be used and are not worth the premium pricing unless you are a power user requiring any of those features.
- For business users: If you are in a small or medium business without a volume licensing agreement, go with the Professional version. If volume licensing is an option, then the Enterprise version will be preferable due to cost and the administrative tools included with this edition.

Once you choose the Windows 7 for your environment you may skip to Chapter 2, "Installing and Upgrading to Windows 7," where we will begin installing and/or upgrading to Windows 7. The New Features section will introduce new features and include a quick reference to help you enable and/or configure those features.

MAJOR CHANGES IN WINDOWS7

This section will serve as a quick introduction to the major changes in Windows 7. You should not skip this section as it introduces fundamental changes that require understanding to avoid issues later. The five primary changes worth noting before we discuss all the new features are:

- Deployment
- DesktopI nterface
- Management
- UserA ccountC ontrol(UAC)
- UserPr ofileD ata

Deployment

Windows 7 has improved desktop and application deployment. One of the toughest jobs in migrating to a different system is the deployment process. Microsoft has considered past issues and improved many aspects of this process for Windows 7, including hardware and application compatibility, new imaging tools and deployment methods/tools, and improved migration tools.

One of the biggest issues in Vista was driver and application compatibility support, and it has been addressed in Windows 7. As one will see when installing Windows 7, most third-party hardware and devices should work from first boot. If not, Microsoft has included multiple new ways to obtain and find solutions to hardware issues; the same is true for application support. New in Windows 7 is Dynamic Driver Provisioning. Drivers may be stored in a repository separate from the images that will be deployed. Then the drivers may be installed from this repository based on the system's hardware requirements. This feature lowers driver conflicts and speeds up installation and setup times of new machines, an administrator's dream.

Deployment tools and methods have also been improved to ease deployment headaches. The Deployment Image Servicing and Management (DISM) tool has been introduced to provide a centralized location to build and maintain Windows 7 image files. Multicast Multiple Stream Transfer allows for deploying these images from multiple locations, speeding up the deployment time. Windows Easy Transfer and the User State Migration Tool (USMT) have been improved to assist migrating user profiles, data, and settings from one system to another. Lastly, Windows 7 now supports VHD image management and deployment allowing for deployment of the same VHD image to a virtual or physical machine. This allows for standardization across all Windows 7 systems in your environment.

DesktopI nterface

The Windows 7 desktop interface, also known as the graphical user interface (GUI), has been significantly improved. The difference will be more noticeable for end users migrating from Windows XP than Windows Vista as the latter introduced Windows Aero. The Windows 7 user interface will be very familiar to any previous Windows user as it continues to include a Start menu, taskbar, notification area, and desktop. However, most of these features have been changed and improved.

Believe it or not, many of these changes do have end-user productivity in mind as opposed to being purely focused on eye candy. Many end users had significant issues with the changes in the desktop environment from Windows XP to Windows Vista and the migration to Windows 7 will not be any easier. It is extremely important to learn and understand the new Windows 7 desktop environment features and properly educate the end users. As you will see, the planning and preparation process of a Windows 7 deployment is just as important as proper user training and education.

Windows 7 includes more than one user experience option that may be selected through the **Themes** option of the **Personalization** console of the Control Panel. These themes allow for different user experiences:

- Windows Classic – resembles the Windows 95, 98, ME, and 2000 desktop interface. The Start menu, however, does not have the option for a classic style, it can only be set as far back as the Windows XP Start menu.
- Windows Basic and Standard – depending on the edition of Windows 7 and hardware compatibility this is the Windows 7 default user interface without Aero features.
- Windows Aero – this is the new and default Windows 7 user experience, edition and hardware allowing. It includes all the Aero features including Glass, Snap, Peek, etc.

The entire Windows 7 desktop experience will be introduced in the next section and Chapter 3, "Deploying Windows 7 in an Enterprise Environment," will go even more in-depth. Important new and improved features of Windows 7 include:

- Bundled applications – Microsoft has included multiple new and improved bundled applications including the calculator and sticky notes while removing Messenger, Mail, and Photo Gallery, which are now a part of Microsoft Live Essentials.
- Improved Start menu – similar to the default Windows XP and Vista Start menu with an improved search bar and other useful features.

- Jump Lists – allows for quick access to associated tasks of the applications elected.
- Notification area – similar to the notification area introduced in Windows 95, it now has customizable options for more effective notifications of system and application status.
- Taskbar – similar to Windows XP and Vista. Microsoft has removed the quick launch toolbar and now allows programs to be pinned to the taskbar for launching and accessing open windows.
- Themes – multiple new and improved themes to customize the desktop backgrounds, window colors, sounds, screen saver, and power options.
- Windows Aero – multiple features including Aero Peek, Snap, Shake, Glass, etc. This requires compatible hardware and Windows 7 edition.
- Windows Explorer – the shell for accessing Windows Explorer has been vastly improved. The menu bar has been removed and various new and enhanced features such as Libraries, address bar, navigation pane, and search have been added.

Management

Windows 7 includes new management tools to automate and centrally administer Windows 7 machines. The two major additions are Windows PowerShell 2.0 and improvements to the Group Policy settings. These tools are introduced in this section but Chapter 6, "Networking and Mobility," goes much more in-depth on how to use the tools for easier management of Windows environments.

Windows PowerShell is a scripting language that supports multiple functions such as automation, looping, branching, functions, debugging, exception handling, etc. It allows for the centralized and automated management of entire Windows environments. Think of PowerShell as the older command prompt on steroids. It is a real shell with scripting capabilities. Windows PowerShell is also a scripting engine that alongside Windows PowerShell Integrated Scripting Environment (PowerShell ISE) can be used to easily write, debug, and execute scripts. PowerShell is a great new tool for managing Windows environments and should be considered by all administrators.

Group Policy has also been improved to include almost every single Windows 7 setting there is. This allows for policy set by OU in the Active Directory to manage your entire environment from a centralized location. Group Policy has traditionally been used to enforce policies but with Group Policy Preferences, administrators can now select how settings are applied. IE 8 Group Policy has been added and supports over 1,000 group policies for IE configurations in your environment, a great way to enforce security settings.

UserA ccountC ontrol(U AC)

As most administrators know, one of the largest issues with Microsoft Vista was the lack of acceptance by end users. The main attribution for this is believed to be the UAC feature introduced in Windows Vista. Microsoft understood the issues with UAC in Vista and has improved the feature for Windows 7. The UAC is now an even better security feature and should never be disabled.

The UAC level may be modified through the Action Center, which is a new feature introduced in the next section. It is found in the Control Panel. Unlike Vista where you could just disable or enable it without more detailed setting, Windows 7 allows four options for UAC as shown in Figure 1.4:

■ **FIGURE 1.4** Windows 7 User Account Control Settings

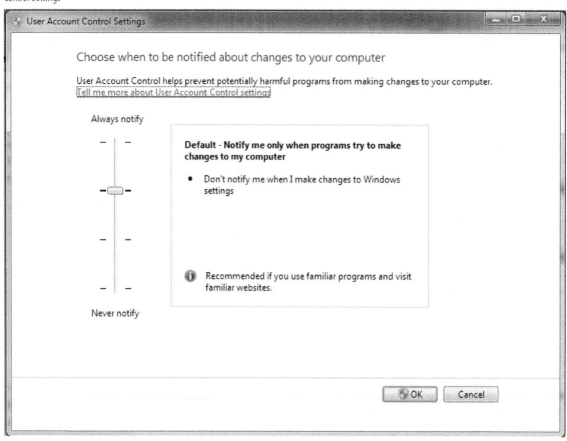

- Always notify me when:
  - ❏ Programs try to install software or make changes to my computer
  - ❏ Im akec hangest oW indowss ettings
- Default – Notify me only when programs try to make changes to my computer
  - ❏ Don't notify me when I make changes to Windows settings
- Notify me only when programs try to make changes to my computer (does not dim the desktop)
  - ❏ Don't notify me when I make changes to Windows settings
- Never notify me when:
  - ❏ Programs try to install software or make changes to my computer
  - ❏ Im akec hangest oW indowss ettings

UserP rofileDa ta

A significant change to Windows 7 over Windows XP is the location of user profile data, the introduction of a brand new feature, Libraries, and a new method of handling a user's local and roaming settings. These are often the primary reason certain applications and software will not work with Windows 7 (especially if the location of these directories is hard coded in the application).

First, the location of the user profile data has been changed from where Windows XP stored user data, %SystemDrive%\Documents and Settings\ %UserName%. Windows 7 user data is now located in %SystemDrive%\ Users\%UserName% as shown in Figure 1.5.

Each user that logs into the Windows 7 system will have a unique personal folder. Generally, the name of this folder is the username used to log into the system or domain. This personal folder is the default location for storing the user's data and files as shown in Figure 1.6. Subfolders in the %User-Name% folder include:

- AppData – user unique application data and settings (hidden folder), more on this ahead
- Contacts – user unique contacts and groups
- Desktop – user unique desktop shortcuts and files stored on the desktop
- Downloads – default folder for downloaded files from IE and soon most third-party browsers
- Favorites – user's favorites or bookmarks from IE
- Links – user's links or bookmarks from IE
- My Documents – main location for users; documents. Note that it is no longer called %UserName%'s Documents.
- My Music – default location to store user's music

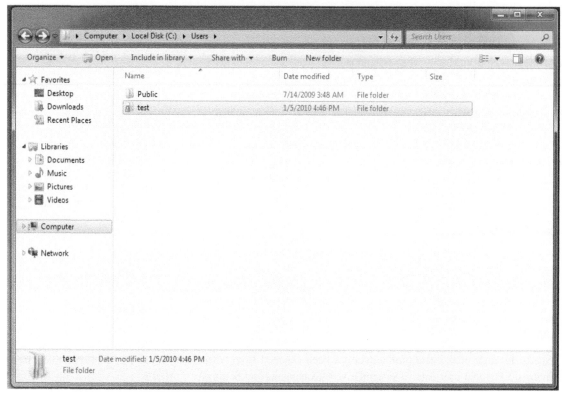

■ FIGURE 1.5 User Profile Folder Locations

- My Videos – default location to store user's videos
- Saved Games – user's default location of Microsoft and Windows saved games. Third-party games will likely adopt this folder as the default folder as well but it depends on the vendor.
- Searches–us er'ss aveds earchque ries

In addition to a new location for the user's data and settings, Microsoft has included a new feature called Libraries. Libraries will be introduced in the next section; however, there are some critical facts you need to know. Libraries are personal collections of user's files and folders grouped together and presented in a common folder, as shown in Figure 1.7. These Libraries are not actual folders but a reference to where the folders and files are actually stored. This can be a great and productive new feature for end users to access data quicker and in a simpler fashion, but education is critical once again.

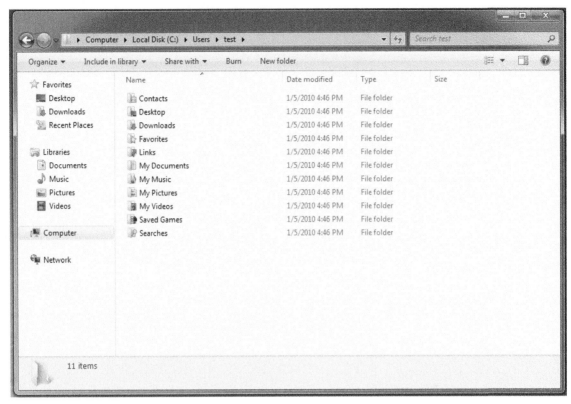

The default Libraries for each user include:

- Documents – collection of the content in the user's My Documents folder and Public Documents folder.
- Music – collection of the content in the user's My Music folder and Public Music folder.
- Pictures – collection of the content in the user's My Pictures folder and Public Picture folder.
- Videos – collection of the content in the user's My Videos folder and PublicV ideof older.

The Public folder is found in %SystemDrive%\Users\Public\ and includes similar folders to the user's personal folder (Figure 1.8).

A new Library may be created by clicking **New Library** from the Library window in Windows Explorer or by right-clicking the Windows Explorer window and selecting **New Library** as shown in Figure 1.9. To edit a

■ **FIGURE 1.7** Libraries View

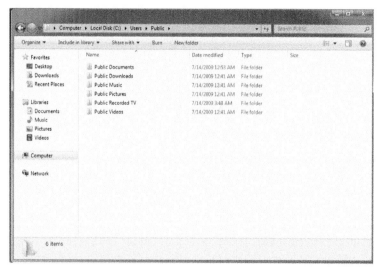

■ **FIGURE 1.8** Public Folder

Library and edit the folders used for the collection, right-click on the Library and select **Properties**. The Properties window allows users to include other folders in the collection or remove a folder from being collected as shown in Figure 1.10.

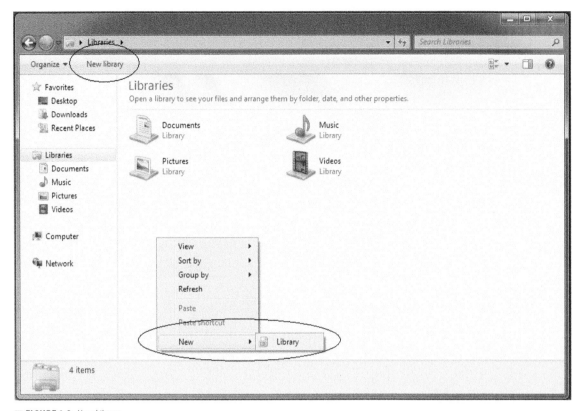

■ **FIGURE 1.9** New Library

Lastly, one of the biggest changes in Windows 7 related to user data compared to Windows XP is the difference in application data folder structure. In Windows XP, the user's application data and settings were stored in %SystemDrive%\Documents, Settings\%UserName%\Application Data\, %SystemDrive%\Documents, and Settings\%UserName%\Local Settings\ Application Data\.

Windows 7 now has move the data and settings in these critical folders to %SystemDrive%\Users\%UserName%\AppData\Roaming and %System-Drive%\Users\%UserName%\AppData\Local as shown in Figure 1.11.

This change is one of the main reasons why some Windows XP software and applications may not function properly, upgrade correctly, and/or be compatible with Windows 7. This should serve as a warning not to skip the planning and preparation phase of Windows 7 deployment as well as a hint to where some application compatibility issues may be.

NOTE
Theu ser'sa pplicationd ataf olders are hidden by default. To enable Windows Explorer to show hidden files, folders, and drives, follow the steps below:

1. Click **Organize** on the upper left section of Windows Explorer.
2. Click **Folder and Search Options**.
3. Clickt he **View**t ab.
4. In advance settings, select the radio button under Hidden files and folders that reads **"Show hidden files, folders, and drives"**.
5. Click **OK**.

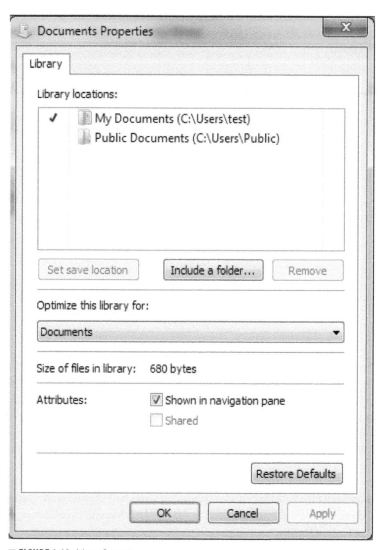

■ **FIGURE 1.10** Library Properties

NEW FEATURES IN WINDOWS7

This section introduces many features of the new Windows 7. Although not meant to go into much detail, it will provide a quick background on how to enable or configure each feature. Most of the features will be elaborated on in later chapters.

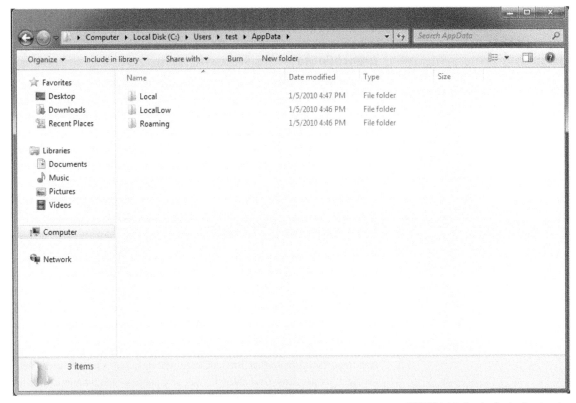

For easier reference, the new features will be divided into different sections: connectivity, entertainment, performance, productivity, and security. The features within these sections will be listed in alphabetical order.

Connectivity

In today's connected world, communication is the most important aspect of business. Microsoft understands this and Windows 7 makes it easier to stay connected. The new connectivity features will be elaborated upon later in this book, and they include:

- BranchCache
- DirectAccess
- HomeGroup
- Internet Explorer 8 (IE 8)
- OfflineD omainJ oin
- VPNR econnect

- WindowsM obilityC enter
- WindowsC onnectN ow

BranchCache

BranchCache is like DNS cache but for files in remote locations. When a Windows 7 user requests a file from a remote location, for example, headquarters or a data center server, the file is pulled from the remote location once and then stored on the requester's machine or a Windows Server 2008 R2 server with BranchCache enabled. Any other user on the same network that requests the same file from the remote site will pull it from the original requester or the Windows 2008 R2 server. This is a great feature introduced in Windows 7 with Windows Server 2008 R2. As the economic trend leads to budget cuts and a push to "do more with less," this feature can assist in lowering bandwidth costs between sites.

BranchCache can work in one of two modes, Hosted Cache or Distributed Cache. With Hosted Cache mode, a server in the remote office running Windows Server 2008 R2 will download the requested file and host it for the other requesters. With Distributed Cache mode, a Windows Server 2008 R2 server is not required in the remote office as the original requester will cache the file and distribute it to other requesters.

It is important to note that BranchCache will only serve files to users with the right permissions. BranchCache will also continue to communicate with the original server to ensure the file is current. As a passive cache, BranchCache will only cache the file once the first user requests the file from the remote location. Furthermore, this feature will only cache read requests, not write requests.

BranchCache supports file caching for Web requests using HTTP and HTTPS protocols as well as SMB. It also works with SSL and IPSec encryption. BranchCache requires Windows Server 2008 R2 in the remote site and Windows 7 clients or another Windows Server 2008 R2 server in the cache site. Enabling BranchCache will be discussed in Chapter 6, "Networking and Mobility," as it requires configuration of the server and client.

DirectAccess

Windows 7 Enterprise and Ultimate editions with Windows Server 2008 R2 introduce a new feature, DirectAccess, which allows remote users to securely access enterprise shared drives, Web sites, and applications without connecting to a virtual private network (VPN). This is possible because DirectAccess establishes a bidirectional connection with a user's enterprise network every time the system connects to the Internet. This connection occurs even prior to the user logging on. Allowing continuous connectivity to the enterprise environment has many benefits, such as simplicity for end users, network, and IT administrators.

DirectAccess uses IPv6 as it uses globally routable addresses. If your organization is not yet moving to IPv6, other options like 6to4, Teredo, and NAT-PT may be configured for similar functionality. This will be expanded on in Chapter 4, "The New Windows 7 Desktop Environment," although most of the configuration is on Windows Server 2008 R2 side.

HomeGroup

As the name suggests, HomeGroup is aimed at home users and networks. This feature allows for easy sharing of files and printers in a home network. HomeGroup uses a password to secure the home network. A user can share pictures, documents, music, printers, and/or videos. Creating a HomeGroup is only possible on Home Premium, Professional, Enterprise, and Ultimate editions while any edition can join a current HomeGroup. More details on HomeGroup will be referenced in Chapter 6, "Networking and Mobility."

Configuring a HomeGroup is very simple and user friendly. When connecting to a home network for the first time, the network configuration wizard will pop up and ask the user what type of network the system is connected to, as shown in Figure 1.12.

It is important that users be trained to select the correct network because the Windows Firewall settings depend on the network that is selected. When Home network is selected, the system will scan the network for a Home-Group. It will then prompt the user to select what items should be shared in the HomeGroup, as shown in Figure 1.13. If there is already a HomeGroup created in the home network, then a password will be requested. Once the user inputs that password once, Windows 7 will detect and connect to that HomeGroup every time the system is on the network. If a HomeGroup is not detected, the step after selecting what to share will create one and create a password as shown in Figure 1.14. This password should be stored safely and only given to trusted users on the network that wish to connect to the HomeGroup.

Internet Explorer 8

IE 8 was released on March 19, 2009 for Windows XP operating systems and above as an optional update. On Windows 7 and Windows Server 2008 R2 systems, it is the default browser. For security reasons alone, it is highly recommended to upgrade to IE 8 on all Windows systems. IE 8 will be further discussed in Chapters 4, "The New Windows 7 Desktop Environment," and

■ **FIGURE 1.12** Choose Network Prompt

■ **FIGURE 1.13** HomeGroup Setup – Select
What to Share

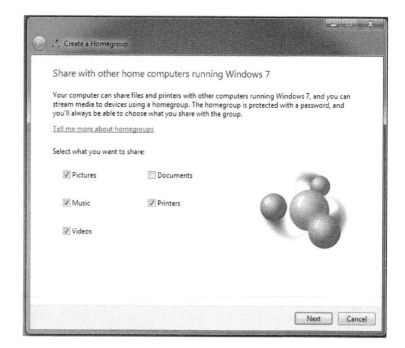

Chapter 8, "Securing Windows 7." This should serve as a brief introduction to the new features of IE 8. It is noteworthy to point out that most of these features can be enabled and disabled from IE options by clicking **Tools** on the top-right corner of the IE 8 window as shown in Figure 1.15.

Following are the few new features that should be understood by administrators and end users for using and configuring IE 8:

- Accelerators – plug-ins or add-ons much like third-party browsers allow users to perform common tasks, such as blogging, e-mail, searching, translating, etc., quicker from within IE.

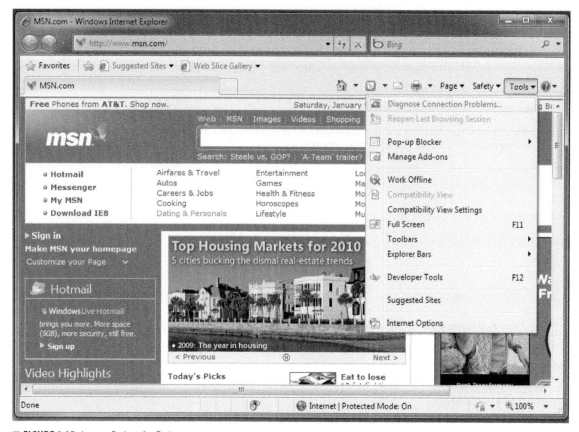

■ FIGURE 1.15 Internet Explorer 8 – Tools

- Compatibility View – toolbar to display Web sites with IE 7 rendering, necessary due to Microsoft not following any standards when it comes to Web browsing.
- Security Features – the most important reason to move to IE 8. End user training is critical for these features to be effective.
  - ❑ Cross Site Scripting (XSS) Filter – XSS is one of the most used attacks against Web browsing users. IE 8 provides a filter for these types of end user attacks by alerting the user and disabling the harmfuls cripts.
  - ❑ DEP – prevents code from being written to executable memory. A feature available for the entire operating system now protects Web users.
  - ❑ Domain Highlighting – a basic feature that highlights the domain name of the site the user is browsing to in the address bar. This assists trained Web users to visually identify the integrity of the site to avoid phishing and malware sites.

- ❏ InPrivate – IE 8 mode that does not leave traces of browsing history, Internet files, form data, cookies, usernames and passwords, and other private data on the computer.
  - ❏ SmartScreen – set of technologies to detect and block possible malicious Web sites and downloads. IE 8 detects such malicious intent and notifies the user and/or blocks the attempt.
- ■ Web Slices – allows for subscribing to compatible Web sites from within IE 8 to later view the site's content without actually visiting the Web site. The Web sites must be compatible by following a standardized HTML markup format. Compatible sites will show a green slice on the top right of the IE 8 window next to the home button.

Offline Domain Join

Since Windows NT4, client machines have been able to join Windows domains as long as a direct connection to the domain controller was present. With Windows 7 and Windows Server 2008 R2, there is now a way to join an offline client to a domain. A new program called djoin.exe has been introduced to perform this task. Like previous versions of Windows, joining a domain is only available on Professional, Enterprise, and Ultimate editions. This feature will be explained more in-depth in Chapter 6, "Networking and Mobility."

VPN Reconnect

Apart from DirectAccess, Windows 7 also introduces a feature called VPN Reconnect. This feature will be useful for the mobile user that must connect to the corporate network from the road. Prior to VPN Reconnect, if the Internet connection experienced connection issues for a mobile worker that was connected to VPN, the VPN would disconnect and not reconnect when the Internet connection returned. VPN Reconnect resolves that issue by automatically reconnecting to the VPN within the network outage time, as shown in Figure 1.16. VPN Reconnect uses IPsec Tunnel Mode that uses IKEv2. This requires configuration of the VPN server and the VPN client. This feature will be fully explained in Chapter 6, "Networking and Mobility."

Windows Mobility Center

Windows 7 has improved the Mobility Center for managing mobile options for laptops, notebooks, netbooks, tablets, etc. The mobility center allows for easy management of display brightness, volume control, power options, wireless networking, external display, sync center, and presentation settings as shown in Figure 1.17. All these options have been available in prior versions of Windows but not in an easy-to-use central console. This

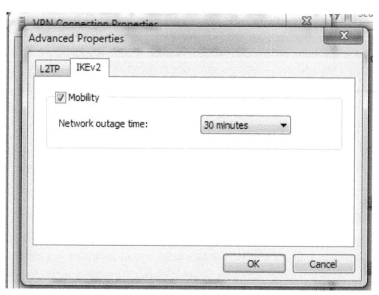

■ FIGURE 1.16 VPN Reconnect – Network Outage Timeout

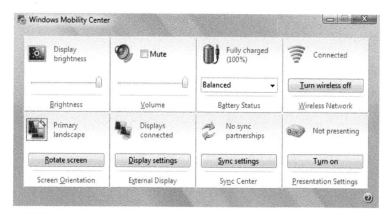

■ FIGURE 1.17 Windows Mobility Center

is definitely a feature that end users should be educated about. This feature is only available on mobile computers and can be started manually from **C:\Windows\System32\mblctr.exe**.

Windows Connect Now

Windows Connect Now was introduced in Windows XP Service Pack 2 but Windows 7 promises more compatibility and easier setup. This feature makes setting up a wireless network quicker and easier for the end user.

The Windows 7 system will connect to the wireless access point or router and automatically set up the device. Once the device is configured, it will automatically set up the computer to connect to the device and save the configuration on USB to easily configure other devices. If the device is already setup, the connection wizard for wireless networking has also been improved for quicker and easier connectivity to already configured wireless networks, as shown in Figure 1.18. This feature will most likely be used by home users and does require the wireless router or access point to be compatible with Windows 7.

Connecting to a network is much simpler in Windows 7:

1. Click the network or wireless logo on the notification area as shown in Figure1.18
2. Click the network that you need to connect to.
3. If it is password protected, input the password and click **Connect**.

Entertainment

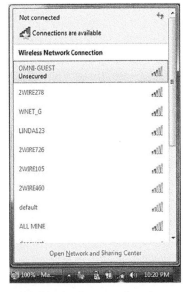

FIGURE 1.18 Connect to a Network

Microsoft Windows operating systems are the standard in PC entertainment. Microsoft continues this trend with many of the new features for Windows 7. Although this is an administrator's reference, we do not want to leave anything out from the end-user's perspective. Most of the features in this section will not be used in the corporate environment and therefore, will not be elaborated on in later chapters. The desktop environment and user interface is discussed in Chapter 3, "Deploying Windows 7 in an Enterprise Environment."

- DirectX11
- Gadgets
- GamesExpl orer
- MultiplayerG ames
- PlayT o
- RemoteM ediaSt reaming
- WindowsM ediaC enter
- WindowsM ediaP layer12

DirectX 11

Windows 7 includes DirectX 11, the latest version of Microsoft's audio and graphics family of APIs. DirectX 11, also known as Direct3D 11 or DX11, will appeal to most gamers and has little to no effect on the business user. Like previous versions, DirectX 11 requires a compatible video card, some of which are set in the second part of 2009 by AMD and NVIDIA, the two largest video card chip makers. Some new features of DX11 include: more efficient leverage of multicore processors for better resource handling, new sophisticated shader technology, enabling the GPU to perform operations other than 3D graphics, more efficient utilization of the processing pipeline, hardware tesselation support for more detailed 3D modeling, and animation.

Independent of what version of DirectX you are capable of running, to make sure DirectX is running correctly you may start the DirectX Diagnostic Tool as shown in Figure 1.19 by typing **dxdiag** in the Start menu Search.

Gadgets

For Windows 7, Microsoft removed the Windows Vista Sidebar and only left the Gadgets feature. The Gadgets in Windows 7 are similar to the Gadgets in Vista as they appear on the desktop but are not mounted to a sidebar. Gadgets were created to integrate the most sought after data from the Internet in a simple and quick fashion.

■ **FIGURE 1.19** DirectX Diagnostic Tool

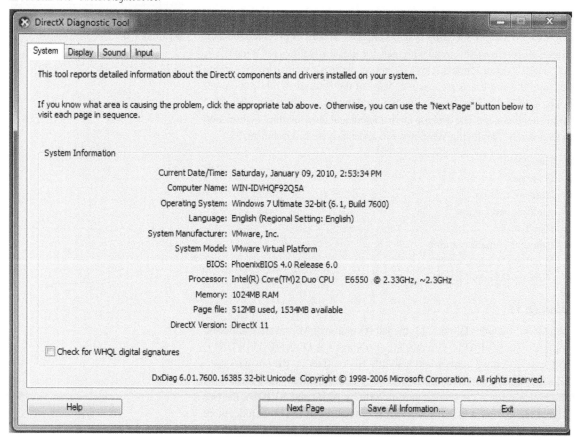

Gadgets are basically mini applications such as a Calendar, Clock, CPU Meter, etc., which provide quick information on the desktop as shown in Figure 1.20. By default, Gadgets are disabled and must be enabled and configured to work. More on Gadgets can be found in Chapter 4, "The New Windows 7 Desktop Environment."

To access and enable Gadgets right-click on the desktop and select **Gadgets** or type **gad** in the Start menu Search.

Games Explorer

Windows 7 is the standard for gaming so Microsoft kept the Games Explorer feature from Windows Vista in this release. The Games Explorer is a quick

■ **FIGURE 1.20** Windows 7 Gadgets

and simple way to launch and organize games as shown in Figure 1.21. It also allows for updates and news feeds and tracks player stats. Third-party games must be compatible with Windows 7 Games Explorer to be automatically added to the Games Explorer. By default, the Games Explorer may be launched from **Start menu | Programs | Games**.

Multiplayer Games

Windows XP multiplayer games are back after being removed from Vista. They can be launched from the Games Explorer and include Internet Checkers, Internet Spades, and Internet Backgammon in 3D as shown in Figure 1.21. This feature may be disabled when deploying or through Group Policy in business environments and will be noted in Chapter 7, "Managing Windows 7 in an Enterprise Environment."

■ **FIGURE 1.21** Windows 7 Games Explorer

Play To

Windows 7 introduces the Play To feature allowing media to be played in other Windows 7 machines or other compatible devices such as an XBOX 360 on the same network. This feature is a part of Windows Media Player 12 and must be enabled for each device.

To set up remote media streaming open Windows Media Player 12, click the **Stream** tab in the Library view, and click More streaming options as shown in Figure 1.22. This may also be accessed through **Control Panel | Network and Sharing Center | Choose homegroup and sharing options**.

Remote Media Streaming

Another feature of Windows Media Player 12 is Remote Media Streaming. This allows for media in a Windows 7 machine to be streamed to other Windows 7 computers in other networks. This feature is similar to devices

■ **FIGURE 1.22** Media Streaming Options

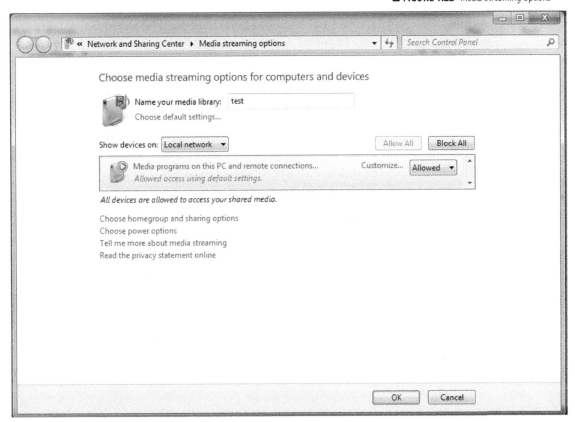

such as Slingbox. Furthermore, this feature requires an online ID to be setup and as of writing it only allows for Windows Live IDs. This feature allows streaming of music, pictures, and video as long as the content is unprotected.

Open Windows Media Player 12, click **Stream** in the top menu and select **Allow Internet Access to Home Media**. A pop-up window will ask you to link an online ID (only Windows Live, as noted above) as shown in Figure 1.23. The same setup must be done from the remote Windows 7 computer.

Windows Media Center

First introduced as its own edition in Windows XP, Windows Media Center is now a feature in Windows Home Premium and Ultimate editions. Windows Media Center lets you watch, pause, and record live TV, listen to music, view pictures, watch movies, and share media, as you can see in Figure 1.24. Windows Media Center promises to be the next TiVo, Moxi, or whatever DVR you use at home. This feature works best with a TV tuner and a remote. Windows Media Center may be launched from **Start menu | All Programs**.

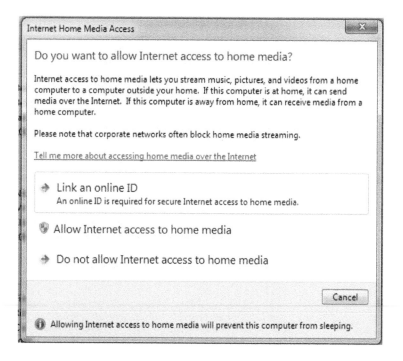

■ **FIGURE 1.23** Internet Home Media Access

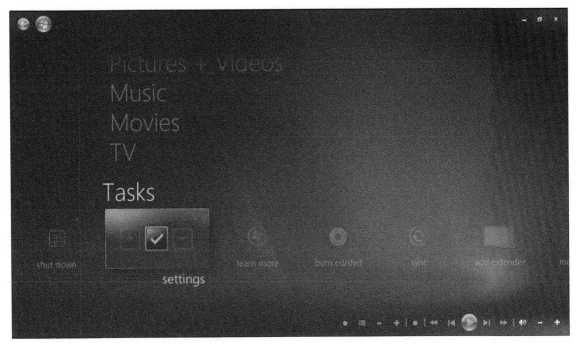

■ **FIGURE 1.24** Windows Media Center

Windows Media Player 12

Apart from some of the streaming features, Microsoft updated Windows Media Player to version 12 on Windows 7. Additionally, Microsoft added default support for many video and audio codecs that in previous versions of Windows would require a third-party installation. This is a great news for administrators and end users alike as many different formats of audio and video will work out of box. There is still a lack of support for the Matroska codec and files in the .mkv format. These can be easily solved by installing the VLC media center as shown in Figure 1.25, available at www.videolan.org/vlc/.

Performance

Microsoft focused most of its development of Windows 7 on performance features. Multiple performance features have been introduced and improved on from Vista. Microsoft realized this was one of the main issues with the Vista release and did not make the same mistake twice. These are some of the new and improved performance features:

- 64-bitC omputing
- ActionC enter

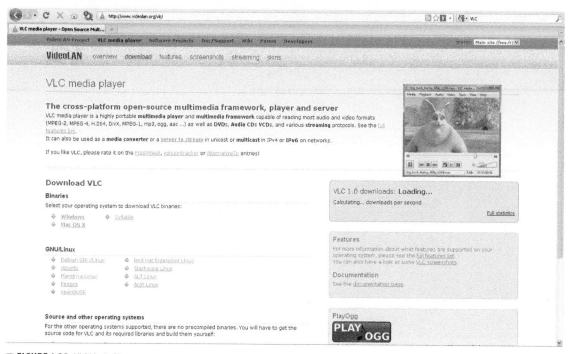

■ FIGURE 1.25 VLC Media Player

- Audioa ndV ideo
- Enhanced Driver and Device Support
- PowerM anagement
- ReadyBoost
- StartupR epair
- SystemR estore
- WindowsA nytimeU pgrade
- WindowsE asyT ransfer
- WindowsE xperienceI ndex(WEI)
- WindowsT roubleshooting
- WindowsU pdate

64-bit Computing

Almost all computers sold in the last few years are 64-bit compatible. In short, this means they have a 64-bit processor. Microsoft has vastly improved 64-bit support in Windows 7. Explained in detail in a previous section, 64-bit computing allows the operating system to handle more than 4 GB of memory so the system can handle larger amounts of information at once.

For 64-bit computing, a 64-bit edition of Windows 7 must be installed. These versions of Windows 7 are available for all editions except for Windows 7 Starter. It is imperative that you install this edition from the start as you will not be able to easily upgrade from a 32-bit to 64-bit version of Windows 7.

Action Center

Microsoft has improved the Security Center from Windows XP SP2 and above and released a new dashboard for Windows 7 called Action Center as shown in Figure 1.26. The Action Center's goal is to be the end users one-stop shop for all security and maintenance needs. Similar to the Security Center, the Action Center notifies the user if there are warnings or issues with the security or maintenance settings of the machine. The user can also choose what alerts to get about these components from the Action Center. Alerts are in two levels distinguished by color. A red warning is an "Important" alert while a yellow warning is a cautionary warning. The Action Center is divided into two parts, security and maintenance.

■ **FIGURE 1.26** Action Center

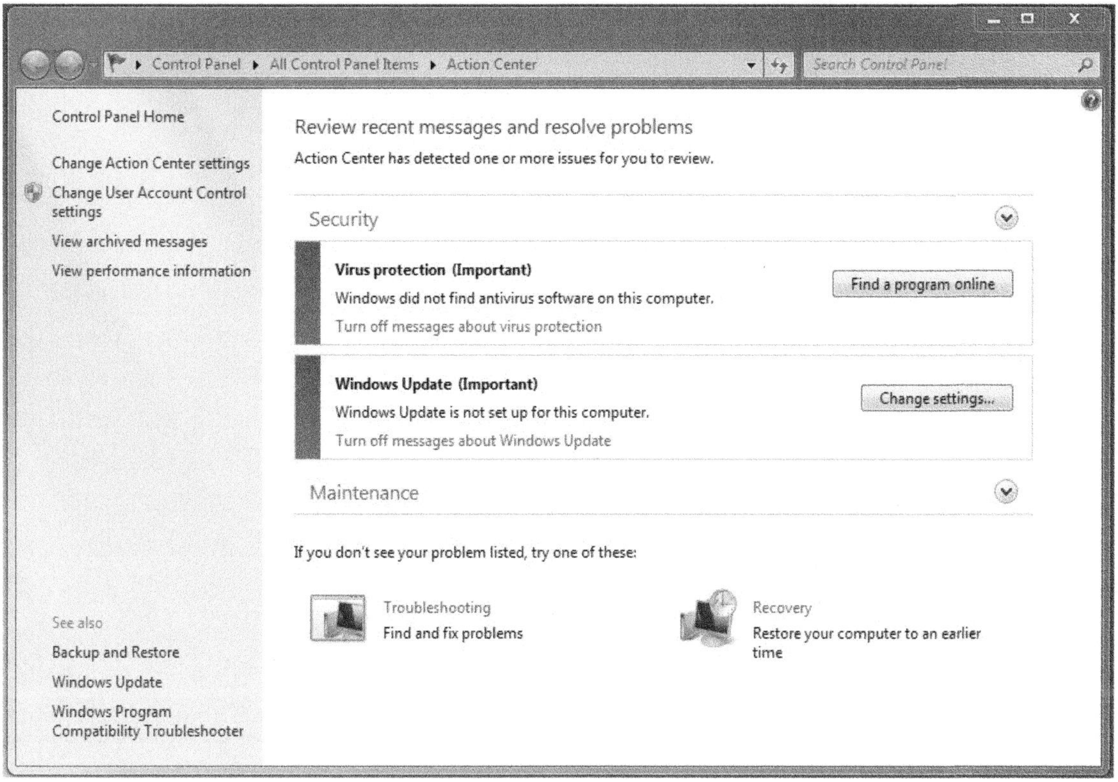

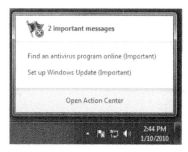

■ FIGURE 1.27 Action Center from
Notification Area

■ FIGURE 1.28 Action Center - Security

The Action Center may be initiated from the notification area through the flag icon as shown in Figure 1.27. It may also be initiated from the Control Panel or by typing **action center** in the Start menu Search.

Security

The security section of the Action Center is the most familiar to Windows XP and Vista users as it is very similar to the Security Center as one can see from Figure 1.28. Here, the user may view and configure alerts of the following security components:

- Network firewall – introduced in Windows XP, the Network firewall is active by default; if turned off the Action Center will display a red warning for this feature.

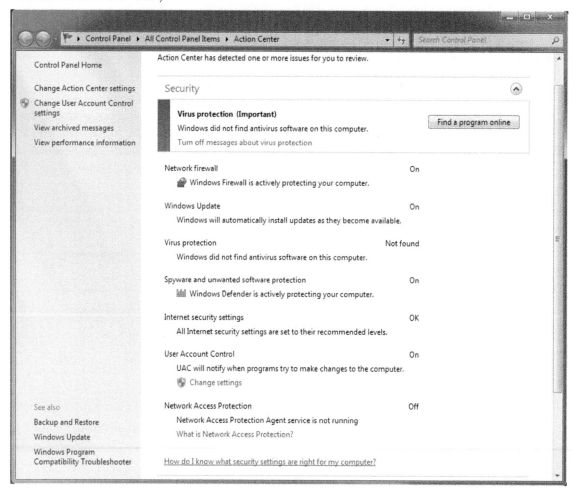

- Windows Update – this feature should always be enabled for automatic install of updates. Choosing anything other than installing updates automatically will yield a yellow or red warning depending on the setting.
- Virus Protection – anti-malware is still required in Windows 7. Not having anti-malware installed will yield a red level warning and not having the software up to date will yield a yellow level warning.
- Spyware and unwanted software protection – this monitors Windows Defender or any other anti-spyware software. Windows Defender is on byde fault.
- Internet security settings – new in Windows 7, this feature monitors the security settings within the Internet browser. This is on by default and Internet settings are set at "recommended levels."
- User Account Control – the famous UAC alert is on by default. In Windows 7, you may change the notification level to four different options. UAC is on by default to alert when programs try to make changes to the computer but not Windows settings. This will be further explored in the Security features section later in this chapter and in Chapter 7, "Managing Windows 7 in an Enterprise Environment."
- Network Access Protection (NAP) – this is for corporate users who use NAP to connect to enterprise networks. This agent is off by default and does not alert of this setting. This setting is activated and alerts by default when the NAP agent is installed and/or not compliant.

Maintenance

The maintenance section of the Action Center is new and should prove to be very useful for the educated user. Here alert settings can be configured and viewed for common maintenance issues such as Backup, Troubleshooting, Updates, and System Maintenance as shown in Figure 1.29. All alerts in this section are on by default and a yellow warning will appear if Backup has not yet been configured. Backup and Troubleshooting will be elaborated on in the Security features section.

Audio and Video

Windows 7 has multiple enhancements to audio and video features. The initial observation should be the automatic enhanced support for audio and video devices, which will be covered when discussing the next feature. Automatic Stream Management has been introduced to route audio to the correct place depending on the device. For instance, Internet calls should be played through a headset instead of speakers while a CD should be played on the speakers instead of a headset. New video features include Display Color Calibration and detection of external video devices such as projectors and televisions.

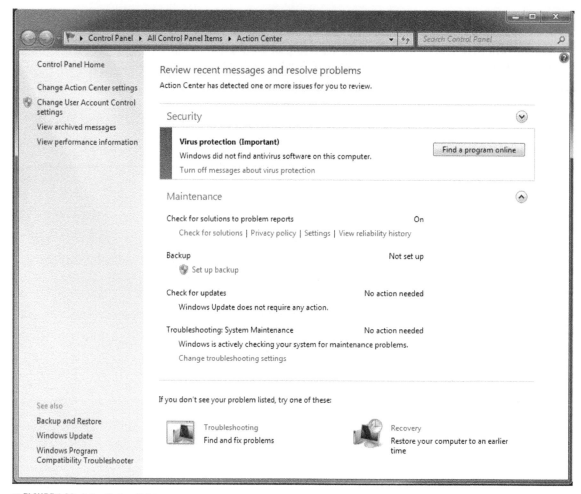

■ **FIGURE 1.29** Action Center - Maintenance

Automatic enhanced audio and video support is on by default but may be adjusted through the **Sound** console in the Control Panel. To configure automatic adjustment of volume depending on the sound, go to the **Communications** tab of the **Sound** console as shown in Figure 1.30.

Video and display options may be accessed by right-clicking the desktop and selecting **Screen Resolution** or choosing the **Display** icon in the Control Panel as shown in Figure 1.31. There are many options for video and display from resolution to themes to color calibration etc., among others. These will all be looked at more in-depth in Chapter 4, "The New Windows 7 Desktop Environment."

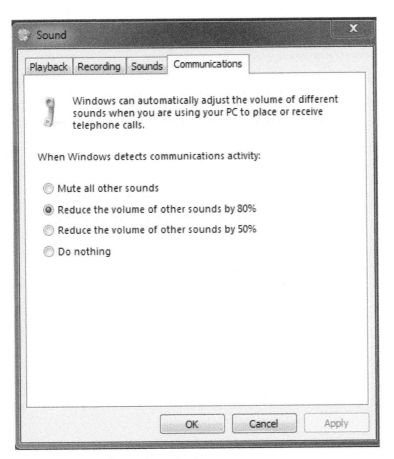

■ **FIGURE 1.30** Sound Options - Communications

Enhanced Driver and Device Support

One of the major issues users and administrators had with Windows Vista was the driver and device support for hardware. Microsoft has concentrated on this issue and believes to have resolved it with enhanced driver and device support. Generally, new releases of Windows have these compatibility issues, however, remember that Windows 7 was built on top of Vista technology. Therefore, Microsoft declares that all hardware should be compatible with Windows 7 if it was compatible with Vista. Apart from using Vista technology, Microsoft seems to have gone out of its way for better driver support by developing the operating system to work better with third-party hardware. As Figure 1.32 shows, all the drivers on this default install of Windows 7 were recognized and installed.

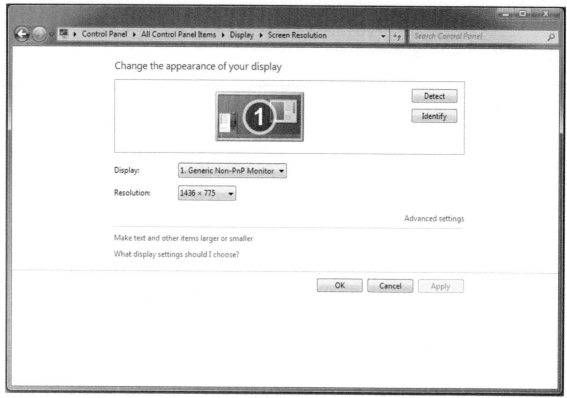

■ **FIGURE 1.31** Display Options — Screen Resolution

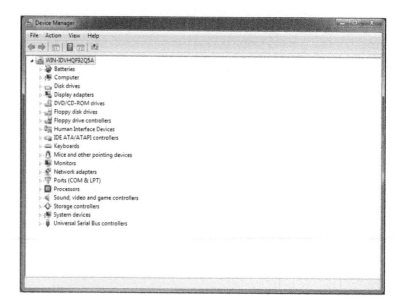

■ **FIGURE 1.32** Device Manager

The Device Manger may be accessed by clicking on **System** in the Control Panel and then **Device Manager** on the left-hand menu. Another way is right-clicking on **Computer**, clicking **Properties**, and then **Device Manager** on the menu on the left.

Power Management

Although power management has been available in Windows from previous releases, Windows 7 has improved the power management feature. As the environmental trends continue to push towards "going green" and organizations realize that the electric bill (overhead) can be lowered, Microsoft has improved the power management of Windows 7 systems to save energy and power. The power options are similar to Windows Vista but have more advanced settings and are defaulted to be energy efficient by dimming the display when it is idle.

Power Management may be accessed from the Control Panel by clicking **Power Options**. The immediate options are Balanced and Power saver as shown in Figure 1.33. To change advanced settings, select **Change plan settings** to the right of these options. More options are available on the left menu.

ReadyBoost

Introduced in Windows Vista, ReadyBoost has been improved to support more flash storage devices and the amount of maximum additional memory. ReadyBoost is for machines that require more memory (RAM) but do not have it available. Generally, Windows will use the hard drive to store files that should be in memory. Accessing files from the hard drive that should be in memory makes applications and the entire system run slower. ReadyBoost offers a solution by allowing the user to use external flash

> **TIP**
>
> TheA ctionC enter'sM aintenance section has a new troubleshooting feature. The troubleshooting options may be accessed from the Control Panel by clicking the **Troubleshooting** icon. By clicking **Check for solutions**, Windows7 will scan the machine for issues and find solutions. This is a first great step to troubleshoot any issue, especially hardware support issues.
>
> Training end users to use these features could prove to be a huge time saver to troubleshoot issues before calling the help desk or openinga t icket.

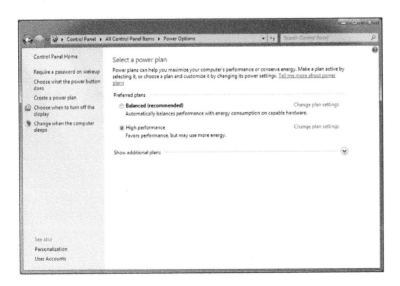

■ **FIGURE 1.33** Power Management

memory such as a thumb drive to emulate RAM and store files there instead of the hard drive. In Windows 7, it has been proven to be faster than using the hard drive for systems with memory limitations. In this version of Windows, up to eight flash devices are able to use ReadyBoost at once for a maximum of 256GB of additional memory.

To set up ReadyBoost, insert the flash device and select **Use as ReadyBoost** on the AutoPlay screen or open Windows Explorer, right-click on the device and select **Properties**. Click on the **ReadyBoost** tab and select **Use this device**. The amount of memory to set as reserved is given as an option to avoid storage limitations as shown in Figure 1.34.

■ **FIGURE 1.34** ReadyBoost Properties

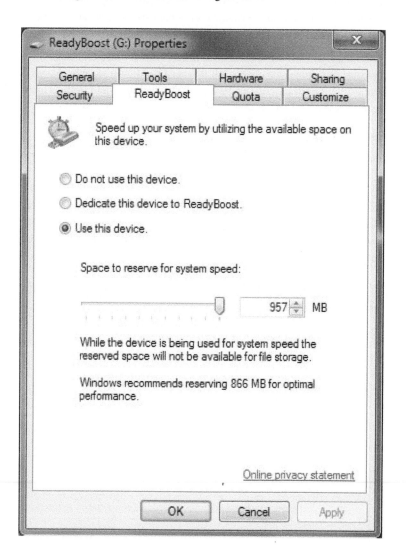

Startup Repair

A Windows system will more than likely experience some sort of issue on a machine during its lifetime. The Startup Repair feature has been refined from its original release in Windows Vista to work better and more consistently. Microsoft has decided to install the Startup Repair tools in a separate partition that is automatically created when you install Windows 7.

If a Windows 7 system is having trouble booting up the first troubleshooting step is to attempt a startup repair. Automatically after a failed startup attempt, Windows 7 will attempt to start the Startup Repair feature to assist with the issue. To access the Startup Repair, you may also press the **F8** key prior to boot after the BIOS prompt as shown in Figure 1.35. This will launch the System Recovery Options as shown in Figure 1.36:

> **NOTE**
> Wheni nstalling Windows7 , Microsoft will automatically set a hidden primary system partition of 100 MB. This hidden partition is used for Windows Recovery Environment, which includes the tools needed for the Windows 7 Startup Repairf eature.

■ **FIGURE 1.35** Launch Startup Repair

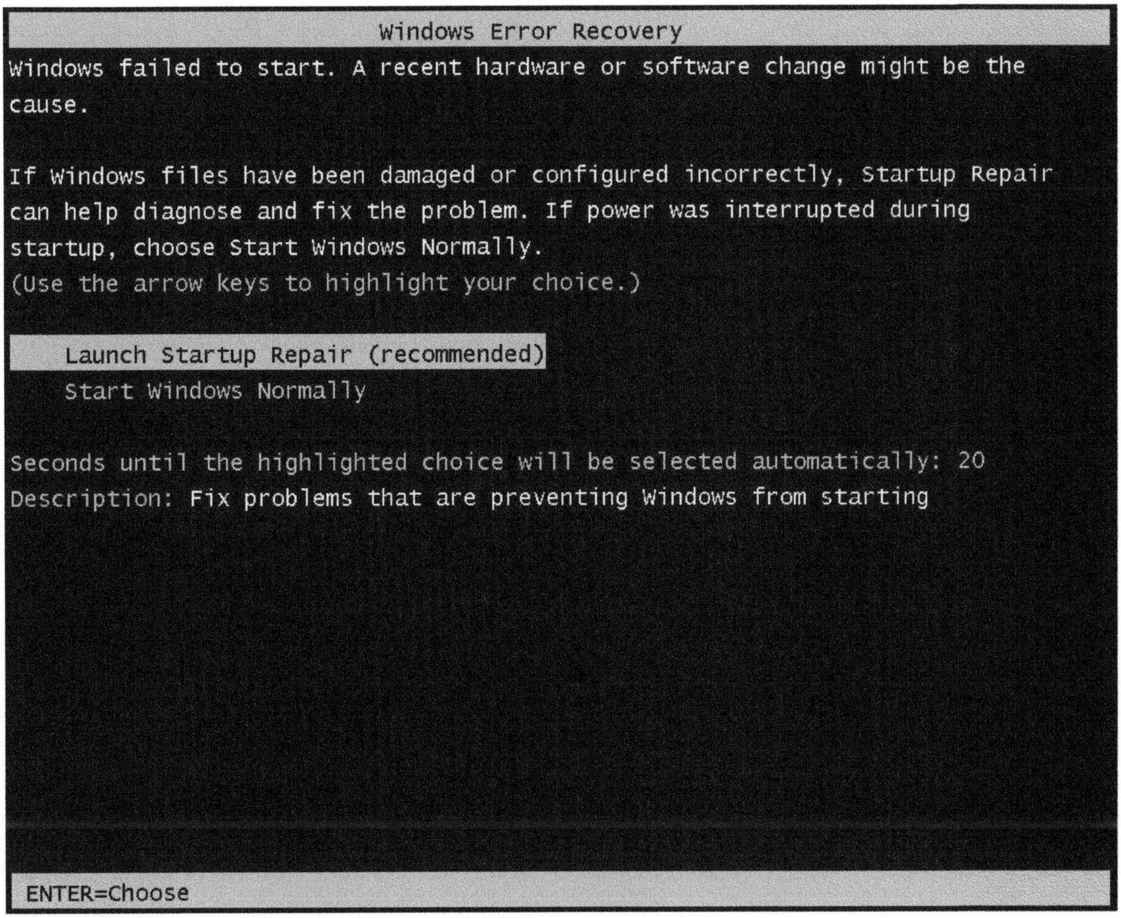

```
                    Windows Error Recovery
Windows failed to start. A recent hardware or software change might be the
cause.

If Windows files have been damaged or configured incorrectly, Startup Repair
can help diagnose and fix the problem. If power was interrupted during
startup, choose Start Windows Normally.
(Use the arrow keys to highlight your choice.)


     Launch Startup Repair (recommended)
        Start Windows Normally


Seconds until the highlighted choice will be selected automatically: 20
Description: Fix problems that are preventing Windows from starting




 ENTER=Choose
```

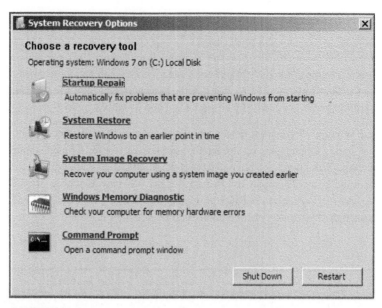

■ **FIGURE 1.36** System Recovery Options

- **Startup Repair** – Windows 7 will attempt to automatically fix any issue preventing Windows from starting. This will start automatically after a failed boot sequence.
- **System Restore** – this feature is available from the System Recovery Options to restore to a previous restore point.
- **System Image Recovery** – this option allows a recovery from a systemi mage.
- **Windows Memory Diagnostic** – this will check your memory for hardwaree rrors.
- **Command Prompt** – a traditional command prompt to troubleshoot Windowsvi ac ommandl ine.

The System Recovery Options and Startup Repair may also be started from a Windows 7 installation disk by booting from the removable media device.

System Restore

The System Restore feature of Windows continues to be improved. This feature assists in restoring a system to a previous restore point. By default Windows 7 will create restore points when software is installed, updated, or patched and at other automatic intervals. This has proven to be helpful for restoring systems infected with malware or corrupted by software installs.

When you are choosing a restore point, Windows 7 will also display the software that will be removed by reverting to the restore point.

System Restore may be started with the System Recovery Options by booting the system and pressing **F8** after the BIOS or booting from the Windows 7 installation media. System Restore may also be accessed from within the system in the Action Center or the **Recovery** icon in the Control Panel as shown in Figure 1.37.

For administrators who have multiple hosts to manage, Windows 7 allows for remotely creating system restore points with PowerShell. This can prove to be helpful to managing remote system restore features.

The System Restore process is a straightforward wizard. The first wizard informs you that System Restore can help fix issues that might make your computer slow or irresponsive. It does not affect your documents, pictures, or other personal data. Clicking **Next** allows you to choose where you would

■ **FIGURE 1.37** System Restore

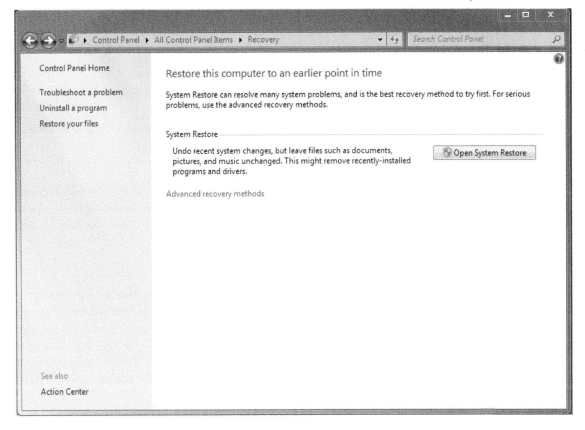

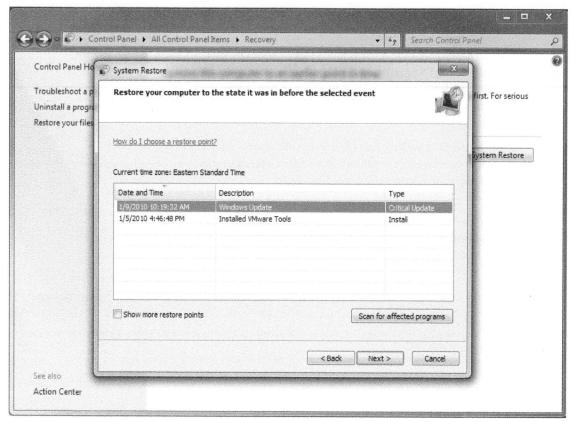

■ **FIGURE 1.38** System Restore – Choose Restore Point

like to restore to as shown in Figure 1.38. The **Scan for affected programs** button looks for the programs that will most likely be removed if the restore point is applied. A confirmation screen requests a final click before beginning the restore process.

Windows Anytime Upgrade

Windows 7 now has the capability to upgrade from a lower version of Windows to a more powerful version at any time. The Windows Anytime Upgrade is an applet located in the Control Panel under **System** and **Security** or by typing **anytime** in the Start menu Search. Through the wizard, you may choose to purchase an upgrade key online or enter the upgrade key that you already obtained as shown in Figure 1.39. The same wizard will update your system to the chosen version.

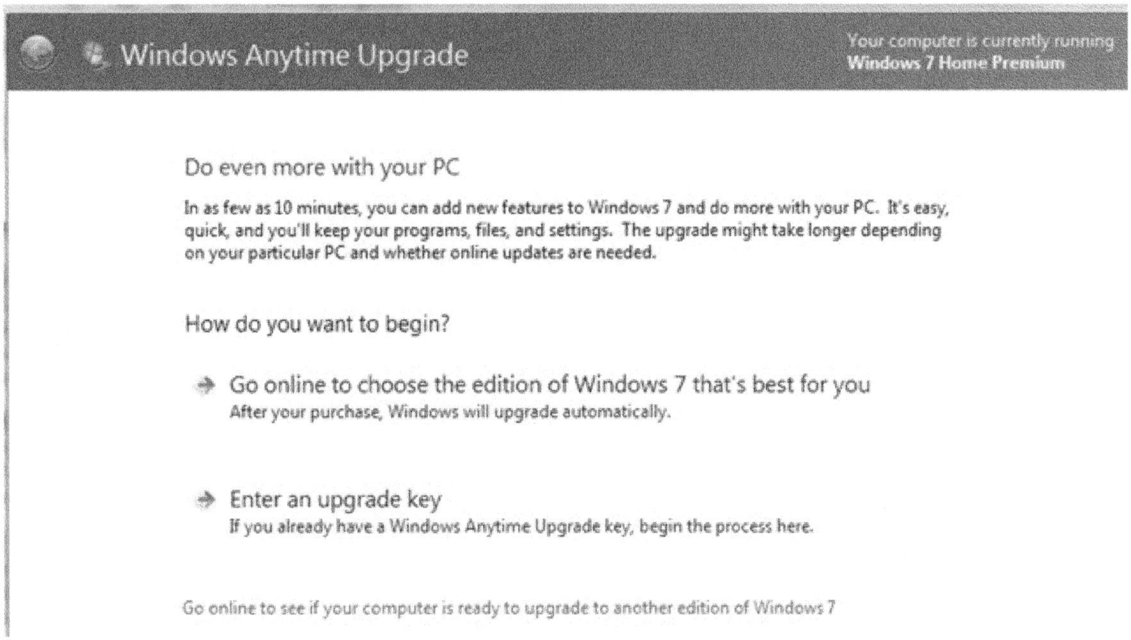

Windows Anytime Upgrade — *Your computer is currently running Windows 7 Home Premium*

Do even more with your PC

In as few as 10 minutes, you can add new features to Windows 7 and do more with your PC. It's easy, quick, and you'll keep your programs, files, and settings. The upgrade might take longer depending on your particular PC and whether online updates are needed.

How do you want to begin?

→ Go online to choose the edition of Windows 7 that's best for you
After your purchase, Windows will upgrade automatically.

→ Enter an upgrade key
If you already have a Windows Anytime Upgrade key, begin the process here.

Go online to see if your computer is ready to upgrade to another edition of Windows 7

■ FIGURE 1.39 Windows Anytime Upgrade – Options

The Windows Anytime Upgrade has restrictions as to what version can be updated to another version. For starters, only 32-bit to 32-bit and 64-bit to 64-bit versions upgrades are possible. From Windows 7 Starter, you may upgrade to Home Premium, Professional, or Ultimate. From Windows 7 Home Premium, you may upgrade to Windows 7 Professional and Ultimate as shown in Figure 1.40; and from Windows 7 Professional you can upgrade to Windows 7 Ultimate. There is no Anytime Upgrade to Enterprise version as it is only obtained through volume licensing.

Windows Easy Transfer

Windows 7 has improved Windows Easy Transfer for more consistent and successful migrations of Windows XP and Vista user data to Windows 7. Windows Easy Transfer is a small application for Windows XP and Vista that assists with migrating user data to Windows 7. In older versions, this process was usually unsuccessful but the new version promises to be better.

Windows Easy Transfer supports transporting user data via USB Easy Transfer Cable, the network, or removable media. A USB Easy Transfer

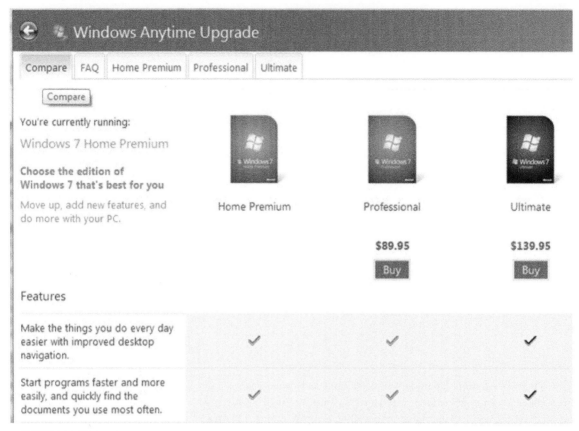

FIGURE 1.40 Windows Anytime Upgrade – Windows 7 Home Premium Upgrade Path

Cable is special male USB to male USB cable used to plug two computers together. We have found the easiest method to be using removable media such as an external hard drive or flash drive or a network share.

Windows Easy Transfer is included in the Windows 7 install media and can also be downloaded for both 32-bit and 64-bit versions of Windows Vista and XP. Windows Easy Transfer is included in all Windows 7 installs under **Start menu | All Programs | Accessories | System Tools** as shown in Figure 1.41. This install file can be found on Microsoft's Web site and users should be cautious about downloading this from other sources. The install is located on the Windows 7 install medium in the support\migwiz folder as migsetup.exe. Once installed, the Windows Easy Transfer is a simple wizard that allows users to migrate data from the machine to a new Windows 7 machine.

Upgrading to Windows 7 through the upgrade option in Windows Setup is very limited as you will see in Chapter 2, "Installing and Upgrading to

■ FIGURE 1.41 Windows Easy Transfer

Windows 7." The Windows Easy Transfer is one of the quickest and easiest ways to migrate data from a single machine to a new Windows 7 system.

Windows Experience Index

The WEI was introduced in Windows Vista and has been improved for Windows 7. The WEI is a Microsoft method of comparing the performance of the hardware capabilities of your system. WEI tests the performance of the processor, memory, general graphics, gaming/3D graphics, and the hard drive. Each component is rated a individually. The weakest score is the system's base score. In Windows 7, the scores may range from 1.0 to 7.9.

To rate your system and obtain your WEI, you must go to **System Properties** through the Control Panel or right-click **Computer | Properties**. Under

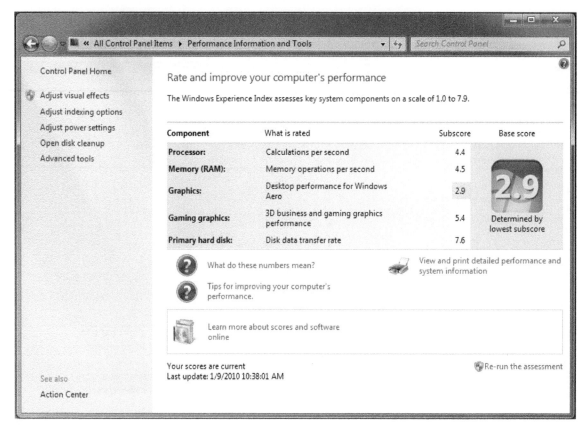

■ **FIGURE 1.42** Windows Experience Index

the System heading is the rating. You may click on the **WEI** to show the scores (Figure 1.42). On the bottom right, you may rerun the assessment to obtain the latest score if new drivers were installed or you have never run the test. You may rerun the test as many times as you would like but the scores do not change unless you change the hardware or drivers.

Windows Troubleshooting

Windows 7 introduces Troubleshooting; troubleshooting should start here. Found in the Control Panel under Troubleshooting or the Action Center as shown in Figure 1.43, Windows 7 provides users a centralized console to troubleshoot the more common issues with networking, Internet, audio, video, program compatibility, and driver issues. Common issues that Windows Troubleshooting has been known to fix are problems with printing, connecting to the Internet, and program compatibility issues.

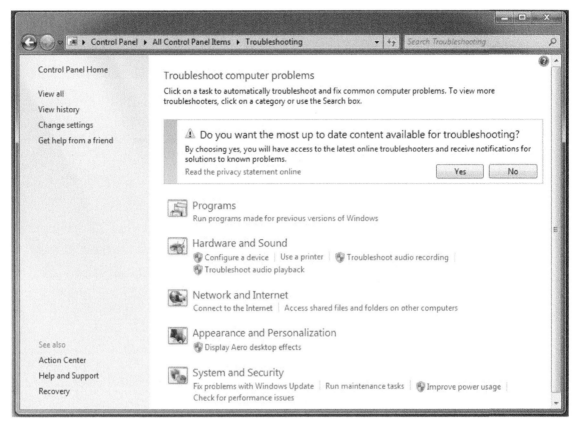

■ **FIGURE 1.43** Windows Troubleshooting

Windows Update

Windows Update should not be new to anyone but the way it works has changed in Windows 7 over Vista and especially over Windows XP. Unlike Windows XP where an IE window was used to check for and install updates, Windows 7 has a Windows Update console to do such tasks as shown in Figure 1.44. If set to automatic, this console will not get much use. Windows Update may be found **Start menu | All Programs** through the Control Panel, or in the Action Center. It should go without mentioning that Windows Update is critical to security and should be enabled for automatic updating. Traditionally, operating system patches and updates were not installed in a timely fashion due to fear of issues. Today, updates for Windows must be installed almost instantly as malicious hackers create exploits for the same vulnerabilitiesa lmosti mmediately.

Windows Update is accessed from **Control Panel | Windows Update**, Action Center, or **Start menu | All Programs | Windows Update**.

WARNING

Make sure to apply all patches and updates to Windows 7 and ALL software installed on the system in a timely fashion. Often the day after Microsoft releases patches for vulnerabilities crackers (malicious hackers) develop exploits for the same. This is critical to keeping a secure operating system.

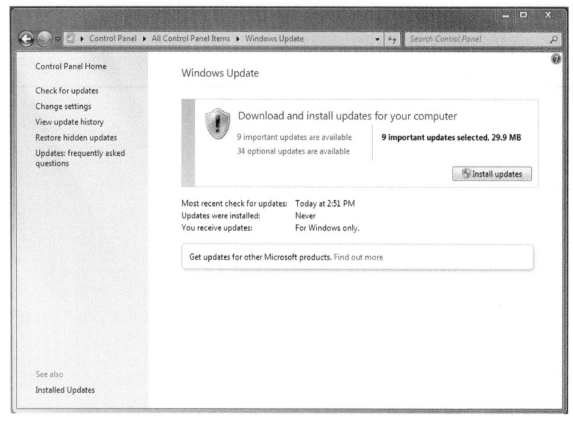

■ **FIGURE 1.44** Windows Update

Productivity

Productivity features are going to be a big highlight of this book. As administrators we must be efficient and productive. Furthermore, we often need to train our users to be more efficient in performing their daily tasks. Most of these new and improved features will be elaborated upon in later chapters:

- Accessibility
- Aero
- Calculator
- Desktop
- DeviceM anagement
- FederatedS earch
- GettingS tarted
- JumpL ists

- Libraries
- LocationA wareP rinting
- MultilingualU serI nterface
- Paint
- ProblemS tepsR ecorder
- SnippingTool s
- StickyN otes
- TabletPC
- WindowsFa xa ndSc an
- WindowsLi veE ssentials
- WindowsSe arch
- WindowsTa skbar
- WindowsTouc h
- WindowsX PM ode
- WordPad
- XPSV iewer

Accessibility

Windows 7 has improved all of the accessibility features from past Windows versions and improved the way users interact with the system. In Windows 7 the Accessibility features are called Ease of Access and are located in **Start menu | All Programs | Accessories**. All of the Ease of Access features are available before login by clicking the **Ease of Access** icon on the bottom left of the screen as shown in Figure 1.45. Additionally, an Ease of Access Center exists in the Control Panel and **Start menu | All Programs | Accessories | Ease of Access** to manage Ease of Access settings and other common related settings as shown in Figure 1.46.

Magnifier

The Magnifier has been improved and users with low vision will enjoy the new features. The Magnifier can enlarge harder-to-see text and pictures when it is enabled. Three view options are available: full-screen mode, lens mode, and docked mode. Each view option then has other options accessible by clicking the **Settings** button to the right of the **Views** button. These options are available by clicking the **magnifying lens** on the desktop as shown in Figure 1.47. Full screen mode enlarges the entire desktop while Lens mode zooms on a particular area, and Docked mode creates a dock on the top of the screen. The Lens mode can be set to follow the mouse or the keyboard focus. Many other options exist depending on the view setting. Figure 1.47 shows options for Full screen view.

■ **FIGURE 1.45** Accessibility at Logon

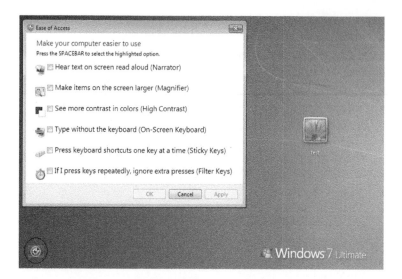

■ **FIGURE 1.46** Ease of Access Center

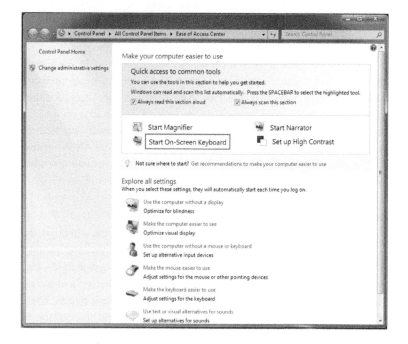

Narrator

Windows 7 includes Microsoft Narrator, which reads on-screen text to the user through the speakers or headset as shown on Figure 1.48. Microsoft Narrator can echo the user's keystrokes, announce system messages, and

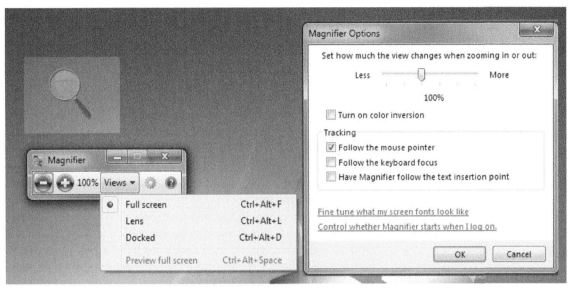

■ **FIGURE 1.47** Magnifier Options

■ **FIGURE 1.48** Microsoft Narrator

announce scroll notifications. This feature can prove helpful to some users and is recommended to at least mention to your users in case they do find this useful.

On-Screen Keyboard

Windows 7 has improved the on-screen keyboard as well. It is visually more appealing as shown in Figure 1.49 and works with multiple inputs such as clicking mode, hovering mode, and scanning mode. Also with the Windows Touch features and the correct hardware you may use touch as an input method.

SpeechR ecognition

By far the most improved Accessibility feature in Windows 7 is Speech Recognition. This feature, bundled with a microphone or headset, allows for the dictating of commands that are understood by Windows and is used to start an e-mail client, surf the Internet without a keyboard, and even dictate your documents.

Like all voice recognition software, this feature requires a bit of training on your part to help the computer's capability to understand you. To access Speech Recognition, go to **Control Panel | Ease of Access | Speech Recognition** or start it through **Start menu | All Programs | Accessibility | Ease of Access**. Once started, a wizard will greet you to easily set up and configure this feature as shown in Figure 1.50. First, you must configure an input device such as a microphone on a headset, webcam, or standalone device. This step also involves testing the microphone location with a sentence you must read aloud. The rest of the wizard asks questions about things such as document review and startup options.

TIP

Theo n-screenk eyboardm ay come in handy if the physical keyboard is experiencing problems or notr esponding.

TIP

Itis hig hlyr ecommendedt he tutorials are used and followed when this feature is first being set up. Like other speech recognition software, the computer needs to "learn" to better understand your voice and commands. You will find that skipping this step results in many errors recognizing your speech.

■ **FIGURE 1.49** On-Screen Keyboard

■ **FIGURE 1.50** Speech Recognition Setup

Aero

Microsoft introduced the Aero desktop experience in Windows Vista and this is by far the most noticeable difference in Windows 7 if you skipped Vista. The Aero desktop features are available in Windows 7 Home Premium and above with a compatible video card. These features are the eye candy of Windows 7 as it mixes cool graphics and a few new features to managing your desktop.

Aero might not be enabled by default if the video drivers were not properly installed during Windows 7 setup. Aero may be enabled in the Control Panel under **Personalization** or by right-clicking the desktop and selecting

Personalize. Once in this menu, select any theme under Aero Themes as showni n Figure1.51 .

Windows Aero include seven themes by default. Each theme has a number of default backgrounds that change every 30 minutes by default, a Windows Color, Sounds, and a screen saver. As you may notice in the Power Options, most screen savers are disabled in exchange for more the efficient energy step of sleeping the display.

Windows also includes six Basic and High Contrast Themes that do not use the Aero features. This might be the default if your video hardware does not meet requirements or you have a version of Windows 7 that does not support Aero features.

■ **FIGURE 1.51** Personalization

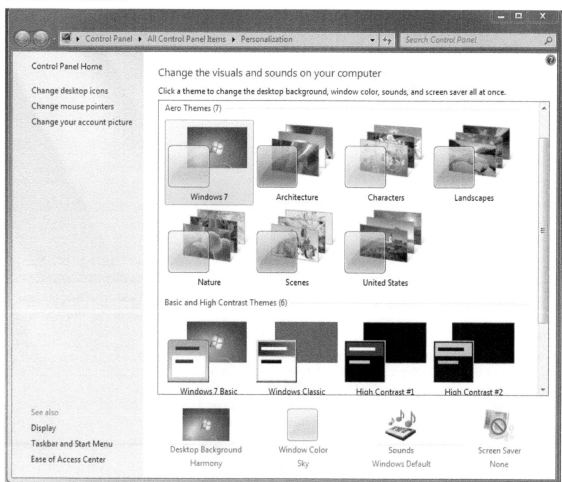

The Windows Aero Experience includes a few other hidden features you should be aware of and can even make users more efficient as they adapt to Windows 7's desktop experience. These features are Aero Peak, Aero Shake, and Aero Snap. A brief introduction follows but these will be elaborated on in Chapter 4, "The New Windows 7 Desktop Environment."

AeroP eek

Aero Peek is enabled by default and is evident by the small bar at the right of the taskbar. Moving your mouse to this area will reveal an X-ray like view of all open windows in the desktop as shown in Figure 1.52. The **Show Desktop** feature that was traditionally in the quick launch bar in prior versions of Windows is now accessible by clicking on this same sidebar to the right of the taskbar as shown in Figure 1.52. Additionally, Aero Peek allows "peeking" at what a program is displaying, even if it is hidden, by placing your mouse over an icon on the taskbar. Some programs even have buttons during the Aero Peek display. An example is iTunes which allows for pausing or changing songs through the pop-up.

AeroS hake

Aero Shake is a simple and hidden feature of the Aero Desktop Experience. This feature allows a user to select a window by clicking on the pane and shaking the

■ **FIGURE 1.52** Aero Peek

mouse to minimize all other windows except the one selected. Another shake of the mouse brings all the windows back. This may be done if the window is maximized or not. This feature can prove to be convenient and perhaps even make users more efficient as they may manage their open applications better.

AeroS nap

Aero Snap is also a hidden feature of the Aero Desktop Experience. This feature allows the user to better organize open windows for reading, organizing, or comparing the content in each window. By grabbing the open window pane with the mouse and moving it to any of the four corners of the desktop as shown in Figure 1.53, the window is resized to take half of the screen. Do this with another open window to another corner and watch both windows be perfectly organized side by side. Also, moving the open window pane to the top of the desktop will open the window in full screen mode. This feature can also assist users in organizing the open windows and applications to almost give a dual monitor effect, allowing the user to be more productive, efficient, and organized.

Calculator

Even the Windows Calculator has been improved in Windows 7. It now contains a new user interface with a cleaner look as well as many new features.

■ **FIGURE 1.53** Aero Snap - Left

It allows for different types of calculations such as Standard, Scientific, Programmer, and Statistics as shown in Figure 1.54. History may also be enabled to see past computations. The Windows 7 Calculator also has added features to calculate fuel economy, mortgages, leases, and can even do unit conversions. On Windows Touch enabled hardware, users will be able to tap calculations on the screen allowing for better usability and efficiency.

The Calculator is found in **Start menu | All Programs | Accessories** or by typing **calc** on the Start menu Search.

Desktop

As you might have already witnessed the Windows desktop has been vastly improved. New Aero features discussed in the previous section such as Shake, Snap, and Peek allow for better desktop management. Additionally, Gadgets have been enabled without a sidebar as they were in Vista making them easier to access and more convenient. The taskbar has also been improved to store shortcuts for the most used programs allowing for quick launching and searching already open windows. Lastly, Microsoft has included a number of new and very good looking wallpapers for themes.

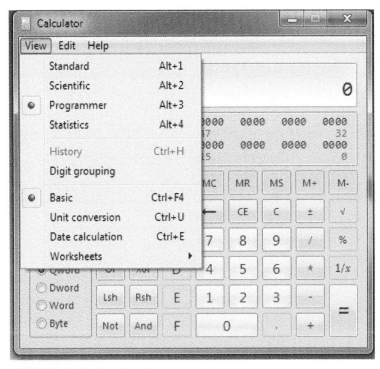

■ **FIGURE 1.54** Calculator – View Options

FIGURE 1.55 Right-Click Desktop Options

Depending on what version of Windows 7 you are running, some of these features may not be enabled. To modify desktop options you may right-click the desktop and select the desired configuration as shown in Figure 1.55 or select the **Personalize** icon from the Control Panel.

Device Management

Windows 7 has improved Device Management tenfold. Vista users and administrators know the headaches cause by Vista's poor device and hardware management offerings. Windows 7 has fixed those issues with two new features: Device Stage and Device and Printers console.

DeviceS tage

The Device Stage is a new feature in Windows 7 designed to be the portal between your hardware device and your system. Depending on the device plugged in the Device Stage will provide the most popular tasks for that specific device. Figure 1.56 displays the Device Stage options for a Nokia N95. For instance, a mobile phone will allow easy managing of music on the device, syncing, and other device-related options. A multifunction office device would allow for easy printing, scanning, and faxing services from

FIGURE 1.56 Device Stage

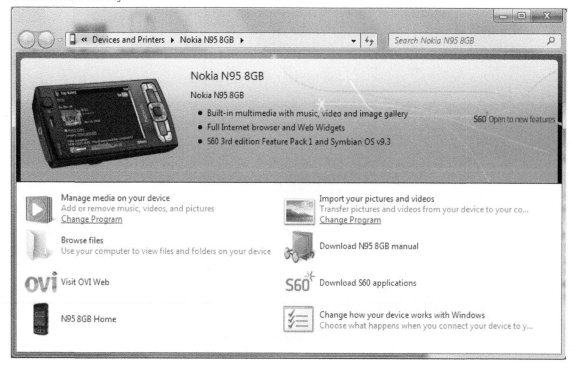

a central console. Additionally, device manufactures can customize the Device Stage options for their specific device.

To access the Device Stage console for a device, simply plug it in and start the Device Stage from the AutoPlay options or by selecting **Hardware and Sound** in the Control Panel.

Devicesa ndP rinters

The Devices and Printers Control Panel feature shows all devices connected to the PC. This allows for checking the status of printers, media players, cameras, mouse, keyboard, display, and digital photo frames to list a few. This new central console for devices should prove to make end users more efficient by providing a single location to perform actions on the desired device. This option may be accessed from the Control Panel by selecting **Hardware and Sound** and then **Devices and Printers** (Figure1.57) .

Federated Search

Federated Search is the simultaneous search of multiple resources. This term originally referred to the searching of multiple Web pages, resources,

■ **FIGURE 1.57** Devices and Printers

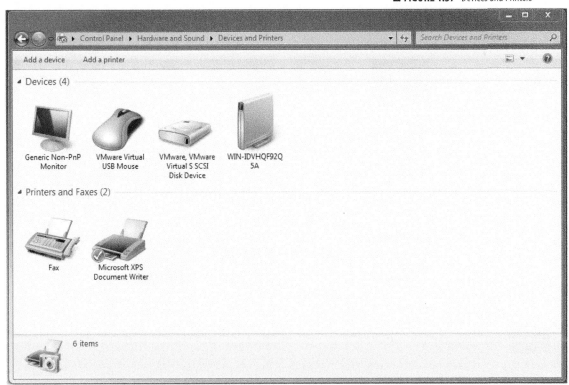

WARNING

Ass earchconne ctorsa rec ustom made and downloaded from the Internet, make sure the creator and site is trusted. Malicious hackers or even spammers could find ways to install malware through the search connectors or even search malicious sites. As always, end user security awareness and training is critical to run a safe computinge nvironment.

databases, etc. While Windows Search allows searching the entire local system and a limited amount of external resources such as shared drives, Federated Search allows searching way beyond the local PC to multiple remote repositories. Based on the open standard OpenSearch and RSS format, custom search connectors can be used to search multiple remote resources. In an enterprise, this can include searching multiple SharePoint sites and other Web applications. This option allows for easier discovery of corporate information and data from within Windows Explorer.

From the end-user's perspective, Federated Search can be used to search multiple external Web sites from within the Windows 7 Windows Explorer. This is possible by installing search connectors that have been custom made and configured for the site the end user wishes to search. As a new feature in Windows 7 there are not many search connectors available as of this writing, however, search connectors are available for searching Twitter, Bing, Google News, and even MSDN forums as shown on Figure 1.58.

■ **FIGURE 1.58** Search Connectors

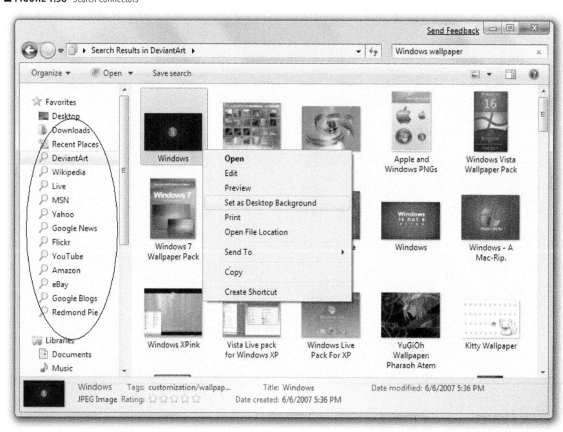

Getting Started

The Getting Started feature was introduced in Windows Vista for desktop users to quickly grasp the new features of the latest Windows operating system. By default, this screen will pop up the first two times a new user logs in. The second time it may be selected to never initialize with the login by clicking the check box on the bottom left of the screen. To open the **Getting Started** console, a user may navigate to the Control Panel and then select **Getting Started**.

The **Getting Started** console educates end users about getting online, personalizing the Windows Desktop Experience, transferring files and settings from other machines, setting up networking, using Windows Live Essentials, and managing users, among other options, as shown in Figure 1.59. This is one of the simplest ways for users to get started with Windows 7 and any new user should check it out the first time they log in to Windows 7 to become more familiar, unless of course you provide the user this book.

■ **FIGURE 1.59** Getting Started

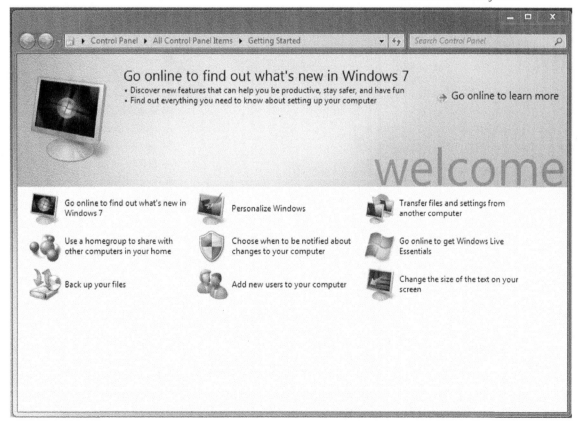

Jump Lists

Jump Lists are new in Windows 7 and can prove to assist users in being more productive. By right-clicking an icon on the taskbar or the arrow in the Start menu as shown in Figure 1.60, the Jump List for that application will pop up. The Jump List options for each application are different. For instance, IE 8 lists tasks such as Start InPrivate Browsing and Open New Tab; also frequently-viewed Web sites will be displayed in the Frequent section. For other applications like Microsoft Word or Media Player options like Recent or Play will be available.

Libraries

Libraries are also a new feature in Windows 7 introduced earlier and referenced in Figure 1.7, Figure 1.9, and Figure 1.10. Libraries are integrated in Windows Explorer and are designed to find and organize files scattered across a PC and/or network. This feature brings all your documents, music, pictures, or videos together into one area that might seem like a folder

■ **FIGURE 1.60** Jump List

although the files are in different locations on the system and/or network. A user can create his or her own Libraries; for instance, a "Work Files" Library can be linked to a folder in the user's profile, a shared network drive, and an external media device bringing all the files in the different locations into a single window.

This feature can prove to make users more productive by easily locating files. Libraries may be accessed through Windows Explorer and creating a new Library is as easy as right-clicking on the window and selecting **New Library** or from the button under the address bar in Windows Explorer. To add locations to the new Library, right-click and select **Properties**. Here a user can add file locations from the local host, network, removal media, etc.

Location Aware Printing

Location Aware Printing is a new feature that will prove very useful to both administrators and end users. Windows 7 has the capability to determine what printers coincide with each network. Whenever a user prints from a network, Windows 7 will remember the printer and network used. Next time the user returns to that network it will automatically set the default printer as the one last used. This will allow for less headaches and steps to printing for laptop users between their work and home environment. Road warriors or any laptop user with Windows 7 Professional and above will be able to use and appreciate this feature.

Multilingual User Interface

Windows 7 Enterprise and Ultimate Editions have multilingual user interface support. This feature allows for a single deployment to systems all over the world. The desired language may then be installed on the system without the need of a separate image. Before Windows 7, administrators had to create separate images for each language supported. Any administrator in that position will attest that it was a daunting process. Not only did the older method require separate images for each language, but also it deviated from the standard image deployed company wide.

The language packs to enable a multilingual user interface can be obtained from Windows Update as shown in Figure 1.61 or included in the image if properly planned for during the preparing and planning phase.

Paint

An older feature of Windows, Windows 7 has finally improved Paint. Now with a ribbon like Microsoft Office 2007 applications, Paint has

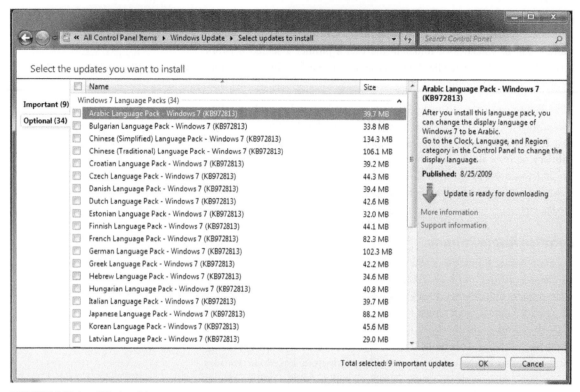

■ **FIGURE 1.61**   Install Windows 7 Language
Packs via Windows Update

been improved with added features and options as shown in Figure 1.62. Light users of imaging programs will be content with the new features. Additionally, Paint is Windows Touch capable allowing users with the correct hardware to finger paint.

Paint may be started from **Start menu | All Programs | Accessories** or typing **mspaint** in the Start menu Search.

Problem Steps Recorder

Windows 7 includes a Problem Steps Recorder. This feature allows the end user to record a screen capture of the system as illustrated in Figure 1.63. If the end user is having problems with an application or the system, he or she can record all the actions as the problem is reproduced. Once recorded, the end user can send the experience to the service desk or support staff. This allows for quicker troubleshooting of issues as the support staff will have the problem documented.

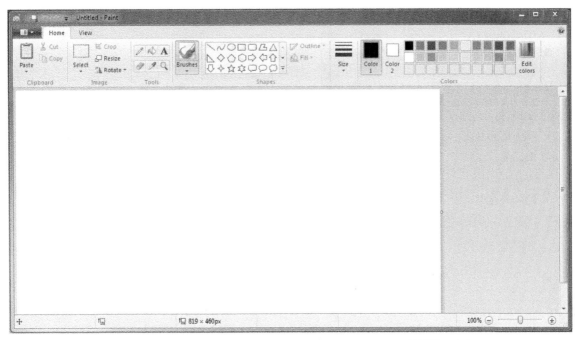

■ **FIGURE 1.62** Paint

■ **FIGURE 1.63** Problem Step Recorder

To start the Problem Step Recorder, type **PSR** in the Start menu Search or go to **Control Panel | Trouble Shooting | Get help from a friend | Problem Steps Recorder.** The tools will pop up in a small window. Clicking **Start Record** will begin to record the sequence of steps and take screen captures. The output will be saved as a zip, which can then be sent to the support staff.

Snipping Tools

Taking screenshots in Windows has always been a bit of a hassle with having to press **Print Screen** on the keyboard then open Paint, paste the image, resize or crop, and then save. Microsoft introduced the Snipping Tool to make this easier in Windows Vista and has included it in Windows 7,

TIP
The Problem Step Recorder is a great feature to train your end users on and have them submit when opening a support call or ticket. Not only does it prove the end user can reproduce the issue, but it also allows time for analyzing and has steps documented for easier troubleshooting by the administrator.

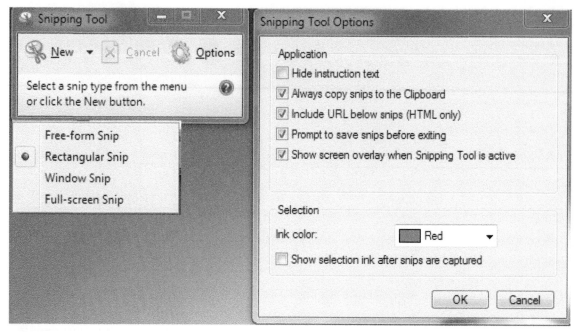

■ **FIGURE 1.64** Snipping Tool

■ **FIGURE 1.65** Sticky Notes

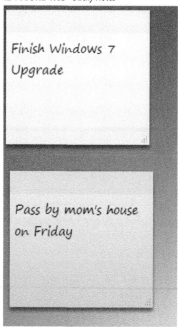

as shown in Figure 1.64. A user must still start this separate and small application, but with it open, a user may select an area of the desktop in free form or rectangle form or take a screenshot of an open window or the entire desktop. Once selected, the screenshot may be saved in various different file formats such as PNG, GIF, JPG, and MHT. Additionally, options such as e-mail to, edit with a pen, or erase are also available.

The Snipping Tool may be started by typing **sn** in the Start menu Search and clicking **Snipping Tool** (in case other results show for the query) or **Start menu | All Programs | Accessories**.

Sticky Notes

Sticky Notes used to be a part of the Gadgets feature but in Windows 7, it has become a standalone application. Look around your monitor or your end user's monitors. What do you see? More than likely, users have sticky notes on the monitor. Prior to Windows 7, either physical sticky notes or a third-party application had to be used to emulate these. Windows 7 includes the Sticky Notes application by default on all versions. This feature can prove handy for end users to remember to do items and other quick text that needs to be jotted down as shown in Figure 1.65.

To open Sticky Notes, go to **Start menu | All Programs | Accessories-Sticky Notes** or Start menu Search for **Sticky Notes**.

Tablet PC

Tablet PCs are nothing new. Since Windows XP, there has been a tablet edition and features aimed at the Tablet PC user. Windows 7 provides improved Tablet PC features for Windows 7 Home Premium, Professional, and Ultimate editions. Improved features include faster and more accurate handwriting recognition, multilanguage recognition, personalized dictionaries, and a new Math Input Panel for mathematical expressions. Tablet PC features require a Tablet PC or Tablet hardware.

Tablet PC tools may be found under the **Start menu | All Programs | Accessories | Tablet PC** folder. This folder includes three application shortcuts the user may select shown in Figure 1.66: **Personalize Handwriting Recognition** to teach the computer to better recognize his or her handwriting technique, **Tablet PC Input Panel** to start the input panel, and **Windows Journal**, a notebook like application for free writing (also available for non-Tablet PC users). Additionally, the **Math Input Panel** may be found in **Start menu | All Programs | Accessories**.

■ **FIGURE 1.66** Tablet PC

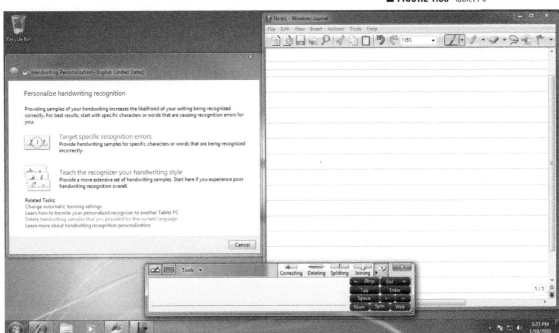

Windows Fax and Scan

Windows 7 includes improved features for using the system as a fax machine. The computer must still be connected to a fax modem and have the appropriate drivers for the device. Once configured, Windows Fax and Scan can be started and configured to receive and send faxes. Windows Fax and Scan may be started from **Start menu | All Programs | Windows Fax and Scan**a ss howni n Figure1.67 .

Windows Live Essentials

Microsoft removed some of the bundled applications that were included in older versions of Windows operating systems. To compensate for removing these applications, they are now available through the Internet. Windows Live Essentials may be downloaded from the Windows Live Web site at www.windowslive.com, and the download includes the option to install the following:

- Family Safety – a tool to filter and block restricted contents from children
- Mail – a simple e-mail client with multiple account support
- Movie Maker – to create movies, edit, and publish movies
- Photo Gallery – to edit, organize, tag, and share photos
- Toolbar – Windows Live toolbar for the Web browser
- Windows Live Messenger – MSN messenger client for chatting

■ **FIGURE 1.67** Windows Fax and Scan

Windows Search

Windows Search is another feature that has been improved from Windows XP and Vista. The Start menu has a Windows Search bar for quick searching and launching of programs and files. Most programs and new features found in Windows 7 can be launched straight from that search. It has come to replace the run command from Windows XP and older versions. By default, this search will search for documents, pictures, music, e-mail, and installed applications. Windows Search is also accessible from the Windows Explorer window on the top right.

Windows Search is improved over the Microsoft Desktop Search application that had to be installed as a third-party program in Windows XP and Vista. Many administrators and end users have issues with Windows Search because of its indexing settings. You may notice that each hard drive on the machine has indexing enabled by default. This can be removed by right-clicking on the hard drive, selecting **Properties**, and unchecking **Allow files on this drive to have contents indexed in addition to file properties** as shown in Figure 1.68. In addition, there is a service running by default called Windows Search that is enabled and started by default. Services can be disabled by typing **services.msc** in the Start menu Search.

Windows Search will be elaborated upon in Chapter 4, "The New Windows 7 Desktop Environment," as well as in Chapter 7, "Managing Windows 7 in an Enterprise Environment," for configuring the options through Group Policy.

Windows Taskbar

The Windows Taskbar was introduced in Windows 95 and will be very familiar to any Windows end user. Windows 7 has provided some modifications to the traditional taskbar. Microsoft has removed the quick launch toolbar and added functionality to the new Windows Taskbar for pinning shortcuts to commonly used applications. Additionally, the taskbar is now more flexible for end users needs allowing for the unpinning and moving of program shortcuts. When a program is started, the application icon on the taskbar appears with a box around it. Multiple open windows appear grouped. If Aero is enabled, moving the mouse over an application icon that is open will preview the window content straight from the taskbar. Lastly right-clicking on application icons will pop up Jump Lists, introduced earlier this chapter.

To pin an application to the taskbar, open the application, right-click on the application icon that appeared on the taskbar, and select **Pin this program to taskbar** as shown in Figure 1.69. If Aero is enabled, right-clicking on the icon will show Jump Lists with options for the specific application. Placing

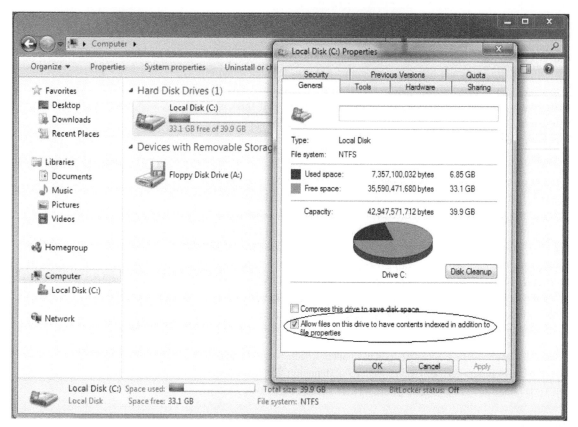

■ **FIGURE 1.68** Index Option on Hard Drive

■ **FIGURE 1.69** Pin Program to Taskbar

the mouse pointer over an open application icon will preview the content of the window if Aero is enabled.

Windows Touch

One-finger touch capabilities have been available in Windows since Windows XP and possibly before with the correct hardware, drivers, and applications. Windows 7 introduces multitouch technology built into the operating system. This technology allows for using more than one finger to perform gestures. Gestures allow for easier manipulation of applications through touch. Windows Touch requires specific hardware technology to function, normally provided by the monitor or an add-on to the monitor. Additionally, Windows Touch is only available in Windows 7 Home Premium, Professional, and Ultimate editions. The new larger Start menu icon, taskbar, Windows Media Player and Center (with a plug-in), and many of the Windows 7 bundled applications support multitouch.

Windows XP Mode

Windows XP Mode is a new feature available to Windows 7 Professional, Enterprise, and Ultimate edition users as they have included Microsoft Virtual PC with these versions. Windows XP Mode provides a separate Windows XP virtual hard drive and license to be used on the system. This is incredibly useful for environments that are upgrading to Windows 7 and/ or 64-bit systems that do not support their current business critical applications. With Windows XP Mode, a virtual Windows XP machine will be installed on the host Windows 7 computer and these incompatible applications may be installed and run from a Windows XP environment as shown in Figure1.70 .

Windows XP Mode and Windows Virtual PC have strict hardware requirements for a hardware virtualization capable CPU, RAM, and hard drive space. Chapter 9, "Virtualization and Windows 7," is dedicated to virtualization and Windows XP Mode as it will be a very valuable feature for environments with incompatible software requirements.

WordPad

An older feature of Windows but very much improved is WordPad. Microsoft has updated this bundled application with the ribbon found on Office 2007 products as shown in Figure 1.71. It has also added new functionality to make the product more of a basic word processing application. It has many formatting options, which previous versions of Windows lacked in the WordPad application, such as bullets, line breaks, text color and highlight, picture insertion, print preview, and zoom.

WordPad is located in **Start menu | All Programs | Accessories | WordPad** and may be used for basic word processing for end users that do not require a full office productivity suite such as Microsoft Office or Open Office.

XPS Viewer

Not only does Windows 7 include an XPS viewer, but it also includes Microsoft XPS Document Writer. This standard format for printing to a file allows

■ **FIGURE 1.70** Windows XP Mode

for a common standard to view documents without the application the document may have been created in. By default, a Windows 7 installation includes Microsoft XPS Document Writer under the **Devices and Printers** console of the Control Panel. This allows for files to be printed from a wide variety of applications such as Word, IE, and virtually any software that allows printing. This is possibly by selecting **Print** from the application and selecting the **Microsoft XPS Document Writer** as the printer. The output is an XPS file that can then be opened with XPS Viewer.

XPS Viewer is a simple application that allows a standard view of XPS documents. The XPS format is similar to the PDF format that is the current standard for sharing read-only files. The XPS Viewer is automatically opened

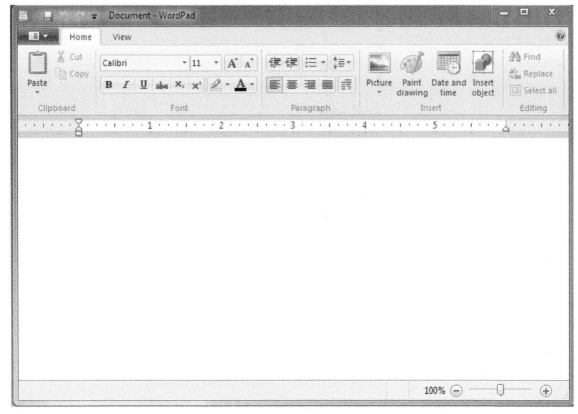

when double-clicking an XPS file in Windows 7 or can be started from the **Start menu Search** by typing **XPS** or from **Start menu | All Programs | XPS Viewer**.

Security

Last but not least, security has been substantially improved over Windows XP and Windows Vista. It might sound surprising but Windows Vista was the most secure operating system Microsoft had released until Windows 7. Windows 7 builds on top of that foundation and architecture to bring many new and improved features:

- AppLocker
- Backupa ndR estore
- BiometricSe curity
- BitLocker
- BitLockerToG o

- EncryptingF ileS ystem
- ParentalC ontrols
- UserA ccountC ontrol
- WindowsD efender
- WindowsF irewall

AppLocker

AppLocker is introduced in Windows 7 as a new application control policy. Essentially, AppLocker allows for application whitelisting or blacklisting. An administrator can specify exactly what applications are allowed to run (whitelisting) or what applications are restricted from running on the system (blacklisting). This feature allows for application standardization in an environment, an ultimate goal of any administrator.

As our users continually beg for local administrative privileges, AppLocker may assist in providing such privileges without the risks that are often attributed. Normally such privileges are necessary to run certain applications and through AppLocker policies they may be granted without full local administrative privileges.

This new feature is only available on Enterprise and Ultimate editions of Windows 7. More in-depth instructions for working with AppLocker are available in Chapter 8, "Securing Windows 7." AppLocker is a policy-based feature and may be configured through gpedit.msc.

Backup and Restore

Windows Vista introduced the Backup and Restore feature and due to its success, Windows 7 also includes the feature. This tool is found in the **Backup and Restore** console of the Control Panel and can be used by end users and administrators to back up the system files, user's files, and even the entire system. This feature is very useful when used correctly and backups are performed regularly. As hard drives tend to fail entire systems with user's files and data can be lost forever. Using Backup and Restore scheduled backups may be configured to back up the system data to another physical hard drive, removable media such as thumb drives, external hard drives, CD, and/or DVD drives, or a network location.

From the **Backup and Restore** console within the Control Panel, a user may choose to create a backup, a system image, a system repair disk, and restore the system from a backup as shown in Figure 1.72. It is recommended that system backups be set up to automatically run as per the configured scheduled configuration. Backup options allow the user to choose what files to back up or alternately Windows can choose, in which case it will back up data files in Libraries and user's profiles, and create a system image.

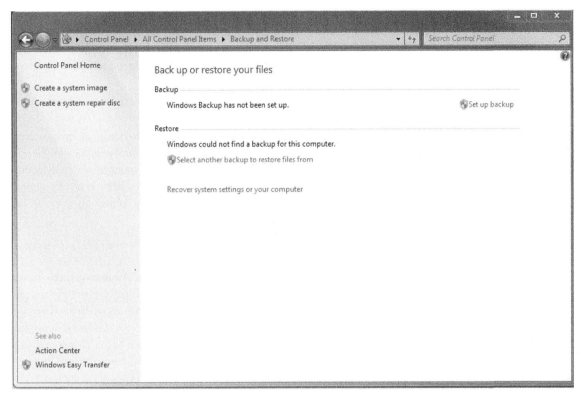

In the event that data is lost or the hard drive fails, Windows Restore is the simplest method to recover the system and user data. From within the same console, a user may **Select another backup to restore files from**. This can be performed from another Windows 7 system and can restore backups performed on Windows 7 or Windows Vista machines.

Biometric Security

Although biometric devices have been available on computers for a few years now, Microsoft Windows 7 is the first operating system to implement biometric security without the need of third-party software. We have discussed that password security should be required for all Windows 7 users. Biometrics takes security to the next level by not only asking the end user to authenticate with something they know but with something they have, the user's fingerprints. Working with multiple biometric devices, Windows 7 now allows the user to login to the Windows 7 system and authenticate with other applications and/or Web sites with the user's fingerprints.

Biometric devices may be configured from the Control Panel. The console states the status of the biometric devices. The end user will first need to

NOTE

It is a best practice to regularly run backups of user's data locally stored on their systems. After a hard drive failure restoring Windows 7 is a simple and accurate task that may be performed to recover the user's system to the point of its last backup.

enroll and follow the Biometric Enrollment wizard, which will assist the end user in configuring the fingers, and which will be used as shown in Figure 1.73. One to ten fingers may be used, and it is recommended to use more than one in case a finger is ever bandaged. Three successful swipes of each figure will conclude the enrollment.

BitLocker

BitLocker was introduced in Windows Vista to provide a full disk encryption solution; however, requirements for specific configurations to the primary partition of the hard drive lead to a small number of deployments. Windows 7 performs the configuration of the hard drive correctly during Windows 7 setup to easily implement BitLocker, a feature only available on Enterprise and Ultimate Editions.

BitLocker requires a compatible Trusted Platform Module (TPM) 1.2 security device. This is a hardware requirement and is a chip included on the motherboard of your system. Some systems may have this device disabled in the BIOS or not have one at all. BitLocker also requires a recovery key to be generated and stored when setting up full disk encryption. This recovery key must be stored in a safe place as it is the only way to unencrypt the hard drive in the event the passphrase is lost. BitLocker integrates with Active Directory to use the domain username and password to boot the hard drive. Active Directory may also be configured to store the escrow recovery keys of the computer.

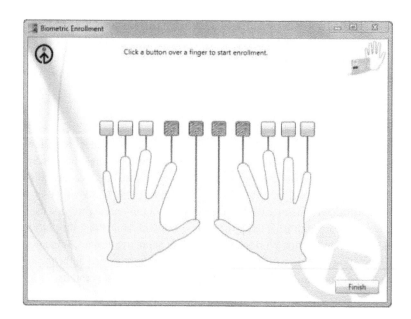

■ **FIGURE 1.73** Biometric Enrollment

To set up BitLocker in Windows 7, select **BitLocker Drive Encryption** from the Control Panel as shown in Figure 1.74. Clicking **Turn On BitLocker** will initiate a wizard to correctly configure and encrypt any hard drive or removable media connected to the system. Full disk encryption is becoming a standard requirement for mobile users. Chapter 8, "Securing Windows 7," elaborates on BitLocker and other full disk encryption solutions for your systems and environment.

BitLocker To Go

BitLocker To Go is new in Windows 7 and builds on BitLocker by allowing users and administrators to encrypt removable media. Many of your end users have USB thumb drives, external hard drives, and other forms of removable media. BitLocker To Go allows for the encrypting of these devices for added security. Reading the data on an unencrypted removable media device is extremely easy and encrypting the device is the safest solution.

Devices encrypted with BitLocker To Go may be read from Windows XP and Windows Vista systems but these systems do not currently support writing

TIP

It is a best practice for all laptops, mobile devices, and removable media to have full disk encryption. It is even suggested to use full disk encryption on desktop and servers. It is extremely easy for an attacker to obtain data from an unencrypted device that has been lost or stolen. With headlines suggesting millions of confidential records lost or stolen from mobile devices and media, full disk encryption can avoid your company appearing in a headline.

■ **FIGURE 1.74** BitLocker Drive Encryption

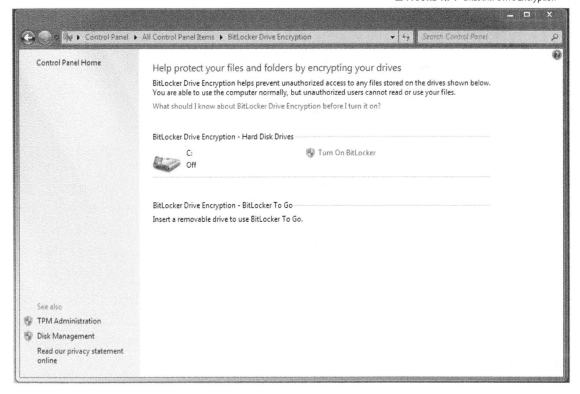

back to the device. As more systems are migrated to Windows 7, this will be a viable option and can be enforced through Group Policy. In other words, an administrator can enforce that removable media be encrypted on Windows 7 hosts prior to functioning. This feature and other full disk encryption solutions are explained in Chapter 8, "Securing Windows 7."

To enable BitLocker To Go on a removable device, right-click the device and select **Turn on BitLocker** as shown in Figure 1.75.

■ **FIGURE 1.75** Enable BitLocker To Go on Removable Media

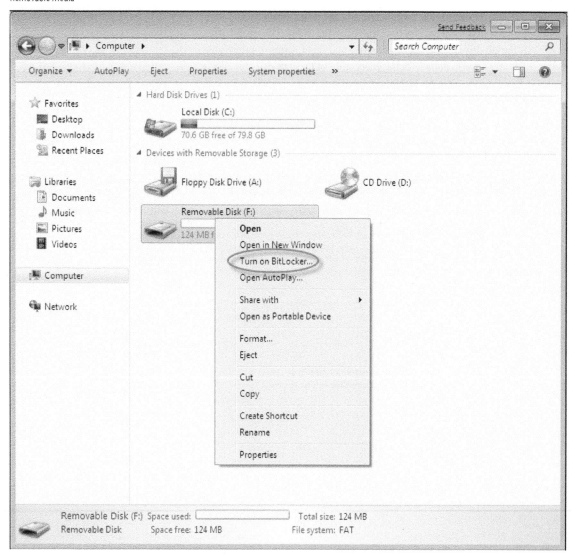

Encrypting File System (EFS)

Windows 7 Professional, Enterprise, and/or Ultimate editions have EFS support. While full disk encryption solutions such as BitLocker allow for the entire disk to be encrypted, these solutions do not protect the user after the system or hard drive has been authenticated and is in use. EFS is useful for user-level file and folder encryption. This is critical for shared systems in use by multiple user accounts. Without EFS, any user can see the other user's data.

EFS adds on to the NTFS security layer by encrypting the data and only letting it be read with the encryption key. Even a system administrator would not be able to access the data without the encryption key.

Using EFS in an environment requires planning, but here is how to encrypt a folder for testing purposes: Right-click on the folder, select **Properties,** click the **Advanced** button on the **General** tab, check **Encrypt content to secure data** as shown in Figure 1.76, and click **OK** twice. A prompt will ask to apply settings to the folder and all other subfolders or just the folder, select your preference, and click **OK**. Once settings are applied, that folder should appear with green letters.

Parental Controls

Windows 7 includes Parental Controls to limit and protect kids' computer use. This feature will most likely not be used in a business environment but could prove popular as a cost-effective solution to home users. This feature allows the limiting of computer use as well as setting restrictions as to what programs and games can be executed by the end user.

Parental Controls may be setup from within the Control Panel. It requires more than one computer user, that is one for the kid and one for the parents. Remember to password protect all user accounts for best security.

User Account Control

Introduced in Windows Vista, UAC has been greatly improved in Windows 7. UAC helps defend the system from malware and malicious hackers. By default, the UAC will prompt for permission before installing any unsigned and approved software. Thanks to Microsoft digitally signing its .dll and executable files in Windows 7, UAC is now much less intrusive.

UAC is explained earlier in this chapter and referenced in Figure 1.4.

Windows Defender

Windows 7 includes Windows Defender for front line defense against spyware and other malicious software. It works much like an antivirus program

WARNING
If a user encrypts his or her hard drive or uses EFS to encrypt a folder, that user will now own the data on that local machine. The encryption key is only on that local machine and should be backed up. If the encryption key is lost, the data in the folder will be very difficult to unlock. When implementing this in Active Directory, environments options are available to back up recovery and encryptionk eysr emotely.

WARNING
Many security features in Windows 7 depend on these UAC settings. The lower the UAC setting is, the more susceptible you or your end users are to running malware without your knowledge or permission. It is recommended to use the highest UAC setting of always notify and to educate users how UAC works. Even if the highest UAC setting is set, if the user gets in the habit to accept every prompt, the machine will be insecure. This security feature relies on user training and proper configuration.

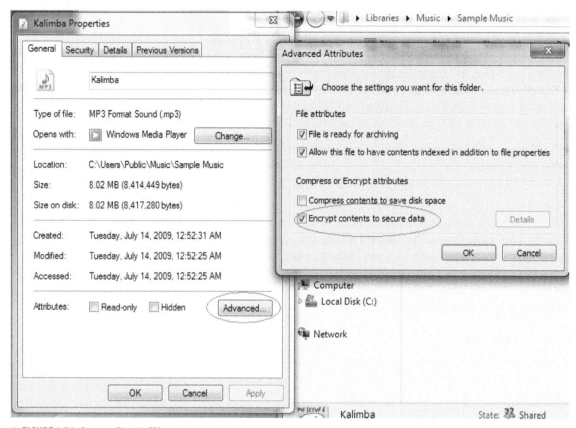

■ FIGURE 1.76 Encrypt a File with EFS

with signatures and some behavioral detections of spyware as shown in Figure 1.77. Window Defender definitions are updated with Windows Update and attempt to scan and clean the system from malicious infection.

Windows Defender can be configured and run from the **Action Center** console within the Control Panel or from **Control Panel | Windows Defender.** It is a best practice to run this software as added protection but should not be the only anti-malware solution, as it does not provide signatures for most viruses.

Windows Firewall

The Windows Firewall was introduced in Windows XP as an inbound only firewall. Windows 7 now configures the Windows Firewall to block both inbound and outbound traffic. Additionally, it is much more flexible to configure custom firewall settings. These settings may be saved as profiles,

WARNING

WindowsD efenderi sn ota replacement for antivirus and other anti-malware solutions. Windows Defender does not have a proven track record of defending against newer spyware attacks and should not be trusted as a security solution to Windows 7.

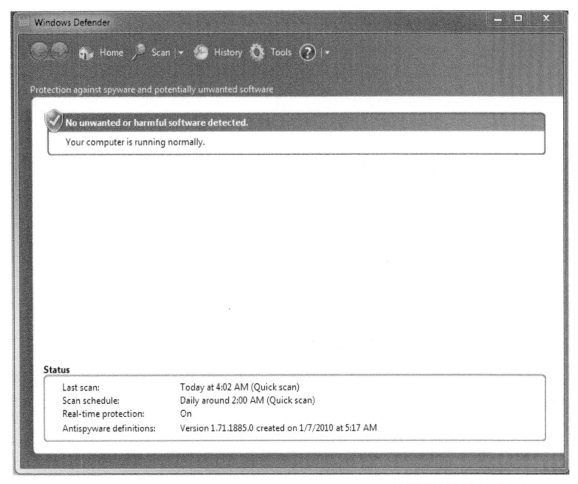

■ **FIGURE 1.77** Windows Defender

another new feature that requires user education. The profile chosen is based on the prompt to **Choose a Network** when the Windows 7 machine detects a connection to a new network. Depending on the end user's choice of Home, Work, or Public, the proper Windows Firewall profile is set. Public network settings block incoming traffic by default, a setting that may be too high for a Home or Work network. Windows 7 will automatically recognize when the machine is connected to a network it was on before, such as a Work or Home network, and apply the correct profile.

The Windows Firewall can be configured from the Control Panel under the **Windows Firewall** or **Systems and Security** consoles as shown in Figure 1.78. The Windows Firewall and other Windows 7 security features and configurations will be discussed in Chapter 8, "Securing Windows 7."

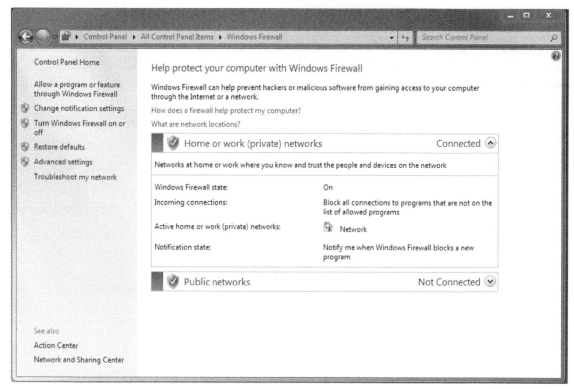

■ **FIGURE 1.78** Windows Firewall

■ SUMMARY

This chapter has introduced you, both the end user and administrator, to Windows 7. Although many end users and administrators skipped Windows Vista, Windows 7 was built on it, and it is important to know this moving forward. Much like Windows Vista, Microsoft has released multiple editions of Windows 7. Understanding the differences between these editions and 32-bit versus 64-bit computing is important to successfully prepare and plan the Windows 7 deployment project. As an administrator in an organization, you will most likely choose between Professional, Enterprise, and Ultimate to deploy in your environment due to the ability to join a domain, while your end users will be using Starter, Home Premium, and even Ultimate on their home systems. As 32-bit and 64-bit versions are available for almost all editions, it is vital to understand what the difference is and the pros and cons to moving to 64-bit. The decision to what edition and version of Windows 7 to use is based on your testing, planning, and preparation phase of a Windows 7 deployment as well as evaluating the features each edition provides or lacks.

The section discussing the major changes of Windows 7 highlighted the most obvious and interesting features included with Windows 7. From an administrator's perspective, the deployment and management methods and tools have been improved making critical administrative tasks easier. For the end user, the desktop environment and user interface has changed from Windows XP and Vista, the UAC feature has been improved and will be less intrusive than Windows Vista, and the user profile data has been moved to a different location. These points require user training, an important part of any information technology or system project.

The last section of this chapter has focused on the new features provided with Windows 7. As an administrator, you are most likely aware of the features but perhaps not aware how to implement or configure them. This chapter should serve as a quick reference to enabling and using all the new features. Some of the features are strictly for the administrator to use and require Windows Server 2008 R2, while other features are for the end user. Most of the new and improved features of Windows 7 assist the end user and administrator to be more productive with his or her daily tasks. Once again, end user training of these new features is critical to seeing productivity go up.

Most of the features and sections in this chapter will be elaborated and further explained in the following chapters. The next chapter will cover installing and upgrading to Windows 7 on a single or small amount of systems, a primary step to the planning and preparation phase of a Windows 7 migration project. Understanding and testing how Windows 7 installs, upgrades, migrates, and works is crucial to planning and performing a successful deployment of Windows 7 in an organization. Once you have Windows 7 installed and deployed on a system, you may wish to jump around this book to reference specific needs.

Installingand U pgrading to Windows 7

INFORMATION IN THIS CHAPTER

- Planninga ndP reparation
- CleanI nstall
- In-placeU pgrade
- Migratet o Windows7
- Virtualizationa ndD ualB oot
- PostI nstall
- Summary

With all the new features described in Chapter 1, "Introduction to Windows 7" you should be excited and ready to get Windows 7 on your machine and/or deployed in your environment. This chapter will focus on the process of installing or upgrading a system to Windows 7. All of the steps explained in this chapter will be addressed in a larger scale in Chapter 3, "Deploying Windows 7 in an Enterprise Environment," for an enterprise-wide deployment. These processes include the planning and preparation phase, installing or upgrading to Windows 7, and the post install steps. As an administrator and/or end user, we must first perform these steps on a single or few systems before deploying Windows 7 to an entire organization. Before preparing and planning to deploy in an enterprise environment, it is crucial to understand how the Windows 7 install, upgrade, and migrations processes work. Initial steps of preparation and planning are very important aspects of a successful deployment of Windows 7, especially for testing purposes.

Although this chapter will focus on deployment of a single system, the same preparation and planning philosophy is applied in an enterprise

DOI: 10.1016/B978-1-59749-561-5.00002-4

93

environment; as you go through this section, begin considering the same points for an organization-wide deployment. The planning and preparation phase of a Windows 7 install include the following:

- Select the Windows 7 Edition to be installed
- Check system compatibility and hardware requirements
- Backupc urrents ystem
- Determinede ployments cenario
- Selecti nstallm ethod
- Obtain Windows7
- Obtain device/hardware drivers *prior to install*

This chapter assumes you have a general idea of what version of Windows 7 will be used on the system and/or environment. Chapter 1, "Introduction to Windows 7," explains the different editions and 32-bit versus 64-bit choices available. Generally, a business will deploy Professional, Enterprise, and/or Ultimate for the ability to join a domain. Windows Starter, Home Basic, and Home Premium do not have the ability to join a domain environment. Regardless of the edition chosen, this chapter addresses installing all versions of Windows 7 as the process is the same for any edition.

Windows 7 introduces many new and easier ways of deploying the operating system in your environment. This chapter will focus only on the Windows Setup deployment option that is initiated with the Windows 7 install media. Chapter 3, "Deploying Windows 7 in an Enterprise Environment," will focus on the other tools available for deploying Windows 7 as they focus on deploying in larger scale.

There are many ways to get Windows 7 on your system. The first is buying a new computer with Windows 7 preinstalled. The second is performing a clean install on the system. A clean install is so called because the install does not touch or modify anything on the hard drive; often a clean install formats the hard drive before installing. The third way is an in-place upgrade from a compatible operating system. The fourth is a migration to Windows 7 from an incompatible operating system, which entails a custom (clean) install with more planning and preparation to avoid losing data and settings. Finally, Microsoft Windows 7 may be installed on a virtual machine and on different operating systems with virtualization technology.

Each of these install methods will reiterate the planning and preparation phase before performing the install as some steps and considerations may be different. Additionally, the post install steps will also be reiterated as certain install methods require different processes to be followed after the install.

- Preinstalled – This is the simplest of deployments as the Windows 7 operating system comes already installed with a new system. This is not recommended for enterprise environments and the section "Preinstalled" addresses these issues.
- Clean install – A clean install is when the Windows Setup installs a new version of the operating system and often means formatting the system for best results. If the partition where the clean install will be performed contains another version of Windows, the Windows and Program Files folders will be renamed but remain on the partition. This install is used when the operating system cannot be upgraded and also for dual booting, creating a virtual machine, or installing from a blank or formatted hard drive. This is the recommended deployment method for best performance with Windows 7.
- In-place upgrade install – An in-place upgrade is an install method from the current, supported operating system that retains applications and user data from the current configuration. The criteria for this type of install are strict, but it is also the easiest method for the end user and administrator to move to Windows 7.
- Migration – This upgrade method is not in place and is used when a nonsupported operating system, such as Windows XP, is used to upgrade to Windows 7. This method will also retain user data but requires a reinstall of the applications. This is the most complex of the deployment methods and will be explained and outlined in the "Migrating to Windows 7" section.
- Virtualization and Dual Boot – Windows 7 may be either installed in a virtual machine or dual booted. There are multiple types of virtualization software that may be used to install Windows 7 on a virtual machine. Additionally, Windows 7 may be dual booted on an existing system by installing on a different disk or partition. Both of these options allow for Windows 7 to run alongside another operating system.

Finally, this chapter will focus on common post install steps that should be followed after Windows 7 installation. These steps include the following:

- Activation – All Windows 7 deployments must have a valid product key and license to activate. Activation is required by Microsoft to ensure all systems are properly licensed. Although a headache for most end users and administrators, Windows 7 has streamlined this process to be less painful.
- Install hardware drivers and devices – Windows 7 does a great job at installing most hardware drivers and devices that are plugged into the machine during setup; however, you will surely encounter having to

install hardware drivers or devices after the setup; this section will guide you through.

■ Update Windows – security and important updates are released by Microsoft every second Tuesday of the month, known as *Patch Tuesday*. These updates should always be performed to ensure the systems are not vulnerable to operating system flaws.

■ Install antivirus – Although the most secure desktop operating system, Windows 7 continues with the Windows tradition of requiring a third-party antivirus. This should be a requirement for all systems especially for untrained end users who can possibly download and run virus from e-mailor Web.

■ Restore user data – As most users will have data that needs to be moved to the new Windows 7 system, this section will explain the methods to restore that data.

PLANNING AND PREPARATION

Although this chapter will focus on deploying Windows 7 on a single system, the planning and preparation phase is still required to ensure a successful deployment of Windows 7. As you go through this section think of the steps taken now and how they would differ in an enterprise-wide deployment plan. This section will explain the basics of the planning and preparation method including the following:

■ Select Windows 7 edition – This step requires evaluating differences between Windows 7 editions and 32-bit versus 64-bit computing to determine what edition of Windows 7 will be installed. Standardizing the edition in an environment is a best practice.

■ Check system compatibility and hardware requirements – It is critical to determine the system in which Windows 7 will be installed meets the system requirements and hardware compatibility *before*de ploying Windows7.

■ Back up current system and user data – For those deployments that require migrating data or upgrading from a current system, it is considered a best practice to perform a full system backup, as well as a user data and setting backup to ensure data is not lost during the migration.

■ Determine deployment scenario – There are four different scenarios for Windows 7 deployments: new system, upgrade system (in-place upgrade from Windows Vista), system refresh, and system replacement. Determining this is important in selecting the install method.

■ Select install method – Determine and select what deployment method is available and will be used to deploy Windows 7 based on current operating system, requirements, selected Windows 7 edition, and scenario.

- Obtain Windows 7 – This step involves acquiring the Windows 7 license, install media, and product key.
- Obtain device/hardware drivers – Obtaining the proper device and hardware drivers *prior to installing* Windows 7 is recommended to save time and headaches when Windows 7 is running but drivers may bem issing.

Select the Windows 7 Edition

Selecting the correct edition of Windows 7 to install in your environment is a critical first step in the preparation and planning stage. A Windows 7 edition comparison may be found in Chapter 1, "Introduction to Windows 7." It is recommended to first determine the needs of the organization and end users. Based on the needs, determine what features address those needs and choose that edition. Many times Windows editions are chosen based on other factors such as upgrade patch and cost instead of the features that are required for the business.

For deployments in an organization or enterprise environment that has a domain, Windows 7 Professional, Enterprise, and/or Ultimate are required. All other versions will not be able to join a domain. It is recommended that an environment run the same edition of Windows 7 for standardization. Testing before choosing what version to deploy in an entire environment is also recommended, and this chapter will assist in getting any version you choose to be installed and running on your system(s).

SystemC ompatibility

Ensuring the computer(s) in which Windows 7 will be deployed meets compatibility requirements is critical to the successful deployment of Windows 7. The easiest method of ensuring the system is compatible is by using the Windows 7 Upgrade Advisor on the current system. The tools and methods required to make this determination involve the following:

- Confirming the hardware requirements are met – making sure the computer meets the minimum requirements for the Windows 7 edition and features that are planned to be used is a major first step. Computers purchased in the last two years should meet these requirements without any issues and even be able to run 64-bit editions. Your specific hardware may be determined on Windows machines through the **System Properties**i nt he ControlP anel.
- Confirming devices and hardware have correct drivers – although Microsoft did a great job in providing a large amount of hardware and device drivers this time around, it is wise to ensure that all your hardware

and devices are compatible with Windows 7. This could be done manually by visiting the computer manufacturer's Web site and verifying whether hardware drivers are available for the version of Windows 7. Pay particular attention to the 32-bit versus 64-bit versions of drivers and devices supported.

- Confirming whether the software required runs on Windows 7 – many of the issues with Windows Vista came from the lack of software compatibility. Windows 7 has fixed this issue, and a wide range of applications are now compatible. This planning phase should not be ignored, especially for the business critical applications being run on your environment. It is recommended that all applications be tested on multiple systems before doing a large deployment of Windows 7.

These three aspects were one of the main reasons for Windows Vista's failure and lack of deployments in the enterprise. When deploying systems organization wide, ensuring software compatibility is a huge factor. The Windows 7 Upgrade Advisor should be run on multiple machines that have business critical applications. Furthermore, testing of these applications should be conducted on Windows 7 to confirm compatibility.

Windows 7 Upgrade Advisor

By far the easiest method to determine whether a single system meets compatibility requirements is with Microsoft's Windows 7 Upgrade Advisor. This software may be installed on any Windows operating system. The purpose of the Upgrade Advisor is to check your PC to see if it can run Windows 7. Information is sent to Microsoft and checked against their database to ensure that the system is compatible. All of the critical items expressed in this section are checked.

The results of the Windows 7 Upgrade Advisor should be able to assist you in the planning and preparation phase. It will let you know if you can do an in-place upgrade or have to do a custom install. It will also let you know of any issues your system, devices, or programs may have with Windows 7.

Install Windows 7 Upgrade Advisor

1. Download the executable named as Windows7UpgradeAdvisorSetup.exe from Microsoft's official Web site.
2. Double-click the executable file that you just downloaded to initiate the setup. You may be prompted by user account control (UAC) if on Vista.
3. Read the license terms and accept them. Click **Install**.
4. Once the installation is complete you may close the setup wizard, or if it prompts you to run the advisor, you may do that as well.

NOTE

Windows7 U pgradeA dvisorm ay be downloaded straight from Microsoft as seen on Figure 2.1 at www.windows.microsoft.com/en-us/windows/downloads/upgrade-advisor

Be careful searching online for Windows 7 Upgrade Advisor as malicious Web sites may attempt to provide software by the same name that will not be as nice to your system as the Microsoft release.

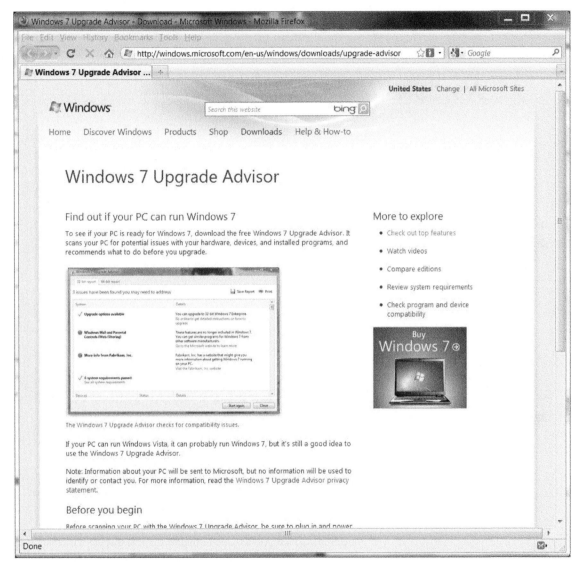

■ **FIGURE 2.1** Download Windows 7 Upgrade Advisor from Microsoft.com

Run Windows7 U pgradeA dvisor

1. The setup should have created a desktop shortcut named *Windows 7 Upgrade Advisor.* Initiate the application by double-clicking the shortcut. The application was installed at %SystemDrive%\Program Files\ Microsoft Windows 7 Upgrade Advisor\ and may be initiated by running WindowsUpgradeAdvisor.exe in this folder.

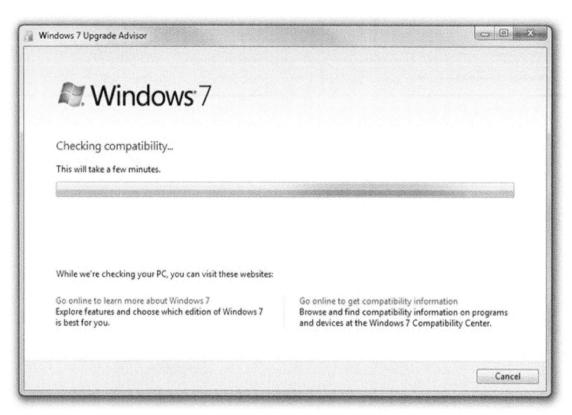

■ FIGURE 2.2 Windows 7 Upgrade Advisor-
Checking Compatibility

2. A pop-up will initiate with instructions. Read these instructions and make sure that all the hardware the system currently uses is plugged in. Click **Start check**w henr eady.
3. The application will scan your computer's hardware, applications, drivers, and so on and communicate with Microsoft's servers to ensure compatibility of all scanned items. This scan as shown in Figure 2.2 will take a few minutes to check for compatibility.
4. Once finished a report as seen in Figure 2.3 will display with insightful information on your system and the problems and/or compatability issues it may have by installing Windows 7. The reports should be easilyr eada ndunde rstood.

BackU pC urrentS ystem

There are multiple methods to back up the user data before migrating to Windows 7. These steps should be performed on a regular basis and are essential before migrating to Windows 7. Although there are multiple methods of migrating user data, this section will focus on migrating user data of a single

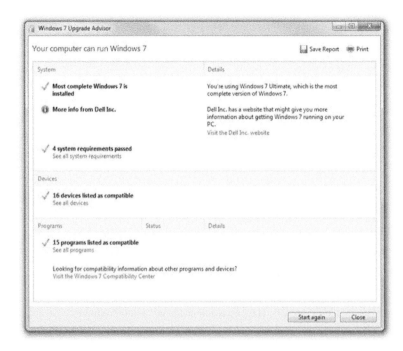

system. This section also focuses on performing a backup with free tools provided by Microsoft and mentions third-party tools that may be used as well.

Windows Easy Transfer

Windows Easy Transfer is a wizard for transferring one or multiple user's files and settings from one Windows computer to another. The easy-to-use wizard allows the administrator or end user to choose what files and settings to transfer and from what users, selects a transfer method to use, performs the transfer, and then creates a report. This tool cannot be used to transfer installed programs or applications to the new system. All programs and applications will need to be reinstalled. The wizard will generate a report suggesting what applications need to be installed on the new system. The transfer methods that Windows Easy Transfer can use are an easy transfer cable, a network share, an external hard disk, or a universal serial bus (USB) flash drive.

Windows Easy Transfer is free and available for Windows XP and Windows Vista from Microsoft.com or from the Windows 7 installation media in the folder %MediaDrive%\support\migwiz\migsetup.exe Windows 7 systems include Windows Easy Transfer installed by default and may be launched from **Start menu | All Programs | Accessories | System Tools | Windows Easy Transfer**.

As mentioned there are three methods of transferring user data and settings:

1. USB easy transfer cable – transferring data from the old functional, powered on computer to the new powered on computer with a male to male USB cable.
2. Using the network – transferring data from the old functional, powered on computer to the new powered on computer that are both connected to the same network.
3. Removable media or a network share – from any old computer to a new computer using a storage repository.

This section focuses on backing up user data using only the third method. For using the first two methods refer to the subsection "Manually Restoring User Data" in the "Post Install" section of this chapter.

Performing a Backup with Windows Easy Transfer

To back up user data with Windows Easy Transfer:

1. Start Windows Easy Transfer from the computer that will be backed up as seen in Figure 2.4. The executable is included in the Windows 7 installation media in the folder %MediaDrive%\support\migwiz\migsetup.exe.

■ FIGURE 2.4 Windows Easy Transfer

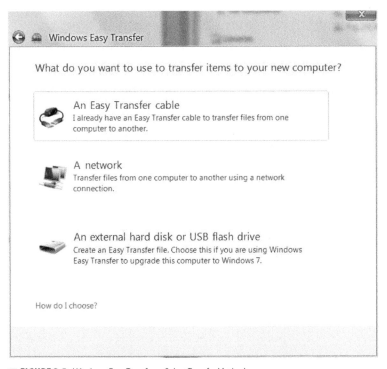

FIGURE 2.5 Windows Easy Transfer – Select Transfer Method

2. Read the introduction and click **Next**.
3. Select the method of transferring the user's data and settings: **An external hard disk or USB flash drive** as seen in Figure 2.5.
4. Click **This is my old computer**, as seen in Figure 2.6.
5. The application will scan all the users and shared items that it believes must be backed up. When completed, the usernames and shared items will be checked. You may click **Customize** to view the selected files that will be backed up as demonstrated in Figures 2.7 and 2.8. Click **Next** when done.
6. Input a password for the Easy Transfer file. This allows for integrity and security of the backup file. When done click **Save**.
7. A standard save dialog will pop up. Choose the shared network resource, removable media location, or any location to save the file to.
8. Click **Next** and **Close**.

Windows Vista File Backup

Certain Windows Vista editions have built in backup capabilities. These backup capabilities are the easiest method of saving end user data without a third-partya pplication.

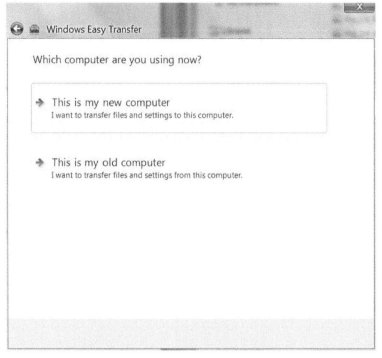

■ FIGURE 2.6 Windows Easy Transfer – Select Which Computer You Are Using

1. There are two easy ways to start backing up files in Windows Vista.
   a. Start the Backup Status and Configuration wizard from **Start menu | All Programs | Accessories | System Tools | Backup Status and Configuration**. Click **Set up automatic file backup**a s showni n Figure2.9 .
   b. Selectt he **Backup and Restore Center console** from the Control Panel, and then click **Back up files**,a ss howni n Figure2.10 .
2. The Back Up Files wizard will pop up. Here you may decide to back up files to a hard drive, CD, or DVD; or back up to the network, as shown in Figure 2.11. Select the option that you would like and click **Next**.
   a. On a hard disk, CD, or DVD – This option will back up the files to a hard drive, external hard drive, flash drive, or any other removable media such as CD and/or DVD.
   b. On a network – This option allows you to choose any network drive available that the user has write access to. It is common to do a backup to the network to avoid removable media disadvantages.
3. On the next screen you may decide what file types to backup. Note the message under *Which file types do you want to back up?*c learly

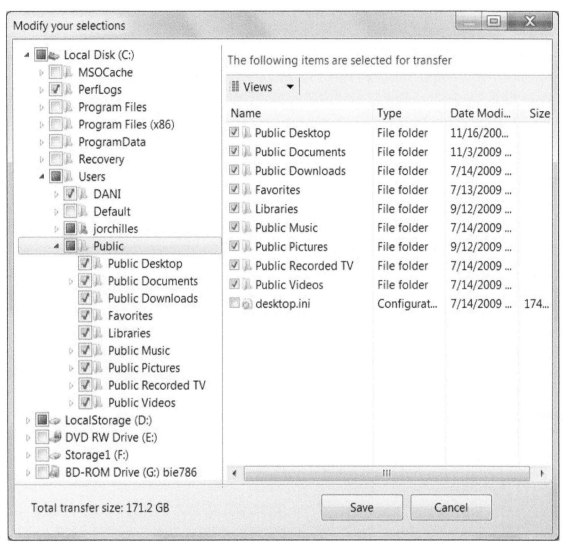

■ **FIGURE 2.7** Windows Easy Transfer —
Search Results and Customize Options

states that all files on the system from *all* users will be backed up. This
excludes system files, executable files, and temporary files. Moving
the mouse over each file type will describe what type of files will be
backed up. It is recommended to select all the file types as shown in
Figure 2.12. Once you make your selection select **Next**.

4. If you have selected to create a scheduled backup, you will be asked
   when to do this. Select the automated backup time and click **Next**. The
   backup will begin, and depending on your system, it will take some time.

■ **FIGURE 2.8** Windows Easy Transfer –
Advanced Selection

■ **FIGURE 2.9** Backup Status and
Configuration – Automatic File Backup

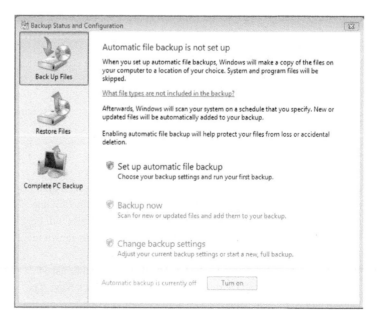

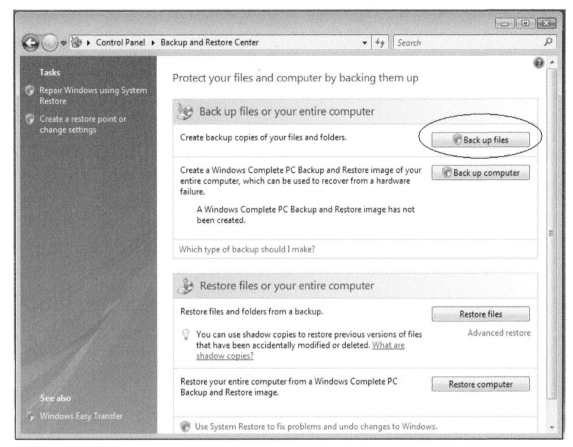

■ **FIGURE 2.10** Backup and Restore Center –
Back up Files

Windows Vista Complete Backup

As noted above, certain Windows Vista editions have backup capabilities. A complete system backup of a Windows Vista machine will ensure the user's data and the entire system is backed up before performing any changes onthe system.

1. There are two easy ways to start a full system backup in Windows Vista.
   a. Start the Backup Status and Configuration wizard from **Start menu | All Programs | Accessories | System Tools | Backup Status and Configuration**. Click on **Complete PC Backup** on the left followed by clicking **Create a backup now** as shown in Figure 2.13.
   b. Selectt he **Backup and Restore Center console** from the Control Panel and then click **Back up computer**a ss howni n Figure 2.10.

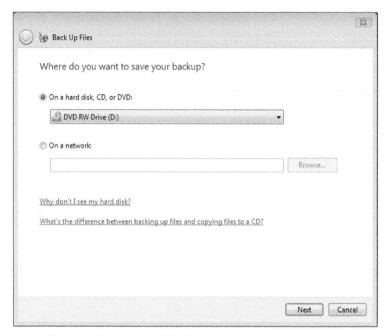

■ **FIGURE 2.11** Back Up Files — Select Backup Location

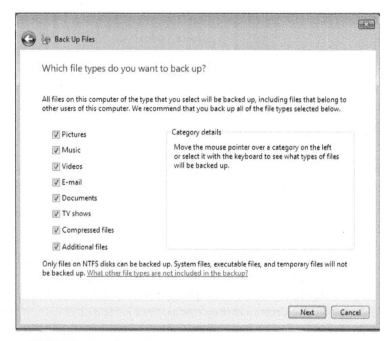

■ **FIGURE 2.12** Back Up Files — Select File Types to Back Up

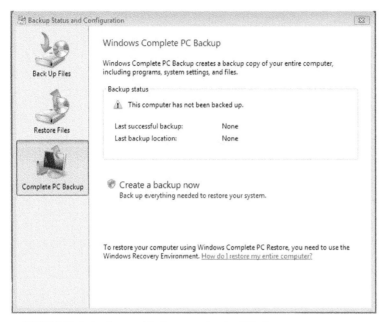

■ **FIGURE 2.13** Backup Status and Configuration — Complete PC Backup

2. The Windows Complete PC Backup wizard will appear. Here you may select **On a hard disk** or **On one or more DVDs** as shown in Figure 2.14. Depending on the size of your system and the hardware available to you, the best option should be chosen.

   a. On a hard disk – This is the recommended option for storage reasons. Make sure to plug in an external hard drive or that you have another physical hard drive in the system. Backing up to another partition is also possible but if the hard drive has physical damage the backup may be corrupted.

   b. On one or more DVDs – This option is available depending on what type of writable media is available on the system. This option generally takes longer and requires a large amount of removable media.

3. Click **Next** and confirm the backup settings on this screen. Click **Start backup** as shown in Figure 2.15. Depending on how much data your system this step varies in time required.

Manual Backup of User Data

User data may be manually backed up by the end user or administrator. Manually backing up user data requires knowledge of the operating

■ **FIGURE 2.14** Windows Complete PC
Backup – Backup Location Selection

■ **FIGURE 2.15** Windows Complete PC
Backup – Start Backup

system and the file system in use. User data backup entails copying the user's files and folders from the system drive to another hard drive, external device, removable media, or network location. User data is generally located in the user's profile folder although it can really be anywhere on the hard drive the user may have saved a file. It is best practice to ask the end user where he or she saves data and what file locations and folders the data is on.

This process may be performed straight from Windows Explorer on Windows XP or Windows Vista. Open a Windows Explorer window and

NOTE

Many folders and files in the user profile folder are hidden. Make sure to show hidden files and folders before copying and backing up to ensure nothing is missed. To show hidden files and folders in Windows XP:

1. Open **Windows Explorer**.
2. Click **Tools | Folder Options**.
3. Clickt he **View**t ab.
4. Select the radio button in **Advanced Settings | Files and Folders | Hidden files and folders** that reads **Show hidden files and folders**,a s showni n Figure2 .16.
5. Click **OK**.

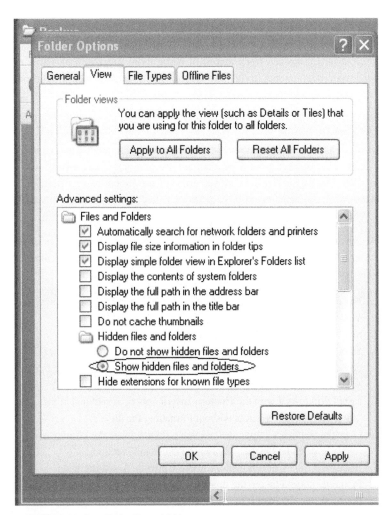

■ **FIGURE 2.16** Show Hidden Files and Folders

> **WARNING**
>
> The manual process of backing up and moving user's data to another storage location is the same process most automated tools perform. By performing a manual backup, you can ensure the back up of all of the user's data that might be in different locations other than the user's profile. Unfortunately, as the process is manual it is prone to human error such as forgetting to back up certain data so be sure to double check with the user, especially if the system where the data is currently stored will be formatted.

> **WARNING**
>
> Remembert hatm ovingu ser data, settings, and applications that were previously installed may not be completely success-ful. Furthermore, if software is not configured correctly, not approved, or contains malicious code it will be moved to the new system. This might not be the best option to maintain a standardized environment.

navigate to the backup location. This may be another hard drive folder, external hard drive, USB key, a blank CD or DVD, or a network-shared drive. Open another Windows Explorer window and navigate to the user's profile folder. On Windows XP look in %SystemDrive%\Documents (Figure 2.17) and Settings\%UserName% and on Windows Vista look in %SystemDrive%\Users\%UserName%, right-click on the entire user folder and select **Copy** (Figure 2.18). Navigate to the Windows Explorer window of the backup location. Right-click and select **Paste**. Repeat for all files and folders that will be backed up.

Other Tools

There are a number of third-party tools available that promise to properly move user data, settings, and even applications. Most of these tools are not free but have a proven track record of being more successful and able to copy more components to the new system. For a single system migration, LapLink PCmover has proved to be successful.

LapLink PCmover

LapLink Software has been around the PC industry for years. The PCmover program has also been around for years and had a major rewrite for Windows 7, as shown in Figure 2.19. PCmover does all the functions of Microsoft's Windows Easy Transfer with the additional feature of migrating installed applicationsa sw ell.

PCmover must be installed on the current operating system before attempting to migrate to Windows 7. The general process works something like the following, but please see the product documentation for exact steps:

1. Install LapLink PCmover on the current Windows XP or Windows Vista machine.
2. Start PCmover and choose the **Upgrade Assistant**.
3. Scan the computer for an inventory of the user data, settings, applications, and other information. An inventory file will be saved on the current system.
4. Install Windows 7 with the **Custom Install** option, as outlined in the "Migration Install" section, without formatting the drive.
5. Once the Windows 7 upgrade completes, do not delete the Windows.old folder, as described in the "Migration Post Install" section.
6. Install and run PCmover again. Choose **Upgrade Assistant** again.
7. PCmover should locate the upgrade file and move the data and application from the old install to the new Windows 7 install. This includes moving settings and registry keys.

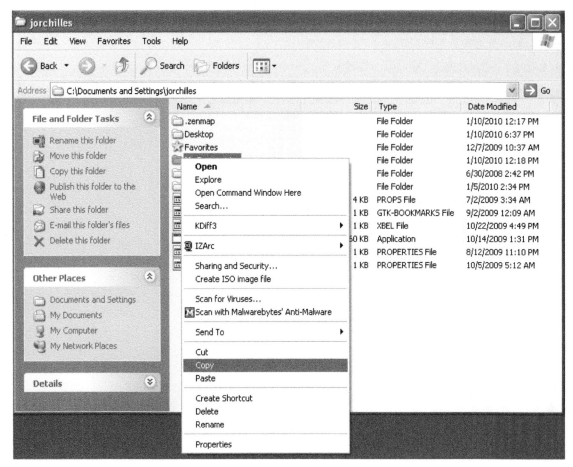

■ **FIGURE 2.17** Windows XP Manual Backup

DetermineD eploymentS cenario

There are four different scenarios for Windows 7 deployments: new system, upgrade system (in-place upgrade from Windows Vista), system refresh, and system replacement. Based on the scenario that applies to your single deployment or organization-wide deployment, one will be better prepared to address other sections in the planning and preparation phase. It is possible that you have each scenario in a large organization, depending on the organizational needs and requirements.

■ New system – This method involves a brand new computer with a formatted or blank hard drive. There is no user data or operating system on the device before installing Windows 7.

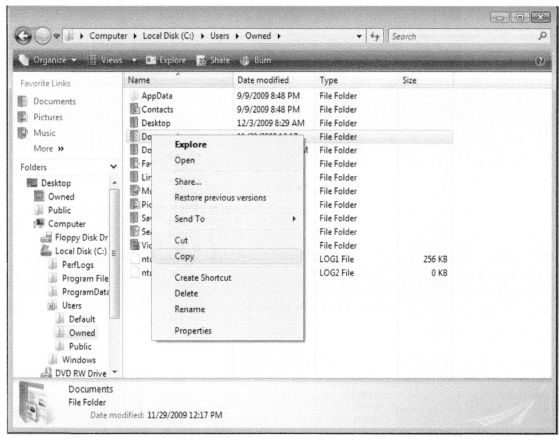

■ **FIGURE 2.18** Windows Vista Manual
Backup

- Upgrade system – This method involves performing an in-place upgrade of a current Windows Vista system on the same machine. Windows Vista is upgraded and no longer accessible once the upgrade completes.
- Refresh system – This method is similar to the new system method except the hard drive contains an operating system that cannot be upgraded and user data.
- Replace system – This migration technique is used when a user from an older machine with an operating system and user data will be migrating to a new computer with Windows 7.

New System Scenario

A new system scenario is the simplest and most recommended scenario for deploying Windows 7. This method involves a clean install of Windows 7

■ **FIGURE 2.19** LapLink PC Mover Web Site

on a new or formatted hard drive. This scenario is the most reliable deployment method as it does not involve any old user data or settings that may be incorrect or corrupt. A new system install allows for a clean configuration from the start. A new system scenario is a great start to a standardized environment. It does not necessarily mean a new computer as Windows 7 can be installed on a virtual machine or on a different partition or hard disk of a current system. Although virtualization or dual booting is involved, the scenario would still be new and the install type clean.

Upgrade System Scenario

An upgraded system scenario involves an in-place upgrade from Windows Vista to Windows 7. This method preserves all of the user's data and settings, as well as installed applications. The in-place upgrade, as you will see in the next section, has strict requirements. Only Windows Vista SP1 and above may be upgraded in place to Windows 7. Additionally, the same edition and 32-bit or 64-bit version must be used. This is another simple method of deploying Windows 7 as data migration and the reinstallation of drivers, devices, or applications is not necessary. However, this method also upgrades all of the data, settings, and applications even if they contain malware, are unauthorized, or are not configured correctly. This could trouble future management and standardization initiatives. Upgrading a nonstandard deployment to Windows 7 does not change the fact that it is not standardized. This method is not recommended in the organization and it is best to consider a new system or refresh scenario.

System Refresh Scenario

> **WARNING**
>
> By migrating user data and settings to a new, clean Windows 7 install, you risk the possibility of copying incorrect configurations or even malware from the user's old computer. It is recommended to scan all user files and folders before migrating them to the new system to ensure this is not the case.

A system refresh is similar to a new system scenario as the system will receive a clean install of Windows 7 as well. However, the system currently contains another operating system such as Windows XP or Windows Vista and end user data, settings, and applications. The system refresh involves performing user backup techniques explained previously to ensure the user's data and settings are saved/preserved and then loaded back on to the clean Windows 7 system. Microsoft provides multiple tools to perform this step on a single or multiple systems. This process is explained in the "Manual Backup of User Data" section and will be elaborated for larger deployment scenarios in Chapter 10, "Windows 7 Troubleshooting and Performance Tools."

System Replace Scenario

The last scenario you may encounter for deploying Windows 7 is moving a user from an old computer to a new computer. Like the refresh scenario, this method involves backing up the user's data and settings from the old computer and transferring them to the new, clean Windows 7 install. This method allows the old computer to still be accessible in case files or settings were not copied correctly. This is also the only method in which a Windows easy transfer cable may be used.

Select Install Type

Microsoft Windows 7 Setup specifies only two install methods as shown in Figure 2.20: **Upgrade** and **Custom**. The upgrade option is what we refer to

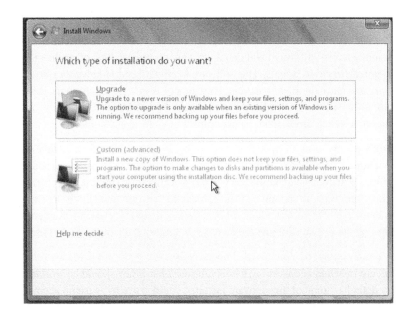

■ **FIGURE 2.20** Windows 7 Install Types — Upgrade or Custom

as an *in-place upgrade*. The custom option is also known as a *clean install*, which installs Windows 7 regardless of what is on the hard drive. However, we will address a few other install types because Microsoft thrives in confusing the end user and administrators.

The first install type that we will discuss does not require an install at all; it is obtaining a new system with Windows 7 already installed or preinstalled. The second install type is performing a clean (or custom as Microsoft calls it) install on a new system. The third involves performing an in-place upgrade (or upgrade as Microsoft calls it) from a compatible Windows Vista machine to a compatible Windows 7 edition. The fourth install type involves migrating to Windows 7 from another Windows operating system (considered an upgrade from Microsoft licensing perspective but a custom install through setup). Finally, Windows 7 may be installed on top of another operating system using virtualization technology or alongside another operating system by using hard drive partitioning or a different hard drive.

Preinstalled

Purchasing a new computer with Windows 7 preinstalled is, and will continue to be, very common in the home, office, and enterprise. This install method addresses the new system scenario and the system replace scenario. It is by far the easiest method of deploying Windows 7; however, administrators frown heavily on this method. Most administrators will tell you that it is not

WARNING

Almostal ls ystemst hatb ring Windows 7 preinstalled will also bring a suite of software often called bloatware or crapware. It is recommended that this software be removed and/or disabled from running at boot. The best solution is a clean install of the operating system; be cautious of the software licensing issues while performing a clean install on an original equipment manufacturer (OEM)s ystem.

TIP

Removeal lap plicationst hat came preinstalled on the system and those that will not be used. This is done by going to the Control Panel and then selecting **Programs and Features**. This should be the first step if choosing to run preinstalled Windows 7 deployments.

recommended to use any preinstalled operating system. The issue with preinstalled systems is that the software manufacturers install by default. Most manufacturers will install additional software on the machine other than the required hardware drivers. This software is often called *bloatware* or *crapware* and normally runs by default, bogging down your system from the start. Not only will the system have unsupported software but also it is the worst start to a standardized desktop environment in your organization.

From an end-user perspective, this is the simplest method of obtaining Windows 7 in a working fashion. Therefore, most end users at home, home offices, and even small businesses will buy systems with a preinstalled operating system version, and run them in a production environment. If this decision is made then the correct edition of Windows 7 should be chosen before purchasing the system to ensure the correct features are available to the end user.

A positive point of a preinstalled operating system is that all hardware drivers are installed and working by default (or at least they should be working by default). Some of the software installed could prove to be useful such as antivirus; however, they will usually ask for payment after three months. Additionally, the manufacturers usually have the correct drivers on their respective Web sites.

Preinstalled Windows 7 licenses are OEM licenses issued by the manufacturer. The next subsection on obtaining Windows 7 will reiterate these points: performing a clean install on these systems might require another license; support is only given by the OEM manufacturer.

Finally, as a preinstalled Windows 7 could be addressing a replace computer scenario, it would be required to load the user's data and settings on this new machine. Steps to moving user's data to the new system are explained in the "Post Install" section of this chapter.

Clean Install

A clean install of Windows 7 is the most recommended method of installing Windows 7 as the hard drive will only have Windows 7 on the disk when the install is completed. This involves a new system scenario only. If the system contains another version of Windows and data and settings must be moved from the user's old computer to the new computer, it is considered a migration, which will be addressed in the "Migration" subsection. A clean install will, generally, be on a blank hard drive or involve formatting the hard drive during the setup phase. This ensures there is no other data on the system that could cause issues later.

A clean install involves booting the computer from the Windows 7 install media, not from within a current operating system. A clean install requires a Windows 7 retail full version license. As you will see in the "Migration" section, it is possible to migrate with an upgrade license and format the hard drive.

Because a clean install will result in a Windows 7 default install, hardware devices and drivers may need to be installed post install. Microsoft has done a pretty good job at providing a large amount of hardware support, but it is possible that some devices might not work.

In-place Upgrade

This install type is the only install type available for the upgrade system scenario. An in-place upgrade is called so because Microsoft Interactive Setup will upgrade the computer from a compatible version of Windows Vista to an allowable edition of Windows 7. An in-place upgrade will upgrade all of the user's data, settings, applications, and hardware devices and drivers. As a result of the upgrading process, the in-place upgrade will take much longer than a clean install; depending on the amount of data, this process can take hours to complete. This method can prove to be efficient for some end users and administrators with fewer machines and enough time as it does not require many post install tasks. However, if the system is using unauthorized software or contains malicious files they will also be upgraded. This makes the process of standardizing the environment much harder.

The in-place upgrade install type requires the Windows 7 upgrade version and media, which will be addressed in the next subsection discussing obtaining Windows 7. The upgrade must be performed from within the system, which will also be addressed in the "In-place Upgrade" section of this chapter.

Microsoft has provided the in-place upgrade install type for easier deployment and migration to Windows 7. However, there are strict guidelines defining what Windows Vista editions may be upgraded to Windows 7 editions. First, 32-bit versions of Windows Vista may only be upgraded to 32-bit versions of Windows 7; the same is true for 64-bit versions. Second, the Windows Vista edition can only upgrade to the same Windows 7 edition. Third, only Windows Vista SP1 and newer versions may be upgraded in place. A chart to better illustrate the strict in-place upgrade criteria is available in Figure 2.21.

Unsupported In-place Upgrade Scenarios

As you can deduce from the chart, the following are not supported for in-place upgrades:

- Any Windows operating system earlier than Windows Vista SP1
- Serverop eratings ystems
- Cross-edition (for example, Home Premium to Professional)
- Cross-architecture (32-bit to 64-bit or vice-versa)

Upgrading Your PC to Windows 7

Upgrade FROM :		Windows 7 Home Premium		Windows 7 Professional		Windows 7 Ultimate	
		32-bit	64-bit	32-bit	64-bit	32-bit	64-bit
Windows XP*		Custom Install	Custom Install	Custom Install	Custom Install	Custom Install	Custom Install
Windows Vista Starter	32-bit	Custom Install	Custom Install	Custom Install	Custom Install	Custom Install	Custom Install
	64-bit	Custom Install	Custom Install	Custom Install	Custom Install	Custom Install	Custom Install
Windows Vista Home Basic	32-bit	In-Place Upgrade	Custom Install	Custom Install	Custom Install	In-Place Upgrade	Custom Install
	64-bit	Custom Install	In-Place Upgrade	Custom Install	Custom Install	Custom Install	In-Place Upgrade
Windows Vista Home Premium	32-bit	In-Place Upgrade	Custom Install	Custom Install	Custom Install	In-Place Upgrade	Custom Install
	64-bit	Custom Install	In-Place Upgrade	Custom Install	Custom Install	Custom Install	In-Place Upgrade
Windows Vista Business	32-bit	Custom Install	Custom Install	In-Place Upgrade	Custom Install	In-Place Upgrade	Custom Install
	64-bit	Custom Install	Custom Install	Custom Install	In-Place Upgrade	Custom Install	In-Place Upgrade
Windows Vista Ultimate	32-bit	Custom Install	Custom Install	Custom Install	Custom Install	In-Place Upgrade	Custom Install
	64-bit	Custom Install	Custom Install	Custom Install	Custom Install	Custom Install	In-Place Upgrade

Custom Install: A custom (clean) installation gives you the option to either completely replace your current operating system or install Windows on a specific drive or partition that you select. You can also perform a custom installation if your computer does not have an operating system, or if you want to set up a multiboot system on your computer.

In-Place Upgrade: Keeps your files, settings, and programs intact from your current version of Windows.

Windows Easy Transfer and the Windows 7 Upgrade Advisor are useful tools that can assist your upgrade. For more information about these tools and upgrading your PC to Windows 7, please visit: **http://windows.microsoft.com/upgrade**

Additional Notes:

*If you are upgrading from Windows XP, you will need to back up your files and settings, perform a custom (clean) install, and then re-install your existing files, settings, and programs.

To upgrade an earlier operating system than Windows XP (e.g. Windows 95 or Windows 2000) you will need to purchase a full license of Windows 7 and perform a custom installation.

In the EEA/EU (including Croatia and Switzerland) and Korea, Microsoft will ship Windows 7 editions that do not include certain features such as Windows Media Player, and related technologies such as Windows Media Center. Upgrading to these editions will require a custom installation.

Upgrading Windows Vista from one language (e.g. English) to Windows 7 in a different language (e.g. French), requires a custom install.

■ **FIGURE 2.21** Windows 7 Upgrade Chart

- Cross-language(Englisht oSpa nish)
- Windows 7 prereleases (Beta or Release Candidate [RC])

AnytimeU pgradet o Windows7

Once using Windows 7, Microsoft has a feature called *Anytime Upgrade*. This allows you to easily upgrade a lower edition of Windows 7 to a more feature-filled Windows 7 edition. These are the Anytime Upgrade paths available:

- Starter to Home Premium, Professional, and/or Ultimate
- Home Basic to Home Premium, Professional, and/or Ultimate
- Home Premium to Professional and/or Ultimate
- Professionalt oU ltimate

Anytime Upgrade is available from within Windows 7 by typing **anytime** in the **Start menu Search**. The wizard assists the user in purchasing an upgrade license and performing the upgrade. It is very simple and does not require any of the processes outlined in this chapter.

In-place Repair Upgrade

An in-place repair may also be performed once Windows 7 is installed. This is exactly like an in-place upgrade but can only be done from the current Windows 7 edition to the same Windows 7 edition. In-place repair upgrade works for all editions of Windows 7 as long the architecture is consistent (32-bit or 64-bit). To do an in-place repair upgrade, follow the "Performing an In-place Upgrade" section in this chapter.

Migration

A migration install is performed for a system refresh scenario. This involves a system that currently runs a Windows operating system and will be migrated (because the in-place upgrade is not possible) to Windows 7 on the same system. A migration is considered a custom install by Microsoft, and it involves performing a custom install followed by migrating the user's data and settings. There are three important steps I would like to reiterate for the migration install: backing up the user data for migration, performing a custom install, and restoring the data. Because there is a current operating system with Windows running, an upgrade license may be used for this install type.

> **NOTE**
> Please ensure that you are using the correct licensing methods as we are not held liable for any decisions made that result in unlicenseds oftware.

Virtualization and Dual Booting

Virtualization allows the install of Windows 7 to occur on a virtual machine on top of a host operating system. This means Windows 7 can virtually run on top of any operating system that supports virtualization technology.

There are multiple products for running virtual machines on desktops. For Windows operating systems, there is VMware Workstation, Player, and Server (http://www.vmware.com/solutions/desktop/), Microsoft Virtual PC, and Sun VirtualBox (http://www.virtualbox.org/). For Apple systems, there is also VMware Fusion and Parallels. These applications installed on top of the current operating system can then run Windows 7 as a virtual machine.

Dual booting allows for Windows 7 to be installed on a separate hard drive or partition of the current system. The difference between dual booting and virtualization is that dual booting will install Windows 7 on a separate hard drive, which means that the boot loader will change and allow only one operating system to boot up at a time. Two operating systems will not be able to run concurrently with this option, and the other system's hard drive or partition could be accessed from the other operating system. This is a good option for testing Windows 7 and/or running it alongside another system that does not support virtualization.

The install type for a virtual machine or dual booting is identical to the clean install type explained in the "Performing a Clean Install" section of this chapter. This method addresses the new system scenario for deployment. Virtualization and dual booting install methods for Windows 7 will be addressed in the end of this chapter.

Obtain Windows 7

Each Windows 7 system in your organization or environment requires a license. Licenses can be obtained through one of the three ways: retail, original equipment manufacturer (OEM), or volume licensing. Each method has its own method of activation to consider.

Retail

Windows 7 may be obtained from retail brick and mortar stores or online stores. Each retail version of Windows 7 brings the installation media and an individually licensed product key for activation. The product key is found inside the packaging and should not be seen by others before your acquisition. The product key is requested during the installation of the system or can be inserted after Windows 7 Setup completes. Once Windows 7 Setup is complete, it must activate the installation using the product key. The activation process is similar to Windows Vista and can be done online or by phone.

To check activation status or activate the product after installing, open the Control Panel and select the **System** console. Scrolling down will display a Windows activation section that states the current status, and allows for activation or change of the product key, as shown in Figure 2.22.

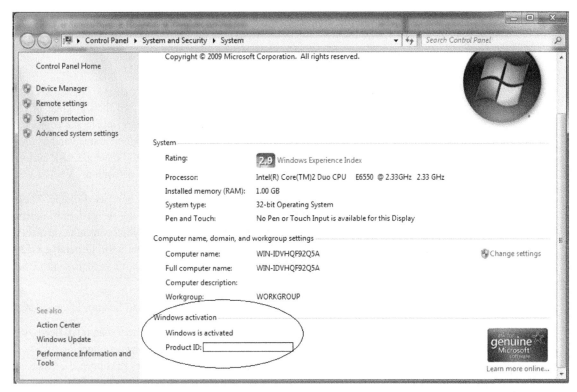

■ **FIGURE 2.22** Activation Status

Two different versions of Windows 7 may be purchased apart from the different editions and 32-bit or 64-bit versions: full version or upgrade version.

Full Version

The more expensive retail version of Windows 7 is the full version. This is for end users who will be installing Windows 7 on a system without Windows XP or Windows Vista. It is the full version of Windows 7, meaning it can perform all types of Windows 7 Setup including upgrade and clean install. Owners of Windows versions earlier than XP or other operating systems must purchase this copy as well.

Upgrade Version

The upgrade version of Windows 7 is for end users who already own a Windows 2000, Windows XP, or Windows Vista license. The upgrade version must be used on the machine with the Windows XP or Windows Vista license to qualify as an upgrade. Microsoft attempts to enforce this by forcing the custom install to be started from within the operating system. However, there is a way to perform a clean install with an upgrade license, and it will be explained later in this chapter in the "Migration Post Install" section.

Original Equipment Manufacturer

OEM licenses are included with a preinstalled Windows 7 system. Computer manufacturers perform the OEM activation on their original image setup on the end users computer before the end user obtains the computer. This method of activation is known as *OEM Activation* and is valid as long as the system has the OEM-provided image on the machine. If a custom image is installed, the OEM key *may* not work for activation.

OEM versions of Windows 7 may be found and purchased online. These versions are aimed at PC builders who intend to sell the system to others. An OEM license obtained online will only come with the installation media, a product key, and possibly a paper describing the item. Generally, OEM licenses can only be purchased with hardware so online vendors send a USB cable with it.

There are a few differences between OEM and retail licenses to consider:

- Cost – Generally, OEM licenses are much cheaper than retail licenses and tend to vary daily. Retail licenses do not change often.
- Support – Microsoft does not offer support for OEM licenses, hence the cost difference. Support must be obtained from the OEM vendor or systemb uilder.
- Gray area – These licenses are only supposed to be sold to PC makers, and vendors are supposed to verify this.

Volume License

Volume licensing is another option for licensing Microsoft products and Windows 7. Volume licensing does not provide a full Windows desktop license. A Windows desktop license must be obtained through an OEM or retail. Volume licensing programs only cover upgrades from an existing Windows product. Benefits of volume licensing include a customized program specific to your organization and size, easier activation through key management services (KMS) or multiple activation key (MAK), and end user activation transparency.

ObtainD evice/HardwareD rivers

Obtaining the device and hardware drivers before installing any operating system is a best practice. Although Microsoft has increased the device and driver support for Windows 7 substantially, there is not a guarantee the drivers will all be installed after a custom install. In the event that Microsoft does not install the hardware drivers by default, you will most likely have to go online and download the drivers manually. If the hardware driver that did not install was the network or wireless card, how will you go online? Hence the reason this step is in the planning and preparation phase.

Depending on your system, the manufacturer, and the hardware components, you may need to do a bit of searching to find the correct drivers. The most important aspect is that you need to find the drivers for the Windows 7 edition you plan to install. It is of utter importance that you obtain the correct 32-bit or 64-bit drivers, depending on the edition. Usually drivers that work for Home Premium will work for Professional, Ultimate, and Enterprise and vice versa. This step can also serve to confirm hardware compatibility.

To find the correct hardware drivers, begin with the manufacturer of the system. Whether it be Dell, HP, IBM, and so on, visit the manufacturer's Web site and search for hardware drivers as shown in Figure 2.23. Often you may put the model of the computer and it will display a list of operating system versions to download all drivers for. Ensure that the 32-bit or 64-bit version is properly chosen.

In the event that you cannot find the drivers from the system manufacturer's Web site, you may search for hardware drivers individually. To determine the individual hardware of your computer, you may visit Device Manager on Windows XP or Windows Vista through **Control Panel | System** or by right-clicking **My Computer | Properties**. In Windows XP, click the **Hardware** tab and then **Device Manager**. On Windows Vista, choose **Device Manager** from the panel on the left. The Device Manager lists all of the hardware components. Clicking on the pane to expand the group will show detailed information about the device as shown in Figure 2.24.

Once you have obtained the hardware and device drivers, store them in a safe location that will not be lost during the deployment. The best place is generally a USB thumb drive, external hard drive, or nonsystem hard drive. In the event the hardware drivers do not install, these devices will not work. A network location might not be the best place if the network drivers do not install correctly.

CLEAN INSTALL

A clean install of Windows 7 is the preferred approach for deploying Windows 7 on a single or few system, even when upgrading from another operating system. The clean install of Windows 7 only installs the default operating system and drivers provided by Microsoft.

WARNING
When searching for drivers, be careful not to fall for fake or malicious driver download sites. It is best to go to the Web site of the manufacturer of the entire computer system or the Web site of the individual hardware device manufacturer. Many sites online advertise having drivers and will ask you to pay or give up information. You should not pay or have to input any information other than the device information to obtain drivers.

WARNING
Ac leani nstalle ntailsi nstalling Windows 7 on a blank or formatted hard drive. The hard drive will be formatted meaning any data on the hard drive will be lost. If you have data that has not been backed up to another system, it will be lost. You may skip to the "Migration" subsection to perform an install that will not remove data from the drive or go back to the planning and preparation phase to back up the data before proceeding.

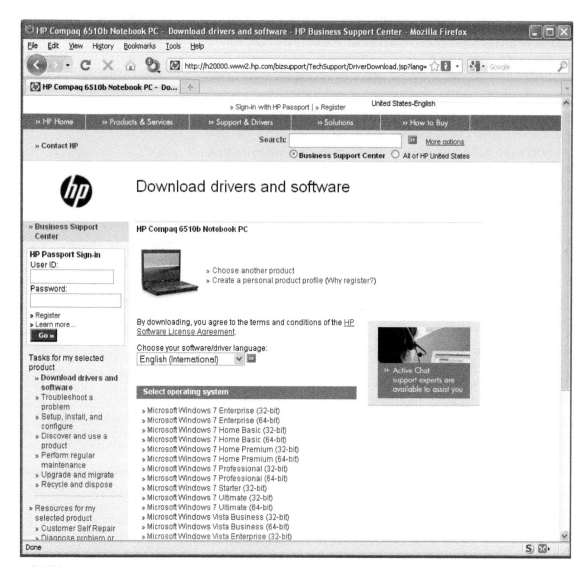

■ FIGURE 2.23 Operating System Drivers for HP Compaq 6150b Notebook PC

Preparation and Planning for a Clean Install

The preparation and planning should have already been conducted if you are on this section, but it is still useful to reiterate the most important aspects of this phase:

- Select the Windows 7 Edition to be installed: 32-bit or 64-bit.
- Check system compatibility and hardware requirements.
- Back up current system if it has data in the hard drive; otherwise, it will be lost when the drive is formatted.

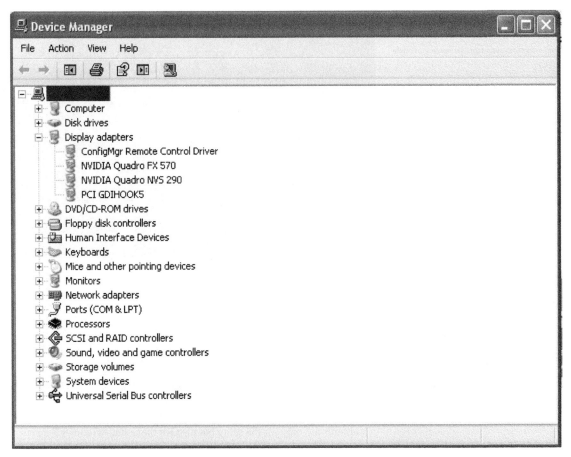

- Determine that the deployment scenario will be a new system scenario.
- Select a clean install method.
- Obtain the Windows 7 media, product key, and license for the edition chosen.
- Obtain the device/hardware drivers *prior to install*.

PerformingaC leanI nstall

A clean install of Windows 7 uses Microsoft's Interactive Setup wizard. The install process has been vastly improved from previous versions of Windows for the most streamlined install process yet. Follow these steps to install Windows 7 as a clean install:

1. Insert the Windows 7 DVD in your system's optical drive and boot the system (or reboot). Depending on your basic input/output system (BIOS) settings, you may need to press a key to change the boot order,

■ **FIGURE 2.25** Windows Logo and "Starting Windows" Text

so the machine boots from the DVD; or you may get a message to press any key to boot from CD or DVD; or you may not get a message at all and see a black screen with a pulsating Windows logo and the "Starting Windows"t exta ss howni n Figure2.25 .

2. The initial setup windows will appear showing Windows 7 and three options as illustrated in Figure 2.26. This is where you may select the language, time, and currency format, and keyboard input type. These options are only for the setup but also for the actual Windows 7 installation as an administrator may install Windows 7 in different language than the end user. Select **Next** when the correct options have been selected.

3. This window will give you the main option to install and two other options. Selecting **Install now** will do just that. Selecting **What to know before installing Windows** will pop up a document that provides general information that you should know before installing Windows 7, including the difference between an upgrade and custom install, all of which is explained in this book. Selecting the **Repair your computer** will bring up the Windows Recovery Environment, which includes Startup Repair. This feature is mentioned in Chapter 1, "Introduction to Windows 7," and explained further in Chapter 9, "Virtualization and Windows 7." Select **Install now** to continue the installation.

4. A Setup is starting… window will appear briefly, depending on your hardware. The next window that requires interaction is the Microsoft End User License Agreement, also known as the EULA. It is recommended

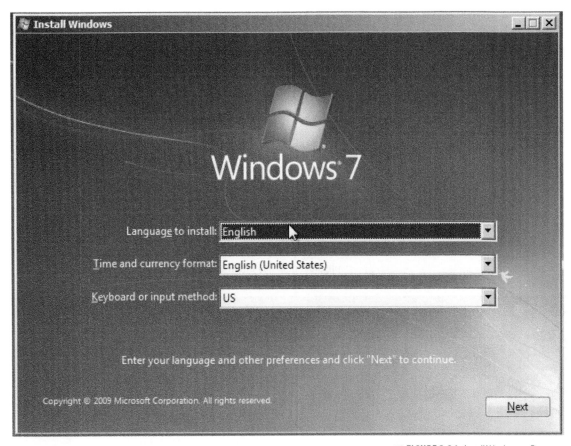

■ FIGURE 2.26 Install Windows – First Screen after Booting from Install Media

that you read this agreement before agreeing to it. In actuality, the end user should also read this. Administrators know this rarely occurs, but for legal purposes we must recommend you read this. If you accept the agreement, check the check box stating **I accept the license terms** and click **Next**.

5. The following screen allows the selection of installation type as shown in Figure 2.20. As we are performing a clean install, the **Custom (advanced)** installation option will be selected. Note that Microsoft reiterates that this option does not keep your files, settings, and programs and includes a recommendation to back up files before proceeding. As this is a clean install to a new hard drive or computer, there should not be data that needs to be backed up. Select **Custom** and proceed.

6. In the next window, you will select where to install Windows 7. This screen varies depending on how many physical hard drives and partitions

WARNING

Selecting **Format** or deleting partitions will delete everything on the hard drive. This option does a quick format, meaning that it is faster but does not "write 0s" to the entire drive. By not performing a full format, the data may still be recovered but, be warned, it will not be easy to recover as this option authorizes new data to be written where the old data was storedont he drive.

are configured in your system. This screen also gives you **Drive options (advanced)** to configure your physical disks and partitions.

a. A new system with a blank hard drive will display Disk 0 Unallocated Space and **Next** may be selected if you do not want to partition the disk and want to let Windows Setup handle it.

b. If there is more than one physical drive, then Disk 0, Disk 1, and so on will display for the number of physical discs. If there is more than one partition on a disk, then Disk 0 Partition 1, Disk 0 Partition 2, and so on will appear for each partition on a physical disc. You may select the disk and partition where you want to install Windows 7 and click **Next**, but clicking **Drive options (advanced)** will provide more options.

c. Selecting **Drive options (advanced)** allows for more options than just selecting where to install. Here you may delete a partition, format a partition, create a partition, and extend a partition if the physical disk has unallocated space as shown in Figure 2.27. It is

■ **FIGURE 2.27** Drive Options

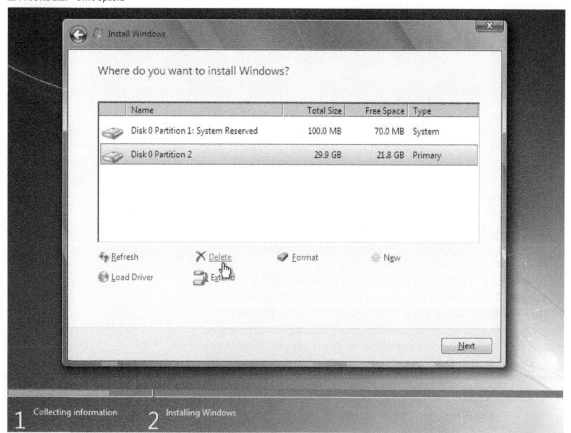

recommended that the partition where you plan to install Windows 7 be formatted before continuing. Once the disk and partition for Windows 7 install is highlighted, select **Next**.

    d. If a disk drive does not show up, it could be because Windows Setup does not have the driver for it. A **Load Driver** option is available to load the driver for the drive as shown in Figure 2.28. This can be found in the hard disk manufacturer's Web site or provided with the drive and/or card used in the system. This may occur if Redundant Array of Inexpensive Disks (RAID), Small Computer Serial Interface (SCSI), or a new type of disk drive is used. Select **Load Driver** and follow the wizard so the drive appears or select **Browse** to manually assign it. **Refresh** can be clicked to refresh the list.

7. Once **Next** is selected from the *Where do you want to install Windows?* screen, Windows 7 will install on your system. A progress window will appear warning of several restarts. Depending on the hardware on this system, this process will take from as little as 10 min up to 45 min; allow more time for slower systems.

8. A few reboots, screen flickers, and other hard work by your system will finish with a final reboot and a greeting welcoming you to Setup Windows.

9. The system will reboot and Windows will ask you for a user name and computer name as shown in Figure 2.29. These two criteria are very important. Please do not skip this part!

    a. User name – The user name setup in this step will be given administrator privileges. Unlike Windows XP but like Windows Vista, only one user will be created in this section and the "Administrator" account is not a visible account for security reasons. A user name of "Administrator" cannot be created for security reasons. Because this user name will be an administrator, you should create an administrative user name that will not be used on a daily basis. We recommend using "OSInstaller" or a similar name.

> **NOTE**
>
> Noticew henc reatinga n ew partition in unallocated space that two partitions are actually created. Partition 1 becomes System Reserved and Partition 2 is the partition specified. The 100 MB System Reserved partition is for the Windows Recovery Environment, which includes the Startup Repair. This feature is mentioned in Chapter 1, "Introduction to Windows 7," and explained further in Chapter 9, "Virtualization and Windows 7." Select **Install now**t o continue the installation. It also allocates space for BitLocker, which is also mentioned in Chapter 1, "Introduction to Windows 7," and explained further in Chapter 7, "Managing Windows 7 in an EnterpriseE nvironment."

> **TIP**
>
> Ast hem achiner eboots,r emember the BIOS settings that might have had to be changed to boot from CD or DVD first, as if this is still set a *Press any key to boot from CD to DVD…* prompt may appear. *Do not* press any key as this will begin Windows Setup from the beginning. You may go back and change this setting to boot from the hard drive first.

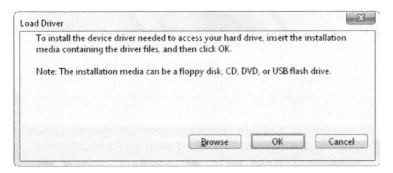

FIGURE 2.28 Load Driver

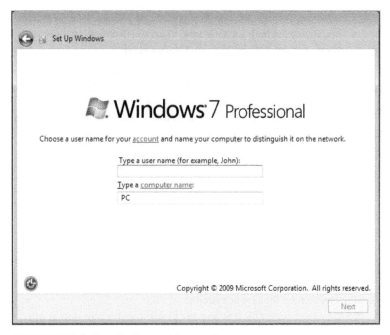

■ FIGURE 2.29 Configure User Name and Computer Name

    b. Computer name – the computer name or host name is how this machine will be identified on the network. Remember that no two like names should exist on the same network. It is a best practice to have a naming convention in place and to follow it. A security identifier (SID) will be created based on the computer name, so changing the computer name later will not change the SID.

    c. Ease of access – Notice the **Ease of Access** button on the bottom left of the screen. This feature, described in Chapter 1, "Introduction to Windows 7," may be used from this point forward to narrate, magnify, see high contrast, and use the on-screen keyboard,s tickyk eys,a ndfi lterk eys.

10. The next screen is to set a password for the account originally created (Figure 2.30). Next to *Type a password* is a (recommended) inference. This is *absolutely necessary*. Recall the user name created previously has administrative privileges. For that user, please create a password that is complex and that only you and/or a limited number of administrators have access to.

11. After setting a password, you may or may not be asked for a product key. This depends on the version and media used to install. If you are prompted for a product key, you may enter it now and select to

■ **FIGURE 2.30** Set a Password

automatically activate Windows after getting online. You may opt out of entering the license key at this point but will only have 30 days to input it later.

12. The following screen will ask whether to enable automatic updates, as illustrated in Figure 2.31. The following are the three options to choose from:

   a. **Use recommended settings** – This option will download and install important and recommended updates automatically by checking every day at 3:00 A.M. by default. It will also allow all users to install updates on the system and get Microsoft product updates for software such as Microsoft Office and other Microsoft applications. *These are the recommended settings* for security purposes.

   b. **Install important updates only** – This option will only download and install important updates, including security updates, automatically by checking every day at 3:00 A.M. by default. This option is recommended as an alternative to the above.

   c. **Ask me later** – This option will allow you to configure automatic updates later and will make the machine unsecure as updates are already out, meaning that your machine will be vulnerable as soon as it gets connected to the Internet. This option is not recommended.

■ FIGURE 2.31 Set Up Automatic Updates

13. The next window will ask for the time zone and setting the correct time. It is a best practice to choose the correct time zone and time for administrativepu rposes.
14. If Windows 7 detected and installed your network hardware drivers correctly and detects a wired or wireless network, the following windows may appear:
    a. Wireless Network Setup – If a wireless network is in range, this window will appear. Here you may select the wireless network to connect to as well as provide the security key if it has one.
    b. Select your computer's current location, as shown in Figure 2.32 – This window will pop up every time the user connects to a new network. It is very important that the end user be trained to select the correct network type the system is connecting to. Depending on this selection, certain networking and security features are configured.
       - **Home network** – The home network is considered a private network for security purposes, meaning that it is trusted. Furthermore, it will ask to set up a *HomeGroup*. AH omeGroup was mentioned in Chapter 1, "Introduction to Windows 7," and will be further explained in Chapter 4, "The New Windows 7 DesktopE nvironment."

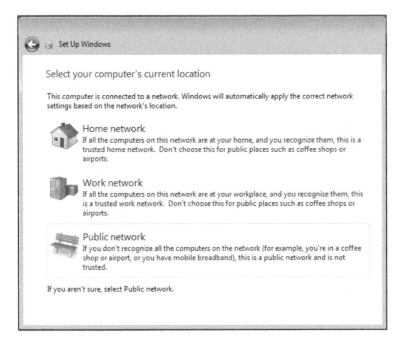

■ **FIGURE 2.32** Select the Computer's Current Location

- **Work network** – The work network is also considered a private network for security purposes, meaning that it is trusted as well. It will not prompt for a HomeGroup but might prompt to join a domain. This feature is mentioned in Chapter 1, "Introduction to Windows 7," and elaborated on in Chapters 4 through 7 as it is thec oreo ft heb usinessu sern etworking capability.
- **Public network** – This network selection is for any public or other network that is not trusted such as cyber cafés, wireless hot spots, and any network that may be hostile. It is extremely important that this is selected when on these networks as the firewall and other security features will be defensively configured.

15. The Windows 7 desktop should now be visible and some of the above steps may have been skipped. Although Windows 7 installation has been completed, there are a few post-setup tasks that need to be completed.

PostC leanI nstall

The post install for a clean deployment of Windows 7 includes the following points described in the "Post Install" section later in this chapter:

■ Install missing hardware and device drivers that Windows 7 Setup missed.

- Run Windows Update to obtain all the latest important and security updates.
- Installa ntiviruss oftware.

Clean Install with Upgrade Media

In every release of Windows, Microsoft attempts to ensure that Microsoft Upgrade licenses are not used for performing clean installs. The reason behind this is that Microsoft needs to prove that the Upgrade license is legit finding another legit version of Windows that is eligible for upgrade. This makes sense from a licensing perspective, but some system administrators and end users have an earlier version of the Windows license and purchased a Windows 7 license, but need to perform a clean install.

The planning and preparation phase of this process still applies. The steps to performing the Windows 7 clean install are all the same with these exceptions:

- Boot the machine with the Windows 7 Upgrade media in the machine and initiate the setup as in Step 1.
- Do not input the product key in Step 11.
- After Windows 7 installation is completed, run Windows Update as explained in the "Post Install" section of this chapter. Install all updates and reboot as needed until no more updates are available.
- Reboot and launch the Activation window by typing **activate** in the Startm enuS earch.

This should work to activate Windows 7. If it does not work, there might be a registry change you must make.

1. Open the registry by typing **regedit** in the Start menu Search. Click **Yes** at the UAC prompt (must have administrative rights).
2. Navigate to: HKEY_LOCAL_MACHINE/Software/Microsoft/Windows/CurrentVersion/Setup/OOBE/ (see Figure 2.33).
3. Right-clicka ndm odify **MediaBootInstall** from the 1 value to 0.
4. Closet heR egistryE ditor.
5. Type **cmd** in the Start menu Search – right-click **cmd.exe** and click **Run as administrator**.
6. Select **Yes** at the UAC prompt.
7. Type **slmgr /rearm** and press **Enter**. Click **OK** on the Windows Script Hostw indow.
8. Reboot and run the activation again by typing **activate** in the Start menuS earch.

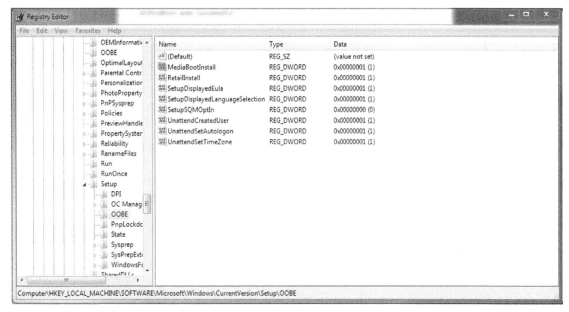

We hope this works to activate the Windows 7 copy. If this still does not work, however, then attempt the following method:

1. Insert the Windows 7 Upgrade media again.
2. Follow the steps in the "In-place Upgrade" section of this chapter (next section).

Now Windows 7 should definitely activate as if an in-place upgrade took place.

IN-PLACE UPGRADE

An *in-place upgrade* is the only upgrade option Microsoft allows during the Interactive Setup wizard. There are two different upgrade methods users and administrators talk of when referring to upgrading to Windows 7. A migration to Windows 7 refers to any process that involves moving from an older version of Windows to Windows 7. This method will be discussed in the next section. This section will focus on the second method of upgrade and what is considered an in-place upgrade.

Preparation and Planning for an In-place Upgrade

An in-place upgrade has a large advantage over the other deployment methods because it promises to keep all applications, user data, and settings installed and functional after the upgrade without further interaction. However, it

> **NOTE**
> Onlyc ertain Windows Vistav er-
> sions are eligible for this type of
> upgrade and only to certain edi-
> tions of Windows 7. The upgrade
> chart is available in the "Planning
> and Preparation" section of this
> chapter for quick reference as
> to what in-place upgrades are
> possible. The Windows 7 Upgrade
> Advisor will quickly tell you if
> your version of Windows Vista is
> upgradablet hrought hism ethod.

is strongly recommended that a full backup is performed before performing this upgrade. Additionally, although Microsoft attests that any hardware and applications that functioned correctly on Windows Vista should function correctly on Windows 7, it is recommended to ensure this by running the Windows 7 Upgrade Advisor tool.

The planning and preparation phases should be completed for the in-place upgrade to ensure it is successful:

- Select a Windows 7 edition that is compatible to perform an in-place upgrade.
- Ensure that all software and hardware is compatible with Windows 7.
- Back up the user's data and settings and/or perform a full system backup to be safe.
- Determine the upgrade system scenario that will be used.
- Select an in-place upgrade install method.
- Obtain a Windows 7 upgrade version of the chosen edition.
- Obtain all Windows 7 device/hardware drivers *prior to install*.

Perform a Full Backup of Windows Vista

It is strongly recommended to do a full backup of the current Windows Vista system before upgrading. Although the track record of the process is good, you do not want to be the one who loses data or even worse, loses someone else's data. Because this will be an in-place upgrade, it is recommended that you back up to another internal hard drive, external hard drive, flash drive, or removable media such as CDs and/or DVDs. A network backup is also advised to put the data in another location. The main point is to move the data from the hard drive that will be upgraded.

NOTE

Once the install media is placed in the system that will be upgraded, the initial screen will ask for a compatibility check. Clicking this option will actually launch the default Web browser to the download location of the Windows 7 Upgrade Advisor. Additionally, once the upgrade process has been selected, the setup wizard will perform a final compatibility check before upgrading. If the system cannot be upgraded, it will not let you continue.

Steps to perform a backup are in the "Planning and Preparation" section of this chapter.

Check Compatibility

Ensuring the software and hardware currently installed on the system is compatible is crucial to ensuring this install method is successful. The easiest way of checking compatibility is by running the Windows 7 Upgrade Advisor. There are multiple checks for compatibility during the upgrade process. The best and most preferred method is to run the Windows 7 Upgrade Advisor before placing the Windows 7 media into the machine. This may be done by downloading the Windows 7 Upgrade Advisor online.

The steps to perform a Windows 7 Upgrade Advisor report are in the "Planning and Preparation" section of this chapter.

Performing a n In-place Upgrade

After you have confirmed that an in-place upgrade is the best deployment method and completed the preparation and planning phase, it is time to upgrade. Here is how an in-place upgrade will typically be performed:

1. An in-place upgrade must be initiated from within the Windows Vista operating system. Place the install media in the computer and wait for AutoPlay to pop up, then select **Run setup.exe**. If AutoPlay is disabled, navigate to the media drive and manually run **setup.exe** in the root of the drive. You may be prompted by UAC; allow this program.

2. In the Install Windows screen, you may choose to **Check compatibility online** or **Install now**, as shown in Figure 2.34.

    a. **Check compatibility online** – Clicking this will open the default Web browser and direct it to the Windows 7 Upgrade Advisor. You should have already run the Upgrade Advisor, but if you haven't, now is a very good time to do so. Steps to perform this process are in the "Planning and Preparation" section of this chapter.

    b. **Install now** – Clicking this will take you straight to the next step to continue the in-place upgrade.

3. Once you have clicked **Install now**, the setup will begin copying temporary files.

> **NOTE**
> In order to perform an in-place upgrade, you must be a member of the Administrators Group on the local computer, or run **Setup.exe** by right-clicking the executable and selecting **Run as Administrator**. If the system is joined to a domain, users in the Domain Admin Group may authenticate to run **Setup.exe**.

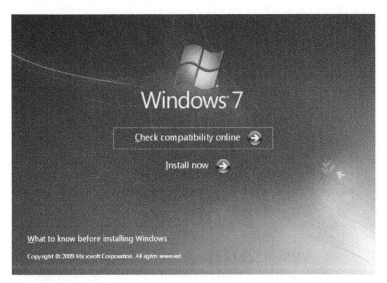

Windows 7

Check compatibility online
Install now

What to know before installing Windows

Copyright © 2009 Microsoft Corporation. All rights reserved.

■ **FIGURE 2.34** Install Windows Screen for In-place Upgrade

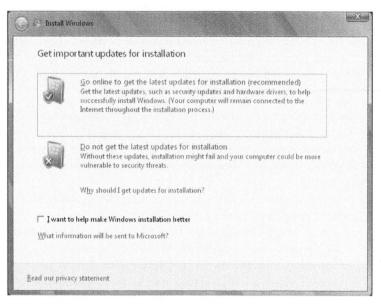

■ **FIGURE 2.35** Get Important Updates for Installation

4. The next screen will ask if you would like to go online to obtain the latest updates for installation as shown in Figure 2.35. It is recommended that this be done, because as Windows 7 goes mainstream, updates will be released to fix any bugs or issues with the in-place upgrade. The Setup wizard will connect to the Internet to obtain these updates, download them, and continue with the in-place upgrade. You may select to not get the latest updates and/or to help make Windows installation better. Selecting to make Windows installation better will send information to Microsoft. You may want to click the link under it to see what exactly is sent to Microsoft by opting to help them.

5. The next window that requires interaction is the Microsoft End User License Agreement, also known as the EULA. It is recommended that you read this agreement before agreeing to it. In actuality, the end user should also read this. Administrators know this rarely occurs but for legal purposes, we must recommend you read this. If you accept the agreement, check the check box stating *I accept the license terms*a nd click **Next**.

6. The next screen will allow you to select between Upgrade or Custom install as shown in Figure 2.20. Click **Upgrade**.

7. A final compatibility check will run and output a report. If your system may be upgraded without issues, you will have the option to select **Next** and continue the upgrade.

8. Depending on the amount of applications, user data, and overall capabilities of the system, this process will take a significant amount of time. The system will reboot a few times, and the screen may or may not flicker. Be patient as this process finishes.

9. If the Windows 7 upgrade was successful, you will see the Windows 7 boot screen followed by a Set Up Windows screen. If you are prompted for a product key, you may enter it now and select to automatically activate Windows upon getting online. You may opt out of entering the license key at this point but will only have 30 days to input it later.

10. The following screen will ask whether to enable Automatic Updates as shown in Figure 2.31. There are three options to choose from:

    a. **Use recommended settings** – This option will download and install important and recommended updates automatically by checking every day at 3:00 A.M. by default. It will also allow all users to install updates on the system and get Microsoft product updates for software such as Microsoft Office and other Microsoft applications. *These are the recommended settings* for security purposes.

    b. **Install important updates only** – This option will only download and install important updates, such as security updates, automatically by checking every day at 3:00 A.M. by default. This option is recommended as an alternative to the above.

    c. **Ask me later** – This option will allow you to configure Automatic Updates later and will make the machine insecure as updates are already out, meaning your machine will be vulnerable as soon as it gets connected to the Internet. This option is not recommended.

11. The next window will ask for the time zone and the correct time. It is a best practice to choose the correct time zone and time for administrativepur poses.

12. The next screen you should see is a login screen for the username used during the upgrade. If you do not have a password, you may land ont hede sktop.

> **WARNING**
>
> If you do not have a password set, please create one immediately. This may be done by going to **Control Panel | User Accounts** and selecting **Create your password**. It is best practice to have a password for all accounts. Passwords should be complex, at least six to eight characters with a combination of upper case, lower case, numbers, and/or symbols.

In-placeU pgradeP ostI nstall

Once you have successfully upgraded to Windows 7, skip to the "Post Install" section of this chapter. As it was an in-place upgrade these will be the steps you do not want to skip:

- Verify that all hardware and device drivers were upgraded correctly.
- Verify that all applications are working correctly.
- Install antivirus if it was not installed previously or if it was removed and verify if it is working properly.
- Perform a Windows Update as there are updates available already.

Issuesw ithI n-placeU pgrade

In the event that the Windows 7 Upgrade is not successful, setup will begin restoring the system to the state it was in before attempting the upgrade. Thankfully, Microsoft has done an incredible job at restoring your current system to the state it was before attempting an upgrade. This process will most likely occur after Step 8 of the "Performing an In-place Upgrade" section.

The first and simplest troubleshooting step to take is to uninstall any applications that were reported as having compatibility issues in the planning and preparation stage. Removing all these applications should be straight forward from within the **Programs and Features** console of the Control Panel.

If the antivirus software running on the system was considered compatible and the in-place upgrade process still failed, it is recommended to remove the antivirus and all other modules of this security product. Remember to save the activation and/or product key for this software as it will be required after the upgrade to reinstall the antivirus software.

MIGRATE TO WINDOWS7

This section will explain how to migrate from any unsupported upgrade version of Windows to Windows 7. This includes all versions of Windows XP and Vista that cannot be upgraded to the version or edition of Windows 7 chosen. Microsoft calls this process a "custom install." The reason this is a custom install is because you must first back up the user data for migration and then perform a custom install on top of the current operating system.

Preparation and Planning for Migration

This section is critical for a successful upgrade from an existing Windows system to Windows 7. It is vital to know that a custom install will need to be performed almost exactly how the "Clean Install" section suggests with the exception of the format, which is optional. These are the planning and preparation steps that should have already been considered and selected:

■ Select that the Windows 7 Edition to be installed.
■ Check the system compatibility and hardware requirements.
■ Back up the current system and user data (this is critical).
■ Determine if the deployment scenario is more likely a refresh or replace systems cenario.

- Select the custom install method with or without a format.
- Obtain an upgrade license for Windows 7 if upgrading from Windows.
- Obtain all device/hardware drivers *prior to install.*

Back Up Current System

Backing up the user's current data and setting defines what makes this a migration instead of a clean install. For system refresh scenarios, it is very important to make sure this process was correctly done. If the hard drive is formatted during the custom install, the data may be lost forever. It is recommended that the backup be placed in a safe place and possibly more than one location to ensure the user's data and settings are not lost.

It is also a good idea to scan these files for malware as you will be placing them back into a refreshed Windows install. The steps to back up the user's data and prepare for the migration are outlined in the "Planning and Preparation" section of this chapter.

Software Compatibility

One of the biggest headaches for administrators and end users alike is the lack of compatibility of mission critical software. Making sure the critical software of the end users works is very important, especially in the refresh scenario as the old system will no longer be available. For this reason, an entire system backup and extensive testing of the software on the system is critical.

To perform a complete system backup and check system and hardware compatibility refer to the "Planning and Preparation" section of this chapter.

PerformM igrationI nstall

Once the preparation and planning steps have been completed, you may begin the upgrade from Windows XP or Windows Vista to Windows 7 as follows:

1. From within the current operating system, insert the Windows 7 Upgrade media and run **Setup.exe** from the AutoPlay window. If Auto-Play does not start you may navigate to the device and select **Setup.exe** from the root folder.
2. The next screen will ask if you would like to go online to obtain the latest updates for installation as shown in Figure 2.35. It is recommended that this be done, because as Windows 7 goes mainstream, updates will be released to fix any bugs or issues with the in-place upgrade. The Setup wizard will connect to the Internet to obtain these

updates, download them, and continue with the in-place upgrade. You may select to not get the latest updates and/or to help make Windows installation better. Selecting to make Windows installation better will send information to Microsoft. You may want to click the link under it see what exactly is sent to Microsoft by opting to help them.

3. On the next screen, illustrated in Figure 2.20, select **Custom** to perform the upgrade.

4. The following step asks for the partition where Windows 7 will be installed as shown in Figure 2.36. Select the partition where Windows 7 will be installed and click **Next**. Windows Setup may ask

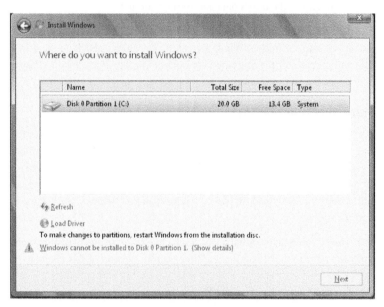

■ **FIGURE 2.36** Where Do You Want to Install Windows?

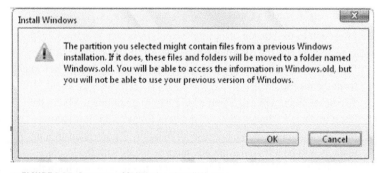

■ **FIGURE 2.37** Renaming of Old Windows Install Warning

for drivers in which case you will need to click **Load Driver** and select the drivers for the hard drive manually or if you have the media, plug it in and click **OK**.

5. Click **Next** and then **OK**. This will install Windows 7 on the chosen partition and not require further interaction.

MigrationP ostI nstall

After installation, the "Post Install" section of this chapter should be followed. However, one difference with a migration that did not format the hard drive during the setup process is that the old install will be renamed to Windows.old. This directory is no longer useful as it contains the old Windows installation.

Delete the Windows.old Directory

The Windows.old directory, which is the old Windows folder renamed during the upgrade, may now be removed. This may be manually removed by opening Windows Explorer, right-clicking on the folder, and selecting **delete**. Or it may be removed with the Disk Cleanup wizard.

1. Open Disk Cleanup by going to **Start | All Programs | Accessories | System Tools | Disk Cleanup**.
2. If you have multiple drives, select your current system drive and click **OK**.
3. Click **Clean up system files**. A scan will occur as shown in Figure 2.38.
4. If prompted for a drive selection, select the drive or partition where Windows 7 was installed and click **OK**.
5. Check **Previous Windows installation(s)** and any other categories you may want to delete. Click **OK** and then click **Delete Files**.

NOTE

Performinga c ustomu pgrade of Windows 7 will change the location of where the previous version of Windows is stored to a folder called Windows.old on the %systemdrive%. This is illustrated in Figure2 .37.

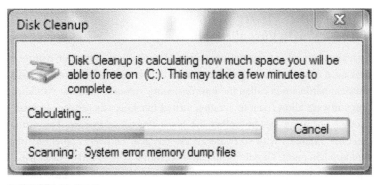

■ **FIGURE 2.38** Disk Cleanup

VIRTUALIZATION AND DUAL BOOT

Virtualization and dual booting are two options for running Windows 7 on a current operating system. Virtualization is becoming more and more popular by the day as it allows virtual machines to run on top of a current operating system. Dual booting has been available for years to run multiple systems on the same computer from different hard drive partitions or different physical hard drives. These options are not only available to run Windows 7 and test a new operating system, but are also available for end users who prefer other operating systems but require a Windows operating system for the corporate image or other software.

This section will address how to use virtualization to create a virtual machine with Windows 7 and how to perform a dual boot to run Windows 7 alongside another operating system.

Virtualization

A virtual machine emulates, or simulate if you will, the hardware function of a physical computer. In short, it lets an entire operating system run as an application on top of a host. In today's diverse technological environments, we are seeing many different systems in any given environment. With Apple, Linux, and/or Unix users in your environment, it may still be a necessity to provide them with a corporate/business system to keep standards. As an administrator, testing Windows 7 settings and applications without housing your current system is also required. Creating a virtual machine on these systems with Windows 7 is the solution. Virtualization and virtual machines can provide many solutions, as well as many new challenges. This section will introduce you to virtualization, describe the different types of virtualization software that may be used, plan and prepare a virtual machine deployment, and show how to perform a Windows 7 install on a virtual machine.

Introduction to Virtualization

Virtualization allows for the emulation of a physical computer within an operating system. The operating system that is currently running on the physical hardware is called the *host operating system*. Installing virtualization software allows you to create a virtual machine where you can install another operating system called the *guest operating system*. The virtual machine emulates with software all the physical hardware functions of a standard computer. Therefore, an entire operating system can be installed on a piece of software that believes it is a physical computer. Because the virtualization technology emulates the hardware, it runs without issues. Because the virtualization technology is essentially software installed on your physical machine, it creates individual files for the guest operating system's hard drive and memory. These are, generally, larger files of the size you specified to make the virtual hard drive and memory.

Virtual machines can prove to be extremely helpful in the testing process of a new operating system, like Windows 7, or any kind of software testing. Because the guest operating system has a virtual hard drive and memory that is a file on the host or physical system, it may be copied, backed up, or reset at any time. Depending on the virtualization technology being used, snapshots can be taken of the current state of the machine. In case something happens later on down the road, say it is infected with malware, you may reset it back to the snapshot. This saves hours in testing that would generally include reinstalling an operating system.

Virtualization Software

There are many products available to run virtual machines on other desktop operating systems. These products are installed on top of the host operating system as applications. Depending on the operating system on the physical machine there are different products available, some free and some for a charge:

- Microsoft Virtual PC – The successor of Virtual PC 2007.
- VMware – A leader in the virtualization arena with different products available.
  - Workstation – For Windows but it is not free. Currently, it has the most advanced features.
  - Server – For Windows and it is free. It has limitations and is slightly more complex.
  - Fusion – For Apple Mac OS X, but is not free. Currently, it has the mosta dvancedf eatures.
- Sun VirtualBox – It is free and available for multiple operating systems.
- Parallels Desktop, is available for Mac, Windows, and Linux but is not free.

Planning and Preparation for Virtual Deployment

Although a virtual machine might seem like an easier feat than a physical computer, the planning and preparation phase should still be followed:

- Selecta Windows7 edition.
- Ensure that all software and hardware are compatible with Windows 7 – most likely they are compatible.

- Back up data – this is not necessary if creating a new virtual machine andd isk.
- Determine the scenario – generally a new system scenario.
- Select the install method – clean install.
- Obtain Windows 7 – a virtual machine requires its own product key andl icense.
- Obtain Windows 7 device/hardware drivers *prior to install* –m ost likely included when installing the virtual machine.

Performing a Windows 7 Install on a VM

Installing Windows 7 on a virtual machine uses the new computer scenario and clean install method. However, it is necessary to create a virtual machine first within the virtualization software. This is different depending on the software, but generally involves the following:

- Selecting the virtual machine hardware compatibility – This depends on the product and its maturity as it may have earlier versions of virtual machines. Remember that a virtual machine is a file, and the virtualization application must be able to understand it to run it.
- Selecting the installer disk – This could be a physical disk in the physical computer that will be emulated in the virtual machine or an installer disc image file.
- Selecting the operating system – This is generally done to automatically configure the virtual hardware.
- Processors – Depending on the processors and cores on the physical system, this may be asked.
- Memory – This is the amount of memory the virtual machine will have. This should be the minimum requirements for the edition of Windows 7 that you will be running. A virtual machine may even run well with less than the required amount of hardware.
- Network connection – This is the configuration of the virtual network card.
  - Bridged – This choice will use the same network as the physical Ethernet card. The virtual machine will appear as another computer on the network.
  - NAT – Network address translation gives the effect of the virtual machine behind a router, where the router would be the host operating system. Generally, Dynamic Host Configuration Protocol will be configured and assigned automatically.
  - Host-only – This will connect the virtual machine to a private virtual network where it will be isolated.
- Virtual disk – You may choose to create a new virtual disk or use an existing one, for this example creates a new one.

- Virtual disk type – This chooses between Integrated Drive Electronics (IDE) or SCSI emulation.
- Virtual disk size – This is the size of the virtual hard drive. Choose wisely as it is difficult to change this later.
- Disk file – You may choose where and how to save the virtual machine harddr ivefi le.

Once the virtual machine is created, the virtualization software will generally boot the system as shown in Figure 2.39. To install Windows 7 on a virtual machine follow the "Performing a Clean Install" section in this chapter.

Virtual Machine Post Install

If you are using VMware, you must install VMware tools after the Windows 7 Setup is finished. This allows for better hardware support within your virtual

■ **FIGURE 2.39** New Virtual Machine Wizard – VMware Workstation 7

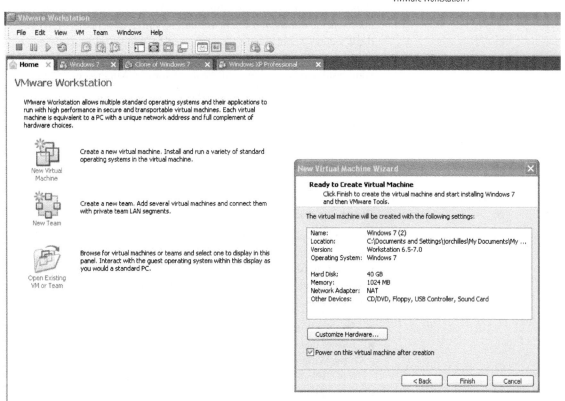

machine, as well as other nice features provided by VMware. All post install options are recommended after the install as this install type is similar to a clean install on a new system deployment scenario.

DualB ooting

Dual booting is a more difficult installation method as it requires installing Windows 7 on a different hard drive or hard drive partition. If the system does not have a second hard drive and/or only one partition on the current drive, then a second partition will need to be created. This section will explain the differences in the planning and preparation phase required to meet the dual boot criteria. It will then explain how to perform the partitioning and clean install of Windows 7. Finally, differences in the post install phase are explained.

Before continuing it is important to understand Window 7's boot scheme. Boot Configuration Data (BCD) was introduced in Windows Vista and is more complex and incompatible with the previous boot schemes of Windows operating systems. Although the Windows 2000 and Windows XP boot scheme allows you to choose among different versions of Windows, the Windows 7 boot menu only lets you select Windows Vista or Windows 7 versions or other operating systems. As a result of these changes, setting up your system to boot several different versions of Windows or other operating systems needs to follow these guidelines:

■ Each operating system should be installed on a different volume or partition.
■ To run Windows versions earlier than Windows Vista, install those systems first and then install Windows 7.
■ Linux or Unix operating systems will need a separate boot manager.

Planning and Preparation

The steps for planning and preparation of a dual boot system are similar to those of a clean install with the exception that a second hard drive or partition needs to be available on the system with at least 16 GB of free space. This section will explain how to correctly partition the hard drive to dual boot Windows 7 from a single hard drive.

■ Selecta Windows7e dition.
■ Ensure that all software and hardware are compatible with Windows 7 – the Windows 7 Upgrade Advisor may be run from the other system if it is a Windows operating system.
■ Back up data – it is not necessary but recommended as the hard drive will be partitioned.

- Determine the scenario – it is generally a new system scenario.
- Select the install method – clean install.
- Obtain Windows 7 – it requires a full version of Windows 7, product key, and license.
- Obtain all Windows 7 device/hardware drivers *prior to install.*

Create a Second Partition with Windows Vista

Windows Vista allows for managing partitions much better than previous versions of Windows. It has the capability to shrink a volume and create another partition, exactly what is needed to dual boot. Ensure that the hard drive that will be used has more than 16 GB of free space. Additionally, you will want to defragment the hard drive before shrinking the volume and creating a new partition.

The following steps defragment a Windows Vista hard drive as illustrated in Figure 2.40 :

1. Ensure all running applications are closed and nothing is being written or read from the hard drive which will be defragmented.
2. Click **Start | Computer**.
3. Right-click the hard drive with more than 16 GB free space that will be used to install Windows 7. Click **Properties**.

■ **FIGURE 2.40** Windows Vista Hard Drive Defragment

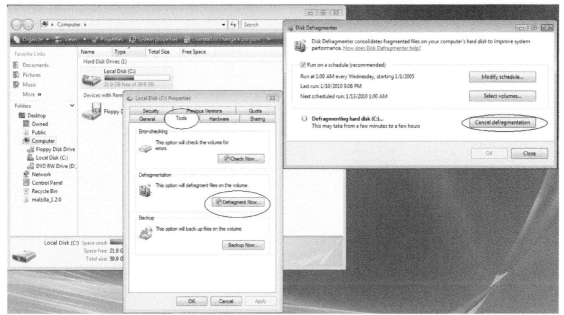

4. Clickt he **Tools**t ab.
5. Click **Defragment Now…** Select **Yes** to the UAC prompt.

Once defragmentation has completed, create a new partition in Window Vista:

1. Click **Start**, right-click **Computer**, and select **Manage**.
2. Click **Disk Management** on the left pane under Storage.
3. Right-click the physical hard drive that will be used for Windows 7 and click **Shrink Volume**a ss howni n Figure2.41 .
4. Input the size, in megabytes, to shrink the partition by Windows 7 needs at least 16, 384 MB. Click **Shrink**.
5. Right-click **Free Space** in the physical hard drive and select **New Simple Volume**.
6. Click **Next**.

■ **FIGURE 2.41** Shrink Volume in Windows Vista

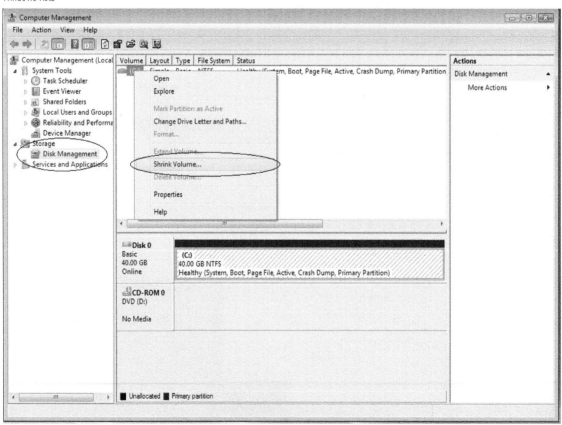

7. Select the volume size, which should be the entire space available by default and click **Next**.
8. Assign a drive letter to the drive and click **Next**.
9. Select to format the volume as new technology file system (NTFS) and assign a volume label. This can be done by Windows 7 Setup as well. Click **Next**.
10. Click **Finish**.

Creatinga N ewP artition

Windows XP and other Windows operating systems before it do not have built-in partitioning support. Other operating systems may have tools available. The general best practice before repartitioning an existing hard drive with data is to ensure that the free space is available and defragment the hard drive before partitioning. Additionally, it is best that the drive not be in use, with the current operating system running while the partitioning is being performed. Defragmenting the hard drive will move the data to the front of the drive, allowing the end of the disk to be partitioned into a different volume. Performing partitioning on a nonempty disk may be risky, and it is recommended that the drive be backed up before attempting this.

As Windows XP and other Windows operating systems before it do not have built-in support for partitioning, a third-party application is necessary. GParted is a free application that can perform this from a boot CD, meaning the operating system on the hard drive will not be running during the partitioning process. GParted is available from http://gparted.sourceforge.net/ with detailed information and explanation on how to perform this process. Another application for partitioning is PartitionMagic (www.symantec.com/norton/partitionmagic). This third-party application is not free but is simpler and can be performed from within the running operating system.

Performing a Dual Boot Install

Installing Windows 7 on a second partition to allow dual booting is the same process used in the "Performing a Clean Install" section. Be sure to select the correct hard drive and partition that was created for Windows 7 and not a partition or hard drive with data that is not empty. Windows 7 Setup will also modify the master boot record to display the two operating system options during the startup.

Dual Boot Post Install

Once Windows 7 Setup finishes, you will notice a choice during startup to boot the Windows 7 operating system or the other operating system on the computer. The "Post Install" section of this chapter should be followed as this system is

WARNING
Make sure to select the correct partition and hard drive when installing Windows 7 in a dual boot scenario. If a Windows operating system is running on the partition selected then a migration install will occur making the current operating system inoperable.

similar to a clean install. As mentioned previously, this is a newer boot menu scheme. This section will explain how to edit Windows 7 boot menu entries.

Edit Windows 7 Boot Menu

The Windows 7 boot menu options are very simple. If multiple Windows 7 versions are installed, there is no way of telling which is which other than the install order. Sometimes nonworking operating systems are still in this menu as well. This is how to edit the Windows 7 Boot Menu:

1. Boot into the Windows 7 instance whose boot menu entry needs to be edited.
2. Start a command prompt by typing **cmd** in the Start menu Search. Right-click and select **Run as administrator**. Click **Yes** on the UAC prompt.
3. Type **bcdedit** and press **Enter**. This will display the Windows Boot Manager and Windows Boot Loader on the system.
4. To edit the boot menu entry for the installation of Windows 7 currently running, type: **bcdedit /set description "Boot menu text here"**.
5. Press **Enter**. The output should return with *The operation completed successfully* a ss eenon Figure2.42 .
6. Perform the same steps for other versions of Windows 7.

> **WARNING**
>
> Be careful not to edit any boot menu entry other than the Windows 7 install that is running. This could edit the options in the boot.ini used by earlier versions of Windows or a different operating system'sb ootl oader.

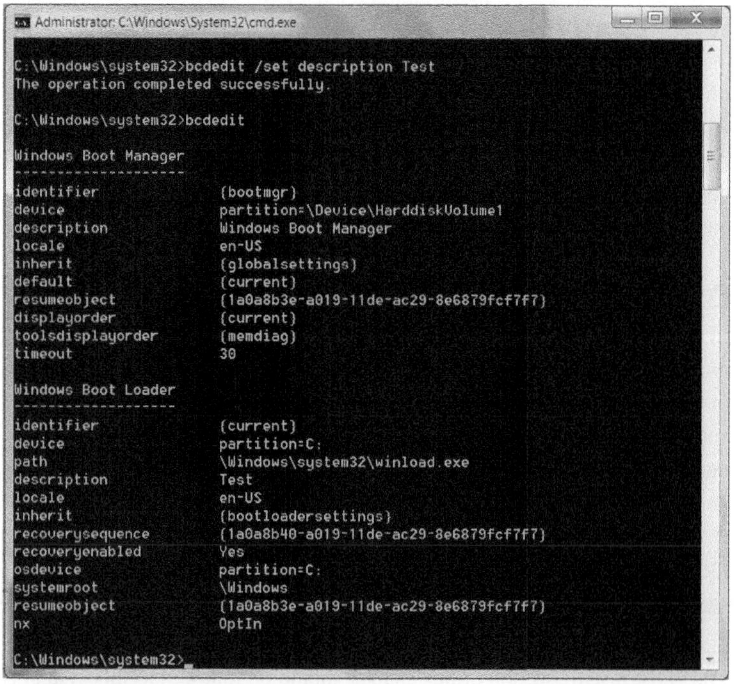

■ **FIGURE 2.42** Bcdedit to Rename Windows 7 Instance

POST INSTALL

The post install process of Windows 7 is generally the same no matter what deployment method was followed. Generally, the first thing Microsoft will ask for is activation. You have 30 days to do this before constant nagging begins. Next and perhaps before activation is possible, you may need to install hardware and device drivers that Microsoft missed. Once the Internet connection is working, you will *need* to install all available Windows Updates for best security and performance. As soon as you connect to the Internet, you may be vulnerable to malware so install antivirus software. Finally, various methods for copying files to the new Windows 7 system will be explained in this here. This section will define all these processes to ensure a good start to the Windows 7 journey.

Activation

Microsoft introduced activation to stop piracy of its operating system. Windows 7 has improved the activation process and streamlined it to an extent. By default, Windows 7 will attempt to activate as soon as the install completes if the product key was entered. The user has 30 days to input the product key and activate the Windows 7 license. After 30 days, the operating system will begin nagging that activation is required.

Activation ensures that the product key and license is valid. Microsoft Windows 7 activation works by creating a hash of the system it is installed on and the product key. This is then sent to Microsoft during the activation process. In other words, the product key is linked to the hardware configuration on the system. If for any reason Windows 7 must be reinstalled, there should not be any problems activating the product again.

The system will automatically attempt activation when the operating system finishes installing; otherwise, it will try in three days. To activate manually or check activation status:

1. Open the activation console by
   a. Typing **activate** on the Start menu Search
   b. **Control Panel | System**a nds crolldo wn.
2. The system console will reveal the activation status as shown in Figure 2.43. Click **Activate Windows now**.
3. Click **Activate Windows online now**.

Windows 7 includes a Windows Software Licensing Management Tool that may be initiated by typing **slmgr.vbs** from the Start menu Search. This tool allows for managing activation for local or remote machines. Running slmgr.vbs will return an invalid combination of command parameters and list the usage and available options in a number of separate screens. This

> **NOTE**
>
> Windows7 A ctivationw illn ag the user with delayed logons, balloon pop ups, and a reset background if the product has not been activated after 30 days. Unlike Windows Vista, the reduced functionality mode and nongenuine Windows mode will not affect Windows 7. It is recommended to activate all Windows 7 systems duringp osti nstall.

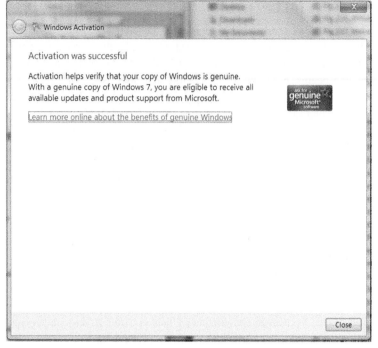

■ **FIGURE 2.43** Windows Activation Status

TIP
Althought heg racep eriodM icro-
soft allows Windows 7 to run without activation is 30 days, there is a
work-around to extend this grace
period to 120 days. This is possible
by resetting the activation time.
Microsoft allows the activation
time to be reset a total of three
times giving the end user 120
days to activate Windows 7. This is
done by typing **slmgr –rearm**in
the Windows 7 command prompt.
The command prompt may be
started from the Start menu
Search by typing **cmd**.R ight-click
the **Command Prompt**and
select **Run as Administrator**t o
ensuret hisw orks.

tool allows for all the types of activation explained in the "Obtain Windows 7" section of this chapter.

```
Usage for local computer: slmgr.vbs <Option>
Usage for Remote Computer: slmgr.vbs [MachineName
[User password] [<Option>]
MachineName: Name of the remote computer
User: Account with required privilege on remote com-
puter to run activation
Password: password for the user account
```

Install Hardware and Device Drivers

The post install tasks involve installing any hardware or device drivers that Windows Setup missed or did not have. Ideally, all hardware that was plugged into the system during the setup should be installed and working. The ideal scenario has occurred multiple times with Windows 7, but it might not have for you. Microsoft does not make drivers for most of the hardware on your system; therefore, it should not be held liable for not supporting the hardware from a clean install. As many of you may have witnessed, these incompatibility issues arose somewhat frequently with Windows Vista, and Microsoft really tried to get it right this time.

To see how well Microsoft installed your hardware in Windows 7, you must visit what has traditionally been called the *Device Manager*. The Device Manager may be started in the Start menu Search bar by typing **device man** and pressing **Enter**. The Device Manager should look familiar if you have ever used earlier versions of the manager. Another way to get to the Device Manager is by clicking the Start menu, right-clicking **Computer**, and selecting **Properties**. On the **System** screen of the Control Panel, select **Device Manager** on the top left.

Once the Device Manager has been opened, you will see a list of all the hardware on your system, and any open tree or node with a yellow exclamation or bang will indicate a driver that was not correctly installed, as shown in Figure 2.44. You may or may not be able to determine what hardware did not install correctly based on the tree and name of the entity. Thankfully, Windows 7 does introduce the following new and improved built-in ways of finding the correct driver for your hardware and installing it:

■ Action Center – the Action Center has an option under **Maintenance** to **Check for solutions** for problems with your machine. This feature is

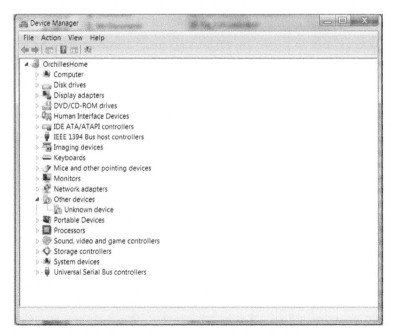

■ **FIGURE 2.44** Device Manager with Yellow Exclamation for Uninstalled Driver

introduced in Chapter 1, "Introduction to Windows 7," and further discussed in Chapter 10, "Windows 7 Troubleshooting and Performance Tools."

- Automatically – by right-clicking the device and selecting **Update Driver Software**, Windows 7 will search the local system and any media connected to find the correct driver. This will rarely work correctly after a clean install.

- Manually – the traditional way of installing drivers still exists by right-clicking the device and selecting **Update Driver Software**. Manually select the driver for this device by navigating to the folder it is located in. If you did not skip the planning and preparation stage and downloaded all the device drivers for the Windows 7 edition you installed, then you may be able to do this depending on the packaging by the manufacturer.

- Run executable driver package – this option is available if you followed the preparation and planning stage and downloaded the drivers for your devices before installing Windows 7; otherwise, you may download the drivers online if your networking works. If the networking drivers are not installed, you may download the drivers from another device and plug the device into the Windows 7 machine. Installing the driver should be as easy as double-clicking the executable and following the wizard.

- Windows Update – difficult to do if the network drivers were not installed, Windows Update also scans your computer for device drivers andfi ndsupda tesonl ine.

Remember the introduction to 32-bit versus 64-bit computing in Chapter 1, "Introduction to Windows 7"; you must obtain the correct driver for the version of Windows 7 you are running. A Windows 7 Home Premium 32-bit driver will work on Windows 7 Professional or Ultimate 32-bit, but it will not, unless otherwise stated, work on any 64-bit version. The same applies the other way around; a Windows 7 Ultimate 64-bit driver will work on a Windows 7 Home Premium 64-bit version but not on a 32-bit version.

Update Windows

Once you have all your drivers working, which thanks to proper planning and preparation should not have taken long, it is time to update Windows. Like all earlier Windows operating systems, Windows 7 *must* be updated with security and important updates. Thanks to Microsoft's security initiative and secure coding and development lifecycle, Windows 7 should not have or need as many Windows Updates as earlier versions of Windows. However, there are already Windows 7 security and important updates available and not doing a Windows Update will leave your new clean install of Windows 7 vulnerable.

TIP

Thel atestd eviced riversa re often released by the actual manufacturer and available on their Web site first. If you bought a system from a manufacturer, it is best to try their Web site for your specific model for updated drivers. Many system builders have released Windows 7 drivers for older systems even if they did not have Windows 7 originally. If you built your system or know the components, you may also check the manufacturer's Web site of the individual hardware, device, or part. Remember, you must get the 32-bit or 64-bit version of the driver depending on the system you are running. Sometimes as a last case scenario, Windows Vista drivers for the respective bit may also work on Windows 7.

To perform a Windows Update, you may go to **Start menu | All Programs | Windows Update**. Another method to get to Windows Update is through the Action Center, which can be found on the bottom right of the screen, also known as the *notification center*.

As you will see, Windows Update is no longer accessed through an Internet Explorer window but through the system itself. This change was implemented in Windows Vista and slightly improved. For instance, Windows Updates no longer trigger UAC prompts. From the Windows Update console select **Check for updates** on the top left and update your new system ass howni n Figure2.45 .

InstallA ntivirus

Although Windows 7 has many new and improved security features including Internet Explorer 8, Windows Defender, Action Center, UAC, and so on, it still *requires* an antivirus solution. Choosing what antivirus solution to go with is entirely your company's decision. No single antivirus product will be able to catch *every* form of malware, so choose the one that you

■ **FIGURE 2.45** Windows Update Checking for Updates

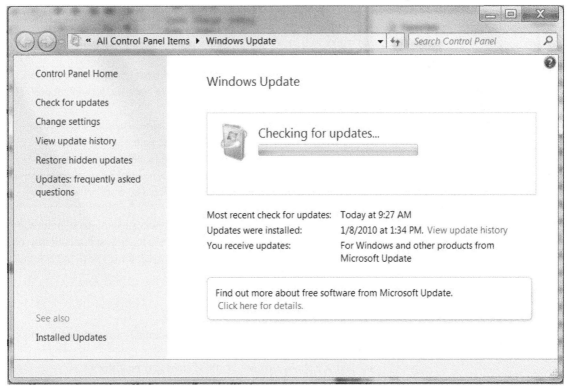

believe will best protect your end users and yourself. There are many free and commercial applications for antivirus and most allow trial periods. Most organizations enforce antivirus solutions on all images, and it is strongly recommended. Home user's often do not want to pay for antivirus and are the most affected. As an administrator and knowledgeable end user, you will most likely be asked to recommend antivirus solutions to friends, family, and even small businesses. There are many free solutions available so no Windows 7 system should go unprotected.

Free Antivirus

There are many free antivirus solutions that are very good. Always verify that you are obtaining the antivirus from a trusted host as there are many Web sites that advertise free antivirus but end up providing you and your users with malware. Also, some free antivirus solutions are only for home and/or personal use. Please ensure you respect these company's licensing policies. The following are a few free antivirus solutions for Windows 7 that wer ecommend.

- GriSoft AVG Free Antivirus – This is a very popular antivirus solution and can be found at http://free.avg.com.
- Avira – A very fast and consistent antivirus solution that also works well in Windows 7. Avira is free and can be found at http://free-av.com/.
- Panda Cloud Antivirus – Although still in beta as of this writing, this solution had a very high-detection rate in our tests. It can be found at www.cloudantivirus.com.
- Avast Home Edition – Another free antivirus solution with a proven track record of maintaining secure home systems. This solution requires a license but it is free. It can be found at www.avast.com.
- Microsoft Security Essentials – This is a free and relatively new antivirus solution from Microsoft. It can be obtained from www.microsoft .com/Security_Essentials/.
- Comodo Internet Security – This offers both an antivirus solution and a firewall solution for free. Although it has the lowest detection rate of all the free solutions it should be considered. It may be found at http:// personalfirewall.comodo.com/.

RestoreU serF ilesa ndS ettings

Restoring the user's files and settings is essentially what makes the migration to Windows 7 a migration instead of a clean install. Depending on what method you choose to back up, these steps may be different.

Using Windows Easy Transfer

Windows Easy Transfer is a wizard for transferring one or multiple user's files and settings from one Windows computer to another. The easy-to-use wizard allows the administrator or end user to choose what files and settings to transfer and from what users, select a transfer method to use, performs the transfer, and then creates a report. This tool cannot be used to transfer installed programs or applications to the new system. All programs and applications will need to be reinstalled. The wizard will generate a report suggesting what applications need to be installed on the new system. The transfer methods that Windows Easy Transfer can use are an easy transfer cable, a network share, or an external hard disk or USB flash drive.

Windows Easy Transfer is free and available for Windows XP and Windows Vista from Microsoft.com or from the Windows 7 installation media in the folder %MediaDrive%\support\migwiz\migsetup.exe. Windows 7 systems include the Windows Easy Transfer installed by default and it may be launched from **Start menu | All Programs | Accessories | System Tools | Windows Easy Transfer**.

As mentioned, there are three methods of transferring user data and settings shown in Figure 2.5, which are as follows:

1. USB easy transfer cable – Transferring data from the old functional, powered-on computer to the new powered-on computer with a male-to-male USB cable.
2. Using the network – Transferring data from the old functional, powered-on computer to the new powered-on computer that are both connected to the same network.
3. Removable media or a network share – Transferring data from any old computer to a new computer using a storage repository.

Depending on what deployment scenario you chose to deploy Windows 7, the Windows Easy Transfer will be different.

Windows Easy Transfer with USB Cable

The USB cable method of running Windows Easy Transfer to migrate files is available with the replace computer scenario. This involves having the old and new computer on, operational, and within close proximity to each other. It also requires a male-to-male USB cable.

1. Install Windows Easy Transfer on the old computer from the Windows 7 install media or by downloading it from www.microsoft.com.
2. Connect both computers with the USB cable. Install any drivers that the cable requires.

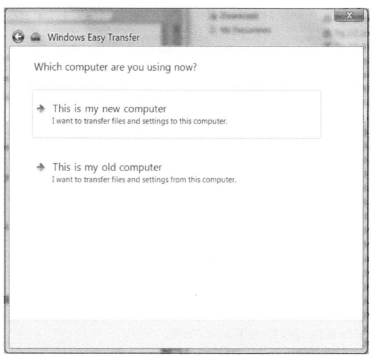

■ FIGURE 2.46 Windows Easy Transfer – Which Computer Are You Using?

3. If Windows Easy Transfer did not start automatically, start it on the oldc omputer.
4. Read the overview of the application to better understand it and click **Next**.
5. Click **An Easy Transfer cable** and **This is the old computer**a s shown in Figure 2.46. Click **Next**.
6. On the new Windows 7 computer, start Windows Easy Transfer by typing **Windows Easy Transfer** in the Start menu Search.
7. Click **Next** on the overview page.
8. Select the method you will use to migrate data | **An Easy Transfer Cable** | **This is my new computer** (Figure 2.46) | **I already installed it on my old computer** | then click **Next**.
9. Once the connection is established, click **Transfer** to transfer all files and settings automatically or **Customize** to choose what files to migrate or what user profiles to migrate.
10. The transfer should occur fairly quickly. When finished, click **Close**.

Windows Easy Transfer with Network

The network method of running Windows Easy Transfer to migrate files is available with the replace computer scenario. This involves having the old and new computer on, operational, and on the same network.

1. Install Windows Easy Transfer on the old computer from the Windows 7 install media or by downloading it from www.microsoft.com.
2. Ensure that both computers are connected to the same network.
3. Start Windows Easy Transfer on the old computer.
4. Read the overview of the application to better understand it and click **Next**.
5. Click **A network** and **This is the old computer** as shown in Figure 2.46. Write down or remember the Windows Easy Transfer key. Click **Next**.
6. On the new Windows 7 computer, start Windows Easy Transfer by typing **Windows Easy Transfer** in the Start menu Search.
7. Click **Next** on the overview page.
8. Select the method you will use to migrate data | **An Easy Transfer Cable** | **This is my new computer** (Figure 2.46) | **I already installed it on my old computer** | then click **Next**.
9. Enter the Windows Easy Transfer Key and click **Next**.
10. Click **Transfer** to transfer all files and settings automatically or **Customize** to choose what files to migrate or what user profiles to migrate.
11. The transfer should occur fairly quickly depending on the amount of data that needs to be transferred. When finished, click **Close**.

Windows Easy Transfer with Removable Media

The removable media or network share method of running Windows Easy Transfer to migrate files is available with all deployment scenarios as long as the Windows Easy Transfer was already running in the old computer or before the system was migrated to Windows 7. This involves having the Easy Transfer file available:

1. Connect the removable media or ensure that the network location of the file is available.
2. Start Windows Easy Transfer in the new computer by typing **Windows Easy Transfer** in the Start menu Search.
3. Read the overview of the application to better understand it and click **Next**.
4. Select **An external hard disk or USB flash drive** | **This is my new computer**(Figure2.46) | **Yes, open the file**.
5. Navigate to the location where the Easy Transfer file is located, select it, and click **Open**.
6. Click **Transfer** to transfer all files and settings automatically or **Customize** to choose what files to migrate or what user profiles to migrate.
7. The transfer should occur fairly quickly. When finished, click **Close**.

Restore Windows File Backup

Certain Windows 7 editions have built-in backup and restore capabilities. These capabilities are the easiest method of saving and restoring end user data without a third-party application. If you backed up data in Windows Vista or Windows 7, you can restore the data like this:

1. Start the **Backup and Restore Center** from the Control Panel and then click **Select another backup to restore files from** as shown in Figure 2.47.
2. The Restore Files wizard will pop up. If the restore files are in a removable media device insert the device now.
3. Click **Refresh** or **Browse network location…**
4. Click **Next** once the wizard finds the backup file to restore.
5. Click the check box next to **Select all files from this backup** or select **Search, Browse for files**, or **Browse for folders**.
6. Click **Next**w henr eady.
7. Select whether to restore to files to the original location or in a specified location. If the original location is selected, the computer should have the same user name as the old system.

■ **FIGURE 2.47** Windows 7 Backup and Restore

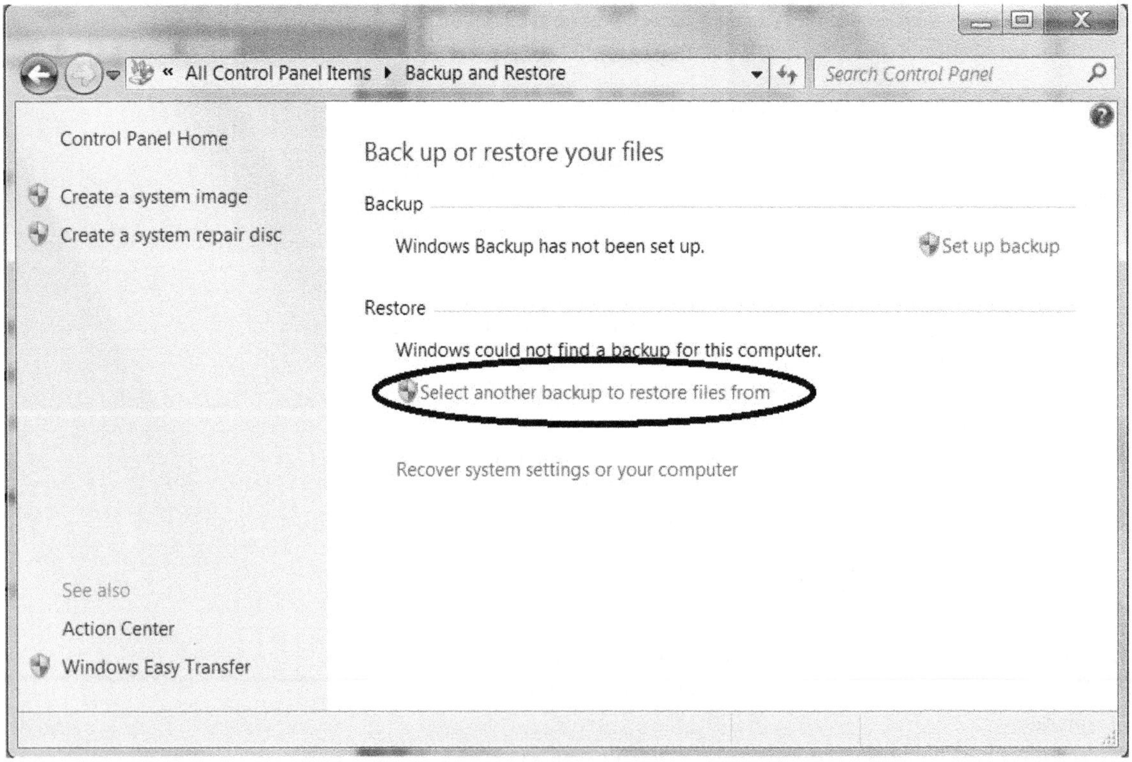

8. Read any errors indicating the status or folder where the restore was made.
9. Click **Finish**w henyoua redone .

Manually Restore User Data

Administrators or end users who manually moved their data to a removable media device or network share can manually move the data back to the respective Windows 7 user folder. Remember that Chapter 1, "Introduction to Windows 7," explained some major changes in Windows 7 over Windows XP in regard to user profile data location. Windows 7 stores user profile data in %SystemDrive\Users\%Username%\ as shown in Figure 2.48.

■ **FIGURE 2.48** Windows 7 User Profile Folder

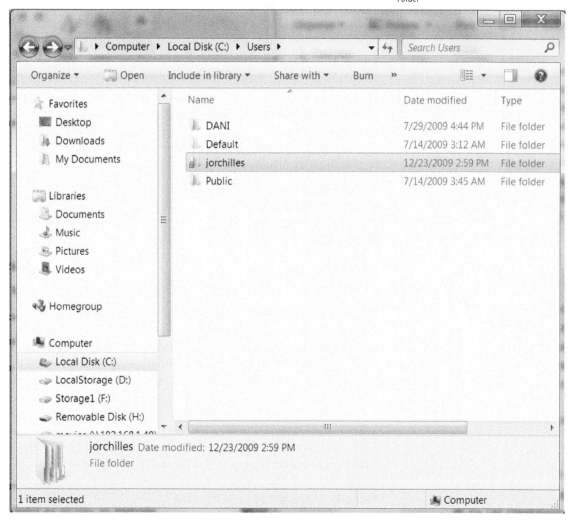

TIP

Ift hes ystemi sr unning Windows Aero, the end user or administrator performing the manual restore can take advantage of *Aero Snap*. Grab one of the Windows Explorer windows and drag it to the bottom right of the screen. It should snap into place taking up exactly half of the screen. Do the same with the other Windows Explorer window but on the bottom left of the screen. Now you can see both folders that you transfer data to andfr om.

Different file types should be moved to their respective folders on the new system. This will allow the Libraries to find the correct data for easier searching and locating of user files. The easiest method is to open two Windows Explorer windows straight from the taskbar. On one navigate to the backup location and on the other to the user's profile folder: %SystemDrive\Users\%Username%\. Transferring files should be as easy as dragging and dropping.

■ SUMMARY

This chapter has introduced the administrator and end user to the steps required to deploy Windows 7 in a single system. The methodologies explained in this chapter are the basis for deploying Windows 7 in an organization or environment. Irrespective of the size of the organization and deployment, it is critical that administrators first use and understand Windows 7 before beginning the deployment process.

The chapter first introduced the planning and preparation phase that is required for any Windows 7 deployment. Although at a much higher level, these steps are required before even obtaining Windows 7 to install on a single system. The planning and preparation phase of a Windows 7 deployment includes the following:

- Select the Windows 7 edition to be installed
- Check system compatibility and hardware requirements
- Backupc urrents ystem
- Determinede ployments cenario
- SelectI nstallm ethod
- Obtain Windows7
- Obtain device/hardware drivers *prior to install*

The following sections took the results of the planning and preparation phase and explained how to perform each install method. The planning and preparation phase would need slight modifications for the selected install type and these processes were explained in each install section. The recommended installation is a clean install as it begins the Windows 7 journey from a clean system without old files or settings. Most users will require their data and some even their settings, a process explained in the migration and upgrade sections. Remember that moving over user files and settings could mean moving wrong configurations and even malicious files. Deploying Windows 7 in an environment is a great way to standardize the applications and settings in the organization. Steps should be followed to ensure this goal is met during the deployment phase of Windows 7.

This chapter concludes by explaining the most important post install steps that should be taken before using Windows 7 for production or even testing purposes. Activation is one of the first steps that should be followed. However, if the system is being used for testing purposes, this step may be skipped. The section provides a tip for testing Windows 7 for a total of 120 days before having to activate. Windows Updates are highlighted and explained as very important to all Windows 7 systems. It is critical to keep these systems updated and secure by setting Windows Updates to occur automatically. Although Microsoft has provided a huge repository of hardware and device drivers, it is possible that some hardware was not installed during setup. The "Post Install" section walks the end user or administrator through many different ways that Microsoft has facilitated the install of drivers. Antivirus was referenced, including a request that all Windows 7 systems include an antivirus solution. Most organizations require and enforce this but home users and small businesses often do not. As the main target for hackers, home and small office users must ensure their systems are secure to avoid an attacker taking advantage of or stealing their data. Six different free antivirus solutions were recommended to assist end users and administrators in providing not so savvy users with a solution. Finally, the chapter suggests different methods to restore data from an old system that was migrated to Windows 7. Remember this requires that the planning and preparation steps were followed or data could have been lost.

The next chapter will use this chapter's primer for deploying a Windows 7 system and explain various different deployment methods for an enterprise environment. As an administrator and end user, perhaps the next step is to experiment and test Windows 7. In that case, skip to Chapter 4, "The New Windows 7 Desktop Environment," which will explain the new desktop environment and how to configure it.

Deploying Windows 7 in an Enterprise Environment

In Chapter 2, "Installing and Upgrading to Windows 7," we covered the numerous ways in which Windows 7 can be installed on a single system, whether as a full installation or as an upgrade; however, in a larger environment, it is less likely for system administrators to perform individual installations given the multiple computers that the operating system would need to be rolled out to. In the past, this may have proved to be a challenging task, but today, there are several tools available to facilitate the deployment. In this chapter, we will look into conducting volume deployment for Windows 7 and how to address the most important considerations.

DEPLOYMENT OVERVIEW

In a nutshell, the deployment process intends to get Windows 7 on the specified target computers. Whether it is being installed on one or many systems, the general approach would be as follows:

- Prepare to build master installation – This step encompasses setting up a technician computer with the necessary tools, Windows 7 source files, applications, device drivers, and additional software packages.

© 2010 Elsevier Inc. All rights reserved.
DOI: 10.1016/B978-1-59749-561-5.00003-6

In this step, you would also prepare the setup automation by creating answer files and configuring a source distribution share.

- Build, test, and capture image of master installation – You will designate a reference or master computer in which you will use the answer file that was previously generated to run and test the Windows 7 installation from the distribution share and ensure that the setup automation works properly. After setup is complete, you can perform the necessary customizations to meet the needs of your business. Once you are satisfied with the master installation, you can then prepare it for duplication and thereafter capture your progress.

- Prepare deployment media and network distribution – In this step, you will make the captured image available on a network share that may be accessed by the destination computers to which the image will be deployed. Alternatively, the images may be stored on other media including a DVD, an external mass-storage device, or *Windows Deployment Services*(WDS).

- Run setup/transfer images on to destination computers – By accessing either the network share or the prepared media, you ultimately will deploy the prepared source media to get Windows 7 on the target computer.

DeploymentS cenarios

In Chapter 2, "Installing and Upgrading to Windows 7," we briefly discussed some of the scenarios in which Windows 7 can be deployed. In this chapter, we will review them from a different perspective as now we are shifting the focus to multiple rather than individual systems. The deployment scenarios are the following: *upgrade* (in-place), *new installation*, *refresh*, and *replace*.

Upgrade Scenario

This scenario allows an installation of Windows Vista Service Pack 1 (SP1) or later to be upgraded to Windows 7 while preserving the user state and all transferrable settings and files, as well as maintaining the installation of existing applications. As discussed in the previous chapter, there is no direct upgrade path for Windows XP, and therefore, the *refresh* method must be used (which keeps files and settings but not installed applications). This deployment method is also assessed by the Windows Compatibility Wizard, which helps determine if any components need to be individually addressed before performing the upgrade.

Performing an upgrade may be one of the easiest and least complex methods for deploying Windows 7; however, there is a certain risk attached to this operation as all settings are imported "as-is" from the earlier version and the administrator does not have much control on what gets transferred. Unless the state and condition of the system are known, it may be preferable to opt for a scenario that allows for selectively preserving the settings.

New Installation

The *new installation* involves deploying a clean copy of Windows 7 on the target computer through a straightforward setup process. It is assumed that the hard drive and system volume have been properly partitioned and formatted. This type of installation will deliver the most consistent result because all settings are either the setup defaults or set by the administrator.

Refresh Scenario

Similar to the *new installation*, the *refresh* scenario contemplates performing a clean setup with the difference being that the target computer already contains a Windows operating system for which files and settings will be preserved (note that as a difference with the upgrade method, the installed applications are not taken into consideration). This scenario is especially useful in the event that preserving the user state is a priority as it still leverages the benefits of consistency that come through a *new installation*. This scenario can be automated with the latest version of the User State Migration Tool (USMT 4.0), which will collect the pertinent data for each user state found in the system and consequently restore it after the clean installation is performed.

Replace Scenario

This is very similar to the *refresh* scenario except that the target system is a new computer, which does not contain any files or settings. The scenario consists of conducting a new installation on the target computer, and then using the USMT 4.0 to transfer files and settings from the old computer. This scenario can be run side-by-side with an older system running Windows XP or Windows Vista.

Understandingt heS etupP rocess

In comparison to Windows XP, there are numerous differences in the deployment technologies that are now available with Windows 7 as new and improved tools have been developed based on technologies that were first introduced with Windows Vista. Before Windows Vista was released, Microsoft did not have robust tools to facilitate mass deployment. If you are unfamiliar with Windows Vista or your organization passed on it altogether, you might as well unlearn everything you know on Windows XP deployment and start from scratch.

Before we are able to prepare for volume deployments of Windows 7, it is important to understand the underlying processes of the installation so that we make the best use of the tools. There have been significant changes to the way the Windows operating system is now deployed. Let us first glance at the following list of things that have changed in deploying Windows since the Windows XP days:

- Booting up the Windows installation occurs through the Windows preinstallation environment (Windows PE), which replaces any DOS-basedboot di sk/media.
- Windows Setup is now a file-based image deployment.
- Installation source files may be 2 GB or higher.
- All Windows installations need to be activated.
- The Boot.ini is no longer used for boot configuration.
- *Setup.exe* is now the new command that launches the Windows installation process, replacing winnt32.exe.
- The Windows installation is independent from the *Hardware AbstractionL ayer*(HAL.dll).
- Windows 7 is not language specific, whereas for Windows XP/2003 or earlier each language had its own build of the operating system. Languages are now separate packages.
- The Windows 7 DVD contains the source Windows Image (WIM) file containing all of the editions of this operating system's version. The installer determines which product to install based on the license key.

The Windows 7 installation is now conducted through file-based images. What comes to mind when we talk about "imaging" is what in the industry is more commonly known as *sector-based imaging*. Numerous administrators have probably worked with third-party utilities for imaging such as Symantec Ghost (http://www.symantec.com/norton/ghost) or Acronis TrueImage (http://www .acronis.com/enterprise/) to take snapshots of a system volume in order to capture the desired system state and installation. The images these products capture are different from the WIM file format that is file-based. The main difference is that sector-based images copy indiscriminately sector-by-sector at a low level from a hard drive to build a snapshot of storage volume; file-based images such as WIM images are captured by taking snapshots at a higher level of files and folders. The bottom line is that even though sector-based images are very flexible because they can ignore the type of file system in use, they are somewhat unpractical to maintain and manage; in order to modify and edit a sector-based image, it would require deploying the image, making the changes, and recapturing it. In the case of WIM files, the action to modify and update the images can be performed by instantly "mounting" the captured image, applying the changes at the file system level, and then committing the changes immediately.

The image-based Windows setup process that was first introduced with Windows Vista greatly facilitates the deployment of the operating system to disparate hardware architectures without requiring building separate installation packages/images. This same behavior can also be found in Windows 7, and it may come as good news to some administrators who did not have much exposure or were unable to deploy Vista. The way the new Windows 7 setup is designed streamlines many portions of previous operating system installations that would usually encounter obstacles when being deployed, especially from captured images.

There were many limitations when Windows XP images were deployed as these would not necessarily restore successfully on to any computer with a hardware architecture different than that of the system from which the image was captured. This created a lot of additional work for system administrators, including managing multiple images and developing custom scripts to force things to work properly. Important system components such as the HAL were tied to the specific installation device and would usually require additional steps/tools to allow a restored image to be reconfigured properly. Some of the known issues for Windows XP images include the following:

- The imaged computer is expected to boot from the same storage controller as the reference computer.
- The imaged systems need to use the same HAL as the reference computer.
- The sector-based imaging process is destructive; thus, it replaces all contents of the destination computer and could complicate some Windows deployment scenarios including in-place upgrades and other types of migrations.
- Maintaining the image to include updates and new applications was time consuming as directly modifying the image was not possible.
- The need for third-party imaging utilities that incurred additional licensing, training, and operational costs.

Windows 7 has several editions; however, all editions of Windows 7 use the same installation image (install.wim which may be found in the *Sources* folder of the installation media). What varies is that Microsoft packaged media that is specific to one edition, which means that if the setup is executed normally, it will allow the installation of just the edition that was purchased through the user interface; nevertheless, by using the unattended setup answer file (unattend.xml), it is possible to install any edition (provided that there is a license key available). By knowing this it is easier to understand that despite the many flavors of Windows 7, there is a universal image from which the setup is based. Depending on the need of a particular system/user, the deployed OS can be any of the needed editions, and it will be installed without the need for additional source files.

Deployment Tools

The tools that are now available to streamline the Windows deployment include the Windows Automated Installation Kit version 2.0 (Windows AIK 2.0), Windows System Image Manager (Windows SIM), and the Windows Preinstallation Environment (Windows PE). In addition to these tools, Microsoft now offers additional solutions that further assist IT professionals in organization-wide deployment such as the Microsoft Deployment Toolkit (MDT) 2010, which we will cover in this chapter. The following is a list of deployment components that play an important role in this chapter:

- **Sysprep** – This is a tool that enables you to remove user and computer-specific data from the operating system image. This enables you to have the reference system ready to capture its image and deploy it to otherc omputers.
- **Windows PE 3.0**
- **Windows Imaging** – This is the technology for storing system images in files with the WIM format and .wim extension.
- **ImageX** – This is the Windows Imaging command-line tool included with Windows Automated Install Kit (WAIK) 2.0 and is used to capture and edit images for deployment.
- **DISM** – Deployment Image Service and Management tool is a command line tool to manage WIM files.
- **WSIM** – Windows System Image Management tool is a tool that allows you to customize an existing WIM file.
- **DiskPart** – DiskPart is a command line tool that allows you to manage diskpa rtitions.
- **USMT** – User State Migration Toolkit is part of WAIK and is used to migrateda taf romt hee xistingc omputert ot hene wc omputer.

Setup Stages

In terms of familiarizing yourself with setup milestones and progress, we were accustomed to different stages in the setup process with Windows XP and earlier editions, which marked points or milestones in getting the operating system deployed onto the computer. It was a notorious step to go from the text-based portion of the setup interface to the graphical user interface (GUI) or mini-setup phase. These stages gave the administrator a general understanding of what types of operations were being performed (that is, copying setup files, installing drivers, customizing user settings, and so on). The Windows 7 installation process can similarly be divided into three stages which mark a point in the setup:

NOTE
Windows Vistaa nd Windows7 with their entirely image-based installations and the richness of the Windows preinstallation have no need for the administrator to necessarily run any "DOS-based" or "DOS-like"t ext-baseds etup.

- Preinstallation (Windows PE) – This phase consists of the environment that is loaded on initial boot of the installation media. This is the stage when you prepare the hard drive for the installation (partitioning and formatting). This is the phase when the Windows 7 image and source files are copied to the hard drive.

- Online configuration – After the system files have been copied to the target hard drive, the Windows 7 setup performs configuration routines or passes that customize the applied installation to use the most suitable drivers and to set system-specific information including networking configuration and other essential properties.

- Windows welcome – This phase consists of delegating control to the end user and providing a welcome to the newly installed system.

Additionally, Windows Setup also undergoes configuration passes within these previously highlighted stages that provide the system with specific configuration functions applying related settings that were set in the Unattend.xml answer file. The following list cited from the Windows 7 Resource Kit describes the passes the Windows Setup runs:

1. WindowsPE – This configures Windows PE options and basic Windows Setup options. These options can include configuring a disk (partitioning and formatting), and configuring networking.

2. OfflineServicing – This applies updates to a Windows 7 image and also applies packages, including software fixes, language packs, and other securityupda tes.

3. Generalize – The generalize pass runs only if you run **sysprep/ generalize**. In this pass, you can minimally configure Windows 7, as well as configure other settings that must persist on your master image. The **sysprep/generalize** command removes system-specific information. For example, the unique security identifier and other hardware-specific settings are removed from the image.

4. Specialize – This creates and applies system-specific information. For example, you can configure network settings, international settings, and domain information.

5. auditSystem – This processes unattended setup settings while Windows 7 is running in system context before a user logs on to the computer in audit mode. The auditSystem pass runs only if you boot in audit mode.

6. auditUser – This processes unattended setup settings after a user logs on to the computer in audit mode. The auditUser pass runs only if you boot in audit mode.

7. ObeSystem – Applies settings to Windows 7 before Windows welcome starts.

Each of these configuration passes can be customized with specific instructions to automate the setup and mold it to the organization's needs. Although these setup passes can be individually configured through the use of an answer file, later in this chapter, we will be covering how to accomplish the automation of the Windows installation using the MDT. For now, take into account that if you were to accomplish automation without the help of the MDT, you would have to use the WAIK to create the Unattend.xml answer file that describes particular settings for Windows 7. The information on this file includes parameters and values for these settings in order to automate the "answers" that a user would interactively provide to move from one phase of the setup to another.

WINDOWS IMAGE MANAGEMENT

The Windows 7 WIM files have the capability to be easily manipulated in order to customize the installation to your needs. Additionally, Windows 7 Enterprise and Ultimate can be configured to boot from virtual hard disk (VHD) files, which allow for increased flexibility in an enterprise environment where virtualized desktops are becoming more common. The VHD file format was initially introduced with Microsoft Virtual PC and Virtual Server. Both of these formats may contain operating systems and may be serviced to contain the necessary software to fulfill your organization's needs. We will discuss how to work with both formats.

Windows 7 has the capability to allow administrators to prepare an image for capture even when the operating system is not running. Typically, the process of prepping an image would be conducted online. Now, you are able to perform offline servicing by mounting a WIM image or VHD.

Through online servicing, building and servicing the image would usually imply conducting a Windows installation on a reference computer, installing all the necessary drivers and applications while the computer is running, and ultimately running Sysprep to leave the system in a state that will allow it to be ready for deployment. By using Sysprep in this manual image-building scenario, the installation is stripped from any unique identifiers and set to boot up the next time as if it had just completed Windows Setup. At this point, the computer's installation can be captured to the Windows Imaging format (.wim file) using ImageX. This could be performed in numerous ways by either booting into Windows PE and performing the image capture on the same machine, or attaching the hard drive from the reference computer onto another system and performing the capture.

With offline servicing, you are able to take a base image and manipulate it further by including additional changes like recently released updates, feature packages, applications, or drivers. To update and modify the image, you may utilize the Windows SIM, which is a GUI-based tool to author WIM image files, or the Deployment Images Servicing and Management (DISM) tool.

For Windows 7 imaging, you can opt to either build images manually or leverage the automated image-capture feature and authoring tools that the MDT provides. With either of these approaches you may be able to manage files, drivers, update packages, language packs, applications, and other settings. Either method is perfectly valid, although opting for manually building an image may be time consuming even though it may provide a higher degree of customization; more administrators will probably favor the streamlined way in which MDT handles imaging.

Building an image for a Lite-Touch Installation (LTI) using MDT 2010 can automate most of the manual preparation, capture, and management of the images through its interface; it even allows for an easy image capture through the network with the *Capture Task Sequence*. We will discuss how to accomplish this later in the chapter.

In order to properly prepare to build our system images, it is recommended to set up a lab that contains the following:

- Windows 7 source files/media and volume license keys
- Target computers – These are selected computers on which to create, install, and test Windows 7 images. It is recommended to have an assortment on the different makes and models in your organization in order to better tailor the images to the business needs.
- A build server for MDT 2010 – This is a computer that hosts MDT 2010 and the deployment share. The build computer should have a DVD-RW drive and should be networked with the target computers. You can install MDT 2010 on a desktop or server computer.
- WDS – The lab environment should contain a server running WDS. Using WDS to boot destination computers is much faster than burning DVDs and starting computers with them.
- Additional source files – Source files include device drivers and hardware-specific applications for each computer in the production environment. Additionally, the team should begin assembling any security updates and operating system packages that must be added to thedi stributions hare.

With a lot of the technical improvements that Windows 7 offers, the process of image engineering has become a lot simpler with the inception of MDT 2010. The approach to building Windows 7 images using MDT2010 is as follows:

- Create a build server – The build server is the host for MDT 2010 and its distribution share.

- Configure a deployment share – The deployment share contains the source files (Windows 7, applications, device drivers, and so on) from which you build operating system images.
- Create and customize task sequences – After stocking the deployment share, you create task sequences. Task sequences associate source files from the deployment share with the steps necessary to install and configuret hem.
- Build initial operating system images – With MDT 2010, building a custom Windows 7 image is as simple as installing the operating system from a deployment share by using the Windows Deployment Wizard. This is an LTI installation process that requires minimal user interaction; it automatically captures a Windows 7 image and stores it back in the deployment share.

For most deployment scenarios, you will probably use LTI. Depending on your needs, you may wish to create a reference or master system, which will allow the capture of a "thick" or "fully-loaded" image, which is packed with as many customizations as you may choose to include. This approach can greatly simplify a lot of the customizations that your image needs. This custom image can then be prepped and generalized to deploy to the target computers. Alternatively, you may choose to keep images "thin" and perform minimal customizations that may not necessarily be accomplished through the automated setup task sequences, or you may use "hybrid" images that can benefit from being tailored to remain relatively lighter than the "thick" images as they are configured to install applications on first run, giving the illusion of a thick image but installing the applications from a network source when needed. Hybrid images have most of the advantages of thin images. However, they aren't as complex to develop and do not require a complex software distribution infrastructure.

NOTE

Depending on your network's capacity and the number of images that you may have to manage, opting to build thick images may not always be the best option because this type of image may be significantly larger in size and take longer periods of time to transmit over the network to client computers. This in turn can hinder the effectiveness of deployment.

The advantages of thick images are deployment speed and simplicity. You will basically create a disk image that contains all the main applications and thus have only a single step to deploy the disk image and core applications to the destination computer. Thick images can also be less costly to develop, as advanced scripting techniques are not often required to build them. In fact, you can build thick images by using MDT 2010 with little or no scripting work. Whichever type of image you decide to build, you can provide it manually, and then capture the image of this reference computer or include the items through the MDT 2010 Deployment Workbench wizards.

Planning a Windows 7 Deployment

Planning is an essential component of any deployment strategy as it encompasses prior considerations that need to be addressed to ensure a successful project. Whether it is a high-volume or low-volume deployment, an important part of planning is determining how many and what type of resources are needed to complete a company-wide rollout of Windows 7. In addition to listing resources and roles your teams will comprise, you also have to reassess your environment to determine infrastructure readiness. You could either spend some time figuring out how to come about the orchestration for this effort or use some readily available references that Microsoft has developed.

From a technical operations perspective, Microsoft's documentation in MDT 2010 addresses many aspects of the deployment planning process in the form of a *planning checklist*, which will help you better foresee important considerations. The following questions are referenced directly from the MDT Documentation Library:

- What is your imaging and source file strategy?
- Will you deploy a full set of operating system files or a custom image?
- How will you handle product keys and licensing?
- Where will you store your distribution files?
- Will you deploy across the network, with removable media, or both? Will you use multicast deployments?
- Are you going to allow users to choose their own operating system, applications, locale, time zone, and administrative password?
- Will users upgrade their current computer in place, migrate settings to a new operating system installation, or get a new computer?
- Which users will be able to install which applications?
- Are you going to migrate user state?
- Do you want to back up computers before deployment?
- Do you want to use BitLocker™ Drive Encryption?
- Will you deploy 32-bit and 64-bit operating systems?
- Will you deploy different product editions (such as Professional, Ultimate,or B usiness)?
- What type of deployments will be performed (for example, deploy a new computer, replace an existing computer)?

Answering these questions will help getting a clearer picture of what needs to be prepared in terms of infrastructure readiness and what may be done depending on your organization's needs, strategy, time, and resources.

One of the first things you must do as you prepare to plan for a Windows 7 deployment is to assess your organization's business needs in order to clearly define the project scope and objectives. After you have conducted this assessment, you may then decide how to leverage Windows 7 to fulfill these needs. By doing this, you will have a more accurate view of current network and computer configurations and determine if there is any need or justification for upgrading hardware or software. Additionally, it will also aid you in selecting the most suitable tools and methods for deploying Windows. With this information, you should now be able to plan your deployment. An operating system deployment plan should include the following:

- A deployment schedule – A timeline to track your project is highly recommended. You should create either a simple schedule by using a spreadsheet or a more detailed and complex one, using a project management tool such as Microsoft Office Project 2007.
- A detailed list of important files/settings – You should have an inventory of applications, device drivers, system features, updates, and settings according to your organization's requirements. This list will ensure that you avoid leaving out any important component that your organization may require.
- A documented assessment of your environment's current configuration – You should create a testing environment or sandbox in which you can practice deploying Windows 7 by using the features and options in your plan. If possible, have your test environment be a mirror of your production environment including network architecture, hardware, and business applications. Be sure to include information about types of users, permissions, structure of the organization, network infrastructure, frequently used software, and available hardware.
- User testing plans – When you're satisfied with the results in your test environment, roll out your deployment to a specific group of users to test the results in a controlled production environment.
- A rollout plan – Finally, roll out Windows 7 to your entire organization.

Preparing the deployment plan is a continuous process. Be sure to review and update your plan as needed. By doing this, you will ensure that the final roll out runs smoothly and is aligned with the scope and objectives.

Current Environment

Document your existing computing environment, looking at your organization's structure and how it supports users. Use this assessment to determine your readiness for desktop deployment of Windows 7. The three major areas of your computing environment to assess include your hardware, software, andne twork.

- Hardware – Do your desktop and laptop computers meet the minimum hardware requirements for Windows 7? In addition to meeting these requirements, all hardware must be compatible with Windows 7.
- Software – Are your applications compatible with Windows 7? Make sure that all of your applications, including line-of-business (LOB) applications, work with computers running Windows 7.

- Network – Document your network architecture, including topology, size, and traffic patterns. Also, determine which users need access to various applications and data, and describe how they obtain access.

Microsoft Assessment and Planning Tool 4.0

When it comes to planning an operating system deployment, you need to begin with an inventory of what you have in place, from hardware to software. Knowing what you have is the key; you wouldn't want to get started down the deployment path only to find that a custom line of business application doesn't work or that your computers don't meet the minimum system requirements, would you?

Microsoft provides a free tool for you to use to plan your Windows 7 deployment. The Microsoft Assessment and Planning Toolkit 4.0 (MAP) is an agentless inventory, assessment, and reporting tool that will simplify your Windows 7 deployment planning. MAP will assess workstations running Windows 2000, Windows XP, Windows Vista, and Windows 7, as well as Windows Server 2000, 2003, and 2008 including R2.

Installing MAP 4.0

Installing MAP 4.0 is a pretty straightforward process; install it on a computer that has network connectivity with the systems you want to inventory. The setup wizard guides you through the process of installing MAP and SQL Server 2008 Express Edition. The discovery computer needs to have Word 2007 (or 2003 SP2) and Excel 2007 (or 2003 SP2) installed as well in order to generate and view the reports.

Map uses Microsoft SQL Server 2008 Express Edition to store collected data. If you don't have it installed, the installer will download, install, and configure a new instance for you (Figure 3.1).

Once the installation is complete, you are ready to start your inventory and analysis. The first time you launch the MAP tool, you will be prompted to create an inventory database, enter any name you like, and click **OK** (Figure 3.2).

Discovering Network Computers

MAP can discover network computers through a variety of methods, which are as follows:

- Active Directory Domain Services (ADDS)
- WindowsN etworkingP rotocols
- Internet Protocol (IP) Address Range scans
- Manuallyi nputtingc omputerna mes
- Importingc omputerna mesf roma fi le

> **NOTE**
> Youc and ownloadt heM icrosoft Assessment and Planning Toolkit 4.0 from http://technet.microsoft.com/en-us/library/bb977556.aspx. MAP does require a Structured Query Language (SQL) database, and the installer will download and install Microsoft SQL Server 2008E xpressE dition.

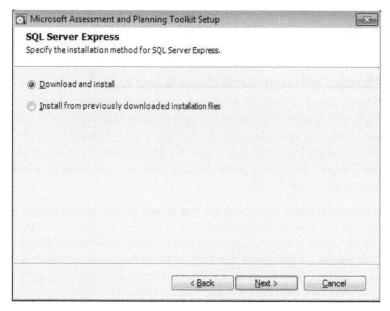

■ **FIGURE 3.1** SQL Server Express Installation

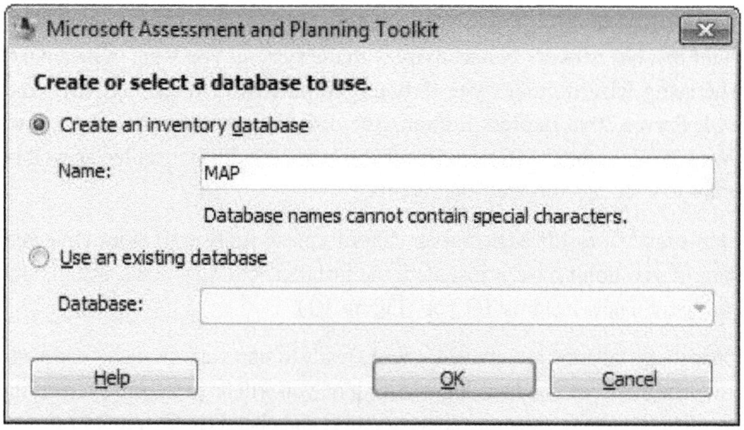

■ **FIGURE 3.2** Create an Inventory Database

Using ADDS, you will be able to customize the computers scanned by domains, containers, or organizational units, and this will discover all computers that are joined to the domain. You can use this method to scan up to 120,000 computers at one time.

You can also use Windows networking protocols that utilize NetBIOS to discover the computers on the network. The computer browser service must be running on all computers; otherwise, they will not be discovered. There is no limit to the number of computers that can be scanned using this method; however, the more computers you scan, the longer it takes to complete. It should be noted that you cannot run a scan using ADDS and Windows networking protocols at the same time.

Additionally, you can scan based on an IP address range. Again there is no limit to the number of computers scanned, but the more you include in the scan, the longer it will take to complete. Finally, you can input the name of a single computer or import a file containing the names of the computers you wish to scan up to a maximum of 120,000 computers. You can use the computer name, NetBIOS name, or the fully qualified domain name (FQDN) as long as each computer name is on a new line and you don't use any delimiters.

MAP uses a number of methods to gather information from the computers being scanned including Windows Management Instrumentation (WMI), which collects hardware, software, and device information from the remote computer, and Remote Registry Service, which collects roles installed on a server. There are a few caveats you need to be aware of regarding WMI:

- The local account on the remote computer must have a password for WMI to be successful.
- The Remote Administration exception (Transmission Control Protocol [TCP] port 135) must be enabled if Windows Firewall is enabled.
- The File and Print Sharing exception (TCP port 137, 445, and User Datagram Protocol [UDP] port 137, 138) must be enabled if Windows Firewall is enabled.
- If the computer is part of a workgroup, the Network Access: Sharing and Security Model for Local Accounts policy setting must be set to **Classic**.

Inventory and Analysis with MAP

Once MAP has been installed and you have launched the tool, you will be presented with the Discovery and Readiness node of the MAP tool (Figure 3.3).

To begin, click on **Inventory and Assessment Wizard** to launch the wizard. You will be required to select your discovery method and provide WMI credentials. Depending on what method you chose, you may also be required to provide ADDS credentials, IP addresses, and/or computer names (Figure3.4).

Once your scan begins, you will see a review that includes how many computers were scanned, how many scans have been successfully completed, and how many failed to connect (Figure 3.5).

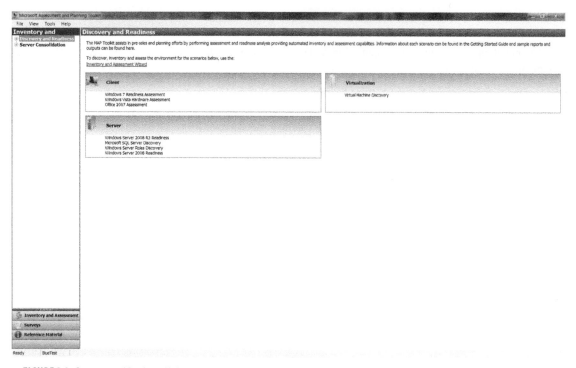

FIGURE 3.3 Discovery and Readiness Node

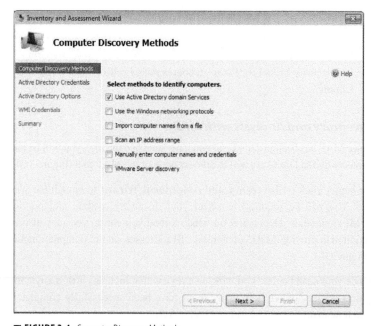

FIGURE 3.4 Computer Discovery Methods

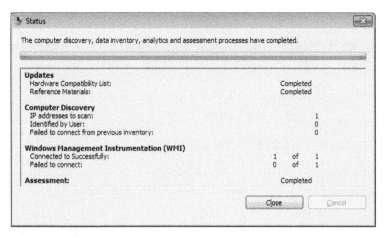

■ **FIGURE 3.5** Inventory Status

Analyzing MAP Data

When your scan is complete, it is time to analyze the data. To begin, expand **Discovery and Readiness** in the left pane and then choose **Windows 7 Readiness Assessment**. You will be presented with a number of pie charts highlighting the inventory summary, computers ready for Windows 7 before hardware upgrades, computers ready for Windows 7 after hardware upgrades, and a list of devices and their compatibility (Figure 3.6).

You can get more detailed reports by clicking on **Generate report/proposal** in the right pane. This will generate a Word document (.docx) and an Excel document (.xlsx) with greater detail on the inventory data collected.

The Excel spreadsheet will give you detailed hardware and device information for each computer scanned along with hardware upgrade recommendations. The Word document will be a proposal outlining the enterprise features of Windows 7, a summary of hardware that is ready for Windows 7 and a summary of hardware that requires upgrades to support Windows 7. Finally, the proposal will also offer some resources on further steps.

NOTE

Youc and ownloada s ample set of MAP reports and proposals for all the inventory and analysis options available with MAP at www.microsoft.com/downloads/details.aspx?displaylang=en&FamilyID=67240b76-3148-4e49-943d-4d9ea7f77730.

DEPLOYMENT SOLUTIONS

Now, we'll discuss some Windows 7 deployment solutions.

Working with MDT 2010

By strengthening best practices and reliable methodologies to facilitate repeatable and consistent deployment with MDT 2010, Microsoft has made it more manageable to create standardized configurations and considerably reduced administrative effort and errors. It is now easier to deploy an

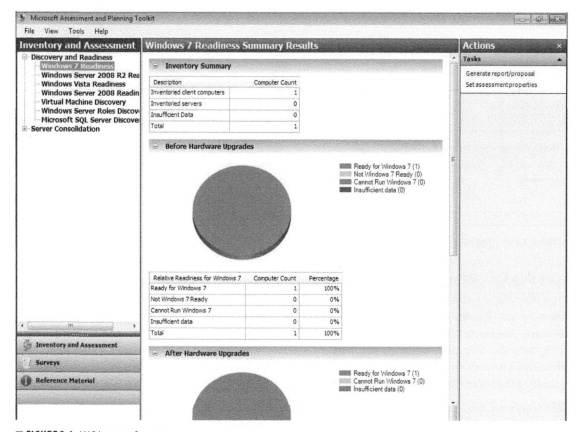

■ FIGURE 3.6 MAP Inventory Summary

operating system in an organization because there is a framework that can guide the administrator through the process from start to end. With MDT 2010, you can determine which components need to be deployed on new systems and start a process for packaging or scripting those applications, so that you can reinstall them quickly and consistently without user intervention. Through the use of the MDT you can do the following:

- Create an imaging process to produce a standard enterprise image of Windows 7 to aid in configuration management and to speed deployments.
- Establish a process for capturing user state from existing computers and for restoring user state on the newly deployed computers.
- Provide a method for backing up the current computer before deploying Windows7.
- Provide an end-to-end process for the actual deployment of the new computers. The guidance includes LTI and Zero-Touch Installation(ZTI).

Although it is certainly very possible to undertake a massive deployment project using the basic tools, MDT 2010 bridges the gap to many challenges that arise when taking the basic approach. By not using MDT 2010, there are still other alternatives that can be explored; however, we will not look into them as these other approaches are typically more complex and require a significant amount of work (that is, writing answer files, manually provisioning images, developing custom scripts, and so on). Most cases may be handled by MDT 2010, and its capabilities can be extended if there is need for additional scenarios.

As mentioned previously, earlier versions of MDT provided detailed planning guidance and job aids; however, because of the overwhelming size of the documentation in MDT, Microsoft has reduced it to essential technical guidance only. Additionally, MDT now includes quick-start guides that provide end-to-end instructions for LTI and ZTI deployment (ZTI can be performed through Microsoft System Center Configuration Manager 2007 with the integration of MDT 2010).

The GUI of MDT 2010 provides numerous wizards to configure the different portions of Windows Setup that can be customized and automated. The toolkit itself will implement the designated settings when it runs, executing instructions in the background that will take care of the many typical and time-consuming tasks that would typically be performed while using standard deployment utilities.

Installing MDT 2010

In order to use MDT 2010, the following components are required to be present in your system:

- Windows PowerShell – Depending on which operating system you are using, you may need to either download or add Windows PowerShell as a feature. If you are installing MDT 2010 on Windows Server 2008 or Windows Server 2008 R2, it is already bundled with your system, and you must install Windows PowerShell from the Add Features Wizard. If you are installing it on any other previous version of Windows, it must be downloaded from the Microsoft Download Center site or from Windows Update from the optional components section.
- MSXMLServices 6.0 – Microsoft Core XML Services (MSXML) 6.0 release provides standards-conformant implementations of common XML standards.
- Window AIK 2.0 – Although this kit can be used by itself to build low-volume automated installations, MDT 2010 leverages its features and requires it to run.

> **NOTE**
> Although it is not a required component to provide higher scalability of the deployment architecture, it is recommended to have an available SQL Server instance or to install SQL Server 2005 with SP2 or later in order to leverage the advanced configuration features with the MDT 2010 database.

- Microsoft Application Compatibility Toolkit 5.5 – A set of tools to test for, and mitigate, application compatibility issues on Windows Vista and Windows7.
- USMT 4.0 (or USMT 3.0 for operating systems earlier than Windows XP SP3) – User State Migration Toolkit is a set of tools to capture and restoreus ers tateda tadur inga de ployment.

To install MDT 2010, you must first download it from the Microsoft Downloads Center site (www.microsoft.com/downloads) or directly through the following URL: www.microsoft.com/downloads/details.aspx?FamilyID= 3bd8561f-77ac-4400-a0c1-fe871c461a89&displaylang=en.

Once you have obtained and installed the required components, you may proceed to launch the MDT 2010 installer. The product's documentation outlines how to complete its setup through the following steps:

1. Double-click **MicrosoftDeploymentToolkit_x86.msi** (or alternatively the **MicrosoftDeploymentToolkit_x64.msi** file if you are running a 64-bit operating system), and then click **Install**.
2. On the Welcome to the Microsoft Deployment Toolkit 2010 Setup Wizard page, click **Next**.
3. On the End-User License Agreement page, review the license agreement, click **I accept the terms in the License Agreement**, and then click **Next**.
4. On the Custom Setup page, click **Next**.
5. Click **Install**. The Installing Microsoft Deployment Toolkit page appears. The installation process status displays and eventually finishes.
6. On the Completing the Microsoft Deployment Toolkit Setup Wizard page, click **Finish**.

After setup is completed, a program group is created; to launch the application click **Start**, and then point to **All Programs**. Point to **Microsoft Deployment Toolkit**, and then click **Deployment Workbench**.

To download and install/update Deployment Workbench components, perform the following steps:

1. In the Deployment Workbench console tree, go to **Deployment Workbench | Information Center | Components**.
2. Int he **Components** pane, in the **Available for Download**s ection, click **component_name** (where *component_name* is the name of the component you want to download).
3. In the details pane, click **Download**. After downloading the component from the Internet, the component is listed in the **Downloaded**s ection in the details pane.
4. In the details pane, in the **Download** section, click the component, and then click **Install**.

NOTE

Ift hereis no **Install** button, the component cannot be installed or the installation is not necessary. Be sure to check frequently for updated components. On the Deployment Workbench main menu bar, from the **Action**m enu, click **Check for Updates**. On the **Check for Updates** page of the Check for Updates wizard, select **Check the Internet**, and then click **Check**.

TIP

At this point, be sure to reboot your build computer (where you have just installed MDT 2010). You may get errors importing images if you fail to do so because there is a great dependency on other components.

Preparing an LTI Deployment with MDT 2010

The following section will provide an overview of an LTI in a *new computer* scenario. This type of installation requires user intervention to a certain degree, yet it can be automated to a point where end users can comfortably go through the setup without major complications, with little or no orientation. The ZTI is entirely automated and requires no end-user input after the setup starts; however, infrastructure considerations are more demanding. To conduct a ZTI, you need to configure the integration with MDT 2010 and System Center Configuration Manager 2007. For more information on ZTI, consultt heM DT2010doc umentation.

Before we begin, we need to gather the necessary items that are required by the LTI deployment process. To prepare for LTI in MDT 2010, you will need to provision the deployment shares by importing or adding the following:

- Windows 7 source files or image files for each operating system to be deployed to the reference and target computers
- Windows 7 packages for the operating systems, such as *security updates*, *feature packs*, or *language packs*a sne eded
- Device drivers for the reference and target computers that are not included as a part of the operating system
- Applications that are to be installed as a part of the operating system image or during the deployment of the reference image

The purpose of a MDT 2010 Deployment Share is not only to host the images of the operating systems that will be distributed over the network, but also to provide the applications, drivers, and other packages that your organization's systems require to correctly function. The Deployment Workbench is the tool that will facilitate the authoring of system configurations into the OS installation images, which will include the aforementioned components. These images, after careful development and testing, will be ultimately rolled out to the client computers on the production environment; however, for the purpose of following a more organized methodology of planning, building, testing, stabilizing, deploying, and supporting the Windows 7 images, it is highly recommended to configure an initial deployment share for development and then merge changes to additional deployment shares for production.

Creating a New Deployment Share in Deployment Workbench

After MDT 2010 is fully installed and updated with all the necessary components, you may launch the Deployment Workbench from the Microsoft

NOTE
Theo therd iscussedd eployment scenarios at the beginning of this chapter (upgrade, refresh, replace) can be accomplished through LTI. For more information on how to prepare task sequences for these types of deployment scenarios, review the MDT 2010 documentation.

NOTE
Additionally,f ort hep urpose of facilitating distribution, advanced options in the Deployment Share allow you to synchronize with *Linked Deployment Shares*. The use of a Distributed File System (DFS) is encouraged in larger organizations to even further facilitate replication of the deployment imagesa ndc onfiguration.

Deployment Toolkit program group. The MDT 2010 documentation outlines how to create a new deployment share, performing the following steps:

1. Click **Start** and then point to **All Programs**. Point to **Microsoft Deployment Toolkit**, and then click **Deployment Workbench**.
2. In the Deployment Workbench console tree, go to **Deployment Workbench | Deployment Shares**.
3. Int he **Actions** pane, click **New Deployment Share**. The **New DeploymentS hare Wizard**s tarts.

Complete the New Deployment Share wizard by going through the following pages of the wizard:

1. **Path** – In **Deployment share path**, type *path* (where *path* is the fully qualified path to an existing folder on a local drive or a network-shared folder created earlier in the deployment process), and then click **Next**. Alternatively, click **Browse** to find the existing folder on a local drive or network-shared folder.
2. **Share** – This page is displayed only if you entered a path to a folder on a local drive on the **Path** wizard page. In **Share name**, type *share_name* (where *share_name* is the share name for the folder on a local drive specified on the **Path** wizard page). Note the fully qualified to Universal Naming Convention (UNC) path to the share being created listed immediately below the **Share name** box, and then click **Next**. The wizard grants the local group Everyone Full Control access at the share level. Based on your security requirements, you may want to restrict the security of the share.
3. **Descriptive Name** – In **Deployment share description**, type *description* (where *description* is a descriptive name that for the deployment share specified on previous wizard pages), and then click **Next**.
4. **Allow Image Capture** – Select or clear the **Ask if an image should be captured** check box based on requirements, and then click **Next**. This check box configures the Windows Deployment Wizard to allow the user to optionally capture an image of the target computer, which is usually the reference computer. If the check box is selected, the path for storing the image and the image name can be configured in the Windows Deployment Wizard. If the check box is cleared, an image is not captured or the image-capture information must be set in the MDT 2010 configuration file or database. By default, this check box is selected.
5. **Allow Admin Password** – Select or clear the **Ask user to set the local Administrator Password** check box based on requirements, and then click **Next**. This check box configures the Windows Deployment Wizard to allow the user to provide the password for the local Administrator account during the deployment process. If the check box is selected, the password can be configured in the Windows Deployment Wizard.

If the check box is cleared, the password must be set in the MDT 2010 configuration file or database. By default, this check box is cleared.

6. **Allow Product Key** – Select or clear the **Ask user for a product key** check box based on your requirements, and then click **Next**. This check box configures the Windows Deployment Wizard to allow the user to provide a product key for the target operating system during the deployment process. If the check box is selected, the product key can be configured in the Windows Deployment Wizard. If the check box is cleared, the product key must be set in the MDT 2010 configuration file or database. By default, this check box is cleared.

7. **Summary** – Review the information in the **Details** box, and then click **Next**.

8. **Confirmation: Tip** – Click **Save Output** to save the output of the wizard to a file, or click **View Script** to view the Windows PowerShell scripts used to perform the wizard tasks. Click **Close**.

Upon completion, the new deployment share is created in the target folder you selected in the wizard and appears in the Deployment Workbench (see Figure3.7).

Configuring and Provisioning the Deployment Share in MDT 2010

Once the deployment share is created, you will need to configure and provision it through the Deployment Workbench. The next thing to do is add the

> **NOTE**
> Ad eployments hared oesn ot have to be located on a specific computer – it can be stored on a local disk volume, a shared folder on the network, or anywhere in a stand-alone DFS namespace. (Windows PE cannot access domain-basedD FSn amespaces.)

■ **FIGURE 3.7** View of the Created Deployment Share within the Deployment Workbench

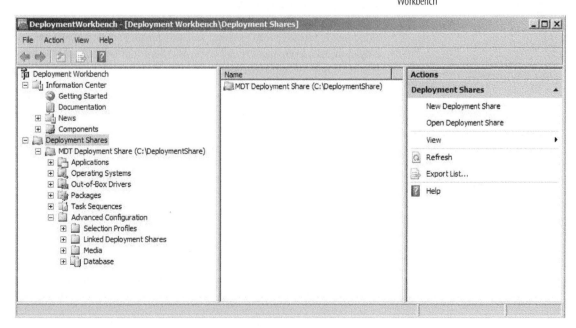

Windows 7 operating system files to the deployment share. The following steps from the MDT 2010 documentation indicate how you must proceed to import an OS:

1. Click **Start**, and then point to **All Programs**. Point to **Microsoft Deployment Toolkit**, and then click **Deployment Workbench**.
2. In the Deployment Workbench console tree, go to **Deployment Workbench | Deployment Shares | MDT Deployment Share (C:\DeploymentShare$) | Operating Systems**.
3. Int he **Actions** pane, click **Import Operating System**. TheI mport OperatingS ystemw izards tarts.

Complete the Import Operating System wizard using the information in the following list:

1. **OS Type** – Click **Full set of source files**, and then click **Next**. In the event you wanted to import a custom installation from a reference computer, you could choose the captured WIM Image.
2. **Source** – In **Source directory**, type *source_path* (where *source_path* is the fully qualified path to the Windows 7 distribution files), and then click **Next**.
3. **Destination** – Click **Next**. (A new folder for this OS will be created.)
4. **Summary** – Click **Next**.
5. **Confirmation** – Click **Finish**.

Creating Task Sequences

Task sequences are necessary to perform the automated deployment of Windows 7. You will need to create task sequences so that they may be displayed on the deployment menu when you boot into the custom Windows PE image built by MDT 2010.

A task sequence defines the steps that are performed for an installation. These may either be bound to a specific operating system or to an unattended setup answer file (Unattend.xml). The answer file can provide information to the task sequence, for example, a product key, organization name, and information necessary to join the computer to a domain; nevertheless, it is preferable to allow MDT 2010 to control the settings in Unattend.xml and use the MDT 2010 database to configure destination computers. Task sequences can also be created to perform other actions during the installation such as automating user backup and restore operations (to perform a user migration). To simplify and reduce the need for custom scripting in the event of a straightforward deployment, MDT 2010 includes task sequence templates that you can use for common deployment scenarios. In many cases, you can use the templates without any modification to the task sequence; however, it is possible to modify these task sequences created from the templates to meet the requirements of your organization. The following are the task sequence templates available in MDT 2010:

- **Capture Only** – It will only capture an image of the reference computer and store it on the Deployment Share under the *Captures*f older. This image can then be further serviced with MDT 2010.
- **Standard Client Task Sequence** – This creates the default task sequence for deploying operating system images to client computers, including desktop and portable computers.
- **Standard Client Replace Task Sequence** – This backs up the system entirely, backs up the user state, and wipes the disk.
- **Custom Task Sequence** – This creates a customized task sequence that does not install an operating system.
- **Standard Server Task Sequence** – This creates the default task sequence for deploying operating system images to server computers.
- **Litetouch OEM Task Sequence** – Preloads operating system images on computers in a staging environment before deploying the target computers in the production environment (typically by a computer Original Equipment Manufacturer [OEM]).
- **Post OS Installation Task Sequence** – This performs installation tasks after the operating system has been deployed to the target computer.

To create a new task sequence, perform the following steps:

1. Click **Start**, and then point to **All Programs**. Point to **Microsoft Deployment Toolkit**, and then click **Deployment Workbench**.
2. In the Deployment Workbench console tree, go to **Deployment Workbench | Deployment Shares |** *deployment_share* **| Task Sequences** (where *deployment_share* is the name of the deployment share to which you will add the task sequence).
3. Int he **Actions** pane, click **New Task Sequence**. The New Task Sequencew izards tarts.

The New Task Sequence wizard finishes. The package is added to the list of packages in the details pane of the Deployment Workbench.

Once you are done servicing the Deployment Share in MDT 2010, it is necessary that you commit the changes by clicking **Update Deployment Share**. This action will then automatically build a custom Windows PE that once booted on a client computer will allow you to connect over the network to the Deployment Share and have access to the task sequences and image

NOTE

Form orei nformationa bout Volume Activation and product keys in MDT 2010, see Windows 7 Volume Activation 2.0 Technical Guidance at http://go.microsoft .com/fwlink/?LinkID=75674.

files; additionally, it will incorporate the files and settings corresponding to the drivers, applications, and packages you added in MDT 2010 to the image.

DELIVERY

In this section, you will learn how to configure WDS to use it in your deployment and also learn how to leverage the images you have prepared using MDT 2010 and ultimately deploy them.

Configuring WDS

WDS is a feature that is included with Windows Server 2008 to provide on-demand deployment of operating systems to bare-metal clients; it accomplishes this through provisioning of the OS images stored in a network repository or share, which will host the Windows 7 and Windows PE images. This feature replaces Remote Installation Services (RIS), which was the solution bundled with Windows Server 2003. WDS is also available for Windows Server 2003 as an add-on. For Windows Server 2003 SP1 and later, you may obtain WDS by installing the Windows AIK 2.0.

WDS enable client computers with Pre-Executable Environment (PXE)-capable network adapters to boot into a customized Windows PE image, which will display a menu from which the user can choose what installation image to deploy. Client computers that are not PXE-compliant can also make use of WDS with the use of boot disks. You will leverage the capabilities of WDS and MDT 2010 by using the custom Windows PE boot files (prepared from MDT 2010) while WDS manages the client's connection and begins transmitting the chosen image files. According to the MDT 2010 documentation, you can use WDS in LTI deployments in the following ways:

■ **Start Windows PE on the target computers** – The beginning of the *new computer* deployment scenario and the second half of the *replace computer* deployment scenario both start the target computer in Windows PE. For these scenarios, you can automate starting Windows PE using WDS.
■ **Install images created in the Deployment Workbench on the target computers** – You can create custom WIM images in the Deployment Workbench that you can deploy directly to target computers using WDS.

To install WDS in Windows Server 2008, you must add it as a role from the Service Manager console (see Figure 3.8).

The installation will prompt you to select which role services to install for WDS; these are the **Deployment Server** and **Transport Server** services. You may choose to install both of them.

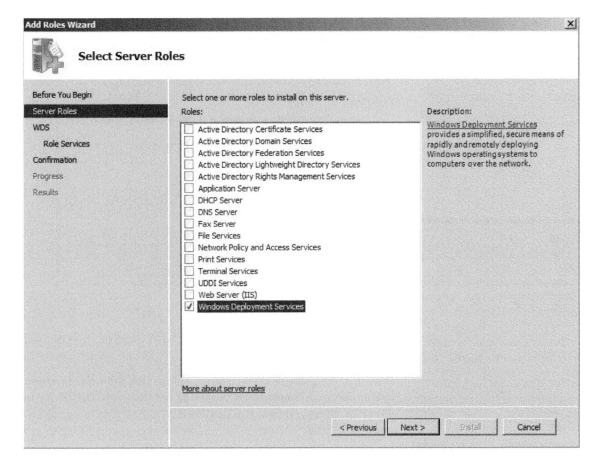

■ **FIGURE 3.8** Selecting **Windows Deployment Services**

Once you have finished installing WDS, you need to authorize and configure the server (in a similar manner as you would do for a Dynamic Host Configuration Protocol [DHCP] server).

You may now find a Microsoft Management Console snap-in for WDS, which will be added within the **Administrative Tools** group. Expand servers, right-click on the server name in the list, and click on **Configure Server**.

Before activating WDS services, you need to ensure that the server is set up with the following parameters (see Figure 3.9):

■ The server that is running WDS is a member of an Active Directory domain.
■ You have a DHCP server (it can be on this same server).
■ Domain Name System (DNS) is configured and running.
■ A location to store images exists (this location should be on a nonsystem volume).

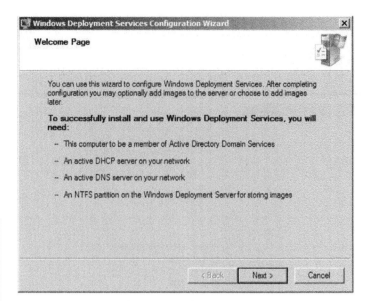

■ FIGURE 3.9 Activating Windows

Specify the path to the location to store your Windows PE images. Once you have chosen the location, click **Next**.

If you are configuring WDS on a server that has DHCP installed, you will need to check the **Do not listen on port 67** and **Configure DHCP option 60 to PXE Client** options so that DHCP and WDS/PXE services can coexist (see Figure 3.10). This way client computers that request to PXE boot can bes erved.

Now you must specify the answer policy, which controls the computers that canbe s ervedbyt he WDSs erver(see Figure3.11).

In the subsequent screen, you can choose to uncheck the option to add images to the WDS as you will add them later. The infrastructure is in place; however, there are couple of additional things you must do before you are able to have computers booting over the network.

If you right-click on the **Server name** and then click **properties**, and finally navigate to the **boot** tab, you'll notice that this panel lists the programs that should be used when a computer connects to the WDS server and requests the boot loader. These programs that are listed are the network boot loader. Now, notice that when we click on the **browse** button, we're actually missing those programs.

If you search your remote install directory, you won't find them either. In order to get these programs, we actually need to add a boot image. Click **Cancel** on the **browse** dialog. Click **Cancel** again on the **properties** dialog box.

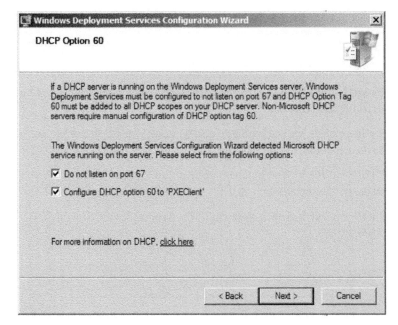

■ **FIGURE 3.10** Configuring Windows Deployment Services on a Server with DHCP Installed

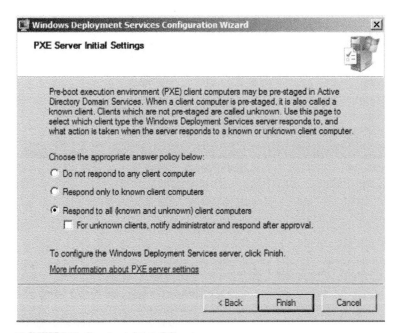

■ **FIGURE 3.11** Choosing an Answer Policy

NOTE

Dependingony ouri magings trategy, more advanced configuration settings allow administrators to perform staged deployments. Prestaged clients may be already named and identified within an Active Directory and may be allowed to PXE boot. This can be a security measure that prevents unauthorizedP XEb ooting.

In the main Microsoft Management Console (MMC) right-click **Boot Images** and click **Add**. We want to add a boot WIM image. We can get this image in two places. In the BDD structure, if you have created and populated a deploy point, there will a file called:

[Business Desktop Deployment (BDD) DRIVE]\Distribution\Boot\Lite-TouchPE_x86.wim

For this example, we will use the PE on a Windows Vista CD. It can be found in the *Sources* folder. Choose the **Boot.wim** file and click **open** (see Figure 3.12).

Click **Next**. If you want to modify the name of the boot image to suit your needs, go ahead (see Figure 3.13).

Click **Next** and then click **Next** again. The wizard adds the boot image (see Figure3. 14).

■ **FIGURE 3.12** Selecting the Windows Image File

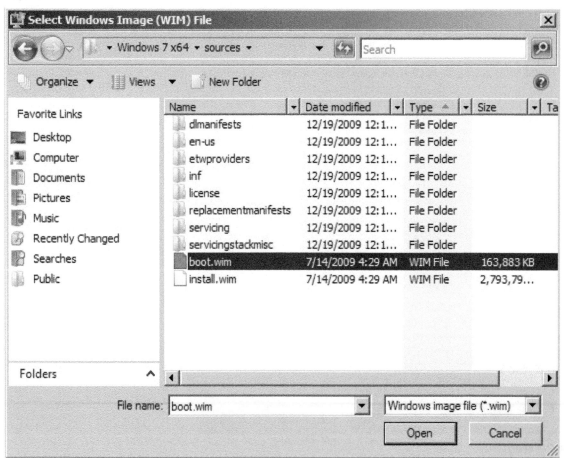

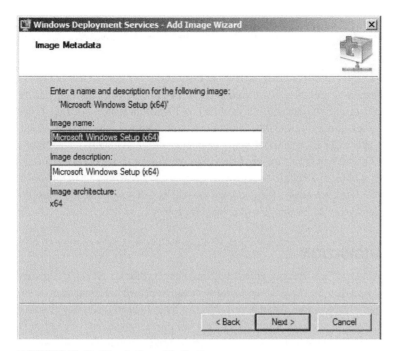

■ **FIGURE 3.13** Modifying the Name of the Boot Image

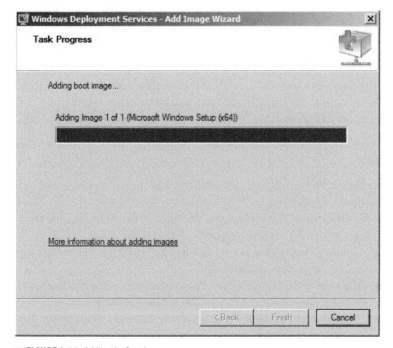

■ **FIGURE 3.14** Adding the Boot Image

Once it's done, check the properties in the **boot** tab again. Notice when you click **browse**, the needed file is there along with several others.

Multicast

Once you are able to get computers to PXE boot, you may conduct the network deployments using the MDT 2010 custom images for Lite Touch Installation; however, this method may take a toll on your network bandwidth and performance if many computers are individually undergoing a LTI. The Windows 7 images that will be deployed over the network can easily add up to a couple of gigabytes being transferred from the deployment shares to each client. The good news is that by using multicasting transmissions you may be able to overcome this problem.

MIGRATION

Windows Easy Transfer provides a convenient method for allowing end users to save their files and settings to transfer them from their old computer to a new one. This Windows 7 tool is very effective for individual cases; however, it is not very robust in performing migrating tasks for a high volume of computers. When it comes to preparing a migration strategy within your Windows 7 deployment plans, whether you are planning to perform *refresh computer* or *replace computer* installations, there are resources available that will make the task of preserving user's settings and files much more manageable.

UserS tateM igration Tool

Included in Windows AIK 2.0 is USMT 4.0. After downloading and installing Windows AIK, the USMT source files will be located in C:\Program Files\ Windows AIK\Tools\USMT*Platform*, where *Platform* is either x64 or x86.

There are a few files included with USMT that you should become familiar with:

- **Scanstate.exe** This tool scans, collects, and uploads user-state data during a migration.
- **Loadstate.exe** This tool imports the collected user-state data into the user profiles on the new computer.
- **Usmtutil.exe** This tool is used to delete the Hard Link migration data once the import is complete.
- **MigApps.xml** This file defines the location for user-specific data for common programs for the source and destination computers.
- **MigUser.xml** This file defines the location for user-specific profile data for the source and destination computers.

- **MigDocs.xml** This file defines the location for document-specific data for common programs for the source and destination computers.
- **Config.xml** This is a custom XML file that you can create to customize what data gets transferred, to perform domain migrations, and to create custom error codes and behaviors.

You will use USMT on computers for which you wish to preserve the user state and additional files/settings. Depending on your environment's configuration, the volume of information that needs to be preserved will vary as follows:

- For instance, if you have leveraged the use of network storage to redirect the user's *My Documents* folder and have enforced this setting using Group Policy, you may have to use less space and time to migrates ettings.
- In a different case, if you are migrating settings to new hardware, USMT can use a remote storage location to temporarily store the user state while the OS is being installed.
- You can also run USMT on a machine on which you intend to perform a *refresh computer* installation (in-place migration), for instance, in the case of a Windows XP computer migrating to Windows 7 on the same hardware. In this scenario, USMT can use Hard-Link Migration to maintain the data on the same volume while the OS image is applied to the computer; subsequently, the preserved user state will be imported to the new OS from the local computer.

You can stage USMT directly on each client computer or on a network share. If you're using MDT 2010, it can install USMT in deployment shares automatically. MDT 2010 already contains logic for using USMT to save and restore user-state data on each computer.

You use USMT in a number of ways: on a network share, on Windows PE media, on an MDT 2010 deployment share, or with Configuration Manager. The last two options enable migration during LTI- and ZTI-deployment projects.

Hard-LinkM igration

A *hard-link migration store* enables you to perform an in-place migration where all user state is maintained on the computer while the old operating system is removed and the new operating system is installed; this is why it is best suited for the *refresh computer* scenario. Use of a hard-link migration store for a *refresh computer* scenario drastically improves migration performance and significantly reduces hard-disk utilization and deployment costs, and enables entirely new migration scenarios.

When to Use a Hard-Link Migration

You can use a hard-link migration store when your planned migration meets both of the following criteria:

- You are upgrading the operating system on existing hardware rather than migrating to new computers.
- You are upgrading the operating system on the same volume of the computer.

You cannot use a hard-link migration store if your planned migration includes any of the following:

- You are migrating data from one computer to a second computer.
- You are migrating data from one volume on a computer to another volume, for example from C: to D:.
- You are formatting or repartitioning the disk outside of Windows Setup, or specifying a disk format or repartition during Windows Setup that will remove the migration store.

The hard-link migration store is created using the command-line option, */hardlink*, and is equivalent to other migration-store types. However, it differs in that hard links are utilized to keep files stored on the source computer during the migration. Keeping the files in place on the source computer eliminates the redundant work of duplicating files. It also enables the performance benefits and reduction in disk utilization that define this scenario.

Using USMT 4.0

After downloading and installing Windows AIK, the USMT source files will be located in C:\Program Files\Windows AIK\Tools\USMT*Platform*, where *Platform* is either x64 or x86. USMT does not need to be installed on every computer, you can simply share the USMT directory or copy the files onto a network share and run the commands from there.

Before you start collecting user-state date, it is a good idea to create a custom Config.xml file to control the type of data being migrated. Now is the perfect time to rid the network of unnecessary data like MP3s and such. It is very easy to do this with a custom Config.xml. To create this XML file simply run the following command:

Scanstate.exe /i:migapp.xml /i:miguser.xml /genconfig:Config.xml

This will create the Config.xml file. You can now browse to the USMT directory and open it with Notepad.

At first look, the Config.xml file can seem daunting, but there really isn't much you need to change here. At the start of the XML file, you will see a list of user-profile data locations for applications, documents, and Windows components. To prevent a type of data from being migrated simply change *migrate="yes"* to *migrate="no"*(see Figure3.15).

Scanstate.exe

There is a long list of command-line options available with both **Scanstate. exe** and **Loadstate.exe**. You don't need to know them all, but we will list the important ones in Table 3.1 to get you started. We encourage you to take a look at them all as there are some powerful options.

```
config - Notepad
File   Edit   Format   View   Help
  </Applications>
  <Documents>
    <component displayname="My Pictures" migrate="no" ID="ht
    <component displayname="My Documents" migrate="yes" ID='
```

■ **FIGURE 3.15** Changing Migration Settings

Table3. 1 Command-Line Options for Migrating Data

Command Line Interface (CLI) Switch	Description
StorePath	Defines the location where the migration file will be stored
/o	Overwrites any existing migration file
/nocompress	Prevents the migration file from being compressed. You must use this switch when using the */hardlink* switch
/encrypt	Encrypts the migration file using a key string (/key:*keystring*) or a file (/keyfile:*path/filename*)
/i	Defines the path to the XML file location
/config	Defines the path to the custom XML file location
/genconfig	Used to generate the custom XML file
/targetXP	Used when collecting user-state data from a Windows XP source computer
/ui	Specifies the user accounts to include in a migration
/ue	Specifies the user accounts to exclude in a migration
/efs: (abort, copy, raw, decryptcopy)	Used to define how to handle Encrypted File System (EFS) encrypted data ■ *abort* stops the migration ■ *copy* copies the data and the EFS certificate ■ *raw* copies only the data ■ *decryptcopy* decrypts the data and migrates it
/hardlink	Used to create a hardlink store on the local machine

A typical user state scan command line to copy the migration store to a share on a file server would look like this:

Scanstate.exe \\servername\share /i:migapp.xml /i:miguser.xml /config:config .xml /encrypt /key:SecureKeyString /efs:copy

If you wanted to run the same command but store the data in a local hardlink store, the command would be as follows:

Scanstate.exe c:\hardlinkstore /nocompress /i:migapp.xml /i:miguser,xml /config:config.xml /efs:copy /hardlink

Once your user-state data is migrated and Windows 7 has been deployed, you can use **Loadstate.exe** to restore the user data (Table 3.2). Again, there are a lot of command-line options, but we will list the most common ones.

The command-line options used to restore the user state we saved in our scanstate examples above would be:

Loadstate.exe \\servername\share /i:migapp.xml /i:miguser.xml /confi g: config.xml /decrypt /key:SecureKeyString

Loadstate c:\hardlinkstore /nocompress /i:migapp.xml /i:miguser.xml /config:config.xml

Although **Scanstate.exe** is a tool that you will use with a login script or some other process to start the data collection, you will probably want to

> **NOTE**
>
> Ify ouu set he */hardlink* switch the hardlink store is not deleted once the user-state data is restored. The hardlink store must be manually deleted using **USMTUtil.exe**w ith the following switch:
>
> *Usmtutil.exe c:\hardlinkstore /rd*

Table3 .2 Command-Line Options for Restoring Migrated Data

CLI Switch	Description
StorePath	Defines the location of the migration file
/decrypt	Decrypts the migration file using the key string or key file used to encrypt
/nocompress	Specifies that the store is not compressed. Must be used with the */hardlink* option
/i	Defines the path to the XML file location
/config	Defines the path to the custom XML file location
/ui	Specifies the user accounts to include in a migration
/ue	Specifies the user accounts to exclude in a migration
/md	Used to move migration data from one domain to another
/mu	Used to move migration date from one user account to another
/lac	Used to create a new local account
/lae	Used to enable the newly created local account.

incorporate your import of user state into the operating system deployment. There are many options available in MDT 2010 and System Center Configuration Manager 2007 SP2, as well as **Unattend.xml** and **RunOnce** options.

■ SUMMARY

Deployment technologies have come a long way from the days of Windows 2000 and XP. In the past, you were forced to rely on a combination of third-party tools, custom scripts, and changing deployment technologies (RIS, WDS, and so on) to deploy Windows. Thankfully that has changed, and using the tools mentioned in this chapter, you can plan your deployment, build your images, and start rolling out Windows 7 in days rather than weeks. Combined with the integration with other Microsoft technologies like WDS or System Center Configuration Manager 2007 SP2, deploying Windows will no longer be the chore that it once was.

The New Windows 7 Desktop Environment

In the Þrst chapter, you were introduced to Windows 7 and many of its new features. Chapter 2, ÒInstalling and Upgrading to Windows 7Ó and Chapter 3, ÒDeploying Windows 7 in an Enterprise EnvironmentÓ referenced how to deploy Windows 7 from a single system to an entire enterprise. This chapter focuses on the new Windows 7 desktop environment from the moment the Windows 7 install Þnishes to the new Windows Explorer and Internet Explorer 8 (IE 8). Finally, this chapter will also reference what makes Windows the leader in the desktop environment, applications, from understanding the new User Account Control features to installing third-party applications and Windows features.

The new Windows 7 user interface is the Þrst new feature both you and your users will notice. The Welcome Screen and Log In is similar to Windows Vista but immediately the user will notice a difference. Once the user is logged in, the user will land on the desktop. The desktop has been changed substantially from Windows XP. The most important factor for user acceptance is that the user learns the new desktop and user interface. The new Aero themes are mostly related to eye candy and making Windows 7 look prettier. However, some Aero features will prove to make end users more

DOI: 10.1016/B978-1-59749-561-5.00004-8

efÞcient with everyday tasks. For example, Aero Snap allows users to put two screens side-by-side for multitasking or referencing. New display and screen resolution options will allow the desktop layout to be conÞgured for any userõ preference. The Start menu and taskbar have also been changed in Windows 7. The new Start menu and taskbar look different but also have new features such as Jump Lists to allow users to execute commands in applications much quicker, making them more efÞcient. All of these new features and others related to the user interface will be referenced and illustrated in this chapter.

Windows Explorer has not changed as dramatically as the desktop and user interface but a user will Þnd some differences. Navigating the Þle system and searching for Þles and folders is now easier and quicker than ever. Microsoft introduced Libraries, which make locating and centralizing Þles and folders easier for the user. Users will no longer spend much time locating Þles and more time using them. The second section of this chapter will introduce the new features of Windows Explorer and describes how to conÞgure it for the best use.

IE 8 is also new and comes with Windows 7. As users and businesses move applications to the cloud and users begin to spend more time on the Internet, the Web browser becomes one of the most critical applications in the computer. IE 8 packs many new features not only for usability but for security as well. Microsoft understands the user is the weakest link in security and Web browsing is the simplest and easiest method for malicious hackers to attack. Thankfully, IE 8 is more secure and has made many improvements to the included features and support. These new features and options will be explained and referenced in this chapter.

Finally, applications in Windows 7 will be tackled. The reason Windows dominates the desktop market is because of the application support. Windows Vista had many problems with software compatibility and Microsoft learned the hard way. With Windows 7, Microsoft has improved how it handles third-party applications by increasing compatibility options and Þne tuning the User Account Control feature. Additionally, Microsoft has included many features in Windows 7 that simply need to be turned on or off. Installing applications, turning on and off Windows features, and understanding software compatibility are a few of the tasks we will tackle in the Þnal section of this chapter.

This chapter focuses on the new desktop environment from an end user and power user perspective. Most of the conÞguration and managing tasks referenced in this chapter are related to the user interface, Windows Explorer, IE 8, and applications. The next chapter will focus on managing the desktop environment.

THE USER INTERFACE

The user interface is the most important aspect of the end user experience. It includes all of the components that an end user will see and use everyday. As an administrator and end user, it is important to understand the user interface to be able to conÞgure and teach end users how to conÞgure and understand these critical components. The Windows 7 user interface has been changed quite a bit from earlier versions of Windows. For end users moving from Windows Vista, the change may not be too drastic. However, Windows XP and prior end users will notice many changes in Windows 7. Remember education is key for end users to understand and learn the new features that Windows 7 brings along with the new interface. Mastering the Windows 7 interface will make the users more productive and the desktop experience much better.

This section focuses on the user interface which includes:

- LogI n
  - WelcomeSc reen
- Desktop
  - Themes
  - DesktopO ptions
  - Modify Window Views
  - DesktopC ontent
  - Windows Aero
  - ScreenR esolutiona ndD isplay
  - Gadgets
- StartM enu
  - Pint oSt artM enu
  - StartM enuS earch
  - JumpL ists
  - Customizet heS tartM enu
  - StartM enuM enusa ndO ptions
- Taskbar
  - TaskbarO ptions
  - Pin a Shortcut to the Taskbar
  - Change Size and Position of Taskbar
  - Customizet he Taskbar
  - NotiÞcation Area
  - Toolbars

LogI n

The Windows 7 Welcome Screen will be the Þrst user interface that most end users will see prior to the new Windows 7 desktop. The Welcome Screen was introduced in Windows XP for logging into computers that were not part of the domain. For computers that were on a domain, the older Windows 2000 and NT login screen was visible in which **Ctrl+Alt+Delete** was required to log in. Since Windows Vista, the Welcome Screen has been used to locally log into the computer or to a domain. The same is true for Windows 7 without an option to use the older Windows 2000 style login screen. The Windows 7 Welcome Screen allows three different scenarios for logging in:

- For computers that are not connected on a domain, the Welcome Screen will display a list of account names and pictures as shown in Figure 4.1. Click the account to log in. If the user account has a password conÞgured, the Welcome Screen will prompt for it. Type the **password** and press **Enter**.

■ **FIGURE 4.1** Windows 7 Welcome Screen for Computers Not Connected to a Domain

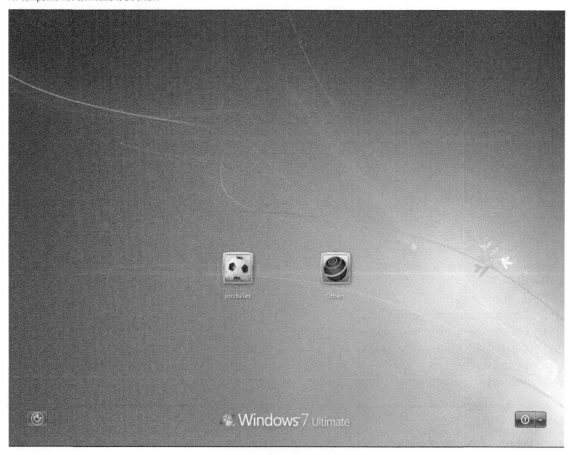

■ For computers that are connected to a domain (as is the case for most business environments), the Welcome Screen will request **Ctrl+Alt+Delete** to be pressed prior to the login screen as shown in Figure 4.2. The name of the last user that was logged in will be displayed and a button to log in as another user will be to its right. Click the **appropriate account**, Þll in the **username**, **password**, and **location (domain name)**, and press **Enter**. To log in to the local computer, input the location name as the hostname of the computer. Clicking **help** reveals the name of the local computer.

■ For computers that are not connected to a domain, only have one account without a password, and/or have been setup to log on automatically, the Welcome Screen may be bypassed landing the user in the Windows7de sktop.

Welcome Screen

The Welcome Screen will generally be the Þrst screen that most end users see every time the machine is booted up, locked, switching users, or waking from sleep, hibernation, or screensaver. The Welcome Screen will most

> **WARNING**
> It is a bad practice to allow automatic login to a Windows 7 computer. It is even worse practice to not have a password on Windows 7 user accounts. It is strongly recommended that passwords be created for all user accounts. Additionally, some features such as Remote Assistance and Remote Desktop require passwordst ofu nction.

■ **FIGURE 4.2** Windows 7 Ctrl+Alt+Delete Screen for Computers Connected to a Domain

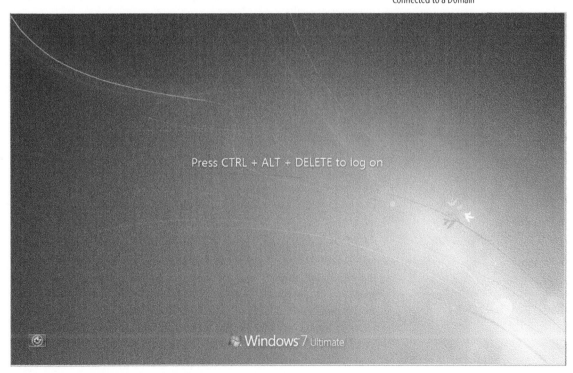

likely contain a button for the last user that logged on, or the users that are currently logged in. Click on the **user account** and enter the **password** to log in. The location will generally be the domain where the computer is joined to or the local computer depending on the user account selected and if the computer is part of a domain (likely in most businesses).

Logging in locally could display a question mark if the user has set up a password hint. This is not available for logging into domains and should only be used to log in locally if the password was forgotten. Another method to recover a forgotten password is with a password reset disk. This is only true if a password reset disk was created for the local computer. For computers that are part of a domain, the user account password may be reset by a system administrator in Active Directory for domain accounts and by connecting with a local administrator group account to the computer with the Manage MMC console for local accounts.

Once the user has logged in, the new Windows 7 user interface will be seen. The next section will explain the new Windows 7 interface's most common components that end users will need to master to become more productive and efficient. Remember you as an administrator are an end user as well, so master these new features so you may train and teach your end users (plus lower service calls).

Desktop

The Windows Desktop has been available in Windows operating systems for years with very little change. In Windows Vista, Microsoft changed the desktop experience and added many new features for Windows 7 with Windows Aero. The Windows 7 desktop is the place where all programs and files will be displayed when opened. It is also a place to display icons or shortcuts to applications, folders, and files. The desktop can even be used as a location for storing items as it is simply a folder in the user's profile folder. The desktop is the base of the user interface and experience. There are many options available to customize almost everything about the desktop.

Themes

Introduced in Windows XP, themes have become a simple way to customize the user interface. In Windows 7, however, the theme sets the base for the user interface. Windows 7 has improved how themes function and what user interface options are applied. A theme in Windows 7 can modify the desktop background, window color, sounds, and screen savers, as well as enable certain features of the user interface. By default, Windows 7 will attempt to load the Windows 7 Aero theme, the option that enables all Windows 7 Aero features; if the hardware is not compatible, then the Windows 7 Basic theme will run. Both the themes are very similar except the Aero theme uses more graphic power to enable the Aero features, transparency, and glassy look. The following three themes are addressed in this section:

- WindowsC lassic
- Windows7B asic
- Windows7 Aero

To change the theme:

1. Opent he **Personalization** console of the Control Panel:
   - Right-clickt he **desktop** and click **Personalize**
   - Open the Control Panel and click **Personalize**
2. Clickt he **desired theme**a si llustratedi n Figure4.3 .
3. To get more themes from Microsoft, click **Get more themes online**.

■ **FIGURE 4.3** Personalize

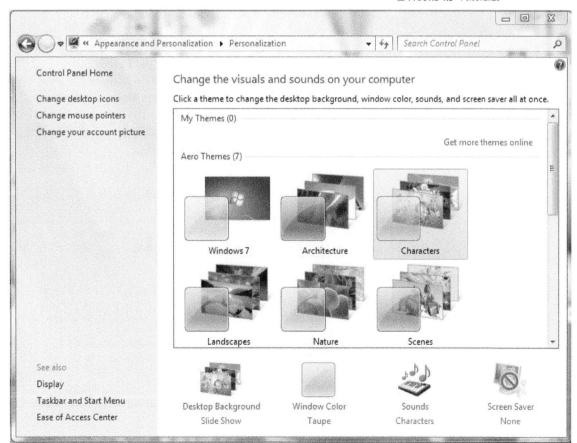

Under the theme selection are links and default settings for the Desktop Background, Window Color, Sounds, and Screen Saver for the chosen theme as shown in Figure 4.3. Although a theme is selected, each component may be chosen creating an Unsaved Theme under the My Themes section of the Themes electionw indow.

■ **Desktop background** ÐThis screen allows the customization of the desktopba ckgrounda ss howni n Figure4.4 .
   ❑ **Picture location** ÐAny location on the local system or network can be chosen to Þnd pictures that can be set as background.
      - **Windows desktop backgrounds** ÐThese are the default backgrounds provided by Windows 7 themes.
      - **Picture Library** ÐThese are all the picture Þles in the Picture Library.
      - **Solid colors** ÐTraditional single color backgrounds used in olderv ersionsof Windows.
   ❑ **Select all, Clear all** ÐThis option allows you to select all the images to cycle through or clear all checks and manually check the pictures that will be rotated.
   ❑ **Picture position** ÐThis is the way the picture will be displayed and the options are **Fill**, **Fit**, **Stretch**, **Tile**, and **Center**.
   ❑ **Change picture every** ÐThis screen allows a time to be set to rotate each picture in the background for Windows Aero themes.

■ **FIGURE 4.4** Desktop Background Configurations

- ❑ **Shuffle** ÐThis allows the pictures selected to be shuffled instead of alwaysf ollowingt hes amer otation.
- ▪ **Windows color** ÐThis option customizes the colors used for the Windows 7 windows as shown in Figure 4.5.
  - ❑ **Change the color of your window borders, Start menu, and taskbar** Ðallows the user to choose a color for the windows, Start menu, and taskbar. Only available in Windows Aero themes.
  - ❑ **Enable transparency** ÐThere is a check box to enable transparency for Windows Aero themes.
  - ❑ **Color intensity** ÐThis is used to set the transparency and color intensity. Shifting the bar to the left is more intense whereas the right is complete transparency. Only available in Windows Aero themes.
  - ❑ **Color mixer** ÐThis allows for a customized window color.
  - ❑ **Advanced appearance settings** ÐThese settings are the traditional settings on earlier versions of Windows. These settings are not availablef or Window Aerot hemes.
    - - **Item** ÐSelect the item to conÞgure
    - - **Size** ÐSet the default size of the window
    - - **Color 1 or Color 2** Ðset the color of the window
    - - **Font** ÐIf the window contains a font, select which font to use
    - - **Size** ÐSet the font size
    - - **Color** ÐSelect the color of the font and whether to use bold or italics

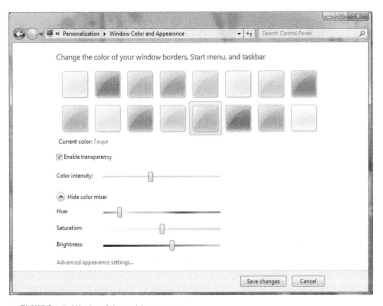

▪ **FIGURE 4.5** Window Color and Appearance

- **Sounds** ÐThis initiates the familiar sound window conÞguration of past versions of Windows as shown in Figure 4.6.
  - ▫ **Sound Scheme** ÐSelect a saved scheme, save the current scheme, or delete a scheme.
  - ▫ **Program Events** ÐSelect the event to conÞgure the sound for.
  - ▫ **Sounds** ÐSelect the .wav Þle to play when the selected event occurs or browse for a custom .wav Þle.
  - ▫ **Play Windows Startup sound** ÐA check box to toggle Windows startups ounds.
- **Screen saver** ÐAll themes have screen savers disabled because Windows 7 uses the improved power management to turn off the display after a few minutes to save more power than a screen saver woulda ss howni n Figure4.7 .

■ **FIGURE 4.6** Sounds

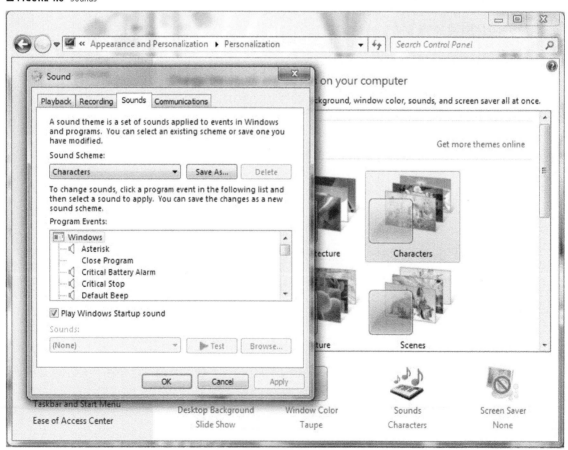

- Select the screen saver from a drop down.
- **Settings** ÐIf 3D text, photos, or a custom screen saver is chosen, there may be options to set.
  - **3D text settings** ÐThis option allows for multiple settings to be set for a 3D text screen saver.
  - **Photos** ÐSet the location of the picture folder, slideshow speed, ands hufßeopt ion.
- **Preview** ÐThis begins the selected screen saver.
- **Wait** ÐThis represents time to wait before the screen saver is activated.
- **On resume, display logon screen** ÐThis locks the computer when the screen saver is activated. A good option for systems that do

■ **FIGURE 4.7** Screen Saver

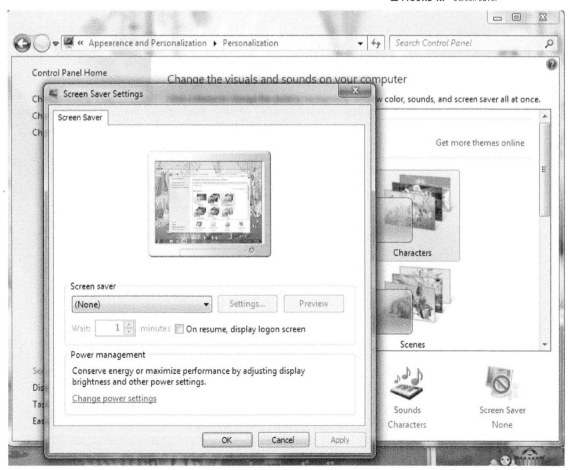

TIP
Microsoft has e nhanced t he power efficiency on the default deployment of Windows 7. By default, the screen saver will not be triggered; instead, the display is put to sleep. This is much more efficient as most of the new monitors go to power saver mode when input is not present. This is the recommended option instead of using screen savers. If a screen saver is required, the blank screen saver consumes less power.

not lock out through Group Policy settings after a certain time for security.

❑ **Change power settings** ÐThis starts the power options in the Control Panel.

To delete a theme:

1. Open t he **Personalization** console of the Control Panel:
   ❑ Right-click t he **desktop** and click **Personalize**
   ❑ Open the Control Panel and click **Personalize**
2. Right-click t he **desired theme** and click **Delete theme**. Themes a re saved by default at %SystemDrive%\%WindDir%\Resources\Themes ass hown i n Figure4.8.

Windows Classic Theme

Windows 7 includes a classic-like user experience for users who enjoy the user interface of Windows 95, 98, ME, and 2000 as shown in Figure 4.9. This interface is available to all Windows 7 editions and is mostly used by users whom have not been trained to use the new user interface of Windows XP, Vista, and now Windows 7. Although Windows Classic resembles Windows 2000 the most, there are still minor changes that require adapting to and possibly training. The biggest feature that Windows Classic does not provide is the classic Start menu.

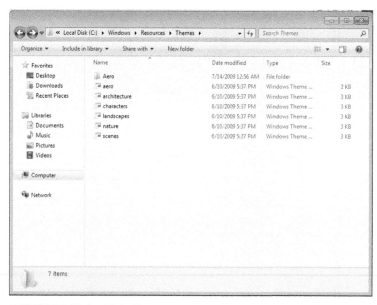

■ **FIGURE 4.8** Windows Theme Directory

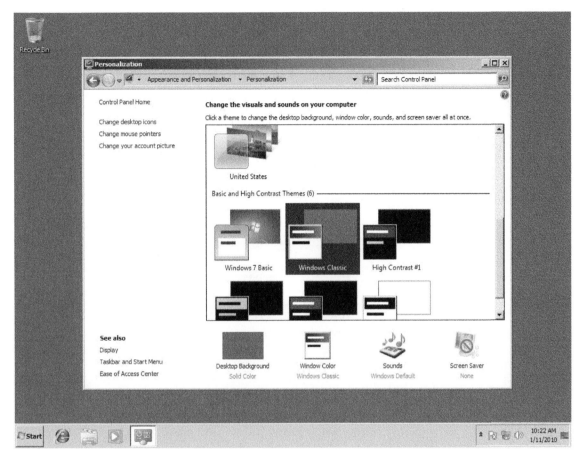

■ **FIGURE 4.9** Windows Classic Theme

To select the Windows Classic theme and user interface:

1. Opent he **Personalization** console of the Control Panel:
   a. Right-clickt he **desktop** and click **Personalize**
   b. Open the Control Panel and click **Personalize**
2. Click **Windows Classic** under the Basic and High Contrast Themes
   section in the main window pane

Windows 7 Basic Theme

The Windows 7 Basic theme is applied by default if Windows Aero hardware
requirements are not met. This theme is essentially the entry-level desktop
theme provided by Microsoft and is very similar to Windows XP user interface as shown in Figure 4.10. The theme is similar to the Windows 7 Aero

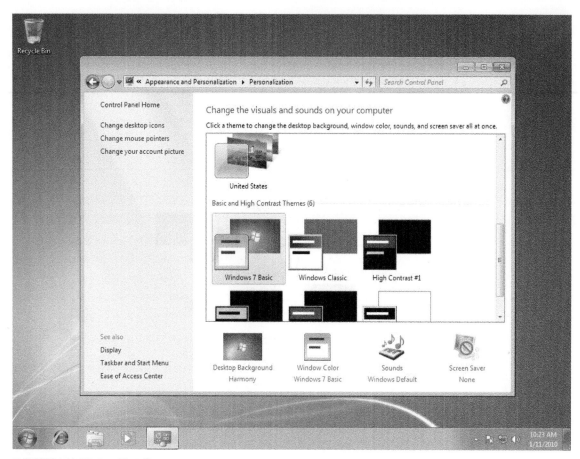

■ **FIGURE 4.10** Windows 7 Basic Theme

theme with the exception of the Aero features and display eye candy. This theme only sets one desktop background, the Windows 7 Basic color for windows, default Windows sounds, and no screen saver.

To select the Windows 7 Basic Theme and user interface:

1. Opent he **Personalization**c onsole of the Control Panel:
   a. Right-clickt he **desktop** and click **Personalize**
   b. Open Control Panel and click **Personalize**
2. Click **Windows 7 Basic** under the Basic and High Contrast Themes section in the main window pane

The Windows 7 Basic theme may be reverted to by applications that are not compatible with Windows Aero. Windows 7 Basic may also prove to increase performance slightly as it does not require the graphical horsepower to display the Aero features, transparency, etc. Using this theme may also enable longer battery life.

WindowsA ero Theme

Windows Aero is the premium desktop theme in Windows 7 that enables all of the Windows Aero features by default. It will attempt to run by default and will most likely be the most used theme by the end user. There are multiple Windows Aero themes to choose from with multiple backgrounds, window colors, sounds, and normally no screen saver option set.

To enable a Windows 7 Aero Theme, user interface, and Aero features:

1. Opent he **Personalization**c onsole of the Control Panel:
   a. Right-click the **desktop** and click **Personalize**
   b. Open the Control Panel and click **Personalize**
2. Pick and click any theme under the Aero Themes section in the main windowpa ne

All Windows 7 Aero themes will enable the Windows Aero features. The most visual feature is Aero Glass; a theme that enables the Start menu, taskbar, windows, and dialogs to have a glasslike transparent look. This feature was introduced in Windows Vista but runs much quicker and smoother (less crashes) in Windows 7. Although mostly eye candy, Microsoft claims this feature moves the end user̃ focus away from the windows themselves and to the content.

Aero Glass may be turned off while keeping Windows Aero features enabled:

1. Opent he **Personalization** console of the Control Panel:
   a. Right-clickt he **desktop** and click **Personalize**
   b. Open Control Panel and click **Personalize**
2. Click **Windows Color**
3. Uncheck **Enable transparency**a ss howni n Figure4.5

Microsoft includes many other features in Windows Aero themes that claim to make the end user more productive and efƀcient performing daily tasks. Features like Aero Snap, Aero Shake, Aero Peak, Windows Flip, Flip 3D, and others will be explained in the Desktop ÐWindows Aero section.

Desktop Options

Right-clicking any item in Windows 7 will usually display a context menu with some common options and options related to the item that was clicked. Right-clicking the **desktop** displays a context menu as shown in Figure 4.11

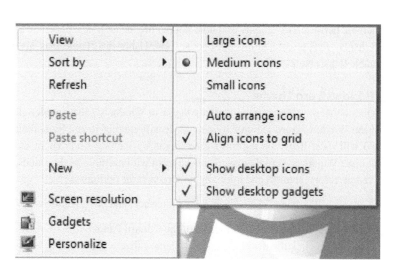

■ **FIGURE 4.11** Desktop Context Menu

with various options that may not be familiar to those switching from Windows XP or earlier systems. The Properties option is no longer available; instead, options for **Screen Resolution**, **Gadgets**, and **Personalize** are available. Additionally, the new context menu available in most Windows Explorer windows is also available to create a new blank Þle of the desired type, including folders and shortcuts. Options available for the desktop are:

- **View** (Figure4.11)
    - **Large icons, Medium icons,** and **Small icons** ÐThis option is for the size of the icons displayed on the desktop. Only one of these options is available.
    - **Auto arrange icons** Ðcheck box function to auto arrange the icons on the desktop
    - **Align icons to grid** Ðcheck box function to align the desktop icons to a hidden grid
    - **Show desktop icons** Ðcheck box function to show the desktop icons
    - **Show desktop gadgets** Ðcheck box function to show desktop gadgets
- **Sort by** Ðchoose to sort the desktop icons by name, size, item type, or datem odiÞed.
- **Refresh** Ðrefreshes the desktop to apply view settings to new items on thede sktop.

Modify Window Views

Windows 7 allows windows to be easily arranged on the desktop for easier view. This can prove to be productive for end users who need to view two

or more windows at a time. To modify the current view of open windows on
your desktop, right-click an empty area of the taskbar:

- **Cascade windows** ÐThis option arranges open windows one on top of
  the other with room to display the title bar on each.
- **Show windows stacked** ÐThis option arranges all open windows to be
  viewed stacked on top of each other horizontally.
- **Show windows side-by-side** ÐThis option arranges all open windows
  to be viewed side-by-side vertically.
- **Show the desktop** ÐThis screen minimizes all windows and
  shows the desktop, similar to the show desktop button in the
  notiÞcationa rea.
- **Show open windows** ÐThis is an available option after clicking
  the **Show the desktop** option to bring all the open windows that
  were previously open before clicking **Show the desktop** back up
  into view.

Desktop Content

The desktop is not only for viewing open windows, but also an area for
shortcuts, folders, and Þles called icons in Windows. Windows XP and prior
versions had multiple desktop icons visible by default, which are now in the
Start menuÕ right pane. Windows 7 only has the Recycle Bin desktop icon
on the desktop by default. The Recycle Bin is a repository for items that
have been deleted and are waiting to be emptied. Other items can also be
placed on the desktop including icons for Computer, UserÕ Files, Network,
and Control Panel. Additionally, shortcuts to programs, Þles, or folders can
be placed in the desktop.

To modify common desktop icons:

1. Right-clickt he **desktop** and click **Personalize**
2. Click **Change desktop icons** as shown in Figure 4.12 on the left pane
   of the **Personalization** consoleof t heC ontrolP anel
3. In the Desktop Icons Settings window, toggle the check box next to
   each desktop icon:
   - **Computer** Ðthe Computer desktop icon allows for quick access
     to the Windows Explorer window for viewing hard drives, devices
     with removable media, and network folders. Right-clicking
     the **Computer** icon on the desktop also enables many
     useful options:
     - **Manage** ÐIt starts the Computer Management MMC console
       for accessing System Tools, Storage, and Services and
       Applications.

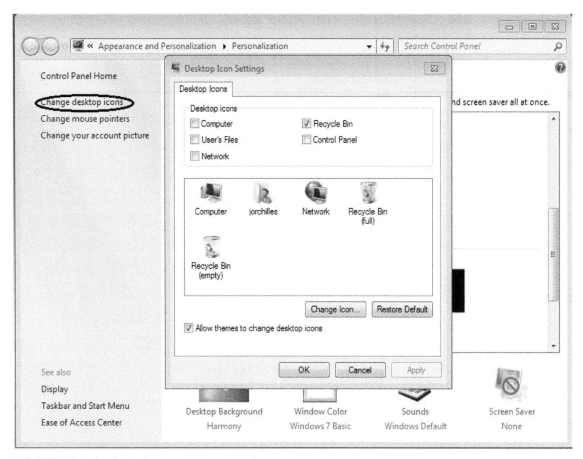

■ **FIGURE 4.12** Desktop Icon Settings

- **Map Network Drive** ÐIt initiates the Map Network Drive wizard to quickly map a network drive to the computer.
- **Disconnect Network Drive** ÐIt initiates the Disconnect Network Drives wizard to quickly remove mapped networkdr ives.
- **Properties** ÐIt starts the System Control Panel console for quicka ccesst oc omputeropt ions.
  - ❑ **UserÕ Files** ÐA shortcut icon to the userÕ proÞle folder located at %SystemDrive%\Users\%Username%\.
  - ❑ **Network** ÐIt adds a desktop shortcut to the Network view of Windows Explorer. Here users can access the Network and Sharing Center, add a printer, add a wireless device, and access network resources.

- **Recycle Bin** ÐIt displays the Recycle Bin on the desktop. The
  Recycle Bin is addressed in the next section.
- **Control Panel** ÐIt adds a desktop shortcut to the Control Panel.

4. You may change the icon or restore it to default by clicking **Change
   IconÉ** or **Restore Defaultm**r espectively.
5. Finally, checking the **Allow themes to change desktop icons check box**
   will let the selected theme change these settings.

As mentioned, shortcuts may be placed on the desktop for quicker access
to programs, folders, or Þles. To create a shortcut for a program, folder,
or Þle:

- Right-click the program, folder, or Þle
- On the context menu, select **Send To | Desktop** (create shortcut)
  (Figure4.13) .

■ **FIGURE 4.13** Send To – Desktop
(create shortcut)

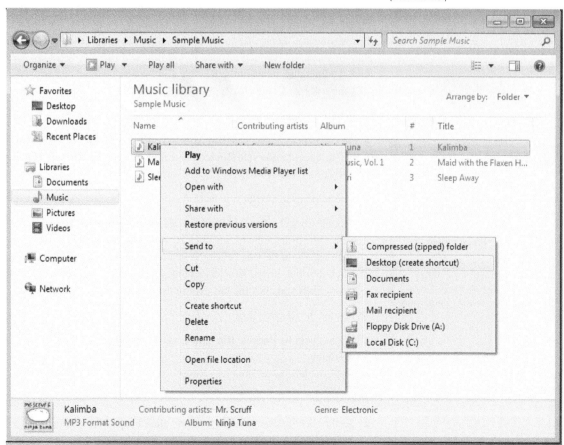

All desktop icons have these options when right-clicked:

- **Open** ÐThis option opens the Windows Explorer window; same as double-clicking the desktop icon.
- **Create shortcut** ÐThis option creates a shortcut on the desktop to open Windows Explorer in the Computer view.
- **Delete** ÐThis option removes the icon from the desktop. If this is a Þle or a folder that is stored on the Desktop, it will be sent to the RecycleB in.

The desktop is also a folder in the userÕ profile folder meaning files and folders may be created and stored on the desktop. The location for items stored on the desktop is: %SystemDrive\Users\%Username%\ Desktop.

Recycle Bin

The Recycle Bin is an analogy to a physical trash can; users place items to be thrown out there, and when the trash can Þlls up it is emptied. The Recycle Bin is similar as items that are deleted are sent there, then the Recycle Bin may be manually emptied or once it is full, it will remove the oldest Þles Þrst. Additionally, items in the Recycle Bin may be restored or retrieved if they are still there, much like a physical trash can.

To empty the Recycle Bin:

- Double-clickt he **Recycle Bin** icon and click **Empty the Recycle Bin**
- Right-clickt he **Recycle Bin** icon and click **Empty the Recycle Bin**a s showni n Figure4.14 .

To restore items in the Recycle Bin:

- Double-clickt he **Recycle Bin** icon and click **Restore All Items**or select one or more items and click **Restore this item**. To pick more than one Þle at the time, click the Þrst one, then hold down **Ctrl** as you click the other items. To select a range, click the Þrst one, then hold down **Shift** and click the last item in the range.

To rename the Recycle Bin:

- Right-clickt he **Recycle Bin** icon as shown in Figure 4.14 and click **Rename**
- Type the new name and press **Enter**

To customize the Recycle Bin:

- Right-clickt he **Recycle Bin** icon and click **Properties** as shown in Figure4.14

WARNING

Itemst hatha veb eend eleted from the Recycle Bin cannot be retrieved using standard Windows tools. To restore files deleted from the Recycle Bin, you must restore the files from a backup or use a third-party recovery tool if the space occupied on the disk by that file has not been overwritten.

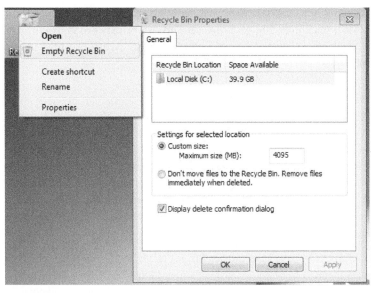

■ **FIGURE 4.14** Recycle Bin Right-click and Properties

■ The Properties window allows the user to customize how the Recycle
Binf unctions:
  ❏ **Recycle Bin Location** Ðthe location of the Recycle Bin and the
    space available at that location.
  ❏ Settingsf ors electedl ocation
    - **Custom Size** ÐIt sets the maximum size of Þles stored in the
      Recycle Bin in MB.
    - **DonÕ move Þles to the Recycle Bin. Remove Þles immediately
      when deleted** Ðbeware that if this is selected, items deleted
      will not be placed in the Recycle Bin and will instead be deleted
      immediately.
  ❏ **Display delete conÞrmation dialog** ÐThis will disable the conÞr-
    mation to move Þles to the Recycle Bin when Þles are deleted. The
    Recycle Bin will still prompt for conÞrmation when being emptied.

Windows Aero

Most of the new Windows 7 features require Windows Aero. The Windows
Aero user experience can make the desktop look nicer but also offers many
productivity enhancements. Windows Aero must be enabled and the simplest method for this is to choose a Windows 7 Aero theme:

1. Right-clickt he **desktop ÐPersonalize**
2. Click a theme under the Aero Themes section of the main window pane

Windows Aero requires additional hardware requirements to run and can cause a small impact in performance. This will be explored in this section. Additionally, Windows Aero provides many new visual and productivity enhancements that will also be addressed.

Windows Aero Requirements

Windows Aero is available with Windows 7 Home Premium and greater Windows 7 editions. It also requires a compatible video card and driver to work properly. Fianlly, it requires a Windows Aero theme to be selected from the Personalization console. Recent computers and video cards should be able to run Windows Aero without any problems. However, Windows Aero does have more requirements than the Windows 7 hardware requirements specify. These requirements are all in reference to the video card hardware:

- DirectX 9.0 and Pixel Shader 2.0
- Supported by Windows Display Driver Model (WDDM) driver Done of the reasons Windows Aero is much more reliable and less likely to crash in Windows 7.
- Dedicated Video Memory Ð512 MB recommended
  - 64 MB for resolutions lower than 1280 × 1024 (less than 1,310,720 pixels)
  - 128 MB for resolutions equal to or less than 1920 × 1200 (up to 2,304,000pi xels)
  - 256 MB for resolutions more than 1920 × 1200 (more than 2,304,000pi xels)

AeroS nap

Aero Snap provides multiple methods to position and resize open windows without buttons or controls on the actual window. This includes maximizing, maximizing vertically, snapping to the left or right, and restoring the window view. Aero Snap does not require the Windows Aero theme to be enabled to work although the name might suggest so.

To maximize the current window, click and hold the **title bar** area of the window and drag the window to the top of the screen. Once it touches the top edge of the screen, it will maximize the entire screen. Another way to do this without Aero Snap is to double-click the **title bar** of the window. Double-clicking the **title bar** of a maximized window will resize it to the previous view.

To maximize a ßoating window vertically, click and hold the top or bottom edge of the window and drag it up or down to the edge of the screen.

To snap a window to the left or right half of the screen, click and hold the **title bar** of the window and drag it to the left or right edge of the display as shown in Figure 4.15. This will make the window view exactly 50% of the screen on the respective side the title bar was dragged to. This feature works best when one window is snapped to the left and another to the right, displaying two separate windows orderly on the desktop.

Restoring a window to its previous size and position is as simple as clicking the **title bar** and dragging the window toward the center of the screen.

AeroP eek

Aero Peek was introduced by Microsoft to assist end users that multitask with multiple windows open at a time. In past versions of Windows, it was

TIP

All of the Aero Snap window views can be performed with keyboard shortcuts:

- Maximize: WindowsK ey (WinKey)+UpA rrow
- Maximize Vertically: WinKey+Shift+UpA rrow
- SnapL eft: WinKey+LeftA rrow
- SnapR ight: WinKey+Right Arrow
- Restore: WinKey+DownA rrow

■ FIGURE 4.15 Aero Snap Left and Right

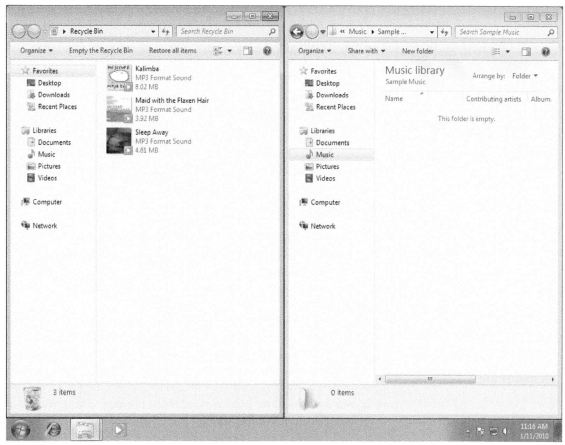

possible to minimize all the windows at once and land on the desktop by pressing the **Show Desktop** button on the Quick Launch toolbar. Windows 7 provides the **Show Desktop** button on the notiÞcation area. At the far right of the notiÞcation area is a rectangular button. Clicking the button will minimize all the windows and show the desktop; clicking the button again will restore the previous view of the open windows.

Aero Peek is a function that allows the end user to peek at the desktop without minimizing the open windows. This is done by placing the mouse cursor over the **Show Desktop** button in the notiÞcation area. This shows the desktop and an outline of all the open windows. This is useful for end users that multitask and need to peek at the desktop or where the windows are located.

Aero Peek is also available when the user is changing windows with the **Alt+Tab** function. **Alt+Tab** will change the view of the window to the one selected. Pausing on an application without releasing the **Alt** button will show the window selected and all other windows with an outline effect:

- Holdingdo wn **Alt** while pressing **Tab** again will move to the next window on the right
- **Alt+Shift+Tab** will switch views to the next window on the left
- Pausing on any window while holding **Alt**do wnw ille nable AeroP eek

Aero Peek is also available to look at windows that are open through the taskbar. Placing the mouse on an open taskbar icon will display the current open windows for that icon. Moving the mouse to one of the open windows will preview the window view and outline the other open windows.

Aero Peek is on by default with Windows 7 Aero themes but can be turned off by the end user:

1. Right-click an empty area of the **taskbar | Properties**
2. Uncheck the option to **Use Aero peek to preview the desktop**a s showni n Figure4.16 .

AeroS hake

Aero Shake is also a new feature of Windows 7 to minimize all open windows except the current window. This could be useful to some end users but is difÞcult to describe without actually performing it. To use Aero Shake, click and hold the **title bar** of the current window and shake the mouse in any direction. All open windows will minimize leaving the current window open and a view of the desktop. Aero Shake can also be triggered with a keyboard shortcut: **WinKey+Home**

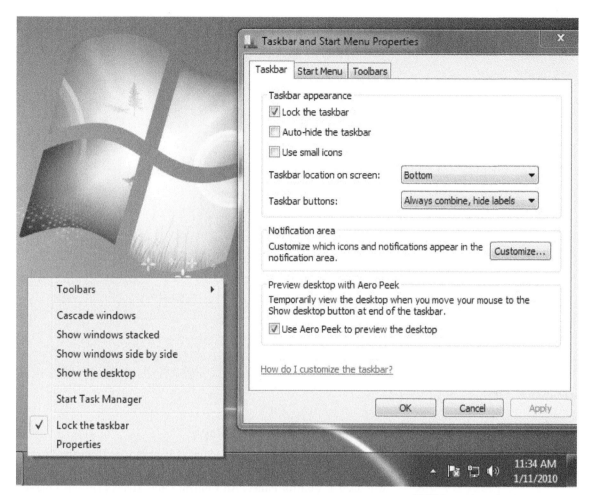

■ **FIGURE 4.16** Toggle Aero Peek

Flip3D

Flip 3D is an enhanced **Alt+Tab**. Using the Aero features, it shows a 3D view of open windows that allows the user to ßip through open windows to the one desired while seeing the window content in a nice manager as shown in Figure 4.17. To use Flip 3D, press **WinKey+Tab**. Without releasing the WinKey, every **Tab** cycles through the open window view. Release the WinKey when the window that you want on top is Þrst. Pressing **WinKey+Shift+Tab** will cycle through the windows in the opposite direction.

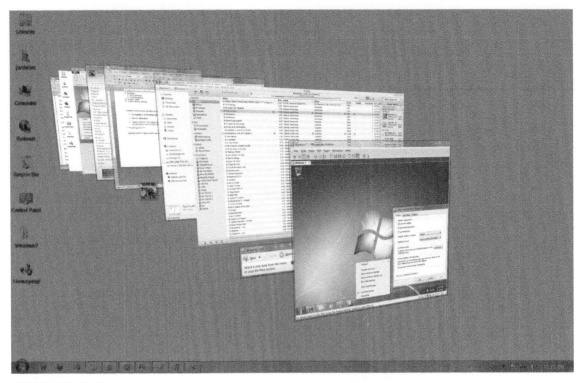

■ **FIGURE 4.17** Flip 3D

Screen Resolution and Display

The screen resolution and display settings can be changed from the desktop. Right-click on the **desktop | Screen Resolution**. A Control Panel window will open at **Control Panel | All Control Panel Items | Display | Screen Resolution**a ss howni n Figure4.18 .

The screen resolution depends on the video card hardware and monitor in use. This window allows the end user to set which display to conÞgure, the resolution, orientation, and multiple displays. Some video card manufactures include another utility for conÞguring screen resolutions, however, the Windows 7 Screen Resolution window should still work correctly:

■ **Display** ÐThis option lets the user choose which display to use. Windows 7 does a pretty good job at identifying the monitor being used and the name shows up in this drop down.
■ **Resolution** ÐThis depends on the video card and monitor. The higher the resolution, the smaller items will look but the larger the display area will be.

■ **FIGURE 4.18** Screen Resolution

- **Orientation** ÐDepending on how the monitor is oriented, this will generally be Landscape, however, options for Portrait and ßipped modes are available.
- **Multiple displays** ÐIf multiple displays are available, this drop down will give the user options for setting them up.

Other display settings may be adjusted from this window by clicking the link **Make text and other items larger or smaller**. This will take the end user to the **Display** console of the Control Panel as shown in Figure 4.19. On the left pane are links to:

- **Adjust resolution** Ðthe simple interface to adjust the display resolutiona ndm onitor
- **Calibrate color** Ða wizard to assist in calibrating the color of the display
- **Change display settings** Ðlink to the Screen Resolution window
- **Adjust ClearType text** ÐThis allows for the turning on and off of ClearType, a software feature made by Microsoft to make fonts look better on LCD screens. The ClearType Text Tuner is easy to use and will often make text more pleasing to the eye.
- **Set custom text size (DPI)** ÐThis is a percentage of the dots per inch (DPI) displayed for the current resolution.

TIP

Changing the text size is a new feature that administrators may find very handy for the end user who may have trouble reading text but does not want to or cannot change the screen resolution.

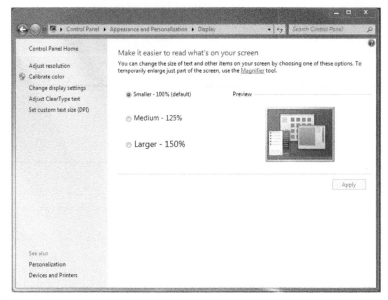

■ **FIGURE 4.19** Display Console – Change Text Size

Advanced Display Settings

Every Windows 7 computer has a monitor and a video driver. These drivers tell the operating system critical information about the capabilities of the hardware. Generally, installing the correct video card driver and the Windows 7 default drivers are enough to run the video settings correctly. However, understanding the properties and how these drivers work is critical for troubleshooting display issues.

Clicking on **Advanced Settings** for the display selected on the Screen Resolution window will display a properties window for the monitor and video cards imilart o Figure4.20 .

The Monitor and Video Card properties have different tabs as shown in Figure4. 20:

■ **Adapter** tab ÐThis tab speciÞes information about the video card adapter. Clicking **Properties** will launch the Device Managerõ Properties window for the video adapter. **List All Modes** will display a screen with all available display settings for that video card.

■ **Monitor** tab ÐThis tab lists the monitor(s) currently connected to the computer. Selecting a monitor and clicking **Properties** will launch the Device managerõ Properties window for the monitor. **Monitor Settings** displays a drop down of available screen refresh rates and a check box to

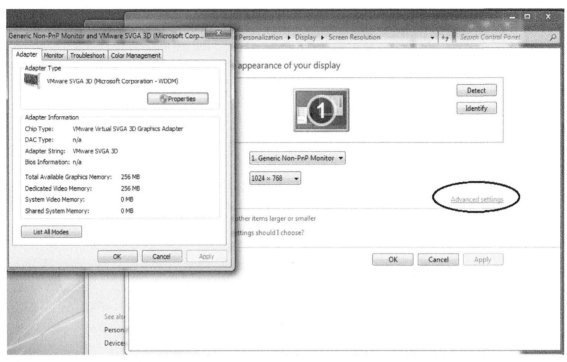

■ **FIGURE 4.20** Display – Advanced Settings

hide rates that the display cannot handle. Choosing the highest refresh rate that works with the monitor is best for the human eye. The **Colors** drop down allows the user to set the color quality. Again the higher the better.

- **Troubleshoot** tab ÐThis tab is very useful for automated assistance for troubleshooting display issues. This launches the **Control Panel Ð Action Center ÐTroubleshooting**a ssistant.
- **Color Management** tab ÐThis tab has a **Color Management** button allows for customization of color management proÞles. Generally, these are set to system by default but may be tweaked if issues with colors are visible.
- **Graphics Card** tab ÐSome graphic card drivers will provide a tab to launch the third-party utility to conÞgure the graphics card.

For more advanced troubleshooting of the display settings, please refer to Chapter 10, ÒWindows 7 Troubleshooting and Performance Tools.Ó

Gadgets

You may have noticed that the sidebar introduced in Windows Vista did not start automatically. This is because the sidebar has been removed from

Windows 7. Instead Windows 7 has desktop Gadgets. Gadgets are simple independent applications that sit on the Windows desktop. The goal of these applications is to provide quick and important information to the user. Desktop Gadgets are off by default and can be enabled by right-clicking the **desktop | View | Show desktop gadgets**.

Adding Gadgets

To add gadgets to the desktop:

- Right-click **desktop | Gadgets**
- Double-click a desired gadget or click and hold the gadget while dragging it to the desktop as shown in Figure 4.21
- **Show Details** Ðgives more information about the selected Gadget

■ **FIGURE 4.21** Gadgets and Options

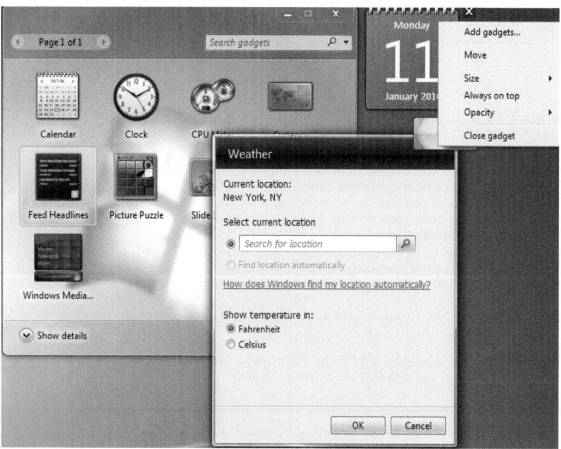

■ **Get more gadgets online** Ða link that launches the default browser to a Microsoft page with the option to view and download other gadgets.

Configuring Gadgets

Gadgets may be placed anywhere in the desktop by clicking and holding the gadget while moving it to the desired location. Each gadget has options that allow them to be conÞgured. Placing the mouse over the gadget displays the conÞguration UI and other gadget-speciÞc controls as shown in Figure 4.21:

■ The **X** button removes the gadget from the desktop.
■ The wrench conÞgures the gadget.
■ The multiple dots move the gadget around the desktop.

Right-clicking a gadget also reveals options for the speciÞc gadget as shown in Figure 4.21. Most gadgets have the option to set it always on top; this option will display the gadget on top of all other windows. The Opacity option allows a user to set a percentage of transparency for that gadget.

StartM enu

The Start menu has been a component of Windows operating systems since Windows 95. This feature should be easily recognized by most users and is located on the bottom left of the screen. Since Windows XP, the visual to launch the Start menu has changed from the word Start to a Microsoft Windows logo. Additionally, the navigation and appearance of the Start menu has been modiÞed to make navigating applications and other features of Windows 7 much easier. Although some users have refused to use the Windows Start menu available in Windows XP and used the classic menu, Windows 7 no longer allows the option to use that classic view. Thankfully, there are many different options and settings to modify the Start menu to Þt the end userÕs needs.

Clicking the **Start menu** button will launch the menu as shown in Figure 4.22. Windows 7 uses a Start menu similar to Windows XP and Windows Vista with slight modiÞcations. It is split into two panels. The left-hand side displays shortcuts that have been *pinned* to the Start menu and recent applications that have been launched. Under this list is the new Start Menu Search, which has been referenced multiple times in this book as a quick method of launching applications, and is circled in Figure 4.22. On the right-hand side are shortcuts to launching common Windows 7 folders and components, by default they include:

■ **%Username%** Ðopens the userÕs default proÞle folder located at %SystemDrive%\Users\%Username%\

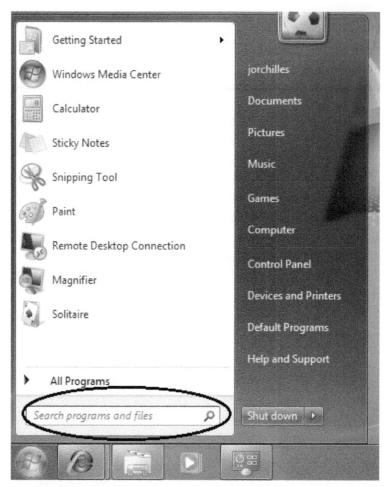

■ FIGURE 4.22 Start Menu

- **Documents, Pictures,** and **Music** ÐThis option opens the Library for each respective option. This by default is the userô personal folder and the public folder for the respective Þle type located at %System-Drive%\Users\%Username%\%LibraryName%\ and %SystemDrive%\ Public\%LibraryName%. There is more on Libraries in the Windows Explorer section of this chapter.
- **Games** ÐThis option launches the Games console mentioned in Chapter1 ,ÒIntroductiont o Windows7. Ó
- **Computer** ÐIt opens a Windows Explorer window for Computer. This used to be My Computer in earlier versions of Windows.
- **Control Panel** Ðlaunches the Control Panel.

- **Devices and Printers** ÐThis option launches what used to be the Printers console but now is used for all hardware devices. This is a Control Panel component.
- **Default Programs** ÐThis launches the Control Panel component to set Default Programs. This will be further explained in the Control Panel section of this chapter.
- **Help and Support** ÐThis launches the familiar Help and Support console from Windows Vista that could be useful for end users.
- **Power Button** ÐThis button can modify the default option to be performed when the power button is pressed and includes a menu for the other options, which include: Switch User, Log Off, Lock, Sleep Shutdown, and Restart the computer.

These default settings are very customizable and although the classic Start menu option is not available, it should be feasible to conÞgure it so that the end users Þnd this menu more productive and efÞcient for launching all applications needed.

Pin to Start Menu

The left-hand side of the Start menu contains pinned shortcuts. These are shortcuts to applications that the user frequently launches. This is a feature of the new Start menu and can prove to be efÞcient for end users to launch applications quicker.

To pin a shortcut to the Start menu, right-click on any shortcut and click **Pin to Start Menu** from the context menu. This could be done from within Windows Explorer, through **Start menu | All Programs** as shown in Figure 4.23, or through the desktop. Any shortcut that is right-clicked or application in the Program Files folder should display the context window when right-clicked to allow **Pin to Start Menu**.

To remove a pinned shortcut from the Start menu, right-click on the pinned shortcut and click **Unpin from Start Menu** or **Remove from this list**.

Start Menu Search

The Start menu Search bar is one of the best features in Windows 7 and is circled in Figure 4.22. Microsoft has integrated the desktop search application that in the past could have slowed system performance and improved it tenfold. The Start menu Search is located on the left panel of the Start menu in the bottom. Typing into this search box will yield results each key stroke to launch applications or files quicker. The search not only returns and launches applications but also searches for documents, pictures, videos, and other file types. The Start menu Search

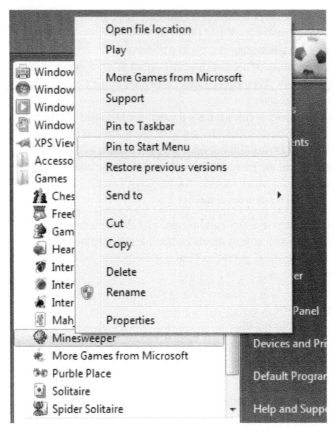

■ **FIGURE 4.23** Pin to Start Menu

has come to replace to older RunÉ command from earlier versions of Windows. The RunÉ command can still be enabled by customizing the Start menu.

JumpL ists

Jump Lists are available in the Start menu and taskbar. Jump Lists allow the end user to quickly access application-speciÞc items. Traditionally, a user opens the application and then from within the application opens the Þle or performs an operation. Jump Lists allow these tasks to be initiated straight from the Start menu or taskbar. The Jump List for each application may be different but most offer a recent or frequently used task display.

To access an applicationÕ Jump List from the Start menu, click **Start** and move the cursor to the arrow to the right-hand side of the application on the left pane. Jump Lists are only available for shortcuts in the Recent and Pinned pane on the left-hand side of the Start menu.

Customize the Start Menu

Even though the classic Start menu cannot be conÞgured to look as it appeared in Windows 2000 and earlier versions, it can be customized to Þt the userÕs most common needs. Start Menu properties are available by right-clicking the **Start menu** button and selecting **Properties**. Note that the only other option when right-clicking the **Start menu** button is to open Windows Explorer as shown in Figure 4.24.

■ **FIGURE 4.24** Right-Click Start Menu— Properties

To change Start menu options:

1. Open the Start menu properties by right-clicking the **Start menu** button and selecting **Properties** or by right-clicking the **taskbar**, selecting **Properties**, and clicking the **Start menu** tab as illustrated in Figure4.24 .

2. This window has a **CustomizeÉ** button to conÞgure all Start menu settings, power button options to conÞgure what happens when the power button is pressed, and privacy options to select where to store and display recent items.

   a. CustomizeÉ Ðclicking this button pops up a window titled Customize Start Menu as shown in Figure 4.25.

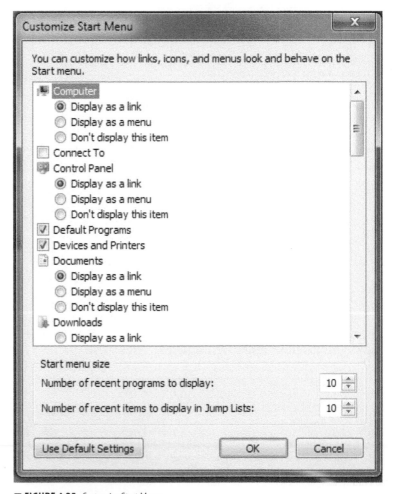

■ **FIGURE 4.25** Customize Start Menu

- The Computer, Control Panel, documents, downloads, games, music, personal folder, pictures, recorded TV, and videos will all have the following three options:
  - ○ **Display as a link** Ðthis will display the name of the respective option in the right-hand side of the Start menu. Clicking on the name will initiate a window in the respective location or application selected.
  - ○ **Display as a menu** Ðthis will display a submenu of folders and options available for the respective folder or feature selected.
  - ○ **DonÕ display this item** Ðthis will remove the respective folder or option from the Start menu completely.
- **Connect To** ÐThis option if checked will provide a link on the right-hand side of the Start menu for easily and quickly launching the Network and Sharing menu for connecting to another network, such as VPN, dialup, or wireless. The same is possible by clicking the **Network**i con in the notiÞcation area.
- **Default Programs** ÐThis option when checked will enable a button on the right-hand side of the Start menu to easily navigate to **Control Panel | All Control Panel Items | Default Programs**. To conÞgure Default Programs, see the Control Panel section of this chapter.
- **Device and Printers** ÐThis option when checked will enable a button on the right-hand side of the Start menu to easily navigate to **Control Panel | All Control Panel Items | Devices and Printers**. Enabling this shortcut could prove to be efÞcient for some users that are used to navigating to the printers console in older version of Windows. To conÞgure Devices and Printers, see the Control Panel section of this chapter.
- **Enable context menus and dragging and dropping** ÐThis option when checked will allow users to right-click on any shortcut to view the context menu available in Windows Explorer. Dragging and dropping simply allows for moving shortcuts around more efÞciently.
- **Favorites menu** ÐThis option if checked will provide a menu on the right-hand side of the Start menu for easily and quickly navigating to shortcuts in the userÕ Favorites folder (usually Internet Explorer (IE) Favorites) located at %SystemDrive%\ Users\%Username%\Favorites
- **Help** ÐThis option when checked will enable a button on the right-hand side of the Start menu to easily navigate to Help and Support. This could be useful for users that often use this feature.

- **Highlight newly installed programs** ÐThis option when checked will highlight all the new applications that have been installed on the system and have shortcuts in the All Programs menu of the Start Menu.
- **HomeGroup** ÐThis option when checked enables a **Home-Group** button on the right-hand side of the Start Menu. The HomeGroup will be explained in detail in Chapter 5 ÒManaging the Windows 7 Desktop Environment.Ó
- **Network** ÐThis option when checked enables a shortcut button on the right-hand side of the Start Menu that navigates to the Network view of Windows Explorer.
- **Open submenus when I pause on them with the mouse points** ÐThis option controls the behavior of menus when the mouse pointer hovers over. When checked, the menu will expand, otherwise a click is necessary to expand the menu.
- **Recent Items** ÐThis option if checked will provide a menu on the right-hand side of the Start menu for easily and quickly navigating to shortcuts of Þles recently opened.
- **Run command** ÐThis option when checked will provide a shortcut on the right-hand side of the Start menu to easily launch the familiar run dialog. This option is standard in older versionsof Windows.
- Searchpr ogramsa ndC ontrolP anel
- **Sort All Programs menu by name** ÐThis option enables the All Programs menu items to be sorted by name or installed date. When checked, the All Programs menu will be sorted alphabetically as opposed to by installed date.
- **System administrative tools** ÐThis setting allows for display of the administrative tools in the Start menu depending on the selected option:
  - ○ **Display on the All Programs menu** ÐThis option will only display on the All Programs menu.
  - ○ **Display on the All Programs menu and Start menu** ÐThis option will display on the right-hand side of the Start menu and All Programs menu.
  - ○ **DonÕt display this item** ÐThis option will not show the items at all. This menu is useful for power users or administrators to quickly access administrative tools.
- **Use large icons** ÐThis option controls the size of the icons in the Start menu. When checked the standard icon size will be used as opposed to a smaller icon next to the program or menu name.

- **Start menu size** ÐThe last two options of the customize
    screen is to set the size of the Start menu depending on the
    amount of recent items the user would like to see. This option
    also depends on the screen resolution and number of pinned
    programs at the top left of the Start menu:
    o **Number of recent programs to display** ÐIt can be between
        0 and 30.
    o **Number of recent items to display in Jump Lists** ÐIt can
        be between 0 and 60. Jump Lists are explained later in this
        section.
- **Use Default Settings** ÐThis option will reset the settings back
    tode fault.

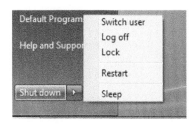

■ **FIGURE 4.26** Power Button Options

b. Power button action Ðthis drop-down list configures the
    default action that occurs when the power button is pressed
    in the Start menu. Although an arrow is available next to the
    default setting for all other options as shown in Figure 4.26,
    this should be configured to what the end user will use the
    button for most.
    - **Switch User** ÐThis option keeps the current user logged in but
        switches to another user proÞle. This is for systems that have
        multiple users and is effective for 24/7 operation environments
        when the computer is never idle.
    - **Log Off** ÐThis option logs the current user off. This is the
        best option for switching users without leaving the current user
        logged in using resources.
    - **Lock** ÐThis option locks the computer with the current user
        that is logged in. This is important when leaving the computer
        unattended even for a short time.
    - **Restart** ÐThis option reboots the computer.
    - **Sleep** ÐThis option puts the computer to sleep. It is great for
        single user system users who leave the computer unattended
        for a period of time. The system will lock and go to a lower
        power state. The current applications will continue to run when
        brought back. This option is more energy efÞcient than locking
        thec omputer.
    - **Shutdown** ÐThis option powers off the system.
c. Privacy ÐThese two check boxes are strictly user preference and
    self explanatory:
    - **Store and display recently opened programs in the Start menu**
    - **Store and display recently opened items in the Start menu
        and taskbar**

The Start menu and taskbar may be customized with Local Group Policy Editor:

1. Open the Local Group Policy Editor as referenced in the Management Tools section of this chapter (by typing **gpedit.msc** in Start Menu Search). Ensure you are logged in as local administrator user or right-click **gpedit.msc** and select **Run as administrator**.
2. Navigate to User ConƉguration\Administrative Templates\Start Menu and Taskbara ss howni n Figure4.27 .
3. Double-click on the desired settings.
4. A pop-up window will appear. The Help: panel on the bottom right of the window provides detailed information for each setting. The Supported on: panel details what systems the setting is supported on. The Options: panel will include options if the Enabled button is selected.

■ **FIGURE 4.27** Local Group Policy Editor – Start Menu and Taskbar

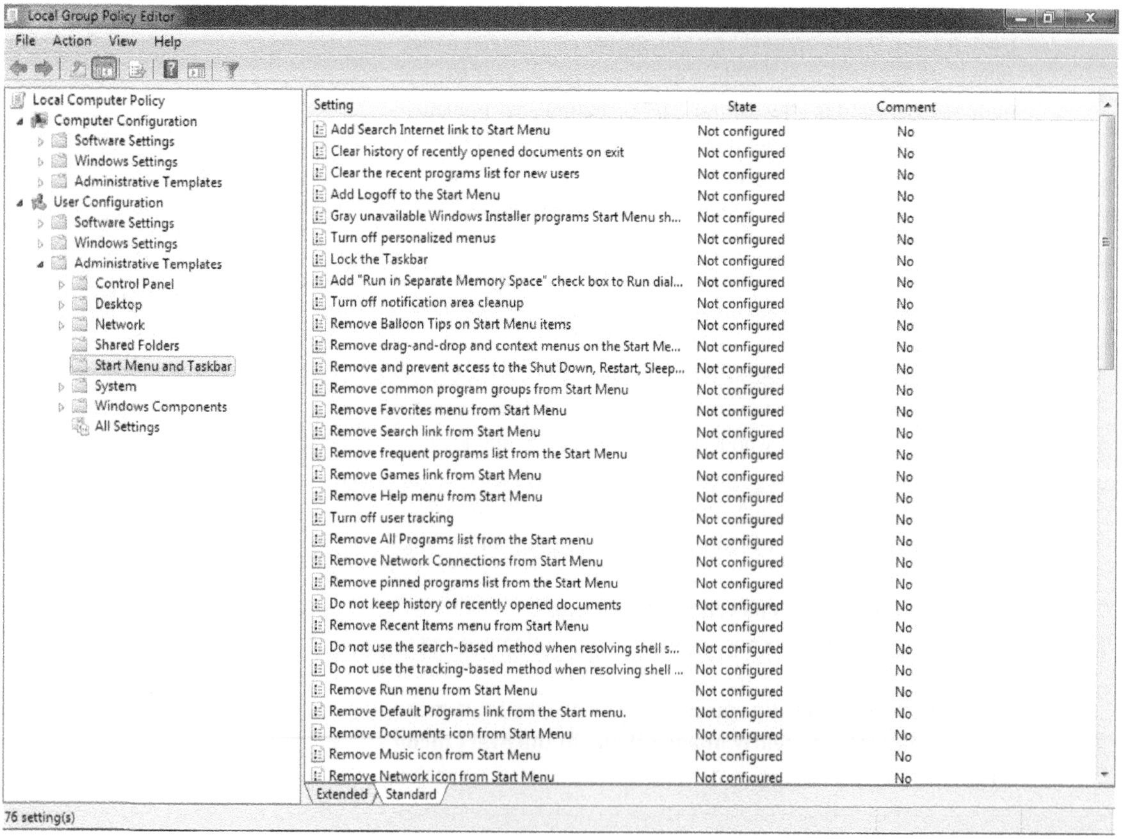

5. Select one of the three options on the top left:
   a. **Not Configured** ÐThe default state, meaning the registry will not bem odiÞed.
   b. **Enabled** ÐThe registry will be modiÞed to reßect the option.
   c. **Disabled** ÐThe registry will be modiÞed to reßect the option.
6. Click **Apply** to apply the settings, **OK** to conÞrm the settings and close the window, or **Cancel** to discard changes and close the window.

The Start menu may also be conÞgured for multiple computers in a domain with Group Policy Preferences:

1. Open the Group Policy Management Editor for the site, domain, or organization unit as referenced in Chapter 7, ÒManaging Windows 7 in an Enterprise Environment.Ó
2. Navigate to User ConÞguration\Preferences\Control Panel Settings.
3. Right-click the Start menu node, click **New**, and click **Start Menu (Windows Vista and Later).**
4. The **New Start Menu (Windows Vista and Later) Properties** dialog box will open.
5. Select the options much like you would with the local machine properties. These settings will be processed by the client computers in the object and applied even if the related value is not set overwriting all existing settings on the end userÕs desktop.
6. The **Common** tab controls how the preferences are applied. This will depend on the speciÞc situation. Generally, setting to Apply Once and Do Not Reapply is best to allow savvy users to change their own optionsl ater.
7. Click **OK** to save. The next time group policy is refreshed in the end userÕs computer, these settings will be reßected.

Start Menu Menus and Options

The Start menu in Windows 7 is represented in the Þle system as a pair of folders named Start menu. Recall in older versions of Windows, there were two Start menu folders, one for all users that log on to the computer and one for each individual user account. Windows 7 is very similar except the Start menu folder locations have changed. The public Start menu folder available for any users that logs on to the computer is located at %SystemDrive%\ProgramData\Microsoft\Windows\Start Menu\. The private Start menu folder for each individual user account is located at %SystemDrive%\User\%Username%\AppData\Roaming\Microsoft\Windows\Start Menu\.

When Windows 7 starts up, it merges both of these Start menu folders to create the Start menu visible by the end user. Each Start menu folder has a

Programs folder, which contain the shortcuts to the installed applications available to the user. Additionally, this folder contains other folders created by the installed application for better organization. Each folder in the Programs folder is a menu in the **Start menu | All Programs**m enu.

Customizing menus can be done within these Þle system folders or from the Start Menu itself.

Rearranging Items

The simplest method for rearranging items in the Start menu is from within the Start menu itself. Administrative privileges are required to move menu items and often require the end user to log off and back on to view the changes. Additionally, the **Enable context menus and dragging and dropping** check box in the **Start Menu Properties** dialog must be checked, whereas the **Sort All Programs menu by name** check box should be unchecked. To rearrange items in the Start menu:

1. Click **Start menu | All Programs**.
2. Click and hold the left mouse button on the shortcut or folder to be moved.
3. Drag the folder or shortcut to the location you want to move it to. Placing the cursor over a folder will expand it. A horizontal line displays where the item will be placed.
4. Drop the item by releasing the left mouse button.

Add, Delete, or Modify Menus

Since the Start menu is made up of two folders in the Windows 7 Þle system, adding, deleting, or modifying the menus is as simple as doing the same in any other Windows Explorer folder. These two folders are hidden so you must enable the **Show hidden Þles and folders** option in Folder View Options.

To add, delete, or modify menus in the Start menu folder for all users, open Windows Explorer and navigate to %SystemDrive%\ProgramData\Microsoft\Windows\Start Menu as shown in Figure 4.28.

To add, delete, or modify menus in the Start menu folder for the current user or a speciÞc user, open a Windows Explorer window and navigate to %SystemDrive%\Users\%Username%\AppData\Roaming\Microsoft\Windows\Start Menu\.

■ Add new menus Ðcreate a folder in the Programs folder or subfolders (except Startup) or create a shortcut to any application. Right-click anywhere in the Windows Explorer window and select **New Folder**or **Shortcut** as shown in Figure 4.28.

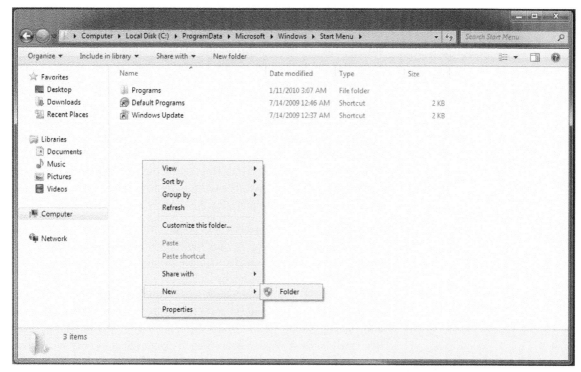

■ **FIGURE 4.28** Start Menu Folder —
All Users

- Modify menus Ðmove or rearrange folders and shortcuts within the Programs menu or subfolders.
- Rename menus Ðright-click on the folder name or shortcut and click **Rename**. This can also be done from within **Start Menu | All Programs** by right-clicking the menu or shortcut and selecting **Rename**.
- Delete menus Ðright-click and click **delete** on any folder or shortcut in the Programs menu or subfolders.

Startup Folder

The Startup folder in **Start menu | All Programs** is the collection of short-cuts in the public Start menu startup folder and the current userÕ startup folder, located at %SystemDrive%\ProgramData\Microsoft\Windows\Start Menu\Programs\Startup and %SystemDrive%\User\%Username%\App-Data\Roaming\Microsoft\Windows\Start Menu\Programs\Startup, respec-tively, that run by default when the user logs into the computer. These programs or shortcut to programs may be modiÞed on the local machine or with Group Policy preferences.

WARNING
Makingc hangesi nt he%S ys-temDrive%\ProgramData\Microsoft\Windows\Start Menu folder affects all user's Start menu. Removing a menu or shortcut that an end user uses could result in a service desk call and loss of end user'sp roductivity.

To add startup shortcuts for all users, navigate to %SystemDrive%\ProgramData\Microsoft\Windows\Start Menu\Programs\Startup, right-click anywhere in the Windows Explorer, click **New-Shortcut**, and select the location of the application or copy and paste a shortcut from any other location to this folder. To remove a program from starting up, right-click the shortcut and click **Delete**.

To add a startup shortcut for a single user, navigate to %SystemDrive%\User\%Username%\AppData\Roaming\Microsoft\Windows\Start Menu\Programs\Startup, right-click anywhere in the Windows Explorer, click **New-Shortcut**, and select the location of the application or copy and paste a shortcut from any other location to this folder. To remove a program from starting up, right-click the shortcut and click **Delete**.

With Group Policy preferences, it is possible to specify what applications start after a user logs on by creating shortcuts in the AllUsersStartup and/or Startup folders. The AllUsersStartu folder sets the startup applications for all users that log on to the system by adding the shortcut to %SystemDrive%\ProgramData\Microsoft\Windows\Start Menu\Programs\Startup while the Startup folder sets the applications to run for the current user that is logged in by adding a shortcut to %SystemDrive%\User\%Username%\AppData\Roaming\Microsoft\Windows\Start Menu\Programs\Startup. For more options and reference to creating menus, shortcuts, and startup applications with Group Policy preferences, refer to the Windows Explorer section of this chapter that focuses on Shortcuts.

Taskbar

The Windows 7 taskbar has been improved from earlier versions of Windows. The easiest way of looking at and explaining the new taskbar is as a combination of the previous taskbar and Quick Launch toolbar. One will notice larger than normal icons by default for IE, Windows Explorer, and Windows Media Player. Clicking any of these icons automatically launches the respective application. The user will quickly notice it did not open another item in the taskbar but simply highlighted the icon that was clicked. Additionally, when other programs that are not on the taskbar are launched, they will be added to the right of the last pinned taskbar icon. Pinning works very similar to the Start menũ pinned shortcuts. Users may right-click a frequently used icon of an application that is running or a shortcut elsewhere in the system and click **Pin to Taskbar** to permanently add the icon to the taskbar whether it is running or not. The pinning feature is similar to adding an icon to the Quick Launch toolbar in older versions of Windows. If Windows Aero is enabled, placing the mouse over an open icon reveals a small pop up of the content of the open window(s). This feature, a live thumbnail preview as shown in Figure 4.29, is very useful for users that run

■ **FIGURE 4.29** Live Thumbnail Preview

multiple applications as they can quickly choose which one to switch to. Aero Peek allows a peek at only the selected window when the mouse cursor is over it. This was explained earlier in the Windows Aero section. Right-clicking on a taskbar icon launches a Jump List for that application. As noted above, Jump Lists are useful for accessing tasks quicker for the speciÞc application. Each applicationÕs Jump List will be different based on the application.

The taskbar has also improved the notiÞcation area. The notiÞcation area is the far right area of the taskbar where application icons and critical features notify the users of their status. This feature has been improved to customization of what applications notify the user and how. The taskbar has moved the **Show Desktop** button to another location as the Quick Launch toolbar is no longer available. The **Show Desktop** button is now a very small rectangular button to the right-hand side of the notiÞcation area as shown in Figure4.30.

Taskbar Options

The taskbar may be modiÞed in various different ways. Users may pin or unpin icons from the taskbar to make launching applications easier. Because it is a new taskbar, users may want to change its size and position, which is also possible. It may also be locked in place, set to auto hide, or even moved to another location on the screen. Finally, the taskbar may be customized to display running applications individually as it did in Windows Vista and Windows XP ungrouped mode.

■ **FIGURE 4.30** Show Desktop Button

Pin a Shortcut to the Taskbar

Pinning a shortcut to the taskbar is similar to adding shortcuts to the Quick Launch toolbar in earlier versions of Windows. End users will appreciate this functionality as they can pin commonly used applications for quicker launching. Although most shortcuts and applications may be pinned to the taskbar, some items simply cannot be pinned. For example, individual Control Panel items such as Network Connections or Personalize settings cannot be pinned.

To pin a shortcut to the taskbar, open the application so the icon is shown in the taskbar, right-click the icon, and click **Pin to Taskbar**. Another method is to right-click the shortcut within the **Start menu | All Programs** and then click **Pin to Taskbar** as shown in Figure 4.23. Any application or shortcut can be pinned by right-clicking and selecting **Pin to Taskbar** from the context menu.

Shortcuts that are pinned to the taskbar may be rearranged by dragging and dropping. Left-click the icon and hold it, then move the cursor with the icon to the new location and release the left mouse button.

To unpin a shortcut from the taskbar, right-click the icon on the taskbar, and click **Unpin this program from Taskbar**.

Change Size and Position of Taskbar

As long as the taskbar is not locked, it may be moved to other positions and resized.

TIP

Pinned shortcuts may be run with keyboard shortcuts by pressing the WinKey and a number between 1 and 0 on the keyboard depending on the location of the shortcut. The first pinned item on the taskbar may be launched by pressing WinKey+1, etc. This is a great tip to share with your end users.

To move the taskbar you may drag and drop it to the new location. Left-click an empty space in the taskbar and hold it, then move the cursor to the new location and release the left mouse button. The taskbar may be moved to any of the monitorⒼ edges. The taskbar location may also be modiÞed in the Taskbar and Start Menu Properties window explained in the next section.

To resize the taskbar, move the cursor to the outer edge of the taskbar, left-click and hold, expand the taskbar towards the other edge of the monitor and release the left mouse button when the desired size is chosen. Do the same towards the monitor edge of the taskbar location to make it smaller.

Customize the Taskbar

The taskbar may also be customized through the Taskbar and Start Menu Properties window. To open the window, right-click an empty area of the taskbar and click **Properties** as shown in Figure 4.31:

- Taskbar
  - **Lock the taskbar** Ðthis locks the taskbar with its current size, location, and settings. This can also be accomplished by right-clicking an open area of the taskbar and clicking **Lock the Taskbar**.
  - **Auto-hide the taskbar** ÐThis will automatically hide the taskbar on the edge of the monitor where it is located. This is a matter of preference for the end user.
  - **Use small icons** ÐThis makes all icons in the taskbar smaller. Windows 7 uses large icons by default to enable Windows Touch users a larger space to select icons and use the Start menu.
  - **Taskbar location on screen** ÐThis positions the taskbar in one of the four edges of the display: bottom, left, right, and top.
  - Taskbarb uttons
    - **Always combine, hide labels** ÐThis is the default, icon only view of shortcut icons and running applications.
    - **Combine when taskbar is full** ÐThis displays the applications with their respective names as Windows XP or Windows Vista did in ungrouped mode. If too many applications are open, it will group the applications. This option may be suitable and provide a more comfortable feel for some end users.
    - **Never combine** ÐThis is similar to the previous option but will never combine the icons or applications together. The Taskbar will get crammed if many applications are running at once.
  - NotiÞcation area ÐThe **Customize** button is for customizing the notiÞcation area explained in the next subsection.

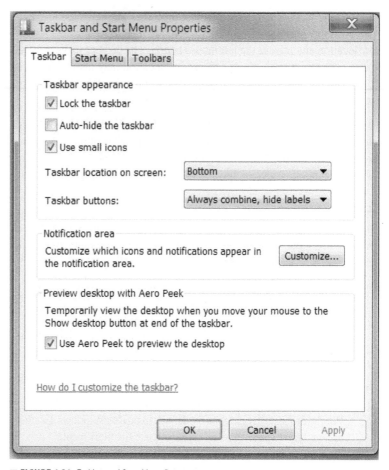

■ **FIGURE 4.31** Taskbar and Start Menu Properties

    ❏ Preview desktop with Aero Peek ÐThis allows the desktop to be
viewed without minimizing all applications when the cursor is
moved all the way to the bottom right of the taskbar on top of the
Show Desktopb utton.

Notification Area

The notiÞcation area was introduced in Windows 95 along with the Start
menu, desktop, and taskbar user interfaces. Windows 7Õ notiÞcation area
has been changed since Windows Vista and Windows XP. A quick glimpse
at the bottom-right of a Windows 7 display will show three components:

- **Show Desktop** button Ðall the way to the right as a small rectangle
- NotiÞcation icons Ðthe icons to the left of the clock
- Windows Clock Ðthe time display on the notiÞcation area

By default, the notiÞcation icons displayed are the Action Center, Network, Volume, and Power Options (only for mobile users). As applications and programs are installed on the computer, more and more icons will begin to appear in the notiÞcation area. These icons may be right-clicked for launching tasks related to the iconÕs application.

The notiÞcation area, as the name suggests, is to notify the user on the status of certain applications. Software developers have turned the notiÞcation area into a taskbar by forcing applications to be minimized and launched from there, so Microsoft has added a few customization options. Windows 7 allows for the customization of notiÞcations so the user may better deÞne what notiÞcation icons to show and what alerts to display. This can be a double-edged sword as critical notiÞcations may be disabled, leaving the system or applications vulnerable. Hidden notiÞcation icons may be viewed by clicking the arrow to the left-hand side of the notiÞcation area.

Customizing the Notification Area

Windows 7 allows the notiÞcation area to be customized by the end user to show only notiÞcations for selected programs. To customize the notiÞcation area, launch the **NotiÞcation Area Icons** console of the Control Panel. This may be done in three different ways:

- Right-clickt he **Windows Clock** and click **Customize NotiÞcation Area**.
- Right-click an empty part of the taskbar, click **Properties**, and then click **Customize** in the notiÞcation area section of the **Taskbar**t ab.
- Open **Control Panel | All Control Panel Items | NotiÞcation Area Icons**.

The NotiÞcation Area Icons screen allows for multiple settings to be set as showni n Figure4.32 .

- Select which icons and notiÞcations appear on the taskbar ÐThe larger pane in this view will show icons and application names on the left and a behaviors drop-down list:
    - **Show icon and notiÞcations** ÐIcons will appear directly in the notiÞcation area and all notiÞcations will be displayed.
    - **Hide icon and notiÞcations** ÐThis option will hide the icon and notiÞcations of this application.
    - **Only show notiÞcations** ÐThis option will hide the icon but displaynot iÞcationsf romt hea pplication.
- **Turn system icons on or off** ÐPressing this button will show options for built-in system icons and notiÞcations:
    - **System Icons** ÐOn the left side are the built-in system icons
    - **Behaviors**ÐO nor O ff

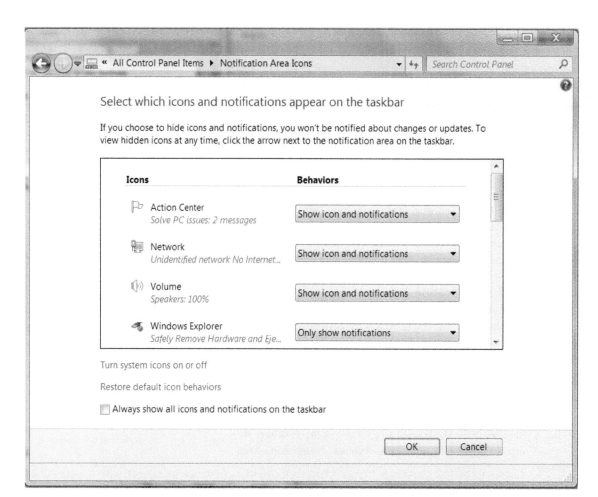

■ **FIGURE 4.32** Notification Area Icons

- **Restore default icon behaviors** ÐThis option will restore all notiÞcations to the default behavior chosen by the software developer.
- **Always show all icons and notiÞcations on the taskbar** ÐChecking this box will show all icons and notiÞcations in the notiÞcation area and will not group the unused icons for access with the Up Arrow. Checking this box disables all other settings.

Windows Clock

The Windows Clock was introduced in the Windows 95 desktop user interface. It changed dramatically in Windows Vista and these changes were carried over to Windows 7. The Window Clock is located on the lower right of the display in the notiÞcation area. Clicking the time once will pop up a calendar view of the current date and analog and digital clock of the current time. Earlier versions of Windows did not pop up a window with a calendar view or clock; instead, it had to be double clicked for the settings. Sometimes, the settings were disabled and users could not take a quick glimpse at the calendar. Thankfully that has changed allowing users to easily see the date and a full calendar.

Changing date and time settings is also a little different in Windows 7. To open the settings, click on the **Windows Clock** and then on the **Change date and time settingsÉ** link or open the **Control Panel | All Control Panel Items | Date and Time**. Three tabs are available to edit date and time settings(see Figure4.33).

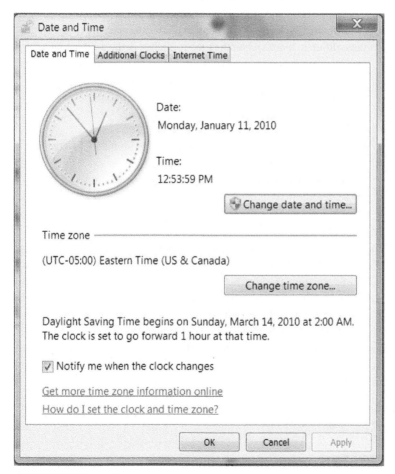

■ **FIGURE 4.33** Date and Time

- **Date and Time** tab ÐThis is the main tab to change the date and time settings as illustrated in Figure 4.33.
  - ❑ **Change date and time** ÐThis option pops up the Date and Time Settings window where the date can be clicked on via a nice calendar and time inputted in the Þeld. The Change calendar settings will open the Region and Language Control Panel options for customizing the date format.
  - ❑ **Change time zone** ÐThis option allows the user to select the appropriate time zone. The check box next to **Automatically adjust clock for Daylight Saving Time** may be checked if the end user is in an area that observes daylight savings time and wants the clock to change automatically.
  - ❑ **Notify me when the clock changes** ÐThis option will notify the end user when the time changes due to daylight savings.
- **Additional Clocks tab** ÐThis option allows the end user to see up to three different clocks when the time is clicked in the notiÞcation area or when the mouse is placed over the time. This is useful for end users who need to know the time in different regions or travel frequently.
  - ❑ **Show this clock** Ðenables the clock
  - ❑ **Set time zone** Ðfor the new clock
  - ❑ Enter display name Ðfor identifying the clock
- **Internet time** tab Ðallows the conÞguration of an Internet Network Time Protocol (NTP) server to synchronize the Windows 7 time. Click **Change settings**, check the box to allow synchronization, and select the server to use from the drop down.

ShowD esktop

The last object of the notiÞcation area is the **Show Desktop** button. In older versions of Windows, this shortcut was in the Quick Launch toolbar. Windows 7 has moved the **Show Desktop** button to the notiÞcation area. If Windows Aero is enabled, moving the mouse cursor over the small rectangle on the far right of the notiÞcation area will enable Aero Peek. Aero Peek displays the desktop with an outline of all the open windows. This allows for a quick glimpse at the desktop without actually minimizing all the open windows. Clicking the same rectangle will minimize all windows and show the desktop. Clicking the button again will bring the windows back to the previous state.

Minimizing all windows to show the desktop can also be done with the keyboard shortcut WinKey+D.

Toolbars

Windows 7 includes different toolbars that may be added to the taskbar (see Figure 4.34). The end user also has the option to create new personal

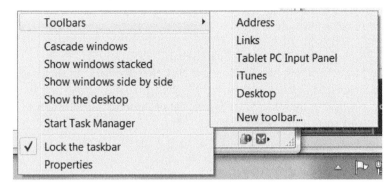

toolbars to enable quicker access to user resources. The included toolbars are:

■ **Address** ÐThis option displays an Address box to quickly launch a URL with the default Web browser or a local or remote folder or Þle location with Windows Explorer. Full Þle paths will launch the default applicationf ort hatÞ le.

■ **Desktop** ÐThis option displays a menu to desktop shortcuts and menus for quicker access without having to minimize windows to access the desktop.

■ **Links** ÐThis option displays a Links menu from the userÕs Favorites folderl ocateda t% SystemDrive%\%Users\%Username%\Favorites\.

Toggle Toolbars

To display or hide a toolbar, do the following:

1. Right-click an empty part of the taskbar.
2. Move the cursor over **Toolbars** and click the toolbar name in the list as shown in Figure 4.34. Clicking a checked toolbar will hide it.

To customize toolbars, right-click the Toolbar and click the selected option:

■ **Show text**
■ **Show title**
■ **View**
■ **Close toolbar**

Createa Toolbar

End users may create a personal toolbar to access folders and Þles quicker. Toolbars may point to any folder on the local computer or network. The folders will appear as menu items and Þles as objects that are quickly launched. To create a toolbar, follow these steps:

1. Right-click an empty part of the taskbar.
2. Move the cursor over **Toolbars** and click **New ToolbarÉ** as shown in Figure4.34 .
3. Navigate to the folder to set as a toolbar on the local computer or network share. Click **Select Folder**.

WINDOWS EXPLORER

Windows 7 has a completely new Windows Explorer. Perhaps the end user will visually see only slight differences, but it has been recoded to not be integrated with IE as it was in earlier versions of Windows. The Windows ExplorerÕ view is different from earlier versions of Windows. At Þrst glance, one will notice the new back and forward buttons, a new Address bar, and a new Search box. Under that bar is a new context-speciÞc toolbar, which we will call the Windows Explorer toolbar. Depending on the folder or view the Windows Explorer window is on, these options will be different: on the left is the navigation pane for easier navigation and manipulation of Þles and folders; on the bottom is a details pane and possibly a status bar; while on the right there may be a preview pane; the middle area of Windows Explorer is the current view of the location the user is on. Each of these views will be explored in this section.

To open Windows Explorer as shown in Figure 4.35, do the following:

■ Click **Start | All Programs | Accessories | Windows Explorer**
■ Click **Start | Computer or %Username% or Documents or Pictures or Music**

WindowsExp lorer Window

The Windows Explorer window is the visual component of Windows Explorer that underwent the most changes. This is the view and window that will open every time an end user needs to manage Þles or folders. It is critical for end users and administrators to understand the basic layout of a Windows Explorer window. This section addresses each part of the Windows Explorer layout shown in Figure 4.35.

Address Bar

The Address bar is right at the top of the Windows Explorer window. There are different components on this bar. On the left is back and forward buttons

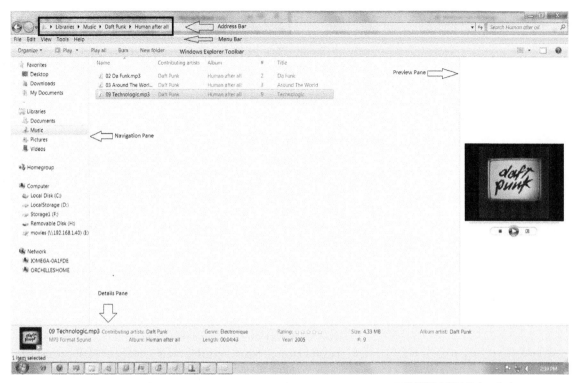

■ **FIGURE 4.35** Windows Explorer

much like IE to navigate back or forward to the location viewed before or after the current view. The buttons will be grayed out if the option is not available. To the immediate right of the forward button is an arrow pointing down. This arrow shows the current location with a dot and the other locations recently viewed for quick access without the forward and back buttons.

The Windows 7 Windows Explorer Address bar is similar to the one from Windows Vista. This may give users coming from Windows XP or earlier versions a bit of a shock and require training. The Address bar no longer shows the location with colons and backslashes. Instead the Address bar shows each location with a drop-down node in between each location. This actually makes it easier to navigate through the Þles and folders. Each location has an arrow next to it which can be clicked to display a drop down used to explore all the folders in that location, as shown in Figure 4.35. Clicking the Address bar at the left-most area or on an empty place will reveal the classic style of viewing the address bar with hard drive letter, colon, and backslashes.

To the far right of the Address bar is a down arrow for navigating to recent locations. To the right of that is a refresh button to refresh the view on the location. Even further to the right is the Search bar. The Search bar can be used for quickly searching within the location Windows Explorer is currently on. Simply click in the Search Bar and type the query. Clicking the **Search box** will also display past search queries, as well as search Þlters for Date ModiÞed and Size. Another way to reach the Search bar is with the keyboard shortcut **Ctrl+F**.

Windows Explorer Toolbar

The Windows Explorer toolbar is located directly under the Address bar or Menu bar (if it is enabled), as shown in Figure 4.35. This is a change from the traditional Windows Explorer task pane from earlier versions of Windows. This toolbar is context sensitive meaning depending on what view or item is selected the buttons and options will be different. There are four consistent buttons to this toolbar:

1. **Organize** Ðcontains functions that would generally be in the Edit Menu bar of Windows Explorer with additional layout and option selections:
   - **Cut, Copy, Paste, Undo, Redo, Select All, Delete**, and **Rename** Ð self explanatory for the current item or view
   - **Layout** Ðcheck boxes to enable the different panes and menu bars in the Windows Explorer view: Menu bar, Details pane, Navigation pane, and Preview pane
   - **Folder and Search Options** Ðquick access to conÞgure Windows Explorer explained later in this chapter
   - **Properties** Ðopens the properties of the selected item. May also be accomplished by right-clicking the item and selecting **Properties**.
2. **View** Ðthis button is the third from last on the right of the Windows Explorer toolbar. It is a button and also has an arrow that displays a drop down. Clicking the button will cycle through the different folder views whereas clicking the drop down will let one pick what view to display.
3. **Preview** Ðtoggles the preview pane
4. **Get Help**Ðope ns Windowsh elp

All other options on the toolbar depend on the view or item that is selected and are relevant to those options. Similar options are available by right-clicking the item. This will display the context menu with multiple options available.

Details Pane

The details pane is enabled by default on the bottom portion of the Windows Explorer window. This pane will display details for the selected item or current view. These details are similar to the details displayed when right-clicking **item | Properties | Details**. As the details pane is enlarged by clicking and holding the top edge and moving the cursor towards the top of the screen, more details of the item are displayed.

To toggle the details pane, click **Organize | Layout | Details** on the toolbar.

Menu Bar

Although the traditional Menu bar is not visible in Windows Explorer, it does not mean it is not there. Pressing **Alt** on the keyboard will temporarily show the Menu bar under the Address bar on the Windows Explorer window. To show the Menu bar at all times, click **Organize | Layout | Menu Bar** on the new task pane. The Menu bar has the same options older versions of Windows had depending on the location in Windows Explorer:

- **File** ÐDepending on what item is selected, this will generally reveal the same context menu as right-clicking the same item. New from Windows XP is a **Share with** option that opens the sharing settings. The option to create new Þles or folders is also available.
- **Edit** ÐThis option allows the typical edit functions such as undo move, redo, cut, copy, paste, paste shortcut, copy to folder, move to folder, select all, and invert selection. Some commands may be grayed out if they are unavailable for the item selected or view in Windows Explorer.
- **View** ÐThis option allows for toggling or selecting multiple Windows Explorervi ews.
  - ❏ **Status bar** ÐThere is a bar at the bottom of the Windows Explorer screen with the status of the view, often the amount of items in the folder or items selected. This is a check box that can be toggled.
  - ❏ **Icon view** ÐThe same views available from the Windows Explorer task pane including extra large icons, large icons, medium icons, small icons, list, details, tile, and content.
  - ❏ **Sort by** ÐThis option allows the user to sort the items in the view by the detailed information available in the view in ascending or descendingor der.
  - ❏ **Group by** ÐThis option allows the user to group the items in the view depending on the details available in ascending or descending order.
  - ❏ **Choose detail** ÐThis option enables detailed information to display about each item in the Windows Explorer view. Name detail cannot be removed from this list.
    - **Details** ÐThere is a huge list available to choose from, but note that some items do not have all details and will simply show blank on the Windows Explorer view

- **Width of the selected column (in pixels)** ÐThis option is available for each detail to better organize the view of the Windows Explorerw indow.
- **Move Up**, **Move Down**, **Show**, **Hide** ÐThis option toggles the position of the detail in the Windows Explorer view. Show and Hide toggle the selected detail to appear or not in the Windows Explorer view. This is the same as toggling the checkmark to the left of the detail name.

❑ **Customize this folder** ÐThis option opens a properties window on the **Customize** tab to edit the speciÞc item selected.

❑ **Go to** ÐThis option allows simple navigation of Windows Explorer to go back, forward, or up a view. A list of recently accessed folders and views will also appear.

❑ **Refresh** ÐThis option refreshes the current view if a change does nota ppeart obe r eßected.

■ **Tools** ÐThis option displays similar tools available in older versions of Windows

❑ **Map network drive** Ðopens the Map Network Drive wizard

❑ **Disconnect network drive** Ðopens the Disconnect Network Drive wizard

❑ **Open Sync Center** Ðopens the **Sync Center** console of the Control Panel

❑ **Folder Options** Ðopens the folder options window explained in thisc hapter.

■ **Help** Ðoffers three options:

❑ **View help** Ðopens Windows Explorer Help

❑ **Is this copy of windows legit?** ÐThis option opens the default Web browser to a Microsoft Web page that assists users on determining if the version of Windows they are running is legit.

❑ **About Windows** ÐThis option displays the About Windows window for information on the operating system version and license.

Navigation Pane

The left window of Windows Explorer is called the navigation pane. As the name suggests this is to enable easier navigation through Windows Explorer. Items with arrows pointed towards them mean that objects exist in them that can be expanded. Expanding an object will display the subobjects within and the arrow will point down and turn black. By default, the navigation pane opens with Windows Explorer and contains the following items:

■ **Favorites** ÐThese are folders that end user commonly visits. Clicking on **Favorites** will navigate the Windows Explorer view to that folder. Items can be added to Favorites by dragging and dropping the item to this area or right-clicking **Favorites ÐAdd current location to Favorites**. To remove from favorites, simply right-click **Remove**. Right-clicking **Favorites** also reveals options to: **Collapse**, **Expand**, **Sort by Name**, **Restore favorite links**, and **open in new window**.

- **Libraries** Ðthe end userß Libraries will be displayed here. Libraries are explained in the next section.
- **Homegroup** ÐIf the machine is part of a Homegroup, quick and easy access is available through here. Right-clicking **Homegroup**r eveals options for the Homegroup. This will be explained in Chapter 5, ÒManaging the Windows 7 Desktop Environment.Ó
- **Computer** ÐThis navigates to components connected to the computer including local hard drives, removable media, network location, and other items that may be added by applications. Right-clicking the computer displays options to:
  - ❏ **Manage** ÐThis option displays the Computer Management MMC console.
  - ❏ **Map network drive** or **Disconnect network drive** ÐThis option initiates a wizard to connect or disconnect a shared network drive.
  - ❏ **Add a new location** ÐThis option initiates a wizard to easily create a shortcut to connect to a network location such as a Web site, FTP server, or shared network resource.
  - ❏ **Properties** Ðopens the **Control Panel | System**c onsole
- **Network** Ðdisplays available network resources. Right-clicking the **Network** icon item reveals:
  - ❏ **Map network Drive** or **Disconnect Network Driv**e ÐThis option initiates wizard to connect or disconnect a shared network drive.
  - ❏ **Properties** Ðopens the **Control Panel | Network and Sharing Center** console

To toggle the Navigation Pane, click **Organize | Layout | Navigation Pane** on the toolbar.

Preview Pane

The preview pane is not enabled by default but can be quickly toggled by clicking the second to last button on the right of the Windows Explorer toolbar. Depending on the item selected a preview will appear in this pane. By default, many folders will have the icons view enabled; this view will be the same as what would appear in the preview pane. The Live Icons feature is enabled by default and previews the content of the item in the actual icon. This can be turned off in the Windows Explorer options as it can prove to slow down navigation on folders that requires rendering of the images.

To toggle the preview pane, click **Organize | Layout | Preview Pane** on the toolbar.

Libraries

Libraries are a new feature introduced in Windows 7. Libraries are displayed on the left-hand side of a Windows Explorer window. Introduced to assist end users with organizing, Þnding, saving, and using Þles and folders, Libraries are a way of locating Þles and folders stored in different locations from a single window. Libraries can be conÞgured to locate Þles and folders in user proÞle data folders, public folders, network shares, removable media devices, external hard drives, and any other location the user has access to. Additionally, Library locations are searchable with Windows 7 built-in search. A Library has a default save location where all Þles and folders created or saved in the Library will be stored. By default, Windows 7 provides four Libraries:

- Documents
- Music
- Pictures
- Video

Each of these Libraries has two default locations set:

- %SystemDrive%\Users\%Username%\%LibraryName%
- %SystemDrive%\Public\%LibraryName%

Only one location in each Library may be set as the save location where Þles and folders that are moved to a Library are stored. The default save location for each location is %SystemDrive%\Users\%Username%\%LibraryName%

To view or edit options of a Library right-click the Library and select **Properties** as shown in Figure 4.36:

- Library locations Ðthis Þeld shows all of the locations that the Library uses to populate and locate Þles.
- To set a save location Ðselect the Library location and click **Set save location**.
    - ❏ If a Library location is removed the next Library on the list, it will be set as the save location.
- To add folders to a Library, click **Include a folder** Ða browsing window will appear so the user may navigate to any location and select the folder as a location. Select the folder and click **Include folder**.
- Optimize this library for Ðthis drop down allows for Windows 7 to better understand and manage the view of the Þles and folders within the Library. The options are:
    - ❏ **General items** Ðfor all types of items
    - ❏ **Documents** Ðfor Þle types related to documents

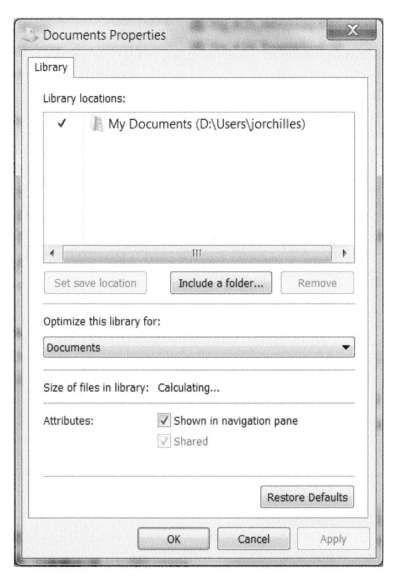

■ **FIGURE 4.36** Library Properties

□ **Music** Đfor music Þles such as .mp3, .wav, etc.
□ **Pictures** Đfor picture Þles such as .jpg, .png, etc.
□ **Videos** Đfor video Þles such as .avi, .mpg, etc.
■ Size of Þles in library ĐIt provides the amount of storage space used for all the Þles in the Library.

- Attributes ÐThere is a check box to show the Library in the navigation pane of Windows Explorer and indicate whether the Library is shared.
- **Restore Defaults** ÐIt restores the default settings of the Library.

Configure WindowsExp lorer

Windows Explorer is, by far, the best tool included with Windows 7 for managing Þles and folders. By default, Windows Explorer is conÞgured to be user friendly for the majority of users. The default settings and options may not be optimal for you or for your end users. Thankfully, there are many different ways to conÞgure Windows Explorer options, menus, and views.

To modify Windows Explorer options:

1. Open **Control Panel | Appearance and Personalization | Folder Options** or from within Windows Explorer click **Organize | Folder and Search Options**.
2. Windows Explorer options are customizable in three different tabs:
   - **General** t aba s (Figure4.37)
     - **Browse folders** ÐThis option allows the user to select between opening each folder in the same window or a new window.
     - **Click items as follows** ÐThis option conÞgures how items interact with the mouse clicks.
       - **Single-click** ÐThis option opens the item on the Þrst click with the option to underline icon titles consistent with the browser or when pointed.
       - **Double-click** ÐThe traditional option to open an item when double-clicked.
     - **Navigation pane** Ðcheck boxes to show all folders or automatically expand to the current folder that is being viewed
     - **Restore defaults** Ðrestore the general Windows Explorer optionst ode fault
   - **View** tab ÐThese are the more advanced options and settings for WindowsE xplorera ss howni n Figure4.38 .
     - **Folder views** ÐYou can apply the current view of Windows Explorer to all folders or reset all folders to default Windows Explorervi ew.
     - **Advanced settings**
       - **Always show icons**, **never thumbnails**Ð Windows Explorer shows large thumbnail images of Þle and folder content. Folders with many Þles take a longer time to render the thumbnails proving to be a waste of time. To disable thumbnail view, check this box. Thumbnail views will still be available when selected in the Windows Explorer view.

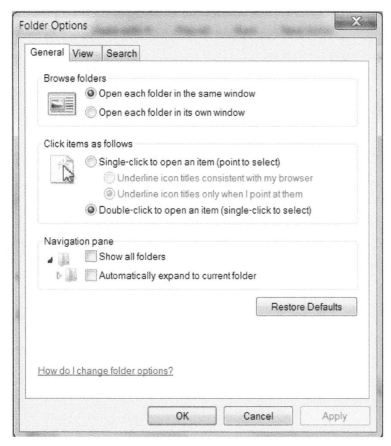

■ FIGURE 4.37 Folder Options – General Tab

- ○ **Always show menus** ÐThis enables the Menu bar to be visible at all times. This can also be toggled in Windows Explorer by clicking **Organize | Layout | Menu Bar**.
- ○ **Display Þle icon on thumbnails** ÐWindows Explorer by default will display a Þle icon on the thumbnail display. To disable, uncheck this box.
- ○ **Display Þle size information in folder tips** ÐPlacing the mouse over a folder in Windows Explorer reveals a pop up display with the folderÕ creation date and time, the size of the folder, and a partial list of Þles. Removing the checkmark from this option will only display the creation date and time, allowing the pop up window to display slightly quicker.
- ○ **Display the full path in the title bar** ÐThe Windows 7 Basic and Aero themes do not display text on the title bar of the Windows Explorer window. Checking this box will

■ **FIGURE 4.38** Folder Options – View Tab

display the full path in the title bar but the Windows Classic theme must be enabled.

○ **Hidden Þles and folders** ÐThis enables the user to see hidden Þles, folders, and drives or to keep them hidden. Administrators need to enable hidden Þles to access and view certain drives referred to in this book.

○ **Hide empty drives in the Computer folderÐ** Windows Explorer by default will show information for empty drives when in the Computer view. Check this option to hide this information.

○ **Hide extensions to known Þle types** ÐWindows Explorer does not display extensions for known Þle types by default. This can be disabled by removing the check next to this option.

○ **Hide protected operating system Þles** ÐRemove the check for this option if you are having trouble viewing operating system Þles. Be careful if this is disabled as modifying a system Þle could hinder the system or worse, cause it to not boot.

- ○ **Launch folder windows in a separate processÐ** Windows Explorer windows run on the same process. If one process locks up or is in a waiting state, it will lock the other open Windows Explorer windows as well. Check this box to open each Windows Explorer window in its own process. This could make opening folders take a little longer.
- ○ **Restore previous folder windows at logon** ÐThis option allows Windows Explorer windows to reopen when the user logs in. The window must have been open when logging off.
- ○ **Show drive letters** ÐThis option will enable the view of drive letters in the address bar
- ○ **Show encrypted or compressed NTFS Þles in colorÐ** Enabling this option will show encrypted Þles and folders in green and compressed Þles and folders in blue.
- ○ **Show pop-up description for folder and desktop itemsÐ** If enabled, a pop-up will display when the mouse is placed on top of a Þle or folder.
- ○ **Show preview handlers in preview pan**e ÐThis option enables items to be previewed in the preview pane. Remove the checkmark to disable this feature.
- ○ **Use check boxes to select items** ÐWindows Explorer allows a single mouse click to select an item and Shift+Click or Ctrl+Click for a range of items. This option will display a check box next to every item and folder for selecting.
- ○ **Use Sharing Wizard** ÐThe sharing wizard is the default setting for sharing folders on Windows 7. Disabling this option will force sharing to occur via the Advanced Sharing properties.
- ○ **When typing into list view** ÐBy default, Windows Explorer allows a key to be typed in certain views to automatically go to the Þrst Þle or folder with that letter. To conÞgure Windows Explorer to **Automatically type into the Search Box** instead of the item, select this option.
- - **Restore Defaults** ÐThis option restores all advanced and folder view settings to default Windows Explorer options and view.
- ❑ **Search** tab ÐThis tab enables search options within Windows Explorer and the Start Menu Search as shown in Figure 4.39.
  - - What to search ÐSelect to only search for content in indexed locations and Þle names in nonindexed locations or to search for content in all locations. The latter takes much longer to perform a search as locations that are not indexed take longer to search forc ontent/

■ **FIGURE 4.39** Folder Options – Search Tab

- How to search ÐThese check boxes allow for customizing how the search is performed:
  - **Include subfolders in search results when searching in Þle folders** Ðwill search within all subfolders
  - **Find partial matches** ÐThis option will search and Þnd Þles and folders that contain the same phrase that is being searched.
  - **Use natural language search** ÐThis option enables search to interpret natural language into the search. For example Ñall Þles before 10/22/2009Ówill be interpreted and search Þles created before 10/22/2009.
  - **DonÕ use the index when searching in Þle folders for system Þles** Ðsearch will not use the index to search making thes earchs lower.

- Whens earchingnon- indexedl ocations
  - o **Include system directories** Ðsearches within the system directories such as %WinDir%
  - o **Include compressed Þles** ÐThis will enable searching within compressed Þles, making the search slower.
- **Restore defaults** ÐThis option restores the search options to Windows7de fault

Shortcuts

In Windows 7, shortcuts and the locations they link to dictate how applications are launched. Shortcuts enable the end user to launch applications much quicker than navigating to the installed location and launching the executable. Shortcuts can point to a local or remote Þle or application or to an Internet location with a URL. A *link* shortcut is used to launch applications, Þles, or folders, whereas a URL shortcut is used to launch the default Web browser to an Internet location. Shortcuts may be created on the local computer with Windows Explorer or through Group Policy.

Creating Shortcuts in Windows Explorer

With Windows Explorer, it is simple to create shortcuts:

1. Log in to the computer as the end user who needs the shortcut or as an administrator.
2. Right-clickt he **Start menu** and click **Open Windows Explorer**.
3. Navigate to the location where the shortcut will be located.
4. Right-click in an open area and click **New | Shortcut** as shown in Figure4.40.
5. Type the location of the item:
   a. Link Shortcut ÐClick **BrowseÉ** and navigate to the install location of the application as shown in Figure 4.40. Click **OK**.
   b. URL Shortcut ÐType the URL of the Internet location into the Þeld.
6. Click **Next**.
7. Type the name of the shortcut Ðusually something familiar to the end user.
8. Click **Finish**.

Configure Shortcut Properties in Windows Explorer

Once the shortcut has been created you may right-click on it and select **Properties**. Depending on if the shortcut is a link or URL shortcut the Properties window will pop up with certain options:

- **General** tab Ðthe general options and information for any Þle. This tab is available by right-clicking any Þle and selecting **Properties**.

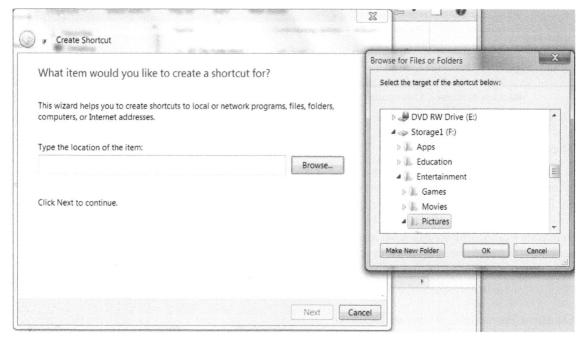

FIGURE 4.40 Create Shortcut

This tab displays the Þle name, type of Þle, description, location, size, size on disk, date created, date modiÞed, date last accessed, and attributes (read-only or hidden).

- **Shortcut** tab ÐIt is the place where the shortcut options may be modiÞed as shown in Figure 4.41:
  - ❑ **Target type** ÐIt is the type of application that will be launched whent hes hortcutr uns.
  - ❑ **Target location** Ðthe folder name of the target location
  - ❑ **Target** Ðthe full path of the Þle where the shortcut will run. Arguments may be added to the end of this line for the speciÞc application.
  - ❑ **Start in** ÐThe location where the Þle is located.
  - ❑ **Shortcut key** ÐA keyboard shortcut can be assigned to launch the speciÞc shortcut for quicker launching of the shortcut.
  - ❑ **Run** ÐIt is the window type to launch when the shortcut is run: normal window, minimized, or maximized.
  - ❑ **Comment** Ðto document the shortcut
  - ❑ **Open Þle location** ÐThis option launches a Windows Explorer window at the Þle location.

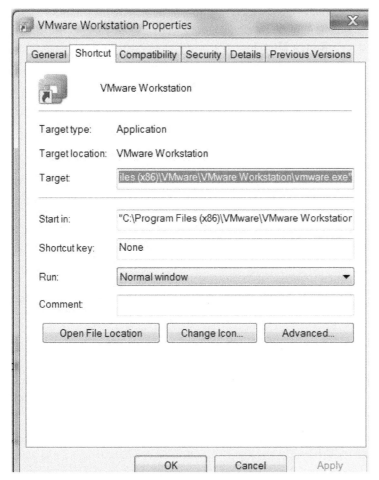

FIGURE 4.41 Shortcut Properties

- ❑ **Change icon** ÐThis option is to change the icon for the shortcut, generally it uses the applicationÕ icon if found.
- ❑ **Advanced** ÐThis option allows you to run the shortcut as and administratora nd/ori ns eparatem emorys pace.
- ■ **Compatibility** tab ÐThis tab sets compatibility options. This is useful when applications will not run by default:
  - ❑ **Compatibility mode** ÐA check box to enable the program to run in compatibility mode for an older version of Windows. Many different versions of Windows are available and it is best to try the latest-known working version to begin troubleshooting why an application will not run.

◻ **Settings** Ðallows for conÞguring the display settings of the application the shortcut points to. The check boxes available are:
  - **Run in 256 colors**
  - **Run in 640 × 480 screen resolutions**
  - **Disable visual themes**
  - **Disable desktop composition**
  - **Disable display scaling on high DPI settings**

◻ **Privilege level** ÐA check box to allow a user to run the application as an administrator when executed through the shortcut.

◻ **Change settings for all users** ÐThis option allows administrators to change the global settings for the shortcut for all user accounts in the computer, so the administrator does not have to modify settings individuallyf ora pplicationsw ithc ompatibilityi ssues

■ **Security** tab ÐThe default security tab for all Þles and folders to set what users and groups have access to the shortcut.

■ **Details** tab ÐA read-only view of the shortcut properties

■ **Previous versions** tab ÐThis option is used to view, open, copy, or restore an older working version of the shortcut.

INTERNET EXPLORER8

IE 8 is included in every version of Windows 7 available in the United States. It is the only Web browser included with Windows 7 and therefore, the default Web browser for all users. Most end users will use a Web browser more than any other application included with Windows 7.

IE 8 will be introduced in this chapter as it is a part of the desktop environment. However, as IE is a complex application, it will be referenced in other chapters as well. Since IE is one of the largest attack surfaces on the Internet, its security will be looked at in Chapter 8, ÒSecuring Windows 7.Ó

FirstR un

To start IE 8, click the **IE** icon on the taskbar or click **Start | All Programs | IE**.

By default, the Þrst time IE 8 is started by a user, a startup wizard is initiated. It is best to understand the questions asked by the wizard and perhaps not press the **Ask me later** button or select the default settings, as many new features are enabled by default.

As usual, Microsoft will Þrst ask if you want to make IE your default browser. Of course, this is your personal preference. Due to security issues, we recommend another browser such as Firefox; however, this will be looked at more in-depth in Chapter 7, ÒManaging Windows 7 in an Enterprise Environment.Ó Under the default browser, another option is a check box for importing settings from another browser for the logged in user. The next screen will ask to turn on suggested sites, explained below. Following the suggested sites option is an option to use express settings or choose custom settings. These settings are:

■ **Choose a default search provider** Ðthis is for the quick search option on the top-right of IE 8. By default, MicrosoftÕ Bing will be used. For more options, select **Show me a Web page after setup to choose more search providers**. This option will take you to another page at the end of the setup to choose from different search providers.

■ **Search provider updates** Ðthis service turns on automatic updates of the IE 8 search box search provider chosen previously. As the search box is an interactive feature with programmable possibilities, search providers might update this automatically. By default this is turned on.

■ **Choose your accelerators** Ðthis feature allows you to select any text and manipulate it through some convenient options. By default this option is on and allows for Blog with Windows Live, Map with Live Search, E-mail with Windows Live, and Translate with Live Search. You can select to choose what accelerators to setup or to turn them off all together, more on this below.

■ **Turn on SmartScreen Þlter** Ðthis is the updated version of the IE 7 Phishing Filter with added anti-malware functionality. This is enabled by default and the reason for the user choice is because IE 8 must communicate with Microsoft servers to check the safety of some Web sites, leading to privacy concerns. More on this feature below.

■ **Compatibility settings** ÐMicrosoft claims to use a standard-based rending engine by default, more on this later. Due to the change, some Web sites might not be compatible with IE 8 and hence this choice. Like SmartScreen Þlter, this feature contacts Microsoft servers for checkingc ompatibility.

Toolbars

IE 8 should look very similar to earlier versions of IE and to any other Web browser as they generally have the same layout. Figure 4.42 illustrates the general layout of the IE 8 window. The top of the browser has the IE 8 toolbar, which has the **Forward** button, **Back** button, navigation arrow, Address bar, and Search bar. The Menu bar may also be displayed if enabled (not enabled by default). The Menu bar is similar to the IE Menu bar of the past with options for File, Edit, View, Favorites, Tools, and Help.

FIGURE 4.42 Internet Explorer 8 Window

IE 8 tries to give the user the most display real estate for viewing Web pages and has disabled this Menu bar by default. Under the Menu bar is the Favorites toolbar. This toolbar is for quick access to favorites, and to add new favorites, suggested sites, more add-ons. Under the Favorites toolbar is the new tabbed browsing view, which shows a tab for the current page or a tab view and tab navigation drop-down arrow. To the immediate right is the **Add Tab** button. To the far right of the tabbed bar is the Command bar. The Command bar is the new Menu bar replacement. Icons can be added and removed from this toolbar; however, it includes the most used icons beginning with the **Home** button and **Page** button, to **Safety** and **Tools**. Finally, the Status bar is included in IE 8 and is located in the bottom of the IE 8 window. All of these toolbars may be toggled by right-clicking the toolbar area and selecting the speciÞc bar.

IE 8 Toolbar

One of the only bars that cannot be removed is the top-most IE 8 toolbar. This toolbar has the traditional back and forward buttons, navigation menu drop-down arrow, Address bar, and Search bar.

The **Back** and **Forward** buttons are standard IE 8 buttons used for navigating through visited Web pages. To the immediate right is a drop-down arrow to display pages that have been navigated to. Clicking any of the options will take the browser to that page. To the immediate right of the drop-down arrow is the Address bar.

The Address bar has been improved for Windows 7. This bar is used to type the URL of the Web page that will be visited. As end users type an address, the Address bar will automatically display a drop down with similar sites that the user is typing drawing from recent sites visited, favorites, and suggestions.

Newl E8 F eatures

This section introduces the administrator and end user to many of the new features in IE 8. The features introduced in this section should assist the user in being more efÞcient when Web browsing and working online.

Accelerators

IE accelerators greatly enhance the usability of IE. Accelerators help you perform common browser tasks much easier than in earlier versions of IE. In many cases, in order to get what you need, you would normally have to copy something from one browser page to another. For example, letÕs say a Web page contains an address for a store you want to visit. Normally, in order to get directions to the store, you would have to copy the address and paste it into a browser session for a Web site that returns driving directions. Well, accelerators can take care of this for you.

To use an accelerator, do the following:

1. Highlightt hede siredt ext.
2. Click on the blue accelerator icon. As shown in Figure 4.43, the Acceleratorm enuw illa ppear.
3. Selectt hede sireda ccelerator.

Accelerators must be enabled for you to use them. When you Þrst conÞgure IE in Windows 7, you have the option to enable accelerators. After the initial conÞguration, you can still enable or disable accelerators. This is done through the Control Panel.

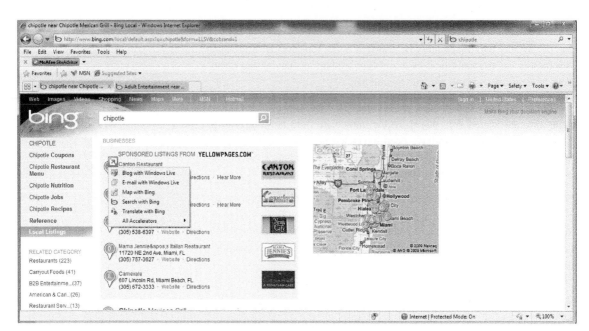

■ FIGURE 4.43 Internet Explorer 8
Accelerator Menu

To enable or disable accelerators, do the following:

1. Opent heC ontrolP anel.
2. In the Control Panel, select **Network and Internet**.
3. Under Internet Options, select the **Programs**t ab.
4. Select **Manage add-ons**.
5. Int he **Manage Add-ons** window, select **Accelerators** in the
   leftpa ne.
6. As shown in Figure 4.44, you can select which accelerators you want
   toe nableor di sable.

Compatibility View

IE 8 Compatibility View can help with Web sites that do not appear properly in IE 8. Compatibility View will allow a Web page to be viewed as it
would be seen in IE 7 and can help Þx simple issue like text formatting and
alignment.

When you navigate to a site that is not displaying properly, simply click the
Compatibility View icon as shown in Figure 4.45 and the site will be seen
in Compatibility View. The entire site will use Compatibility View, not just
that page. Also, the next time you navigate to the site, the Compatibility
View setting is remembered, so you donÕ have to set it again.

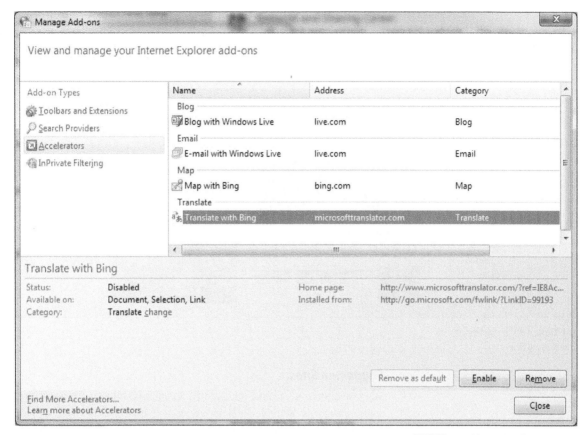

■ **FIGURE 4.44** Manage Add-Ons Window

You can also manually conÞgure Compatibility View. This is done through Compatibility View Settings. From the Tools menu in IE, select **Compatibility View Settings**. As shown in Figure 4.46, the Compatibility View Settings window will appear. In this window, you can conÞgure which sites will be viewed using Compatibility View. You can conÞgure IE to show all sites in Compatibility View, or just certain ones.

Search Suggestions

Search Suggestions is more of a convenience feature of IE. When you start typing words into a search box, IE will offer suggestions on text you could use to Þll out the search request. This is very useful if you have forgotten a part of a name, phrase, or something of that nature that you want to search for. ItÕs also useful in helping to ensure that you supply enough information to the search engine in order to adequately narrow down your search.

■ FIGURE 4.45 Internet Explorer Compatibility View

Suggested Sites

Suggested Sites is a feature added to IE 8 similar to other recommendation engines such as StumbleUpon (www.stumbleupon.com), which suggest other Web sites similar to the ones visited by the user. This is done by the browser sending information to Microsoft, over a secure connection, about the current user's Web browsing.

To toggle suggested sites in IE 8, select **Tools** and check or uncheck **Suggested Sites**.

Tabbed Browsing

In IE 8, Microsoft has enhanced its Tabbed Browsing feature, starting with the New Tab page. The New Tab page has been enhanced to provide more functionality. On the New Tab page, you can reopen closed tabs, browse with inPrivate, or use an accelerator.

Additionally, there are more methods for managing tabs. Right-clicking on a tab will bring up the Tab menu, as shown in Figure 4.47. Using the Tab menu, you can close the current tab, close all other tabs, refresh the current tab, refresh all tabs, and perform many other functions.

WARNING

EnablingS uggestedS itesp otentially sends personally-identifiable information such as user's IP address and browser information to Microsoft over the HTTPS protocol. Microsoft has stated that they do not store this information..

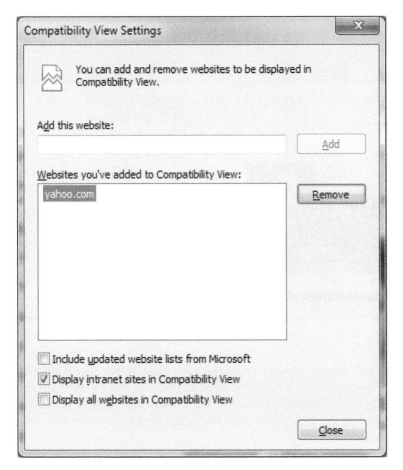

■ **FIGURE 4.46** Compatibility View Settings Window

Microsoft has also introduced the concept of Tab groups. When you open multiple tabs, tabs with related content or from the same site are added to the same group. The group is visually indicated using tab shading or coloring. Now, when you want to close a tab, you have the option to close a single tab or close all the tabs within that Tab group. If you close one tab within a Tab group, you are taken to another tab within that group. This helps to ensure you will be taken to a tab with similar content as the page you were viewing.

Web Slices

Web Slices are another convenient feature of IE 8. Web Slices are used to keep up-to-date with changing Web content. This content could be news,

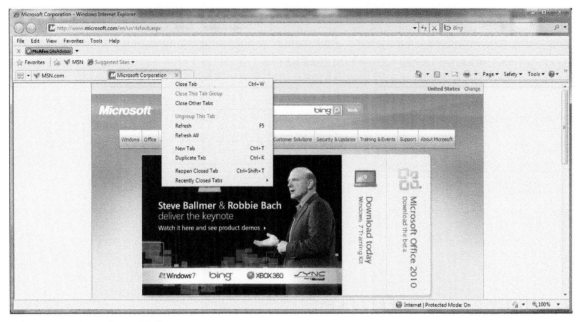

■ FIGURE 4.47 Internet Explorer Tab Menu

e-mail, auctions, or several other types of content. A Web Slice is a sample of this content. Web Slices are added to your Favorites bar. Now you can keep track of this changing content directly from your Favorites bar. IE will automatically highlight the Web Slice when the content of the Web Slice changes.

To create a Web Slice, do the following:

1. Hover over the desired content. If the content is capable of being used with a Web Slice, the green Web Slice icon will appear.
2. Clickt he **Web Slice** icon. You are presented with the Add a Web Slice window,a ss howni n Figure4.48 .
3. Clickt he **Add to Favorites** bar. The Web Slice will be added.

Web Slice settings be conÞgured in **Internet Options | Content | Settings**. Here you can turn Web Slice discovery on or off. You can also conÞgure how often Web Slices are checked for updates, as well as other Web Slice settings.

InternetE xplorerO ptions

As previously mentioned, IE 8 is a complex application included with Windows 7. This application is what most users will be using to navigate

■ **FIGURE 4.48** Internet Explorer Add a Web Slice Wndow

around the Web to external and internal Web sites. Due to all the possibilities the Web has introduced to the end user desktop experience, IE 8 has become a huge and complex application. In this section, we explain the **General**, **Connections**, **Programs**, and **Advanced** tabs. The **Security** tab, **Privacy** tab, and **Content** tab will be referenced in Chapter 8, ÒSecurity in Windows 7.ÓTo access IE 8 options (Figure 4.49):

- Clickt he **Tools** button in the command bar within IE 8 and click **Internet Options**.
- Got o **Control Panel | Internet Options**(iconsvi ew).

General Tab

The Þrst tab, **General**, shown in Figure 4.49, manages the conÞguration of the Home page, browsing history, search, tabs, and appearance.

HomeP age

To conÞgure the Home page, enter the URL of the Web site(s) the user would like to open. To open more than one Web site in tabs, separate each URL by pressing **Enter**. The three buttons in this section allow the user to set the current Web site(s), the default Web site (MSN.com), or a blank page as the Home page.

■ **FIGURE 4.49** Internet Properties

Browsing History

IE 8 downloads and stores all the components of a visited Web page in a folder in the hard drive. For this reason, there are different browsing history options. Browsing history allows the user to delete browsing history by clicking the **Delete** button. The user may then check which options to delete or preserve including: Preserve favorites Web site data, temporary Internet Þles, cookies, history, form data, passwords, and InPrivate Þltering data. The user may also opt to delete the browsing history every time IE is closed by checking the check box with the respective name.

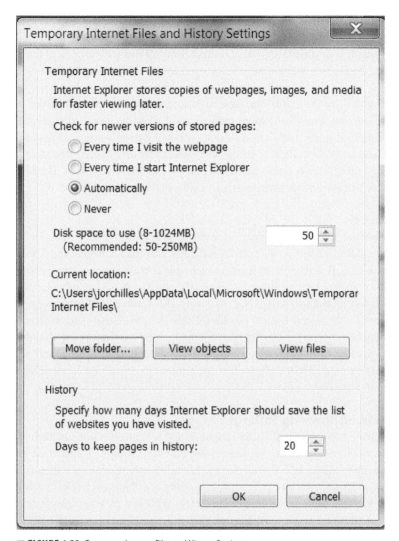

■ **FIGURE 4.50** Temporary Internet Files and History Settings

The **Settings** button allows the user to conÞgure the temporary Internet Þles and history settings as shown in Figure 4.50. Under temporary Internet Þles, the user may select to check for new versions of Web pages every time the Web page is visited, every time IE is opened, automatically, or never. The default option is **Automatically**. This option can cause some Web pages not to show the most current and up-to-date information. Depending on the userÕs Web surÞng habits and the Web sites the user visits, this may need to be toggled. Additionally, you may conÞgure the disk space to use for temporary

Internet Þles. The current location shows where the temporary Internet Þles are stored. By default, temporary Internet Þles are stored in %SystemDrive%\Users\%Username%\AppData\Local\Microsoft\Windows\Temporary Internet Files\. This location may be changed by selecting **Move folderÉ** and selecting in the pop up Windows Explorer window where the Þles should be stored. The current user must have write access to that folder for the folder to be selected. Two other buttons in this section allow the user to view objects and Þles that have been downloaded by standard Web browsing in a Windows Explorer window. Finally, the user may select how long to keep Web browsing history. This is simply the URLs that the user has navigated to. This history will show when partially typing a URL in the Address bar of IE 8.

Search

The Search **Settings** button will launch the Manage Add-ons window for IE introduced earlier in this section. Here, the user may conÞgure the search providers IE 8 uses in the Search bar. In this console, the user may choose the default search provider by clicking the name of the search provider and the **Set as Default** button. The user may also **Enable** or **Disable** suggestions for the selected search provider. The search suggestions URL is shown under this option for security reason. Finally, there is a checkbox to **Prevent programs from suggesting changes to my default search provider**. This may be toggled to not allow other applications to change the userÕs default search provider.

Tabbed Browsing Settings

Tabbed browsing is relatively new to IE and has different settings that can be tweaked by clicking **Settings** in the Tabs section of the **General** tab as shown in Figure 4.51. One of the new features worth mentioning is that each tab in IE now runs its own process of iexplore.exe; this is evident by looking at the Task Manager with multiple IE tabs. This is a great security feature that Microsoft added to IE 8.

The Tabbed Browsing Settings are not very complex. The Þrst tab is to enable or disable tabbed browsing in IE and requires a restart of the application to apply. The user can also conÞgure what page to open, when to open a new tab, what to do when a pop-up is encountered, and where to open links from other programs.

Appearance

The Appearance section allows the customizing of colors, languages, fonts, and accessibility. These options are normally just user preference and do not modify the technical aspect of the Web browsing experience. The

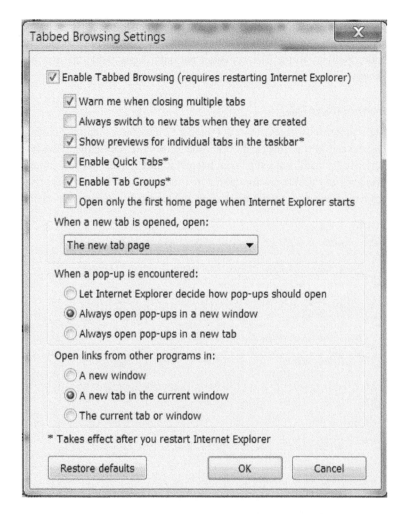

Colors button will bring up color options. By default, IE will use Windows colors. The **Languages** button does affect the Web browsing experience because it is the language that is sent by the Web browser to the site that is being visited. For instance, if the language is set to Spanish (Colombia) [es-CL], some Web sites will display content in Spanish and even for the Colombian audience. The other option in the language preference is to toggle the use of ÒwwwÓwhen typing a Web address and the sufÞx to use when a Web address is typed and **Ctrl+Shift+Enter** is pressed. By default, ÒwwwÓand ÒcomÓare added to Web address. The **Font** button allows the setting of the language script and what Web page font and plain text font to use if the Web page does not specify. Finally, the **Accessibility** button allows the conÞguration of what type of font styles, sizes, and colors the

Web browser will interpret and display. The option to use a user-supplied style sheet is also available. Enabling these options will still download the entire Web site to the user computer but only display what the user has chosen not to ignore.

Connections Tab

The **Connections** tab as shown in Figure 4.52 includes settings to conÞgure Dial-up and VPN settings and Local Area Network (LAN) settings. The Þrst button is the traditional setup for an Internet connection that has been around Windows and IE releases for quite a few versions. In Windows 7, the wizard has improved at setting up devices and hardware detection. This setup

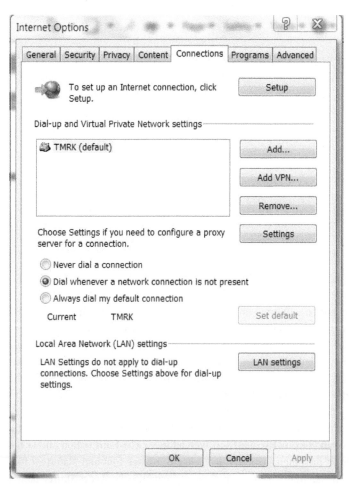

■ **FIGURE 4.52** Connections Tab

wizard will guide a user through setting up a connection on the individual computer. The wizard sets up dial-up connections, VPN connections, and any local area connections.

Under the **Setup** button is the Dial-up and Virtual Private Network settings. If the user has any Dial-up and/or VPN connections conþgured, they will show in this box. From here, the user can click **Add** to conþgure a Dial-up or Broadband (PPPoE) connection. The wizard is straightforward and requires the user to input the username and password provided by the ISP. The **Add VPN** button will initiate the Create a VPN connection wizard discussed in Chapter 5 ÒManaging the Windows 7 Desktop Environment.Ó The **Remove** button will remove the selected connection and the **Settings** button will pop up the settings for the selected device. Under the connections box is the radio button option to **Never dial a connection**, **Dial whenever a network connection is not present**, or **Always dial my default connection**.

Finally, the **LAN settings** button will pop up the LAN Settings. Here, the user can conþgure Automatic conþguration. IE 8, by default, will automatically detect if a connection to the Internet is through the LAN. This option can be unchecked if no automatic detection is necessary. In the proxy server options, the user can conþgure a proxy server to use while Web browsing. Depending on the LAN conþguration in the location the user is, this may need to be conþgured to access the Web. Finally, there is a check box to **Bypass proxy server for local addresses**. This option will not use the proxy server conþgured when accessing an address in the same LAN.

Programs Tab

The **Programs** tab is not as complex as the **General** or **Advanced** tab. Here, the user can set IE as the default Web browser, manage add-ons, and choose what programs to use by default for HTML editing and other Internet services as shown in Figure 4.53.

Under the Default Web browser section, the user may click **Make default** to set IE as the default Web browser. The check box will toggle a prompt when IE is opened and not set as the default Web browser to ask the user to make it so. We recommend this be unchecked for its annoying reputation.

The **Manage add-ons** button will open the Manage add-ons console to manage any add-on that has been installed to IE 8. By default, Toolbars and Extensions, Search providers, Accelerators, and InPrivate Filtering will be enabled as add-ons. As a user installs more add-ons, there will be more options here. Toolbars and Extensions can be enabled or disabled. Generally,

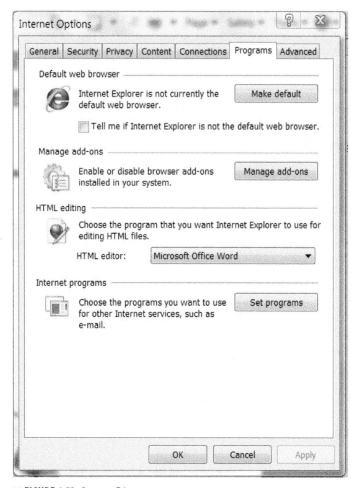

■ **FIGURE 4.53** Programs Tab

when IE 8 has issues, it is due to an extension. Ensuring that only approved extensions are running is critical to maintaining a safe browsing experience for the user. Other add-ons have been addressed previously in this section.

Finally, the HTML editing section sets the default HTML editor when the user chooses to edit a Web page that is being visited. The **Set programs** button will initiate the Default Programs referenced in the next section.

Advanced Tab

The **Advanced** tab in Internet Options is the most complex Internet Options tab (Figure 4.54). The Settings section has a number of check boxes related

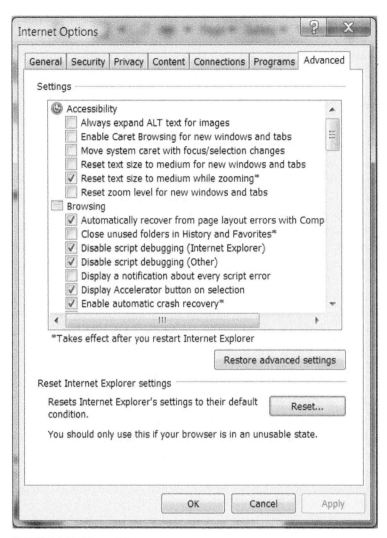

■ FIGURE 4.54 Advanced Tab

to accessibility, browsing, international, multimedia, printing, search, and security settings. These settings generally do not need to be changed unless a business critical application requires it. Additionally, there are two very important buttons: the **Restore advanced settings** and **Reset** buttons. The **Restore advanced settings** button will reset the settings above it to the default value when IE 8 was Þrst initiated. The other **Reset** button will reset all IE 8 settings including: toolbars, add-ons, browser settings, privacy, set-tings, security settings, tabbed browsing settings, advanced options, and pop-up settings. There is also a **Delete personal settings** check box before doing the full reset. These two buttons must be pressed after removing malware from a Windows 7 machine. Most malware on Windows 7 will likely be downloaded via IE 8, and will attempt to change these settings. Resetting IE 8 to the default settings will be very helpful to the administrator when troubleshooting Web browsing related problems.

APPLICATIONS

One of the main advantages of Microsoft Windows operating systems is the availability of endless third-party applications. As an administrator or end user, you will need to install, conÞgure, and maintain applications on Windows 7 computers. Installing and conÞguring applications on Windows 7 prior to deployment is a best practice to ensure a standardized computing environment. However, requests for installing new applications on computers will also surely come from end users. As an administrator, you will also be required to ensure these applications are up-to-date, and run properly for the end user, and even uninstall applications. Although most of the applications have very simple-to-use installations, problems are sure to arise. User Account Control can play a large role when installing, attempting to run, or even uninstalling applications. This chapter focuses on installing, maintaining, and uninstalling applications.

ApplicationU AC

User Account Control, introduced in Windows Vista and one of the main complaints from the end user side (even the main cause of Windows VistaÕs failure), changes the way applications are installed, run, write data, and use permissions. Hence, why UAC is the Þrst topic of this section; it is critical to understand these essentials prior to installing and attempting to maintain stable applications in Windows 7.

Windows 7 divides applications into two categories:

- UAC-compliant Ð Any application written speciÞcally for Windows Vista and/or Windows 7 architecture should be UAC-compliant and even have a UAC-compliant logo. These applications understand the UAC architecture explained below and allow applications to run smoothly with the standard user privilege, and when administrator privileges are required within the application a UAC prompt will display.
- Legacy ÐAny application written for Windows XP or earlier versions of Windows is considered a legacy application, as it does not use or understand UAC architecture, so Windows 7 must compensate with compatibilitym ode.

Whether logged in as an administrator or standard user, Windows 7 UAC runs applications with a standard user token. This is an added security feature to reduce the attack surface on the operating system level. Applications that run with standard user privileges cannot write to system files or system registry locations. If the application must write to a system location, the UAC will prompt the user for credentials or consent. An administrative user can still run the application with an administrator token the entire time but not by default. Running an application with the administrator token requires right-clicking the application or shortcut and selecting **Run as administrator**. From that point forth, the application is running with full administrative privileges and can write to system files and system registry locations.

Legacy applications also run with a user's standard access token. To support the UAC architecture, Microsoft introduced the compatibility mode to use virtualized file and registry locations. When an application attempts to write to a system file or system registry, Windows 7 will give the application a private copy of the requested files and save them in the user's profile folder. When the application requests the same file again, Windows 7 will give it the private file in the user's profile folder.

Windows 7 identifies the publisher of any application that attempts to run as administrator and marks it depending on the publisher:

- Windows7/ Windows Vista
- Publisher verified or signed
- Publisher not verified or signed

Depending on the classification, a color-coded elevation prompt will display a UAC message about the application:

- Administrative application – blue-green background with the message, "Windows needs your permission to continue"
- Signed by Authenticode and trusted – gray background with the message, "A program needs your permission to continue"
- Blocked publisher or blocked by Group Policy – red background with the message, "The application is blocked from running"
- Unsigned or signed by unverified publisher – yellow background with the message, "An unidentified program wants access to your computer"

Run as Administrator

Certain applications need to run as administrator to perform administrative tasks, whereas some legacy applications require administrator privileges to

NOTE

Windows Application Compatibility Toolkit (ACT) can assist administrators in solving many compatibility issues with applications. ACT allows application compatibility shims to be created to trick applications that require specific operating systems or privileges to run by setting application inquiries to True. This solution will address the **Run as administrator issue** for end users.

run at all. An application may be run as administrator once or conþgured to always run as administrator.

To run an application as an administrator once, right-click the application or shortcut and click **Run as administrator**. Depending on the userÕs rights, a UAC prompt will ask for administrative credentials for an administratorÕs account or simple consent.

To set an application to always run as administrator, do the following:

1. Locate the shortcut of the application on the Start Menu, right-click the shortcut, and select **Properties**.
2. Clickt he **Compatibility**t ab.

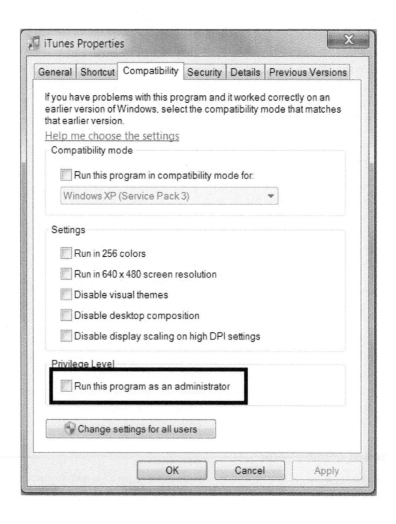

■ **FIGURE 4.55** Run as Administrator

3. If you are setting run as administrator only for the current user, check the **Run this program as an administrator** box in the Privilege Level section as shown in Figure 4.55. Click **OK**.

4. If you are setting run as administrator for all users, click **Change settings for all users**.

   ❑ In the Properties dialog for the applicatioñs executable Þle, check the **Run this program as an administrator** box in the Privilege Level section. Click **OK**.

InstallingA pplications

If you have been using Windows Vista, you woñt see much of a difference when installing applications in Windows 7. If you have been using Windows XP, installing applications in Windows 7 will be a little bit different. The key difference is that in Windows 7, there is no **Add or Remove Programs** applet in the Control Panel. There is simply a **Programs** section of the Control Panel.

Installing applications is still fairly straightforward in Windows 7. The key thing to note is that there are two types of applications. There are applications that come as part of Windows 7, called Windows Features. There are also add-on and third-party applications that can installed. These two types of applications are installed by different methods. In this section, we will go over the different methods for installing each type of application.

Installing Windows Features

Windows Features are programs and applications that are built into Windows 7. These features include applications like games, SNMP support, and telnet support. Some of these programs are enabled by default, whereas some are disabled by default. You can also enable and disable these programs using the Control Panel.

To enable a Windows Feature via the Control Panel:

1. Select **Start | Control Panel**.
2. Once inside Control Panel, select **Programs**.
3. Now in the Programs and Features section, select **Turn Windows features on or off**.
4. As shown in Figure 4.56, the Windows Feature window will appear. From here, simply check the Windows Features you want to enable. You can also uncheck the Windows Features you want tod isable.

■ FIGURE 4.56 Windows Feature Window

Installing Add-on Applications

Add-on and third-party applications can be installed in three main ways: via media (CD,DVD, or USB Drive), via the Internet, or from a network connection. Installing from any of these methods is pretty much the same. You must locate the installation package and run that package.

Installing applications may require escalated privileges. Privilege escalation can be done in two ways. First, if you run the installation package with User Account Control enabled and the installation requires administrative privileges, you may be prompted by UAC to allow administrative access to the installation package. You can also manually escalate privilege at the start of the installation by right-clicking on the installation package and selecting **Run as administrator**. This will cause the installation to initiate using administrator privileges from the beginning.

DefaultA pplications

Windows 7 allows you to set default settings for programs and applications. You can conÞgure default settings for media and devices, and set default programs to use when opening Þles. These settings can be of great convenience to you. They can help remove the amount of manual steps necessary to perform daily tasks.

Change Default Settings for Media or Devices

Windows 7 allows you to set defaults for what happens when certain types of media are inserted into the system, and when certain devices are added to the system. For example, you can conÞgure your system so that Windows 7 attempts to burn an audio CD anytime a blank CD is inserted into the system. This way, you donÕt have to always manually kick off the audio CD wizard every time you insert a blank CD.

To set media defaults via the Control Panel:

1. Select **Start | Control Panel**.
2. Once inside Control Panel, select **Programs**.
3. Now in the Default Programs section, select **Change default settings** for media or devices.
4. As shown in Figure 4.57, the AutoPlay window will appear. From the AutoPlay window, you can conÞgure AutoPlay settings for audio CDs, DVD movies, blank CDs and many other media and device types.

There will be different options available for each media or device type. Some of the more common options are **Take no action**, **Ask me every time**,

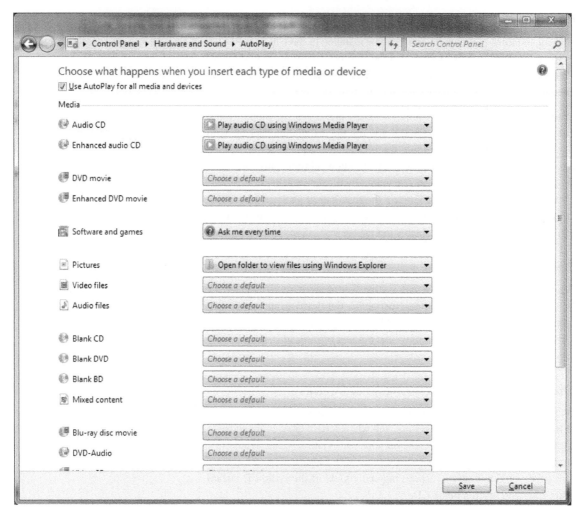

■ **FIGURE 4.57** AutoPlay Window

Play using Windows Media Player, and **Open folder to view Þles using Windows Explorer**.

Make a File Type Always Open in a Specific Program

Different applications can be used to open different types of Þles. Often times, you will have multiple applications on systems that can be set to open a single type of Þle. File Type Association allows you to specify what program to use to open a speciÞc Þle type or protocol. Setting this default association makes opening Þles in the application of your choice a seamless matter.

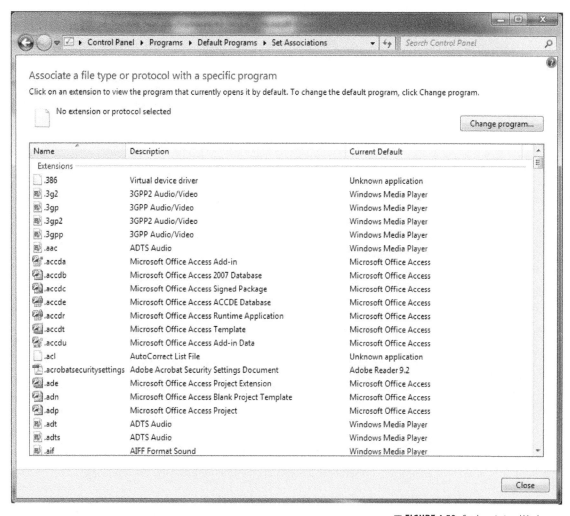

■ **FIGURE 4.58** Set Associations Window

To set File Type Association via the Control Panel:

1. Select **Start | Control Panel**.
2. Once inside Control Panel, select **Programs**.
3. Now in the Default Programs section, select **Make a Þle type always open** in a speciÞc program.
4. As shown in Figure 4.58, the Set Associations window will appear. Select the Þle type you would like to change, and click **Change Program**.
5. As shown in Figure 4.59, the Open with window will appear. This is where you choose which program to use to open the Þle type.

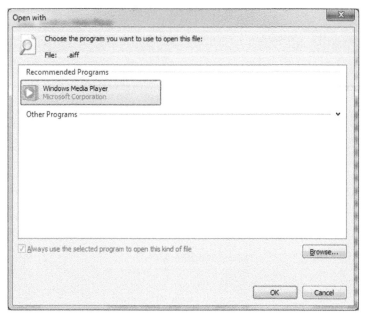

■ **FIGURE 4.59** Open with Window

Set Your Default Programs

This option is similar to the option previously discussed. This option allows you to set Þle type and protocol associations for speciÞc Windows programs. You can choose a speciÞc program and make it the default for all Þle types and protocols it is capable of opening.

To set these defaults via the Control Panel, do the following:

1. Select **Start | Control Panel**.
2. Once inside Control Panel, select **Programs**.
3. Now in the Default Programs section, select **Set your default programs**.
4. As shown in Figure 4.60, the Set Default Programs window appears. In the programs pane, select the program you would like to set defaults for.

Once the program is selected, you have two options:

- **Set this program as default** ÐThis option will set the program as default for all Þle types and protocols it is capable of opening.
- **Choose defaults for this program** ÐAs shown in Figure 4.61, this option allows you to specify which Þle types and protocols the program will be used with by default.

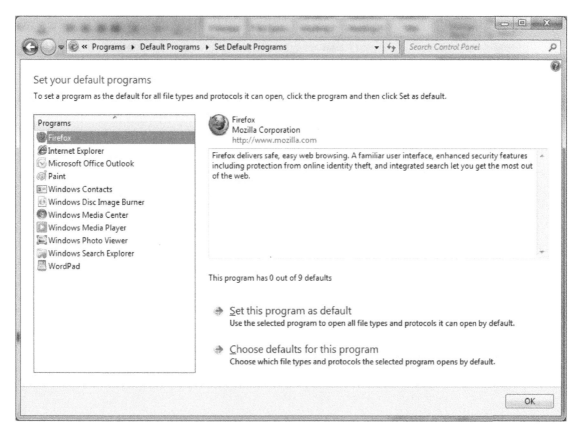

■ **FIGURE 4.60** Set Default Programs Window

■ SUMMARY

This chapter explained the new Windows 7 desktop environment, including the new user interface, Windows Explorer, IE, and applications. This should serve as a reference to better conþgure and manage an end userõ desktop environment. Many of the new features introduced in Chapter 1, Ûntroduction to Windows 7Õwere explained in more detail in this chapter.

While most of this chapter may have appeared as basic knowledge for experienced administrators, it is critical to understand the new features and desktop environment to know exactly what will be managed and conþgured in the next chapters. Additionally, many of the topics introduced in this chapter should be passed on to your end users. Most of the new features explained will make your end users more efþcient and productive. A well conþgured desktop environment will also result in less service and help desk calls.

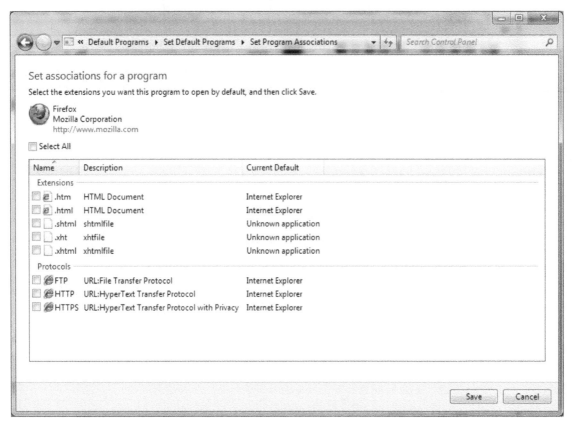

■ **FIGURE 4.61** Set Program Associations Window

Chapter 5, ÒManaging the Windows 7 Desktop EnvironmentÓ will build on this chapter from an administrator perspective as it will include a reference to the local management tools, managing hardware devices and drivers, and managing disk and Þle systems. Chapter 6, ÒNetworking and MobilityÓ will continue to build on this chapter, discussing networking and mobility for the end users. Chapter 7, ÒManaging Windows 7 in an Enterprise EnvironmentÓ will explain how to conÞgure many of these settings for more than a single system and in an enterprise environment.

Managing the Windows 7 Desktop Environment

INFORMATION IN THIS CHAPTER

- LocalM anagement Tools
- Managing Hardware Devices and Drivers
- Managing Disks and File Systems
- Summary

Windows 7 comes with a variety of tools for managing your system. There are tools for managing the local system, managing hardware and devices, and managing disks and file systems. Some of these tools are new, and some have been around for a while. Windows 7 can be a quite complex operating system. So you need to make sure that you understand all the tools that have been created to make the job of managing systems easier.

LOCAL MANAGEMENT TOOLS

Windows 7 includes many management tools to help manage your system. We will review a few of the most commonly used ones. These are as follows:

- ControlP anel
- MicrosoftM anagementC onsole3.0
- ComputerM anagementC onsole
- Local GroupPol icyEdi tor
- WindowsR egistry

Each of these management tools serves a different purpose and provides different functionality. It's important that you have a good understanding of all these tools in order to properly manage your system.

DOI: 10.1016/B978-1-59749-561-5.00005-X

ControlP anel

The Control Panel has long been a central place to go to configure your Windows system. The look has changed over the years, but tools have stayed pretty similar, with a few additions. The Windows 7 Control Panel is broken down into several categories and subcategories. Control Panel is accessed from the Start menu. When you first open Control Panel, you see the main categories and some of the tasks within the subcategories. To see the entire list of subcategories, you must click on a category heading.

The categories and subcategories available in Control Panel are as follows:

- **System and Security** – Action Center, Windows Firewall, System, Windows Update, Power Options, Backup and Restore, BitLocker DriveE ncryption, Administrative Tools
- **Network and Internet** – Network and Sharing Center, HomeGroup, InternetO ptions
- **Hardware and Sound** – Devices and Printers, AutoPlay, Sound, Power Options, Display, Windows Mobility Center, Biometric Devices
- **Programs** – Programs and Features, Default Programs, Desktop Gadgets
- **User Accounts and Family Safety** – User Accounts, Parental Controls, Windows CardSpace, Credential Manager, Mail
- **Appearance and Personalization** – Personalization, Display, Desktop Gadgets, Taskbar and Start Menu, Ease of Access Center, Folder Options, Fonts
- **Clock, Language, and Region** – Date and Time, Region and Language
- **Ease of Access**–E aseof AccessC enter,S peechR ecognition

System and Security

The **System and Security** category in Control Panel contains applets that allow you to secure, fine tune, and optimize your system. The subcategories under the **System and Security** category are Action Center, Windows Firewall, System, Windows Update, Power Options, Backup and Restore, BitLocker Drive Encryption, and Administrative Tools. We will briefly discuss each of these items.

Action Center

The Action Center helps you solve basic system issues. It can help troubleshoot security, maintenance, and performance issues. In the **Action Center** section of the Control Panel, you have four options: **Review your computer's status and solve issues**, **Change User Account Control settings**, **Troubleshoot common computer problems**, and **Restore your computer to an earlier time**.

TIP

The Control Panel consists of two main views: Category view and Icon view. Icon view is further divided into small and large icons. When you set the Control Panel to Icon view, you are able to see all of the applets in the Control Panel.

If you choose **Review your computer's status and solve issues**, the Action Center will open. It will display any issues that your system has detected. These could be issues with security, Windows Update, Windows Backup, or a host of other issues.

If you choose **Change User Account Control settings**, the User Account Control Settings window, as seen in Figure 5.1, will open. User Account Control (UAC) is used to control whether programs can make changes to your system. This is important because you don't want malicious programs to be able to make system changes.

The User Account Control Settings window includes four options:

- **Always notify** – The user will always be notified when either the user or a program attempts to make changes to the system.

■ **FIGURE 5.1** User Account Control Settings Window

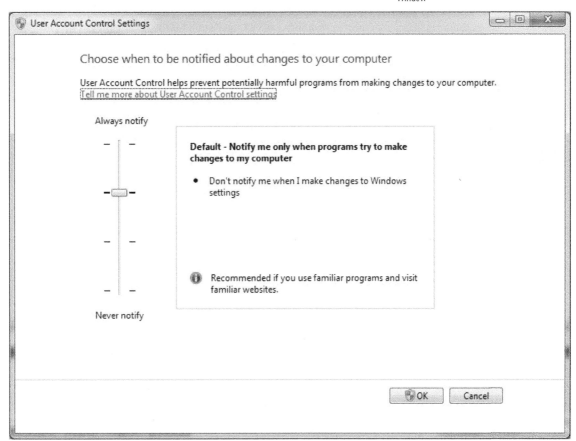

- **Notify me only when programs attempt to make changes to my desktop** – The desktop will be dimmed when these attempts are made. This is the default option.
- **Notify me only when programs attempt to make changes to my desktop (do not dim my desktop)** – The desktop will not be dimmed when these attempts are made.
- **Never notify** – The user is never be notified when either the user or programs attempt to make changes to the system.

If you choose **Troubleshoot common computer problems**, the troubleshooting applet will open. The troubleshooting applet, as seen in Figure 5.2, will allow you to troubleshoot issues with programs, hardware, internet connections, appearance, personalization, and security.

Choosing the option named **Restore your computer to an earlier time** will open the Recovery window. In the Recovery window, you can open the System Restore wizard. The System Restore wizard will allow you to restore system files and settings without losing your personal files and data. The System Restore wizard will allow you to select a restore point, as seen in Figure 5.3. Windows 7 will restore your system to the state it was when the restore point was created.

■ **FIGURE 5.2** Troubleshooting Applet

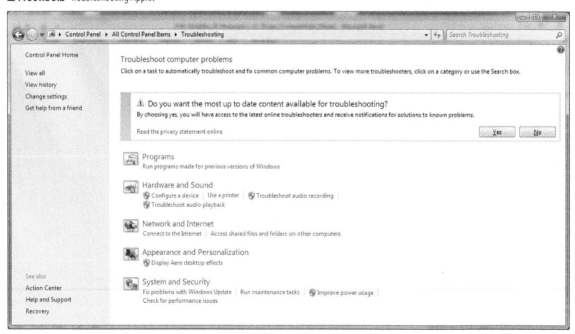

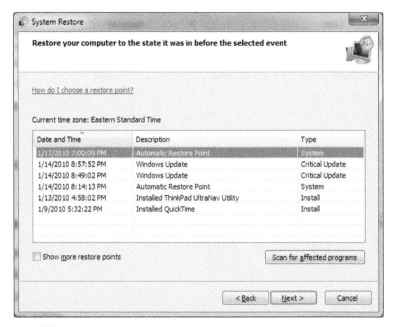

■ FIGURE 5.3 Restore Point Selection Window

The Recovery window also includes an option for **Advanced Recovery Methods**. These **Advanced Recovery Methods** will restore your system, but everything will be replaced, including your personal files and data. You can restore your system using a previously created image. You can also choose to reinstall Windows 7, using the installation media. If you choose either of these methods, you are given the option to back up your important files and data.

Windows Firewall

The Windows Firewall is used to protect your Windows system from network-based threats. You can control who has access to your system, and what access they have. The Windows Firewall applet allows you to configure these firewall settings. In the **Windows Firewall** section of the Control Panel, you have two options: **Check firewall status** and **Allow a program through Windows Firewall**.

The **Check firewall status** option will bring up the Windows Firewall window, as seen in Figure 5.4. This option will allow you to see if Windows Firewall is enabled or disabled on your system. You can also see Windows Firewall settings for incoming connections and notifications.

The option named **Allow a program through Windows Firewall** will bring up the Allowed Programs window, as seen in Figure 5.5. Here, you can see

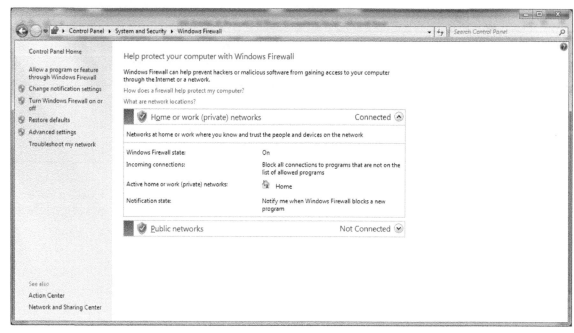

■ **FIGURE 5.4** Windows Firewall Window

■ **FIGURE 5.5** Allowed Programs Window

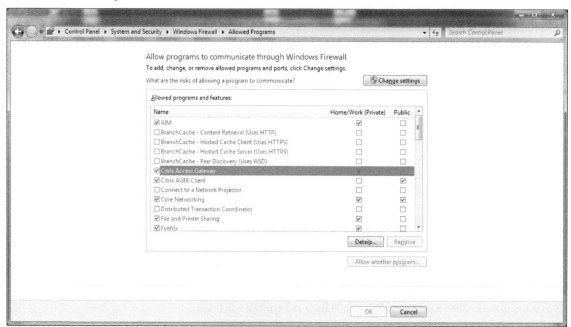

what programs are allowed by Windows Firewall. If you want to change these settings, you must choose the **Change settings** option. You can now select a program to allow and what networks the program is allowed to communicate on. The **Details** option will show you the path to the executable for the application being allowed. If you want to allow a program not listed, you can choose the **Allow another program** option. You can then specify the location of another program you want to allow through the firewall.

System

The **System** section of the Control Panel allows you to view and configure basic system settings. The **System** section has five options: **View amount of RAM and processor speed**, **Check the Windows Experience Index**, **Allow remote access**, **See the name of the computer**, and **Device Manager**.

The option named **View amount of RAM and processor speed** will launch the System window, as seen in Figure 5.6. Here, you can view basic system information. You can see the processor speed, the amount of RAM in the system, the system type, computer name, and other important information.

■ **FIGURE 5.6** System Window

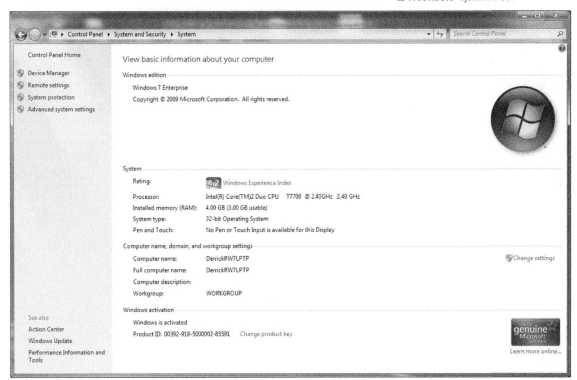

The option named **Check the Windows Experience Index** will launch the Performance Information and Tools window, as seen in Figure 5.7. You can see your system's Windows Experience Index. The Windows Experience Index is a number between 1.0 and 7.9 that represents the overall performance of your system. Your index is based on five components: processor, memory, graphics, gaming graphics, and primary hard disk. Each of these components is given a rating. Your index is based on the lowest individual score for the components. You can rerun the assessment any time you wish. This will help you determine if changes made to the system increased or decreasedo verallpe rformance.

The option named **Allow Remote Access** will bring up the **Remote** tab of the System Properties window. You can use this tab to enable or disable **Remote Assistance**. You can also use it to enable or disable **Remote Desktop**.

Selecting the option named **See the name of this computer** will launch the System window. You can view the name and description of the computer. In addition, you can view the workgroup or domain the computer resides in. You can also use this window to change the name of the computer or change the workgroup or domain the computer resides in.

■ **FIGURE 5.7** Performance Information and Tools Window

This **Device Manager** option will bring up the Device Manager window. Device Manager can be used to manage the hardware devices in your system. You can install, disable, and uninstall devices. You can update drivers. You can also use Device Manager to determine when there is a problem with one of your hardware devices and when one of your devices not functioning properly.

Windows Update

Windows Update is used to keep your system up-to-date with the latest updates and patches. Windows Update can automatically download and install device drivers, OS patches, and application patches. The **Windows Update** section of the Control Panel has three options: **Turn automatic updating on or off**, **Check for updates**, and **View installed updates**.

The option named **Turn Automatic Updating on or off** will bring up the Windows Update Change Settings window, as seen in Figure 5.8.

■ FIGURE 5.8 Windows Update Change Settings Window

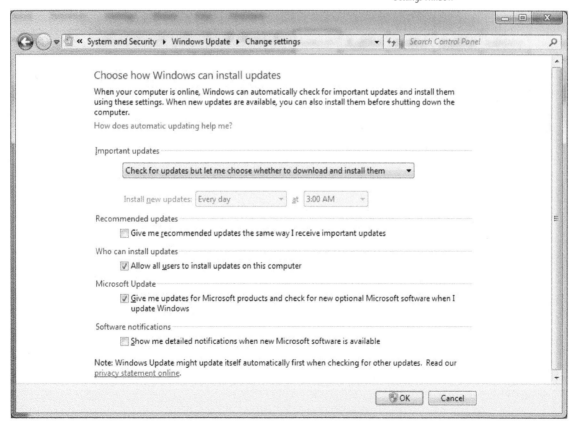

Here, you can enable or disable Windows Update on your system. You can also control how updates are handled. You can set whether updates are automatically downloaded and installed, or whether user intervention is necessary.

The **Check for updates** option brings up the Windows Update window, as seen in Figure 5.9. Windows Update will check and see what updates are available for your system. It will also let you know when your system was lastupda ted.

Selecting **View installed updates** will bring up the Installed Updates window. The Installed Updates window will list all the updates that have been installed on your system. You can see operating system updates, application updates, and security updates. The Installed Updates window also allows you to uninstall updates that you would like to remove from your system.

■ **FIGURE 5.9** Windows Update Window

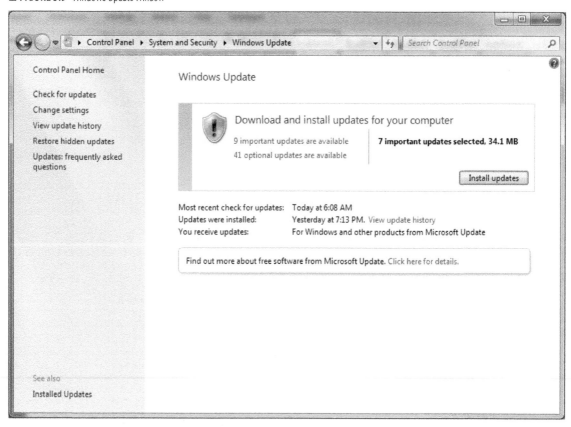

Power Options

The **Power Options** section of the Control Panel includes the following options: **Change battery settings**, **Require a password when the computer wakes**, **Change what the power buttons do**, and **Change when the computer sleeps**.

The **Change battery settings** option will bring up the Power Options window. The Power Options window allows you to choose a power plan. Power plans determine how your system will manage energy consumption, especially when running on battery power. A good power plan will help extend the amount of time your system can run on battery power.

Choosing **Require a password when the computer wakes** brings up the Power Options System Settings window. This window will allow you to configure whether a user has to enter a password when the system comes out of sleep mode. Take note that in order to make changes to this setting, you have to first select the **Change settings that are currently unavailable** option.

Choosing **Change what the power buttons do** also brings up the Power Options System Settings window. You can configure what your system does when you press the **power** or **sleep** buttons. You can also configure what happens when you close the lid on your laptop.

Choosing **Change when the computer sleeps** will launch the Edit Plan Setting window. This window will allow you the change the settings for your current power plan. You can control when the display will dim or turn off. You can configure when the system will enter sleep mode. You can also adjust the screen brightness.

Backup and Restore

The **Backup and Restore** section of the Control Panel includes two options: **Back up your computer** and **Restore files from a backup**.

The **Back up your computer** option will launch the Backup and Restore window, as seen in Figure 5.10. You can use the Backup and Restore window to create a system image, create a system repair, or to perform a backup of your s ystem.

The **Back up now** option will start a new back up of your system. The backup will use your current backup device/location. The **Turn on schedule** option will allow you to set up periodic backups of your system. You should schedule these backups for a time when the system will be online, but not in use. The **Change settings** option will allow you to change the default settings for your backups. For example, you can use this to change the default backup location.

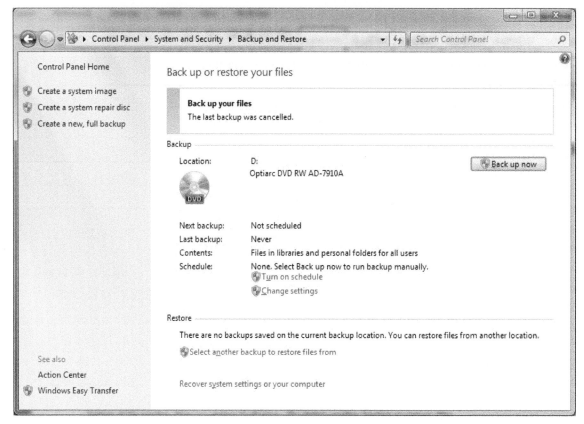

■ **FIGURE 5.10**   Backup and Restore Window

The **Restore files from a backup** option will bring up the Backup and Restore window. At the bottom of the window, there is a Restore section. The **Select another backup to restore files from** option will bring up the Restore Files wizard. The Restore Files wizard will walk you through while doing a restore. You will have to specify the location of the backup to restore from, the files you want to restore, and what you want to do with the restored files.

BitLocker Drive Encryption

BitLocker is covered in depth in Chapter 8, "Securing Windows 7."

Administrative Tools

The **Administrative Tools** section includes the following options: **Free up disk space**, **Defragment your hard drive**, **Create and format hard disk partitions**, **View event logs**, and **Schedule tasks**.

Choosing **Free up disk space** will launch the Disk Cleanup applet, as seen in Figure 5.11. The Disk Cleanup applet will scan your system and determine

■ **FIGURE 5.11** Disk Cleanup

what can be done to free up space on your disks. You can delete Downloaded Program Files, Temporary Internet Files, Offline Webpages, files in the Recycle Bin, Setup Log Files, Temporary Files, Thumbnails, Per user archived Windows Error Reports, and System archived Windows Error Reports.

The Disk Cleanup applet also includes an option to **Clean up system files**. This option will cause the Disk Cleanup applet to open with a tab called **More Options**. On the **More Options** tab you have the option to remove programs that you do not use. You also have to option to remove older system restore points.

Choosing the **Free up disk space** option will bring up the Disk Defragmenter. The Disk Defragmenter can help improve performance of your drives. Fragmentation occurs when files split all over your disks. When this happens, you disk has to do more work to access files. The Disk Defragmenter will move your files to a contiguous location. This will speed disk access performance.

Choosing the **Create and format hard disk partitions** option will bring up the Disk Management console. You can use the Disk Management console to manage your hard disks and disk partitions. You can create partitions and format partitions. You can also configure fault tolerance for your disks.

Choosing the **View event logs** option will open the Windows Event Viewer. You can view the Windows logs: Application, Security, Setup, and System. You can also view individual logs for certain Windows applications and Windows services. You can use Event Viewer to view logs on the local system or a remote system.

Choosing the **Schedule tasks** option will launch Task Scheduler, as seen in Figure 5.12. Using Task Scheduler, you can schedule tasks to run at specified times. This is great for administrative and maintenance tasks that must be run on a regular basis.

Task Scheduler offers great flexibility. You can use the Create Basic Task wizard or manually create a task. You can schedule tasks to run once, daily, weekly, monthly, when the computer starts, when a user logs on, or when a specific event is logged. The task can be to run a program or script, send an email, or display a message. Task Scheduler also allows you to import and export tasks. This is useful if you want to run the same task on multiple systems.

Network and Internet

The **Network and Internet** category in the Control Panel contains applets that let you configure your network settings and your Internet settings. You can connect to wired and wireless networks. You can configure sharing permissions. You can configure the behavior of Internet Explorer and other applications. The subcategories under the **Network and Internet** category are Network and Sharing Center, HomeGroup, and Internet Options.

Network and Sharing Center

The Network and Sharing Center allows you to configure local network settings for your system. You can connect to a network and determine what resources can be accessed by other computers. The Network and Sharing Center contains four options: **View network status and tasks**, **Connect to a network**, **View network computers and devices**, and **Add a wireless device to the network**.

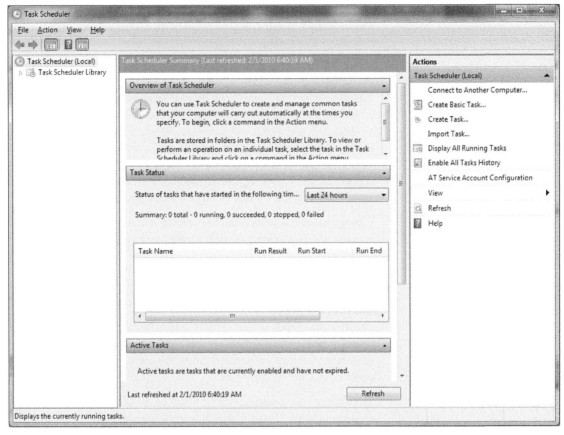

Choosing the **View network status and tasks** option will bring up the Network and Sharing Center. The Network and Sharing Center lets you configure all aspects of your system networking. You can view the status of your active networks. You can also configure settings for your network adapters.

Choosing the **Connect to a network** option brings up the wireless network connection dialog. You can see what wireless network you're currently connected to, if any. You can also connect to a network or disconnect from a network.

Choosing the **View network computers and devices** option will bring up the Network window. You can use this to view the other computers and media devices on your network. You can also use the Network window to connect to these computers and devices.

Choosing **Add a wireless device to the network** will bring up the Add a Device wizard. It will scan your network for wireless devices that you can connect to your system.

HomeGroup

You can configure a HomeGroup on your home network. A HomeGroup is a collection of computer on the network. Your HomeGroup makes it easy to share files and media with other computers. You can configure sharing settings for your HomeGroup, and other computers that are a member of your HomeGroup will be governed by these settings when they attempt to connect to your computer. The **HomeGroup** section of the Control Panel contains one option: **Change homegroup and sharing options**.

Change homegroup and sharing options will bring up the HomeGroup window. The HomeGroup window allows you to configure settings for your HomeGroup. You can configure what libraries and media other members of your HomeGroup can access.

Internet Options

The **Internet Options** section of Control Panel allows you to manage Internet and Internet Explorer settings for your computer. You can configure security settings and access settings. You can control add-ons, Active-X controls, and other components.

The **Change your homepage** option brings up the **General** tab of the Internet Properties window. Here, you can configure the home page for Internet Explorer. You can use the current page, the default, a blank page, or type in a page.

The **Manage browser add-ons** option brings up the **Programs** tab of the Internet Properties window. You can use the **Manage add-ons** option to launch the Manage Add-ons window. Here, you can configure toolbars, search providers, accelerators, and InPrivate Filtering.

The **Delete browsing history and cookies** option brings up the **General** tab of the Internet Properties window. The Browsing History section allows you to view temporary internet files, cookies, and downloaded program files. You can delete your history, form data, and temporary files.

User Accounts and Family Safety

The **User Accounts and Family Safety** section of Control Panel allows you to configure user settings and controls for your system. You can add and edit user accounts. You can also specify what access different members of your family will have.

User Accounts

The **User Accounts** section of Control Panel allows you to control Windows user settings. User accounts determine who can and cannot access the system. User accounts are also used to determine what rights a user will have on the system. The **User Accounts** section of Control Panel has three options: **Change your account picture**, **Add or remove user accounts**, and **Change your Windows password**.

Change your account picture enables you to associate a picture with your user account. This picture will appear on the Start menu and on the Welcome screen next to your user name. The **Change your account picture** option will bring up the Change Your Picture window, as seen in Figure 5.13. You can use this window to change the picture associated with your user account. You can use one of the preselected pictures or add your own picture.

■ **FIGURE 5.13** Change Your Picture Window

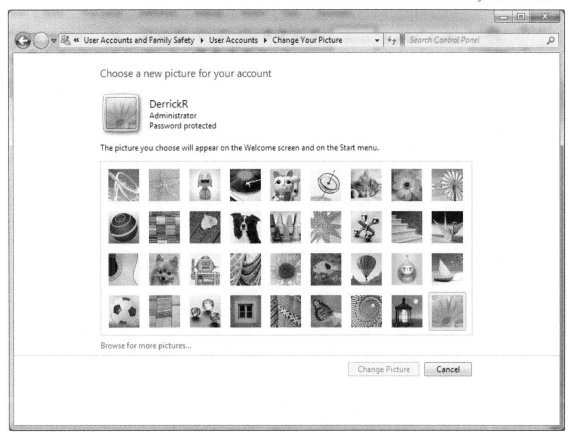

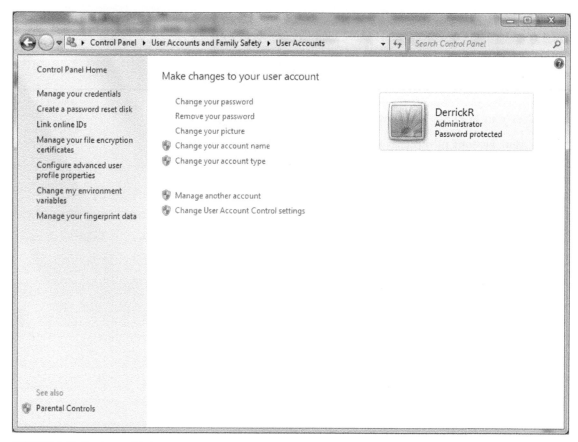

■ FIGURE 5.14 User Accounts Window

The **Add or remove user accounts** option will bring up the User Accounts window, as seen in Figure 5.14. The User Accounts window allows you to change your password, remove your password, change your picture, change your account name, change your account type, manage another account, or changeU ACs ettings.

The **Change Your Windows Password** option will also bring up the User Accounts window. Selecting the **Change your password** option will bring up the Change Your Password window. Here, you can change your current password. You can also set up a password hint, just in case you forget your password.

Parental Controls

Parental Controls are used to limit access on your system. You can limit the access other members of your family have. For example, you can prevent younger members of your family from accessing sites that you might deem inappropriate. The **Parental Controls** section of the Control Panel has one option: **Set up parental controls for any user**.

The **Set up parental controls for any user** option will bring up the Parental Controls window. Here, you can select which account you want to set parental controls for. Once you enable Parental Controls for the user, you can control when the user uses the computer and what games they can play, and you can block the use of specific programs.

Windows CardSpace

Windows CardSpace is a system for managing Information Cards. Information Cards can be used to represent a user's identity to Web sites. Each card has a digital signature that is used to keep the card unique for each user and the Web site it's used for. A single user may have many different Information Cards. That's why it's important to have a system to manage and keep track of these cards. The **Windows CardSpace** section of the Control Panel has one option: **Manage Information Cards that are used to log on to online services**.

The **Manage Information Cards that are used to log on to online services** option will launch the Windows CardSpace window, as seen in Figure 5.15. You must then specify if you want to create a personal card or install a managed card. If you create a personal card, then you will be asked what information you want to have presented with the card. If you already have a card and choose to install a managed card, you will be asked for the location ofthe card.

Once you have the card installed on your system, the CardSpace window will allow you to back them up. You can use this backup to move the card to a different system, or to do a restore if your cards or your system become corrupt.

Credential Manager

Nowadays, in order to ensure security, many sites are password protected. Passwords help prevent unwanted users from accessing confidential or private information. With the abundance of password-protected sites, users are finding it difficult to keep track of all these passwords. Windows 7 makes this a little easier with Credential Manager. Credential Manager is used to store passwords for various sites in one place. Instead of remembering all the passwords, the user can simply store them in Credential Manager, and have Windows submit the passwords to the appropriate site. These could be Web sites or network locations. The **Credential Manager** section of Control Panel has one option: **Manage Windows credentials**.

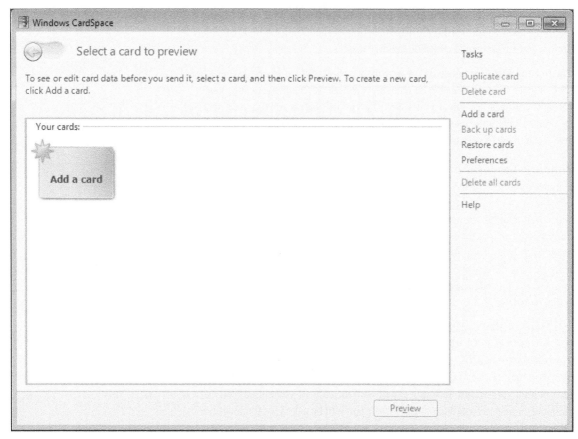

■ **FIGURE 5.15** Windows CardSpace Window

The **Manage Windows credentials** option will bring up the Credential Manager window, as seen in Figure 5.16. Credential Manager will allow you to save Windows credentials, certificate-based credentials, and generic credentials. If you choose to save Windows or generic credentials, you will be prompted to enter the Internet or network address, the user name, and the password. If you choose to save certificate-based credentials, you will have to enter the Internet or network and select the appropriate certificate from yourc ertificates tore.

Credential Manager also gives you the ability to back up and restore your credential vault. This is useful if your credential vault becomes corrupted for any reason. Your vault backups will be protected with a password. This password must be supplied before a restore is allowed. This helps to prevent unwanted users from accessing your credentials.

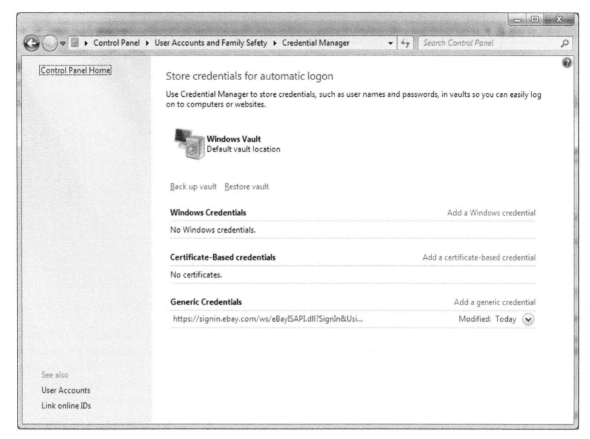

Mail

The **Mail** section of Control Panel allows you to configure Microsoft Outlook profiles. You can have multiple profiles for a single version of Microsoft Outlook. This is very useful if you need to have multiple Outlook identities. Perhaps you want to have one setup for work, and one setup for home. You can have different settings for each of these identities.

If you select the **Mail** option of Control Panel, it will bring up the Mail Setup window, as seen in Figure 5.17. The Mail Setup window allows you to configure e-mail accounts, data files, and profiles. You can associate the e-mail accounts and data files you have created with the desired profile.

Clock Language and Region

Windows 7 is used all over the world. Different regions, countries, and so on have different ways of presenting and displaying information. Different

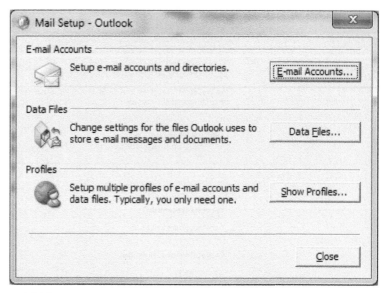

■ FIGURE 5.17   Mail Setup Window

regions have different languages that they communicate in. They have different ways of displaying numbers, dates, and currencies. It's important that Windows 7 allows users to display information in the way that's best for them. The **Clock Language and Region** category of the Control Panel allows you to configure these settings. The **Clock Language and Region** category contains two subcategories: **Date and Time** and **Region and Language**.

Date and Time

The **Date and Time** option in Control Panel allows you to configure time and date information for your system. You can also add the Clock gadget to your desktop, so you can see time from different regions right on your desktop. The **Date and Time** section of Control Panel has four options: **Set the time and date**, **Change the time zone**, **Add clocks for different time zones**, **Add the Clock gadget to the desktop**.

The **Set the time and date** option will bring up the **Date and Time** tab of the Date and Time window, as seen in Figure 5.18. Here, you can change the current date and time. You can also change the time zone of your system. The **Date and Time** tab also allows you to configure whether or not you want to be warned when the clock changes. This is for Daylight Savings Time. Windows will notify you when your clock needs to change for Daylight Savings Time.

Selecting the **Change date and time** option will bring up the Date and Time Settings window. You can use the calendar to change the current date

■ FIGURE 5.18 Date and Time Tab

for the system. You can also change the current time for the system. The Date and Time Settings window also includes an option to change calendar settings. With this option, you can change the format used for the time and the date.

The **Change the time zone** option will also bring up the **Date and Time** tab of the Date and Time window. In the Time Zone section, select the option for **Change time zone**. This will bring up the Time Zone Settings window. Here, you can choose the appropriate time zone and select whether your clock will be automatically adjusted for Daylight Savings Time.

Sometimes, you need to see time for more than one time zone. Let's say your company has multiple offices. You may want to be able to see the time at that office, in addition to the time at your current office. The **Add clocks for different time zones** option allows you to do that. It will bring up the **Additional Clocks** tab of the Date and Time window, as

■ **FIGURE 5.19** Additional Clocks Tab

seen in Figure 5.19. You have the option to add two additional clocks to your system. These clocks will appear when you select the clock area of the system tray.

The **Add the Clock gadget to the desktop** option will bring up the Gadgets window, as seen in Figure 5.20. There is a gadget for the system clock. You can use the Gadgets window to add the Clock gadget to your desktop. If you want, you can add multiple Clock gadgets to your desktop. You can add a gadget for each time zone you would like to see time for.

Region and Language

The **Region and Language** section of the Control Panel allows you to control the format and display of information on your system. You can alter your format and language to be better aligned with the region in which you are most comfortable. The **Region and Language** section of the Control Panel has five options: **Install or uninstall display languages, Change display language, Change location, Change the date, time, or number format, and Change keyboards or other input methods.**

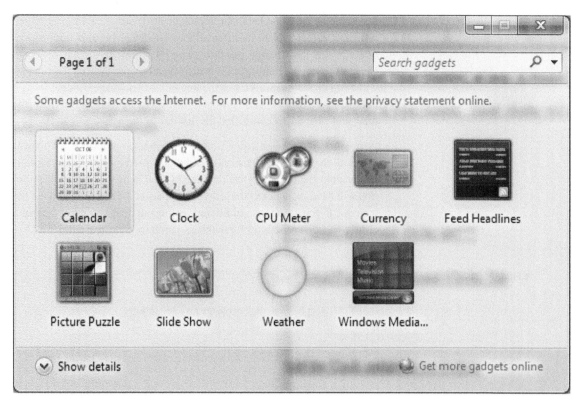

Page 1 of 1

Search gadgets

Some gadgets access the Internet. For more information, see the privacy statement online.

Calendar   Clock   CPU Meter   Currency   Feed Headlines

Picture Puzzle   Slide Show   Weather   Windows Media...

Show details   Get more gadgets online

■ **FIGURE 5.20** Adding a Gadget to Your Desktop

The **Install or uninstall display languages** option will bring up the Install or Uninstall Display Languages wizard. First, you must choose if you want to install or uninstall a display language. If you choose to install a display language, you must select the location of the display language install package. The language pack will be installed and will be available for you to use. If you choose to uninstall a display language, simply select the display language you want to uninstall, and it will be removed for you.

The **Change display language** option will bring up the **Keyboards and Languages** tab of the Region and Language window. Here in the Display language section, you can choose which display language you would like to use. You can choose from any language for which a display pack has been installed. Windows will now be able to display text for that language.

Some applications and Web sites will display specific information based on what location you have selected. You can use the **Change location** option to specify a particular location for your system. This option will take you to the **Location** tab of the Region and Language window. You can change your current location to whatever location best fits your region.

INSTALLING LANGUAGE PACKS

The easiest way to install a language pack is through Windows Update. Langauge packs are listed under the Optional Updates section of Windows Update. You can use Windows Update to download the language pack and then kick off the language package installationw izard.

Dates, times, and numbers can appear in many different formats. Often different regions will have different ways of displaying this information. You can use the **Change the date, time, or number format** option to change the way this information is displayed on your system. This option will bring up the **Formats** tab of the Region and Language window, as seen in Figure 5.21. You can choose what format you want to use for the date, the time, and what day is considered the first day of the week.

First, you can choose a region from the **Format** drop-down list. This will adjust all the formats to those most commonly used by that region. Now, if you want to change the format for an individual item, you can do that also. You will have examples of the different formats in the bottom section of the window. If you select the **Additional settings** option, you will be given a chance to set more settings for numbers, currency, time, and date.

■ FIGURE 5.21 Formats Tab

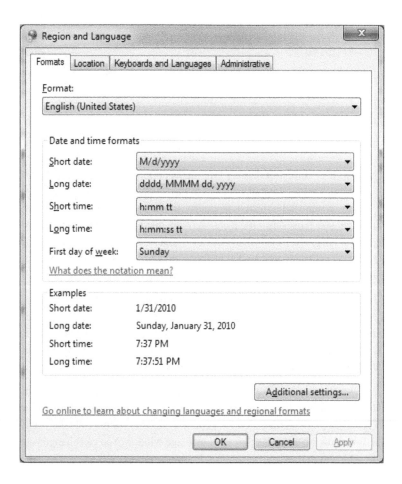

The **Change keyboards and other input methods** option will bring up the **Keyboards and Languages** tab of the Region and Language window. In the keyboards and other input languages section, choosing the **Change keyboards** option will bring up the Text Services and Input Languages window. You can change the input languages used by your devices. You can also change specific items like the keyboard that is used by your system. If you have multiple input languages specified, you must specify the default language for your system to use.

Ease of Access

The **Ease of Access** category of the **Control Panel** does just that. It provides ways of making your computer easier to use. In some cases, these are convenience features. In other cases, without these settings, some people wouldn't be able to use the system at all. The **Ease of Access** category of the Control Panel includes two subcategories: Ease of Access Center and Speech Recognition.

Ease of Access Center

The **Ease of Access Center** section of the Control Panel contains several items for making your system easier to use. You can configure visual modifications, sound modifications, and input modifications. The **Ease of Access Center** section has five options: **Let Windows suggest settings**, **Optimize visual display**, **Replace sounds with visual cues**, **Change how your mouse works**, and **Change how your keyboard works**.

The **Let Windows suggest settings** option will bring up a wizard that Windows will use to determine what settings should be set on your system. The wizard will ask you a series of questions. There will be questions on eyesight, dexterity, hearing, speech, and reasoning. Based on your answers to these questions, Windows will propose a set of settings. Select all the settings that you would like to apply and then click **OK**. The settings will automatically be applied to your system.

The **Optimize visual display** option will bring up the Make the computer easier to see window. Here, you can adjust settings that will make it easier to view information on your screen. You can turn the high contrast theme **on** or **off**. You can have text and descriptions read aloud using **Narrator and Audio Description**. You can make things on the screen larger using **Magnifier**. You can also make the focus rectangle thicker, change the thickness of the blinking cursor, turn off unnecessary animations, and remove background images.

The **Replace sounds with visual cues** option will open the Use text or visual alternatives for sounds window. Here you can set certain visual cues to be used instead of sounds. This is especially useful for the hearing impaired. You can have the system flash the active caption bar, flash the active window, or flash the desktop instead of giving a sound notification. You can also set text captions to be used instead of spoken dialog.

The **Change how your mouse works** option will bring up the Make the mouse easier to use window. You can use this window to configure settings to make it easier to control your mouse. You can change your mouse pointer to something easier to view. You can configure so that you can control your mouse with your keyboard. You can set your system so that a window can be activated by hovering over it with the mouse. You can also set your system so that windows will not be automatically arranged when moved to the edge of the screen.

The **Change how your keyboard works** option will launch the Make the keyboard easier to use window. Here, you can allow the mouse to be controlled by the keyboard. You can turn on sticky keys, toggle keys, and filter keys. You can also have Windows underline keyboard shortcuts and access keys.

Speech Recognition

Speech Recognition can make using your computer much easier. With Speech Recognition, you can control your computer using your voice. You can start programs, dictate into documents, and send e-mails. The **Speech Recognition** section of Control Panel allows you to make this happen, and this section has two options: **Start speech recognition** and **Set up a microphone**.

If Speech Recognition has already been set up, the Speech Recognition application will open. If it has not been set up, then the **Start speech recognition** option will bring up the Set up Speech Recognition wizard. This wizard will take you through a series of questions to properly configure your system. First, your microphone will be set up and then speech recognition will be set up.

To use the Set up Speech Recognition wizard, follow these steps:

1. First, select which type of microphone you will be using. Click **Next**.
2. Properly position your microphone according to the on-screen recommendations. Click **Next**.
3. Read the dialog displayed on the screen. Click **Next**.
4. You should receive a message saying your microphone has been set up. Click **Next**.
5. Enable or disable **document review**. Click **Next**.
6. Choose an activation mode. Click **Next**.
7. View and/or print the **Speech Reference Card**. Click **Next**.
8. Select whether or not to run Speech Recognition at startup. Click **Next**.
9. Speech recognition should now be set up. Select to either run or skip thet utorial.

The **Set up a microphone** option will launch the Microphone Setup wizard. This wizard is the same as the beginning of the wizard used when you first set up Speech Recognition.

MicrosoftM anagementC onsole3 .0

Microsoft has based most of its management applications on the Microsoft Management Console, or the MMC. The MMC provides a framework for building management consoles. This framework has been used by Microsoft and many third-party application vendors for creating their management consoles. In fact, many of configuration tools available in Windows 7 are really MMC consoles with preadded snap-ins. The consoles are then saved in such a way that they cannot be directly altered by users.

The MMC contains snap-ins that are used for system and application management. As seen in Figure 5.22, Windows 7 comes with many built-in MMC snap-ins that can be used to manage the system. These snap-ins can

■ **FIGURE 5.22** Windows 7 MMC Snap-ins

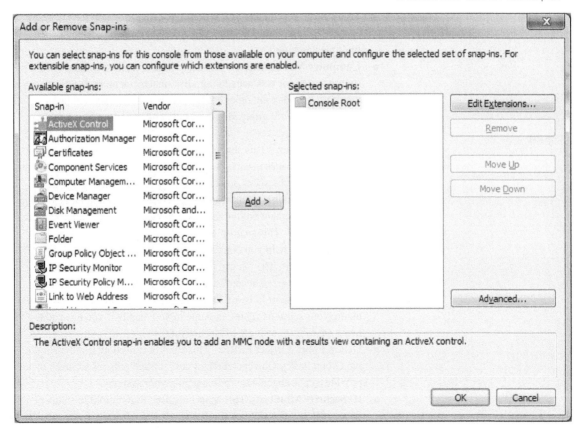

be used to manage user settings, Windows applications, security, and many other vital aspects of the system.

Windows 7 contains the following built-in MMC snap-ins:

- **ActiveX Control** – This snap-in allows you to add individual ActiveX controls to view and configure. ActiveX controls are Internet Explorer plug-ins that are used to add functionality to the browser.
- **Authorization Manager** – This snap-in allows you to set permissions for Authorization Manager-enabled applications.
- **Certificates** – This snap-in allows you to configure the different certificate stores available on the system. Certificates help provide a secure operating environment for your system. You can use them for identification, securing data, and securing communications. There are certificate stores in place for users, applications, and the system itself.
- **Component Services** – This snap-in is used to manage the system's COM+, or Component Services configuration. You can also configure Distributed Computer Object Model (DCOM) and Distributed Transaction Coordinator (DTC) settings using this snap-in. These are especially important when programs need to communicate between multiplec omputers.
- **Computer Management** – This snap-in is actually a collection of snap-ins used for task scheduling, disk management, performance monitoring, and many other configuration and management tasks. These snap-ins are grouped together under **Computer Management** for ease of use.
- **Device Manager** – This snap-in is used for viewing and configuration of hardware devices installed on the system. You disable devices, update drivers, and troubleshoot potential issues with your hardware devices.
- **Disk Management** – This snap-in is used for disk and volume management. You can create volumes, format disks, and enable fault tolerance.
- **Event Viewer** – This snap-in is used to view the system event logs. These logs can help you determine if your system or applications are having problems. The Security log can also be used to determine if there is unauthorized access to your system.
- **Folder** – This snap-in is used to add a folder than can be used for organizing your snap-ins. This can come in very handy if you have added many snap-ins to a single MMC console.
- **Group Policy Object Editor**– This snap-in is used for configuring the Group Policy Objects on the system. Group policies are used to provide a centralized way for managing your systems.
- **IP Security Monitor** – This snap-in is used to monitor the status of your IP Security (IPsec) configuration. IPsec is used to secure

communications between computers. This snap-in can help you determine which IPsec policies are being applied to your systems.

- **IP Security Policy Management** – This snap-in is used to understand and configure the settings in your IPsec policy.
- **Link to Web Address** – This snap-in allows you to add a Web page to the MMC. This can be useful for applications and systems with Web-basedm anagement.
- **Local Users and Groups** – This snap-in allows you to configure users and groups on the local system. You can add user accounts, delete user accounts, and configure various user properties.
- **NAP Client Configuration** – This snap-in allows you to configure Network Access Protection (NAP) client configuration settings. NAP is a security feature that is used to limit who can gain access to your network.
- **Performance Monitor** – This snap-in allows you to monitor your system performance, including memory, hard disks, processors, and many other components.
- **Print Management** – This snap-in is used to manage print servers and printers connected to the system.
- **Resultant Set of Policy** – This snap-in is used to show what settings will be applied to the system after all policies have been applied. This helps when you want to test out your Group Policy settings without actually applying them to the system.
- **Security Configuration and Analysis** – This snap-in provides configuration and analysis of security templates being applied to the system.
- **Security Templates** – This snap-in allows you to edit the security templates that can be applied to the system.
- **Services** – This snap-in allows to you view and configure the properties for services running on the system. You can disable, start, stop, or restart services. You can also configure authentication and fault tolerance for services.
- **Shared Folders** – This snap-in allow you to view properties and status information for file shares that exist on the system. You can see what folders are beings shared and who is accessing them.
- **Task Scheduler** – This snap-in allows you to schedule tasks to be automatically run at specified times and/or at specified intervals.
- **TPM Management** – This snap-in allows you to configure the Trusted Platform Module, if one exists in the system. Trusted Platform Modules are used to generate keys for cryptographic operations.
- **Windows Firewall with Advanced Security** – This snap-in allows you to configure Windows Firewall settings on the system. You can control what processes, applications, and systems can access your system or generate network traffic from your system.

- **WMI Control** – This snap-in allows you to configure and manage the Windows Management Instrumentation (WMI) service. WMI is used for management and monitoring of Windows systems.

To add snap-ins to an MMC console, do the following:

1. Run the command **MMC.exe** from a command prompt or from the Windows 7 Search bar.
2. If prompted by UAC to allow the MMC to make changes to the computer, click **Yes**. This should bring up a blank MMC console.
3. Fromt he **File** menu, select **Add/Remove Snap-in**.
4. From the Add or Remove Snap-ins window, choose the snap-in you want to add. Click **Add**. Depending on the snap-in you add, you may be prompted for additional information.
5. After you have added all your snap-ins, click **OK**. You snap-ins should now appear in the MMC.

The MMC can be very flexible. You can add whatever snap-ins you want to a blank MMC console. You can also modify one of the predefined management tools that use the MMC. After you have modified an MMC console, you have the option to save your changes. Simply select **File | Save** or **File | Save As**, whichever is appropriate.

There are also other options available for controlling what can and cannot be done inside an MMC console. If you choose **File | Options**, you will be presented with the MMC Options window, as seen in Figure 5.23. Here, you can change the icon used for console, or set the console mode. The console mode determines what users can and cannot see within the console and what changes they can make. The following are the four basic console modes available for the MMC:

- **Author mode** – This mode gives you full access to do anything in the MMC. You can add and remove snap-ins, create views, and open new windows.
- **User mode – full access** – This mode give you full access to the tree within the MMC. But, you cannot add or remove snap-ins.
- **User mode – limited access, multiple window** – This mode prevents you from being able to view contents of the tree that are not visible in the console window.
- **User mode – limited access, single window** – This mode opens the console with just a single window. Users cannot view items that do not appeari nt hatw indow.

The Options window allows you to specify if changes to the console can be saved. There is also an option for whether or not to allow the user to customize the console views.

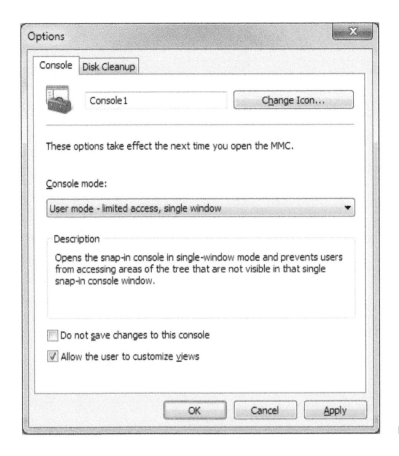

■ **FIGURE 5.23** MMC Options Window

ComputerM anagementC onsole

The Computer Management console is a predefined MMC-based management tool. It contains several snap-ins that aid in managing your system. These snap-ins are available individually, but are put together in one console to make management easier. The Computer Management console can be accessed by right-clicking on **Computer** on the Start menu and selecting **Manage**. Or you can add the Computer Management snap-in to your own customized MMC console.

As seen in Figure 5.24, the Computer Management console contains three categories that contain the actual snap-ins: **System Tools**, **Storage**, and **Services and Applications**.

- **System Tools** – Task Scheduler, Event Viewer, Shared Folders, Local Users and Groups, Performance, Device Manager
- **Storage** – Disk Management
- **Services and Applications**–Se rvices, WMIC ontrol

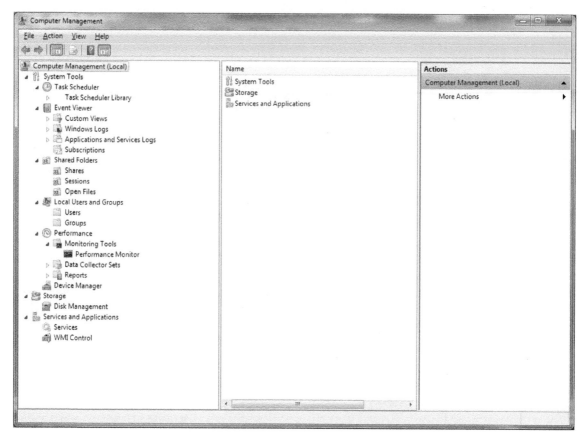

■ **FIGURE 5.24** Computer Management
Console

These snap-ins are used to manage the system. Again, these snap-ins can
be used individually. The Computer Management console just puts them
all together to make management easier. If you need to, you can create a
custom MMC console with these snap-ins in addition to others.

LocalG roupP olicyEdi tor

Setting individual settings can be quite cumbersome. To help Windows
uses the concept of group policies. Group policies can be used to easily set
multiple settings. Windows 7 comes with an MMC snap-in called Group
Policy Object Editor. You can add this snap-in to the MMC and choose
Local Computer when asked which Group Policy Object to edit. Now, you
can edit the computer's local group policy.

As seen in Figure 5.25, the local computer policy is divided into two main
sections: **Computer Configuration** and **User Configuration**.

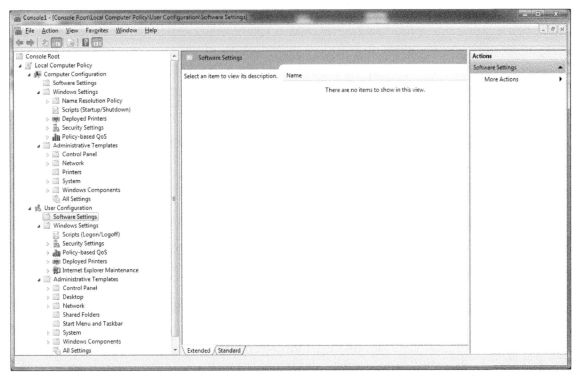

Computer Configuration

The **Computer Configuration** section is used for computer-wide settings. Many of these settings are applied when the system first boots up. These settings will apply to any user who logs into the system. The **Computer Configuration** section contains three subfolders:

- **Software Settings** – By default, there is nothing to be configured here.
- **Windows Settings** – These are general Windows settings that can be configured for all users. There are subnodes for **Name Resolution Policy**, **Scripts(Startup/Shutdown)**, **Deployed Printers**, **Security Settings**, and **Policy-based QoS**.
- **Administrative Templates** – These are registry-based settings that can be set for the system. There are subnodes for **Control Panel**, **Network**, **Printers**, **System**, and **Windows Components**.

User Configuration

The **User Configuration** section is used for user-specific settings. Most of these settings are not applied until a user logs into a system. These settings will apply no matter what system a user logs into. The **User Configuration** section contains three subfolders:

- **Software Settings** – By default, there is nothing to be configured here.
- **Windows Settings** – These are general Windows settings that can be configured for all users. There are subnodes for **Scripts(Logon/ Logoff)**, **Security Settings**, **Policy-based QoS**, **Deployed Printers**, and **Internet Explorer Maintenance**.
- **Administrative Templates** – These are registry-based settings that can be set for the system. There are subnodes for **Control Panel**, **Desktop**, **Network**, **Shared Folders**, **Start Menu**, and **Taskbar**, **System**, and **Windows Components**.

WindowsR egistry

The registry has long been the central configuration store for Windows systems. The registry is divided in categories called *hives*. These hives are where the actual configuration settings are stored.

There are five main hives in the registry are as follows:

- **HKEY_CLASSES_ROOT** – This maintains file type associations.
- **HKEY_CURRENT_USER** – This maintains user settings for the user currently logged into the system.
- **HKEY_LOCAL_MACHINE** – This maintain system-wide settings.
- **HKEY_USERS** – This maintains user settings for all users.
- **HKEY_CURRENT_CONFIG** – This maintains information about thec urrentha rdwarec onfiguration.

The registry can be modified directly or indirectly. You must be careful when modifying the registry directly. Any misconfigurations or typos can severely affect the functioning of your system. Regedt32 is the primary tool provided with Windows 7 for modifying the registry. You can use Regedt32 to configure registry settings and to set registry permissions.

SimplifiedC onfigurationa ndM anagement of Desktops

Microsoft developers included an undocumented method for simplying administration by combining shortcuts. It is a simple and single container with multiple shortcuts to Windows 7 options that are available through other methods as seen in Figure 5.26. This may be helpful for administrators and power users alike to configure and manage single Windows 7 desktops.

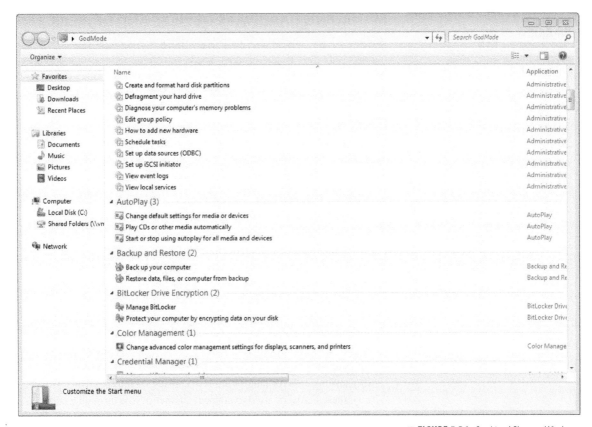

■ **FIGURE 5.26** Combined Shortcut Window

To create a Combined Shortcut window:

1. Right-click on the desktop or anywhere in Windows Explorer where you would like this shortcut.
2. Select **New | Folder**
3. Name the folder: <Name>.{ED7BA470-8E54-465E-825C-99712043E01C}
4. The folder icon will change to a **Control Panel** icon, as seen in Figure5.27 .

■ **FIGURE 5.27** Control Panel Icon

To use the combined folder, simply double-click the **Control Panel** icon just created for your new applet. A Windows Explorer window will open with shortcuts for many different configuration options in Windows 7. All of these options are available through other methods, mostly through the standard Control Panel shortcuts.

MANAGING HARDWARE DEVICES AND DRIVERS

Windows 7 provides several tools and utilities for configuring and managing hardware devices and printers. You have several options for configuring devices and installing the necessary drivers. Without the proper drivers and the proper configuration, your devices will not function properly.

InstallD evices

Installing hardware devices and drivers is much simpler in Windows 7 than in previous versions of Windows. There are several different types of hardware devices that may be installed on Windows 7 computers:

- **Internal Drives** – hard drives, CD drives, DVD drives, Blu-Ray drives, floppy drives, Zip drives, and any other internal drive that is released can be installed on Windows 7. These devices generally include a data cable (Integrated Drive Electronics [IDE], Serial Advanced Technology Attachment [SATA]) that attaches to the motherboard and a power cable that attaches to the power supply.
- **Internal Cards** – Adapters or expansion cards that are plugged into the desktops motherboard's expansion slots (Peripheral Component Interconnect Express [PCIe], Peripheral Component Interconnect [PCI], Accelerated Graphics Port [AGP]) including video cards, Redundant Array of Inexpensive Disks (RAID), and SATA controllers. Expansion cards for laptops are also considered internal cards. Generally, these cards are used to connect another device through a cable.
- **External Devices** – Any external device that connects to the computer through the available ports including universal serial bus (USB), IEEE-1394 (FireWire), Line Printer Terminal (LPT), Computer Object Model (COM), and so on. These ports can be connected to printers, scanners, external hard drives, media devices, and so on through the appropriate cable.
- **Memory** – Memory may be added to the computer's motherboard to expand the amount of memory the computer has access to.

Windows 7 automatically detects any hardware recently installed and attempts to automatically install the driver. Additionally, after Windows 7 Setup completes, if some drivers were not installed by default, Windows 7 will attempt to find the device and respective driver. This is possible through Windows Update. This section will cover basic methods of installing hardware devices including internal and external devices, printers, wireless devices, and so on.

Install Drivers with Windows Update

Windows 7 detects hardware that was not automatically installed with Windows 7 Setup; most of the time this will occur if the Windows 7 media did not include the driver for the hardware. The built-in hardware diagnostics will, generally, detect that hardware that is installed on the computer that has no drivers are installed for it. It will attempt to identify the hardware and then use Windows Update to search for the correct driver. Windows Update will automatically download the driver but will not install it.

Open Windows Update in any of the following ways to check for new drivers or updated drivers:

- Click **Start | Control Panel | System and Security | Windows Update**
- Click **Start | Control Panel | Windows Update**
- Type **windows update** on Start menu Search.
- Right-click **Action Center | Open Windows Update** on the notification area.
- After opening Windows Update, click **Check for updates** on the leftpa ne.

Essential drivers for video, sound, or hard disk controllers may appear as important updates. Other device drivers will appear in the optional updates section. Click the link on the main Windows Update console titled **[X] optional updates are available,**a ss howni n Figure5.28 .

By default, optional updates will not be selected to install. Check the box to the left of each driver you wish to install, and then click **OK** to download and install the update. Once the driver is installed, Windows will automatically detect the hardware device and install it.

■ **FIGURE 5.28** Windows Update Console – View Optional Updates Available

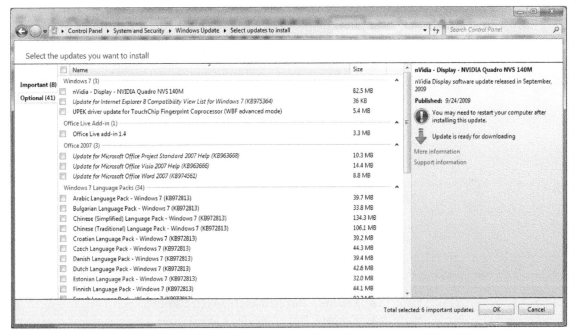

DeviceM anager

Device Manager is the central location to view, configure, and manage hardware devices. It is critical to understand how the Device Manager works before working on hardware devices.

There are multiple ways to open the Device Manager:

- In the Start menu, right-click **Computer | Manage**, expand **Computer Management** on the console tree, and then select **System Tools | Device Manager**.
- Enter the Start menu, right-click **Computer Properties**, then click **Device Manager** on the left pane.
- **Control Panel | Device Manager**
- **Control Panel | Hardware and Sound | Device Manager**

Notice the Device Manager is a MMC 3.0 Console. Expanding the device view is similar to any other MMC 3.0 console, simply click the arrow to the left of the device to expand the node. Devices with issues are displayed with a small symbol next to the device icon. A red X indicates the device is not installed correctly or disabled by the user or administrator. A yellow exclamation point indicates a problem with the device.

To change the view select **View** on the **Menu bar**.

- **Devices by Type** – This is the default view, which displays the devices by the type of hardware; devices are under the name of the devicet ype.
- **Devices by Connection** – This displays devices by the connection each device is connected to.
- **Resources by Type** – This displays the devices by resource type. There are four resource types: direct memory access (DMA), input/output (IO), interrupt request IRQ, and memory.
- **Resources by Connection** – This displays the devices by the type of resource it is connected to. There are four resource types: DMA, IO, IRQ, and memory. This allows for tracing resources by the connection.
- **Show Hidden Devices** – This displays devices that have been removed but drivers have not been uninstalled, as well as non-plug-and-play devices.

To view options or actions for each device, either right-click the device or click on the device, and then click **Action** on the Menu bar. The options for each device are as follows:

- **Update Driver Software** – This initiates the Hardware Update wizard.
- **Disable** – This disables the selected driver.
- **Enable** – This enables the selected driver.

- **Uninstall** – This uninstalls the device and respective driver.
- **Scan for Hardware Changes** – This initiates a Windows 7 scan for new hardware devices or changes.
- **Properties** – This initiates the Properties window for the selected device.

Devicesa ndP rinters

The Devices and Printers applet allows you to configure devices and printers attached to your system. You can configure device properties, your default printer, and many other settings. The Devices and Printers applet gives you the ability to **Add a device** or **Add a printer**.

Add a device – Selecting this option will kick off the Add a Device wizard as seen in Figure 5.29. Windows 7 will automatically attempt to detect devices that have been added to the system. If the system cannot automatically detect the device, you will be given the option to manually add it.

Add a printer – Selecting this option will kick off the Add Printer wizard, as seen in Figure 5.30. You can use it to install a local printer, network printer, wireless printer, or Bluetooth printer.

There are two sections in the applet: **Devices** and **Printers and Faxes**.

■ **FIGURE 5.29** Add a Device Wizard

■ **FIGURE 5.30** Add Printer Wizard

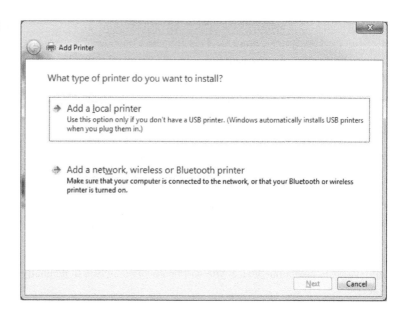

Devices

The **Device** section is used to configure devices attached to the system. The system seen in Figure 5.31 has a biometric coprocessor and an integrated camera. There is also a device listed representing the system itself.

If you select the device representing the system, you get two device options:

> **Browse files** – You can use this option to view files on the disk drives attached to the system. These could be hard drives, disk drives, or removablem edia.
> **Eject** – You can use this object to remove hot-pluggable hardware and removablem edia.

Printers and Faxes

The **Printers and Faxes** section contains all of the printers connected to the system. You can configure printer properties and your default printer.

If you select one of the printers you have configured, you get four options:

> **See what's printing** – This option allows you to view print jobs being serviced by the printer. You can view, cancel, or restart print jobs.
> **Manage default printers** – This option will bring up the Default Printers window, as seen in Figure 5.32. The Default Printers window allows you to set an overall default printer. Or you can set a different default printer for each network your system connects to.

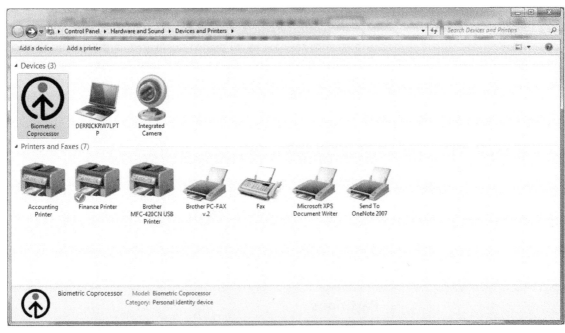

■ **FIGURE 5.32** Manage Default Printers Window

Print server properties – The Print server properties application allows you to configure system-wide print server properties. These print server properties are used by all printers configured on the system. You can configure printer forms that are available and configure printer ports to be used on the system. You can also add and remove printer drivers.

Remove device – This option allows you to remove a printer from the system.

MANAGING DISKS AND FILE SYSTEMS

The disks and the file system are at the center of Windows 7. It's important that your disks and file system are correctly configured. If not, you system might not function properly, or it may not function at all. The disks are where all your information is stored; the operating system files, the applications, your data, everything. The file system determines how this information is stored on your disks.

Partitions

Partitions are basically used to divide and segment your disks. Your disks can have either a single partition or multiple partitions. Even though having a single partition is the simplest way to configure your disk, there are several reasons why you might want to have more than one partition. Having multiple partitions can allow you to separate your operating system files, applications files, and data files. Sometimes, you must have multiple partitions because of size limitations for a partition. You may also need multiple partitions to run a multiboot system. This would especially be the case if different operating systems used different file systems. You would need to have a different partition for each of the different file systems.

MBR and GPT

MBR stands for Master Boot Record. Most legacy disks are MBR disks. MBR disks store partition information in the MBR, hence the name. This information is generally stored in the first sector of the disk.

GPT stands for GUID Partition Table. GPT disks store partition information in the GPT header. For compatibility with MBR systems, GPT disks continue to store the MBR entry as the first sector of the disk. After this entry is the start of the GPT. It is called the *Primary Partition Table Header*. For redundancy, the GPT header and partition table are also written at the end of the disk.

Choose between MBR and GPT

In Windows 7, you can have MBR or GPT disks. When a new disk is first added, you must choose between making it an MBR or GPT disk. It's important that you understand the differences between these two types of disks. Because the GPT format is newer, you may run into compatibility issues if you choose this format. MBR disks have a wider range of compatibility. GPT disks, however, support larger partition sizes.

Convert from MBR to GPT

You can convert a MBR disk to a GPT disk. In order to convert a disk to GPT format, the disk cannot have any volumes. If the disk has volumes, you should remove them.

To convert a MBR disk to a GPT disk, do the following:

1. Opent he **Disk Management MMC**s nap-in.
2. Right-click on the disk and select **Convert to GPT disk**.
3. The disk will be converted, and should show as Online.

Convert from GPT to MBR

You can also convert a GPT disk to an MBR disk.

To convert a disk from GPT to MBR, do the following:

1. Opent he **Disk Management MMC**s nap-in.
2. Right-click on the disk and select **Convert to MBR disk**.
3. The disk will be converted, and should show as Online.

Basic and Dynamic Disks

There are two types of disks available in Windows 7: *basic disks* and *dynamic disks*. You can think of basic disks as the traditional technology used for Windows disks.

When disks are first created, they are created as basic disks. In the original Disk Creation wizard, you can covert the disk to a dynamic disk. You can also convert to a dynamic disk later.

To convert a basic disk to a dynamic disk, do the following:

1. Opent he **Disk Management MMC**s nap-in.
2. Right-click on the disk and select **Convert to Dynamic Disk**, and as seen in Figure 5.33, the Convert to Dynamic Disk window will appear.
3. Select the basic disks you want to convert to dynamic disks.
4. Click **OK**. Thedi sksa rec onvertedt odyna micdi sks.

CONVERTING BETWEEN MBR AND GPT FORMAT
When you convert a disk from MBR format to GPT format, you will notice the amount of unallocated disk space on the disk decreased. This is because of the additional space used to hold disk and partition information on GPT disks. When you convert from GPT format to MBR format, you will notice a reverse effect.

WARNING
It is possible to convert a basic disk with a volume configured on it, but you will receive the Disk Management warning as seen in Figure5 .34.

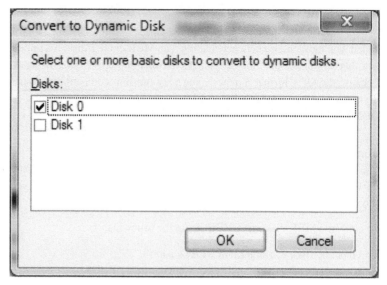

■ **FIGURE 5.33** Convert to Dynamic Disk Window

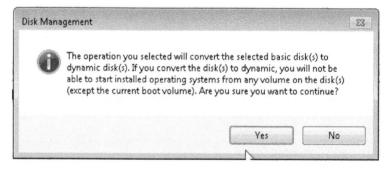

■ **FIGURE 5.34** Disk Management Warning Window

To convert a dynamic disk back to a basic disk, do the following:

1. Opent he **Disk Management MMCs** nap-in.
2. Right-click on the disk and select **Convert to Basic Disk**.
3. Click **OK**. The disk is converted back to a basic disk.

If the disk has a volume on it, you cannot convert it back to a basic disk. You must delete the volume before attempting to convert the disk back to a basic disk.

Volumes

Once you have your disks created and configured, you need to create volumes on them. You cannot store information on your disks until volumes are created. There are several different types of volumes you can choose to create. You can create simple volumes, spanned volumes, striped volumes, or mirrored volumes.

Create a Simple Volume

Creating a simple volume is easy. Just do the following:

1. Right-clickon **Unallocated space**. Select **New Simple Volume**.
2. The New Simple Volume wizard appears. Click **Next**.
3. On the Specify Volume Size screen, enter the desired size of the new volume. Click **Next**.
4. On the Assign Drive Letter or Path screen, choose the desired drive letter for the new volume. Click **Next**.
5. On the Format Partition screen, choose the option for **Format this volume using the following settings**.
6. Chooset he **NTFS file system**. Enter a volume label. Select the option for **Perform a Quick Format**. Click **Next**.
7. On the Completing the new Simple Volume Wizard screen, click **Finish**. The new volume will be formatted and should show a status of *Healthy*.

Create a Spanned Volume

To create a new spanned volume, do the following:

1. Right-clickon **Unallocated space**. Select **New Spanned Volume**.
2. The New Spanned Volume wizard appears. Click **Next**.
3. As seen in Figure 5.35, the Select Disks screen appears.
4. Select the disk you want to add to the spanned volume. Click **Add**.
5. Once the disk is added, you can specify how much disk space from the disk you want to add to the spanned volume. Click **Next**.
6. On the Assign Drive Letter or Path screen, choose the desired drive letter for the new volume. Click **Next**.
7. On the Format Partition screen, choose the option for **Format this volume using the following settings**.
8. Chooset he **NTFS file system**. Enter a volume label. Select the option for **Perform a Quick Format**. Click **Next**.
9. On the Completing the new Simple Volume Wizard screen, click **Finish**. The new volume will be formatted and should show a status of *Healthy* on each of the disks it was added to.

Create a Striped Volume

Striped volumes and spanned volumes are similar to each other, but there is one big difference. Both types of volumes can stretch across multiple

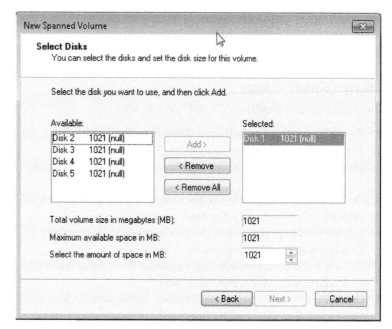

■ **FIGURE 5.35** Select Disks Screen

disks. Striped volumes, however, use the same amount of disk space on all disks, whereas spanned volumes can use a different amount of space on each disk.

To create a new striped volume, do the following:

1. Opent he **Disk Management MMC**s nap-in.
2. Right-click **Unallocated space**. Select **New Striped Volume**.
3. The New Striped Volume wizard appears. Click **Next**.
4. The Select Disks screen appears. Select the disks you want to add to the spanned volume. Click **Add**.
5. Once the disks are added, you can specify how much disk space from the disk you want added to the striped volume. (Note: This will be the same for all disks.)
6. Click **Next**.
7. On the Assign Drive Letter or Path screen, choose the desired drive letter for the new volume. Click **Next**.
8. On the Format Partition screen, choose the option for **Format this volume using the following settings**.
9. Chooset he **NTFS file system**. Enter a volume label. Select the option for **Perform a Quick Format**. Click **Next**.

10. On the Completing the new Striped Volume Wizard screen, click
Finish. The new volume will be formatted and should show a status
of *Healthy* on each of the disks it was added to.

Create a Mirrored Volume

Windows 7 has the ability to create mirrored volumes. Mirroring volumes is
done for fault tolerance and redundancy. When a volume is mirrored, a copy
of the data written to one volume is also written to a second volume. This way,
if one of the volumes becomes corrupted or a disk fails, you can still access
your files and data using the copy of the data stored on the other half of the
mirror.

To create a new mirrored volume, do the following:

1. Opent he **Disk Management MMCs** nap-in.
2. Right-clickon **Unallocated space**. Select **New Mirrored Volume**.
3. The New Mirrored Volume wizard appears. Click **Next**.
4. The Select Disks screen appears. Select the disks you want to add to
the mirrored volume. Click **Add**.
5. Once the disks are added, you can specify how much disk space from the
disks you want to be mirrored. (Note: This will be the same for all disks.)
6. Click **Next**.
7. On the Assign Drive Letter or Path screen, choose the desired drive
letter for the new volume. Click **Next**.
8. On the Format Partition screen, choose the option for **Format this
volume using the following settings**.
9. Chooset he **NTFS file system**. Enter a volume label. Select the option
for **Perform a Quick Format**. Click **Next**.
10. On the Completing the new Mirrored Volume Wizard screen, click
Finish. The new volume will be formatted and should show a status
of *Healthy* on each of the disks the mirror was added to.

> **WARNING**
> Dynamicd isksa rer equiredt o
> create spanned volumes, striped
> volumes, and mirrored volumes.
> If you attempt to create any of
> these volume types on basic disks,
> the disks will automatically be
> converted to dynamic disks.

Resize a Volume

Sometimes, when you create a volume, you will later be faced with the need
to change the size of that volume. Luckily, once you have created a volume
with a certain size, you are not limited to that size. You can either extend or
shrink a volume, if necessary.

To extend a volume, do the following:

1. Opent he **Disk Management MMCs** nap-in.
2. Right-click on the volume to be extended. Select **Extend Volume**.
3. The Extend Volume wizard appears. Click **Next**.

WARNING

If you choose to extend a volume to another disk, a spanned volume will be created. If the disk is a basic disk, it will be converted to a dynamicd isk.

4. The Select Disks screen appears. You can choose to extend the volume on the current disk or extend it to another disk.
5. Click **Next**.
6. Click **Finish**. The volume is extended and maintains the same file system as the original volume.

To shrink a volume, do the following:

1. Opent he **Disk Management MMCs** nap-in.
2. Right-click on the volume to be shrunk. Select **Shrink Volume**.
3. As seen in Figure 5.36, the Shrink Volume window appears. Enter the amount of space by which you would like to shrink the volume.
4. Click **Shrink**. The volume is shrunk and the freed up space is seen as unallocateds pace.

Delete a Volume

There are several instances where you may have to remove a volume. For example, you may need to remove a volume if you want to convert a disk to a different format.

To delete a volume, do the following:

1. Opent he **Disk Management MMCs** nap-in.
2. Right-click on the volume to be deleted and select **Delete Volume**. You will receive a warning that all your data will be erased.
3. Click **Yes** to continue. The volume will be deleted and the freed disk space will be returned to unallocated space.

■ **FIGURE 5.36**   Shrink Volume Window

Shrink G:

Total size before shrink in MB:	1021
Size of available shrink space in MB:	630
Enter the amount of space to shrink in MB:	630
Total size after shrink in MB:	391

ⓘ You cannot shrink a volume beyond the point where any unmovable files are located. See the "defrag" event in the Application log for detailed information about the operation when it has completed.

See Shrink a Basic Volume in Disk Management help for more information.

Shrink   Cancel

Virtual Hard Disk

The Virtual Hard Disk or VHD format is basically a hard drive that actually exists as a file. VHDs are generally used with virtual machines. But, they can also be used with physical machines. VHDs have the .vhd file extension.

Create VHD

VHDs can be created in the **Disk Management MMC**s nap-in.

To create a VHD, do the following:

1. Right-clickt he **Disk Management MMC** snap-in and select **Create VHD**. As seen in Figure 5.37, the Create and Attach Virtual Hard Disk window will appear.
2. Specify a location for the hard disk file.
3. Specify a size for the VHD.
4. Choose whether you want to create a dynamically expanding VHD or a fixed-size VHD.
5. Click **OK**. The VHDi sc reated.

■ **FIGURE 5.37** Create and Attach Virtual Hard Disk Window

Use VHD

Before a VHD can be used by a system, it must be attached to the system. VHDs that you create on a system, like in the previous example, are automatically attached. But, you must manually attach other VHDs to your system.

To attach a VHD to a system, do the following:

1. Right-clickt he **Disk Management MMC** snap-in and select **Attach VHD**. The Attach Virtual Hard Disk window will appear.
2. Specify the location of the VHD you would like to use.
3. Specify whether you would like the VHD to be mounted as read-only ornot .
4. Click **OK**. The VHD will be attached to your system.

Once VHDs are attached to your system, they appear in the **Disk Management** snap-in, just like any other disk. If the VHD is new, it will have to be initialized. After the disk is initialized and Online, you can create a volume on the disk. The disk is then ready for use.

FileS ystemF ragmentation

Disk fragmentation occurs when files or pieces of files get scattered throughout your disks. Not only do hard disks get fragmented, but removable storage can also become fragmented. This can cause poor disk performance and overall system degradation.

Windows 7 includes a disk defragmentation utility that can defrag your disks and restore system performance. The tool is called *Disk Defragmenter*. Disk Defragmenter can be accessed from **Start | All Programs | Accessories | System Tools**. Disk Defragmenter can also be accessed by right-clicking on a disk in Windows Explorer, selecting **Properties**, and then going to the **Tools**t ab.

Disk Defragmenter, as seen in Figure 5.38, allows you to defragment your disks now, or schedule defragmentation for later, or schedule periodic defragmentation. Disk Defragmenter also includes an option for **Analyze Disk**. If you choose this option, Disk Defragmenter will determine if your system can benefit from running the defragmentation process. This is important because, sometimes, defragmentation can take a very long time to complete. If it's not going to benefit your system, there is no reason to run a defragmentation.

SymbolicL inks

A *symbolic link* is a pointer that redirects to another location. When a symbolic link is accessed, a user or system is automatically sent to the file or folder referenced in the symbolic link. Symbolic links are generally done for ease of use or application compatibility.

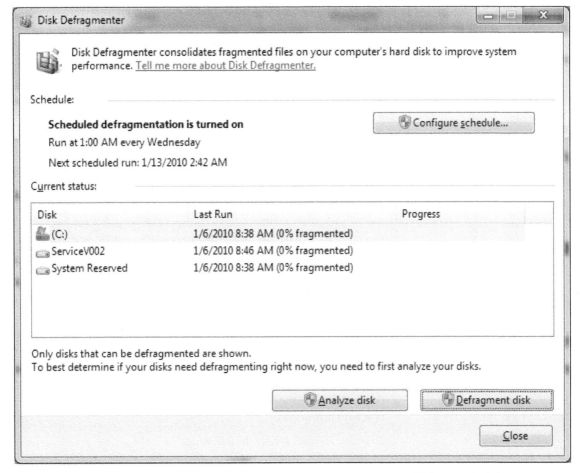

■ **FIGURE 5.38** Disk Defragmenter

Create Symbolic Links

The *mklink* command is used to create symbolic links in Windows 7. The syntax and usage of mklink is as follows:

MKLINK [[/D] | [/H] | [/J]] Link Target
/D – creates a directory symbolic link. Default is a file symbolic link.
/H – creates a hard link instead of a symbolic link
/J – creates a *Directory Junction*
Link – specifies the new symbolic link name
Target – specifies the path (relative or absolute) that the new link refers to

Create Relative or Absolute Symbolic Links

Symbolic links can be either absolute or relative. Absolute links specify the entire path in the link. Relative links only contain the latter portion of the link. With relative links, the beginning portion of the link is based on the location of the link.

Relative links generally begin with one of the following or use one of the following formats:

- **Dots** – Either (.) or (..). For example, .\test.txt or ..\test.txt
- **Root relative** – For example, \test.txt
- **Current directory relative** – For example, c:test.txt
- **Just the file name**–F ore xample,t est.txt

Use Hard Links

A *hard link* is a link between two files on a hard disk. When you click a hard link to a file, the operating system and applications will behave as though you are accessing the file itself. Hard links can be used to link files on the same volume only.

WindowsR eadyBoost

Windows ReadyBoost can be used to speed up the performance of you Windows 7 system. When your system runs out of RAM, it begins using the hard disk to store files it needs to use. This disk access can impact the performance of your system. To help with this, Microsoft developed ReadyBoost. ReadyBoost allows Windows 7 to use a flash drive instead of the hard disk for this storage. This flash drive access can be much faster than hard disk access.

To enable ReadyBoost, do the following:

1. In Windows Explorer, right-click the drive representing the flash drive and select **Properties**.
2. Go to the **ReadyBoost**t ab.
3. Select **Use this device**.
4. Specify how much of the drive you want to set aside for ReadyBoost.
5. Click **OK**.

WARNING

WindowsR eadyBoostr equiresa t least 235 MB of free space on the flash drive. Without it, you will not be able to configure ReadyBoost on the drive. It is recommended, however, that you set aside at least 1 GB of space for ReadyBoost usage.

DiskQ uotas

Disk quotas allow you to specify a limit to the amount of disk space a user can use. This is very useful if you have limited disk space available for use. You can control how much disk space is used by everyone, and ensure that you have enough space left over for the system to use for things like application installation, system file storage, and paging.

Configure Disk Quotas

You can configure Disk Quotas on the various disk volumes within your system. You can actually have two volumes on the same disk with different quotas.

To enable Disk Quotas, do the following:

1. In the **Disk Management** MMC snap-in or Windows Explorer, right-click the volume you want to enable quotas for and select **Properties**.
2. Go to the **Quota** tab. (Note: If you are using Windows Explorer, you will also have to click **Show Quota Settings**.)
3. Check the box for **Enable quota management**.

Once you have enabled quota management, there are several possible configuration options:

-   **Deny disk space to users exceeding quota limit** – If you select this option, once a user exceeds their quota, they will no longer be able to write to the disk. This will help prevent users from going over their quota. But, it can cause applications not to perform properly.
-   **Limit disk space to** – By default, disk space is not limited. You can specify the limit for the amount of disk space the user can use.
-   **Set warning level to** – Once you set a disk space limitation, you can then set a warning level. The option allows you to specify at what level of disk usage the user will begin receiving disk-space warnings.
-   **Log event when a user exceeds their quota limit** – This option specifies whether an event will be logged to the system log when the user exceeds his or her amount of allocated disk space.
-   **Log event when a user exceeds their warning level** – This option specifies whether an event will be logged to the system log when a user exceeds the amount of disk space usage designated at the warning level.
-   **Quota Entries** – This option allows you to specify quota options for differentus ersa ndgr oups.

■ SUMMARY

Windows 7 includes a variety of local management tools. There is Control Panel, the MMC, the Computer Management Console, the Local Group Policy Editor, and the Windows Registry. Each of these management tools provides a different function. They all come together to provide a total management solution for your Windows 7 system.

It's important that your system hardware is properly installed and configured. Malfunctioning hardware can really be a hassle to fix. Windows 7 includes applications like Device Manager and the Devices and Printers applet to help ensure that your hardware is properly installed. Device Manager and Windows Update can help ensure that your devices are configured with the most up-to-date drivers.

Everything in your system relies on your disks and file systems. This is where all of your files are stored. If your disks and file systems are not properly configured, you system may not run at all. Windows 7 volumes can provide convenience through disk spanning or fault tolerance through RAID 5. You need to make sure that you choose a configuration that best suitsyou rne eds.

Networking and Mobility

INFORMATION IN THIS CHAPTER

- TCP/IP
- Network Location and Network Discovery
- NetworkE xplorer
- Network and Sharing Center
- Set Up a New Connection or Network
- Wireless
- Connect to a Network
- NetworkC onnections
- HomeGroup
- Mobility
- PowerM anagement
- Enhancements with Windows Server 2008 R2
- Summary

Microsoft significantly improved networking and mobility from Windows XP and previous versions with Windows Vista. Windows 7 takes many of the changes in Windows Vista and improves them a bit more. Networking and communication is almost required today for all computer systems. Keeping your environment and end users connected is a major task for system administrators. With Windows 7, Microsoft makes it simpler for end users to stay connected and for administrators to manage them. This chapter will look at configuring and managing networks in Windows 7 and mobile user connectivity.

This chapter will first explain the new TCP/IP network stack of Windows 7. Windows 7 uses both IPv4 and IPv6 in what Microsoft is calling Next

DOI: 10.1016/B978-1-59749-561-5.00006-1

Generation TCP/IP Stack. It is critical to understand this for the recent migrations to IPv6 that should be underway. Network Location and Network Discovery are also new networking features in Windows 7 that base network and security settings on the location the user is connected to.

The Network and Sharing Center is a centralized location to manage and troubleshoot networking in Windows 7. Here, the administrators can create new network connections via wired, wireless, dial-up, and/or virtual private network (VPN) methods. The user can also connect or disconnect from a network simpler than ever through the Network and Sharing Center or by clicking the **Network** icon in the notification area. The HomeGroup can also be configured from this area for locations set to Home.

Mobility in Windows 7 has also been improved with a new centralized area to manage and configure settings easily for the end user called Windows Mobility Center. The menu has many different options including Power Management, which is also a topic in this chapter. Power plans can be configured on the desktop or remotely with group policy or command lines. Finally, this chapter will look at added features to Windows 7 when using Windows Server 2008 R2 including DirectAccess, BranchCache, and offline domain join.

TCP/IP

Windows 7 uses TCP/IP as the default network protocol. These protocols allow computers to communicate across networks and the Internet through the installed network adapters. Windows 7 uses a dual IP-layer architecture in both IPv4 and IPv6 for common Transport and Frame layers. IPv4 uses 32-bit addresses and is the primary version of IP used on the Internet and most networks. IPv6 uses 128-bit addresses and is the next generation of IP.

IPv4

IPv4 addresses have been used for years and continue to be the dominant IP protocol used in networks and Internet. An IPv4 address is 32-bit and looks like 192.168.1.1 and 10.1.1.2. The four separate decimal values are called octets because each represents 8 bits of the 32-bit number. Of the 32-bit IP, a part of it represents the network ID, whereas the other part represents the host ID. There is no relationship between an IPv4 address and a network adapter's Media Access Control (MAC) address. The MAC address of an adapter is a unique identifier assigned to the network adapter by the manufacturer. In TCP/IP networks, the Address Resolution Protocol (ARP) is used to discover a host's MAC address when only the IPv4 address is known. ARP has been used in networking since 1982 and now is one of the most unsecure network protocols in use.

IPv6

IPv6 is the new IP protocol, which is being rolled out as you read this. IPv6 are 128-bit addresses divided into eight 16-bit hexadecimal numbers separated by colons. Unlike IPv4, the first 64 bits are the network ID, whereas the last 64 bits are the network interface. An example of an IPv6 IP is 2002:4a33:e2a8: 1234:7829:9c7b:3edd:435f. IPv6 does not require ARP but its functionality is provided by the Neighbor Discovery Protocol (NDP), which has proven much more secure.

NextG eneration TCP/IPS tack

Windows 7 introduces what Microsoft calls the Next Generation TCP/IP Stack. This simply means that when a network adapter is installed, both IPv4 and IPv6 are enabled by default. Therefore, when installing a network adapter in Windows 7, there is no need to install either TCP/IP for IPv4 or TCP/IP for IPv6. Microsoft is priding itself in this great interoperability in Windows 7 for TCP/IP. The Next Generation TCP/IP Stack allows both IPv4 and IPv6 to work on the same network making it much easier for network and system administrators to deploy IPv6.

NETWORK LOCATION AND NETWORK DISCOVERY

As stated in Chapter 1, "Introduction to Windows 7," when a Windows 7 computer first connects to a network, it will scan and attempt to determine what network it is connected to. If the computer cannot identify the network, it will prompt the user to select what kind of network the computer is connected to as shown in Figure 6.1. Network discovery settings work with the Windows Firewall settings and depend on the type of network that the computer connects to. It is critical for end users to be educated to select the correct network. If a Home or Work network is selected in a public network, then the Windows Firewall will be configured incorrectly and might allow a potential malicious user access to the system.

The Windows Firewall and networking settings are dependent on the location chosen by the user. There are four categories of network locations:

- **Home** – Computers that are connected to a home network. This enables HomeGroup and easy configuration of a home network.
- **Work** – Computers that are connected to a workgroup where some sharing may occur.

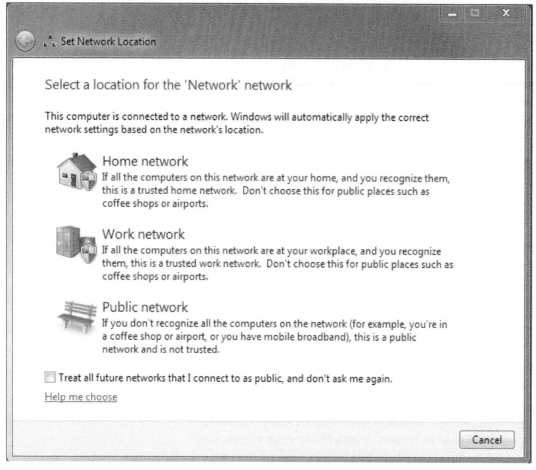

■ FIGURE 6.1 Select Network Location

- **Public** – This is for any location that is not trusted. This location has the most secure firewall settings.
- **Domain** – This is for computers connected to a domain infrastructure. The user is not prompted to connect to these as the computer uses the domain relationship to auto discover.

Depending on the location chosen by the user, network discovery may be on. To toggle network discovery, ensure the location is set for Home or Work:

1. Click **Change advanced sharing settings** on the left panel of the Network and Sharing Center.
2. Expand Home or Work settings by clicking the **down arrow**.
3. Click the radio button to **Turn on network discovery**.

NETWORK EXPLORER

Network Explorer has been a feature in Windows since we can remember. It is accessed through the Windows Explorer window and when selected, it shows all computers and devices connected to the network as shown in Figure 6.2. For Windows 7, Microsoft has improved the network discovery feature to find more devices and computers on your network. Once a device is found and given the user has the correct sharing permissions, the device or computer may be clicked, and access to the shared resources granted.

The Windows Explorer toolbar has three options in the Network Explorer view. A user can launch the Network and Sharing Center, add a printer, or add a wireless device. All of these actions are explained in the corresponding section of this chapter. Additionally, right-clicking a device or computer that is shown in the Network Explorer gives the option to open the device to see shared resources, create a shortcut, or open a remote desktop connection.

■ **FIGURE 6.2** Network Explorer

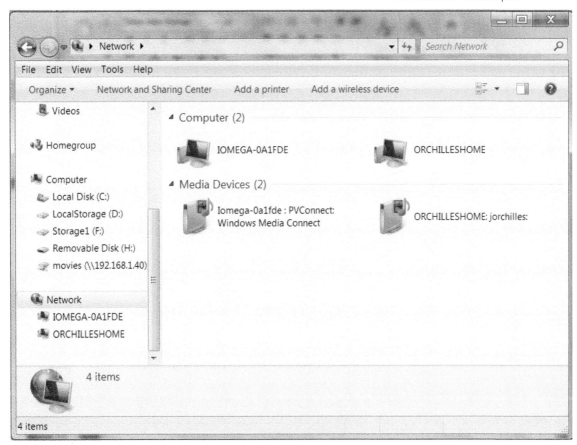

NETWORK AND SHARING CENTER

The Network and Sharing Center is a console within the Control Panel that provides the current network status and an overview of the current network configuration as shown in Figure 6.3. The Network and Sharing Center is

■ **FIGURE 6.3** Network and Sharing Center

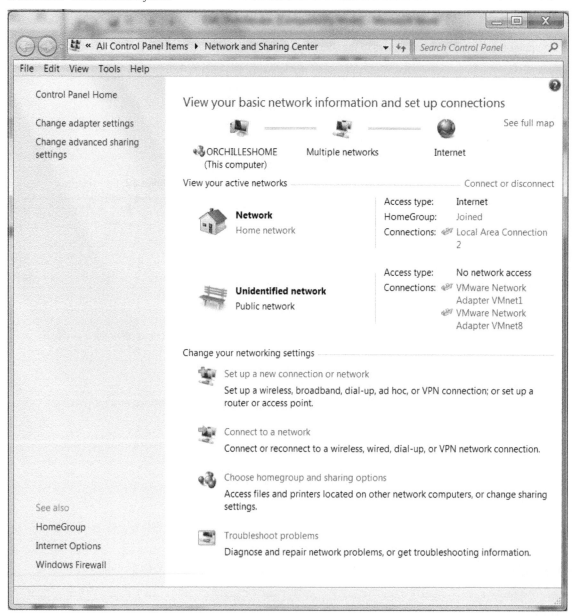

also the central location to manage everything that is related to networking from creating connections to configuring adapters. The Network and Sharing Center can be accessed in a number of ways:

- **Start | Control Panel** (icon view) | **Network and Sharing Center**
- **Start | Control Panel** (category view) | **View network status and tasks**
- Click the **Network** icon in the notification area and select **Network and Sharing Center**
- Right-click the **network** icon in the notification area and select **Network and Sharing Center**

The Network and Sharing Center is an overview of your current network status. Starting at the top is an abridged view of your network map. Clicking **See full map** will take you to the Network Map console to see a full view of all connected computers and devices on your network. Under the abridged map in the Network and Sharing Center are active connections. The active connections will provide the network the computer is connected to (Home, Work, or Public), access type, HomeGroup status, and Connections being used. Under the active networks section is the section where you can change networking settings. From here, it is simple to set up a new connection, connect to a network, choose HomeGroup and sharing options, or troubleshoot problems. On the left panel of the Network and Sharing Center are links to manage wireless networks, change adapter settings, and change advanced sharing settings.

NetworkM ap

The network map is a new feature of Windows 7 that scans the entire network and maps it in an easy-to-understand console. For the network map to work, network discovery must be enabled. This feature is helpful in providing a graphical layout of your network as shown in Figure 6.4. To view the Network Map, one must click **See full map** in the Network and Sharing Center. This will initiate a network discovery of devices and computers currently connected to the same network as the Windows 7 system.

Computers and devices that are found as a part of the network will be shown with lines connecting to network devices such as a switch, router, access point, gateway, or directly to the Internet. Some devices that could not be mapped will be shown at the bottom of the window. If Windows 7 detects any issues after the network discovery process, the user will see warning icons in the network map. A yellow warning icon suggests a configuration issue. A red X suggests a network is missing a connection point. Clicking on the **Warning** icon will initiate the Windows Network Diagnostic to automatically find and resolve the problem.

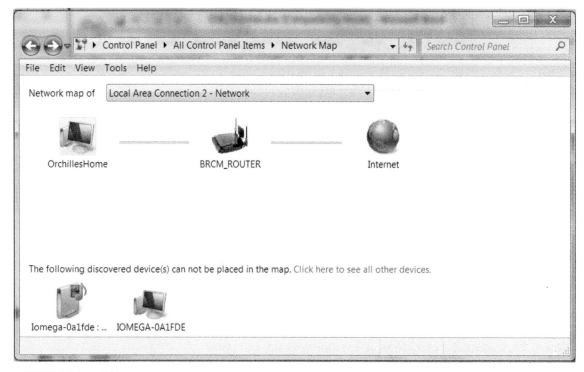

■ **FIGURE 6.5** Connect to a Network

ActiveN etworks

In the Network and Sharing Center, under the basic/abridged network map, is a section where you can view your active networks. To the immediate right of the text is the **Connect** or **Disconnect** link that pops up the Connect to a network pop up as shown in Figure 6.5. This is the same connect or disconnect console that pops up when clicking the **Network** icon in the notification area and **Connect to a network** in the Network and Sharing Center.

Under the view your active networks section is a list of current active networks by name. The network name is listed in bold and is to the right of the **Network** icon. Clicking the **Network** icon will pop up a console to change the name or icon of the selected connection. Under the network name is the profile the active connection is using: Home, Work, or Public. Clicking the link will pop up the network location console shown in Figure 6.1 to change the network profile.

The access type indicates if there is Internet access or not. If there is Internet access, the access type will read *Internet*. If Internet access is not available, the access type will read *No Internet Access*. Below the access type may be the HomeGroup status depending on what profile is selected. If the Home-Group is connected, the status of the HomeGroup will be shown. Clicking **status** will lead the user to the HomeGroup settings console. The Home-Group will be discussed later in this chapter.

Finally, the Connections will list the network adapters related to the active network. Clicking the name of the network adapter (usually Local Area Connection X) will pop up a window with the status of the network adapter, as shown in Figure 6.6. The status of the network connection will display the basic information about the connection. In the Connection setting is the

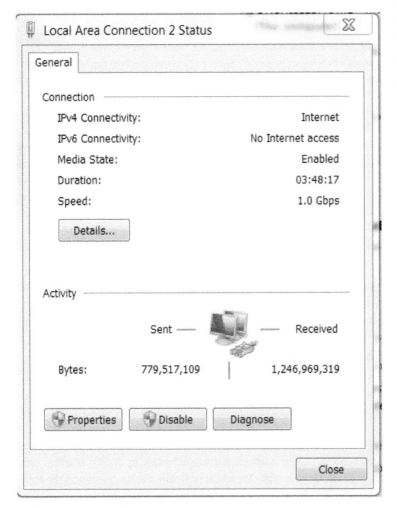

TIP
Ensuring the end user is connected to the correct network and setting the correct network profile is one of the first steps to troubleshooting network issues. If the user is on the wrong network, then it will be difficult to connect to devices on the network. The user should disconnect from the incorrect network and connect to the trusted, correct one. If the user is connected to a work network and has a public profile selected for the location, then many required work functions might not work.

■ **FIGURE 6.6** Local Area Connection Status

IPv4 Connectivity, IPv6 Connectivity, Media State, Duration, and Speed. Clicking **Details…** will pop up a more detailed view of the network connection. The same details can be viewed from the command prompt by typing **ipconfig /all**. The other section in the Local Area Connection Status window is Activity. Here the amount of bytes that have been sent and received by the connection is displayed. Under the amount are three buttons. The **Properties** button will bring up the network adapter settings, which will be discussed later this chapter. The **Disable** button will disable the network connection. The **Diagnose** button will launch Windows Network Diagnostics, which will automatically scan for network issues and attempt to resolve them.

SET UP A NEW CONNECTION OR NETWORK

More and more users need to connect to remote networks such as an office, remote office, or even an ISP. Setting up a connection to the Internet, workplace, or dial-up is easier than ever on Windows 7. Dial-up networking allows a user to connect with a modem to a business network or ISP. Broadband connections allow users to connect to the Internet and then possibly to the organization's network. VPN connections allow secure VPN connections to organizations as well. Finally, wireless connections are everywhere to allow Internet connection and network connectivity to anyone's mobile almost anywhere. Thankfully, most of these networks work with Dynamic Host Configuration Protocol (DHCP), which assigns the network adapter an IP address and other network configuration settings so it can automatically connect to the network. In case that DHCP is not setup, a static IP and options may be set, which will be explained in the Network Connections a part of this chapter.

To access the network connection setup, click **Set up a new connection or network** in the Change you networking settings section in the Network and Sharing Center. A wizard will pop up as shown in Figure 6.7.

Connect to the Internet

The first option in the Set Up a Connection or Network window is the **Connect to the Internet** option. This is one of the new and improved features of Windows 7. It allows users and administrators to easily set up a connection to the network and Internet. Selecting this option and clicking **Next** will scan the Windows 7 system for current network adapters including local area network (LAN) adapters, wireless adapters, or dial-up adapters such as modems. Once it scans for adapters, it will attempt to connect the LAN adapter to the Internet if present. Depending on what other adapters it finds, it will give the user options to configure and connect to the Internet via

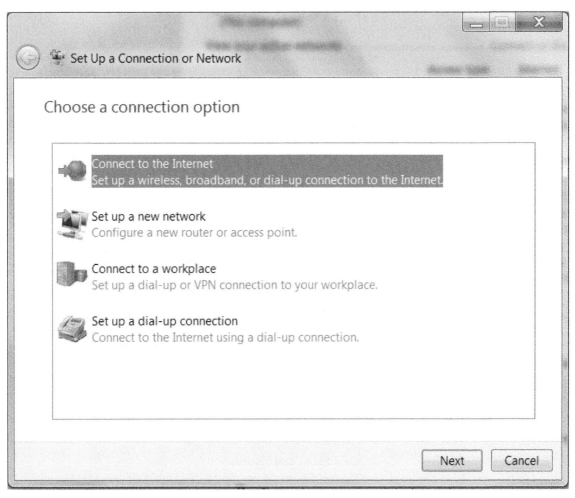

■ **FIGURE 6.7** Set Up a Connection or Network

whichever adapter it finds. If the wizard finds a wireless adapter and wireless networks, it will ask which network to connect to. If it finds a modem, it will walk the user through setting up a dial-up connection. All of these connection types will be explained in this section.

In the case that the LAN is connected to a broadband connection, then this wizard will be the easiest method of configuring a PPPoE connection for Windows 7 to use the broadband connection. In the How do you want to connect screen, click **Broadband (PPPoE)**. The next screen will ask you for the username, password, and connection name for this connection. The username and password should be supplied by the ISP. Click **Connect** to test the connection.

Set up a New Network

This new feature is for novice home users to assist them in setting up a router or wireless access point. Windows 7 has added support for a number of routers and wireless access points. The wizard will attempt to automatically find any networking device that is directly connected to the Windows 7 system. Then the Windows 7 computer will walk the user through configuring the device. Once the device is configured, the user will be able to download the configuration to easily connect other devices to the same network. This feature will most likely never be used in a place of business.

Dial-UpC onnection

Windows 7 allows two types of dial-up connections: a dial-up connection to an ISP and a dial-up connection to a workplace. Both the dial-up connections require an initial first step of setting up a default location and dialing rules.

Locations and Dialing Rules

A location specifies a profile with dialing rules. The dialing rules determine how the phone, modem, or fax will use the phone line to establish a connection. The first time a dial-up connection is setup, a default location will be chosen. Then, through the Phone and Modem console, locations and dialing rules will be added, edited, or deleted.

To set the default location for the first time:

1. Open the Control Panel in icon view.
2. Click **Phone and Modem**.
3. The first time the Phone and Modem console is opened, a Location Information panel will pop up, as shown in Figure 6.8.
4. Answer the questions to configure the default location:
   a. **What country/region are you in now**? Select the country or region from the drop-down menu.
   b. **What area code (or city code) are you in now**? Input the area code of the area you are in.
   c. **If you need to specify a carrier code, what is it**? A carrier code may be needed to dial out or long distance.
   d. **If you dial a number to access an outside line, what is it**?S ome phone lines require a nine or other number to dial out.
   e. **The phone system at this location uses**: Most systems in the UnitedS tatesus e Tonedi aling.
5. Click **OK**.

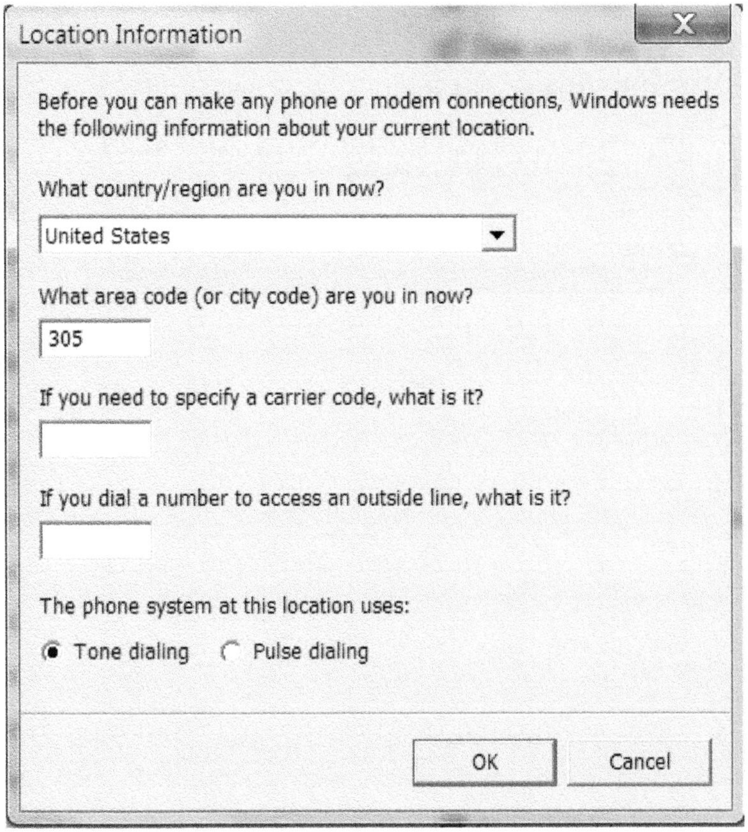

■ **FIGURE 6.8** Location Information

Once the default location is set, the Phone and Modem console will appear, as shown in Figure 6.9. Since the default location has been created, this is the screen that will open when Phone and Modem is chosen in the Control Panel. Options in this dialog box allow for the creation of other locations for users that travel and will be in other locations for dialing out. Locations can bede leted,a dded,or e dited.

Dial-Up Connection to an ISP

One of the types of dial-up connections Windows 7 allows to easily be setup is connecting to an ISP. For setting up this connection, some information must be known and provided by the ISP including the dial-up phone number, username, and password. A dial-up connection to an ISP does not use the Client for Microsoft networks and does redial the ISP if the line is dropped by default.

TIP
Show your users how to configure the Phone and Modem locations and dialing rules so they can easily connect when in a remote location. Often users have everything configured for home and work but when they travel offsite they can no longer connect. These are often the toughest service calls for administrators.

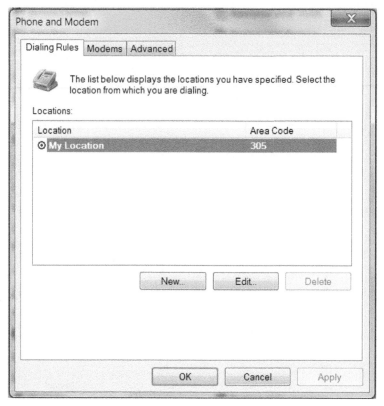

■ **FIGURE 6.9** Phone and Modem

To set up a dial-up connection to an ISP:

1. Open the Network and Sharing Center.
2. Click **Set up a dial-up connection** and click **Next**.
3. Input the dial-up phone number, username, and password provided by the ISP, as shown in Figure 6.10.
4. Input a name for this connection that best describes it such as the name of the ISP.
5. Select if this connection may be used by all users by clicking the checkbox.
6. To configure dialing rules for this connection, click on **Dialing Rules** to the right of the phone number input.
7. Click **Create**.

Connectt oa Workplace

Connecting to a workplace allows the user to set up dial-up or VPN to a workplace. A dial-up connection to a workplace is different than a dial-up connection

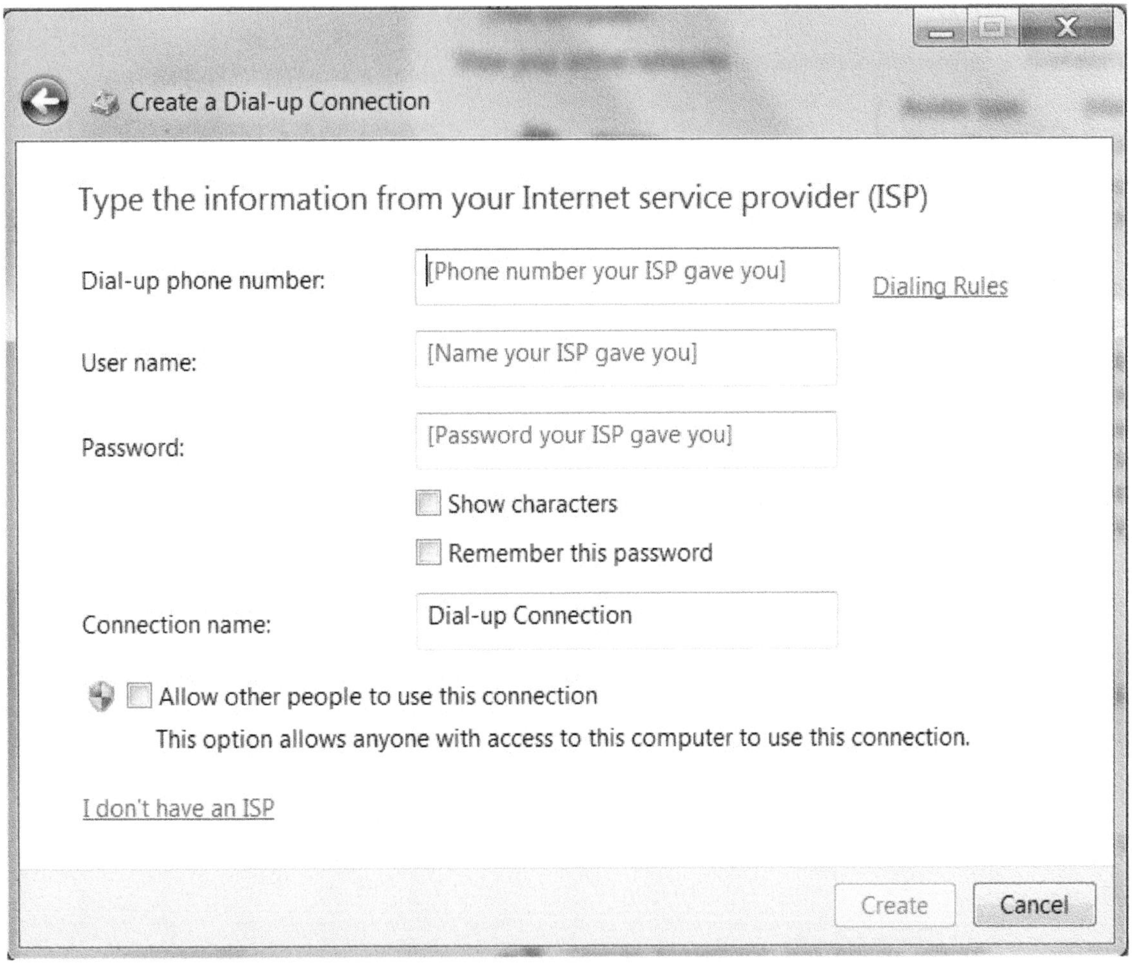

■ **FIGURE 6.10** Create a Dial-up Connection

to an ISP. The dial-up connection to a workplace uses Client for Microsoft Networks components and does not allow redialing if the connection is dropped.

To create a dial-up connection to a workplace:

1. Open the Network and Sharing Center.
2. Click **Set Up A New Connection Or Network**.
3. Click **Connect to A Workplace** and click **Next**.
4. If a connection is already setup, select **No, create a new connection**.
5. Click **Dial directly** as shown in Figure 6.11.
6. Input the telephone number to dial to connect to the workplace and the destination name that describes the connection, as shown in Figure 6.12.
7. To allow other users to use the connection, check the box. If the user will use a smart card, check the other box. Then, click **Next**.

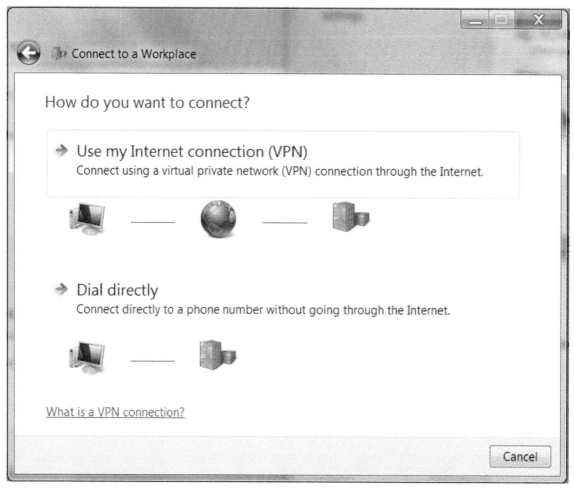

■ **FIGURE 6.11** Connect to a Workplace –
VPN or Dial-Up

8. The next screen will ask for user credentials. It is not a good practice to save these credentials. Simply educate the user to input the username, password, and/or domain to connect to the network.
9. Click **Connect** to test the connection. If this is being setup within the network that the user will be connecting to, it may not work. Have the usert estf roma di fferentl ocation.

Dial-up connections can be created, edited, or removed with Group Policy:

1. Open Group Policy Management Editor.
   a. For computers navigate to: **Computer Configuration | Preferences | Control Panel Settings | Network Options**.
   b. For users navigate to: **User Configuration | Preferences | Control Panel Settings | Network Options**.

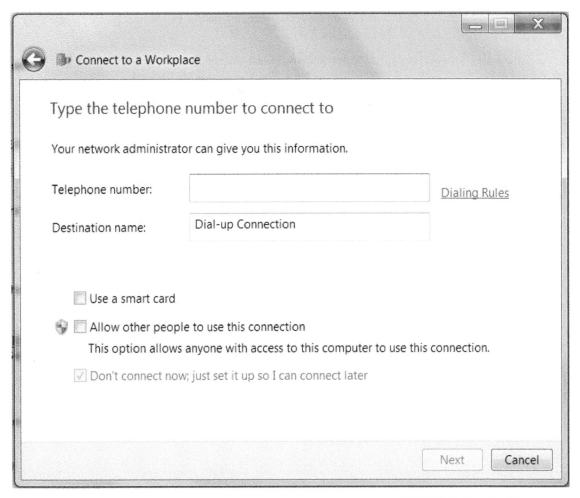

■ **FIGURE 6.12** Connect to a Workplace –
Dial-Up Setting

2. Right-click **Network Options | New | Dial-up Connections**.
3. In the pop up of Network Options Properties, select **Create, Update, or Replace**.
4. Select **All Users Connection** or select the **User Connection** to apply only to the users specified by the policy.
5. Entert he **telephone number** and **name of the connection**.
6. Ont he **Common** tab, select how to apply the policy.
7. Click **OK**t os ave.

A VPN connection is used to connect to a workplace through the current Internet connection. A VPN creates a secure tunnel to the workplace and is one of the safest ways to connect to a workplace. To create a VPN connection:

1. Open the Network and Sharing Center.
2. Click **Set Up A New Connection Or Network**.
3. Click **Connect to A Workplace** and click **Next**.
4. If a connection is already set up, select **No, create a new connection**.
5. Click **Use my Internet connection (VPN)**, as shown in Figure 6.11.
6. Enter the IP address or fully qualified domain of the remote access server and a name for the connection as shown in Figure 6.13.
7. If the user will use a smart card, check the **Use a smart card** check box.

■ **FIGURE 6.13** Connect to a Workplace – VPN Setting

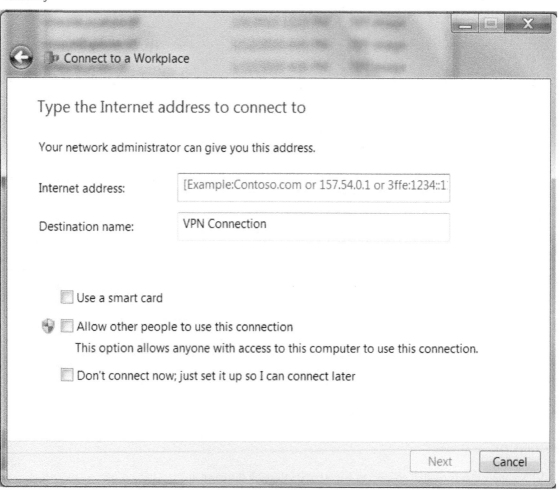

8. If all the users need access to the connection, check the **Allow other people to use this connection**c heckbox.

9. Click **Next**. Educate the user to input the username, password, and/or domain to connect to VPN. Do not choose to save the password for the user as this is insecure and will allow access to your network if that machine becomes compromised.

10. Click **Connect** to test or **Close**t os ave.

VPN connections can be created, edited, or removed with Group Policy:

1. Open Group Policy Management Editor.
   a. For computers navigate to: **Computer Configuration | Preferences | Control Panel Settings | Network Options**.
   b. For users navigate to: **User Configuration | Preferences | Control Panel Settings | Network Options**.

2. Right-click **Network Options | New | VPN Connection**.

3. In the pop up of Network Options Properties, select **Create, Update, or Replace**.

4. Select **All Users Connection** or select the **User Connection** to apply only to the users specified by the policy.

5. Enter the IP address or fully qualified domain and a name for the connection.

6. Int he **Security** tab, click **Advanced** and configure the Data Encryption that matches that of the server.

7. Ont he **Common** tab, select how to apply the policy.

8. Click **OK**t os ave.

WIRELESS

Setting up and connecting to a wireless network has been improved in Windows 7. Wireless networking is being deployed in many organizations and is available to mobile users in their homes, coffee shops, hotels, and almost anywhere else an Internet connection is available. Almost all of notebooks and laptops sold today include a wireless network adapter. A wireless network adapter is like a LAN adapter but uses an antenna to connect to a network instead of a cable. The wireless network adapter connects to a wireless access point or router by finding the Service Set Identifier (SSID) and authenticating with it, as shown in Figure 6.14.

This section describes all things wireless from wireless basics including 802.11 specifications to connecting to a wireless network. This section also shows the administrator how to setup a wireless access point using a Windows 7 computer and wireless network adapter.

■ **FIGURE 6.14** Connect to a Wireless Network

WirelessB asics

The most used wireless network adapters and access points use the Institute of Electrical and Electronics Engineers (IEEE) 802.11 specification. Most wireless devices are based on this specification and are therefore Wi-Fi certified. There are several different IEEE 802.11 specifications:

- **802.11a** – Wireless speed up to 54 Mbps using the 5GHz transmission frequency with effective indoor ranges between 25 and 75 feet depending on obstacles.
- **802.11b** – Wireless speed up to 11 Mbps using the 2.4GHz transmission frequency with effective indoor ranges between 100 and 150 feet. 802.11b is compatible with 802.11g running at 11 Mbps.
- **802.11g** – Wireless speed up to 54 Mbps using the 2.4GHz transmission frequency with effective indoor ranges between 100 and 150 feet. 802.11g can operate with 802.11b at 11 Mbps.
- **802.11n** – Wireless speed up to 600 Mbps using either 2.4GHz and/or 5GHz transmission frequency with effective indoor range between 200 and 300 feet. 802.11n can operate with 802.11b at 11 Mbps or 802.11g at 54 Mbps. 802.11n is the newest standard for wireless networking and has improved on previous standards by adding multiple-input multiple-output(MIMO).

Most organizations with wireless networking choose to use 802.11g or 802.11n for the speed and backwards compatibility with older devices. Configuring the wireless access point is not within the scope of this book but once it is configured, as long as the Windows 7 system is compatible with the access point specification, there should not be problems connecting.

Connectt oa WirelessN etwork

Connecting to a wireless network in Windows 7 is very simple. Click the **Network** icon in the notification area or click **Connect to a network** on the Network and Sharing Center as shown in Figure 6.14. Click on the wireless network to connect to as shown in Figure 6.14. The wireless network name is the SSID set on the wireless access point during setup. Then click **Connect**. If the wireless access point has security enabled, which it should, Windows 7 will ask for a security key, as shown in Figure 6.15, and automatically authenticate with the security protocol configured on the access point. Input the security key and click **OK**. This will connect the Windows 7 system to the access point.

Once connected to an access point, most of the Network and Sharing Center options are the same as a local area connection or any other connection for

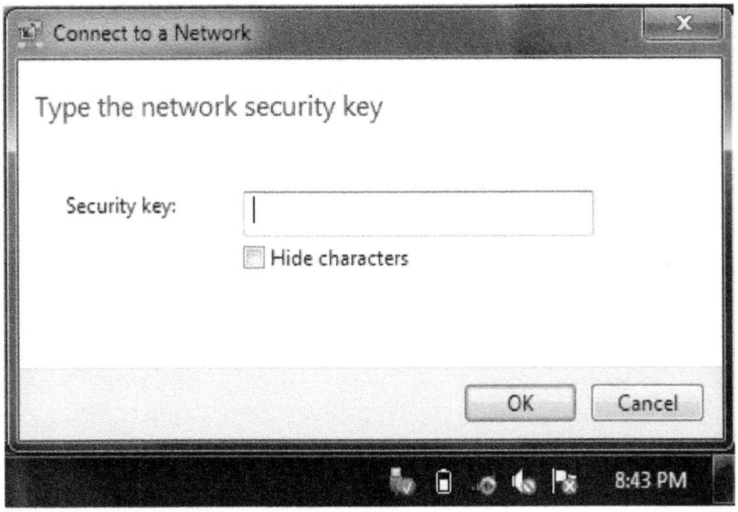

■ **FIGURE 6.15** Input Security Key of Wireless Access Point

that matter. Some differences in the status of the Wireless Network Connection include displaying the SSID, speed, and signal quality of the wireless connection as shown in Figure 6.16. This can be easily accessed by right-clicking the SSID in the Connect to a network pop up and clicking **Status** or as explained in the Network and Sharing Center.

WirelessP roperties

In the Wireless Network Connection Status window shown in Figure 6.16, one can see a **Wireless Properties** button that is not available to LAN or dial-up network connections. Clicking on the **Wireless Properties** button will pop up a window similar to Figure 6.17. Here, the user can see connection properties and make a few changes to settings for this specific wireless network connection. The network type informs the user if the connection is to an access point or an ad-hoc connection. An ad-hoc connection is when the wireless network adapter is configured to connect directly to another computer's wireless adapter. The access point network type actually refers to an infrastructure mode connection where the wireless network adapter is connected to an access point, which in turn is connected to a network. Network availability states if the wireless network connection is configured for all users or the logged on user. By default, any wireless connection added by an administrator account will be available for all users, whereas a standard user will only make the connection available for that user.

■ FIGURE 6.16 Wireless Network Connection Status

The next options in the **Connection** tab of the Wireless Network Properties window are check boxes:

- **Connect automatically when this network is in range** – This is the default setting when configuring a wireless network. This will enable the Windows 7 system to connect to the wireless network whenever it is in range. This is convenient for some end users but can pose a security threat by an attacker spoofing the SSID to match one configured on the Windows 7 system.
- **Connect to a more preferred network if available** – If more networks are available and set to automatically connect, this can be checked and Windows 7 will connect to the network with the higher preference. Setting preferences is looked at in the next section.

■ FIGURE 6.17 Wireless Network Properties – Connections Tab

- **Connect even if the network is not broadcasting its name (SSID)** – This will enable Windows 7 to attempt to connect to saved networks even if the SSID is not broadcasting.

The last option in the **Connection** tab of the Wireless Network Properties is to copy the network profile configured on the Windows 7 system to a USB flash drive to later configure another machine much quicker. This is helpful for administrators setting up multiple computers to connect to a wireless network. The administrator needs to only configure one Windows 7 system and then copy the configuration to a flash drive using the user-friendly wizard. The administrator can then plug the USB drive into other Windows systems to automatically configure those systems with the same properties.

The **Security** tab as shown in Figure 6.18 in the Wireless Network Properties allows for a number of security settings to be configured for the wireless network. These settings work with a top–down approach. Depending on the security type configured on the wireless access point, different encryption types may or may not be required, as is true for the network security key. This is a good time to look at wireless security.

■ **FIGURE 6.18** Wireless Network Properties — Security Tab

No wireless security is the worst security as anyone can connect to the wireless access point and the traffic sent to and from the access point can be read by anybody. These types of access points are considered open and show a yellow shield. Attempting to connect to an open network will show a message of *Information sent over this network might be visible to others.* Often users will connect to these types of wireless networks in public locations. It is critical for the user to choose a **Public** network when connected to open networks. The **Security type** for an insecure wireless access point is **No authentication(Open)** and the **Encryption type** is **None**.

The most basic wireless encryption is Wireless Equivalency Protection (WEP). WEP uses a symmetric key derived from the WEP key that may be 40 bits, 128 bits, 152 bits, or higher. Although this may sound secure, it is extremely easy for an attacker to crack a WEP key by sniffing wireless traffic to and from the wireless access point. To make this encryption more insecure, the WEP key does not change, allowing an attacker unlimited access. The **Security type** for WEP can be set to **No authentication (Open)** or **Shared** and the **Encryption type** is **WEP**.

Wi-Fi Protected Access (WPA) and Wi-Fi Protected Access Version 2 (WPA2) are the much better securities for wireless network encryption. WPA was created as an interim security solution until WPA2 was finalized. WPA2 uses the IEEE 802.11i specification for security. Both of these solutions may be used in personal or enterprise mode. Personal mode authenticates with the access point with a preshared key. The preshared key is the initial key used to authenticate and begin rotation of session keys. Enterprise mode uses IEEE 802.11X and EAP, which uses two sets of keys: session keys and group keys. The session keys are used to authenticate with the access point, whereas group keys are shared among the clients connected to the access point. Both the keys rotate to make it harder for an attacker to crack. Depending on the WPA method used, the **Security type** would be chosen, followed by the **Encryption type**, and then a network authentication method.

Clicking **advanced settings** for the configured security setting will allow the user to configure advanced settings for the security settings applied. Some of these settings allow Federal Information Processing Standards (FIPS) to be enabled for federal compliance.

Manage WirelessN etworks

Most mobile users will have more than one wireless network connection configured on their Windows 7 system. Managing the different wireless network connections and profiles has been improved in Windows 7. The Manage

Wireless Networks console can be accessed from the Network and Sharing Center by clicking **Manage wireless networks** on the left panel. The Manage Wireless Networks console is relatively simple, as shown in Figure 6.19. In the center area, there are the wireless network connections that have been configured for the user to log into. If an administrator is logged in, most of the wireless network connections should be shown unless a user has a private one. When the Windows 7 system scans for wireless networks to connect, it will connect to an available network in the order listed here. You can select a network and move it up or down the list on the Windows Explorer toolbar.

Connections can be deleted by clicking **Remove** or right-clicking the **connection** and selecting **Remove network**. Other options for a connection are in **Adapter properties**. This will pop up the same Wireless Network Properties window referenced in the previous section. **Adapter properties** will show

■ **FIGURE 6.19** Manage Wireless Networks

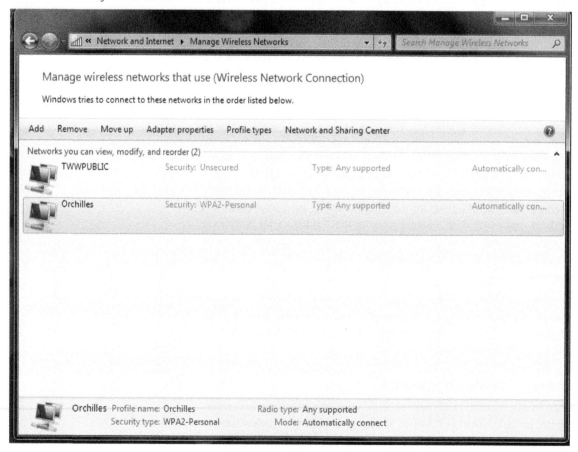

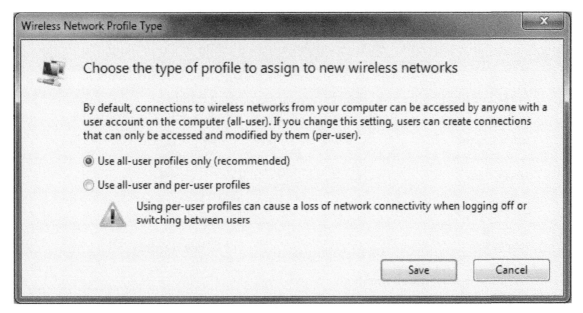

the properties for the network adapter, which will be discussed in this chapter in the "Network Connections" section. Clicking **Profile type** will pop up the Wireless Network Profile Type window shown in Figure 6.20. Here, an administrator or a user who created the wireless network connection can set a connection profile to be an all-user profile or an all-user and per-user profile. Selecting the all-user and per-user profile option will cause the computer to not automatically log on to the wireless network connection when no users are logged in. This is an added security feature, but can cause connection problems in certain scenarios.

The **Add** button in the Manage Wireless Networks toolbar allows a user to create a manual connection to a wireless network that may not be in range or is not broadcasting the SSID or an ad-hoc network to connect two computers together with a wireless connection. To manually create a wireless network connection, click **Add** and **Manually create a network profile** on the console that pops up. The next screen will ask for the **Network name**, which is the SSID of the network that the system will be connecting to and the **Security type, Encryption type**, and **Security Key** that the administrator should already have as shown in Figure 6.21. Reference the Wireless Properties section for an in-depth explanation of these fields.

The second option when clicking **Add** in the Manage Wireless Networks toolbar is to set up a wireless ad-hoc network. In ad-hoc mode, the wireless adapter is configured to connect directly to other computers. This wizard will

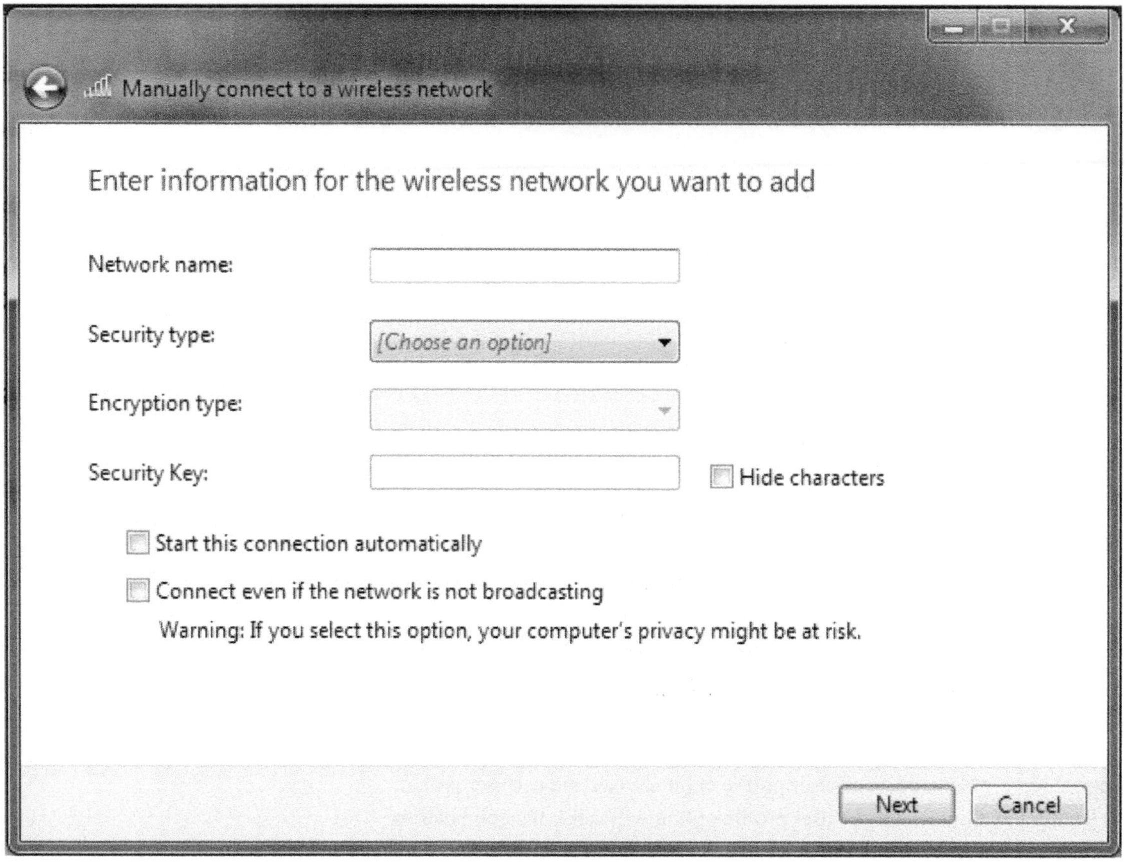

■ FIGURE 6.21 Manually Connect to a Wireless Network

create the ad-hoc network on the system and allow other computers to connect to it using the steps to connect to a wireless network referenced in this section. Since the process is similar to an infrastructure mode (access point) setup, the setup of an ad-hoc network will ask for a **Network name** (the SSID of the network) to be created, as well as a **Security type** and a **Security key** (Figure 6.22). It is the best practice to choose WPA2-Personal as the security type to only allow users with the key to connect to this network.

SoftA ccessP oint

A feature that Microsoft was going to include with Windows 7 but didn't make it is using the Manage Wireless Networks wizard to create a wireless access point. The ad-hoc network setup will allow users to connect computers together with wireless and share an Internet connection coming from another adapter. However, if a Windows 7 user is connected to a wireless access point and wants to share that connection via the same wireless adapter, it is now possible.

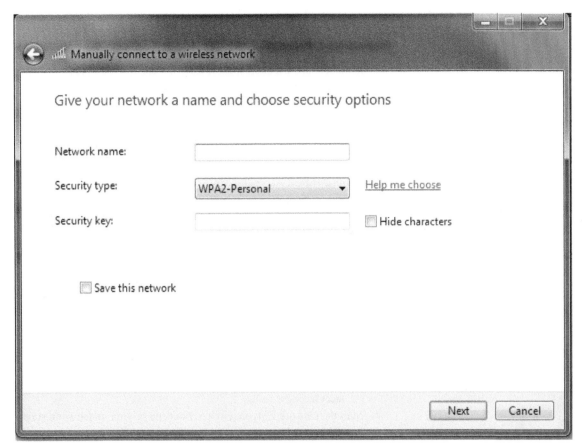

FIGURE 6.22 Set Up Ad-Hoc Wireless Network

Users and administrators will find value in this hidden feature when connected to a hot spot that must be paid for. The user can connect with the wireless adapter and then create a wireless access point with the same adapter to connect other devices. This way the user will end up using only one connection to the hot spot but have more devices on the same connection. Creating a wireless access point may be done manually with the command prompt (administrator privileges required) or with a third-party application called Connectify.

Windows 7 can create a virtual wireless adapter based on the physical wireless adapters with a unique MAC address and all the other network components. This is called *Microsoft Virtual WiFi Miniport Adapter.* Configuring this is simple and this section will walk you through:

1. Configure an SSID and WPA password.
2. Configure Internet Connection Sharing to bridge the virtual adapter with the physical adapter.
3. Startt hew irelessa ccesspoi nt.

A requirement to run an access point in Windows 7 is having a Windows 7 certified wireless network adapter. All wireless network adapters can run in ad-hoc mode in Windows 7 but only these certified cards can run the Access Point mode. For a list of compatible cards, please visit the Connectify site at www.connectify.me/docs/supportedcards.html

Manual Configuration

To manually configure a soft access point:

1. Type **cmd** in the Start menu Search. Right-click and select **Run as administrator**. Accept the UAC prompt or authenticate.
2. Configure the hosted adapter with SSID *Test* and Security key *wpak-eywpakey* by typing: **netsh wlan set hostednetwork mode=allow ssid=Test key=wpakeywpakey**.
3. Configure Internet Connection Sharing for the device that has the Internet connection by:
   a. Clicking **Change adapter settings** in the Network and Sharing Center.
   b. Right-click the adapter with the Internet connection and select **Properties**.
   c. Clickt he **Sharing tab**.
   d. Check **Allow other network users to connect through this computer's Internet connection**.
   e. In the Home networking connection, choose the new hosted interfacet hatw asc reated.
4. Start the network by typing in the command prompt: **netsh wlan start hosted network**.

Connectify

Connectify is a third-party tool that performs the manual steps automatically and with a nice user interface. To create a wireless access point with Connectify:

1. Download and install Connectify from the Web site: www.connectify.me/.
2. When running Connectify it will appear in the notification area. Click oni t.
3. Fill in the WiFi Name as the SSID, Password to connect, and connection with Internet.
4. Click **Start Hotspot**.

Connect to a Soft Access Point

Connecting from any other device to the Windows 7 access point is as simple as connecting to any other wireless network. Select the SSID from the list of scanned networks. Then input the password that was set. Once connected, the device will use the Windows 7 access point as the gateway to the Internet.

CONNECT TO A NETWORK

Microsoft has improved the usability and user-friendliness of connecting to a network. Whether an end user needs to connect to a wireless connection, VPN, or dial-up, connecting to a network is very easy in Windows 7. Figure 6.5 shows the simple Connect to a network pop up. This may be accessed by clicking the **Network** icon on the notification area or clicking **Connect to a network** in the Network and Sharing Center.

The Connect to a network pop up will show any wireless network connection in range that is broadcasting the SSID to connect or any connection that has already been created in the Set up a connection or network area of the Network and Sharing Center. The previous section in this chapter focused on creating these networks. Connecting to a VPN or dial-up connection requires clicking the drop-down arrow in the pop up to display the connections available. Once the connection is selected, click the **Connect** button. If a username or password is required, a pop up will request for it and the connection will initiate.

Disconnecting from a network is just as easy. Click the **Network** icon on the notification area or click **Connect to a network** in the Network and Sharing Center, choose the network to disconnect from and click **Disconnect**.

NETWORK CONNECTIONS

The Network Connections console of the Network and Sharing Center is similar to the Network Connections from Windows since TCP/IP was introduced. To access the Network Connections console, click **Change adapter settings** on the left pane of the Network and Sharing Center. This console will show all of the configured network adapters and connections as shown in Figure 6.23. Here is where administrators and users can manually configure all of the features explained in this chapter and more. Depending on the adapter or connection chosen, different options will appear in the toolbar. Right-clicking the adapter will also bring up options.

Network adapters may be disabled on the hardware level by right-clicking the device and selecting **Disable** or clicking **Disable this network device** on the toolbar. Disabling the device will automatically disconnect any connection to that device. This can be seen in the Device Manager as well.

To check the status of a device, right-click the adapter and select **Status** or select the device, and click **View status of this connection** on the toolbar. This is the same window referenced in the Network and Sharing Center.

The **Diagnose this connection** button or right-clicking the adapter will bring up the Windows Network Diagnostics. This wizard scans the network adapter and connections for problems. This is a great tool to use for troubleshooting a network connection.

■ FIGURE 6.23 Network Connections

Renaming a device is as simple as right-clicking the device and selecting **Rename** or clicking the device and selecting **Rename this connection**.

To create a shortcut to the connection as was done to easily connect to dial-up and VPN in older versions of Windows, right-click the connection or adapter and select **Create shortcut**.

Properties

Right-clicking on an adapter or connection and choosing **Properties** will bring up the more advanced properties of network connections and adapters. This can also be initiated by selecting the adapter and clicking **Change settings of this connection**. This section focuses on local and wireless area connection properties as shown in Figure 6.24. The Network Properties window will have two tabs, a **Networking** tab where all the networking protocols and items installed can be configured and a **Sharing** tab to enable Internet Connection Sharing of the selected device.

Networking Tab

The **Networking** tab will show the network adapter that is used for the selected connection. Clicking **Configure...** will bring up the Device Manager properties for the device. It is not recommended to make changes to the

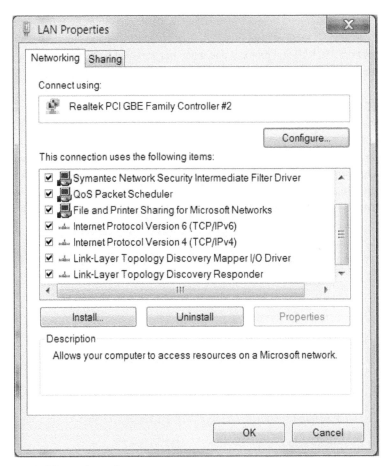

■ **FIGURE 6.24** Network Properties

device unless the administrator knows exactly what is being changed. Under the **Configure**… button is a list of the items used by the selected connection that includes various clients, services, and/or protocols. By default, Windows 7 will install Client for Microsoft Networks, QoS Packet Scheduler, IPv6, IPv4, Link-Layer Topology Discovery Mapper I/O Driver, and Link-Layer Topology Discovery Responder.

To install a client, service, and/or protocol:

1. Click **Install**…
2. Select **Client**, **Service**, or **Protocol** and click **Add**.
3. Select the network feature to add. If you have a disc, select **Have Disk**.

To uninstall an item, select the item, and click **Uninstall**.

The most important item for networking to work correctly is TCP/IPv4 and TCP/IPv6. If these are not installed, they are most likely required by your network. TCP/IP is a protocol and when not installed will show up during the install of the protocol steps.

TCP/IP Properties

The TCP/IP properties are where an administrator can configure the IP settings of the connection, DNS, Gateway, and WINS. These options are very similar for IPv6 and IPv4. The **General** tab is the simpler configuration where an administrator can configure the connection to obtain an IP address and DNS automatically through DHCP or set the connection to static where it is configured manually as shown in Figure 6.25. Most networks use DHCP either

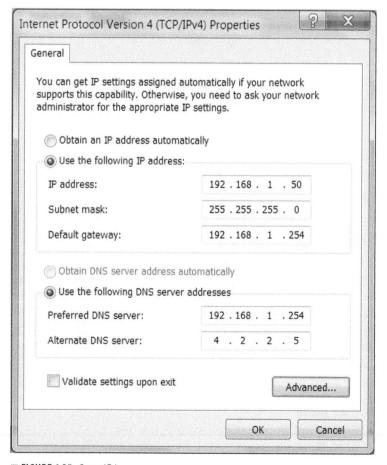

■ FIGURE 6.25 General Tab

through a dedicated DHCP server or a router. In the event that DHCP is not available or the computer needs to be set up with a static IP, it can be set here. The same IP address cannot exist more than once in a network so ensure the IP address assigned is well documented. The subnet mask is the subnet mask of the network depending on what network scheme is being used in the environment. The default gateway needs to be configured to access outside of the network or the Internet. DNS can be configured to be static even if the IP address is automatically assigned. Generally, a DHCP server will assign a DNS but in the event that it does not it may be assigned manually. Only the preferred DNS server is required but having a backup DNS server is always a good practice.

The **Advanced**… button will initiate the Advanced TCP/IP Settings window where more IP, DNS, and WINS settings may be applied. The **IP Settings** tab allows a user to add more than one IP address to the device by clicking **Add…**. IP addresses may also be removed or edited. Note that each IP address requires a subnet mask to be configured. More than one default gateway may also be added by using the **Add…** button in the Default gateways section. The same is true for editing a gateway or removing it.

The **DNS** tab is more complex as there are more settings for DNS as shown in Figure 6.26. Generally, these settings are set on the DHCP server and do not have to be manually configured each computer. However, if DHCP is not available on the network, manually setting DNS is possible through this tab:

- **DNS Server addresses** – The DNS server addresses allow the user to add many DNS servers and select the order for them to be used. This is done by clicking the **Add…** button and adding DNS servers. Selecting a DNS server and moving it up or down will set the order that Windows 7 will use the DNS server to resolve hostnames.
- **Append primary and connection specific DNS suffixes** – On by default, this option is used to resolve unqualified computer names in the domain. If the computer name is OrchillesHome and the domain is orchilles.com, then the computer name will resolve to OrchillesHome.orchilles.com
- **Append parent suffixes of the primary DNS suffix** – On by default, this option enables resolving unqualified computer names using the parent/child domain hierarchy. If the computer name is OrchillesHome and the domain is test.orchilles.com, then the computer name will first resolve to OrchillesHome.test.orchilles.com and if not available to OrchillesHome.orchilles.com
- **Append these DNS suffixes (in order)** – This option is used to resolve DNS suffixes in the order selected. This is useful after a domain migration or when other child domains are available.

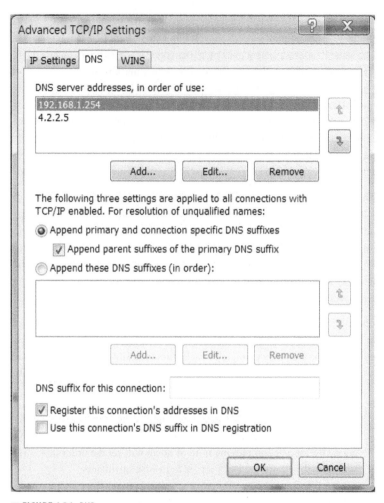

■ **FIGURE 6.26** DNS

- **DNS suffix for this connection** – This option allows an administrator to set a specific DNS suffix for the connection that overrides DNS names already configured.
- **Register this connection's address in DNS** – On by default, this option will register the connection in the DNS with the computer's fully qualified domain name.
- **Use this connection's DNS suffix in DNS registration** – This option will register all IP addresses for the selected connection in DNS under thepa rentdom ain.

The **WINS** tab is used to configure the WINS settings to resolve NetBIOS computer names to IPv4 addresses. This option is not available for IPv6. If

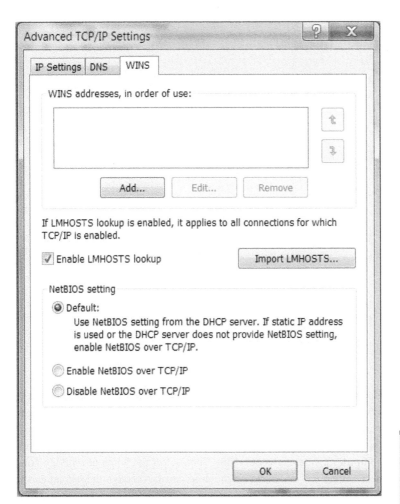

■ **FIGURE 6.27** WINS

WINS is configured in your environment, this tab will allow the configuration of the WINS server. WINS requires NetBIOS Over TCP/IP service installed, which was discussed earlier in this section. To add WINS addresses is similar to DNS, click **Add…** and input the address. Other options include enabling LMHOSTS lookup and NetBIOS settings as shown in Figure 6.27.

Sharing tab

Internet Connection Sharing can be enabled for almost any network connection. It is simple to enable using the **Sharing** tab of the Network Properties window (Figure 6.28). The Windows 7 system must have more than one connected connection for this to work. The theory is to Internet

NOTE

Afterm akingc hangest o advanced settings, in particular DNS, it may be required to flush and register the DNS. This may be done in the command prompt:

1. Opena c ommandp rompt with elevated privileges.
2. Type: **ipconfig/flushdns**
3. Type: **ipconfig/register dns**

The **ipconfig** command can also be used to release DHCP and renew by using the **ipconfig /release** command to release the DHCP settings and **ipconfig/ renew** to obtain a new DHCP configuration. **ipconfig/all**w ill show all settings for all adapters.

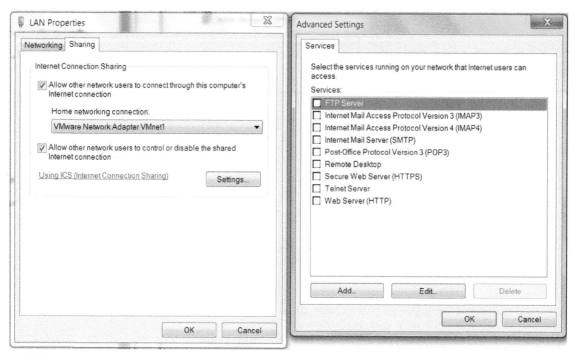

■ **FIGURE 6.28** Sharing Tab

Connection Sharing to share the connection coming into the Windows 7 system from one adapter with another connection on that same system that may be connected to a switch or a hub. To enable Internet Connection Sharing, simply check **Allow other network users to connect through this computer's Internet connection.** Then select the home networking connection that will be shared on the drop down. Although the second check box is on by default, we recommend disabling the option to **Allow other network users to control or disable the shared Internet connection.** Finally, the **Settings**… button will bring up a window that allows services to be passed through the Windows 7 host from the Internet. This is similar to a router that allows certain services to be accessed from outside, as shown in Figure 6.28.

HOMEGROUP

HomeGroup is a new feature in Windows 7 and was introduced in Chapter 1, "Introduction to Windows 7." This feature is more for end users at home to easily create a Windows network. This feature is based on the fact that the user selects the network location as Home when first connected. When a Windows 7 computer connects to a network and selects Home as the location, the system will scan the network for a HomeGroup. If the system finds a HomeGroup that was already created in the network, it will ask for the password as shown in Figure 6.29. The user then simply enters the HomeGroup password and is connected to the HomeGroup. The password can be seen from the computer that created the HomeGroup by going to **Control Panel | HomeGroup** and clicking **view or print the homegroup password**unde r **Other homegroup actions**.

Creating a HomeGroup is as simple as following the wizard, also referenced in Chapter 1, "Introduction to Windows 7." Once the computer is connected to a HomeGroup, either by joining one or creating one, the HomeGroup

■ **FIGURE 6.29** Join a HomeGroup

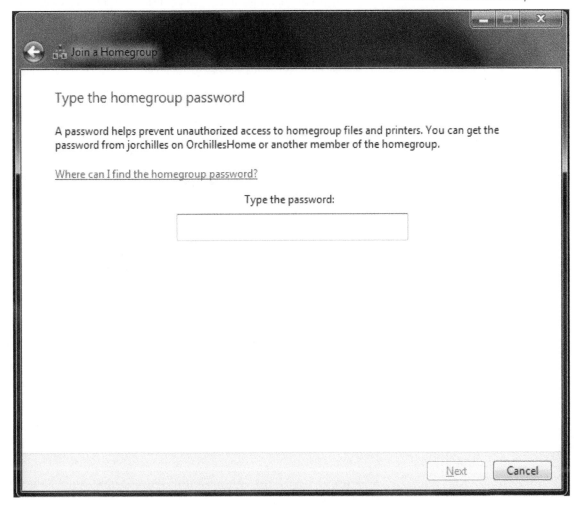

settings may be changed in the HomeGroup console found in the Control Panel as shown in Figure 6.30. In this console, the user can choose what libraries and printers to share by clicking on the check boxes next to Pictures, Music, Videos, Documents, and Printers. Keep in mind these options will share all the items in the respective Library. Other options in the HomeGroup console are:

- **Share media with devices** – This enables the ability to stream the shared items with all devices in the same location.
- **View or print the HomeGroup password** – This console will show the HomeGroup password so other devices can join.
- **Change the password** – This will allow a user to change the Home-Group password. Ensure if it is changed that it be something complex.
- **Leave the HomeGroup** – This can be used to disassociate a computer from the HomeGroup.
- **Change advanced sharing settings** – This initiates the console to change advance sharing settings by location.

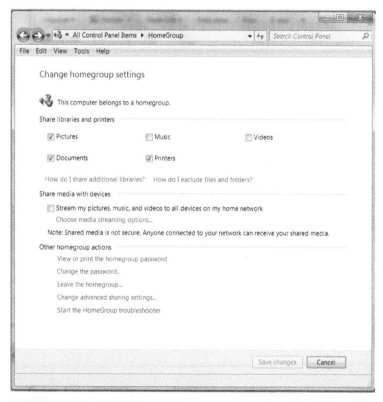

■ **FIGURE 6.30** HomeGroup Settings

- **Start the HomeGroup troubleshooter** – This wizard is helpful for troubleshootingi ssuesw itht heH omeGroup.

MOBILITY

Road warriors, the term used for the mobile workforce, have always been the most problematic end user in an organization. Before Windows 7 and the addition of the enhanced mobility center, location aware printing, and VPN Reconnect features, the mobile worker always had issues with connectivity, making it even more difficult for an administrator to assist. Windows 7 brings many new features to assist the end user in staying connected and to make it easier to configure settings suitable for the enviroment they are working in. This section looks at the Windows Mobility Center, Location Aware Printing, and VPN Reconnect, all great new features to make it simpler for the end user when on the road.

WindowsM obilityC enter

Microsoft introduced the Windows Mobility Center (Figure 6.31), which is available to all laptop, netbook, and Tablet PC users. This console may be accessed by right-clicking the **Power** icon on the notification area and selecting **Windows Mobility Center** or started manually by running **C:\Windows\ System32\mblctr.exe**, It is a centralized place to manage all the settings mobile user will likely need, including:

- **Brightness** – The user can easily slide the Display brightness bar left and right for more or less brightness. The brighter the display, the more battery is drained.
- **Volume** – The user can easily slide the volume bar left and right to adjust the volume or completely mute the sound from the system.

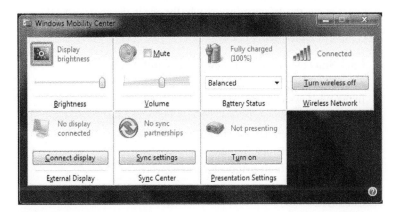

■ **FIGURE 6.31** Windows Mobility Center

- **Battery Status** – This shows the status of the battery whether the system is charging or using the battery. The user can select the power options High performance, Power Saver, or Balanced, which will be referenced later in this chapter.
- **Wireless Network** – This provides the status of the wireless connection and can shut it off to preserve power when not in use.
- **External Display** – A user can easily connect another display that is detected from here without having to go through the traditional **Control Panel | Display | Screen Resolution**.
- **Sync Center** – This allows the user to view the status of file synchronization or start a new sync. The Sync Center can be accessed through the **Control Panel | Sync Center**.
- **Presentation Settings** – This allows the user to easily set up a project to display or present what is on the desktop.

As one can see, the new features that Microsoft provides the mobile user are great. However, if the users are not educated that these options and features are available, they will bring no value to them. All of these settings are simple and showing a user how to access the Mobility Center will be beneficial for the end user and the administrators.

LocationA wareP rinting

Location Aware Printing is a great new feature in Windows 7. Often mobile users have issues every time they are in a different location and have to print. Most users are used to printing to a default printer. In the past, only one printer could be set as the default printer and this printer was only in one location. Now, thanks to the Network Locations feature, printers may be set as default printers depending on the location. Therefore, a user when connected to the office network will have an office printer as the default printer and when the user goes home, the default printer will be the one in the home network.

To set up Location Aware Printing:

1. Click **Start** menu and then click **Devices and Printers**.
2. Selecta **printer** by clicking it.
3. In the Windows Explorer toolbar, click **Manage Default Printers**.
4. In the Manage Default Printers console, click **Change my default printer when I change networks**, as shown in Figure 6.32:
   a. Selectt he **network** from the dropdown list.
   b. Selectt he **default printer** for that network.
   c. Click **Add**.
5. Click **OK**.

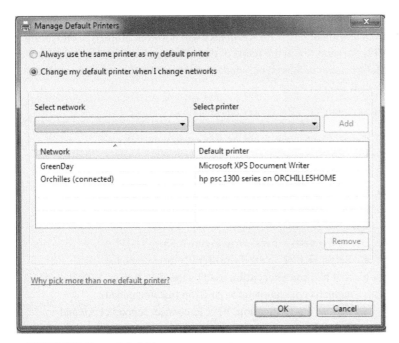

■ **FIGURE 6.32** Manage Default Printers

VPNR econnect

VPN connections are one of the primary methods mobile users use to connect to an organization when offsite. As explained earlier in this chapter, a VPN connection requires an Internet connection to be established for the VPN connection to connect through. In the past, if the Internet connection was interrupted for a few seconds or more, the VPN connection would drop closing any connection established with the business network. Microsoft attempts to resolve this issue, which is very common for mobile users, by introducing VPN Reconnect.

Technically, VPN Reconnect is built on IPsec Tunnel Mode, which uses IKEv2 for key negotiation and transmits ESP packets. MOBIKE is used to switch the tunnel end points when the Internet connection drops or is changed. Therefore, a user can be using VPN from a wired LAN at a remote office and then switch to a wireless hotspot without the VPN connection dropping causing the user to reconnect. Other variations that VPN Reconnect addresses are switching from IPv4 to IPv6 on the Internet connection, switching when the IP address of the Internet interface changes, and persistent connection to VPN when the Internet connection drops frequently.

The VPN server must be configured to use IPSec Tunnel Mode, which uses IKEv2; without this, VPN Reconnect will not work properly. Configuring a VPN Server is not in the scope of this reference but note that IPSec Tunnel Mode can be configured on Windows Server 2008 R2 and many other commercial VPN Servers.

To configure VPN Reconnect on a Windows 7 client:

1. Create a VPN connection, as referenced in this chapter.
2. Navigate to Network Connections by clicking **Change adapter settings** on the Network and Sharing Center.
3. Right-clickt he **VPN connection** and select **Properties**.
4. Ensure the IP or Fully Qualified Domain name of the VPN server is filled out properly.
5. Ont he **Security** tab shown in Figure 6.33:
    a. Select **IKEv2** on the **Type of VPN** drop-down list.
    b. Sett he **Data encryption** used by the VPN Server. VPN Reconnect supports encryption up to AES256 (recommended).
    c. Sett he **Authentication**. VPN Reconnect supports EAP and X.509 Machine Certificates. For Authentication properties select **Properties** under the drop down list.
6. Click **Advanced settings** under the **Type of VPN**dr op-downl ist.
7. Ensure **Mobility** is checked and **Network outage time** is set according to policy. 30 min is the default. If **Mobility** is not checked, then tunnel switchingw illnot oc cur.

WorkingO ffline

Like older versions of Windows, Windows 7 allows users to work with files that may not be immediately available. For instance, a user has a home drive on a file server but needs access to the files in that drive when not in the office or connected to the file server. This feature is used mostly by mobile users but may also benefit other users. Configuring offline files involves multiple steps. First Group Policy must be configured with the correct settings, then the offline folders must be configured, and finally the local user settings for working offline must be set.

Offline files allow the user to store network files and folders on the local computer and access them when the network resource is not available. Windows 7 will automatically use the offline files when the resource is not available making it much easier for the user. Once the resource is available, Windows 7 will automatically synchronize the files with the network resource. This feature has been in Windows prior to Windows 7 but there

■ **FIGURE 6.33** VPN Security Tab

are two new enhancements: change-only syncing and unavailable file and folder ghosting. The user also has control to manually synchronize the files and folders through the **Sync Center** available in the Control Panel.

Offline file policy may be configured on the computer or user level in both domain Group Policy and Local Group Policy in the **Computer or User Configuration | Administrative Templates | Network | Offline Files**. The first item to enable is **Allow or Disallow use of the Offline Files**. Other policies related to offline files may be set here and applied to users or computers. These options depend on the environment and all include a description to assist the decision of enabling or disabling. Once offline files is enabled, an administrator must choose what shares may be used offline. Sharing files and folders is referenced in Chapter 8, "Securing Windows 7."

The offline files options may also be edited through the Sync Center by clicking **Manage offline files** on the left pane. The offline files properties are:

■ **General** – The user can disable or enable offline files and view offline files on the current computer through a Windows Explorer window.

■ **Disk Usage** – The user may configure how much space on the disk is allocated and may be used for offline files. Clicking **Change Limits** allows the user to set the maximum amount of space for offline and temporary files. Finally, it allows deleting of all temporaryfi les.

■ **Encryption** – This allows encrypting or decrypting offline files. Encryption will be referenced in Chapter 8, "Securing Windows 7."

■ **Network** – This allows the user to work offline on slow connections and to set how often to check the connection speed.

The end user will most likely not be involved in the first two steps of enabling offline files and then sharing files or folders with offline files enabled. The mobile user may enable offline files from a shared resource. The end user may right-click on the shared **file** or **folder** in Windows Explorer and select **Make Available Offline**. If the policy allows, this will add a sync partnership to the end user's computer. The mobile user will also be able to manually sync offline files and manage other sync-related tasks through the **Sync Center**. A user may view current sync partnerships by clicking **View sync partnerships** on the left pane of the **Sync Center**. From this console, the user may also choose to sync files manually with either method:

■ **Sync all offline files and folders** – This will sync all partnerships that are currently connected by clicking **Sync All**.

■ **Sync a specific network share** – Clicking the **individual partnership** and selecting **Sync** will sync only that shared folder.

Automatic synchronization may also be configured for a specific partnership if not done so with policy. The automatic sync times are:

■ **At a specific scheduled time** – The user or administrator can create a New Sync Schedule by right-clicking the partnership and selecting **Schedule for Offline Files**.

■ **When the user logs on** – If the user logs on and the resource is available, the synchronization will occur. This often slows the log on process.

■ **When the computer is idle** – This is sometimes not the case for the mobileus er.

■ **When the user locks or unlocks Windows**

A user may also resolve any synchronization conflicts that may occur with files. The user may click **View Sync Conflicts** on the left pane of the Sync Center. This will display all conflicts. Double-click the conflict to resolve and select which version of the file to keep or the option to keep both files. Be careful to not overwrite the wrong file.

POWER MANAGEMENT

Power management has been around in Windows since Windows XP. However, Windows 7 has improved the options and controls the user and administrator have of the power options. Today, saving energy has become a large issue, not just for the environment but for the organization's power bill. Mobile users have always cared about saving energy to ensure the laptops do not run out of juice at the most critical time. Power management in Windows 7 is configured based on power plans. These options are available in the **Control Panel | Power Options**.

PowerPlans

Windows 7 includes three power plans by default. The power plans can be viewed and selected on all Windows 7 computers in **Control Panel | Power Options**. Laptop and mobile device users can also choose a power plan by clicking the **Battery** icon in the notification area and either selecting the desired plan or **More power options** for the Control Panel console shown in Figure 6.34. By default, Microsoft includes three plans:

- **Balanced** – As the name suggests, this plan balances energy usage and system performance. Depending on the task being performed and applications running the processor will speed up when resources are required and slow down when they are not. By default, the display is turned off after 10 min of no activity and the computer is put to sleep after 30 min of inactivity.
- **Power Saver** – This is the default low-power usage plan designed to make laptop batteries last longer. The plan slows the processor down and can impact the use of more resource intensive applications. By default, the display is turned off after 5 min of no activity and the computer is put to sleep after 15 min of inactivity.
- **High Performance** – This option runs the processor at full speed all the time even when idle. This plan will drain a laptop battery the quickest but ensure the best performance. By default, the display is turned off after 15 min of no activity and the computer is never put to sleep.

Changing plan settings are divided into basic and advanced options. When a user clicks **Change plan settings** in the **Power Options** console of the

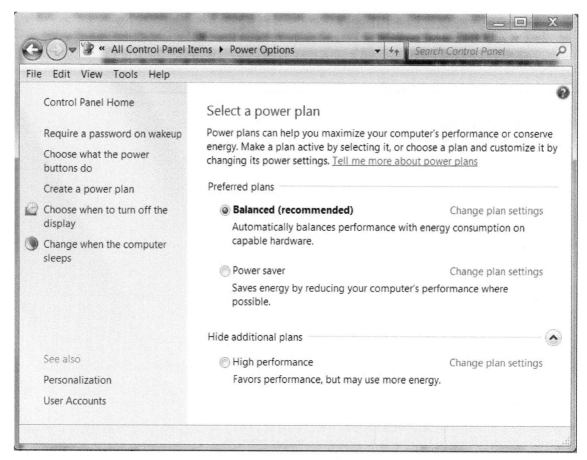

■ **FIGURE 6.34** Power Options

Control Panel, the only two basic options that appear only allow setting the time to turn off the display and put the computer to sleep. These are often the options the end user cares the most about but as an administrator, the advanced power settings let one customize the individual power settings. Clicking **Change advanced power settings** will pop up the advanced settings of the Power Options as shown in Figure 6.35. From here, the user may choose what power plan to modify from the drop-down menu. Below that, the advanced settings may be configured:

■ **Require a password on wakeup** – This option should always be set to **Yes** for security reasons but can be set to **No** on computers not on a domain and with only one user account.

■ **Hard disk** – The hard drive may be set to be turned off after the selected number of minutes. Setting the minutes to 0 will set the option to Never.

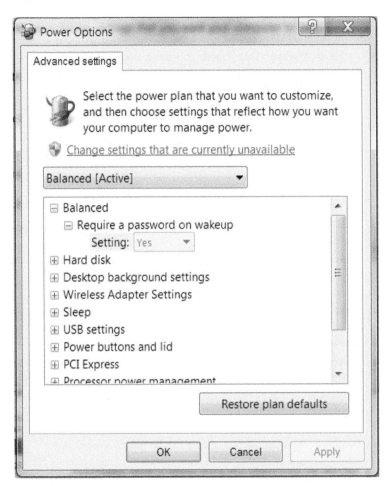

FIGURE 6.35 Advanced Power Options

- **Desktop Background Settings** – This option enables or disables the slide show feature of the desktop.
- **Wireless Adapter Settings** – This option allows the configuration of the power saving mode of the wireless adapter. The options include Maximum Performance, Low Power Saving, Medium Power Saving, and High Power Saving.
- **Sleep**
  - **Sleep After** – This option allows setting the amount of minutes to sleep the entire computer after the set amount of minutes. Setting the minutes to 0 will set the option to Never.

- ❑ **Allow hybrid sleep** – This option allows the use of the new Windows 7 sleep feature instead of the traditional Windows sleep mode. The hybrid sleep mode puts the computer in low-power consumption state until the user resumes it. This means the computer is still using power but not as much as if it were on.
- ❑ **Hibernate after** – This option enables the traditional hibernation from older versions of Windows. When the computer is put into hibernation, a snapshot of the memory is taken and then restored when the computer comes back up. Setting the minutes to 0 will set the option to Never.
- ❑ **Allow wake timers** – This option enables timed or scheduled events that can wake the computer from sleep.
- ■ **USB Settings** – This option enables the USB selective suspend feature whena vailable.
- ■ **Power buttons and lid** – These two options set what occurs when the power or sleep button is pressed. Options are to do nothing, sleep, hibernate, or shut down.
- ■ **PCI Express** – This option allows the user to configure PCI Express devices. Options are Off, Moderate Power Saving, or Maximum Power Saving.
- ■ **Processor Power Management** – These options set the minimum and maximum processor state based on a percentage of the CPU usage. The system cooling policy will enable the fan speed to increase or decrease based on the processor state. Options for the cooling policy are Active orP assive.
- ■ **Display** – This option sets how long to wait before turning off the display in minutes. Setting the minutes to 0 will set the option to Never.
- ■ **Multimedia settings** – These options set the computer to not sleep, prevent idling, or enter away mode when sharing media. When playing video, the options are to optimize the video quality, power settings, or balanced.

Now that the advanced settings are understood, it is simple to create a new power plan. In the **Power Options** console, select **Create a power plan** on the left panel. A window similar to Figure 6.36 will prompt the user to choose a power plan to copy when creating the new one. On the bottom, a **Plan Name** must be chosen. Clicking **Next** will ask for the basic power options to be configured. Once the user selects the basic power options and clicks **Create**, the new power plan will appear in the **Power Options** console. From here, a user or an administrator may change advanced settings and apply the power plan.

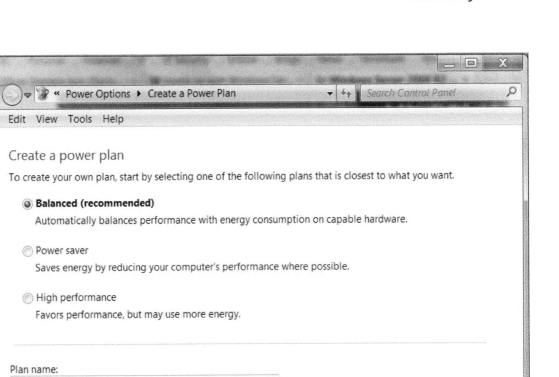

GroupP olicy

Managing a single or a few system's power options is not very difficult using the previous reference. However, administrators will need to modify, create, and apply power plans to more than a few computers. Thankfully, power management can be done via Group Policy on a domain:

1. In the Group Policy Management Editor, expand **Computer Configuration | Preferences | Control Panel Settings** and select **Power Options** for computer policy or **UserC onfiguration\Preferences | Control Panel Settings** and select **Power Options** for user policy.
2. Right-click **Power Options**, click **New**, and then click **Power Plan** (Windows Vista and later).

3. On the Action list, select **create**, **update**, or **replace**, depending on youri ntent.
4. In the selection list, choose the **power plan** that is being worked on.
5. To set the plan as active, select the **Set As the Active Power Plan** checkbox.
6. In the Options, select the options for the plan.
7. Click **OK** to close. Once Group Policy is refreshed, the setting will takee ffect.

You may also open the Group Policy object that you would like to edit from **Administrative Templates System | Power Management | Computer Configuration**.

CommandL ine

Windows 7 also includes a Power Configuration utility for managing power options from a command line. Start a command prompt with elevated privileges and type **powercfg /?** for a list of commands. There are many commands that can be used with powercfg. For example:

- **powercfg –energy** will scan the computer for energy efficiency problems and return a report in HTML format. This may be useful for energyc ompliance.
- **powercfg –l** will display existing power plans with an * on the one beingus ed.
- **powercfg –a** will query the computer for what power features are availableont heha rdware.

ENHANCEMENTS WITH WINDOWS SERVER 2008 R2

Windows 7 and Windows Server 2008 R2 were released at around the same time by Microsoft. This was purposefully done as some of the new features of Windows 7 do not work with prior versions of Windows Server. On the other hand, some features of Windows Server 2008 R2 do not work on clients other than Windows 7. For this reason, this section focuses on configuring Windows 7 as a client to the enhanced features in Windows Server 2008 R2. This section will not focus on configuring the server side as it is not within the scope of this book.

BranchCache

Many organizations have more than one office connected together via resources that are not optimal. Many users from a remote office may require working on files from the data center, or corporate office. Traditionally, each user will download the files from the other location independently. BranchCache solves this issue by allowing data downloaded by one user at a remote site to be accessed by any other user in that same site. There are two ways to do this:

■ **Hosted Cache** – One Windows Server 2008 R2 server at each location has BranchCache installed, enabled, and configured. The server will cache the data on behalf of the entire location when it is requested from a remote location for the first time. When more users request the same file from the remote location, the server at the location will provide the cached file eliminating the resources needed to download across sites again.

■ **Distributed Cache** – No dedicated server is used on site. Once a user requests data from the remote location, the file is downloaded and cached on that user's system. When another user requests the same file from a remote location, it will be distributed by the first user who obtained it and has it cached.

The most complex configuration for BranchCache is on the Windows Server 2008 R2 system. Configuring BranchCache on the Windows 7 system is fairly simple and done through Group Policy:

1. In the Group Policy Management Editor, expand Computer Configuration\Policies\Administrative Templates\Network\BranchCache.
2. Double-click **Turn on BranchCache** and set to **Enabled**.
3. Depending on the cache mode, enable **Turn on BranchCache – X Caching Mode**.
4. Configure the latency required for caching to not cache if the latency is less than a certain threshold (option) by double-clicking **Configure BranchCache for network files,** setting it to **Enabled**, and setting the latency.
5. Configure the amount of disk space to be used for the cache on the clients by double-clicking **Set percentage of disk space used for client computer cache**.
6. Navigate to **Computer Configuration | Policies | Windows Settings | Windows Firewall with Advanced Security | Inbound Rules**.
7. Right-click and select **New Rule**.
8. Depending on the environment, under HTTP, Port, TCP 80, create a rule to allow all profiles or only a domain.
9. Depending on the environment, create a rule under WS-Discovery, Port, UDP 3702 to allow all profiles or only a domain.
10. Close **GPO** and refresh the policy on the computers.

BranchCache may also be enabled in an elevated command prompt:

1. Open an elevated command prompt.
2. For distributed mode type: **netsh branchecache set service mode=distributed**
3. For hosted mode type: **netsh branchecache set service mode=hostedclient location=<hosted cache server>**

DirectAccess

DirectAccess, like BranchCache, is a new feature in Windows 7 and Windows Server 2008 R2. DirectAccess allows remote users to always be securely connected to a corporate environment via an Internet connection without the need of a VPN. In other words, DirectAccess is an always-on connection for employees inside and remote to the organization infrastructure. This new feature is a great news for both end users and administrators as the end users will not have trouble connecting and administrators will be able to connect to the end user wherever they are.

Deploying DirectAccess is not as simple, however. It requires IPv6 infrastructure or alternatives like Teredo, 6to4, or IP-HTTPS. Most of these protocols have not been deployed in most work environments. Deploying the infrastructure for IPv6 is a huge project on its own and once DirectAccess is running, it will only work for Windows 7 systems.

Depending on the environment, infrastructure, and DirectAccess setup, the Windows 7 client may be configured. Generally, this will involve adding the computer account to a security group for DirectAccess, confirming IPv6 is properly configured on the client computer, and configuring certificates on the client computer. Due to all of these reasons, configuring a Windows 7 client for DirectAccess will not be referenced in this book.

Microsoft is providing free of charge a DirectAccess Step-by-Step guide for a Test Lab. This document provides configuration and step-by-step references to configuring DirectAccess in a lab. The file is hosted on Microsoft. com servers at www.microsoft.com/downloads/details.aspx?displaylang= en&FamilyID=8d47ed5f-d217-4d84-b698-f39360d82fac.

DomainJoi n

Joining a Windows 7 computer to a domain does not require Windows Server 2008 R2 as a Windows 7 system can join any Active Directory domain. Windows Server 2008 R2 does provide the most Group Policy settings for Windows 7 but is not required. The **System** console of the Control Panel provides information under the Computer name, domain, and workgroup

■ **FIGURE 6.37** Computer Name

settings. Clicking **Change settings** to the right of the information will pop up the System Properties as shown in Figure 6.37. This is the classic view of the **Computer Name** tab. Windows 7 introduces a new way to connect to a domain or home network with the **Network ID...** button. This initiates the Join a Domain or Workgroup wizard, which asks the end user or administrator a series of questions to set up either a home network or workgroup, or connect to a domain.

The traditional way of joining a computer to the domain is clicking the **Change...** button as shown in Figure 6.37. In the Computer Name/Domain Changes pop up shown in Figure 6.38, the user can change the computer name or hostname of the machine. A restart is required after changing the computer name. The user can also join the computer to the domain by selecting the radio button next to **Domain** and inputting the domain that the machine will be joining. The user must have rights to join the computer to the domain in the Active Directory as credentials will be required. A computer that is already

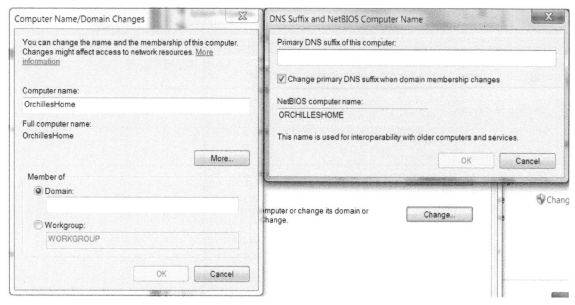

■ **FIGURE 6.38** Computer Name/Domain Changes and DNS Suffix and NetBIOS Computer Name Configuration

on a domain may be removed by selecting **Workgroup** and filling out the workgroup name. The user removing the computer from the domain must also have rights to do so in Active Directory as credentials will be required. Clicking the **More...** button under the Computer Name will prompt the DNS Suffix and NetBIOS Computer Name window as shown in Figure 6.38. Here, the user may fill out the Primary DNS suffix of the computer if it is different than the computer name. Most changes in these options require a reboot.

OfflineDom ainJoi n

Offline domain join is a new feature in Windows 7 and Windows Server 2008 R2 that lets you join a computer to a domain without contacting a domain controller directly. This feature can add computers to a domain when network connectivity is not available. When a computer joins a domain, trust relationships change between both the computer and the Active Directory domain. Prior to Windows 7 and Windows Server 2008 R2, there was no application to make these relationship changes on the computer unless it was directly connected to the domain controller at the time it joined the domain. Windows 7 and Windows Server 2008 R2 include the application djoin.exe located on %SystemDrive\Windows\System32\djoin.exe to perform this task. The general process for using offline domain join is simple:

1. Create the computer account on the Active Directory.
2. Force the replication of the secrets of the computer that is going to join thedom ain.

3. Use djoin.exe to output the relevant state information that the computer will use to connect to the domain to a text file.

4. Run the text file on the computer using djoin.exe and when it reboots, itw illbe j oinedt ot hedom ain.

This tool can be used to deploy Windows 7 computers using the unattended .xml file as it now includes a section for offline domain join.

Djoin.exe must be run with an elevated command prompt. Running djoin. exe /? will display the available commands as shown in Figure 6.39. As the examples show, to provision a computer account to a domain, you will need to use **djoin.exe /PROVISION /DOMAIN <DomainName> /MACHINE <ComputerName> /SAVEFILE <FilePath>** on a computer that is on the

■ **FIGURE 6.39** djoin.exe /?

```
C:\Windows\system32\cmd.exe

C:\Users\jorchilles>djoin /?
Usage: djoin.exe [/OPTIONS]

  /PROVISION  - Provision a computer account in the domain
      /DOMAIN <Name> - <Name> of the domain to join
      /MACHINE <Name> - <Name> of the computer joining the domain
      /MACHINEOU <OU> - Optional <OU> where the account is created
      /DCNAME <DC> - Optional <DC> to target for account creation
      /REUSE - Reuse any existing account (password will be reset)
      /SAVEFILE <FilePath> - Save provisioning data to a file at <FilePath>
      /NOSEARCH - Skip account conflict detection, requires DCNAME (faster)
      /DOWNLEVEL - Support using a Windows Server 2008 DC or earlier
      /PRINTBLOB - Return base64 encoded metadata blob for an answer file
      /DEFPWD - Use default machine account password (not recommended)

  /REQUESTODJ  - Request offline domain join at next boot
      /LOADFILE <FilePath> - <FilePath> specified previously via /SAVEFILE
      /WINDOWSPATH <Path> - <Path> to the Windows directory in an offline image
      /LOCALOS - Allows /WINDOWSPATH to specify the locally running OS.
                 This command must be run as a local Administrator.
                 This option requires a reboot for changes to be applied.

Examples:

To provision a computer account in the domain:
djoin.exe /PROVISION /DOMAIN <DomainName> /MACHINE <MachineName>
          /SAVEFILE <FilePath>
          Note: Other parameters are optional

To request the local machine to perform an offline domain join:
djoin.exe /REQUESTODJ /LOADFILE <FilePath> /WINDOWSPATH <Path>
          Note: Other parameters are optional
```

domain or the domain controller itself. Ensure the computer name has been added to the domain. Then on the local machine that is offline or on the domain run in an elevated command prompt: **djoin.exe /requestodj / loadfile <filepath> /windowspatch <%WindowsDirectory%>**

■ SUMMARY

This chapter addressed Windows 7 networking and mobility. First, TCP/IP was referenced as Windows 7 uses the Next Generation TCP/IP stack, which uses both IPv4 and IPv6 to ease the deployment of IPv6 in environments. TCP/IPv6 is installed on all Windows 7 machines and the deployment in organizations should be underway or in the planning stages. Windows 7 uses network locations when a network connection is established. The first time a user connects to a new network the correct location should be chosen as the choice influences the network profile and firewall rules. Network discovery is enabled in Home and Work locations to scan and find other Windows hosts in the network for either a HomeGroup or domain. The Network Explorer also uses network discovery to find computers and devices in the network to connect to for sharing resources.

This chapter then explained and referenced the Network and Sharing Center. This is the central location for managing everything related to networking. The network map is the first view that shows the devices in the network and how the computer is connecting to the Internet. Under the network map is the active networks. Here, the user can determine what network and adapter is connecting to what, if Internet access is available, and if the computer is connected to a HomeGroup. Additionally, the user may view the connection status. The Network and Sharing Center also can set up new connections or networks through easy-to-use wizards or connecting to or disconnecting from an existing network. Adapter settings may also be launched to manually configure networks and adapters. HomeGroup settings may also be launched from the Network and Sharing Center.

Next, this chapter focused on mobility and power management. Windows Mobility Center allows mobile end users to quickly tweak settings related to mobility including display brightness, external display, presentation, volume, wireless, and power plans. The power management section went further in depth with the power plans, describing how to modify both the basic and advanced setting and create a new power plan. Managing power plans in enterprise environments is more difficult and this chapter explained how to do so in Group Policy or the command line.

Finally, the chapter explained enhanced features with Windows Server 2008 R2 and Windows 7. These features require the combination of both operating systems to work and include BranchCache for caching files in remote locations, DirectAccess for an always on connection to the organization's infrastructure, and offline domain join to join remote machines to the domain.

Chapter 7, "Managing Windows 7 in an Enterprise Environment," requires the end user computers to be connected to the network and joined to the domain to efficiently manage the computers from a central location. The chapter will introduce many tools available to the administrator to perform everyday tasks as well as set policies to ensure that Windows 7 clients remain configured correctly.

Managing Windows 7 in an Enterprise Environment

INFORMATION IN THIS CHAPTER

■ Management Tools

■ Roaming

■ Administrative Templates

■ Summary

Since the introduction of Microsoft's Active Directory system in Windows 2000 Server, the management of client computers within the enterprise has become more and more streamlined allowing more and more control of the client. Microsoft has also been releasing more and more automation features with each release to make control of the clients easier with each release. The release of the Windows 7 client operating system (OS) and Windows Server 2008 R2 is building on this foundation to include even more control for the IT Administrator over the enterprise.

In this chapter, we will be focusing on the changes to Group Policies in Windows 7 and Windows Server 2008 R2, some of the improvements which are included in Windows PowerShell v2. We will also look into the improvements in Windows 7's remote management capabilities and the improvements in the Windows 7 implementation of remote desktop. We will also be highlighting the Windows 7 remote user capabilities and the improvements to Administrative Templates, which are included with Windows 7.

MANAGEMENT TOOLS

When it comes to managing Windows 7 within your enterprise environment, the most common tools you'll be looking at are the components of the Remote Server Administration Toolkit (RSAT) such as the Group Policy Editor. This

© 2010 Elsevier Inc. All rights reserved.
DOI: 10.1016/B978-1-59749-561-5.00007-3

allows you to edit your Windows Server 2008 R2 Group Policies and push those changes to your client computers. By applying Group Policies to specific organizational units (OUs), you can affect only a subset of the computers in your environment, specifically the users or computers within that OU. For even greater control, you can also use Windows Management Instrumentation (WMI) filters to specify a further subset of computers to apply the OU to.

Microsoft has extended the power of the Group Policy Editor by including some PowerShell Cmdlets, which allow you to control your Group Policies without having to open the Microsoft Management Console (MMC) and the Group Policy Editor.

Group Policy

Group Policies were introduced in Windows Server 2003 as a way to allow systems administrators to manage a large number of settings in a quick and easy way. Settings within the Group Policy are broken down into Computer settings and User settings.

Windows PowerShell Cmdlets for Group Policy

The new Windows PowerShell Cmdlets are extremely powerful tools, which can be used to make your Group Policy editing and scripting much easier to perform, especially when you have to make large numbers of Group Policy changes. One of the biggest benefits of being able to use Windows Power-Shell to make these changes is that you can first test the changes in a lab environment, then run the exact same script against your production domain and get the exact same results.

All the Windows PowerShell Cmdlets, which are available for Group Policy editing, are broken down into the following five categories:

1. Maintaining your Group Policy Objects (GPOs) – This subset includes the creation, import, deletion of your Group Policies, as well as the ability to back up your Group Policies.
2. Linking GPOs with OUs – This subset includes the creation and deletion of the link between the GPO and the OU.
3. Rights and Inheritance – This subset includes editing the permissions on the GPO itself, as well as editing the Inheritance flags on each GPO.
4. Configuring of settings – This subset includes the ability to view, update, and deconfigure the Group Policy settings.
5. Starter GPOs – This subset includes the ability to create and edit the starterG POs.

To use the new Group Policy Cmdlets, you must be connected either to a Windows Server 2008 R2 domain controller or to a Windows Server 2008

R2 member server with the Group Policy Management Console (GPMC) or a Windows 7 client with the Remote Server Administration Tools (RSAT) installed. (All demo scripts for this chapter were taken while running on a domain controller in the lab.local Windows Server 2008 R2 domain.) The Group Policy Cmdlets are not automatically imported when you start Windows PowerShell. Before you can begin, you will need to import the Group Policy Module. To do this, you will need to run the **Import-Module** Cmdlet as shown in Figure 7.1.

The **– verbose** flag can be omitted if you don't wish to have the status of each Cmdlet displayed in the screen, as shown in Figure 7.2. Once the Group Policy Module has been loaded, you can access the help screen for each Cmdlet by using the **Get-Help** Cmdlet followed by the name of the Cmdlet.

■ **FIGURE 7.1** Running the **Import-Module** Cmdlet within Windows PowerShell

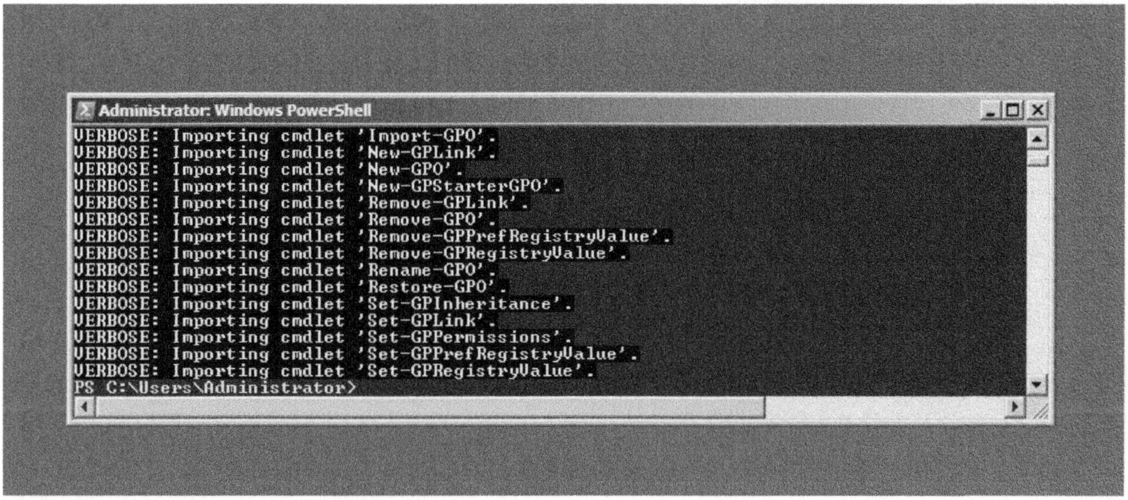

■ **FIGURE 7.2** Output from Running the **Import-Module** Cmdlet in Windows PowerShell

Before we begin with the various GPOs, let's first look at the GPOs that are provided with Windows Server 2008 R2 for the purpose of managing your GPOs. Table 7.1 lists all 25 Cmdlets and describes the function of each Cmdlet.

Table7. 1 Cmdlets

Cmdlet Name	Description
Backup-GPO	It backs up some or all GPOs in a Windows Server 2008 R2 domain to a file on a local or networked hard drive.
Copy-GPO	It creates a duplicate GPO in the target Windows Server 2008 R2 domain from the source GPO in the source domain. These domains do not need to be the same.
Get-GPInheritance	It returns inheritance information for the specified OU or Windows Server 2008 R2 domain.
Get-GPO	It gets basic information about either a single GPO or all GPOs in the specified Windows Server 2008 R2 domain.
Get-GPOReport	It gets detailed information about either a single GPO or all GPOs in the specified Windows Server 2008 R2 domain in either an XML or HTML format.
Get-GPPermissions	It gets the access control list information about a single GPO or all GPOs in the specified Windows domain.
Get-GPPrefRegistryValue	It allows you to retrieve one or more registry preference items from either the Computer or User configuration of a GPO.
Get-GPRegistryValue	It allows you to retrieve one or more registry-based policy settings from either the Computer or User configuration within a GPO.
Get-GPResultantSetOfPolicy	It retrieves the Resultant Set of Policy information for a user, computer, or both to a file.
Get-GPStarterGPO	It retrieves one or all starter GPOs in a Windows Server 2008 R2 domain.
Import-GPO	It imports a GPO from a file into a Windows Server 2008 R2 domain.
New-GPLink	It creates a new link between a GPO and an OU.
New-GPO	It creates a new GPO.
New-GPStarterGPO	It creates a new Starter GPO.
Remove-GPLink	It removes a link between a GPO and an OU.
Remove-GPO	It removes a GPO from the Windows Server 2008 R2 domain.
Remove-GPPrefRegistryValue	It removes one or more registry preference items from either the Computer or User configuration of a GPO.
Remove-GPRegistryValue	It removes one or more registry-based policy settings from either the Computer or User configuration of a GPO.
Rename-GPO	It renames a GPO.
Restore-GPO	It restores one or all GPOs in a domain from one or more GPO backup files.
Set-GPInheritance	It changes the inheritance settings for a specified domain or OU.
Set-GPLink	It changes the settings of an existing GPO Link.
Set-GPPermissions	It changes the permissions of an existing GPO.
Set-GPPrefRegistryValue	It changes one or more registry preference items from either the Computer or User configuration of a GPO.
Set-GPRegistryValue	It changes one or more registry-based policy settings from either the Computer or User configuration of a GPO.

The syntax for most of these policies is very similar, but you can always find the syntax by using the **get-help** Cmdlet. As an example, we can see the **New-GPO** Cmdlet being used to create a GPO called "Sample GPO" in Figure 7.3. After the GPO is created, PowerShell outputs the information about the GPO to the screen.

Once you have created the new GPO, you can begin to edit the various settings of that GPO using the **Set-GPRegistryValue** and **Set-GPPrefRegistryValue** Cmdlets. In Figure 7.4, you can see the syntax to set the default screen saver time-out value to 15 min. You can then verify that the setting has been set in the GPO by using the **Get-GPRegistryValue** Cmdlet or by using the Group Policy Management Editor MMC snap-in.

■ **FIGURE 7.3** Command and Output from **New-GPO**

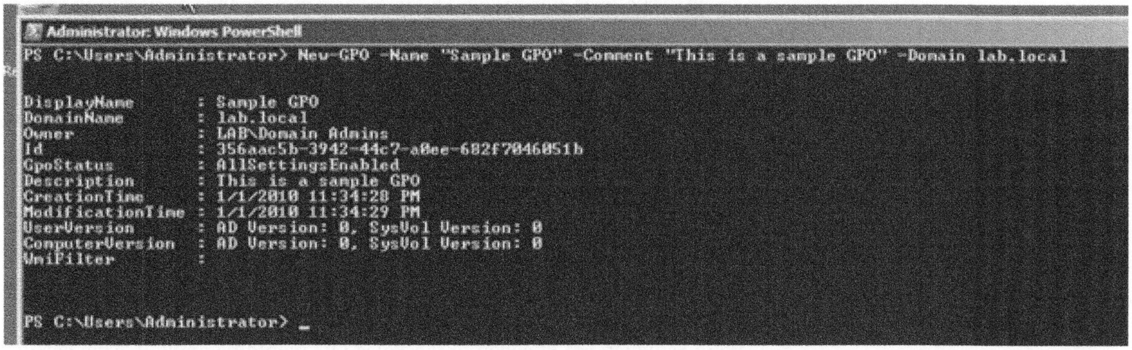

■ **FIGURE 7.4** Changing the Screen Saver Time-Out Value

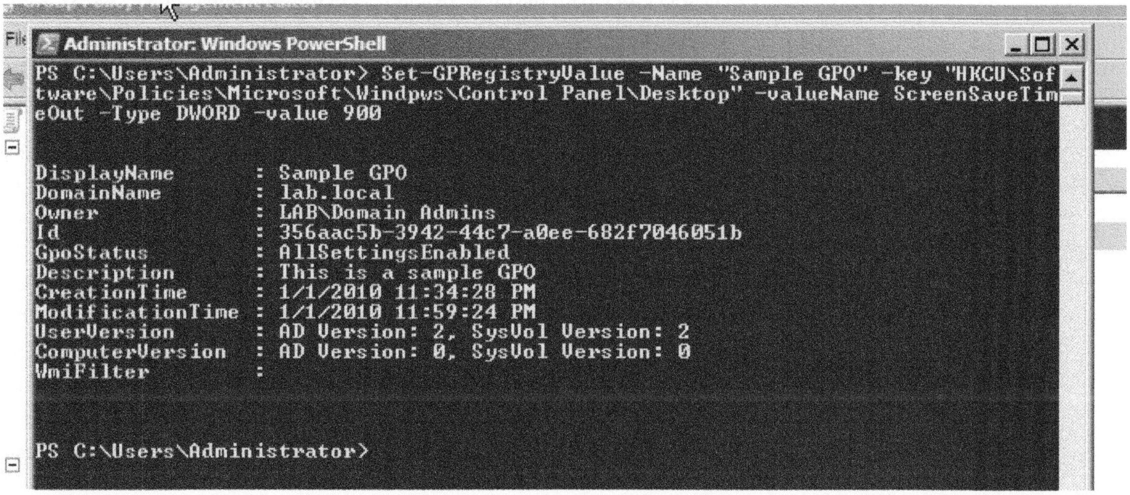

Group Policy Preferences

Group Policy Preferences let you manage many settings on the client machine without the need to learn a new scripting language for each one. These settings can all be controlled through your Group Policies. There are a large number of settings that you can control through the Group Policy Preferences including drive mappings, registry settings, local user account creation, local group membership, service startup configuration, and file and folder security.

You can create one or many Group Policies at the domain level, the site level, and each OU within your domain. Group Policies are applied to a computer in a predictable order so that you know the order in which they will be applied. Group Policy settings can override each other or block the override, depending on how the settings of each Group Policy are set.

At each level within the Active Directory structure, you can specify the order in which the policies are applied. This is done by moving the policies up and down in the Group Policy Management application. As you can see in Figure 7.5, our sample domain has two Group Policies applied to the root of the domain.

When Group Policies are applied, any Group Policies that have been applied at the site will be applied first, in the order specified. After the site policies are applied, the policies which have been applied at the domain level will be applied. After that, the policies will be applied one OU at a time until the computer or user has been reached. If a user account was located in the **Accounts | Sales OU** structure as shown in Figure 7.5, any Group Policies which are attached to the Account OU would be applied, then any Group Policies which are attached to the Sales OU would be applied. This nesting allows you to simplify your Group Policy structure because without it, for a policy to apply to all the OUs under the Accounts OU, you would need to link the same GPO to all the OUs. In addition to filtering what objects have Group Policies applied to them by using OUs, you can also configure GPOs to only apply to specific computers based on WMI filters. This allows you to configure specific GPOs to only apply to a subset of computers within that GPO.

Now also keep in mind that User Configuration settings can override Computer Configuration settings, but typically Computer Configuration settings won't override User Configuration settings. This is because there are two times during the day when Group Policies are applied. The first time is when the computer first boots up and authenticates against the Windows domain and the client computer requires the list of GPOs that need to be applied to it. The second time is when the user logs into the computer. At this time, the computer will request all the GPOs for that user and apply them to the computer. If the user settings override the computer settings, which were already downloaded from the domain, then the user settings

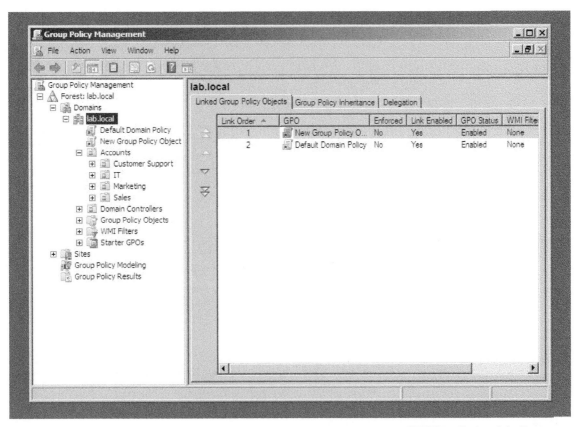

will be put into place. When the user logs off of the computer, the user settings are removed so that when the next user logs in, his or her settings will
then take effect.

WMI filters are an extremely powerful, yet underused, feature of the Group
Policy Management part of Active Directory. Through WMI, you can filter
Group Policies to only run against specific machines using just about any
metric about the computer that you can think of. You can query off of the
machine name, disk drives which are installed, type of CPU that the computer has in it, number of CPUs, the amount of RAM, and so on. However,
you need to be sure to always test your WMI filter before putting it into production because a slightly incorrect WMI filter will prevent the GPO from
being applied to any computer as no computers will fulfill the WMI filter.

With the release of Windows 7 and Windows Server 2008 R2, the settings
that can be controlled have been increased to include the Power settings,

NOTE

One place where the use of WMI filters can come in very handy is to stagger the Windows Update schedules of computers so that not all computers get the updates at once. This will reduce the stress on your Windows Update server (or Internet connection if you don't have a Windows Software Update Services [WSUS] server).

If your workstation computers are numbered, you could group the computers into five groups so that only 20 percent of the workstations attempt to patch itself. To do this, create one master Group Policy over the OU that has your workstations in it. In this OU, set all of your Windows Update settings except for the time when the computers should install the updates. Then create five additional OUs. In each of these OUs (linked to the same GPO), schedule the Windows Update time to update. A typical example would be to have each group an hour apart starting at 10 P.M., then at 11 P.M., and so on, until the last group patches at 3 A.M. Then create a WMI filter for each group. The queries will be identical, just changing the WHERE part of the query. For the first group, use the query: SELECT * FROM Win32_ComputerSystem WHERE Name like "%1" or Name like "%2." The second query would use names ending in 3 and 4, and so on. Now, when your computers go to patch themselves at night, only 20 percent of the workstations will attempt to patch themselves at a time.

Scheduled Task settings, Immediate Task settings, and Internet Explorer 8 settings. All of these new settings can also be applied to Windows Vista and Windows Server 2008 client computers within your Windows Server 2008 R2 domain.

The **Power Options, Schedule**, and **Immediate Tasks** are all configured under **Preferences** then **Control Panel Settings** under either the **Computer Configuration** or **User Configuration** nodes of the Group Policy Management Editor. The **User Configuration** menu is shown in Figure 7.6. The Internet Explorer 8 settings (as well as the Internet Explorer 5 through 7 settings) can only be set through the **Internet Settings** node under the **User Configuration** node.

In addition to these new settings, there are hundreds of additional settings that can be controlled through a Group Policy. If you dig into the policy enough, you will find that you can control just about every setting that the Windows 7 computer has available. From little things like if Internet Explorer shows the home page or a blank page when a new tab is opened (found under **Users Configuration | Policies | Administrative Templates | Windows Components | Internet Explorer**) to important security-related policies such as if auditing should occur when a failed login is attempted (found under **Computer Configuration | Policies | Windows Settings | Security Settings | Local Policies | Audit Policies**).

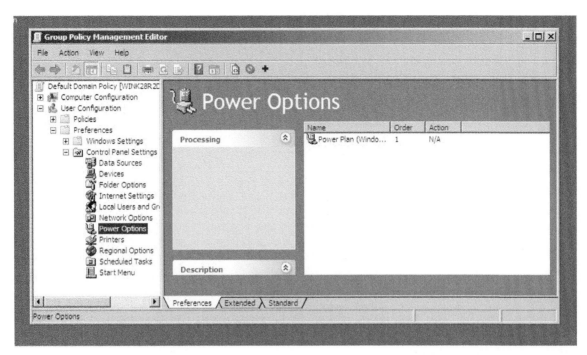

■ **FIGURE 7.6** The Group Policy Editor in the Power Plan Section of the **User Configuration** Node

With the great power of the Group Policy Editor, comes great responsibility to use that power correctly. The last thing you want to do is to create a large number of Group Policies as that will not only slow down your user's log-in process but also make resolving problems and conflicts within your Group Policies much harder to resolve.

Power PlanS ettings

It used to be that power-saving settings were something that only laptop users needed to deal with. But power costs are of big importance in today's world, and desktop computers take up a lot of power when they are running. Fortunately, Windows Server 2008 R2 and Windows 7 give the power-conserving Windows administrator the ability to reduce the amount of power being used by the desktops and extend the lifetime of laptop batteries. This is done through creating and using Power Plan settings on a user's computer.

For desktops, we want to reduce the power costs of keeping those computers running all night, and with laptops, we want to make the batteries last as long as possible. The first step in doing this is to spin down the hard drive when it isn't in use.

> **TIP**
>
> For desktops, it may not seem like power-saving settings could save a company any real money, but the standard desktop computer has a 500 kw power supply in it (yours may have smaller or larger power supplies in them, but mine has a 500 kw power supply in it). That same computer is left running 24 h a day, but is only used for 9 to 10 h of that day. Companies can be charged up to $0.50/kW·h of power that they use (depending on a variety of factors, but we'll use $0.50/kW·h to make the math easier to deal with), so the 14 h/day that the computer isn't in use is costing the company about $7/day. Now, in a company with 1000 workstations, it costs $7000/day. During the 5-day work week, it costs the company $35,000. Weekends are even worse because the computer is running for 48 h with no one using it. Then, those 1000 computers cost $24,000/weekend, plus the $35,000 that they cost during the week for a total cost of $59,000/week just to keep the computers running. Multiply these numbers out per month (roughly $247,800), and yearly (roughly $3,068,000), and the numbers start looking rather large.
>
> Now, will you save this amount by putting your computers to sleep at night, only waking them as needed? No, because the computer has to stay on to some extent so that it can wake up as needed. However, you can realize easily 30 to 50 percent of these numbers; of course, your mileage may vary.

You can use the new power plan settings to control the **Power Plan** options, which will be available on your client computers when in the **Power Management** console of the Control Panel. You can also edit or remove (not recommended) the existing default power plans, which Windows Vista or Windows 7 create. As you can see in Figure 7.7, we are creating a new power plan called **Long Life Plan**, in which we set the hard drive and monitor to power down as quickly as possible so that the computer battery lasts as long as possible.

In Figure 7.8, you can see the new power plan has been applied as the default plan. If the setting doesn't apply right away, this is normal as GPOs aren't immediately updated. You may need to wait several hours for the new settings to be downloaded. If you wish to speed up this process, you can run **gpupdate** on your client computer to manually refresh the GPO settings.

Scheduled and Immediate Tasks

You can now create and run scheduled and immediate tasks from a central GPO so that the task is run against all Windows Vista, Windows 7, Windows 2008 and Windows Server 2008 R2 computers in your Windows Server 2008 R2 domain. When you open the Group Policy Editor to the **Scheduled Tasks** node and right-click, you will get a menu, similar to the one shown in Figure 7.9, which allows you to create a scheduled task for older operating systems or for Windows Vista and later.

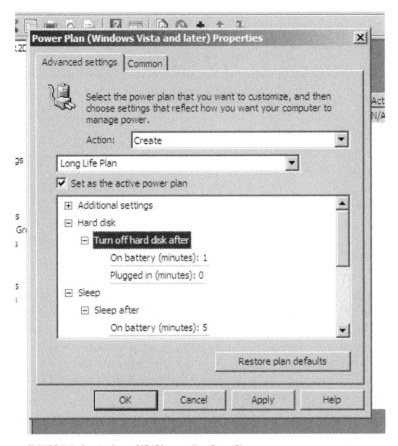

■ **FIGURE 7.7** Creating **Long Life Plan** as a New Power Plan

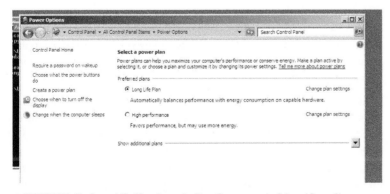

■ **FIGURE 7.8** The **Long Life Plan** Set on the Client Computer as the Selected Power Plan

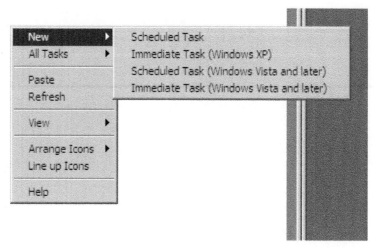

■ **FIGURE 7.9** Menu and Submenu When Creating a New Scheduled or Immediate Task

A policy-created scheduled task will be accepted by computers running client OSes as old as Windows 2000, while immediate tasks can only be run on Windows XP and later OSes. Windows Vista and later OSes have a separate menu item as their task schedulers are quite a bit different from the Windows XP and Windows 2000 task schedulers. As you can see in Figure 7.10, the task creation window in the Group Policy Editor looks very similar to the one shown in the client OS.

Running a GPO-controlled scheduled task allows you to run an application against each computer in the site, domain, or OU that the GPO has been specified against on a regular basis. You can run a local application such as a third-party spyware application, or you can launch an application from a network share hosted on your network. To run a scheduled task against an application hosted on a network share, you'll need to specify a domain user account to run the task.

When you create a scheduled task through Group Policy, you can control all the settings of the scheduled task. You can even hide the task from the Windows clients so that they cannot see that you have a scheduled task configured to run on their machine.

A hidden scheduled task is extremely useful for practical jokes, when the victim of the joke has a good sense of humor. A task which throws a dialog box up on the screen can be highly entertaining. That's all I am going to say on the subject.

Unlike the task scheduler that was included in order versions of Windows, the task scheduler that was introduced in Windows Vista allows you to schedule multiple actions for each task. This allows you to run multiple applications in sequence all through a single task. When the first application has completed, the scheduled task will then start up the next task on the list, until all the tasks have been completed. In earlier versions of Windows,

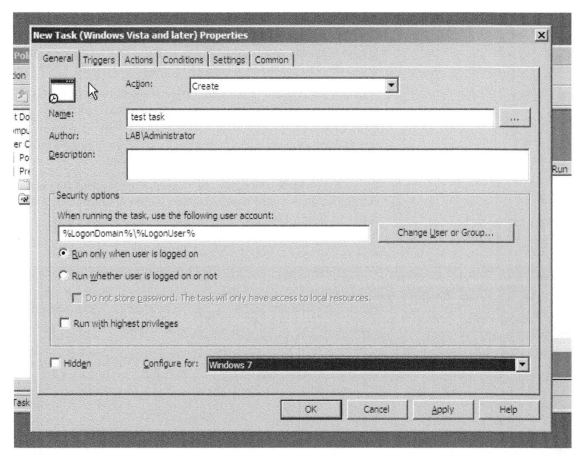

getting this same level of flexibility required either a third-party scheduler or the use of flag files, which would be written to look if the next task was ready to execute upon completion of the previous task.

You will see the biggest difference between scheduling a task on one machine and on the domain when you schedule a task on the domain through Group Policy, as you have the option to synchronize the run time across time zones. Normally, when you schedule a task to run at 3 P.M. (15:00 h), it will run at 3 P.M. at the local time of the workstation. When you select the **Synchronize across time zones** check box, as shown in Figure 7.11, the task will be scheduled against the coordinated universal time instead of the local time. This option allows you to have all computers in your Windows Active Directory domain run the same task at the exact same moment.

Another nice feature of a scheduled task is the ability to randomize the start time. You can randomize the start time by as little as 30 s in either direction to up to 1 day. This delay is controlled by the **Delay task for up to (random delay)** check box as shown in Figure 7.11.

After you have configured the when (triggers) and the what (actions), you can specify some additional conditions for the scheduled task. These additional conditions found on the **Conditions** tab allow you to delay execution until the computer is idle, ensure that the computer is plugged into the power, or that a specific network connection is available.

By selecting the **Idle** option, you can ensure that the computer isn't in use, and that the use won't be impacted by the scheduled task running. This is useful for running tasks such as a defragmentation of the hard drive.

■ **FIGURE 7.11** The New Trigger Screen of the Task Scheduler Shown through the Group Policy Editor

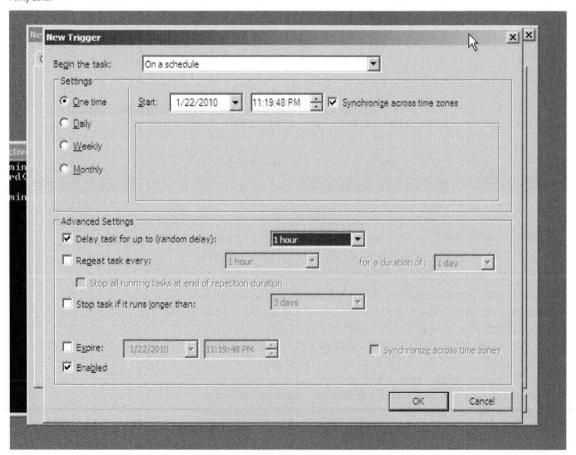

Within the power settings area, you've got a couple of different independent settings. The first allows you to start the task only if the computer is plugged into the power outlet. This is useful for laptops as you probably don't want to start defragging a user's laptop when it is running on battery power. You can also stop the task if the user switches from AC to battery power. The second power option allows you to wake up the computer if it is sleeping so that the task can be run. This would be useful if you configured all your user workstations to sleep automatically at night, but you still wanted some process to be run against the workstations at night.

On the **Settings** tab of the window you have some additional settings, which can be configured to control the restart options of the task (among other settings). You can control if the task can be started by the user or not (if the task is marked as hidden on the **General** tab, checking this box would be kind of pointless). You can configure the job to start up as soon as possible after a job schedule is missed. This would allow the job to start up when the computer was first turned on if the computer was powered off when the job was supposed to have started running. You can control the **Restart** options for the job including how often the task restarts and how many times it will restart. You can also stop the task after it has been running for a long period of time. You can also configure the job to automatically remove itself from the user's computer after the job is no longer scheduled to run (assuming that you have configured an Expire date on all the triggers which start this task).

Probably the most important setting on this tab is the last one, which tells the task scheduler what to do if the scheduled task is already running when it is time to start the task up again. You can choose the default which is to not to start a new instance of the task, start up a second instance of the task running in parallel, queue the new task so that it starts when the already running task is complete, or stop the currently running task. For tasks which could run for a long time and take a lot of resources like the disk defragmentation example discussed earlier, you'll probably want to select the **Default** option to not to start a new instance of the task. Otherwise, the user's computer could be running the disk defragmentation program in an endless loop, slowing down the user and causing help desk calls.

One tab you won't see when creating scheduled tasks on the client directly through a GPO is the **Common** tab as shown in Figure 7.12. This tab allows for some settings that are specific to being created through a Group Policy.

The first option **Stop processing items in the extension if an error occurs** tells the Windows 7 computer that if this task fails, then do not run any other tasks that have been created on the computer by this same GPO. The second

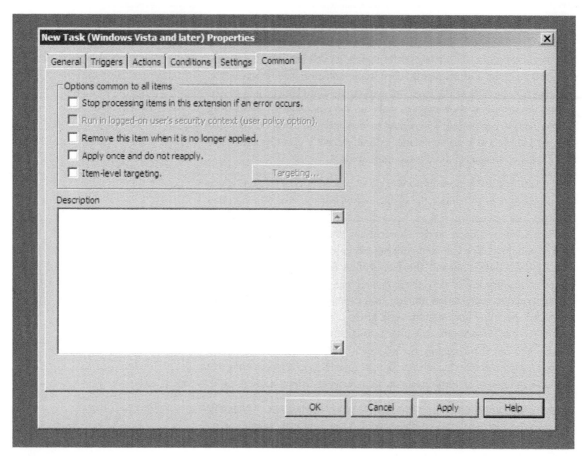

■ **FIGURE 7.12** The **Common** Tab Shown
When Creating a New Scheduled Task through
Group Policy

option, which is only available when you are creating a user policy (the
screenshot was taken when creating a computer policy), allows you to run
the task under the logged in user's credentials. The third option tells the client computer to remove the scheduled task from the client computer if it is
removed from the Group Policy or when the Group Policy no longer applies
to the client computer because the computer has been moved to another OU
within the domain structure. The fourth option on the screen tells the client
computer to create the task once and not to update it if the Group Policy
changes.

The last item is the **Item-level targeting**. This allows for an extra layer
of filtering when applying this scheduled task to the client computer. You
can select a wide variety of computer side settings to match before the

scheduled task will be applied to the computer. Just some of the items that you can use to filter against include the following: if the computer does or does not have a battery (machines with a battery are most likely a laptop or netbook), the speed of the CPU, how large the disks are, the value of an environment variable, what OU the computer is in, if the computer is docked or not, the amount of RAM installed, or the site that the computer is in. You can even use a WMI query that allows you to match against anything that isn't configured as a default options. As you can see from the sample targeting filter shown in Figure 7.13, there is a lot of power available in the targeting selector. In this case, we have selected to only apply this task to computers that have at least 2 GB of RAM and 1 Ghz CPUs, and the computers must have at least 80 GB of available disk space on their system drive and must be running Windows 7 but not Windows 7 64-bit Business edition.

■ **FIGURE 7.13** The Targeting Editor

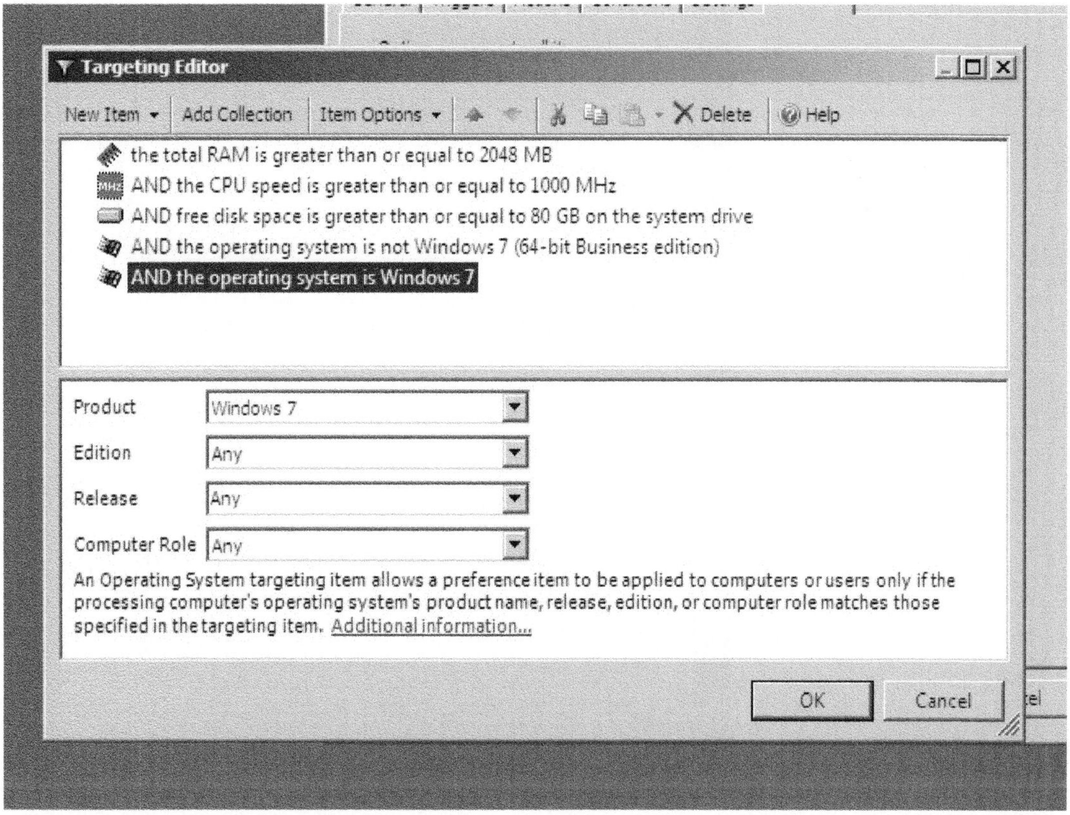

The Immediate Task creation window will look identical to the Scheduled Task creation window with the single exception that the **Triggers** tab has been removed. That is because this task is run once when the client gets the updated copy of the GPO and then removed, so the **Triggers** tab would be irrelevant to configuring the immediate task.

Internet Explorer 8

Internet Explorer 8's properties can be set much in the same way the settings for Internet Explorer 5 through 7 can be set as part of a GPO. Because the Internet Settings window for each version of the browser are different, each one gets a different settings page that must be set. As you can see in Figure 7.14, when you create a new Internet Explorer 8 policy, the settings screen will match the settings screen that you would see when opening the

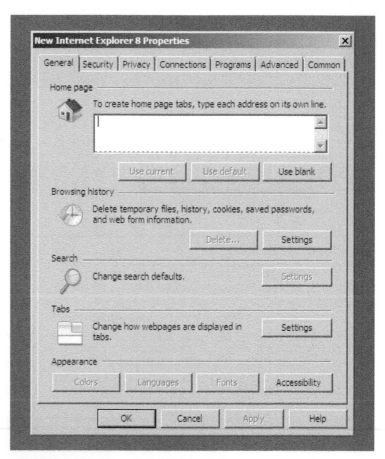

■ **FIGURE 7.14** Default Internet Explorer 8 Settings Window

Tools drop-down menu and then clicking the **Options** menu within Internet Explorer8.

This settings window gives you control over almost every setting that the user could modify from within Internet Explorer themselves. Any settings you wish to prevent them from adjusting beyond these settings can be controlled through **User Configuration | Policies | Administrative Templates | Windows Components | Internet Explorer | Internet Control Panel** node within the same Group Policy or another Group Policy.

If you wish to manage the default settings for multiple versions of Internet Explorer within your enterprise, you will need to create multiple Internet Settings items within the policy. You can create one for Internet Explorer 5 and Internet Explorer 6, then a separate set of settings for Internet Explorer 7. If you create only a single set of settings, then those settings will not switch between versions.

On the first tab of the Internet Explorer 8 Properties window, you can create one or more home pages for your users. For multiple home pages, simply put each URL on a different line. When Internet Explorer is opened, each URL will be opened in a new tab. You can also adjust the cache settings and location of the cache by clicking on the **Settings** button of the browsing history section. You can adjust how Internet Explorer handles tabs (if multiple tabs should be an option) by clicking the **Settings** button within the tabs section. You can also control the accessibility options by clicking on the **Accessibility** button at the bottom of the window.

On the **Security** tab, you can control the levels for each of the four zones, but you can't assign sites to each zone. That is controlled through **Policies | Administrative Templates | Windows Components | Internet Explorer | Internet Control Panel | Security Page | Site to Zone Assignment List setting**. For each of the four zones listed (Internet Zone, Local Intranet Zone, Trusted Zone, and Restricted Zone), you can adjust the default security level, and then customize the settings within that zone so that you can fine tune what users can and can't do within each zone.

On the **Privacy** tab, there isn't much available to do. You can enable and configure the Pop-Up Blocker, and allow specific sites to allow pop-ups, which would be useful for any internal Web-based applications that require pop-ups. However, on this tab, you cannot configure the privacy settings for the Internet zone.

On the **Connections** tab, you can configure what connection if any should be used to get to the Internet. You can also configure if a dial-up connection should never be used, should always be used, or should be used if the local

TIP

Remember that these settings will only apply to Internet Explorer, and not to any other Web browsers that your users have installed. If your network allows direct Internet traffic and your users are able to download and install FireFox, Chrome, and so on, then they will have direct Internet access without going through your proxys erver.

NOTE

Oncet heu pperm anagement learns that you can control all these settings, there is a good chance that they will want you to lock down every setting possible, so that everyone has the same user experience every desktop looks and acts the same. However, keep in mind that many users consider Web browsing as a very personal experience, and little things like the ability to see animations in Web pages may keep the users happy when they browse the Web during their breaks or lunch.

Just because every possible setting can be controlled, doesn't mean that they should be controlled for the bulk of your user base. Giving the users some level of personal expression can make their work experience a much more pleasant experience, and if employees like their job, they are more willing to come back to it everyd ay.

area network (LAN) isn't detected. You can also configure the proxy settings for Internet Explorer by clicking on the **LAN Settings** button within the Local Area Network settings section.

On the **Programs** tab the only setting which you can configure is if Internet Explorer should check to see if it is the default Web browser when it starts or not. You can not through this screen configure the default applications to use for e-mail, newsgroups, and so on. If you need to set these settings, you can enforce them through registry settings directly.

On the **Advanced** tab, you can control all the advanced options that are available through the **Internet Control Panel** in Internet Explorer 8.

The **Common** tab, which you wouldn't normally see on the Windows 7 desktop, looks much like the **Common** tab that we saw in Figure 7.12 and has the same effects, including the advanced capabilities of **Item-level targeting**, which we saw in Figure 7.13.

StarterG POs

Starter GPOs are preconfigured GPOs that are stored is a specific folder on each domain controller. These GPOs cannot be linked to OUs themselves. They are templates which the Domain Administrator can create and use later when creating other GPOs. Starter GPOs can be found within the Group Policy Management MMC snap-in under the local domain in a special folder called **Starter GPOs**a ss howni n Figure7.15 .

You can create Starter GPOs by right-clicking on the **Starter GPOs** node in the menu and selecting **New**. Name the Starter GPO in the pop-up window. After the Starter GPO has been created, you can edit it by right-clicking on the Starter GPO and selecting **Edit** from the context menu. This will open the Group Policy Starter GPO Editor. It will look very similar to the GPO Editor except that only the **Administrative Templates** options are available.

You can set as many settings as are needed for your Starter GPO and then close the Group Policy Starter GPO Editor. You can reedit the Starter GPO or use the Starter GPO to create new GPOs within your Active Directory environment. To create a new GPO from a Starter GPO, right-click on the Starter GPO and select the **New GPO From Starter GPO...** menu option from the context menu. This will bring up a dialog box that allows you to name your new GPO as shown in Figure 7.16.

After you click **OK** on the window shown in Figure 7.16, you can create links between your new GPO by using the Group Policy Management window, or using the **New-GPLink** PowerShell Cmdlet, which was described in Table 7.1.

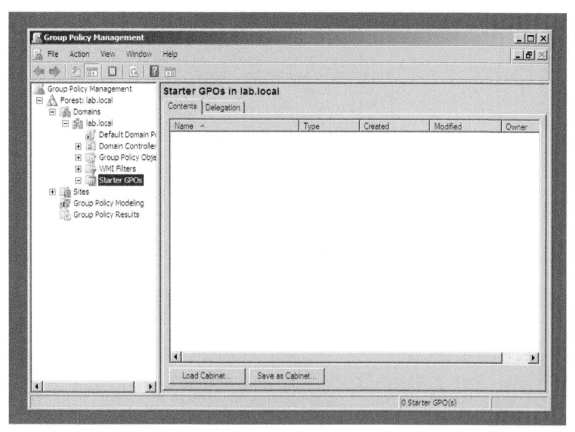

■ **FIGURE 7.15** Starter GPOs Location within the Group Policy Management MMC Snap-in

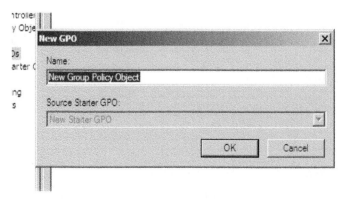

■ **FIGURE 7.16** Copy GPO from Starter GPO Window

Creating Shortcuts through Active Directory

Windows Server 2008 Active Directory includes the ability to create short-cuts as part of the Group Policy, so that all users within your enterprise environment have the same shortcuts no matter what computer they log in to. This allows you to preconfigure new users, so that when a new user is brought into the environment or when that user account is moved from one OU to another, the shortcuts are consistent with the other users in the department. It allows prevents users from removing the shortcuts that would be required to do their job.

You can create shortcuts by the computer or the user. Edit a GPO and navigate to **Computer Configuration** or **User Configuration** then to **Preferences**, then **Shortcuts**. Right-click on **Shortcuts** and select **New**. You'll then be presented with a window as shown in Figure 7.17. You can create the shortcut to a File System Object, a URL, or a Shell Object.

■ **FIGURE 7.17** Creating a New Shortcut to Deploy through an OU

A File System Object can be a document or an application. If pointing to a document, image, and so on, the computer will need to have the correct application installed, and you'll need to have the correct file association configured. If the file association is not configured, you can call the application directly and pass the file in as an argument, assuming that the application supports the file being opened through an argument as shown in Figure 7.18 .

You'll note that the only difference between the two examples is the inclusion of the full path to the file as an argument. Different applications accept arguments differently, so you'll need to know how the application that you wish to use works.

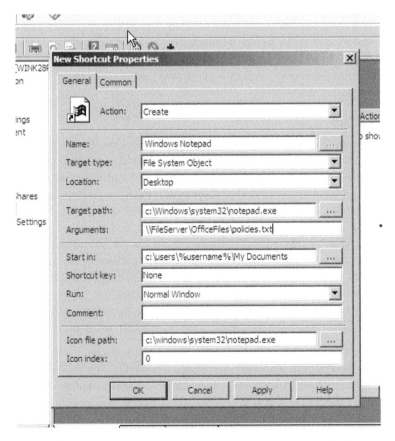

■ **FIGURE 7.18** Configuring a Newly Deployed Shortcut to Launch an Application and Passing It a Filename to Display as an Argument

PowerShell

Back with Windows Server 2003, Microsoft introduced a new scripting language called *Windows PowerShell*. PowerShell has gone from an add-on to a core part of the Windows Management Tools. Starting with Windows 7 and Windows Server 2008 R2, every management tool that has a user interface to work with also has a set of PowerShell Cmdlets, which can be used to automate the management of that system. The current policy at Microsoft with regard to PowerShell is that the PowerShell Cmdlets are written first, and then the management interface is written to use the PowerShell Cmdlets. This way, they can be sure that you can script every function that can be done in the user interface.

The initial implementation of Windows PowerShell was very rough in that the editor was Windows Notepad. The implementation of Windows PowerShell included with Windows 7 is much more user friendly. It includes a nice three-pane editor, as shown in Figure 7.19, which gives you a command window at the bottom that allows for tab completion of your commands. The middle pane of the application shows the results of the run command, and the top pane of the application is the script which you are editing.

Cmdlets

There are hundreds of Cmdlets available in Windows PowerShell, so it is not possible to review all of them here. Cmdlets are small commands that can be called from PowerShell either by themselves or with other commands. To get a list of the available Cmdlets on your system, run *get-help* * in Windows PowerShell and it will output a list of the available Cmdlets, as well as any aliases setup on your system. Microsoft has created, by default, several dozen aliases so that normal DOS commands will work within PowerShell. As an example, there is no PowerShell command called "dir"; however, there is an alias called "dir," which points to the **Get-ChildItem** Cmdlet, so that when you type **dir** into PowerShell, you get back results that you are looking for. You will also find alias for *nix* commands as well, such as the command *ls*, which is also mapped to the **Get-ChildItem**C mdlet.

PowerShell Cmdlets are small applications, which can be run from the Windows PowerShell interface. PowerShell Cmdlets are loaded within modules, which can be loaded manually by using the **Import-Module** Cmdlet. These PowerShell Cmdlets can perform all the management functions of the Windows management interface.

Some Cmdlets return data from the system, whereas other Cmdlets make changes to the system. You can combine these in a single command by using

---

TIP

If you administrate an Exchange 2007 Server, you will notice that the Exchange team has included many Cmdlets that do not have a UI version making the PowerShell Cmdlets essential to managing an Exchange 2007 implementation. Hopefully, this won't become the case for every Microsoft application as this would be a very steep learning curve for many people. However, it is something to keep in mind, and if you can't find a way to do it in the UI, check PowerShell because there might be a way to do it through script.

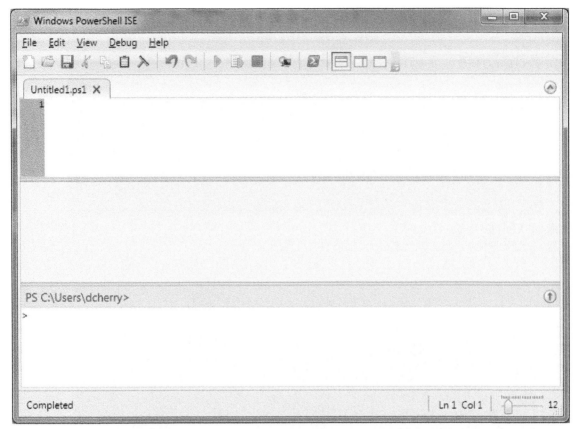

■ **FIGURE 7.19** New Windows PowerShell Editor

the pipe symbol (|) between the commands. For example, you could use a Windows PowerShell command to query the computer for a list of the network shares on the computer, and then change the comment on the network share all within a single command.

The most important Cmdlet that you can send objects to is the **Where** Cmdlet. This allows you to filter the output from another Cmdlet. As an example, you could use the **WmiObject** Cmdlet to query the list of network shares from the current computer. In order to return only the administrative shares, you would pipe the output from the **WmiObject** Cmdlet to the **Where** Cmdlet looking for names that end in a dollar sign as shown in Figure 7.20.

However, if you take this same command and change the – *like* command to – *notlike* command, it will return any network shares on the server that aren't administrative network shares. When run against our sample domain control, you'll get an output similar to the one shown in Figure 7.21.

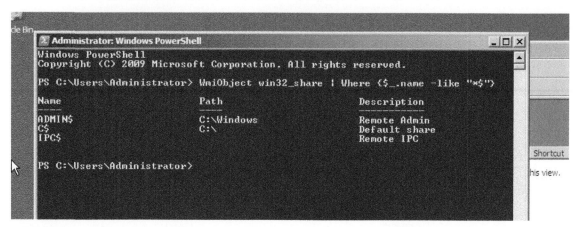

■ **FIGURE 7.20** Using Windows PowerShell to Query for Hidden Network Shares on the Local Server

■ **FIGURE 7.21** Using Windows PowerShell to Query for Nonhidden Network Shares on the Local Server

Remote Management

With the introduction of Windows PowerShell 2, which was introduced with Windows 7 and Windows Server 2008 R2, you now have the ability to run PowerShell Cmdlets against remote machines. Until this time, Windows PowerShell Cmdlets could only be run against the same machine in which the PowerShell script was run. This is done by adding the – *computername* parameter to the first command as shown in Figure 7.22.

Integrated Scripting Environment

The initial version of Windows PowerShell included the shell environment as shown in figures such as Figure 7.22. Windows Server 2008 R2 and Windows 7 introduced the *Integrated Scripting Environment*, which provides you with a more user-friendly interface as shown as Figure 7.23.

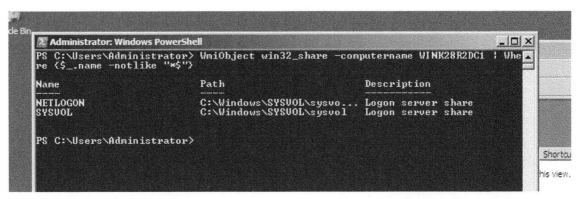

■ **FIGURE 7.22** Accessing a Remote Computer's Network Shares through PowerShell

■ **FIGURE 7.23** Windows PowerShell Interactive Scripting Environment

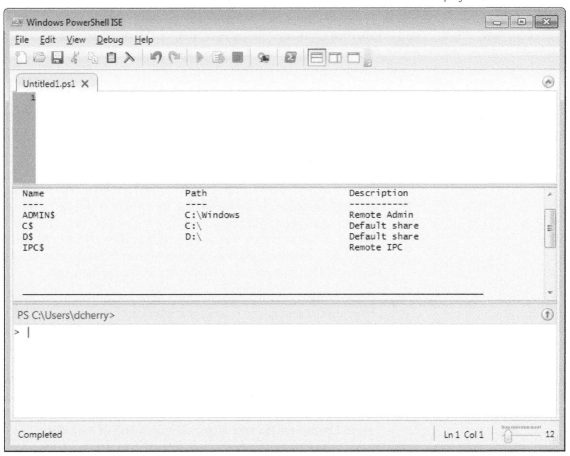

The top of the interface allows you to open, save, and run the scripts. The middle window shows any output from the script that you are currently running. The lower part of the window is an immediate run window, which allows you to run commands in a more interactive application like the prior PowerShell V1 application. This lower window includes tab completion of both the command and the parameters for the command.

RemoteM anagement

You have a lot of options when it comes to managing your Windows 7 clients.

You can use the native graphical tools, such as Computer Management, Event Viewer, Performance Monitor, and so on, to interactively work with the tools through the new Microsoft Management Console 3.0. You can use PowerShell to write highly powerful scripts, which can be used to control the user's environment and change the same settings that are available through the native tools. You can also use Group Policy through Active Directory to control thousands of computer settings on the client computers so that your users have a consistent, streamlined, and secure desktop environment to work within.

RemoteD esktop

The Windows 7 remote desktop functionally has changed quite a bit from earlier versions.

In earlier versions of remote desktop, copying files from the computer to which you were connected could be a challenge, to say the least. This is no longer the case. When connected to a Windows 7 computer through remote desktop from another computer running Windows 7, simply copy a file on the remote machine, then minimize the remote desktop window and paste that file to your local computer's hard drive. The file will be automatically copied from the remote computer through the secure remote desktop connection to the local computer with no extra drive mapping required.

If you frequently use the */console* switch to remote desktop to the physical console of servers, you'll notice that this switch no longer works in the Windows 7 version of the remote desktop client. The */console* switch has now been replaced by the */admin* switch. The reason for this change is that Windows 7 and Windows Server 2008 R2 don't have what is considered a console connection any more. If you are logged in to the physical console and you then remote desktop into that server, the console session will be moved to a virtual session, so that you are then using the same session that you had before with the same applications open that you had before.

If you have multiple monitors and you like to have the remote desktop window spread across all your monitors, you can now do this with the */multimon* switch. This switch will configure the remote session monitor layout to match your current physical monitor configuration.

Some of the other Remote Desktop 7.0 features that are introduced in this new version include using a Remote Desktop Connection Broker to access personal virtual desktops and virtual desktop pools. Personal virtual desktops allow users to have their own virtual desktop that they can use. Personal virtual desktops are assigned to users on a one-to-one basis. However, the virtual desktop pools are the complete opposite of the personal virtual desktop. When the users connect to a virtual desktop pool, they are connected to a stateless virtual desktop, which could be used by any user. The virtual desktop is stateless, so when the user logs off of the virtual desktop, all changes are rolled back and the next time the user connects to the virtual desktop pool, the session will look just like it did when they logged on the previous time.

Another great new feature (at least users think so, managers and the network team that have to pay for bandwidth may not agree) is the Windows Media Player redirection. This new feature allows users to watch video within Windows Media Player on a remote machine without any real loss in video or audio quality. This is because the video encoding is now processed on the local computer and not on the remote computer allowing for Windows Media Player to maintain audio and video sync when viewing video over an Remote Desktop Protocol (RDP) window. This works for both Windows Media Player, as well as Windows Media Player controls hosted within Web pages; however, it won't work with third-party media players unless they are built using Windows Media Player controls.

Remote Desktop 7.0 on Windows 7 now includes bidirectional audio support. You have always been able to hear sounds being played on the remote machine on your local speakers, but now with bidirectional audio support, you can turn on your microphone on your local computer and use remote voice-activated software and/or recording software on the remote machine. Of course, the success that you have with both the Windows Media Player redirection and the bidirectional audio support will depend completely on the amount of network bandwidth that is available between the computer you are connecting to and your local computer.

Because remote desktop is an add-on, you can get support for some of these features on your down-level clients today by installing the Remote Desktop Connection 7.0 client on down-level clients. Remove Desktop Connection 7.0 client is available for Windows XP running Service Pack 3 or later, and

> **TIP**
>
> There are many new features that are introduced in Windows 7 and Remote Desktop 7.0. You can find a complete list of these features in the Microsoft Knowledge Base under article 969084, which can be found at http://support .microsoft.com/kb/969084.

Windows Vista running Service Pack 1 and later. However, in order for these new features to work, the down-level client will need to remote desktop to a computer running Windows 7 or Windows Server 2008 R2. There are a handful of known issues with the down-level client versions that are all documented in the MSKB article 969084, which is referenced in the preceding note.

RemoteS erverA dministration Toolkit

The RSAT is the replacement for the adminpak.msi, which was introduced in Windows 2000 and stayed through Windows 2003. Like its predecessor, the RSAT is used so that you can fully manage your entire Windows Server 2008 R2 domain from the comfort of your Windows 7 desktop. With Windows 2008 and Windows Vista, there was no real remote-administration toolkit released when the operating systems were released. This lack of remote-administration capabilities meant that to perform many domain-level administrative functions, you had to remote desktop to a server to gain access to the tools. This hurt productivity and increased the overhead on the servers as you would constantly have people logged into production domain controllers doing routine work.

With the RSAT, you no longer have to work from the server's console to get your administration work done. You can now work from your desktop more easily utilizing multiple monitors and having your other applications such as Outlook and your internal ticketing application available to you for easy reference.

In order to get started with the RSAT, you'll need to download the installer from Microsoft. You can download the file by searching for the RSAT on http://download.microsoft.com or by navigating to http://bit.ly/MS-RSAT. The file that you download will be a Windows Update Microsoft Software Update (MSU) file, which you can publish in a GPO through Active Directory or add to your WSUS server for easy deployment to the workstations of your administrative staff. After you have installed the RSAT, you'll notice that you don't actually have it available to you. You must now activate the component on the Windows 7 workstation. To do this, open the Control Panel, then open **Programs** (**Programs and Features** if you are using the Control Panel in list mode), then click on **Turn Windows features on or off**. In the Windows Features window that opens, navigate to the RSAT and select the tools that you that to have access to on your workstation as shown in Figure 7.24.

After you have selected the tools you wish to have activated, click the **OK** button to begin the installation. Depending on the tools that you have selected, this can take several minutes or longer to complete. After you have

NOTE

Although itw ouldn'tn ecessarily be recommended that you install RSAT on every user computer, there is no harm in doing so because any changes to Active Directory or to the other services, which can be managed through the services managed by the RSAT MMC snap-ins (also called applications during this chapter), all authenticate the remote user using Windows Authentication before any read or write operation to the service can be performed. The user will only be able to perform the actions which the domain account that they are using to connect to the remote server has access to perform. In addition, the specific tools need to be turned on through the **Programs and Features** section of the Control Panel, which can be disabled through Active Directory GroupP olicy.

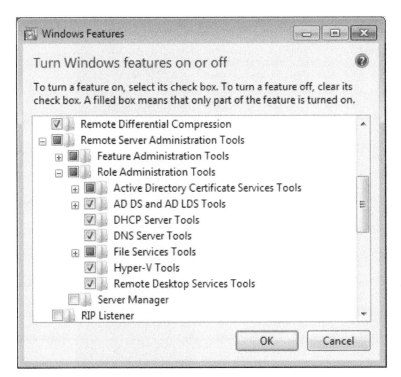

■ FIGURE 7.24 Windows Features Screen with Required Tools Selected

turned on the RSAT tools that you want, your **Start | Programs | Administrative Tools** folder will be similar to the one shown in Figure 7.25.

When you open the tools installed by the RSAT, you'll get the same tools that you would be presented with when launching them from a Windows Server 2008 R2 server. You can create, edit, or delete the OUs and user and computer accounts through the Active Directory Users and Computers application. You can create or delete domain trust relationships with the Active Directory Domains and Trusts application. You can create, edit, or delete sites and set domain controllers as global catalogs from the Active Directory Sites and Services application. Using the applications for Dynamic Host Configuration Protocol (DHCP), domain name system (DNS), and Hyper-V, you can control the DHCP, DNS, and Hyper-V services through their respective RSAT applications.

Most of the applications can be used to administrate a Windows Active Directory domain that is not a Windows Server 2008 R2 domain; however, there are some applications such as the Active Directory Administrative Center that require at least one Windows Server 2008 R2 domain controller to be installed within your domain.

NOTE
If you follow security best practices and your daily use Windows account does not have domain administration rights, you will need to perform an additional step when launching the tools. When you go to run RSAT, hold down the **Shift** key and right-click on the item. From the context menu that pops up, select the **Run as a different user** option and you will be prompted with the Run as window so that you can type in your account credentials that have domain administration rights. If your desktop account doesn't follow this best practice and does have domain administration rights, you do not need to perform this additional step.

NOTE
Although we will touch on the bulk of these applications (which are actually MMC snap-ins) in this chapter, not all of the advanced functionality will be covered as this full functionality is beyond the scope of this book.

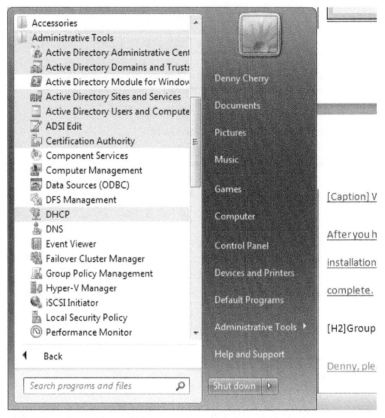

■ **FIGURE 7.25** Administrative Tools Program Group after Installing RSAT

Active Directory Administrative Center

The biggest change between the Administration tools of Windows Server 2008 and Windows Server 2008 R2 is the Active Directory Administrative Center. This application gives you a single place where you can manage a lot of your environment. First-time domain administrators may find this new application to be more user friendly than the Active Directory Users and Computers application. In addition to a much sleeker user interface (as shown in Figure 7.26), it provides a much more powerful search engine for searching through your Active Directory objects.

Reset Password Widget

The first thing that you notice when opening the Active Directory Administrative Center is that you can easily reset a user's password. When using the Active Directory Users and Computers, you would first need to find

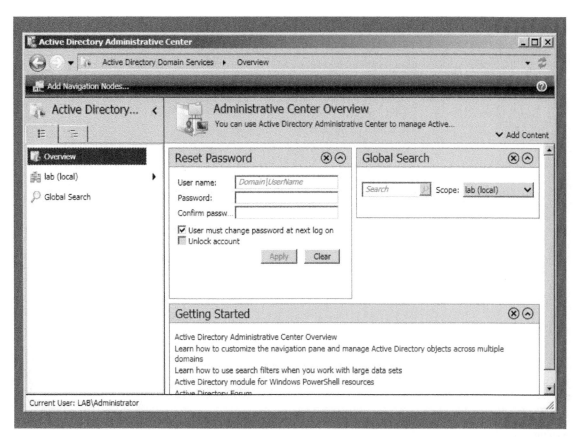

the user's account, then right-click on it, select **Reset Password** from the context menu, and type in the new password. When you open this new application, the first thing that you are greeted with is the ability to change a user's password.

Global Search Widget

From this same home screen, you can quickly perform a search against any object in the entire Active Directory database by using the **Global Search** widget on the upper right. By simply typing your search query into the search box and pressing **Enter**, you will search all objects in the Active Directory database for the string you typed in as shown in Figure 7.27. Once the results have shown, you can then perform whatever administrative action that needs to be completed.

As you can see in Figure 7.27, after you search for an object, you get a menu of tasks that can be performed against that object. Selecting objects

> **TIP**
>
> Microsoft chose to put the **Reset Password** widget on the Active Directory Domain Services screen for a simple reason; password reset tickets make up anywhere between 15 and 35 percent of all help desk tickets throughout the day (depending on which report you read). By making this simple task much faster, administrators can get through those tickets that much faster leaving them free to work on other tickets that much quicker.

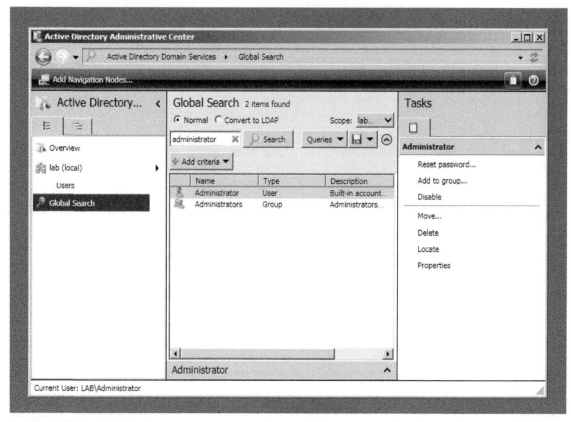

■ FIGURE 7.27 Searching the Active Directory Database for the Phrase "administrator" Using the Active Directory Domain Services Application Returns Two Results by Default

of different types will give you different options on the tasks pane on the right-hand side as only the tasks that are relevant to the object type are useful to you.

Object Properties in Active Directory Administrative Center

The first time you edit the properties of an object in the Active Directory Administrative Center, you'll see a major difference from the Active Directory Users and Computers application. In the Users and Computers application, you'll see a tabbed window similar to the one shown in Figure 7.28 with a bunch of tabs on it that you have to hunt through to edit all the options you are able to edit.

However, when you edit the same object in the Active Directory Administrative Center, you'll see just a single long screen, which you can scroll up and down as shown in Figure 7.29. You no longer have to hunt through over a dozen tabs looking for the field you are looking for.

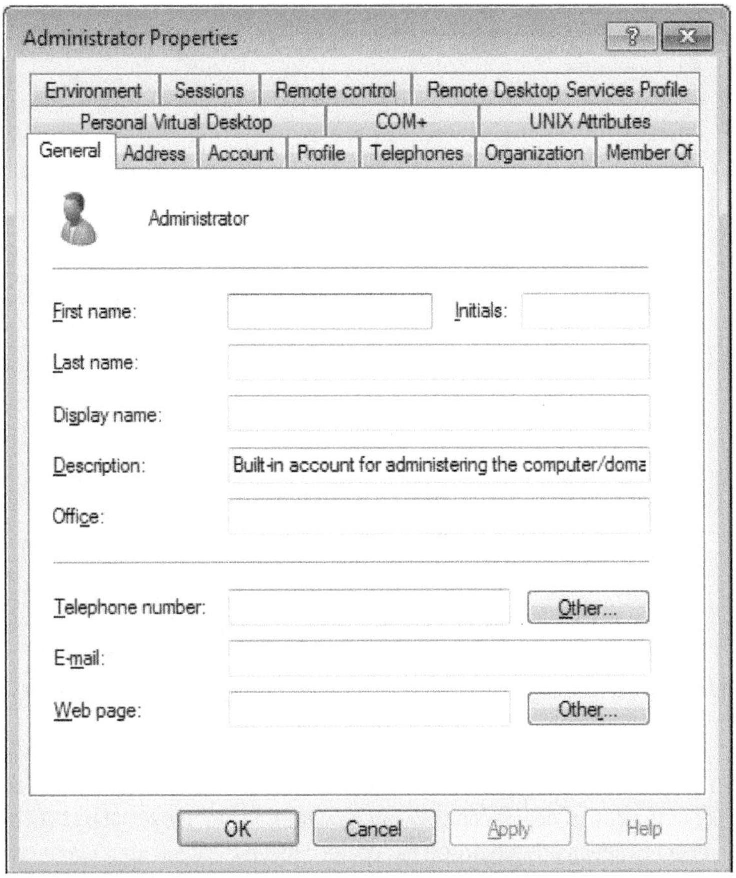

■ **FIGURE 7.28** **User Properties** Dialog Box from Active Directory Users and Computers Showing the Administrator Account

The user account editing screen, for example, no longer has the basic information for the account spread between the **General** and **Account** tabs; instead all the same information is shown under the **Account** heading. The biggest reduction in clicking between tabs will be seen under the **Organization** heading. This heading combines the old **Address**, **Telephones**, and **Organization** tabs and includes other new features such as a way to add all of a person's direct reports without having to go and edit every direct report's Active Directory object one by one.

The **Member Of** and **Profile** headings look very similar to the **Member Of** and **Profile** tabs in the old Active Directory Users and Computers application. At this point, you might be asking yourself where all the other tabs are?

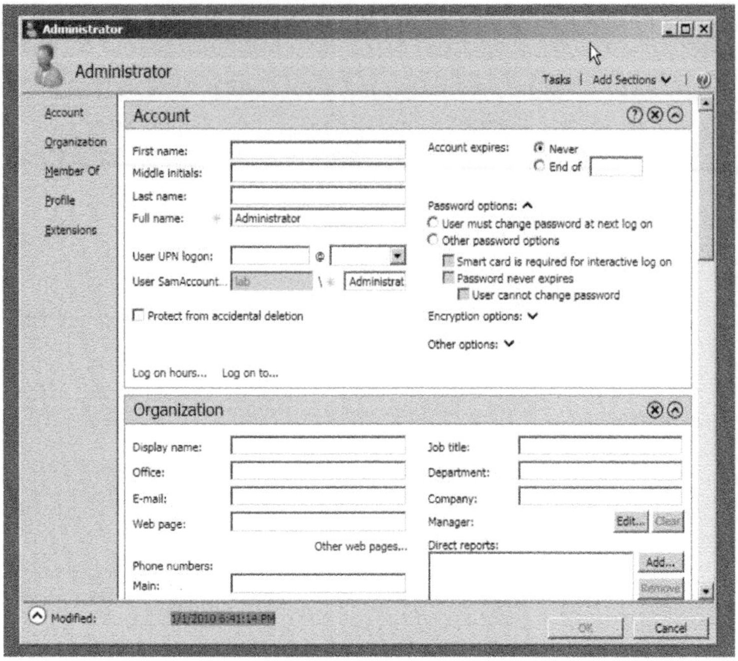

■ FIGURE 7.29 Properties of the Administrator Account as Shown in the Active Directory Administrative Center

They are all hidden under the **Extensions** heading where someone got a bit lazy in the design department. We are now back to our classic tabbed environment as apparently Microsoft has decided that these items aren't going to be used very often (see Figure 7.30).

Out of the box Active Directory Administrative Center does require at least one domain controller in each domain that you wish to administrate to be running Windows Server 2008 R2. This is because this tool requires the use of the Active Directory Web Service (ADWS), which was introduced in Windows Server 2008 R2.

If you wish to use this tool without installing a Windows Server 2008 R2 domain controller on your domain (which requires upgrading the Active Directory schema and shouldn't be done without proper planning), you can download and install the Active Directory Management Gateway Service on a Windows Server 2003 Service Pack 2 through Windows Server 2008 domain controller. The Active Directory Management Gateway provides the same functionality as the ADWS. More information can be found about this on the TechNet Web page at http://technet.microsoft.com/en-us/library/dd391908(WS.10).aspx#BKMK_1.

TIP

Now to be perfectly honest, I didn't see all that much use for the Active Directory Administrative Center for a Systems Administrator, unless you spend your day processing password reset requests (and if you do I'm sorry). Now for help desk employees, I can see this as being an invaluable tool that will increase productivity and decrease the time to resolve those password reset tickets. And in this economy of do more with less, anything that can help us achieve that goal has to be a good thing.

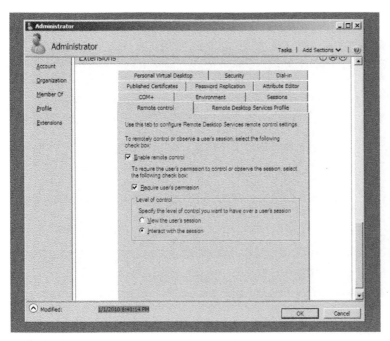

■ **FIGURE 7.30** The **Extensions** Heading of a User Object in the Active Directory Administrative Center

Active Directory Module for Windows PowerShell

The second truly new feature that you will see as part of the RSAT is the Active Directory Module for Windows PowerShell. This icon, which can be found in your **Start | Administrative Tools** folder after installing the RSAT (the third item on the list in Figure 7.23), opens your traditional Windows PowerShell v1 command window. However, unlike your normal Windows PowerShell command window, it comes preloaded with the Active Directory modules, so you don't have to manually import them using the **Import-Module**C mdlet.

Like the Active Directory Administrative Center, the Active Directory Module for PowerShell requires a Windows Server 2008 R2 Domain controller running the ADWS to be functional, as the PowerShell modules use the ADWS to interact with Active Directory. If you don't have a Windows Server 2008 R2 domain controller in your domain, you can install the Active Directory Management Gateway on a Windows Server 2003 or Windows Server 2008 domain controller. This is covered earlier in the chapter. If you don't have ADWS or ADMG installed or the servers aren't available when you open the Active Directory Module for Windows Powershell, you'll receive

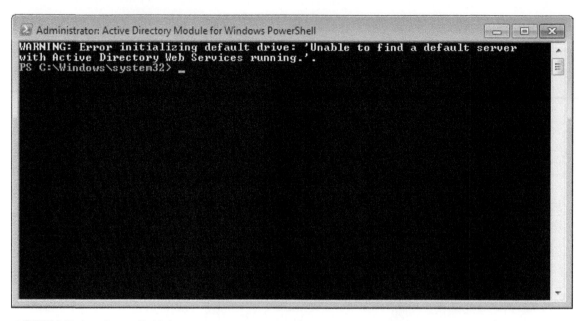

■ FIGURE 7.31 Active Directory Module for Windows PowerShell with the ADWS Server Unavailable

an error message as shown in Figure 7.31. If you open Windows PowerShell without the Active Directory module, you can import the module using the **Import-Module** Cmdlet. The module name is ActiveDirectory so the command would be **Import-Module ActiveDirectory**.

You can use the Active Directory Module for Windows PowerShell to manage just about any domain objects or settings that you would normally make from the other MMC snap-ins that are included as part of the RSAT.

From within this PowerShell environment, you can manage your users completely if you prefer the command line over the Windows user interface. Each object type has a separate Cmdlet for creating the object. Users can be created through the use of the **New-ADUser** Cmdlet, whereas new computer accounts can be created through the use of the **New-ADComputer** Cmdlet. You can create new domain groups by using the **New-ADGroup** Cmdlet, while adding a user or computer to a domain group is done through the **Add-ADGroupMemberC** mdlet.

Each of these Cmdlets has similar parameters, some of which are optional and some of which are required. Looking at the **New-ADUser** Cmdlet, you'll want to use at least four parameters: – *SamAccountName*, – *Name*, – *AccountPassword*, and – *Enabled – Path*. The – *SamAccountName* parameter allows you to set the log-in name for the account. This would be the name that the user types in when logging into the account. The – *Name*

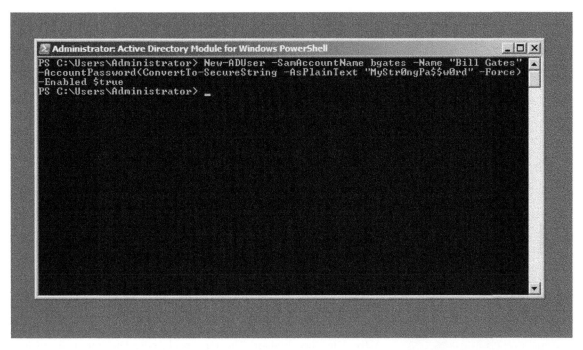

■ **FIGURE 7.32** Using Windows PowerShell to Create a New Domain Account for a New Employee

parameter is the display name for the user and should be surrounded with double quotes if you are specifying both a first and last name. The – *AccountPassword* parameter has a fairly complex syntax to allow for both encrypted and unencrypted passwords to be specified from the command line (the syntax for the plain text password is shown in Figure 7.32). The – *Enabled* parameter allows you to tell Active Directory if the account should be enabled or not. The –*Path* parameter is the path to the user's home directory.

To create a new computer account, the syntax is similar to the syntax to create a new user account. You use the **New-ADComputer** Cmdlet and specify the – *SamAccountName*, – *AccountPassword*, and the – *Enabled* flag. Once this command has been run, the computer with that name can be connected to the domain.

The **New-ADGroup** Cmdlet used to create new domain groups is slightly more complex as there are more parameters that must be included. We are already familiar with the – *Name* and – *SamAccountName* parameters because of the **New-ADUser** and **New-ADComputerC** mdlets.

However, to create a domain group, first, you have to decide if this domain group will be a *Security* group or a *Distribution* Group. This requires the use

NOTE

In truth, you don't need to specify much more than just the – *SamAccountName* parameter when creating accounts. The other parameters are recommended as a minimum set of parameters to use so that you don't have accounts created with just a username floating around your domain that someone later on needs to modify and attach the rest of the descriptive information.

of the – *GroupCategory* parameter, which accepts either *Security* or *Distri-bution* as a parameter value. Second, you need to define the scope of the group, whether the group should be a domain local group, a domain global group, or a universal group. This requires the use of the – *GroupScope* parameter, which accepts *Local*, *Global*, or *Universal* as parameter values. You can optionally include the – *DisplayName* and *–Path* parameters so as to control the name shown in Active Directory and the location within the Active Directory schema that the new group will be saved into.

There are hundreds of more Active Directory Cmdlets that can be accessed from Windows PowerShell. We have shown just a few here to give some examples of the power of the Active Directory Module for Windows PowerShell. For a full listing of the available modules and their full syntax, you should refer to Microsoft's TechNet site, specifically article 378785 that can be found at http://technet.microsoft.com/en-us/library/dd378785(WS.10).aspx.

Active Directory Users and Computers

The Active Directory Users and Computers application is used to create objects, move those objects between OUs, and delete objects from the Active Directory database. This traditional Active Directory tool was first introduced in Windows Server 2000 as the primary Active Directory man-agement tool. In addition to managing objects, the Active Directory Users and Computers application is the noncommand-line tool to use when creat-ing and deleting the OUs from your Active Directory database.

The first thing that many administrators will do when opening the Active Directory Users and Computers application is turn on the advanced features. This allows you to see all the optional information and some additional tabs within the properties for each object. You can turn on the advanced features by clicking on the **View** drop-down menu and selecting the **Advanced Fea-tures**m enui tem.

The Active Directory Users and Computers application, by default, does not allow you to edit every attribute of an object. This is because editing the attributes directly can be very dangerous, and Microsoft didn't want people destroying their Active Directory database by accident. However, if you turn on the **Advanced Features** option from within the main menu, every object's properties page will get an Attribute Editor screen. On this tab, you can view and, in some cases, edit the attributes of the object. Without this attribute editor, your only other options for editing the attributes would be to write an application that would update the Active Directory database, or use Windows PowerShell to handle the updates.

WARNING

The Active Directory Users and Computers application goes by another name as well. Many people will call it "Active Directory Users and Confusers." Two of the reasons that it got this nickname is one that not all information is shown by default, requiring that the **Advanced Features**op tion be enabled, the other being the absolutely silly number of tabs that are shown when editing a user's domain account. With **Advanced Features** turned on the properties page of a user's account has no less than 19 tabs shown in five rows.

ROAMING

Windows 7 supports some amazing roaming capabilities. With Windows 7 on the client and Windows Server 2008 R2, you can effectively remove the need for users to manually remote desktop into the office for anything. Windows 7 automatically connects to the corporate network through a secured Internet Protocol Security (IP-Sec) tunnel when corporate network resources are needed, and then automatically disconnects when those network resources are no longer needed.

This support can greatly simplify network topologies and reduce the learning curve for employees who need to be able to virtual private network (VPN) into the office for the first time as they will simply access the internal resource and the computer will automatically and seamlessly connect them to the office network.

The typical example of using this technology would be sending out an e-mail with a link to the internal SharePoint portal. In today's world, either the SharePoint portal would need to be publicly accessible or the external or home user would need to VPN into the office in order to view the document, which means that the user would need to know how to VPN into the office to view the document. Using the new roaming capabilities of Windows 7 and Windows Server 2008 R2, the client computer would see that a URL is being opened on a Web site that is inside the company. The user's computer would automatically make a secure IP-Sec-encrypted tunnel between the user's computer and the corporate network. Once this tunnel was established, the Web browser would be able to access the SharePoint portal and display the document. After the user is done viewing the document, the secure tunnel will automatically be closed until the next time it is needed, preventing unauthorized applications from attempting to access company resources.

The other great thing about this technology is that the client computer will automatically check in with the domain every few hours looking for GPO changes, just as any other computer within the network, so that it can download and apply new settings. You could then automatically install or upgrade the software on a home user's computer as it checks in even if the user doesn't access company resources that day.

Now, you might be concerned that this will route additional network traffic between the home user and your corporate network as it routes normal Internet traffic on this secure link, but it won't. Windows uses DNS to figure out what resources are corporate resources and which ones are Internet resources. What this means is that it now becomes very important for your internal domain name structure to not be a valid Internet domain name; otherwise, this new remoting system won't be able to identify which requests are for the internal network and won't be able to create that automatically encrypted connection between the home user and the office.

You can read more about this functionality, as well as how to configure it, in the section, "Enhancements with Windows Server 2008 R2," of Chapter 6, "Networking and Mobility."

ADMINISTRATIVE TEMPLATES

When working with Group Policies, the Administrative Templates are where you will end up making the most changes. The Administrative Templates section of the Group Policy contains more settings that can be adjusted than any other group of settings in the Group Policy. You can apply Administrative Templates at both the Computer and User level of the Group Policy, with some settings being found in both areas; however, some settings can only be found in one area or the other. In fact, the Computer Configuration branch has 1644 settings available, whereas the User Configuration branch has 1453 settings available.

The thing to remember when editing these Administrative Templates is that they are applied in order and settings can be overwritten, so just because you adjust a setting in a Group Policy in a higher OU or at the domain level doesn't mean that new setting will make it to the client as the setting could be overridden by another policy closer to the user or computer object.

Group Policies are always applied in a fixed order so that the results of the application can be very predictable. The first GPOs that will be applied will be the site-specific GPOs. After those have been applied, then any domain-specific GPOs will be applied. After those have been applied, Windows will traverse the OU tree between the domain and the computer (or user) object, applying all the GPOs starting with the OU closest to the domain in the structure and ending with the OU that the computer or user object resides in. With the release of Windows 7 and Windows Server 2008 R2, Microsoft has made several improvements to the Administrative Templates (ADMX files). The biggest change that you will face is that the interface has changed. Instead of the traditional three-tab properties window, which has been used previously, we get a single screen with all the options on it as showni n Figure7.33 .

We now have the **Not Configured**, **Enabled**, and **Disabled** radio buttons on the top left of the screen, with the options section expanded with the available options shown to the lower left. What used to be the **Explanation** tab

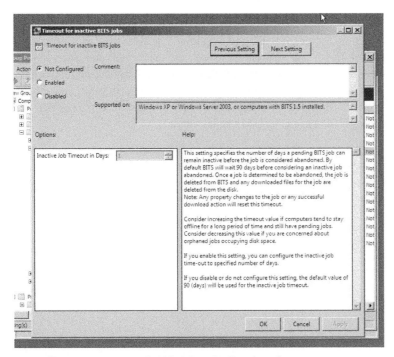

■ FIGURE 7.33 Properties Page of an **Administrative Templates** Option

is now the Help section with the Comment and Supported on boxes prominently displayed in the upper middle and right of the screen.

Another major change that you will see, although it may take you longer to notice it, is that the Administrative Templates now support multistring (REG_MULTI_SZ) and QWORD registry value types. This allows you even greater control over the client operating systems as some settings simply weren't controllable through the old Administrative Templates in Windows 2003 and Windows 2008 because multistring registry settings couldn't be modified. The QWORD support enables you to use Administrative Template policy settings to globally manage 64-bit applications, which wasn't possible without the QWORD support.

With Windows Server 2008 R2 and Windows 7, there have been more than 300 Administrative Template policy settings additions. There is information available about each of the new policy settings within TechNet; however, you will need to navigate to the specific technology section to find out if there are any new policy settings for that technology you are interested in.

■ SUMMARY

Windows Server 2008 R2 and Windows 7 provide you with some very powerful tools that you can use to remotely manage the computers in your enterprise. Depending on the tool that you use, you can manage and configure a single computer using the Computer Management MMC snap-in or a number of computers contained in a single OU of your entire company by editing a GPO using the group policy editor.

In order to manage both a single group and multiple computers, you'll want to ensure that you are familiar with Windows PowerShell, which can be used to remotely access a single computer and change settings on the computers within your domain through Group Policy.

Securing Windows 7

INFORMATION IN THIS CHAPTER

- User and Group Accounts
- Action Center
- Encryption
- AppLocker
- Summary

Securing Windows has traditionally been a daunting task due to Microsoft's lack of security awareness and consideration when making the operating system. However, since Windows XP SP2, Microsoft has made a commitment to improve the security of their products and Windows 7 is proof of that. There are many new and improved features in Windows 7 that make the system secure but they must be understood and configured correctly. Like Microsoft became aware of security, all your users must do so as well. The best line of defense is a knowledgeable and security-aware end user. Unfortunately, as systems become more secure, attackers are targeting the individual and there is little Windows 7 can do to protect a user who ignores its warnings.

This chapter focuses on configuring Windows 7 securely to allow the most productive working environment. First, user and group accounts will be explained. All users must have a complex password that meets password policy. A computer with a single user account without a password could be the only hole an attacker needs to get in. The first section will also look at User Account Control (UAC), an improved feature from Windows 7 to enforce standard users instead of administrative users. The Credential Manager will be referenced as a feature to store passwords and Parental Controls to control kids and even users at certain levels. Biometric security has been added to Windows 7 to allow users to use two-factor authentication: a

DOI: 10.1016/B978-1-59749-561-5.00008-5

password that the user knows and a fingerprint that the user has. Then file system security and sharing files and folders will be referenced.

The Action Center section will look at the features the Action Center monitors including Windows Updates. Not only must the operating system be up-to-date, but also all the applications must be up-to-date as well. As Microsoft has done a great job securing the operating system level, attackers are targeting the third-party applications that tend to be updated rarely. Antivirus and anti-malware will continue to be a requirement in Windows 7 and should be centrally managed for security and compliance in enterprise environments. The Windows Firewall has also been improved allowing specific rules to be configured and filtering both inbound and outbound traffic as well as adding Internet Protocol Security (IPsec). Internet Explorer 8 (IE 8) has many new security features and options that will be referenced in this section. Finally, Network Access Protection will be introduced as Windows 7 includes an agent to support the security solution.

The final sections will discuss encryption using BitLocker and BitLocker To Go, and encrypting file systems. While most of the security features in Windows 7 defend against network and software attacks, full disk encryption will defend against physical attacks through lost or stolen laptops, hard drives, and USB devices. AppLocker will also be referenced as a great solution for whitelisting and/or blacklisting at the application level. This will prove to be a great solution to defend against malware and other unauthorized software at the payload level.

As one can see from this brief introduction, Windows 7 has many security features. The best or worst security feature will end up being the human element. These features must be configured correctly and the end users must be educated to use the systems correctly. Deploying Windows 7 with all the security in place will do nothing if the end user ignores the Internet Explorer warnings and runs a malicious file. Security will be a never-ending battle and staying current will be the best solution for your organization.

USER AND GROUP ACCOUNTS

Many of the security features in Windows 7 are based on user accounts. It is an importing starting point to understand how user and group accounts work because proper user and group configuration is necessary to configure a number of security features. A user account with no password on a local system can compromise an entire organization. It is very important that all user accounts have a password.

UAC relies heavily on differentiating administrator and standard users for running and installing applications. UAC was introduced by Microsoft to battle the increased malware installing and running in administrator mode in older versions of Windows. It is critical that the user not be given administrative privileges to avoid malware outbreaks in an organization. Other topics related to how users log in such as biometric security and Credential Manager are introduced in Windows 7. It is critical that an end user understands password policy and uses it correctly to avoid malicious hackers logging in with their credentials. Additonally, file system and sharing security relies on user accounts to access shared resources on the network and on the local system.

This section will reference all of these important aspects of user and group accounts in Windows 7:

- User and Group Account Basics
- Manage User and Group Accounts
- UAC
- CredentialM anager
- ParentalC ontrols
- BiometricSe curity
- FileSys temSe curity
- SharingFi lesa ndF olders

User and Group Account Basics

Windows 7 systems can be configured to be members of a HomeGroup, workgroup, or domain. When a computer is configured to be a part of a HomeGroup or a workgroup, the user access and accounts are configured on the system itself through user accounts and groups. When a computer is a part of a domain, the user access is configured both on the Windows 7 system and on the Active Directory level. This section focuses on managing local user accounts and access.

Like other versions of Windows, Windows 7 has user accounts and group accounts. User accounts are designed for individual users, whereas group accounts, also known as groups, are designed to simplify administration of multiple users. Users can log on to a Windows 7 system but groups cannot. Furthermore, Windows 7 works with two types of user accounts:

- **Local user accounts** – These are defined on the local Windows 7 system and only have access to that one system. User administration can be performed in the **Control Panel | User Accounts** console or in the Computer Management MMC.
- **Domain user accounts** – These are defined in the Active Directory. A domain user account can login to a computer that is on the domain with credentials although a local user account does not exist. Managing Active Directory users and computers is available on Windows 7 with the RSAT tool referenced in the previous chapter.

Both of these user accounts types may be assigned as Standard or Administrator accounts. The Standard account has limited privileges, whereas the Administrator account has administrative privileges. All user accounts are identified by a logon name made up of two parts: the username and the user computer or domain. The logon name may be used in two different ways:

- The user computer or domain and the username separated by a back-slash (\) for example ORCHILLESHOME\jorchilles when the computer name is OrchillesHome and the username is jorchilles. The same is true for a domain account.
- Domain accounts can also log in with the username and the domain separated by an At sign (@) for example jorchilles@orchilleswork where jorchilles is the username and orchilleswork is the domain name. This does not apply to local user accounts.

The logon name is only used for logging into a computer or domain because what really holds the account privileges and permissions are the security identifiers also known as SIDs. SIDs are unique and the same SID should never exist in the same environment. SIDs are used for user accounts and computer accounts. The computer SID is created when a hostname is given to it the very first time it boots. For this reason, cloning Windows machines require changes the SID of the new machine. The user SID is created with the computer or domain SID prefix and a relative ID of the user. When access controls are set in Windows file system, the account SID is used instead of the username. This allows for changing the username easily and stops a malicious user from deleting an account and creating a new one with the same username to have access to the old user files.

User accounts can authenticate with a password or a certificate. A password is something the user knows, whereas a certificate is something the user has. A password is more secure than no password at all and a certificate is more secure than a password. Certificate authentication uses a smart card that has a private key, whereas the computer has the public key.

Default User and Group Accounts

Windows 7 comes with default user and group accounts. These are built-in accounts that are rarely modified but can be for various reasons. When installing Windows 7, one may have noticed that creating an account with the name **Administrator** or **Guest** was not allowed. This is because those accounts are already built-in and disabled by default. There are also a number of built-in group accounts that an administrator should be aware of.

There are two types of built-in user accounts: the standard local user accounts and the pseudo-accounts. The standard local user accounts built into Windows 7 are:

- **Administrator** – This account is disabled by default and a new security measure by Microsoft to not allow systems to have a generic Administrator username with full access to the system.
- **Guest** – This account is also disabled by default and has very limited privileges. This account should not be enabled as it will put the systems securitya tr isk.

The pseudo-accounts are built in to perform specific system tasks. They are only available on a local system. An administrator cannot change settings for these accounts or log in with these accounts. The built-in pseudo-accounts may all use the right to log on as a service and they are:

- **LocalSystem** – It is used for running system processes and tasks. Services that use this account to run have the most privileges.
- **LocalService** – It is used for running services that do not require full privileges and run on the local system.
- **NetworkSerivce** – It is used for running services that do not require many privileges on the local system but do require network resources.

Group accounts are created to make administrating user accounts easier. Group accounts can be given access privileges as a user account would. If the user is a part of a group with access to a resource that user also has rights. Group accounts also use SIDs for the same security reasons as computer and user accounts do. There are three types of group accounts:

- **Local groups** – These groups are only on the local system and can have rights assigned only on the local system.
- **Security groups** – These groups only work with Active Directory and are used for granting access to resources.
- **Distribution groups** – These groups are used in Active Directory as e-maildi stributionl ists.

Windows 7 includes many built-in groups that may be accessed through the Computer Management MMC by right-clicking **Computer | Manage**. In the Computer Management MMC expand **System Tools | Local Users and Groups | Groups** as shown in Figure 8.1. The built-in group accounts are:

- **Administrators** – This account has access to everything on the local computer. End users should not be a part of this group.
- **Backup Operators** – Members of this group can backup and restore files and folders on the local computer. Members of this group can

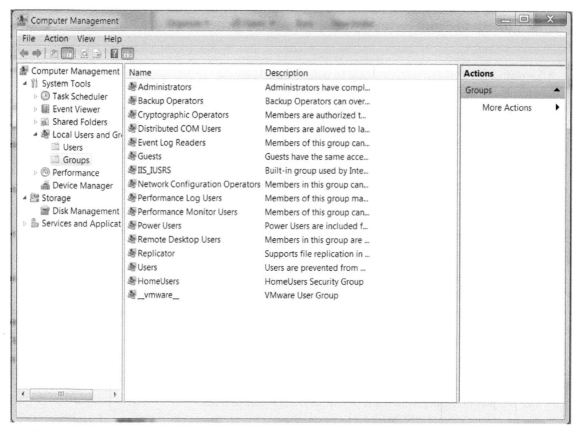

■ **FIGURE 8.1** Computer Management – Groups

access all files on the computer regardless of their access level to perform the backup and restore duties but they cannot change access permissions to files or perform other administrative tasks.

- **Cryptographic Operators** – Members of this group can manage encryption, IPsec, digital IDs, and certificates on the local system.
- **Distributed COM Users** – Members of this group can launch, activate, and use distributed COM objects on the local computer.
- **Event Log Readers** – Members of this group can view Event Logs on the local system.
- **Guests** – Members of this group have very limited privileges mostly based on using resources but are not allowed to modify anything.
- **Network Configuration Operators** – Members of this group can manage network settings and configure manual network configurations including network connections and adapters.
- **Performance Log Users** – Members of this group can view and manage performance counters and logs.

- **Performance Monitor Users** – Members of this group can view performance counters and logs.
- **Power Users** – This group is only maintained in Windows 7 to ensure compatibility with legacy applications and systems.
- **Remote Desktop Users** – Members of this group can log on to the computer remotely. Once logged in, all other privileges are based on other group memberships and the user account. Users in the administrators group are automatically allowed to connect remotely.
- **Replicator** – Members of this group can manage the replication of files and folders for the local system.
- **Users** – Members of this group can log on locally and work on the system without modifying system settings or configurations. Users in this group can access and create a user profile.

ManageU sera ndG roupA ccounts

This section focuses on managing local user and group accounts. The Basic User Management section will reference the easier and friendlier way of managing users on a local system using the **Control Panel | User Accounts** console. The Advanced User and Group Management section will reference using the Computer Management MMC for managing local users and groups. The basics of local user and group accounts were covered in the previous section, as well as the difference between local and domain accounts.

Basic User Management

The **Control Panel | User Accounts** console is the most user-friendly account management console in Windows 7. Most simple tasks including creating a user, creating or changing a password, changing account type, changing account name, and changing the account picture can easily be done from this console. However, more administrative tasks such as adding users to groups cannot be done from here.

To access the **User Accounts** console open Control Panel in icon view and click **User Account**. The **User Account** console is shown in Figure 8.2.

Create a New Account

To create a new account through the Control Panel, ensure a local administrator is logged in to the Windows 7 system:

1. Click **Manage another account** in the **User Accounts**c onsole.
2. Click **Create** a new account.
3. Type the **username** for the new user in the text box, as shown in Figure8.3 .

■ **FIGURE 8.2** Control Panel – User Account

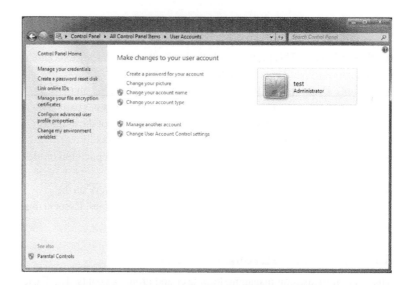

■ **FIGURE 8.3** Create a User Account

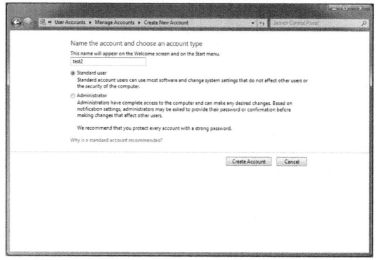

4. Select the type of account the user will be from the radio button selection:
   a. **Standard user** – Most of the users should be standard users while an administrator account should exist only administrator purposes like installing applications or making system-wide changes.
   b. **Administrator** – This user will have complete access to the Windows 7 system. Only one administrator account is recommended.
5. Click **Create**.

Createa Password

Every user should have a password, no excuses. Passwords should also be complex. This can be set in Local Group Policy referenced later in this section. To create a password for the logged on user or for another user, do the following:

1. Click **Create a password for your account** in **Control Panel | User Accounts** for the logged in user or click **Manage another account**, click the **account**, and click **Create a password**.
2. Input the desired password twice. Ensure it is complex by having at least eight characters, a number, symbol, and an upper- and/or lowercase letter. Click **How to create a strong password** for more information on creating a secure password.
3. Input a password hint if required by policy. Although a password hint may assist a user it can also assist a malicious hacker.
4. Click **Create password**.

> **NOTE**
> Allu sera ccountss houldh ave a complex password assigned. Reference the Local Security Policy section of this chapter for information on enforcing passwordst hroughp olicy.

Change Account Name, Password, Picture, or Type

The other changes a user can make to his or her account or an administrator can make to other accounts is changing the account name, account password, account picture, and account type. From the **User Accounts** console, click **Manage another account**. This window shows user accounts on the Windows 7 system. Click the **user account** that will be modified to display the **Change an Account** console as shown in Figure 8.4.

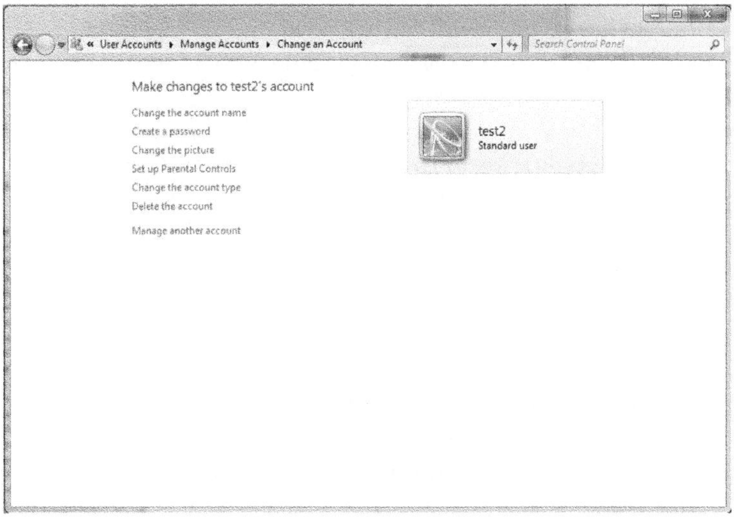

■ **FIGURE 8.4** Change an Account

Select what modification will be made:

- Account name – The account name is the name that will appear on the Welcome Screen and Start menu. This will not change the name of the user's profile folder in %SystemDrive%\Users\%Username%.
- Account password – A user may change their own password by typing the current one and then the new one. An administrator can change any user's password without knowing the current password.
- Account picture – A user or administrator can set a picture for the account when selecting it in the logon screen and Start menu. Clicking browse for more pictures allows the user to choose any image file as the account picture.
- Account type – The administrator can set the user as a standard user or administrator. More options are available through the computer management console and they are referenced in the next section.

Deletea n Account

Local user accounts may be deleted through the Control Panel as well. The user account that will be deleted cannot be the user logged in and an administrator must be logged in to delete another account through the Control Panel. When deleting an account, the administrator will be prompted to delete the user files or keep the files. The user files are stored at %SystemDrive%\Users\%Username%.

To delete a user account, do the following:

1. Fromt he **User Accounts** console in the Control Panel, select **Manage another account**.
2. Select the user account that will be deleted.
3. Click **Delete the account** in the **Change an Account**c onsole.
4. Select **Delete** or **Keep files**.

Create a Password Reset Disk

A user may create a password reset disk for his or her local user password. A password reset disk may be created on a floppy disk or removable media. Once the password disk is created, it must be stored in a safe place as anyone with access to it will be able to reset the password.

To create a password reset disk:

1. Click **Create a password reset disk** in the left panel of the **User Accounts** console of the Control Panel.
2. Read the information on the Forgotten Password wizard and click **Next**.

3. Select the device to create the password reset disk from the drop-down menu and click **Next**.
4. Typet he **current user password** to ensure no one unauthorized is creating the disk.
5. Click **Next** and then **Finish**.
6. Store the password reset disk in a safe, secure location.

The Forgotten Password wizard will create a userkey.psw file in the root of the device chosen. This file is then used to reset the password in the event the user forgets it in the future. The userkey.psw is encrypted using RSA2.

To reset the user password using the password reset disk:

1. After a failed login attempt in the Welcome Screen, a **Reset password…** link will appear under the password prompt. Click the link to initiate the Password Reset wizard.
2. Click **Next**.
3. Select the device with the password reset file from the drop down and click **Next**.
4. Create a new password that meets complexity requirements and click **Next**. A password hint may be set.
5. Click **Finish**.
6. Logi nus ingt hene wpa ssword.

LinkO nlinel Ds

Windows 7 can link online IDs with the local user account. This may make it easier for a user to share files or connect to other computers. The process for linking an online ID with a local user account involves adding an online ID provider and then linking that online ID to the user account. Adding an online ID provider entails downloading a third-party application like the Windows Live ID Sign-in Assistant, installing the application, and then using it to link the account.

To add an online ID provider:

1. Click **Link online IDs** in the left panel in the **User Accounts**c onsole within the Control Panel.
2. Click **Add an online ID provider**, which will open the default Web browser to http://windows.microsoft.com/en-US/Windows7/OnlineIDProviders.
3. Download the third-party application for the ID provider that will be linked to the user account.
4. Install the third-party application and follow any other instructions uniquet ot hepr ovider.

To link the user's online ID to the local user account:

1. Click **Link online IDs** in the left panel of the **User Accounts**c onsole within the Control Panel.
2. Click **Link Online ID** on the online ID provider that will be linked.
3. Entert he **username** and **password** to sign in to the third-party service and follow any unique instructions by the provider.
4. Click **OK**.

ProfileP roperties

User profiles in Windows 7 store user-related settings for the user. Generally, each computer a user uses will have an independent user profile on the local computer. In an enterprise environment, some users may need or enjoy the same settings on multiple systems. This is possible with a roaming profile. A roaming profile is required for advanced infrastructures such as the Virtual Desktop infrastructure referenced in the next chapter.

To view user profiles and set user profiles as local or roaming, do the following:

1. From the left panel in the **User Accounts** console in the Control Panel, click **Configure advanced user profile properties**.
2. Select the profile to change or view profile information.
3. Clickt he **Change Type...** button to change a profile between local profile to roaming profile or vice-versa.
4. Select the radio button for the change and click **OK**.
5. Click **OK**.

UserEn vironmental Variables

Environmental variables may be added, removed, or edited for a single user account even if the account is a standard user. The same console used to make changes for user environmental variables is also used for system environmental variables as shown in Figure 8.5. There are multiple ways to open the **Environmental Variables** console:

- Type **environment** in the Start menu Search and select **Edit environmental variables** for your account or **Edit the system environment variables**.
- From the left panel in the **User Accounts** console in the Control Panel, click **Change my environment variables** (user variables only).
- Int he **System** console of the Control Panel or right-click **Computer | Properties**, select **Advanced system settings** on the left panel, click the **Advanced** tab, and click the **Environment Variables...**b utton.

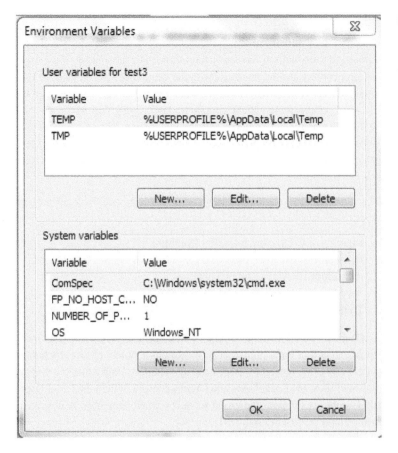

Allow Domain User Local Logon

Sometimes an administrator may need to add a domain user as a local user to log on to the Windows 7 system locally. This is possible in Windows 7 as long as the computer is already a member of the domain:

1. In the **Control Panel | User Accounts** console, select the **Change accountt ypel** ink.
2. Click **Add...**
3. Inputt he **domain username** and **domain** in the Add New User wizard.
4. Select the type of user account:
   a. **Standard user** – It will add the user to the Users group.
   b. **Administrator** – It will add user to the Administrators group, which is not recommended.
   c. **Other** – Select which group the user will be a member of.
5. Click **Finish**.

Advanced User and Group Management

Although the **Control Panel | User Accounts** console is friendly and easy to manage users with, it has many limitations. For this reason, local users and groups may also be managed with the Computer Management MMC. This method offers many more options for managing user and group accounts related to the local computer. User and group accounts may be added, managed, or deleted from the Computer Management MMC. Working within the Computer Management MMC for managing users and groups is much like managing users and groups in Active Directory Users and Computers.

The Computer Management MMC may be accessed in a variety of ways:

- Right-click **Computer** and select **Manage**.
- Int he **Administrative Tools** console within the Control Panel, click the **Computer Management**s hortcut.
- Type **Computer Management** on the Start menu Search.
- Through MMC by adding the **Computer Management**s nap-in.

As Chapter 5 mentioned, the Computer Management MMC is a great local management tool for administrators. It contains a variety of tools including system tools, storage, and services and applications. Expanding the system tools will show the Local Users and Groups console. Within the Local Users and Groups are the user and group accounts, where they may be managed, as shown previously in Figure 8.1.

Create, Rename, and Delete a User Account

A new local user may be created in the Computer Management MMC as shown in Figure 8.6:

1. Right-click **Users in Computer Management | System Tools | Local Users and Groups** and select **New User…** or right-click the **open area** in the details pane of users and select **New User**.
2. Fill in the fields:
   a. **Username** – The logon name the user will use to log on. The name should follow the username policy convention.
   b. **Full Name** – The full name of the user for proper documentation and identification. This field is optional.
   c. **Description** – A description of the user, generally, this is the title of the user. This field is optional.
   d. **Password** – Create a password for the user ensuring complexity andpol icyr equirementsa rem et.

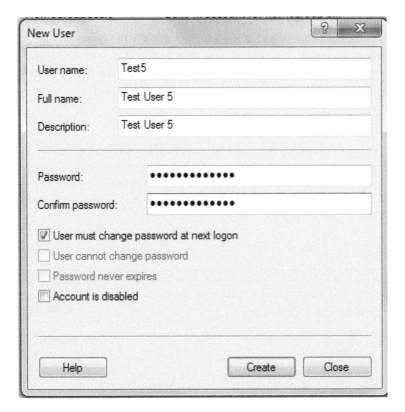

3. Select the appropriate check boxes:
   a. **User must change password at next logon** – If checked, the user will be prompted to change his or her password at logon. This is standard when an administrator is creating an account for another user.
   b. **Userc annotc hangep assword** – If checked, the user will not be able to change the password. Generally, this is not recommended but cases may arise when necessary.
   c. **Password never expires** – if checked, the password will not expire per policy settings. Generally, this is not recommended, but cases may arise when necessary.
   d. **Account is disabled** – If checked, the account will be disabled and the user will be unable to log on.
4. Click **Create**.

A user account may be renamed. Renaming the user account will change the user's logon name and input required for credentials, but it will not change the user's SID meaning all settings will remain. To rename a user, right-click the **username** and click **Rename** in the Users view.

A user account can be easily deleted from this view as well. Deleting the user will remove the SID for the user, and it will be very difficult to restore, by design. Deleting the user from here will not delete the user's profile folder or files. Ensure prior to deleting the user that there is another local administrator account or you may lock yourself out. To delete a user, right-click the **user** and click **Delete**.

UserP roperties

Local user accounts may also be managed from this area much like managing users in Active Directory except with fewer options. To access the user properties, right-click the **user** and select **Properties**. As shown in Figure 8.7, there are fewer tabs in the local user properties than in Active Directory user properties:

■ **FIGURE 8.7** User Properties

- **General** tab
  - ❑ **Full name** – Modify the full name of the user. This should be filled correctly for documentation.
  - ❑ **Description** – A field for a short description of the user. This is often set to the user's title or role.
  - ❑ **User must change password at next logon** – Makes the user change the password on next logon.
  - ❑ **User cannot change password** – This does not allow the user to change his or her own password.
  - ❑ **Password never expires** – Overrides policy forcing passwords to be changed after certain time.
  - ❑ **Account is disabled** – To disable an account, check this box. The user will not be able to log in to the system or access resources.
  - ❑ **Account is locked out** – Used to unlock or lock a user account.
- **Member Of** tab – This tab displays the groups the user is a member of.
  - ❑ Add user to a group:
    - Click **Add...**
    - **Object type** – This is the type of object, in this case **Groups**.
    - **Location** – This can be the local computer expressed as the computer name or a domain.
    - **Object Names** – Here you may type the **group name** and click **Check Names to validate**.
    - **Advanced** – This allows searching through locations for groups.
    - Click **OK**.
  - ❑ **Remove user from group** – Select the **user** and click **Remove**. This will remove the user from the group and any access allowed through that group.
- **Profile** tab – Here, the administrator may set the user profile path, logon script, home folder, and a connected network drive.

Secure Guest Account

The guest account is disabled by default, but some environments may require a secure guest account on the system. A standard user account will most likely be too much access for the guest so creating a guest account could be a bit tricky:

1. Create a new user as referenced in the previous section.
2. Create a secure password for the new account.
3. In the user properties, remove the user from the Users group and add to the Guest group.
4. For more secure access, apply User Rights Assignment from the Local Security Policy section referenced in this chapter.

Create, Rename, and Delete a Group Account

A new local group may be created in the Computer Management MMC as shown in Figure 8.8:

1. Right-click **Groups** in **Computer Management | System Tools | Local Users and Groups** and select **New Group...** or right-click the **open area** in the details pane of Groups and select **New Group**.
2. Fill in the fields:
   a. **Group name** – The name of the group, using proper conventions.
   b. **Description** – A clear description of the group that illustrates itspur pose.
   c. **Add...** or **Remove...**m embers.
3. Click **Create**.

Group accounts may also be renamed. Renaming the group account will not change the group's SID meaning all settings will remain. To rename a group, right-click the **group** and click **Rename** in the Groups view. A

■ **FIGURE 8.8** New Group

group account can be easily deleted from this view as well. Deleting a group will remove the SID for the group and it will be very difficult to restore, by design. Deleting the group will remove all users from the group and the security access allowed to that group is deleted. To delete a group, right-click the **group** and click **Delete**.

Add User Accounts to Local Groups

Administrators will often need to add domain user accounts to local groups to grant access on the local computer. Users that have not logged on to the local computer can be added to groups to ensure productivity later. It is not recommended to add domain users as administrators in the local system.

To add a user to a group:

1. Expand **Computer Management | System Tools | Local Users and Groups | Groups**.
2. Double-clickt he **group** the user will be added to.
3. Click **Add...**
   a. **Object type** – This is the type of object, in this case **Groups**.
   b. **Location** – This can be the local computer expressed as the computer name or a domain.
   c. **Object Names** – Here, you may type the **group name** and click **Check Names to validate**.
   d. **Advanced** – This option allows searching through locations for groups.
4. Click **OK**.

UserA ccountC ontrol

Working on any operating system on a day-to-day basis with an account that has administrator privileges is bad practice and insecure. A huge problem with Windows security is that most of the user accounts are members of the administrative group. Prior to Windows Vista, any process that required administrative privileges would simply run without notifying the user. This flaw allowed all types of malware to be installed on Windows systems and caused huge problems with the systems as the malware was running with full rights. For this reason, Microsoft introduced UAC. UAC is a significant new feature in Windows Vista and improved in Windows 7. Chapter 1, "Introduction to Windows 7" introduced UAC and Chapter 4, "The New Windows 7 Desktop Environment," expanded on it for installing and running applications, which is one of the biggest effects UAC has on Windows 7 usability. UAC affects what user privileges standard and administrator users have. Understanding UAC will help you become a better administrator as many issues and solutions will revolve around this feature.

UAC has redefined the administrator and standard user role. All applications run in a standard user mode and when administrative access is required, the user is prompted to accept the process or authenticate as an administrator to run what is called Admin Approval Mode. The Admin Approval Mode is the component of UAC that determines what and who can run what.

The standard user role in Windows 7 has been changed to allow standard users to perform daily tasks without needing administrator rights. This should allow administrators to deploy Windows 7 systems to domain users without requiring membership to any other groups for access. Some of the tasks standard users can now do are:

- View system clock, calendar, and change time zone
- Installf onts
- Change display and power settings
- Install printers and devices as long as drivers are installed
- Downloada ndi nstall WindowsU pdate
- Create VPNc onnections
- Setup WEPonw irelessc onnections

User Account Control Settings

Unlike Windows Vista, UAC settings can be set instead of simply turned off. Setting the UAC to a setting lower than default will disable the secure desktop. It is not recommended to turn off UAC. Turning off UAC will disable many security settings in Windows 7 including some in IE 8.

UAC settings may be accessed in different ways:

- Got o **Control Panel | Action Center** and click **Change User Account Control Settings** on the left pane.
- **Control Panel | User Accounts | Change User Account Control Settings**
- Type **uac** in the Start menu Search

There are four options in the UAC Settings (Figure 8.9):

- Alwaysnot ifym ew hen:
  - ❏ Programs try to install software or make changes to my computer.
  - ❏ I make changes to Windows settings.
- Default – Notify me only when programs try to make changes to my computer.
  - ❏ Don't notify me when I make changes to Windows settings.
- Notify me only when programs try to make changes to my computer (does not dim the desktop).
  - ❏ Don't notify me when I make changes to Windows settings.

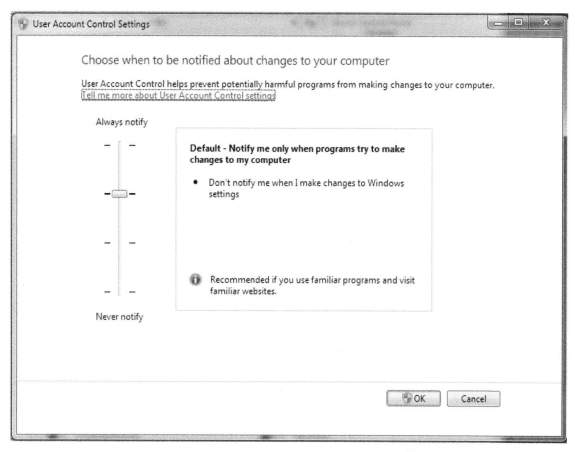

- Nevernot ifym ew hen:
  - Programs try to install software or make changes to my computer.
  - Im akec hangest o Windowss ettings.

UAC settings may also be managed through Group Policy in the Local Security Policy console or Local Group Policy editor as shown in Figure 8.10 by expanding **Computer Configuration | Windows Settings | Security Settings | Local Policies | Security Options**:

- UAC: **Admin Approval Mode for the Built-in Administrator account** – Enabled by default, this feature requires the built-in administrator, which is disabled by default, to require elevation prompt and Admin ApprovalM ode.
- UAC: **Allow UIAccess applications to prompt for elevation without using the secure desktop** – Disabled by default, this allows User

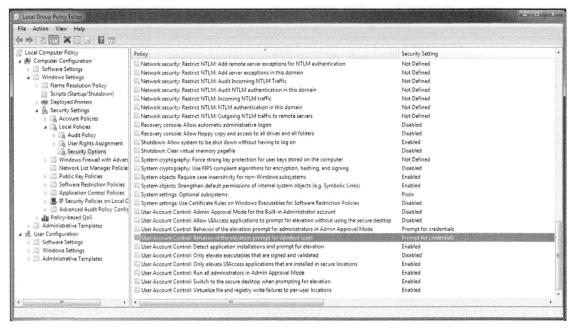

■ **FIGURE 8.10** Local Group Policy
Editor – UAC

Interface Accessibility (UIAccess) programs to automatically disable the secure desktop for elevation prompts on standard users.

- UAC: **Behavior of the elevation prompt for administrators in Admin Approval Mode** – This option sets how the elevation prompt receives consent from the administrator. The options are:
  - ❏ **Elevate without prompting**
  - ❏ **Prompt for credentials on the secure desktop**
  - ❏ **Prompt for consent on the secure desktop**
  - ❏ **Prompt for credentials**
  - ❏ **Prompt for consent**
  - ❏ **Prompt for consent from nonWindows binaries**
- UAC: **Behavior of the elevation prompt for standard users**– This option sets how the elevation prompt receives consent from the standard user. The options are:
  - ❏ **Automatically deny elevation requests**
  - ❏ **Prompt for credentials on the secure desktop**
  - ❏ **Prompt for credentials**
- UAC: **Detect application installations and prompt for elevation** – Enabled by default, this configures whether Admin Approval Mode or elevation prompt are enabled when attempting to install an application.

- UAC: **Only elevate executables that are signed and validated**–
  Disabled by default, this setting will only elevate executables and
  DLLs that are signed and validated in the Trusted Publisher store.
- UAC: **Only elevate UIAccess applications that are installed in
  secure locations** – Enabled by default, this setting will only elevate
  UIAccess applications located in %SystemRoot%\%ProgramFiles%\ or
  %WindowsDirectory%\system32\.
- UAC: **Run all administrators in Admin Approval Modes** – Enabled
  by default, this requires all administrators to use elevation prompts and
  Admin ApprovalM odes.
- UAC: **Switch to the secure desktop when prompting for elevation**–
  Enabled by default, this setting sets whether secure desktop (dimmed
  display) is initiated for elevation prompts.
- UAC: **Virtualize file and registry write failures to per-user
  locations** – Enabled by default, this should remain enabled for
  softwarec ompatibility.

Thankfully, Microsoft included different settings for UAC for administrators to tweak for each environment. As each environment is different
especially in reference to applications, it is difficult to recommend settings.
We recommend enabling and using the most UAC settings that don't inter-
fere with user productivity.

CredentialM anager

Windows 7 includes a Credential Manager where end users can save credentials for Web sites, applications, and servers that support the feature.
The credentials are stored in Windows Vault and provide easy and quick
logon to any of the saved resources. This may benefit users who have trouble logging into resources, writing passwords down insecurely, or using
the same password for every resource. Ensure your organization has the
correct policy set for passwords and how they are managed and stored.
User awareness of password policy will go a long way in running a secure
environment.

Credential Manager can store three types of credentials:

- Windows credentials – Any resource that uses Windows authentication
  such as NTLM or Kerberos.
- Certificate-based credentials – Any resource that requires a certificate.
- Generic credentials – Any resource that uses basic authentication such
  asus ernamea ndpa ssword.

This section will reference adding, editing, backing up, restoring, and
removing credentials to the Windows Vault. Credential Manager may be

accessed from the Control Panel or by typing **credential** in the Start menu Search and is illustrated in Figure 8.11.

To add credentials to a user account for automatic logon, do the following:

1. Click **Add a Windows credential**, **Add a certificate-based credential**, or **Add a generic credential** in the **Credential Manager** console of the Control Panel.
2. Fill the text boxes with the proper data:
   a. **Internet or network address** – Enter the server host name, IP address or fully qualified domain name. Wildcards may be used by using the asterisk (*).
   b. **Username** – The username used for the resource. For the default domain, one may use the username alone. For other domains, use %domain name%\username or username@%domain name%. Web sites may require an e-mail, which may be used as well.
   c. **Password** – The password for the username and resource.
   d. **Certificate** – Click **Select certificate** and select the correct certificateor de vicef ora uthentication.
3. Click **OK**t os avec redentials.

■ **FIGURE 8.11** Credential Manager

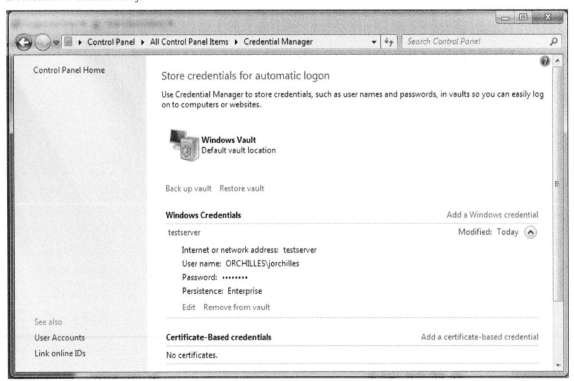

To edit an entry in the vault, simply click the **credential** and click **Edit** as shown in Figure 8.11. This must be done when passwords are changed. To remove credentials is similar except you must click the **Remove from vault** link as shown in Figure 8.11. Backing up a user's vault and restoring it back are also features of the Credential Manager. This is useful for moving the user to another system as well as protecting data loss.

To back up credentials in the vault:

1. Click **Back up vault** in the **Credential Manager**c onsole.
2. Click **Browse** to select a location to backup the vault. Saving in the system drive will impede recovery when the drive fails.
3. Click **Next**.
4. Press **Ctrl+Alt+Delete** to enter a secure desktop to create a password for the vault file.
5. Typet he **password** twice and click **Next**. Ensure the password meets policyr equirements.
6. Click **Finish**.

To restore credentials from a backup file:

1. Click **Restore vault** in the **Credential Manager**c onsole.
2. Click **Browse** to select the backup file.
3. Click **Next**.
4. Press **Ctrl+Alt+Delete** to enter a secure desktop to authenticate the password for the recovery file.
5. Typet he **password** and click **Next**.
6. Click **Finish**.

ParentalC ontrols

Parental Controls is a console within the Control Panel allowing administrators or parents to control the access of users or kids on the system. Although this may not be used in a business environment, we will reference it briefly as it is a part of Windows 7 security features and can be used to limit local user access.

Parental Controls requires at least two user accounts on the computer. One must be an administrator, whereas the other should be a standard user. Each account should have a password, but it is required the administrator set a password.

To enable and configure the Parental Controls, do the following:

1. Ensure you are logged in as an administrator account.
2. Click **Parental Controls** console in the Control Panel.

3. Clickt he **user** to set parental controls for. This will be the standard user account for the child.
4. Click **On**, **enforce current settings** on the **User Controls**c onsole.
5. Select **Windows Settings** to configure Parental Controls:
   a. **Time limits** – This allows the parent to control at what time the user may log on to the computer. This is similar to options in Active Directory for users. Click the **time** to allow or block based on day of the week and time. Blue boxes will not allow the user to log on at those times, whereas white or clear boxes will.
   b. **Games** – Here the administrator can block games completely or allow certain types by game rating or individual game. Selecting **No** will block all games, whereas selecting **Yes** will allow the administrator to configure the block by rating, content type, or name.
      - **Set game ratings** – Here the administrator may allow or block games with no rating. These ratings are done by the game rating system put in place by the Entertainment Software Rating Board (ESRB), which is the standard in computer game ratings. The administrator may choose the highest-rated game the user can play, as well as block individual content based on the game ratings ystem.
      - **Block or Allow specific games** – Here the user may choose to always allow access to a specific game, always block access to a specific game, or condition access to the specific game based on the user rating settings. The game must support Windows 7 to be on this list.
   c. **Allow and block specific programs** – This console configures allows the administrator to manually choose which programs the user can an cannot use or allow the user to use all programs on the system. If the program is not on the list, clicking **Browse** will allow form anuali nput.

To change the game rating system, click **Game Rating Systems** on the left panel of the **Parental Controls** console, select the radio button to the left of the system which is preferred, and click **OK**.

BiometricS ecurity

Windows 7 has added biometric devices and support for using finger scanning devices to log in to the system, domain, and other resources. This is possible using the Windows Biometric Framework (WBF), which is a framework for supporting biometric authentication devices. For years, computer makers have released computers with biometric devices, which

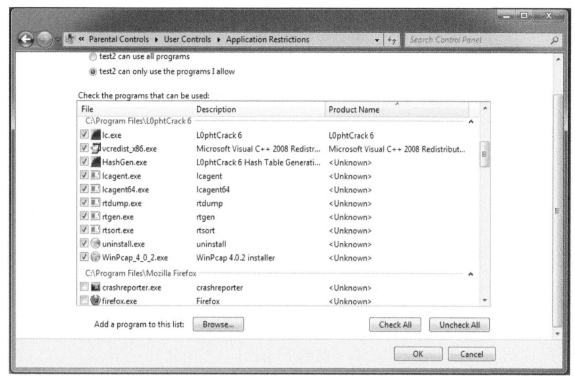

FIGURE 8.12 Application Restrictions in Parental Controls

relied on a third-party application to log in. These applications often had security holes in the implementation or technology itself, which allowed attackers to break into systems. Biometric security uses a different form of authentication then passwords. A password is something a user knows, whereas a fingerprint is something a user has. If biometric security is to be deployed, consider deploying two form factor authentication requiring a username, password, and biometric instead of just a biometric. As with all security features, this must be evaluated, written into policy, and then deployed.

Windows Biometric Framework

Microsoft redesigned the winlogon process in Windows Vista by removing the Graphical Identification and Authentication (GINA) infrastructure and adding the Credential Provider extension model. This infrastructure is a set of interfaces that allows consistency with third-party devices and applications around how users enter credentials. In Windows 7, Microsoft added the WBF to the winlogon process as well to support biometric authentication devices (only supports fingerprint readers).

The WBF uses these components:

- Windows Biometric Drive Interface (WBDI) – Provides a common driver for biometric devices. Biometric device drivers must use Windows Driver Model, Kernel Mode Driver Framework, or User-Mode Driver Framework (recommended).
- Windows Biometric Service (WBS) – This component interfaces WBF with the driver and the WBF API to integrate with applications. It uses a GUID or SID much like user and group accounts to keep the fingerprint content secret. WBS manages pools of biometric devices to enable how they may be used:
  - System pool – This uses biometrics to authenticate with any Credential Dialog including UAC Admin Approval Mode, elevation prompt, and logon.
  - Private pool – It does not allow applications to integrate with Windowsa uthentication.
  - Unassigned pool – Any device that does not fit in the prior two pools.
- WBF API – This set of APIs is known as the WinBio* APIs and allows applications and user mode components to directly interact with the biometric device. This is to support third-party devices and applications as well as Control Panel enrollment, which will be looked at in thene xts ection.

The WBF may be used by end users in the **Control Panel | Biometric Devices** console or by a third-party application and by system administrators through Group Policy. The **Biometric Devices** console in the Control Panel allows a user to configure logging into a system and other applications with a biometric device, whereas an administrator can manage the entire framework from Group Policy, including disabling the framework or only allowing certain types of logins and authentication through biometric devices.

Biometric Devices – Control Panel

End users may configure biometric devices in the Control Panel to enable log in to the system, UAC prompts, and other applications that support it. The system must have a fingerprint scanning device connected and drivers correctly installed.

To configure biometric devices:

1. Ensure the user configuring the fingerprint device is logged in.
2. Open the **Biometric Devices** console from the Control Panel. If it is not available, ensure the proper drivers are installed in the Device Manager.
3. Click **Use your fingerprint with Windows**.

4. Authenticate at the UAC prompt.
5. Select which finger(s) will be used by clicking the **finger** in the Enrollment wizard. You may setup all ten.
6. Swipe each finger three times. The icons on the right will determine successfuls wipes.
7. Click **Finish**.

This will enable use of the biometric device as the only method to log in to Windows. The **Biometric Device** console in the Control Panel also has options that the end user may configure:

- Enableor di sablebi ometrics
- Enable or disable local logon
- Enable or disable domain logon
- Deletefi ngerprintt emplatesa ndpa sswordda ta

FileS ystemS ecurity

Windows 7 uses New Technology File System (NTFS), which was the standard file system for Windows NT. Although NTFS has several improvements over the File Allocation Table (FAT) file system, it is not the most secure file system available. Unfortunately, Microsoft has yet to build or decide to use a more secure file system so everyone is stuck with this. NTFS will offer mediocre security when configured correctly and this section will focus on that. NTFS can control access to files and folders by assigning permissions that specifically allow or deny access to user or group accounts.

Windows 7 must be installed on NTFS, but it supports mounting other file systems. To determine what file system the hard drive you are accessing has, you may right-click the **drive** and select **Properties**. The file system will indicate the type as shown in Figure 8.13. FAT file systems do not offer access control lists and anyone with access to the file system may read, write, or remove data without restrictions or auditing.

Basic Permissions

NTFS offers basic permissions that are fairly user-friendly and provide basic security. It is critical to understand the basics of NTFS security to administer file system security. The owner of a file or a folder has the ultimate right to allow or deny access to that file or folder. Users with administrative privileges or full control of the file or folder may also grant or deny other users or groups permission to access the file or folder. An entry that denies permission to an account takes precedence over entries that allow permission. If a user is a member of two groups, one with access and one with denied access to a folder, the user will not be able to access the resource.

■ **FIGURE 8.13** Hard Drive Properties

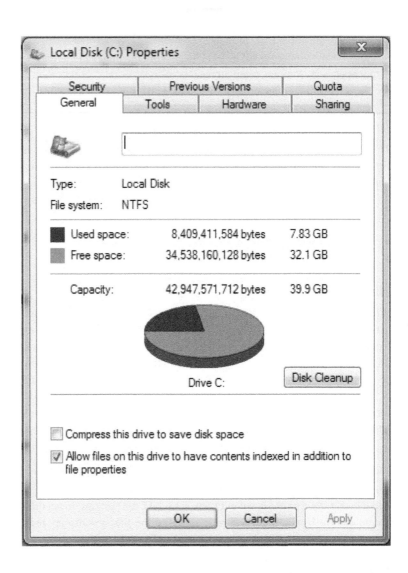

To view basic file or folder permissions as shown in Figure 8.14:

1. Right-clickt he **folder** or **file** in Windows Explorer or on the desktop.
2. Click **Properties**.
3. Clickt he **Security**t ab.

The **Security** tab shows the object name at the top and the group or user accounts with permissions set on this file or folder. Clicking on a **user** or **group** will show the permissions for that account in the Permissions For list. Check marks that are shaded indicate the permission is inherited from a parent folder. Clicking **Edit...** will pop up the basic permissions for the

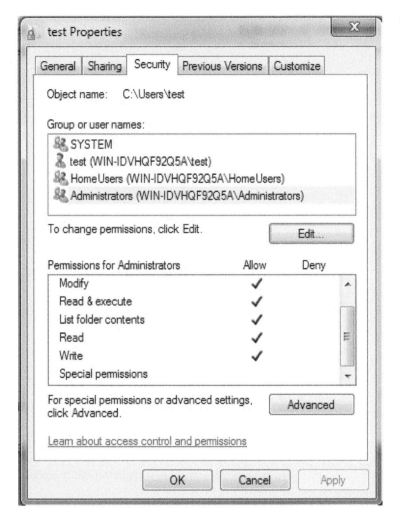

selected file or folder as shown in Figure 8.15. There are six basic permissions for a folder and five for a file:

- **Full Control** – This option allows user or group to read, write, modify, execute, and delete permissions. A user with full control can take ownership of the file or folder.
- **Modify** – This allows users or groups to read, write, change, execute, and delete permissions. It does not allow user to take but allows for the user to create folders and subfolders.
- **Read & execute** – This option allows the user or group to view and execute files. This setting is applied to subfolders. This permission enables the List folder contents and Read permissions.

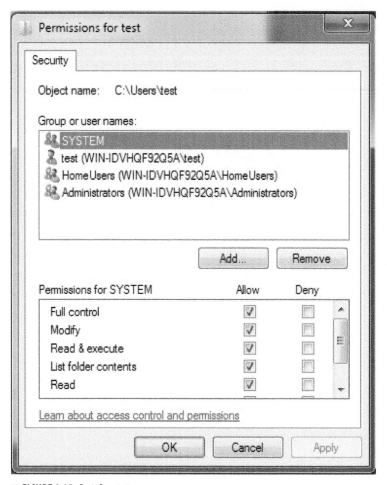

■ **FIGURE 8.15** Basic Permissions

- **List folder contents** (folder only) – This option allows a user or group to view and list files and subfolders as well as execute files. Permission is inherited by subfolders but not by files within the folder or subfolders.
- **Read** – This option allows users or groups to view and list the contents of a folder, view file attributes, read permissions, and synchronize files.
- **Write** – This option allows the user or group to create new files and write to existing files, view file attributes, read permissions, synchronize files, and delete files and folders.

Selecting a user or a group in the Permissions console shows the access that object has in the Permissions for list. An administrator may check or uncheck the allow or deny box for each permission. Keep in mind that using group accounts for administering file system security is often the better choice as individual accounts in groups may be managed easier. Denied permissions have precedence over any other permission so any group or user account that has denied access will be denied. Other scenarios for denying permissions:

- A group is granted permission, but a certain user within that group should not have permission: allow access to the group and deny access to the user.
- Inherited permissions from a parent folder: deny the user or group accessi nt hes ubfolder.

Adding permissions for other user or group accounts that are not shown here is simple:

1. Click **Add...**
    a. **Object type** – This is the type of object, in this case **Users**, **Groups**, or **Built-in security principals**. On a domain, other objects may exist.
    b. **Location** – This can be the local computer expressed as the computer name or a domain. Always double check this value as it will generally be the domain the user is logged in on.
    c. **Object Names** – Here you may type the **username** or **group name** and click **Check Names**t ov alidate.
    d. **Check Names** – Validates the object names and underlines the user when correct. If the object is not found, a **Name Not Found** prompt will ask to ensure the object type, location, and object name arec orrect.
    e. **Advanced** – This option searches through locations for users and groupsa ss howni n Figure8.16 .
2. Click **OK**.
3. Now you may allow or deny permissions using the check boxes for eachobj ect.

An administrator can also add permissions for special identities. Special identities are members of some groups automatically and may assist an administrator in assigning permissions. Some of the special identities are shown in Figure 8.16 and they are:

- **Anonymous logon** – Any logon, including network, for which credentials were not provided. This will allow access to anyone and is often used for public Web sites or FTP servers.
- **Authenticated users** – Any user logged on with a username and a password excluding members of the Guest group.

■ **FIGURE 8.16** Select Users or Groups

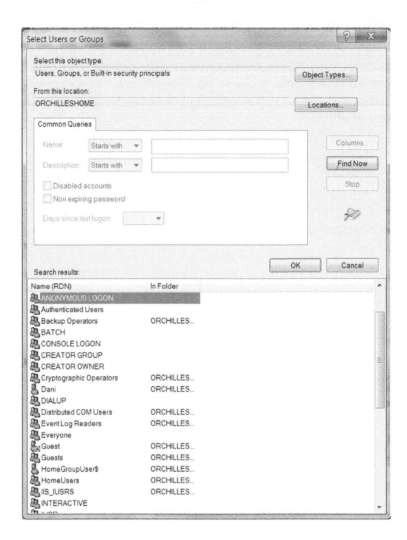

- **Creator Owner** – The user account that created the file or folder has full authority over the resource.
- **Dialup** – Any user accessing the resource through a dial up connection.
- **Everyone** – All users including guests.
- **Interactive** – Any user logged on locally or via remote desktop.
- **Network** – Any user logged on over the network.
- **Users** – For authenticated and domain users only. This is preferred over **Everyone**.

Users and groups may also be removed from the Permissions window by selecting the user or group and clicking **Remove**. This will not necessarily block the user from using the selected resource but will remove the Permissions. If a user needs to be denied permission to a resource, it is better to add the permission and select deny.

Advanced Permissions and Ownership

One may have noticed a special permissions object in the permissions lists of the resource's **Security** tab shown in Figure 8.14. The special permissions represent one of the advanced permissions we will be discussing in this section. The advanced permissions can be accessed by clicking **Advanced** in the **Security** tab of the file or folder properties.

Special permissions represent more granular control of permissions for users and groups. These are an extension of the basic permissions to set better control on a certain resource. The special permissions are automatically assigned when using the basic permissions method:

- Read
    - **List folder** – This option allows the viewing of file and folder names.
    - **Read data** – This option allows the viewing of file contents.
    - **Read attributes** – This option allows the viewing of basic attributes of a file or folder including Read-Only, Hidden, System, and Archive.
    - **Read extended attributes** – This option allows the viewing of extended attributes for a file.
    - **Modify** – This option allows the viewing of folder and file permissions.
- Read& Ex ecute
    - All special permissions for Read
    - **Execute file** – This option allows the running of a file.
- ListF olderC ontents
    - All special permissions for Read
    - **Traverse folder** – This option allows access to subfolders even if read access is not allowed (not denied).
- Write
    - **Create data** – This option allows the adding of items to a folder.
    - **Write data** – This option allows a user or group to overwrite but not add new data to an existing file.
    - **Create folders** – This option allows for the creation of folders within a subfolder.
    - **Append data** – This option allows one to add data to a file but not overwrite the file.
    - **Write attributes** – This option allows the changing of attributes of a file or folder including Read-Only, Hidden, System, and Archive.
    - **Write extended attributes** – This option allows the changing of extended attributes on a file.

- Modify
  - All special permissions for Read
  - Alls pecialpe rmissionsf or Write
  - **Delete** – This option allows for the deleting of a file or folder as long as the files within the folder have the appropriate permissions.
- FullC ontrol
  - All special permissions listed above
  - **Delete subfolders and files** – This option allows the deletion of the contents of a folder.
  - **Change permissions** – This option allows the changing of basic and advanced permissions.
  - **Take ownership** – This allows a user to take ownership of a file or folder. Administrators can always take ownership.

To modify special permissions:

1. Right-clickt he **file** or **folder** and select **Properties**.
2. Clickt he **Security** tab and select **Advanced**.
3. Click **Change Permissions** in the **Permissions**t ab.
4. Click **Add...** to add a new user or group or **Edit** to edit the selected user or group as shown in Figure 8.17. For adding a new user or group:
   a. **Object type** – It is the type of object, in this case **Users**, **Groups**, or **Built-in security principals**. On a domain, other objects may exist.
   b. **Location** – This can be the local computer expressed as the computer name or a domain. Always double check this value as it will generally be the domain the user is logged in on.
   c. **Object Names** – Here you may type the **username** or **group name** and click **Check Names**t ov alidate.
   d. **Check Names** – Validates the object names and underlines the user when correct. If the object is not found, a **Name Not Found** prompt will ask to ensure the object type, location, and object name arec orrect.
   e. **Advanced** – This option searches through locations for users and groups as shown in Figure 8.16.
   f. Click **OK**.
5. Allow or deny the permissions for the user or group. Shaded permissions are unavailable because they are inherited from a parent folder. To override the inherited permission, you must deny access.
6. In the **Apply to** drop down you must choose how to apply the permissions:
   a. **This Folder Only** – only applies to selected folder
   b. **This Folder, Subfolders And Files** – applies to current folder, all subfolders, and all files within folders and subfolders

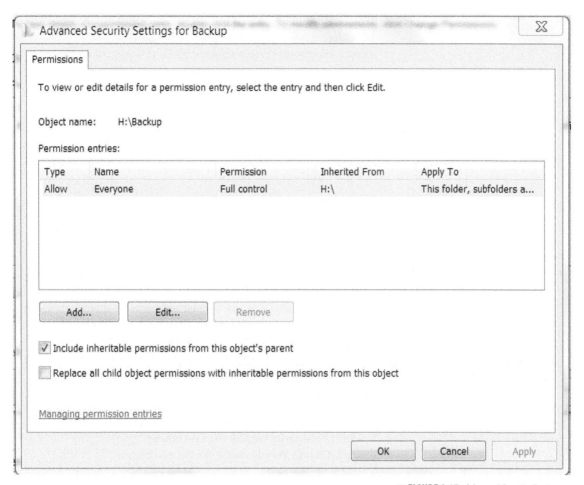

    c. This Folder and Subfolders – applies to current folder and all subfolders

    d. This Folder and Files – applies to current folder and files within thatf older

    e. Subfolders and Files Only – applies to any subfolders within the folder and files in all folders

    f. Subfolders Only – applies to subfolders within the current folder but not the folder itself

    g. Files Only – applies only to the files

7. Click **OK**.

The Permissions window of the Advanced Permissions console has a check box to **Include inheritable permissions from this object's parent** and/or

Replace all child object permissions with inheritable permissions from this object as shown in the bottom of Figure 8.17. Inherited permissions are used every time a new resource is added to a parent folder. Therefore, whatever permissions the parent folder has, the new file or folder will have. This is not the most secure way of setting permissions when sharing files and folders. Keep this in mind in the next section.

To view if a file or folder is using inherited permissions, look at the Advanced Security settings in the Permissions entries window. The Inherited From column will show where the permission has been inherited from or state <not inherited> if it is not inherited.

To remove inherited permissions for a file or folder:

1. Right-clickt he **file** or **folder** and select **Properties**.
2. Clickt he **Security** tab and select **Advanced**.
3. Click **Change Permissions** in the **Permissions**t ab.
4. **Uncheck** the box named **Include inheritable permissions from this object's parent**.
5. Read the Windows Security warning and select the appropriate option:
    a. **Add** – This option will convert the permissions that have been inherited and set them for the current file or folder.
    b. **Remove** – This option will remove all inherited permissions.
    c. **Cancel** – Thisopt ionw illc ancelt hea ction.

To restore inherited permissions for a file or folder from the parent folder:

1. Right-clickt he **file** or **folder** and select **Properties**.
2. Clickt he **Security** tab and select **Advanced**.
3. Click **Change Permissions** in the **Permissions**t ab.
4. Check the box next to **Replace all child object permissions with inheritable permissions from this object**
5. Click **Yes**i nt he WindowsS ecurarypr ompt.

The **Owner** tab in Advanced Security settings displays the current owner of the file or folder. The owner of the resource has the right to allow or deny access to that resource. In other words, the owner has full control of the resource. The owner, by default, is the creator of the file or folder. The owner also has power to remove all user and group access to a resource in which case no one will be able to access it. This can be overridden by another administrator or anyone in the Restore Operators group by taking ownership of the resource.

Allowing administrators and members of the Restore Operators group access to take ownership of a resource is a good idea in case a resource is locked out. However, it may be used to force access to an unauthorized user. For instance, a hard drive is taken from a computer. Once it is booted into

NOTE

If all inherited permissions are removed and no other permissions are applied, the only user with access to the resource will be the owner. All other users and groups will be denied access.

another Windows instance, the user can take ownership and access the entire file. This is one of the flaws of NTFS and can be mitigated by using full disk encryption, explained later in this chapter.

To take ownership of a file or folder:

1. Ensure you are logged in as an administrator, backup operator, or restoreope rator.
2. Right-clickt he **file** or **folder** and select **Properties**.
3. Clickt he **Security** tab and select **Advanced**.
4. In the **Owner** tab, select **Edit**.
5. Select the user to make the owner in the **Change owner** window or click **Other users or groups** and add a user or group to be the owner.
6. Select **Replace owner** on sub containers and objects if required.
7. Click **OK**.

The **Effective Permissions** tab lists a user's effective permissions for the selected file and resource. Simply click **Select…** and choose a user or group in any location to see what permissions that object has on the selected resource. This is good for troubleshooting access issues.

Auditing

This section has focused on setting user and group permissions to secure data. However, the permissions only act as a control list of who has access and who doesn't. The permissions do not log or indicate who accessed files or folders. Auditing can be configured for files and folders to determine exactly who accessed what for a resource. This is important to do before a file or folder is mysteriously deleted or an incident occurs where data is stolen!

Auditing must first be enabled in the Group Policy level for a local system through Local Group Policy or Enterprise Policy. To enable auditing through Group Policy:

- Local Group Policy – Open **Local Security Policy** and expand **Local Policies | Audit Policy**. Select **Audit object access**. Select to audit success and/or failure.
- Group Policy Management Editor – Expand **Computer Configuration | Administrative Templates | Local Policies | Audit Policy**. Select **Audit object access**. Select to audit success and/or failure.

Now that auditing is enabled for object access an administrator must configure what objects to audit. To specify files and folders to be audited by users or groups:

1. Right-clickt he **file** or **folder** and select **Properties**.
2. Click the **Security** tab and select **Advanced**.

3. Click the **Auditing**t ab.
4. Click **Continue**.
5. Click **Add...**
   a. **Object type** – This is the type of object, in this case **Users**, **Groups**, or **Built-in security principals**. On a domain, other objectsm aye xist.
   b. **Location** – This can be the local computer expressed as the computer name or a domain. Always double check this value as it will generally be the domain the user is logged in on.
   c. **Object Names** – Here you may type the **username** or **group name** and click **Check Names to validate**. To choose all users type **Everyone** or alternately specifically type each user or group to audit.
   d. **CheckN ames** – Validates the object names and underlines the user when correct. If the object is not found, a **Name Not Found** prompt will ask to ensure the object type, locations, and object name are correct.
   e. **Advanced** – This option searches through locations for users and groups as shown in Figure 8.16.
   f. Click **OK**.
6. In the Auditing entry shown in Figure 8.18, choose what permissions to audit by checking **Successful** or **Failed** check boxes for the corre-spondingpe rmissions.
7. Select the appropriate **Apply onto** setting explained earlier in this section.
8. **Allowi nheriting** if required. The inheritance of objects works the same as in the advanced permissions referenced earlier in this section.
9. Click **OK**.

The auditing logs may be viewed in the Event Viewer by expanding **Windows Logs | Security**. The Event Viewer is referenced in Chapter 10.

SharingF ilesa ndF olders

Sharing files and folders is a great way of collaborating with other users in any network. Windows 7 attempts to make sharing files and folders as simple as possible for the home user using a HomeGroup and allows advanced sharing for business environments. Unlike Windows XP, Windows 7 allows you to use both sharing models at the same time. The two sharing models are:

■ Standard folder sharing – Enables sharing files and folders on a system. Two sets of permissions are used to determine access to a resource: file system permissions (referenced in the previous section of this chapter) and sharing permissions.

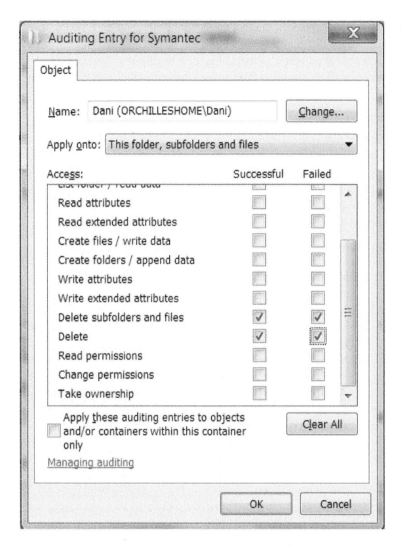

- Public folder sharing – Enables users to share anything in %System-Drive%\Users\Public\. If a user copies any file or folder to this folder, the Public folder permissions will be inherited allowing everyone access to the files and folders.

Sharing is a three-step process. First, sharing of files and folders must be enabled on the Windows 7 system. This may be done in the Control Panel or through Group Policy. Next, the sharing must be enabled and configured correctly to allow other users access. Finally, the remote user will need to know how to access the shared resource. This section will reference enabling sharing on a computer through the Control Panel and Group Policy. It will explain the different ways to share a file or folder on a computer as well as how to grant access to users or groups. Finally, it will reference how to access network resources from an end user and administrative standpoint.

Enable Sharing

Sharing files and folders is extremely easy for an end user in Windows 7. This may be a benefit for home users but can also cause a security issue in an organization if the user does not set the proper permissions. Before sharing a file or folder, the Windows 7 computer must have sharing enabled. This may be done in the Control Panel under the Advanced Sharing settings or through Group Policy.

To change sharing settings for a network location:

1. Open the Network and Sharing Center from the notification area or ControlP anel.
2. Click **Change advanced sharing settings** on the left pane.
3. Select which network location profile to change settings for as shown in Figure8.19 :
   a. **Networkd iscovery** – This option searches for other devices on the same network and allows the computer to be visible to others. This should be disabled in a Public locations and enabled or disabled in a Home or Work network depending on policy.
   b. **Filean dp rinters haring** – This option allows files and printers to be shared. This should be disabled in Public locations and enabled or disabled in Home or Work networks depending on policy.
   c. **Publicf olders haring** – This option allows anyone on the network to read Public folders. This should be disabled in Public locations and enabled or disabled in Home or Work networks depending on policy (recommend disabled).
   d. **Medias treaming** – This option allows anyone on the network to view pictures, music, or videos that are streaming. This should be disabled in Public locations and enabled or disabled in Home or Work networks depending on policy (recommend disabled).
   e. **Files haringc onnections** – This option sets the encryption for file sharing. 128-bit encryption is recommended but may cause issues when sharing files or folders to devices that do not support 128-bit encryption.
   f. **Password protected sharing** – This option allows only user accounts with passwords to access shared files or folders on the computer. This should be disabled in Public locations and enabled or disabled in Home or Work networks depending on policy.

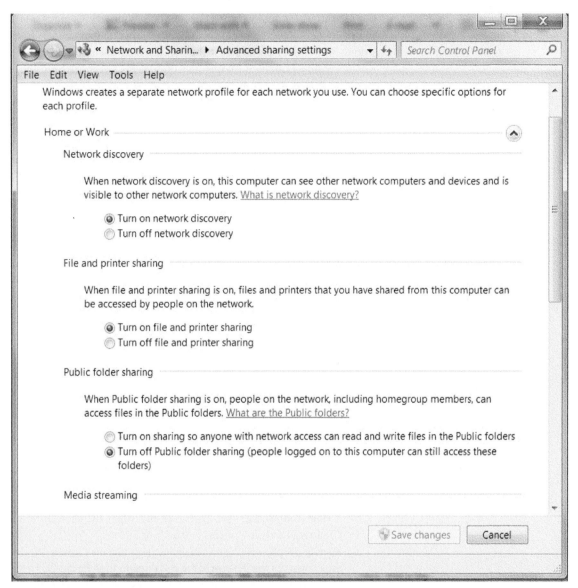

■ **FIGURE 8.19** Advanced Sharing Settings – Control Panel

g. **HomeGroup connections** – This option allows Windows to manage HomeGroup connections allowing anyone in the same HomeGroup access to resources. Using user accounts and passwords is a littlem orec omplexb utm uchm ores ecure.

These settings may also be applied through Group Policy. Preventing a computer from joining a HomeGroup may be a good and secure idea for corporate systems and is an option in Local Group Policy by expanding **Computer**

Configuration | Administrative Templates | Windows Components | HomeGroup. Another option in Local Group Policy is to prevent users from sharing files within their profile, found by expanding **User Configuration | Administrative Templates | Windows Components | Network Sharing**.

Configuring and Managing Shares

Once sharing is enabled in the current network location, a user or an administrator can easily setup a shared resource. As stated previously, sharing is based on the sharing access and the file system access. Therefore, the user or group who will have access to the share must have access in the file system as well. There are different ways to share and manage shares for files and folders:

- **Windows Explorer** – This is the simplest method for sharing files and folders.
- **Computer Management** – This can create shares, view configured shares, view sessions, and view open files as well as disconnect or removes hares.
- **Net Share** – The net share command line tool is used to share files or folders from the command line, usually using scripts. It allows many options and commands, which may be viewed by typing **net share /?** ina c ommandpr ompt.

To configure basic sharing for a file or folder with Windows Explorer:

1. Selectt he **file** or **folder**i n WindowsE xplorer.
2. Right-click it and select **Share with** or click **Share with** from the Windows Explorer toolbar.
3. Select the appropriate option:
   a. **Nobody** – This will disable sharing for the chosen resource.
   b. **HomeGroup\read** – This will allow any user in the same Home-Group read access to the file or folder.
   c. **HomeGroup\write** – This will allow any user in the same Home Group read and write access to the file or folder.
   d. **Specify people** – Here you can choose user accounts from a drop down or type the **username** and **domain** to share the file or folder. To the right of the user is the Permission level, which may be set to Read, Read/Write, or Remove user from the share.

An administrator or user can also configure file or folder sharing within the **Properties** window of the file or folder in Windows Explorer. This allows custom permissions to be applied to the shared resource:

1. Right-click the **file** or **folder** in Windows Explorer and select **Properties**.
2. Click the **Sharing**t ab.

3. Click **Advanced Sharing…** as clicking **Share…** will initiate the basic sharing wizard to specify the users and basic sharing options.
4. Select the check box to **Share this folder** as shown in Figure 8.20:
   a. Typea **name** for the share. This will be the folder when accessing the resource remotely.
   b. **Limit the number of simultaneous users to** – Set the amount of users that may be logged on at once to the resource.
   c. **Permissions** – Here a user may add the users or groups who have access to the shared resource. This is very similar to the file system permissions referenced in the previous section. Notice that there are more options than through basic sharing.
   d. **Caching** – Configure the offline settings for users. This will allow the user to access the resource on the remote system even when the local computer is offline or restrict the users from making the resource available offline. This is also a part of BranchCache, which wasr eferencedi n Chapter6 .
5. Click **OK**.

Once the first share is enabled, Windows 7 will automatically create the appropriate Windows Firewall rules to allow sharing. The firewall rule will

■ **FIGURE 8.20** Advanced Sharing

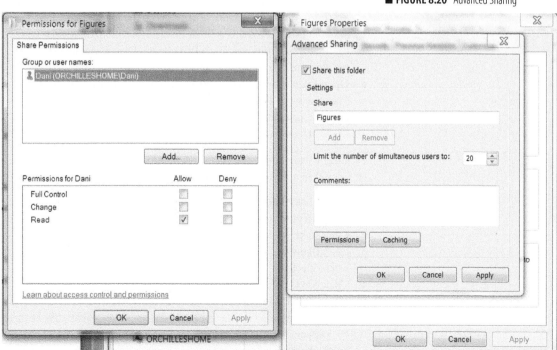

apply for the network location the user is on. These are the changes automatically made in the Windows Firewall:

- File and Printer Sharing Exception
- Allow inbound Server Message Block (SMB) traffic
- Open UDP port 137 for NetBIOS name resolution
- Open UDP port 138 for NetBIOS datagram transmission and reception
- Open TCP port 139 for NetBIOS Session service

To stop a file or folder from sharing through Windows Explorer simply right-click the **file** or **folder** and select **Share With | Nobody** or in the Sharing Properties, remove the check mark to share this folder. This is useful to remove one shared resource, however, the Computer Management MMC offers many more options to manage shared resources. By expanding **System Tools | Shared Folders** in the Computer Management MMC, an administrator can view the following:

- **Shares** – Displays all the shares configured on the local system. To remove a share, right-click the **share** and select **Remove**. To add a share, right-click the **Shares folder** and select **New Share**. Thent he Create a Shared Folder wizard will walk the user through a more advanced setup referenced in this section.
- **Sessions** – Displays all current sessions on the local computer of users accessing shared resources. To disconnect a session, right-click it or right-click **Sessions** and select **Disconnect**. Disconnecting users may result in the remote user losing work.
- **Open Files** – Displays open files being accessed by remote users. These may be disconnected one by one or all at once by right-clicking the **open file** or **Open Files** folder and selecting **Disconnect**. Disconnecting users may result in the remote user losing work.

Creating a share through the Create A Shared Folder wizard is a little more complex than doing so through Windows Explorer:

1. Right-click **Shares** in the **Computer Management | System Tools | Shared Folders** and select **New Share**.
2. Click **Next**.
3. Click **Browse...** to select the folder that will be shared. Click **OK** whens elected.
4. Click **Next**.
5. Name, Description, and Settings. Click **Next** when done:
   a. **Share name** – Type the name of the share. Share names may be up to 80 characters. Ending the share with a $ will make the share hidden.
   b. **Share path** – This will be the path when accessing from another computer.

c. **Description** – Type a description to identify the share,

d. **Offline settings** – Set the offline settings for users to be allowed to cache the files when the local system is offline.

6. **Shared Folder Permissions** – These options are only for shared permissions. File system permissions must still be set. **Custom...** can set advanced permissions for sharing and the file system for the selected folder as referenced in this section. Click **Next**w hendone .

7. Click **Finish**.

In the Shares folder of the Computer Management console, there are a number of shares ending with a $. This means the share is hidden and not displayed to users when accessing the shared resource. To create a share that is hidden, simply add the $ to the end of the share name. Windows 7 has a few hidden default shares that may be viewed through the Computer Management console:

■ C$ and every other local disk – This allows administrators and backup operators to log in to the root of the local disk. This is for performing administrative tasks but poses a security risk.

■ ADMIN$ – This administrative share can access the Windows directory where the operating systems files and folders reside. This is meant as a convenience for remote administrators to access the operating system folder. This may also pose a security risk.

■ IPC$ – This administrative share is used for named pipes that applications use for interprocess communication as they may be redirected through the network.

■ PRINT$ – This share is for sharing printer drivers when a system does not have the printer installed.

To determine hidden shares on a remote computer, an administrator needs to connect to that computer with the Computer Management MMC by right-clicking on **Computer Management** and selecting **Connect to another computer**. An administrator may input the IP address, fully qualified domain name, or **Browse...** to find the computer and connect. Viewing and managing the shares is the same as on the local computer as referenced in this section.

Accessing Shared Resources

Now that file sharing has been enabled and shares have been configured, users on other devices may access the shared resources. Users and administrators can connect to a device that is sharing resources in different ways:

■ **Network Explorer** – The user may look for the device through the Network Explorer within Windows Explorer. Once the device is visible, if double-clicked, it will reveal the shared resources.

■ **Windows Explorer** – The user may manually type the resource name in Windows Explorer Address bar preceded by two backslashes

(\\) such as \\ORCHILLESHOME\. If the user knows the shared resource, it may be included after the last backslash. Hidden shares must have the $ after the name. For example, \\ORCHILLESHOME\C$.

■ **Network Drive** – A shared resource may be mapped allowing the user to access it as a resource through Windows Explorer. This will assign a drive letter allowing users to access the drive when needed.

■ **Net Use** – Net use is a command used in the command prompt or for scripts to connect to shared resources. Type **net use /?** in a command prompt for options and commands.

Connecting to a shared resource through the Network Explorer and Windows Explorer manually can make end users waste time and possibly experience problems when connecting. For this reason, mapped network drives are used. A network drive may be mapped manually through Windows Explorer, Group Policy, or the net use command.

To map a network drive in Windows Explorer:

1. Click **Map network drive** from the Windows Explorer toolbar window or right-click the resource name when manually accessing the resource and select **Map network drive**.
2. The Map Network Drive wizard is simple as shown in Figure 8.21:
   a. Drive – Select the **drivel etter** to map as the resource.
   b. Folder – Type the resource manually or **Browse…** for it.
   c. Reconnect at logon – This option is to automatically connect the drive next logon.
   d. Connect using different credentials – In case the logged-in user does not have access to the resources.
3. Click **Finish**.

To disconnect a mapped drive, simply right-click it in the Computer view of Windows Explorer and click **Disconnect**.

An administrator can also setup one or more mapped network drives through Group Policy. This is efficient when many users need to have mapped shared resources. To create a mapped network drive in Group Policy:

1. Expand **User Configuration | Preferences | Windows Settings**.
2. Right-click **Drive Maps** and select **New | Mapped Drive**.
3. **Select**, **Create**, **Update**, **Replace** or **Delete** in the Action list of the New Drive Properties window.
4. In **Location**, type the path of the resource or click **Browse** to locate it.
5. Click **Reconnect** if this drive will need to be reconnected each time the user logs in.

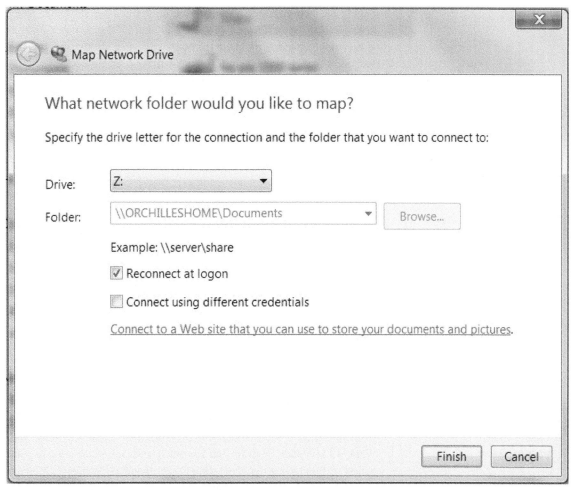

■ **FIGURE 8.21** Map Network Drive

6. Select a starting point for the Drive letter and select **Use First Available** if you are not sure what other drives are on the computers applying this policy.
7. Configure any other options in this dialog box.
8. Clickt he **Common** tab to select how to apply the preference.
9. Click **OK**.

ACTION CENTER

The Action Center is derived from the Security Center in previous versions of Windows. The Action Center provides a centralized location for end users and administrators to check security and maintenance alerts and issues. The action center also alerts the user when certain maintenance tasks need to be performed or require attention. The Action Center is always running and is visible in the notification area as the flag icon. This section, although titled Action Center, will look at the components the Action Center monitors and other related components specific to securing Windows 7 including:

- ActionC enterC onfiguration
- Keep SystemsU p-To-Date
- Antivirusa nd Anti-malware
- NetworkF irewall
- InternetE xplorer8
- Network AccessP rotection

After a clean install of Windows 7, running Windows Update should be the first step after connecting to the Internet. Keeping Windows up-to-date is a critical first step for securing the operating system. Once other applications are installed, it is also **VERY** important to keep them up-to-date. Microsoft has improved the Windows Update feature in Windows 7 and allowed for other Microsoft Updates to install via the console. However, third-party applications are left out and it is up to the administrator or end user to update them. This section focuses on keeping Windows 7 systems up-to-date.

Once Windows Update completes the Action Center will notify the user of a missing third-party application that is also **VERY** important in Windows 7, virus protection. Although Microsoft has taken many steps to secure their latest and most secure operating system, antivirus software is still required. Microsoft does provide some sort of protection against malware with Windows Defender. Spyware and unwanted software protection is a component of Windows 7 that the Action Center monitors. Windows Defender is a simple-to-use anti-spyware application that scans the system for certain malware. Its definitions are nowhere near that of antivirus or third-party anti-malware tools. This section focuses on virus protection and why it is still required and critical that all Windows 7 systems run it.

The Action Center also monitors the network firewall, which may be Windows Firewall by default or a third-party firewall. Unlike Windows XP firewall, the Windows 7 firewall provides both inbound and outbound protection. This is a major step forward as many of the new threats do not force their way through the inbound rules but infect the machine and call out (outbound) to a command and control server or attacker. The importance of a soft firewall will be explained in this section as well as firewall basics to configure the Windows Firewall or a third-party firewall for your system(s).

IE 8 security settings are monitored by the Action Center. The reason Microsoft did this is because most spyware, adware, or browser hijacks modify the Internet security settings. IE 8 was referenced in Chapter 4, "The New Windows 7 Desktop Environment" as an end user tool and Web browser. This section focuses on the security settings and many new security features including SmartScreen filter, XSS filter, domain highlighting, InPrivate browsing and filtering, and Data Execution Prevention (DEP).

Finally, this section will reference Network Access Protection (NAP). NAP, or Network Access Control (NAC) depending on the vendor, is a platform used to ensure that systems connecting to the network comply with policy. When the computer connects to a networking using NAP, it is checked to ensure all required software is installed and up-to-date including antivirus, Windows Updates, firewalls, etc. Once the computer complies with the policy, it is allowed access to the network. If it does not, it either forces compliance or puts the computer in a separate network until compliance is met.

ActionC enterC onfiguration

The Action Center provides status and information related to security and maintenance tasks. It is always running on Windows 7 in the notification area as the flag icon. When issues or possible problems are found with any task monitored by the Action Center, it will inform the end user and offer the simplest method to fix the issue. The Action Center may be accessed through the notification area's flag icon by clicking it and selecting **Open Action Center** or through the **Control Panel | Action Center**. The Action Center is illustrated in Figure 8.22. As one can see, the Action Center has two sections: security and maintenance. If there is an issue or a problem, the Action Center will show a yellow or red notification with options related to that issue.

To configure what the Action Center should alert the user about, click **Change Action Center settings** on the left pane of the Action Center console. In this window, one may check or uncheck the component the user will be alerted about. The Related settings on the bottom allow you to change settings for the Customer Experience Improvement Program, problem reporting, and Windows Update. The Customer Experience Improvement Program is used by Microsoft to collect information about the Windows 7 system and certain usage information. This information is then sent to Microsoft. If this is enabled, Windows 7 will also periodically download a file to collect information on problems in Windows. In other words, this is a legit method Windows 7 uses to call home. The two options are either **Yes, I want to participate in the program** or **No, I don't want to participate in the program**. The problem

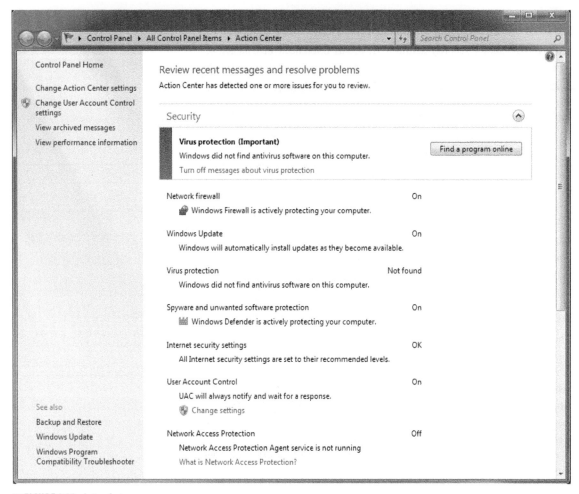

■ **FIGURE 8.22** Action Center

reporting service is used to send problem reports to Microsoft as well. Periodically, Microsoft will send solutions to problems that have been reported by the system. This is also a call home type service and the various settings are:

- Automaticallyc heckf ors olutions
- Automatically check for solutions and send additional report data, if needed
- Each time a problem occurs, ask me before checking for solutions
- Neverc heckf ors olutions

Other options in the Problem Reporting Settings console change report settings for all users and select programs to exclude from reporting. Microsoft has a privacy statement for both of these call home features that should be read and understood prior to enabling these features.

The Action Center also has other options on the left pane as shown in Figure8.22 i ncluding:

- **Change** UAC **settings** – Feature, settings, and configuration options were addressed in the User Accounts section of this chapter.
- **View Archived Messages** – This option displays past messages from the Action Center that have been archived.
- **View Performance Information** – This option view the computer's performance rating. This feature was introduced in Chapter 1, "Introductiont o Windows7. "

KeepS ystemsU p-to-Date

Keeping computers up-to-date is a difficult task for administrators but can prove to be one of the best lines of security for an entire environment. Most worms propagate through vulnerabilities in the operating system or third-party applications. Many of these attacks can bypass antivirus and anti-malware signatures and compromise the computer in seconds. An example of a major worm outbreak in recent times is Conficker, which targeted a vulnerability in various Windows operating systems. Microsoft knew of the vulnerability and had patched it months before Conficker was created with MS08-067. However, it still managed to infect over 35 million computers. This worm could have been avoided if all those systems had been up-to-date.

Microsoft has improved how Windows Update works in Windows 7 and it should be enabled to automatically update systems. Windows Update can also update certain Microsoft software but does nothing for third-party applications. Third-party software must be updated using the software or whichever means are made available by the software developer. For administrators, this is a daunting task especially when the end users do not have administrator privileges to update software. For this reason, Microsoft and other vendors have released tools like System Center Configuration Manager, Systems Management Server, and Windows Server Update Services to track software assets and automatically update Windows systems to the latest software releases. Although these tools are not part of the scope of this book, we recommend evaluating software to manage Windows Update and third-party software updates to ensure a secure environment.

Windows Update

Microsoft improved how Windows Update and Microsoft Updates work from Windows XP. Windows XP required Internet Explorer and ActiveX to search for available patches and updates to the operating system and then download and install them. In Windows 7, Windows Update is a part of the Control Panel and all updates are done through the console without requiring Internet Explorer. Windows Update now supports distribution of the following:

- **Critical Updates** – Updates that are critical to the stability of the operatings ystem
- **Security Updates** – Updates that make the operating system more secure
- **Update roll-ups** – Updates that include various updates at once
- **Service Packs** – Larger updates to the operating system including critical, security, and roll-up updates
- **Optional Updates** – Updates that are not required and include drivers andl anguagepa cks

Windows Update should be enabled to automatically check for updates and install them. In larger environments, other software may be used to distribute Windows and software updates. In the past there were case where a Windows Update broke something in the operating system or a third-party application. More and more, Microsoft has improved its track record when releasing patches so as not to cause these issues. Given the amount of third-party applications, Microsoft cannot test every application against every patch or update that is released. For this reason, enterprise environments should have a patching policy that first distributes a new patch to a small test group to ensure the Windows Update does not break anything in your environment.

Even if an administrator or an environment does not possess a budget for such software, Windows Update may be configured on the local system to any of these options:

- **Install updates automatically** – When enabled, the system will check the update server every 22 h by default and install the update at 3:00 a.m. This is recommended for most end users and environments.
- **Download updates but let me choose whether to install them–** When enabled, the system will check and download new updates. The user will then need to install them through Windows Update or Action Center.
- **Check for updates but let me choose whether to download and install them** – When enabled, the system will check for updates, however the user will need to download and install them.

- **Never check for updates** – This disables automatic updates and the user will have to check for updates manually. This is not recommended.

Computers on a domain may be configured using Group Policy under-**Computer Configuration | Administrative Templates | Windows Components | Windows Update**. As one can see from Figure 8.23, there are many policy settings that may be applied. To reiterate, Windows Update should be enabled on all Windows computers to ensure computers are secure.

Windows Update is accessible from the Control Panel or from the **Start Menu | All Programs | Windows Update**. The main window displays the Windows Update status depending on the configuration set on the local computer. The left-side pane is where most of the options for Windows Update are available:

- **Check for updates** – This will contact the update server and find any available updates. If updates are found, one may view them by clicking the link of the updates found or they may be installed by clicking **Install updates**. Clicking the link will show available updates in the followingc ategories:
  - ❑ **Important updates** – These updates include critical, security, roll-ups, and service packs for the operating system and built-in applications.
  - ❑ **Recommended updates** – These updates include updates to drivers and optional updates.

■ **FIGURE 8.23** Local Group Policy Editor – Windows Update

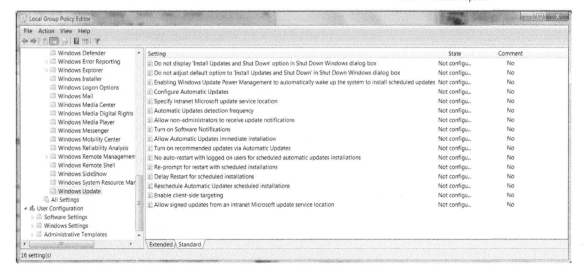

- ❏ **Microsoft product updates** – These updates include Microsoft products and software not built-in to the operating system.
- ❏ **Point and Print drivers** – These updates include drivers for printers and other devices.
- ■ **Change settings** – In this console, the end user or administrator can change settings for Windows Update:
  - ❏ **Important updates** – These settings were mentioned previously in this section including setting the date and time for automatic updates.
  - ❏ **Recommended updates** – This allows recommended updates to be shown like important updates.
  - ❏ **Who can install updates** – This sets permissions for standard users to install updates. A great new feature for remote users. Recommended.
  - ❏ **Microsoft update** – Provides updates for optional Microsoft products and software.
  - ❏ **Software notification** – Provides notifications for other Microsoft software.
- ■ **View update history** – Displays a list of installed updates. Clicking **Installed Updates** will navigate the Control Panel to **Programs and Features | Installed Updates** where updates may be uninstalled and features turned on and off.
- ■ **Restore hidden updates** – This will allow you to restore updates that were hidden and not installed when checking for updates.

As one can see, setting up Windows Update to automatically check and install updates is simple and will ensure the computer is more secure. Thankfully, Microsoft has made it easier to update the Windows operating system and through its security-focused initiative also has less patches released monthly compared to all previous operating systems.

Software Updates

Due to Microsoft and end users being more consistent in patching the operating system with the latest patches, attackers are finding it harder and harder to exploit the operating system. For this reason, attackers have shifted the attack from Windows operating system vulnerabilities to third-party software vulnerabilities. Traditionally, updates to third-party applications are only applied when issues or new features arise with the end user. However, this must change to manage a more secure environment. For example, most organizations use Adobe Reader, which is installed when the computer is deployed. Hackers then find a hole in Adobe Reader and target your end user to open a malicious PDF file. The malicious PDF is not detected by the antivirus and has now opened an outbound connection to the attacker's machine.

Most software that is installed on computers has a **Check for Updates** function that connects to the developer's Web site and finds new updates. However, users must manually do this and then have administrator privileges to install the update. This will not work well unless administrator rights are granted to the users, which is not recommended, and they are taught to perform these actions at regular intervals. This is not a good solution. The better solution to ensure third-party software is up-to-date is to allow an administrator to remotely push out updates and patches with a patch management or software deployment solution. These administrator solutions allow administrators to push out updates and updated software packages to computers in an environment. It will then be the administrator's responsibility to stay current with software updates for the environment. It is recommended this be evaluated and considered in all environments to ensure software is up-to-date, ultimately making the computer and environment more secure.

A great resource for managing software updates and ensuring systems are up-to-datei s www.appdeploy.com.

Antivirusa ndA nti-malware

Although Microsoft has made huge improvements to Windows 7 concerning security, antivirus software is still recommended and should be required in most environments. Virus and other types of malware (malicious software) are one of the main security problems faced by organizations and end users. At a minimum, a computer should have an antivirus and the day-to-day user should be a standard user. Home computers have many options for antivirus that are free or commercial. Chapter 2 discussed installing an antivirus as one of the first steps after installing Windows 7 and provided a few free antivirus products that may be used in the home. However, most administrators are concerned about antivirus in the enterprise environment and these all require licenses. There are many antivirus solutions available and we will not recommend a single one, as each solution is slightly different and so is each enterprise's policy and enviroment requirements.

> **WARNING**
> Look out for rouge antivirus software often called scareware. This is a type of malware that begins scaring the end user of possible problems with the computer system including viruses, corrupt files, etc. The user then clicks the link and installs the rouge software on the machine. This software is difficult to fully remove and can cause other security issues.

Evaluating Antivirus Solutions

When evaluating an antivirus solution, there are different aspects that need to be addressed. For starters, the antivirus solution should be compatible with Windows 7. Many security features are different in Windows 7 and this will ensure the antivirus properly communicates with the system and runs smoothly. Second, many antivirus products provide other features to add value. These features can be anything from spyware and phishing protection, system and network firewalls, host-based intrusion detection and/ or prevention, browser protection, e-mail and instant message protection, identity theft protection, and even PC tune-up capabilities.

It is important to note that more security features a product may not translate to a more secure computer. These security solutions need to be properly configured and managed by the administrator. For this reason, a centralized management console should be included in all those features. Some solutions will take more system resources than others making the end user have productivity issues as well. All of these features need to be assessed by an administrator before deploying an antivirus solution. What should not be an option, however, is not running an antivirus solution at all. On that note, ensure that the antivirus is frequently updated with the latest definitions as an out-of-date antivirus is like having no antivirus at all.

We also recommend a solution that has host-based intrusion detection and prevention. These systems used at the server infrastructure and network level have proven to be very effective on endpoints. Many of the new threats are not detected by antivirus as they use signature-based security. Some antivirus solutions are heuristic-based and these are also recommended as they may detect unknown viruses, which signatures are not available for. All of these solutions will detect viruses when they are on the hard drive. It is also important for an antivirus solution to scan the memory for malware, as attackers are now using exploits that do not touch the hard drive. Scanning live memory is difficult without crashing the system, so most solutions take snapshots of the memory and then scan it for malware.

We hope these recommendations may assist an administrator in choosing the best solution for the particular environment. Most enterprise solutions that are already deployed should be compatible with Windows 7, as most large vendors should be keeping up-to-date with technology. If they are not, it may be time to change them.

Antivirus Policy

Once an antivirus or similar solution has been chosen for Windows 7, it is critical to define the policy that will be used and deployed. This is one of the reasons a centralized management console is important. Policy for antivirus includes, but is not limited to:

- Signature updates – How often will signature be updated? Will it be through the vendor directly or through the centralized server?
- Scan frequency – How often will systems be scanned? Full system scans? Quick scans?

- Exceptions – What programs, applications, databases, or Windows directories should not be scanned?
- Default actions – What will be done when a threat is detected?

Depending on the antivirus and the amount of features included, the size of the policy will vary. These policies will ensure easier compliance with regulatory agencies and a well-documented secure endpoint environment. Some users may complain of scan times and falling back on policy sponsored by management is the safest route for an administrator to take.

Windows Defender

Anti-malware and antivirus solutions for businesses almost go hand in hand. Windows 7 does include a specific solution for spyware, Windows Defender. This feature found in the Control Panel acts much like an antivirus solution. It downloads updated signatures from Microsoft and scans the computer for any matching characteristics. The Action Center will monitor Windows Defender for updated signatures and notify when scans have not been performed. Opening Windows Defender from the Control Panel will open a new window as shown in Figure 8.24. The main screen of Windows Defender shows the status of Windows Defender. Normally, this will read **No unwanted or harmful software detected**.

Running a scan is simple and involves clicking **Scan** from the top menu and selecting which type of scan: **Quick Scan**, **Full Scan**, or **Custom Scan**. The **History** button will show malware found in the past and the action taken. The most functionality will be in the Tools and Settings section shown in Figure 8.24. Here, the user may customize options, join the Microsoft SpyNet, view Quarantined items, allow items and view allowed items, and access other Microsoft resources. The options in Windows Defender are very similar to basic options in an antivirus product. They are:

- **Automatic Scanning** – This option enables automatic scanning and sets the frequency of each scan. It also enables checking for definitions automatically and sets when to run the scan.
- **Default Actions** – This option sets what action to take with the detected malware depending on the severity.
- **Real-time Protection** – This option enables Windows Defender to run in real-time, checking any new process that is initiated for malware.
- **Exclusions** – This option sets excluded files, folders, and file types.
- **Advanced** – This option allows settings to be enabled including: scan archive files, scan e-mail, scan removable drives, use heuristics, and create a restore point prior to taking action.
- **Administrator** – This option can enable or disable Windows Defender and showing items from all users.

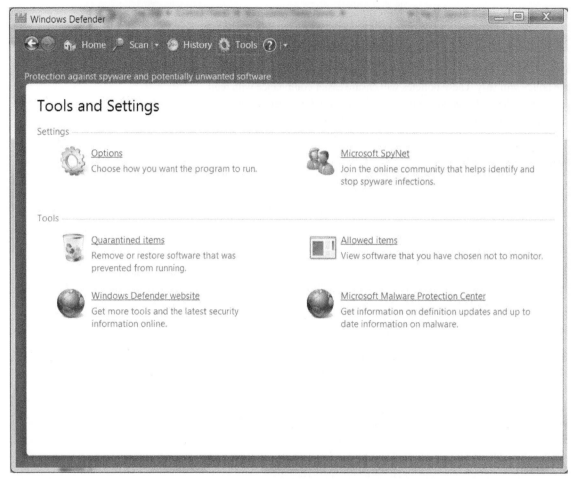

■ **FIGURE 8.24** Windows Defender Tools and Settings

Microsoft SpyNet is a new online community that sends detected spyware threats to Microsoft. Please read the privacy statement before enabling this. Other tools and settings include links to the Windows Defender Web site and Microsoft Malware Protection Center. These are useful for end users to become educated about malware and the threats they may cause. The **Allowed items** link shows the exclusions configured by a user or administrator, whereas the **Quarantined items** link shows the items Windows Defender believes are malicious and has moved to a location that may be more secure.

There are many other third-party spyware and malware removal tools as well as real-time protection tools. These tools tend to be used after a computer has been compromised by malware to remove the actual malicious files. The best defense against malware is user awareness and education.

NetworkF irewall

A firewall is traditionally used in the network infrastructure to only allow certain traffic in and out of the network. Firewalls are configured by rules for inbound and outbound traffic. When an application needs to send or receive traffic to or from the Internet, the firewall will inspect the traffic and if it matches a rule for the specific traffic, allow or deny it. Microsoft introduced the first built-in firewall on Windows for Windows XP and called it Internet Connection Firewall. This was a small attempt at endpoint security and only allowed filtering inbound traffic. Prior to Windows XP and today, third-party vendors released and encouraged the use of a software firewall in Windows. Microsoft introduced a much better firewall than Windows XP in Windows Vista appropriately called Windows Firewall, which uses Windows Filtering Platform and added the much needed filter for outbound traffic. For Windows 7, Windows Firewall supports multiple active firewall policies to support the growing mobile user group.

Remember that Chapter 6 explained the importance of choosing the correct network location when a user connects to a network. This is because depending on the network location, the Windows Firewall will choose and use the correct profile. A new feature included in Windows 7 is the capability to use multiple active profiles at once. For example, a wireless connection in a public location will use the public firewall policy, whereas a wired Ethernet connection in the work location will use the work firewall policy. This is a great new feature for mobile users.

The Window Firewall status may be accessed through the **Control Panel | Windows Firewall**. This main console will show the firewall status and settings by network location as shown in Figure 8.25. Notice the different network locations have different firewall policies: domain networks, home or work networks, and public networks. The status shown in the main Windows Firewall console is:

- **Windows firewall state** – This shows whether Windows Firewall is enabled or not.
- **Incoming connections** – This shows the action to take with incoming networkc onnections.
- **Active networks** – This shows the active network that is currently connected.
- **Notification state** – This shows how the user will be notified of WindowsFi rewalla ctions.

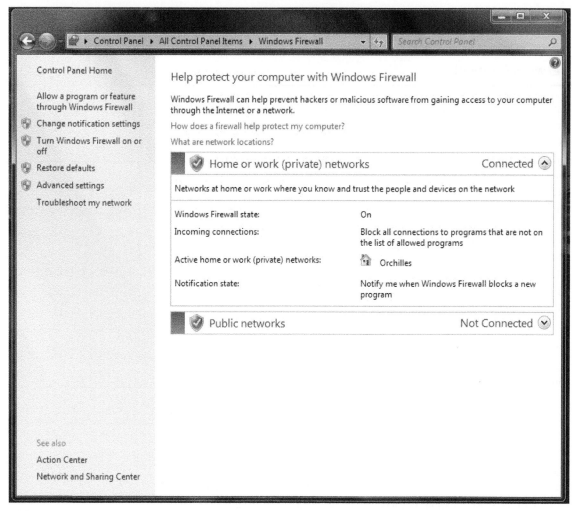

■ **FIGURE 8.25** Windows Firewall

In the event that another software firewall is installed and enabled in the Windows 7 system, the Windows Firewall console will state this information and provide the vendor application that is managing the firewall. As there are a multitude of software vendors for Windows firewalls, this section focuses on using Windows Firewall. Keep in mind that most firewall configurations are similar and this section may serve as a reference for configuring a third-party firewall that is not specifically mentioned.

This section will be divided in basic firewall settings, which will reference Windows Firewall settings through the Control Panel and advanced firewall settings, which will reference the Windows Firewall with Advanced Security MMC.

Basic Firewall Settings

The basic Windows Firewall settings may be accessed and configured straight from the Control Panel console for the Windows Firewall. On the left panel are links to:

- **Allow a program or feature through Windows Firewall**– This configures the rules for applications and features to go through the Windows Firewall depending on the network location.
- **Change notification settings** – This turns the Windows Firewall on or off, can block all incoming connections, and can be set to notify the user when something is blocked.
- **Turn Windows Firewall on or off** – Same as above.
- **Restore defaults** – This restores the Windows Firewall rules and settings to default.
- **Advanced Settings** – This will be referenced in the next section.

To turn the Windows Firewall on or off and change notification settings, do the following:

1. Open Windows Firewall from the Control Panel
2. Click **Change notification settings** or **Turn Windows Firewall on or off** from the left panel.
3. Select settings for each network location:
   a. **Turn on Windows Firewall** – This is recommended if no other firewall is installed.
   b. **Block all incoming connections, including those in the list of allowed programs.**
   c. **Notify me when Windows Firewall blocks a new program.**
   d. **Turn off Windows Firewall**– Thisi snot r ecommended,e ver.
4. Click **OK**.

Once Windows Firewall is on, an administrator may need to configure certain applications to be allowed access through the firewall. Carefully evaluate the application that will be allowed access as any traffic it sends or receives will not be blocked. To allow incoming connections through the firewall, do the following:

1. Open Windows Firewall from the Control Panel.
2. Click **Allow a program or feature through Windows Firewall** from the left pane.
3. Check or uncheck the program or feature that may communicate through the Windows Firewall.
4. If the program is not in the list, click **Allow another program…**, select it from that list and click **Add**. If the program is still not in the **Add a Program** list, you may click **Browse** to find the executable for it.

5. Check or uncheck the program or feature under the network location as shown in Figure 8.26. A check will allow the communication.
6. Click **OK**.

In the event that Windows Firewall configurations and settings are misconfigured, the Windows Firewall may be reset to default state. Restoring the Windows Firewall to its default state will remove all the custom settings and even cause some programs that require networking to not work correctly. Most programs that require a Windows Firewall rule will automatically create the rule. Therefore, restoring defaults will remove that rule and may require reinstalling the program or manually adding the rule.

■ **FIGURE 8.26** Windows Firewall — Allowed Programs

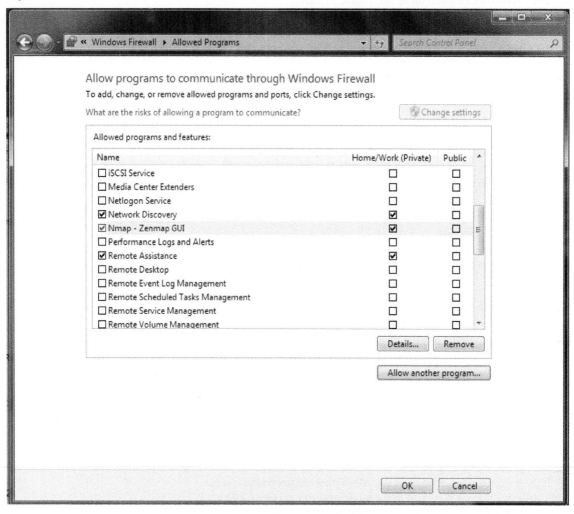

To restore defaults:

1. Open Windows Firewall from the Control Panel
2. Click **Restore defaults** from the left pane.
3. Click **Restore defaults**.
4. Click **OK**.

Advanced Firewall Settings

The basic firewall settings are limited to only allowing certain applications through the Windows Firewall. Microsoft included in Windows 7 an MMC console called Windows Firewall with Advanced Settings for this reason. This console may be accessed from the Local Group Policy Editor, Local Security Policy, or Windows Firewall Control Panel console and is illustrated in Figure 8.27. This MMC allows much more granular configuration of the Windows Firewall, Inbound Rules, Outbound Rules, Connection Security Rules, and Monitoring.

The main window of Windows Firewall with Advanced Security provides an overview of the firewall profiles. As shown in Figure 8.27, there are three different profiles: domain profile for the domain network location, private

■ **FIGURE 8.27** Windows Firewall with Advanced Security

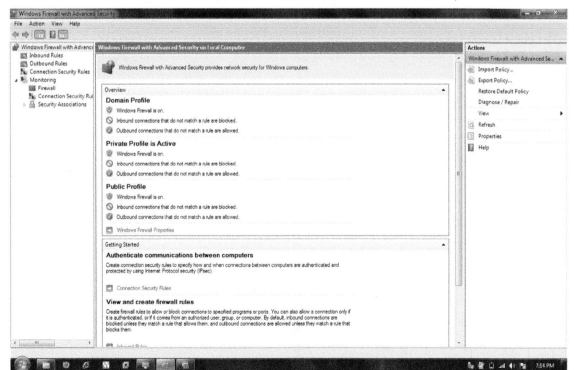

profile for the home and work network location, and public profile for the public network location. Under each profile is the Windows Firewall Properties associated with the profile. On the left panel, there are the different rule sets including **Inbound Rules, Outbound Rules, Connection Security Rules**, and **Monitoring**, which is a simple view of each rule type. The Action menu in the main view allows administrators to import or export firewall policy. This is very important for backing up Windows Firewall Policy and distributing a policy among other computers. The Action menu also can restore the policy to default.

To configure the Windows Firewall Properties:

1. Click **Windows Firewall Properties** from the Overview window or from the Action menu.
2. Select the profile to edit from the tabs: **Domain Profile, Private Profile**, or **Public Profile** (Figure 8.28). Note that the options are the same for each tab.
3. State:
   a. **Firewall state** – This option sets the firewall on or off for the selectedpr ofile.
   b. **Inbound connections** – This option can be set to block all inbound connections, allow all inbound connections, or block (default). Block will block all inbound connections except the ones specifically allowed through a rule.

■ **FIGURE 8.28** Windows Firewall Properties

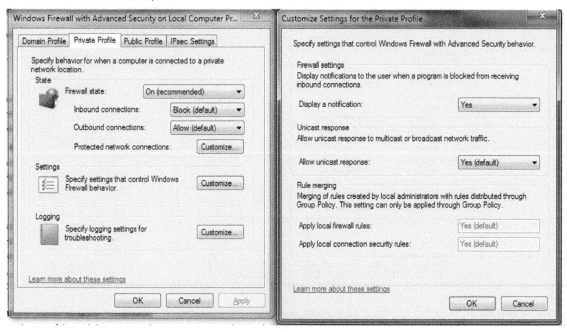

    c. Outbound connections – This option can be set to block or allow outbound connections except the ones specifically allowed or denied through a rule.

    d. Protected network connections – This option chooses what network connections may use the selected profile.

4. Settings – Clicking the **Customize** button will allow you to configure:

    a. Display a notification – This will show a notification in the Action Center when an inbound connection is blocked as shown in Figure8.28 .

    b. Allow unicast response – This allows the sending of unicast responses to multicast or broadcast network traffic as shown in Figure 8.28.

    c. Rule merging – This can merge local policy rules with Group Policyr ulesa ss howni n Figure8.28.

5. Logging – Clicking the **Customize** button will allow you to configure:

    a. Name – The location to store firewall logs. Default is %SystemRoot%\system32\logfiles\firewall\pfirewall.log.

    b. Size limit – The maximum size of the log file. When the log is full, it will begin overwriting the oldest data first.

    c. Log dropped packets – This will log when packets are dropped. This may be useful to troubleshoot network issues.

    d. Log successful connections – This will log every successful connectiont ot hel ocalc omputer.

6. **IPsec settings** – This configures the settings for connection security rules. IPsec settings include Key exchange (main mode), data protection (quick mode), and authentication method.

7. Click **OK**.

The Windows Firewall Properties are important because the Inbound and Outbound Rules depend on the configuration. To view any of these rules, one must expand the Windows Firewall with Advanced Security node in the MMC and select the desired rules to view. Each rule has a number of tabs and configurations. Understanding these properties will make creating Inbound and Outbound Rules much easier. To view the properties of a rule:

- Double-Clickt he **rule**
- Right-clickt he **rule** and select **Properties**
- Select **Properties**f romt he Actionm enu

The Properties for an Inbound or Outbound Rule are:

- **General** – The General rule information and action.
  - ❑ **General** – The name and description of the rule. A check box to enable or disable the rule.

- ❏ **Action** – The options are to allow the connection, allow the connection only if secure, or block the connection. If setting only to allow the connection if secure, the administrator much choose to:
  - - **Allow the connection if it is authenticated and integrity-protected** – This uses IPsec.
  - - **Require the connections to be encrypted** – This requires encryption as well as IPsec.
  - - **Allow the connection to use null encapsulation** – This only requiresa uthentication.
  - - **Override block rules**
- ■ **Programs and Services** – This can configure the rule to a certain program or service or both.
  - ❏ **Programs** – This option is to allow all programs that meet the conditions or specify a program in particular.
  - ❏ **Services** – This specifies a particular service for the rule.
- ■ **Computers** – This can set the rule to only allow connections from certain computers or to skip the rule for certain computers. To only allow connections from certain computers, allow only if secure must be used in the General tab.
- ■ **Protocols and ports** – This is the basic network firewall configuration to select the following:
  - ❏ **Protocol Type** – Any or from a list of protocol types including: HOPOPT, ICMPv4, IGMP, TCP, UDP, IPv6, IPv6-Route, IPv6-Frag, GRE, ICMPv6, IPv6-No Nxt, IPv6-Opts, VRRP, PGM,L 2TP.
  - ❏ **Protocol Number** – This sets if the customer Protocol Type iss et.
  - ❏ **Local Port** – This sets all ports, specific ports (allows ranges), RPC Dynamic Ports, RPC Endpoint Mapper, orI PHTTPS.
  - ❏ **Remote Port** – This sets for all ports or specific ports (allows ranges).
  - ❏ **ICMP Settings** – This can be set to apply to all ICMP types or specificI CMPt ypes.
- ■ **Scope** – This sets the scope to any or specific local or remote IPs.
- ■ **Advanced** – This sets profiles, interface types, and edge traversal.
  - ❏ **Profiles** – This specifies which profiles the rule applies to.
  - ❏ **Interface types** – This applies the rule to all network interfaces or only selected interfaces.

- ❏ **Edge traversal** – Setting for accepting unsolicited inbound packets through an edge device. One may block, allow, or defer to user or application.
- ■ **Users** – Setting to only allow connections from certain users or exceptionsf orc ertainus ers.

As one can see the advanced settings for Inbound Rules and Outbound Rules contain many settings that can be tweaked to a very granular level. This flexibility proves the advances that Windows 7 has made with Windows Firewall from its introduction in Windows XP.

Creating an Inbound Rule or Outbound Rule is very similar and uses the New Rule wizard. Right-click **Inbound Rules** or **Outbound Rules** on the left panel depending on which will be created and select **New Rule…**. The New Rule wizard will ask a number of questions in reference to the rule that will be created. The first screen will ask you to select a **Program**, **Port**, **Predefined connection**, or **Custom** rule type. Custom will allow you to create a more specific rule as referenced in this section.

The Connection Security Rules configure IPsec, which is a newer more secure Internet Protocol (IP). It uses authentication and encryption for each IP packet at the beginning and during the session. IPsec may be enabled between two hosts such as a client and a server or between a security gateway and a host. Configuring IPsec is more complex than an Inbound or Outbound Rule. To create an IPsec rule, right-click **Connection Security Rules** on the left pane and select **New Rule…**. The first screen of the Rule wizard will ask for the rule type to be used. The options are:

- ■ **Isolation** – This bases authentication on domain membership or health status.
- ■ **Authentication exemption** – This does not authenticate from certain computers.
- ■ **Server-to-server** – This authenticates between two hosts.
- ■ **Tunnel** – This authenticates between security gateways.
- ■ **Custom** – This uses any of the above options or a combination of the aboveopt ions.

The monitoring console displays a more detailed view of the current firewall profile and the properties associated with it. Expanding the monitoring node will display Firewall, Connection Security Rules, and Security Associations where each of these may be viewed in a single location.

Finally, Microsoft has changed the command line command for configuring the firewall. The new command is **netsh advfirewall**. For a list of commands use

netsh advfirewall /? as shown in Figure 8.29 or **netsh advfirewall firewall /?** in an elevated command prompt. These commands configure the firewall policy through the command line for scripts or remote management.

InternetE xplorer8

IP 8 is the default and only Web browser included with Windows 7. There are many other Web browsers available for Windows 7 including: Mozilla Firefox, Google Chrome, Apple Safari, and Opera among others. We highly recommend evaluating other Web browsers to deploy in your environment. Internet Explorer has traditionally been insecure as can be confirmed by the number of vulnerabilities and the malware that targets it. Microsoft is aware of this and has attempted to resolve the security issues with IE 8. One of the biggest issues with malware and Internet Explorer was the capability to hijack the browser with spyware and adware that changes the Internet properties. The Action Center

■ **FIGURE 8.29** Firewall Policy Command Line Options

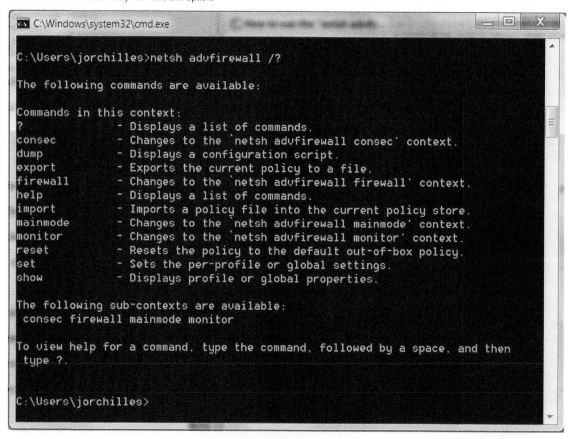

attempts to help the end user avoid these attacks by monitoring Internet options. The security-related Internet options will be referenced in this chapter including the **Security**, **Privacy**, and **Content** tabs. Additionally, IE 8 has many new features to protect end users including SmartScreen Filter and Cross Site Scripting (XSS) Filter, Domain Highlighting, InPrivate Browsing, and DEP. Like all new features in Windows 7, an administrator must understand these features and ensure the user is aware and knows how to use these features. There is no security advantage if the end user continues to click on a possible XSS message and gets their credentials stolen.

Internet Security Settings

The Action Center monitors and ensures the Internet options have not been tampered with by another application or malicious user. Many of the Internet options were referenced in Chapter 4, "The New Windows 7 Desktop Environment" including the General, Connections, Programs, and Advanced options. This section focuses on the Security, Privacy, and Content options. Remember that IE 8 has approximately 1,300 Group Policy settings. An entire book may be written on configuring all these policies so this reference will focus on what the options do and how they affect the end user experience. An administrator who understands these options will be able to configure Internet Explorer Group Policy better for the organization's environment.

Internet Explorer settings for Group Policy are located in **Administrative Templates | Windows Components | Internet Explorer** as shown in Figure 8.30. As referenced in Chapter 4, "The New Windows 7 Desktop Environment", Internet options may be accessed from the Control Panel or from the Tools menu of IE 8 to modify settings for a single end user.

Security Tab

The **Security** tab of the Internet options configures the security for each zone. A zone is defined to allow certain settings for different types of Web sites. The available zones are:

- **Internet** – This is any Web site that is not on the Intranet or added in the Trusted or Rescricted sites list.
- **Local Intranet** – These are all Web sites and portals located within the organization's environment. These include SharePoint sites among others.
- **Trusted Sites** – These are all Web sites the user or administrator has determineda re Trusted.
- **Restricted Sites** – These are all Web sites the user or administrator has determined are malicious and not trusted.

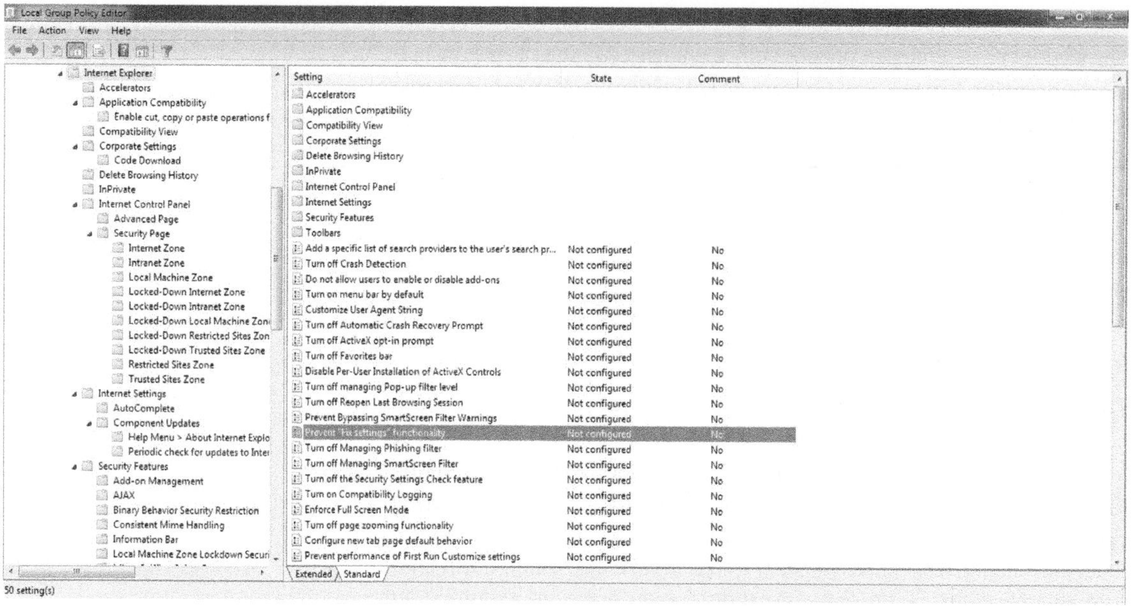

■ **FIGURE 8.30** Group Policy – Internet Explorer

To edit the sites list for each zone, click **Sites**. Local Intranet sites are set to automatically detect the Intranet network by default. This may be unchecked or other options include: **include all local (Intranet sites not listed in other zones, include all sites that bypass the proxy server, and include all network paths (UNCs)**. Trusted sites allow adding any Web site to the zone. By default, only sites using SSL/TLS with https will be allowed. This may be unchecked and used to add HTTP sites. The asterisks (*) may be used as a wild card for all subdomains, for example, *.orchilles.com. Any type of site can be added to restricted sites, whether HTTP or HTTPS. The restricted sites may be used to block malicious Web sites and domains. A great resource for malicious domains is the Malware Domain List: www .malwaredomainlist.com.

For each security zone are security level options. This bar has a range of options based on default settings set by Microsoft including High, Medium-High, Medium, Medium-Low, and Low. A user or administrator may click **Custom Level…** as shown in Figure 8.31 for an advanced window of different settings related to .Net Framework, ActiveX controls and plug-ins, Downloads, Scripting, User Authentication, and Miscellaneous. These options must be tested on business critical sites as disabling an option may not allow the Web site to function properly. As more and more applications move to the cloud and use the software-as-a-service model, more and more Web browser functions will be used.

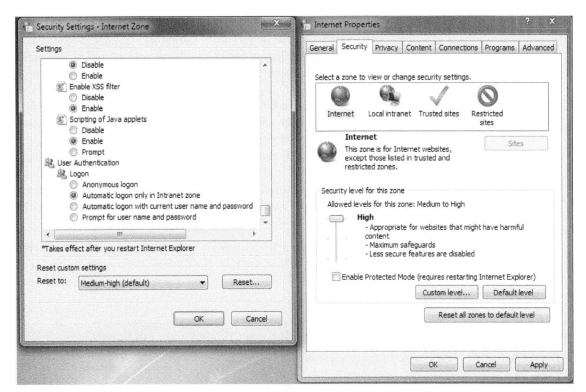

■ **FIGURE 8.31** Internet Explorer 8 – Zone Security Settings

The last important option in the Security tab of IE 8 is Protected Mode. Protected Mode is Microsoft's attempt at blocking malicious software from exploiting the Web browser and accessing other parts of the operating system that should not be accessed including processes, files and folders, and registry keys. Protected Mode should always be enabled and if a file does attempt to access any of the protected areas of the operating system, the user will be prompted for permission. This is another reason users must be educated about Web browsing usage.

Privacy

The **Privacy** tab of Internet options is used to configure the options related to privacy including cookie usage by Web sites, pop-up blocker, and InPrivate Web browsing. The Settings area allows users to choose a security option for how Internet Explorer handles cookies between blocking all cookies or allowing all cookies. Cookies are used by almost every Web site to maintain a user's preferences, shopping cart, and other data to identify and track the end user. Since HTTP is connectionless, the cookie becomes one of the main solutions to maintaining user sessions. The **Sites** button shown in Figure 8.32 allows a user to block or allow cookies for certain Web sites. The **Import** button can import a policy for cookies based on a predefined policy and simply loads the policy file. The **Advanced** button can override the cookie settings and setting options based on first-party cookies and third-party cookies as shown in Figure 8.32. The most secure option is to not use cookies at all; however, that is rarely an option. As mentioned many times in this chapter, these settings must be tested based on the environment and users educated to select the correct option if prompted. The **Default** setting will leave the level in medium where third-party cookies will be blocked if they do not have a compact privacy policy or save information that may be used to contact the end user and first-party cookies will be blocked if they save information that may be used to contact the end user.

The Pop-up Blocker may be turned on and off by using the check box in the **Privacy** tab shown in Figure 8.32. The **Settings** button allows the adding of Web sites that are allowed to use pop-ups. The notification and blocking level

■ **FIGURE 8.32** Internet Explorer 8 – Privacy Tab

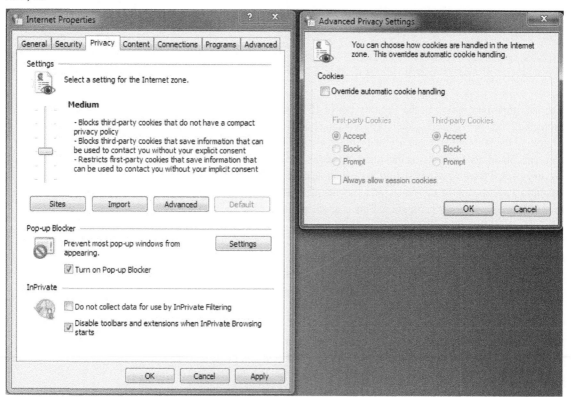

options can set a sound to play every time a pop-up is blocked or display the information on the Information Bar of Internet Explorer. Additionally, the blocking level may be set between High, Medium, and Low.

Finally, the InPrivate Web browsing, which will be looked at in the following section, may be configured to not collect any data when using this browsing mode and to disable all toolbars and extensions. This is the recommended setting for the InPrivate mode to ensure it is the most private Web browsing mode the end user may use. This may make forensics difficult if an incident does occur however.

Content Tab

The **Content** tab of Internet options has different sections for a variety of content-related settings including Parental Controls, Content Advisor, Certificates, AutoComplete, and Feeds and Web Slices. The Parental Controls section has a button that will open the Parental Controls from the Control Panel. These settings are referenced earlier in this chapter. Web Filtering is an additional feature that must be installed to control Web browsing. Instead, the Content Advisor may be used to filter and act as a parental control. These are controls within IE 8 and a third-party application may be more effective. The Certificates area controls SSL certificates and various options related to this. The AutoComplete settings customize what the browser can remember and suggest when using forms and other inputs that support this. Finally, the Feeds and Web Slices settings will configure how often they are updated.

The Content Advisor has a button to **Enable** or **Settings** button depending if it is already enabled or not. The Content Advisor window has four tabs to configure what content the end user may view. The **Ratings** tab has a number of categories. For each category, the setting may be set by adjusting the slider to a setting of **None**, **Limited**, or **Unrestricted**. The **Approved Sites** tab can add sites that will never be viewable or always be viewable no matter what the content is. The **General** tab sets user options to either allow users to view Web sites without ratings or allow a supervisor to use a password to view the blocked content. The Supervisor may create a password that blocks the settings and may be used to view blocked content. The rating system(s) used may be added or administered from here. The rating system is the main control in the Content Advisor. Finally, the **Advanced** tab has an option to add a Ratings bureau or use PICS Rules to define what Web sites may be viewed or not.

The Certificates section can clear the SSL state, which clears any certificate currently in use. The other two buttons manage the **Certificates** and

Publishers. Certificates may also be managed from the Certificates Management MMC. Certificates are used on Web sites that use SSL/TLS to authenticate clients and servers and ensure the communication is secure. The Certificates window has many options related to certificates. The certificates may be sorted by the intended purpose including **Client Authentication**, **Secure E-mail**, **Advanced Purposes**, or **All**. Advanced purposes includes all the certificates selected when clicking the **Advanced** button. The advanced options also can set the export format of certificates when dragging and dropping to a file folder. The tabs separate the certificates based on their criteria: personal, other people, intermediate certification authorities, trusted root certification authorities, trusted publishers, and untrusted publishers. Certificates may be imported by selecting **Import...** and selecting the **certificate** from the Windows Explorer menu. To remove or export a certificate, select it and click **Export** or **Remove**.

The AutoComplete settings set what types of fields will be remembered and then auto completed when filling out a Web site. These include Address bar, browsing history, favorites, feeds, forms, usernames and password forms. There is also an option to use Windows Search for better results and a choice to ask the user before saving the password. Saving passwords is not a good security practice with Internet Explorer as anyone with access to the system may be able to see them. Finally, the **Delete AutoComplete history** button will clear all fields that IE 8 has stored.

The Feeds and Web Slice settings are straightforward and set a schedule for feeds and Web slices to be downloaded. They also include advanced settings related to marking the feed as read, turning feed reading view on or off, playing a sound when feeds or Web slices are updated, and turning on Web Slice discovery.

As one can see, there are many security options available to an end user and an administrator straight from the Internet options. These must be tweaked and configured by the administrator to be the most secure and productive for a user. Although Internet Explorer is the most used Web browser, it is not the most secure and other Web browsing solutions should be evaluated as well.

Internet Explorer 8 Security Features

IE 8 also has new features the end user should be educated about and know how to use. These features are made to protect the end user and their personal information from being sent to a malicious Web site or attacker. The end user should be made aware of these new features and how to use them. Furthermore, some features are not enabled or activated by default so it would be wise to evaluate them and enable them in Group Policy. Features in this section include domain highlighting, InPrivate Browsing, Smart-Screen and XSS Filter, and DEP.

DomainH ighlighting

Domain highlighting can help protect against certain URL attacks like phishing attacks. Internet Explorer will make the user aware that they are accessing a domain that they perhaps did not intend to. It supplies visible notification to the user as to which domain the user is visiting. When a URL is entered into the browser, Internet Explorer will highlight the portion of the URL that corresponds to the domain being accessed. As shown in Figure 8.33, the domain will appear in a darker font than the rest of the URL. When accessing Hotmail, the domain accessed is *live.com*. Therefore, *live.com* is in a darker font than the rest of the URL.

InPrivate

InPrivate Browsing and InPrivate Filtering are introduced in IE 8. InPrivate Browsing prevents browsing history, temporary Internet files, form data, cookies, and usernames and passwords from being retained by the browser, claiming to leave no *easily* accessible evidence of browsing or search history on the user's profile. InPrivate Filtering provides users with an added level of control and choice towards the information that third-party Web

■ **FIGURE 8.33** Domain Highlighting in Internet Explorer

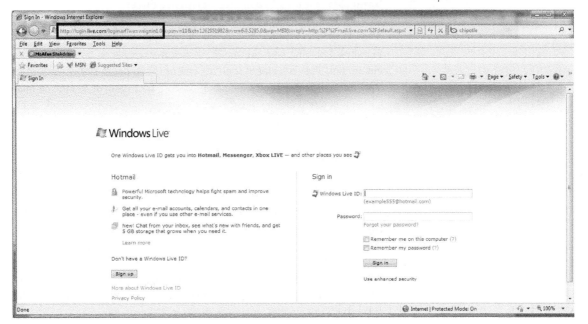

sites can potentially use to track browsing activity. InPrivate subscriptions allow you to augment the capability of InPrivate blocking by subscribing to lists of Web sites to block or to allow.

InPrivate is enabled when the words "InPrivate" show to the left of the Address bar with a blue background.

To start InPrivate Browsing:

- Right-click on the **IE taskbar** icon and select **Start InPrivate Browsing**
- Open a new tab and select **Open an InPrivate Browsing Window**
- Selectt he **Safety** button on the top-right of IE8 and select **InPrivate Browsing**
- **Ctrl+Shift+P**f romw ithinI E8

InPrivateF iltering:

- **Ctrl+Shift+F** from within IE8
- Selectt he **Safety** button on the top-right of IE8 and select **InPrivate Filtering**

Settings for InPrivate can be accessed through the same **Safety** button for Web page Privacy Policy and InPrivate Filtering Settings.

SmartScreen and Cross Site Scripting Filter

IE 7 introduced the Phishing Filter. IE 8 has improved the filter and renamed it to SmartScreen Filter. This contains end-user protection against phishing sites. Phishing sites are the Web sites that appear to be a certain site but are not. They attempt to trick the end user into putting credentials in to steal information. A good example of this is a fake Bank of America e-mail with a link to log in. The link takes the user to http://phishingexample.com/bankofamerica.com and appears to be a Bank of America site. The user then logs in and sends the credentials to an attacker. The SmartScreen Filter, when enabled, will detect many phishing sites and notify the user with a red screen. This again goes back to user education to not click the link in the first place.

IE 8 also added a "Type 1" XSS Filter to protect the end users against XSS attacks. XSS are vulnerabilities on Web sites that allow attackers to inject scripts to bypass access controls and access sensitive data. However, the vulnerability may be used by an attacker to control the connection between the user and the Web site. This is one of the most seen emerging threats and administrators should be aware of them. The XSS Filter will disable the cross site script attempt and notify the user of the attempt.

Data ExecutionP revention(DEP)

DEP is used in Windows 7 not only for IE 8 but also for many other applications. DEP is used to prevent applications or services from executing code from a memory region it does not have access to. This is a great security feature to block virus and other malware from executing or injecting code into other parts of the system. IE 8 benefits tremendously from this by providing software-enforced DEP. Most malware is obtained from a Web browser and then executed through the system. DEP and IE 8 attempt to not allow this.

To determine if an application in Windows 7 is using DEP, do the following:

1. Opent he **Task Manager** by right-clicking the **taskbar** and clicking **Task Manager**.
2. Clickt he **Processes**t ab.
3. Click **View | Columns**
4. Check **Data Execution Prevention** and click **OK**.
5. The DEP column will show the status of the process as shown in Figure8.34 .

NetworkA ccessP rotection

NAP or NAC is an endpoint security solution that is becoming very popular among organizations. The objective is to check every endpoint before it is given network access to ensure it meets certain security criteria. This

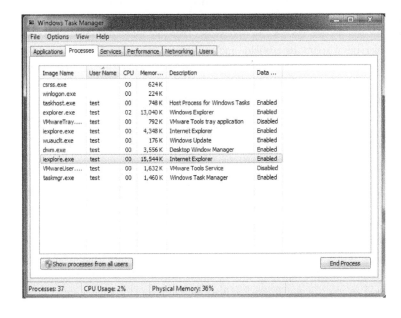

■ **FIGURE 8.34** Data Execution Prevention

solution requires additional network and server infrastructure to validate the endpoint and then allows it to access the entire network. Windows Server 2008 provides a role for this and Windows 7 has improved on the agent. There are other third-party solutions for NAP and NAC that may be evaluated prior to deploying the one supplied by Microsoft.

Windows 7 does include a client agent for NAP, which connects to the NAP server and informs the server what security criteria is met and what is not. If the criteria is not met, the endpoint may be placed on a separate network until it complies or is disconnected. The NAP Agent is monitored by the Action Center and a service in Windows 7.

ENCRYPTION

This chapter has referenced many security solutions and settings for Windows 7, however, none of the solutions protect the computer or removable device if it is lost, stolen, or in the physical possession of a malicious attacker. The user account security will protect the system from being logged on normally, but if the system is booted from a boot CD, then the file system may be accessed. The file system provides security but only within the system. Therefore, any hard drive that may be physically obtained by an attacker is not secure. The solution for this is encryption. Hard drives and removable media may use full disk encryption and the file system may use an Encrypting File System to not allow users without the correct authentication to view the content of the devices. Full disk encryption is a great solution for laptops and USB devices especially when many of the recent data breaches involve lost laptops and USB memory devices. There are many third-party full disk encryption solutions available including TrueCrypt, CheckPoint, and PGP among others. However, Windows 7 Enterprise and Ultimate come with BitLocker and BitLocker To Go for full disk encryption and removable device encryption. This section focuses on these two encryption solutions. Additionally, Windows 7 includes an Encrypting File System to protect sensitive user information within the operating system and this section will reference it.

BitLocker

BitLocker was introduced in Windows Vista but, like the operating system itself, did not get many implementations due to lack of features and control. Microsoft has improved the feature for Windows 7, which now may be used in enterprise environments. BitLocker provides full-volume encryption for the full disk encryption solution. This protects the entire disk from being accessed when a laptop or a computer is lost or stolen. BitLocker may be used on computers with Trusted Platform Module (TPM) and without TPM.

TPM is used to ensure boot file integrity. If TPM is not present, a USB flash drive or smart card may be used to supply the startup key, which is normally stored in the TPM. TPM creates the cryptographic keys, encrypts them, and then decrypts them.

Many of the options available for BitLocker, including whether to use TPM or not, are available in Group Policy. Group Policy can enable TPM, enable BitLocker, and manage the keys with a data-recovery agent to recover encrypted drives if the password or TPM is missing.

Trusted Platform Module

Some systems have TPM but it may be disabled in the BIOS. To enable TPM, an administrator will need to be at the physical system and enable it prior to boot in the BIOS. While here it is a great idea to create a BIOS password to only allow administrators in the BIOS. Remember as easy as it is to enable TPM, it is also easy to disable it. TPM may be managed with two different tools in Windows 7: TPM Management by typing **tpm.msc** in the Start menu Search or TPM Security Hardware by typing **tpminit** in the Start menu Search.

Once TPM is enabled and either of the management tools accessed, the administrator will need to create a TPM owner password:

1. Type **tpminit** in the Start menu Search.
2. The computer may need to reboot to enable TPM or reset TPM firmware through the BIOS.
3. Select **Automatically create the password** or **Manually create a password**. If creating your own network, ensure it is a long passphrase. The longer it is, the more difficult it will be to crack. Include all types of characters.
4. Save the password, print it, or save it to a USB for when the computer needs to be decommissioned or managing TPM in the future.
5. Click **Initialize**.

To manage TPM once it has been initiated for the first time, type **tpm.msc** in the Start menu Search to start the TPM Management MMC as shown in Figure 8.35. TPM may be turned off from the Action panel by clicking **Turn TPM Off**. This will turn off TPM but not clear the owner password. The password should be kept until the TPM is cleared. To clear the TPM, click **Clear TPM** on the Actions panel. This will clear the TPM to factory defaults and all TPM keys and data protected by the keys lost! The TPM owner password may also be changed from the Actions panel and requires the password or user to be logged in by clicking **Change Owner Password**.

TIP

TPM and full disk encryption should be setup by an administrator especially if the system is a corporate asset. If an end user performs this setup and then is let go or decides to leave, it will be very difficult to recover the TPM password or full disk encryption password. Key management is a very important aspect of encryption.

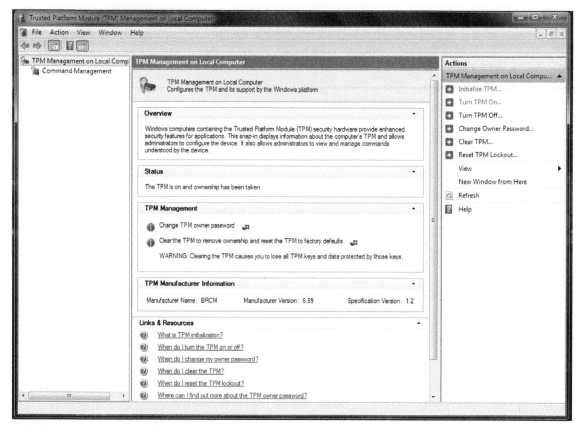

■ **FIGURE 8.35** Trusted Platform Module
Management

BitLocker with TPM may be used for full disk encryption with the following modes:

■ **TPM-Only** – Only the TPM is used to validate the boot files, operating system, and encrypted volumes. This is transparent to the user and will allow other users onto the hard drive. Therefore, this mode is not recommended as it will not provide the key benefits of full disk encryption. If TPM is missing, BitLocker will enter Recovery mode and will require the recovery key or password.

■ **TPM and PIN** – This uses TPM and a user inputted PIN. If either is missing, BitLocker will enter Recovery mode and will require the recovery key or password.

■ **TPM and Startup Key** – This uses TPM and a startup key located in a USB device. The user must have the USB device to boot the system. If either is missing, BitLocker will enter Recovery mode and will require the recovery key or password.

■ **TPM and Smart Card Certificate** – This uses TPM and a smart card provided by the user. If either is missing, BitLocker will enter Recovery mode and will require the recovery key or password.

Computers that do not have TPM may use Startup Key Only or Smart Card Certificate Only mode to decrypt the hard drive and have access to the files. These options are viewed in the next section.

Enable BitLocker in Control Panel

Once TPM has been enabled, BitLocker may be turned on through the Control Panel on the system drive:

1. Click **BitLocker Drive Encryption** in the Control Panel.
2. Click **Turn on BitLocker** on the system drive.
3. Once the checks have completed, you will need to store the recovery key in a USB flash drive, file, or print it. This is very important, in case the PIN or Startup Key is lost.
4. Select **Run BitLocker system check** and/or click **Start Encrypting**.

BitLocker may also be turned on for nonsystem drives:

1. Click **BitLocker Drive Encryption** in the Control Panel.
2. Click **Turn on BitLocker** on the nonsystem drive.
3. Choose **How you want to unlock this drive**.
   a. Use a password to unlock the drive.
   b. Use my smart card to unlock the drive.
   c. Automaticallyunl ockt hisdr iveont hisc omputer.
4. Click **Next**.
5. Click **Start Encrypting**.

Enable BitLocker in Group Policy

Enabling BitLocker in Group Policy is not as simple as on a single host. Deploying BitLocker through Group Policy requires preparation and planning to ensure the correct policy is being applied. An administrator must evaluate the different authentication methods and choose the appropriate one for the organization, determine whether the organizations computers support TPM and what configuration to use, and define how to store and maintain the encryption keys, recovery passwords, and certificates.

An administrator must also become familiar with the options available for BitLocker and TPM in Group Policy. TPM policies are under **Computer Configuration | Administrative Templates | System | Trusted Platform Module Services** and BitLocker policies are under **Computer Configuration | Administrative Templates | Windows Components | BitLocker Drive Encryption**a ss howni n Figure 8.36.

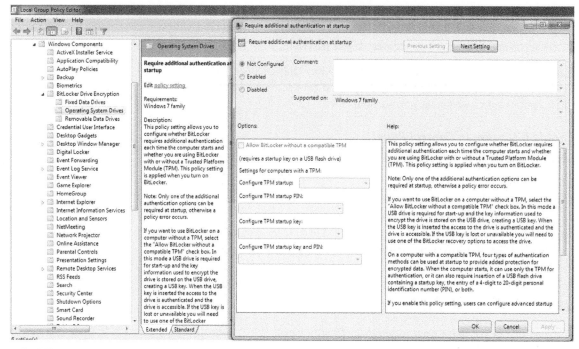

■ FIGURE 8.36 BitLocker Drive Encryption –
Group Policy

To enable BitLocker Drive Encryption:

1. Open the Group Policy Editor to **Computer Configuration |
   Administrative Templates | Windows Components | BitLocker
   Drive Encryption | Operating System Drives**
2. Select **Require additional authentication at startup**
3. Select **Enabled** and the options determined by the preparation and
   planningpha se.
4. Click **OK**.

As one can see, there are many options to setup BitLocker through Group
Policy. As this is a new feature and your environment is unique, it is recommended to test any deployment plan thoroughly to ensure the best security
without issues for the end user.

BitLocker To Go

Windows 7 also supports encrypting removable media drives with
BitLocker To Go. Any USB flash drive that uses FAT, FAT32, or NTFS may
be encrypted with BitLocker To Go. Once a USB drive is encrypted with
BitLocker To Go, it can only be accessed by Windows operating systems.
On older versions of Windows, the drive will be read-only and the user will

not be able to write to the drive as it cannot encrypt but only decrypt. Windows 7 only environments will not have any issues with this limitation. However, users and organizations with multiple operating systems will not find this solution acceptable. BitLocker To Go may be enabled through Group Policy as BitLocker was enabled. Group Policy also has an option to force all removable media to be encrypted. This will protect the organization and data when USB drives go missing.

When BitLocker To Go is enabled on the drive, it will create a virtual volume that will be encrypted and store the encryption key in the other volume. It will also create an autorun.inf file and Read Me.txt for when plugging into other Windows operating systems. When the drive is plugged in, it will ask for a password or the smart card to decrypt the file and use it to read and write.

To enable BitLocker To Go in Windows Explorer or the Control Panel, do the following:

1. Insertt heU SBdr ive.
2. Open **BitLocker Drive Encryption** in the Control Panel and select **Turn On BitLocker** or right-click the drive from Windows Explorer and select **Turn On BitLocker**.
3. Select to use a password to unlock the drive or to use a smart card to unlock the drive. Input the password if necessary or smart card and select **Next**.
4. Select how to store the Recovery key and perform the action.
5. Click **Start Encryption**.

EncryptingF ileS ystem

Users may use Encrypting File Systems for protecting sensitive data so it may only be accessed with the user's public/private key certificate. The encryption certificate is stored in the user's profile and anyone with access to the certificate may decrypt the files. File encryption with EFS is supported on a per folder or per file basis. Any file moved to an encrypted folder will become encrypted as well. Encrypted folders look green by default in Windows Explorer.

By default, Windows 7 uses Advanced Encryption Standard (AES) 128-bit Cyclical Bit Check. Group Policy may be modified to use Triple DES, RSA, or SHA-1 in **Computer Configuration | Windows Settings | Security Settings | Local Policies | Security Options | Public Key Policies**. Like BitLocker, EFS has recovery agents in the event the user's certificates are lost or deleted in the Domain and Local computer level.

To encrypt or decrypt a file or folder:

1. Open WindowsE xplorer.
2. Right-clickt he **file** or **folder** and select **Properties**.
3. Click **Advanced** in the **General**t ab.
4. Check or uncheck **Encrypt Contents to Secure Data**.
5. Click **OK**.

Notice the file or folder turns green. This means the file or folder is encrypted. Windows 7 automatically decrypts the file or folder and then encrypts it when written. Windows 7 also includes a command line tool for EFS called Cipher. Type **cipher /?** in an elevated command prompt for commands and help.

APPLOCKER

AppLocker is also a new feature in Windows 7. It is actually an improved version of Software Restriction Policies in older versions of Windows Server. Like BitLocker, AppLocker is only available on Windows 7 Enterprise and Ultimate editions and requires Windows Server 2008 R2. AppLocker is an application whitelisting and/or blacklisting solution for Windows 7. It specifies what applications and software can and cannot run on a system. This is an added security feature and will prove to be very useful in defending against malware and attackers because it allows or denies content to run based on its payload. Like other features referenced in this book that require Windows Server 2008 R2 including BranchCache, DirectAccess, and even BitLocker, deploying AppLocker takes preparation and planning for the unique environment.

AppLocker may be configured on a local Windows machine through Group Policy for testing purposes. To access AppLocker policy, open Local Security Policy to **Application Control Policies | AppLocker** as shown in Figure 8.37. From here, rule enforcement may be configured as well as Executable Rules, Windows Installer Rules, and Script Rules.

To configure Rule Enforcement in AppLocker Properties:

1. Select **Configure rule enforcement** from the main AppLocker view in the Security Policy MMC.
2. AppLocker rules may be configured for enforcement or audit. Select the rules to be configured from the check boxes: **executable**, **windows installer**, and **script rules**. It is recommended to audit rules first.
3. Int he **Advanced** tab, one may enable the DDL rule collection.
4. Click **OK**.

The administrator must now create rules for each of the categories that were enabled. Microsoft has assisted this process greatly. Right-click on any of the rules and you will see the following options:

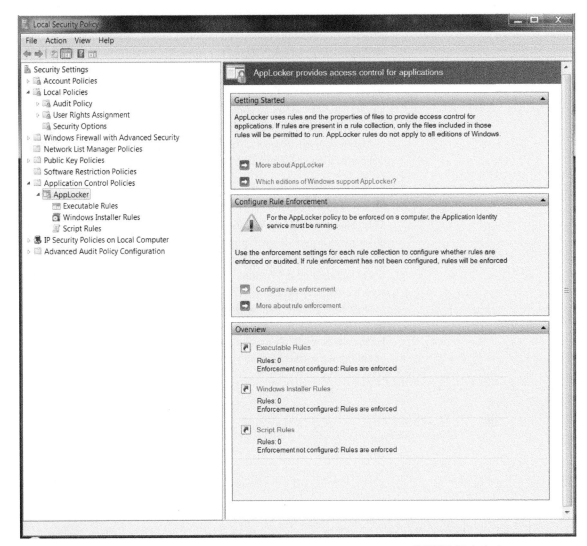

■ **FIGURE 8.37** AppLocker

- **Create New Rule...** – This wizard creates a rule from scratch. It will first ask if the rule is an allow or deny and what user or group to apply it to. Then primary conditions will be chosen whether it be publisher, path, or file hash followed by more granular rules.
- **Automatically Generate Rules** – This wizard will create rules automatically based on the installed applications, for example, running this on a new image will create rules only for the installed applications.
- **Create Default Rules** – This will create default rules that are very lenient but a start for testing.

Once the rules have been created and enforced on a single system, an administrator can extract the policy and import it to other computers. Right-click on **AppLocker** and select **Export** or **Import** to a file. This allows you to test the AppLocker solution prior to deploying across an environment.

We recommend AppLocker to be evaluated and considered because as attacks get more and more sophisticated application whitelisting and blacklisting will likely block a number of malware and applications that should not be in your environment. AppLocker also allows application inventory, standardization, and manageability.

■ SUMMARY

This chapter focused on Windows 7 security from the user account level to physical security with encryption and application whitelisting or blacklisting. The features referenced here should only be the beginning of the security solutions used in Windows 7. There are thousands of policies related to security that may be enabled in an environment. Training your users to be security aware will be one of the best investments in security your organization makes. Windows 7 will do a lot of the work when configured correctly but the attacker will always find the weakest link. Be sure you have methods of finding the weakest link in your infrastructure before they do.

Virtualization and Windows 7

INFORMATION IN THIS CHAPTER

- WindowsX PM ode
- ManyF ormsof Virtualization
- Summary

Windows Virtual PC is an optional component of Windows 7 Professional, Enterprise, and Ultimate editions. Windows Virtual PC allows Windows 7 to run other operating systems as virtual machines. This means the Windows 7 system will be the host where Windows Virtual PC is installed and then guest operating systems may be installed. This feature allows end users and administrators to install legacy applications that may not be compatible with Windows 7 on another operating system and have them appear to be running seamlessly with Windows 7.

WINDOWS XP MODE

Windows 7 Professional, Enterprise, and Ultimate support additional features that both administrators and end users can take great advantage of. One of these features is Windows XP Mode. Windows XP Mode is a virtualization technology that gives end users and administrators the ability to use the new features of Windows 7 while allowing the use of critical and essential applications that may not function correctly on Windows Vista or Windows 7. Window XP Mode functions with Windows Virtual PC, which is available for Windows 7 Professional, Enterprise, and Ultimate. Windows Virtual PC is an evolution of Virtual PC 2007, a stand-alone product for previous versions of Windows.

Windows XP Mode is a separate download from the Microsoft Web site. You will also require Windows Virtual PC, which is also free as a download from Microsoft.

DOI: 10.1016/B978-1-59749-561-5.00009-7

With some limitations, Windows XP Mode is a full version of Windows XP Service Pack 3. Installing a program in Windows XP Mode makes the program available in both Windows XP Mode and Windows 7. This technology allows users and businesses to run legacy applications during the transition to Windows 7. It does not support 3D graphics or applications that require specialized hardware like TV tuners or similar devices.

The following are some specific requirements to run Windows XP Mode:

- Windows operating systems such as Windows 7 Professional, Enterprise, or Ultimate editions.
- A computer that is capable of hardware virtualization. This means your computer has a central processing unit (CPU) with either Intel-VT or AMD-V virtualization features. If it is a fairly new computer, you will probably have this feature in it.
- Virtualization features turned on in your computer's basic input/output system (BIOS). These are not always turned on by default so you may need to enter the setup mode of your computer to enable these features.

> **WARNING**
> Bec areful whenc hangingB IOS settings. The BIOS interface is designed for advanced users; it is possible to make changes that could prevent your computer froms tartingcor rectly.

Verifying Your Windows7 Version

The first part of loading Windows XP Mode is to make sure that you are running the correct version of Windows 7. You must be running the Professional, Enterprise, or Ultimate version of Windows 7. To verify that you are running the correct version, click the **Start button** 🔵 | **Control Panel | System and Security | System**. Confirm the version as shown in Figure 9.1.

■ **FIGURE 9.1** Windows 7 Version

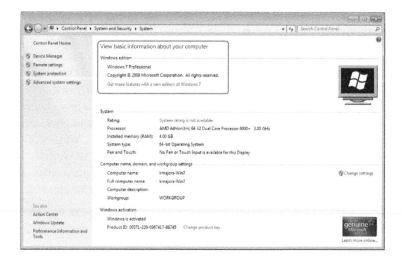

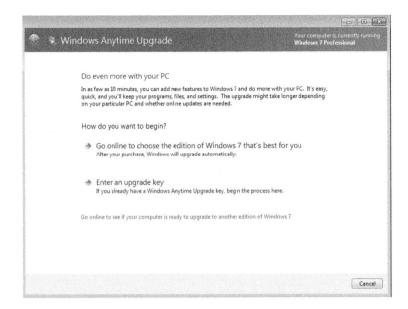

If you need to upgrade your Windows 7 version, you can click the **Get more features with a new edition of Windows 7** hyperlink. This will open a window to ask what you want to do next. This window is shown in Figure 9.2.

Once you select the desired version of Windows 7, you will be prompted for a method of payment. This is the part that is not free, and you will have to pay for the upgrade if you wish to continue with Windows XP Mode. You will receive a license key when the transaction is complete.

Once your new upgrade key is received, you can return to the screen shown in Figure 9.2, and this time select **Enter an upgrade key**.

Enter your upgrade key in the dialog box, as shown in Figure 9.3, and click **Next** to activate the Windows 7 upgrade. Click **Finish** when you have finishedt hea ctivation.

ConfirmHar dware Virtualization

You must have a computer with a CPU that has hardware virtualization capabilities to use Windows XP Mode. This should not be too difficult of a requirement to meet. Most modern processors will have this feature. If you are running a processor from Intel, you will need the Intel-VT feature. AMD processors must have the AMD-V hardware features. Microsoft has created a **Hardware-Assisted Virtualization Detection Tool** for your convenience. This tool can be downloaded at www.microsoft.com/downloads/details.

aspx?FamilyID=0ee2a17f-8538-4619-8d1c-05d27e11adb2&displaylang=en or you can search for **havdetectiontool.exe** at the Microsoft Downloads Web site.

When you select the **Download** button, you will be asked to save or run in a window like Figure 9.4. Select **Run**.

■ **FIGURE 9.3** Anytime Upgrade Key

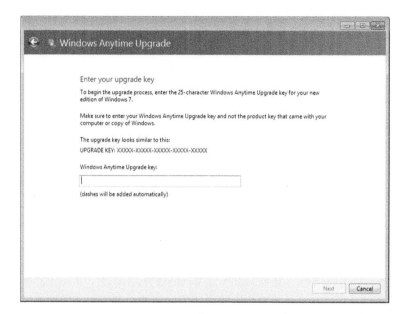

■ **FIGURE 9.4** Security Warning

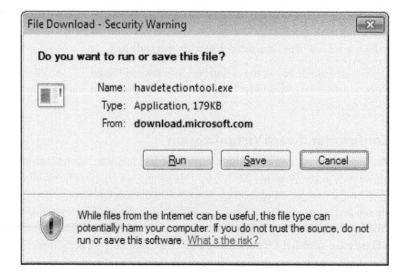

Another security warning may appear as shown in Figure 9.5. Select **Run** toc ontinue.

When the license agreement appears, read the license agreement and then click the **I accept the license terms** box as shown in Figure 9.6. Click **Next** toc ontinue.

You will receive an informational window similar to Figure 9.7 that will tell you if your computer meets the virtualization requirements.

You could receive one of three possible messages:

- *This computer is configured with hardware-assisted virtualization.* This is the message we are looking for. It tells us that we are ready to go!

■ **FIGURE 9.5** Security Warning

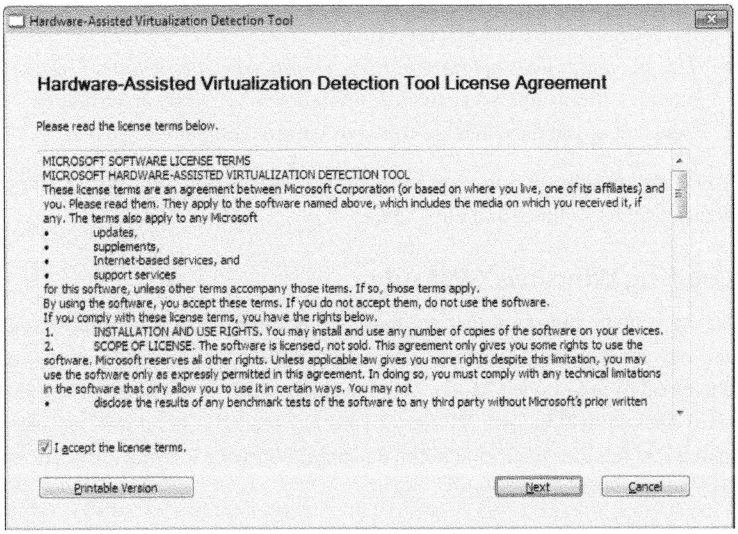

■ **FIGURE 9.6** License Agreement

■ **FIGURE 9.7** Virtualization Detection Message

- *Hardware-assisted virtualization is not enabled on this computer.* This means your computer is capable of virtualization, but you will need to enable the hardware virtual assistance in the system BIOS. Please see the warning above before proceeding.
- *This computer does not have hardware-assisted virtualization.* This message means that you cannot run Windows XP Mode or Virtual PC. You cannot use these features on your current computer.

You can now select if you want to share this information with Microsoft or not. Select your choice and click **OK**.

Loading WindowsX PM ode

We have now confirmed that we have a supported version of Windows 7 and our computer is capable of supporting virtualization. We are ready to download Windows XP Mode. Windows XP Mode is a complete Virtual Hard Disk with Windows XP Service Pack 3 loaded. This download may take a few minutes to several hours depending on your Internet connection, so plan your day accordingly.

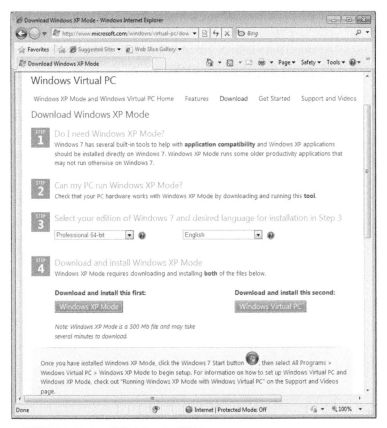

■ **FIGURE 9.8** Windows XP Mode Download Web Site

Follow these instructions to install Windows XP Mode on your Windows 7 computer:

1. Make sure you are connected to the Internet and go to the Windows XP Mode download Web page at www.microsoft.com/windows/virtual-pc/download.aspx. You will see a qualification page similar to Figure 9.8.
2. We have already confirmed Step 1 and Step 2, so select the version of Windows 7 you have running on your computer. Please be careful of the 32-bit or the 64-bit selection. Select your preferred language in the second pull-down list.
3. Click the **Windows XP Mode** download button in step four of Figure 9.8. This is a 500MB file, so it might take a few minutes or longer depending on your Internet connection.

4. You will get a security warning like Figure 9.9.
   a. Click **Save** to save the download for use on several similar Windows 7 desktops. You will be prompted for a location to save the file.
   b. Click **Run** if this is the only desktop that will be running Windows XPM ode.
5. You may be asked for authorization again to start the installation of Windows XP Mode as shown in Figure 9.10. Click **Run**t oc ontinue.

■ **FIGURE 9.9** Security Warning

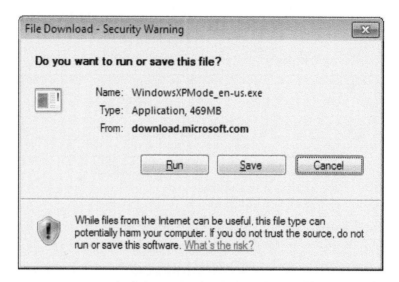

■ **FIGURE 9.10** Security Warning

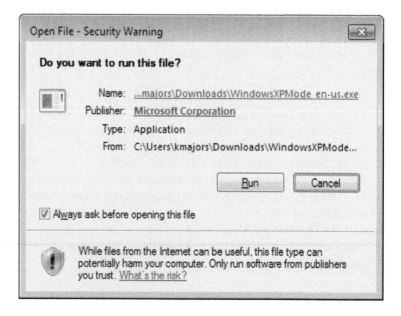

6. Windows XP Mode will start the install process as shown in Figure 9.11. Click **Next**t oc ontinue.
7. Select the location for the install of Windows XP Mode files. The location is shown in Figure 9.12. You can either accept the default or click the **Browse** button to select another location. These files are

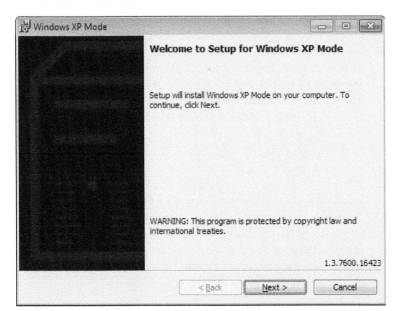

■ **FIGURE 9.11** Welcome Screen

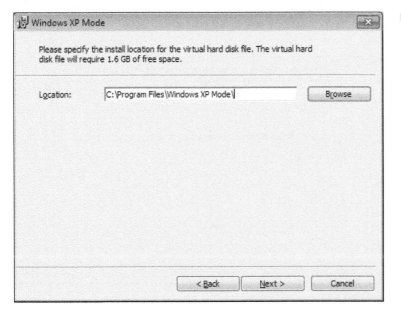

■ **FIGURE 9.12** Installation Location

fairly large, so if you have a larger disk drive that has more space, is faster, or you just want to locate this in a different spot, you may want to select a different location other than the default. Click **Next** when ready to continue.

8. The files will begin to load. The installation progress will be similar to Figure 9.13. The progress line will cross a couple of times, so be patient.

9. Congratulations! You are finished. Click **Finish** as shown in Figure 9.14.

10. Next you need to install Virtual PC on your Windows 7 desktop. Start by going back to the Virtual PC Web site in step 1. Click the **Windows Virtual PC** button as shown in Figure 9.8.

11. Again you will be asked if you want to **Run** or **Save** the download as shown in Figure 9.9. If this is the only desktop you will be loading Virtual PC on select **Run**. If you have more than one desktop, select **Save** and pick a folder to store for file. This is only a 10MB file so it won't take quite as long to download.

12. When the file is finished downloading, you will be asked if it is **OK** to install the update as shown in Figure 9.15. Click **Yes** to continue.

13. The License screen appears. Read the license by scrolling to the bottom or select the printable version and print it out. Click the **I Accept** button as shown in Figure 9.16 when ready. If you do not want to accept the license, click the **I Decline** button. This will prevent you from installing the Windows Virtual PC software.

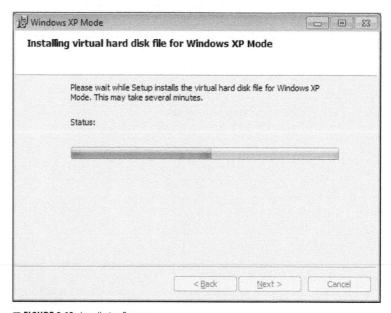

■ FIGURE 9.13 Installation Progress

■ FIGURE 9.14 Installation Complete

■ FIGURE 9.15 Stand-Alone Installer

■ FIGURE 9.16 License Screen

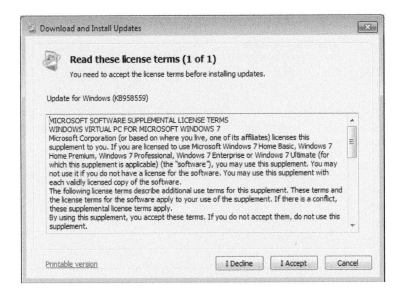

14. The installation will begin. You can track the progress by watching the progress bar as shown in Figure 9.17.
15. Congratulations! You have successfully completed the install of Virtual PC as shown in Figure 9.18. You will now have to reboot your desktop. You can click the **Restart Now** button to reboot the computer. You can click **Cancel**t or ebootl ater.

■ **FIGURE 9.17** Installation Progress

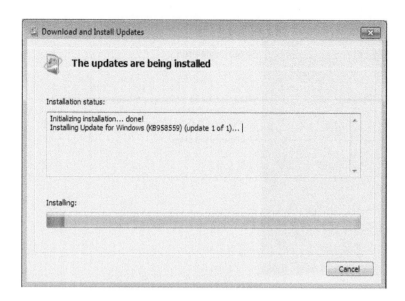

■ **FIGURE 9.18** Installation Complete

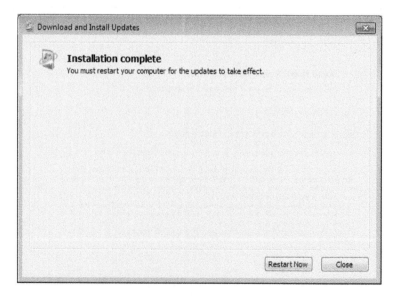

Setup of Windows XP Mode

We now have Windows XP Mode installed, but we still need to set it up. Remember this is a separate implementation of a full operating system. You must go through the first time use setup of Windows XP just like it is installed on a stand-alone computer. The big difference is that, this time, it will be available to both Windows XP and Windows 7. The following steps will get you through it easily.

■ **FIGURE 9.19** Start Menu Selection

1. When your computer has restarted, click the Windows 7 **Start**b utton
   , then select **All Programs | Windows Virtual PC | Windows XP Mode** to begin setup as shown in Figure 9.19.
2. You will be presented with a licensing screen. Please read the licensing terms and click **I accept the license terms** when ready, and then click **Next** as shown in Figure 9.20. You can click the **Printable version**l ink if you want to print the agreement.
3. Next, you must verify the installation folder and set up a password for the XPMUSER account. This is a required account that is automatically created. It is the default account used to run Windows XP Mode and any virtual applications installed in the virtual instance of Windows XP with SP3. You would normally need to enter this password when starting the Windows XP Mode. If you do not want to enter the password each time you start Windows XP Mode, you can store the credentials by checking the **Remember credentials** check box. Figure 9.21 shows the Installation folder and credentials screen.
4. Verify the installation folder listed at the top of this screen. It should be the same folder you selected when you installed Windows XP Mode in the previous section. If not, click the **Browse** button and find the installation files. Enter an appropriate password for your password rules. Reenter the password again. Click **Next** when ready to continue. Any authorized user accessing an application running in Windows XP Mode will use these credentials.

■ **FIGURE 9.20** Windows XP Mode License Screen

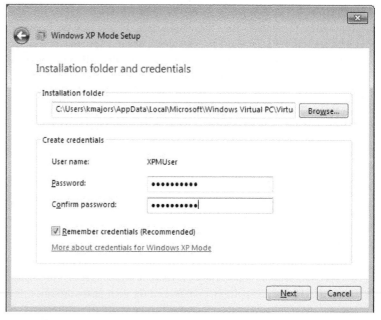

■ **FIGURE 9.21** Installation Folder and Credentials

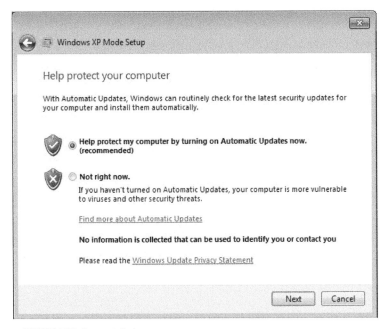

■ **FIGURE 9.22** Automatic Updates

5. You need to set up Automatic Updates next. As shown in Figure 9.22, you can select an option to automatically download and apply the updates or to turn this service off. For this service to function properly, both the host Windows 7 computer and the Windows XP Mode virtual desktop must be able to connect to the Internet. It is recommended that Automatic Updates be enabled. Click **Next**t oc ontinue.

6. Setup will now configure drive sharing. Drive sharing will allow files to be shared between both the Windows 7 operating system and the Windows XP Mode. Applications can pass data between the two operating systems with copy and paste seamlessly. Click **Start Setup**a s showni n Figure9.23 .

7. The setup process will start. Figure 9.24 shows you the progress screen. This may take a few minutes, so be patient.

8. Once the installation is complete, you will be automatically logged on to the new virtual machine. The hardware will be identified as Windows XP Mode starts up. Figure 9.25 shows the virtual desktop for WindowsX PM ode.

9. Next, you will need to apply any additional updates for Windows XP. You should see the **Automatic Updates** icon in the lower right corner. This is shown in Figure 9.26. Double-click this icon to start the update process.

FIGURE 9.23 Setup Drive Sharing

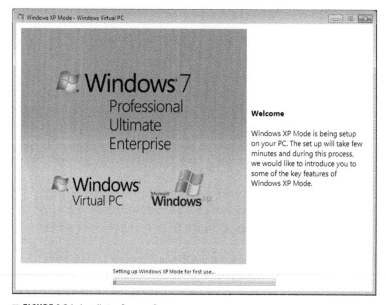

FIGURE 9.24 Installation Progress Screen

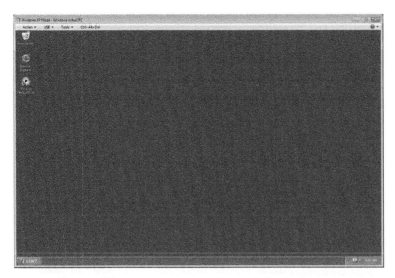

■ **FIGURE 9.25** Windows XP Mode Desktop

■ **FIGURE 9.26** Automatic Update Icon

■ **FIGURE 9.27** Automatic Updates

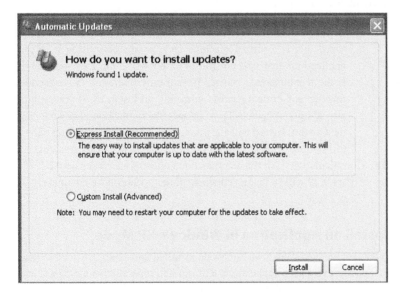

10. You should see the familiar Automatic Updates screen as shown in Figure 9.27. You have two choices:
    a. **Express Install** – This option will install all the recommended and criticalupda tes.
    b. **CustomI nstall** – This option will list all the available updates and allow you to select the ones you want to install.

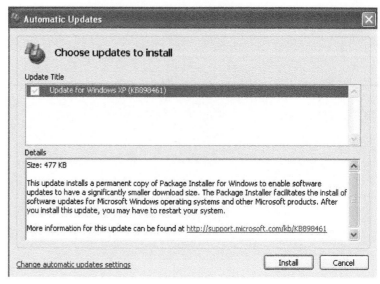

■ **FIGURE 9.28** Custom Install

Since this is a virtual machine and we are only using it to run applications that will not run in Windows 7, the **Express Install** is the recommended choice. We are only interested in the recommended and critical patches in mostly all instances. If you require any additional updates for your specific application, then choosing the **Custom Install** will allow you to be selective. Figure 9.28 shows this option. Click **Install** for either option to install the updates.

11. Congratulations! All the recommended updates have been applied. Figure 9.29 will be displayed when all the updates have completed. Click **Close**.

Install an Application in Windows XP Mode

Now that we have Windows XP Mode installed and setup, we need to load an application. These applications will run in a separate memory space and will be isolated from Windows 7 applications. Although mostly all applications can be configured to work with Windows 7, there are a few that either will not work or work better if they are running on Windows XP. A good example may be that a custom application was built on Microsoft Access XP. This application is the remaining application that has not been migrated to Microsoft Access 2007/2010. You must load Access XP into Windows XP Mode. The following steps will show you the process of loading an application into Windows XP Mode.

WARNING
WindowsX PM oded oesn ot include any antivirus protection. You need to load an antivirus program even if you already have one loaded on the host Windows 7 computer.

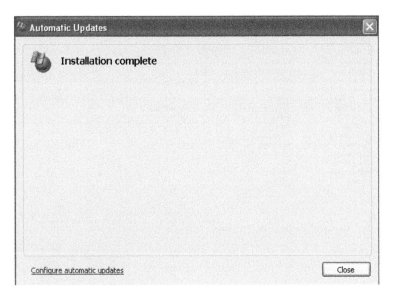

■ **FIGURE 9.29** Installation Complete

1. To start Windows XP Mode, click the **Windows 7 Start button**,t hen select **All Programs | Windows Virtual PC | Windows XP Mode** as showni n Figure9.19 .

■ **FIGURE 9.30** Windows XP Mode Menu Bar

2. Insert the software CD into the CD- or DVD-ROM or mount an International Organization for Standardization (ISO) file to Windows XP Mode. To mount an ISO file click **Tool | Settings…** from the top menu in the Windows XP Mode window as shown in Figure 9.30.
   a. Select the DVD drive from the list of devices as shown in Figure9.31 .
   b. If you have more than one physical DVD drive, you can select the one you want to use by clicking the **Access a physical drive**r adio button and selecting the desired DVD drive letter from the pull-down box. If you have an ISO image you want to use, just click the **Open an ISO image** radio button. Click the **Browse** button. Select the ISO image you want to mount as shown in Figure 9.32 and click **Open**t oc ontinue.
   c. Regardless of your installation media choice, once you have made your selection, click **OK**t oc ontinue.
3. Select the setup program and start the application install. Figure 9.33 shows an application ready to install.
4. Follow the installation instructions for your application.
5. Once the application is completed, you can run the application in Windows XP Mode by clicking **Start | All Programs** and selecting

■ FIGURE 9.31 Virtual Device Settings

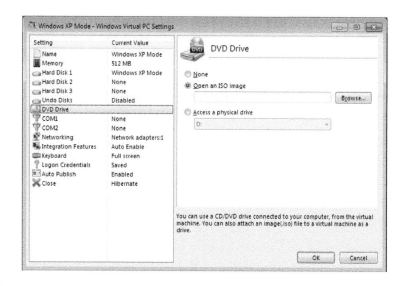

■ FIGURE 9.32 Selecting an ISO Image File

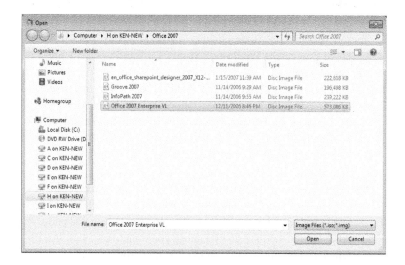

your application. The application should start up as it normally would in a Windows XP desktop. Figure 9.34 shows Microsoft Project 2000 running in the Windows XP Mode desktop.

6. Congratulations! You have loaded an application into a virtual machine. What does this means to you and how does it help your situation? Go ahead and close the application and log off Windows XP Mode and close the window. You will receive a message that *The Windows XP Mode is hibernating.*

■ **FIGURE 9.33** Application Installation

■ **FIGURE 9.34** Application Running in Windows XP Mode

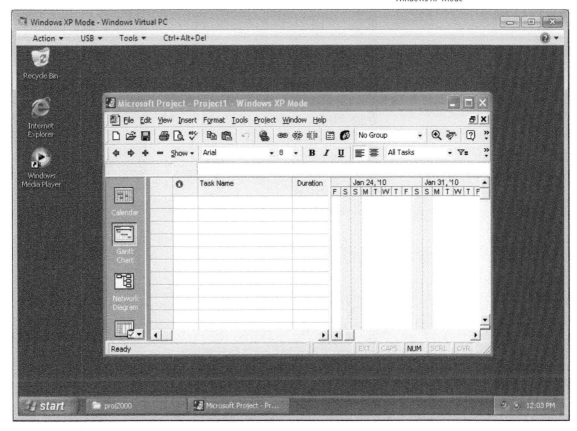

7. Click the **Windows 7 Start button | All Programs | Windows Virtual PC | Windows XP Mode Applications** as shown in Figure 9.35. Notice your application is listed.

8. Double-click this application. You will receive a message that Windows XP Mode is being enabled and your application starts up as showni n Figure9.36 .

9. As you use your application, you will discover that it performs as it normally would if it was installed locally on the Windows 7 desktop directly. Figure 9.36 also shows that this is Microsoft Project 2000 running in Windows XP Mode.

10. Congratulations! You have successfully installed and configured Windows XP Mode and loaded and run an application from both the Windows XP Mode desktop and the Windows 7 Start menu.

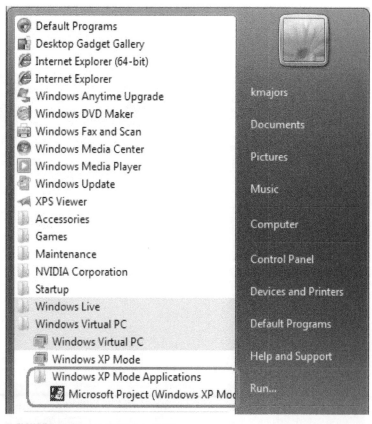

■ **FIGURE 9.35** Windows XP Mode Applications

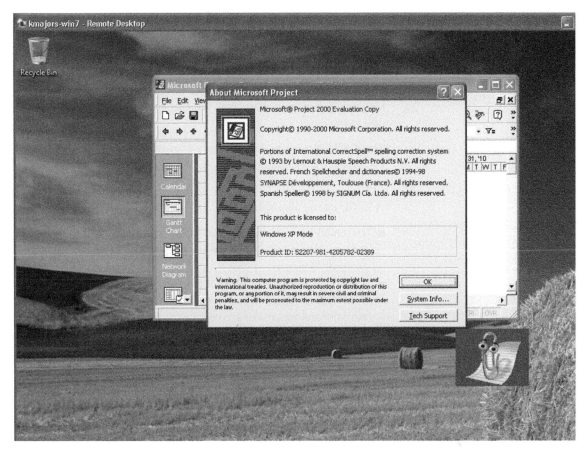

MANY FORMS OF VIRTUALIZATION

Windows 7 can support many different methods of virtualization and leverage them in combinations to meet the deployment needs for yourself or your business. We will next look at some of these methods to give you an idea of what can be accomplished.

Using Windows 7 in combination with Windows Server 2008 and Hyper-V and the System Center Suite can provide your enterprise with a very flexible and robust environment to provide your users with the desktop they require. This can start with the very desktop itself to access to applications or a completely hosted desktop. The key to this is a new licensing model that Microsoft has developed. The Virtual Enterprise Centralized Desktop (VECD) license is the Windows 7 license that allows virtualization of Windows desktops.

VECD Licensing Is a Challenge

The VECD license is the Windows 7 license that allows virtualization. Traditionally, a user only accessed one desktop at a time on a single specific device. When a new desktop device was installed, it typically required a new Windows license. If it relocated an existing license, the previous desktop was taken out of service. With virtualization, this is not the typical use case anymore.

The VECD allows a business to run a copy of Windows 7 in a data center that may provision multiple desktops across several servers in production and for disaster recovery.

A VECD license allows the following:

- *The ability to run a copy of Windows in a data center* – This is required for dynamic provisioning and creating deployment images of Windows 7 for use by your users.
- *Rights to move virtual machines between servers for increased reliability* – With load balancing and disaster recovery, even a virtual desktop may run on several servers in a data center or even multiple data centers. Each instance of Windows 7 would normally need to be licensed, but with the VECD, only the active instance would need to be licensed.
- *Unlimited backup of virtual machines* – This is especially important for distributed disaster-recovery sites. Many companies will back up desktops to multiple disaster-recovery sites for rapid recovery if any one location becomes unavailable. This is different from the normal backup to tape or even a removable disk for desktops. It is not uncommon for servers to maintain a continuous data-protection model, but more frequently desktops now fit the category of a critical system.
- *Ability to access up to four running VM instances per device*– Traditionally, all users needed their own license for a desktop. The VECD will allow the same desktop device to access up to four running virtual machines. We have already loaded Windows XP Mode on our Windows 7 desktop. That is a running virtual machine. You are good for three more. This is possible because we also loaded Virtual PC. You could create a complete data center on just your desktop. You may need to license the other three operating systems but not the connections.
- *Rights to access corporate desktops from home for a user that has already been licensed at work* – If a user normally accesses a virtual machine running Windows 7 at work, they are allowed to access the same virtual desktop from home without requiring an additional license.

- *Availability to volume licensing keys, such as Key Management Service (KMS) and Multiple Activation Keys (MAK)* – This feature allows the enterprise to use the KMS system in Windows Server 2008 to activate and authorize Windows 7 desktops locally without the need to connect to the Internet or contact Microsoft individually.

The key to the VECD license is the desktops *must* be covered under Microsoft's Software Assurance (SA). This is a requirement to even purchase the VECD license. This can save a great deal on the cost of the upgrade and support of the Windows 7 environment. For example,

- Your company has 100 laptops and desktops.
- Your company has 100 thin clients.
- If the laptops do not have SA, you would need 200 VECD licenses (100 thin clients and 100 laptops).
- If the laptops have SA, you would need 100 VECD licenses (100 laptops). You would need to maintain the SA on each of the laptops.

The details and specifics of your exact solution is beyond the scope of this book. You are encouraged to download the latest version of the Virtual Desktop Infrastructure (VDI) licensing brochure at www.microsoft.com/windows/enterprise/solutions/virtualization/licensing.aspx or contact your Microsoft Licensing Specialist.

As you can see from our simple example, you could save a significant amount on your licensing costs if you decide to leverage virtualization in your business. Although it is a bit tricky at first look, it is worth spending a few minutes discussing the benefits and requirements with your licensing provider.

VDI or Centralized Virtual Desktops

VDI is an alternative desktop deployment model for Windows 7. Instead of running a local copy on each user's desktop, a common image is created and stored on one or more servers in the data center. This image is deployed to a server running a hypervisor.

There are several benefits to implementing a VDI infrastructure:

- A common supported desktop environment can be rapidly deployed across your by creating a single Windows 7 desktop image and using that image to deploy virtual machines on your server hypervisor. A single server can support many virtual desktops. Each of these desktops reacts as a stand-alone Windows 7 desktop. Unlike using Remote Desktop Services (RDS), the users connecting to a virtual

WHAT IS A HYPERVISOR?

A *hypervisor* is a layer of software that allows for the running of several operating systems simultaneously on a common computer while maintaining isolation between the different operating systems. Windows Server 2008 has a hypervisor know as *Hyper-V*. There are also several other hypervisors such as VMware vSphere and CitrixX enServer.

desktop can have full access to all features of that virtual machine without impacting the other virtual desktops or the host server. Your users could still use the Remote Desktop Client to connect to their virtualde sktop.

■ Updates and changes to Windows 7 can be done in a centralized fashion by updating the Windows 7 desktop image and then redeploying the updated image to all your users. When they log on the next time, they will have the updated image and all the rest of their settings will bem aintained.

■ If a problem with an update requires a rollback to a previous version of the desktop image, it can be quickly done. Saving a copy of the previous image before performing the update allows for a roll back by redeploying the previous image and having users to log off and then log back on to receive the previous image.

Figure9. 37s howsa s ample VDIde sign.

■ **FIGURE 9.37** Sample VDI Design

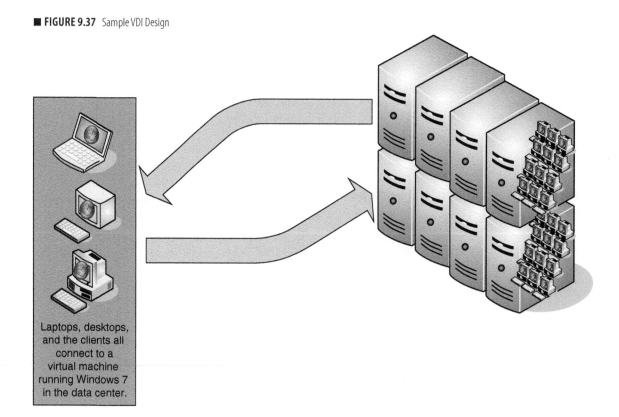

Laptops, desktops, and the clients all connect to a virtual machine running Windows 7 in the data center.

There are some barriers to implementing a VDI. The start-up costs can be high, and the return on investment is longer than it is on a server virtualization project. This is a business decision that should not be taken lightly but instead planned and budgeted before embarking on the project. Some specific areas that need to be considered are as follows:

- VDI may not reduce desktop costs because any saving is typically redirected into server, network, and storage infrastructure. Improvements in desktop management and user management are required to support large numbers of virtual desktops. Applying Group Policies through Active Directory to redirect user folders and implementing roaming profiles will increase the flexibility of a VDI design. VDI should be considered when desktop flexibility is more important than immediate costs avings.
- A user connected to a virtual desktop requires a constant connection to the network. Whether this is through a Local Area Network or across a Wide Area Network (WAN) or a remote connection, the user must be connected to the virtual desktop to be productive. If a user must be able to operate in a disconnected environment, VDI is not a suitable solution for them. If your users are not mobile or only work when they are connected to the network, then this could be a viable solution.
- Planning your VDI deployment is critical to the success of the project because it can be a complex and an investment in infrastructure. Defining which users will benefit the most and the needed virtualization components to deploy is crucial for success.

Distributed VirtualD esktops

A distributed desktop model allows for different desktop images to be deployed to a specific group of users based on their location or user group. This model can be useful if you have a number of different types of users in a single location or you have users in a variety of locations like a branch office. Each group has a different desktop requirement or is connected by a slow or intermittent link. The remote users may have a file server that stores their files and information. Figure 9.38 shows a distributed virtual desktop to a branch office.

Another distributed desktop design may include setting up a Pre-eXecution Environment. This method allows an administrator to deploy an image to a server and a desktop to download and boot that image at start up. Several desktop images can be developed and assigned to a desktop. When the desktop is started, the image is streamed to the device as it starts up. Changing a desktop image is as simple as reconfiguring the device's target image

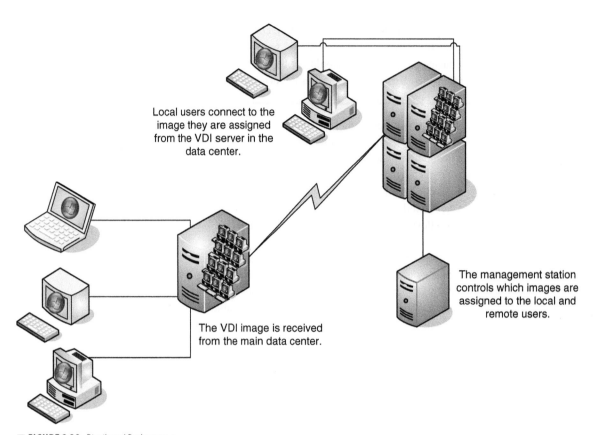

Local users connect to the image they are assigned from the VDI server in the data center.

The VDI image is received from the main data center.

The management station controls which images are assigned to the local and remote users.

■ **FIGURE 9.38** Distributed Desktops to a Branch Office

and restarting the desktop. This is a viable design if applications must be run from the local desktop. Some applications require a hardware dongle or a specific Media Access Control address for licensing. Applications that require special graphics or additional cards or adapters not supported in a virtual environment are also good candidates for this type of deployment.

The drawbacks and benefits are as follows:

- The individual images must be loaded with any applications or drivers required for the individual desktop computers. Unless all the desktops are identical, you may need to add the different drivers for each type of hardware the image is being prepared to run on.
- A different image can be configured to load on a desktop as a shift changes or new updates are configured. This is particularly useful because a new image is loaded each time the desktop is rebooted. Viruses and malware are limited in their effectiveness because the entire desktop image is reloaded each time the desktop is reloaded.

- This model is best used with a local server that holds the desktop images. Loading a desktop image over a WAN is a slow process that will discourage the remote users from rebooting their desktops. In this scenario, you should look at using either a local VDI or a distributed VDIs olution.

Desktops can also be distributed using Microsoft System Center Configuration Manager (SCCM). This product is part of the System Center Suite and can be used to distribute both applications and desktops to user's desktops, both local and remote. This model will actually install the desktop operating system on the targeted desktop. This is a fairly complex product, and planning and testing of the solution is required for optimum success. You can also use this management solution in conjunction with another System Center Suite component, the Virtual Machine Manager 2008, to create, deploy, and manage desktops in a distributed environment.

Remember, when it comes to deploying a user's desktop, there are several options and one design rarely fits all situations. You can see for the different scenarios that a combination of all options can be leveraged to meet the specific needs of your situation.

Application Virtualization

Application virtualization can mean many different things when talking about Windows 7 and Windows Server 2008. We have already used one type with Windows XP Mode when we loaded and ran an application that would not normally run on Windows 7. Although this is an easy answer to application virtualization, there are more advanced solutions.

Remote Desktop Services

RDS (formerly Terminal Services) is the most commonly used method of application virtualization. This method presents applications to connected users. The application actually runs in a session on the server in the data center while it appears to be running on the local desktop. This is a cost effective and reliable method of deploying applications to an enterprise. Figure 9.39 shows a simplified diagram of how RDS works.

Users, whether local or remote, all connect to the RDS server. The application is displayed to the end user while being executed on the RDS server. This gives equal performance to both local and remote users running the application. When the applications need to be upgraded or patched, they are patched only on the RDS servers. When the users next connect and run the application, they receive the updated version. The RDS server is capable

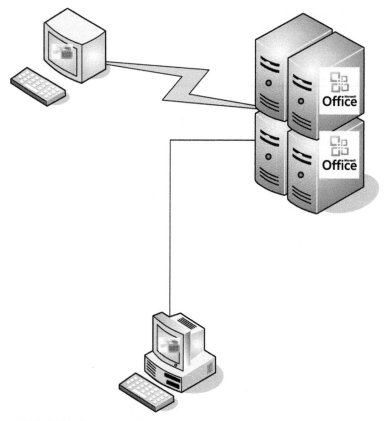

■ FIGURE 9.39 Remote Desktop Services

of supporting multiple users on a single server, and there are many new enhancements in RDS with Windows Server 7 that allow for a variety of connection methods. Web Services, Session Broker, and Network Load Balancing all work together to provide a seamless application virtualization environment for most users.

If your users do not want to connect to a server or a Web page to run their applications, there is a new feature in Windows Server 2008 RDS called *RemoteApp*. A published application can be converted to a RemoteApp and generate a Windows Installer File (MSI) that can be deployed through Active Directory, file download, e-mail, or your SCCM environment to all the targeted users. When installed on your Windows 7 desktop, double-clicking on it will launch the application just like it is installed on the end-user desktop. The connection to the RDS server is automatically established and the application is started. The RemoteApp can add items to the desktop Start menu or desktop icon just like a locally installed application.

Using the advanced features of the Remote Desktop Client in Windows 7 allows for mapping of resources to the RDS server, so files and printers can be shared when a user connects. The advanced features also can authenticate a user before a user session is created to relieve the extra burden on the RDS server and allow for more connections and better performance. The drawback to this solution is the fact that a user must be able to connect to the RDS server in some fashion to be able to run an application.

App-V

App-V (formerly SoftGrid) is a method of application distribution that allows the application to be executed on the local desktop without actually installing the application on the individual desktop. Instead, it is streamed to the desktop as the different features of the application are required. This offers a method of running applications in a disconnected mode and allows applications to run in an isolated environment, so they don't conflict with each other. Figure 9.40 shows this basic design.

When an application is installed on the App-V server, it is sequenced, so the most common program modules are loaded first. The purpose of this sequencing is to allow the application to open faster and to allow the user to begin using the application even before all of it is loaded on the desktop. Because of the sequencing of the applications when the application is

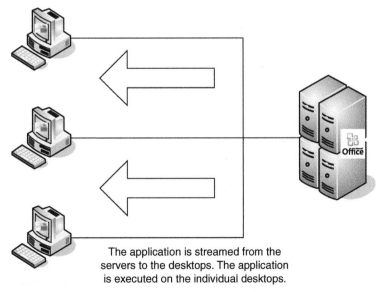

The application is streamed from the servers to the desktops. The application is executed on the individual desktops.

■ **FIGURE 9.40** App-V Design

requested, the server sends the most common modules first or streams the application to the desktop. As more modules are requested by the desktop, they are streamed to that desktop. The application is actually processed on the desktop and not on the server.

The benefit of this design is that each application runs in a separate memory space. Applications that normally conflict with other applications can be configured to run on the same desktop without problems. These application streams can be directed to individual desktops, virtual desktops, or even RDS server sessions.

If a user needs to run an application in a disconnected mode, the application can be checked out for a specific amount of time. The entire application will be streamed to the desktop and will be available to the user even if the desktop become disconnected from the network. An example of this is laptop users. The user needs to download the application and then disconnect from the network to travel. When the application is started in a disconnected mode, it performs exactly the same as when connected to a network. Files and documents can be updated or created as needed. When the user reconnects to the network, the files are synchronized to the file servers and the application is either checked back in or the ticket can be renewed for the next trip. If the application has been updated since the initial check out, the new version is streamed to the laptop. Because this checkout process is similar to checking a book out of the library, there is a time limit on the application. This time limit is configured by the administrator. If the laptop is lost or stolen, the application will time out and become unusable. This helps protect you and your company from losing expensive software when the laptop is removed from the environment.

UserS ession Virtualization

User session virtualization is a newer version of desktop virtualization that works at the operating system level. While normal virtualization of the desktop allows an operating system to be run by virtualizing the hardware of the desktop, RDS and App-V allow for the virtualization of the applications. User session virtualization lies between the two.

A desktop has an operating system loaded on the base hardware. This can be either physical or virtual. The user session virtualization keeps track of all changes to the operating system that a user might make by encapsulating the configuration changes and associating them to the user account. This allows the specific changes to be applied to the underlying operating system without actually changing it. This allows several users to have completely different operating system configurations applied to a base operating system installation.

The most common example of user session virtualization is leveraging folder redirection and roaming profiles with Windows Server 2008. Applying these settings in Group Policies allows for a basic operating system to be loaded on several desktops, and a user can have the same experience and find all their files regardless of the specific desktop they choose to use. Although these settings are commonly used in an RDS environment, it can be just as easily implemented for your desktop environment. The big key to performance is to keep the user data close to the desktop the user will access. Because an RDS environment is centrally located in the data center, having the user-redirected folders and profiles in the data center improves overall performance. The same design could be true for a VDI deployment where all the virtual desktops are located in a data center. All the user-redirected folders and profiles should be located close to the virtual host servers.

If you are in a distributed desktop environment and there are local file servers available at each location, you can deploy virtualized user sessions in the form of redirected folders and roaming profiles.

Folder Redirection

Folder redirection is configured by applying a Group Policy. Windows Server 2008 has several settings that allow you to redirect user folders that would normally be contained in your profile to server-based folders. These settings are contained in the User Setting\Administrator Templates\System\ Folder Redirection section of the Group Policy. You must be on the domain controller to enable these settings.

Common folders that can be redirected are as follows:

- MyD ocuments
- Favorites
- StartM enu
- Desktop
- ApplicationD ata

These are the most common but there may be others you want to redirect. There are normally two settings, *Basic* and *Advanced*.

- Basic – This setting applies the folder redirection to all users to whom the Group Policy applies.
- Advanced – This setting applies to select users and can apply different settings to different user groups.

These folders are normally contained in your profile. They can become very large and take a long time to load when you log on. By redirecting them, you place a pointer in your profile that points to the folder where this information is located. The pointer is not very large and does not change, so your profile remains smaller.

Roaming Profiles

To enable the roaming profiles, you use the Active Directory Users and Computer tool on your domain controller. By modifying your user account, you can point to the location of your profile on a file server. When you log on to a desktop computer, your profile settings will be downloaded to that desktop. When you log off, any changes will be copied back to the folder and your profile will be removed from the desktop.

There are two main types of roaming profile, *Terminal Services* and *Windows* profiles.

- Terminal Services – This profile is only applied to users running a Remote Desktop Session. It can be different from the Windows profile but is typically only set up for RDS users.
- Windows – This is the normal profile. It is set up in the Account Properties of each user account.

To set up a roaming profile you must create a shared folder on a centralized server and configure the path to the share in the user account properties. Using the format of \\Servername\ProfileShareName\%Username% will create a folder and insert the profile for each user configured to use a roaming profile. If for some reason the file share is not available, a default local profile will be created for the users when they log on. They will not have their settings or files.

Using roaming profiles across a slow link is not recommended because of the amount of time to load the file. You should always locate the file server close to the location the user will need it. That means if the roaming profile will be used in a desktop environment, the profile server should be close to the desktop. If this is a VDI, then the desktop is in the data center. If this is a Remote Desktop Service infrastructure, then the desktop is on the RDS server.

MicrosoftE nterpriseD esktop Virtualization

Microsoft Enterprise Desktop Virtualization (MED-V) is Microsoft's new core component of the Microsoft Desktop Optimization Pack (MDOP). Med-V enables the deployment and management of Microsoft Virtual PC images of Windows desktops to address enterprise upgrade and migration scenarios. MED-V helps an enterprise upgrade the version of Windows on the desktop even when some applications are not yet functional or supported on the new version of Windows. Windows XP Mode of Windows 7 is part of MED-V and leverages the Virtual PC on the Windows 7 desktop.

MED-V builds on top of Virtual PC to run two operating systems on one device, adding virtual image delivery, policy-based provisioning, and centralized management. MED-V works with other Windows operating systems like Vista to allow them the same benefits of Windows XP Mode on Windows 7.

Using the MDOP tools, an administrator can build and configure a desktop image with the unsupported application and deploy it to the enterprise desktops as a virtual image that will run as if it was installed on the desktop operating system.

MED-V allows deployment of legacy versions of a Windows operating system like Windows XP or Windows 2000 to any version of Windows desktop operating system. The management server allows for the creation and testing of multiple images. When the image is correct, it can be deployed to all users requiring the application.

Once installed, the application is available to users just like it was locally installed. Figure 9.41 shows the processes of MED-V in action.

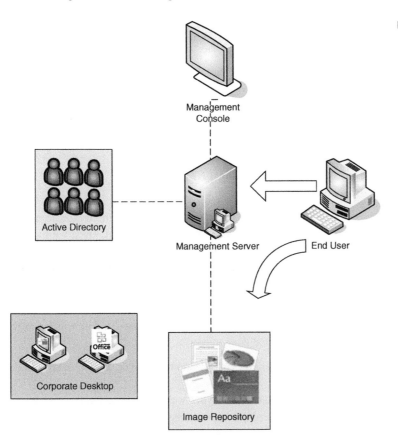

■ **FIGURE 9.41** MED-V in Action

The process works as follows:

1. The Corporate desktop images are prepared.
2. The image is stored in the Image Repository.
3. The Image Repository registers the image with the Management Server.
4. The Administrator uses the Management Console to assign the image to the appropriate Active Directory user group.
5. When the end user signs in, the image is deployed to his or her desktop and stored in the Virtual PC virtual machine folder.

In order to use MED-V, you must use and all managed desktops must be members of the Active Directory domain. Clients can be Windows 7, Vista, or Windows XP SP2. The guest operating system can be Windows XP SP2 or SP3 or Windows 2000 SP4.

The use of MED-V extends the benefits of Windows 7's Windows XP Mode to other desktops. This tool eliminates the barriers to adoption of a current desktop operating system because of application incompatibility.

■ SUMMARY

In this chapter, we learned how to deploy Windows 7's Windows XP Mode feature. To do this, we needed to:

- Verify our Windows 7 operating system was Professional, Enterprise, orU ltimate
- Verify our computer had virtualization hardware assist
- Verify that the computer BIOS was configured to enable the hardware assistf eatures.
- Download and install Windows XP Mode
- Downloada ndi nstall VirtualP C

We configured Windows XP Mode by going through the wizard to assign a password and then performed a reboot of the system. Once we had the Windows XP Mode running, we installed a legacy application. We launched the application from Windows XP Mode and from the Start menu of Windows 7. This demonstrated the integration of the legacy application with the primary operating system.

We discussed several different types of virtualization and how to leverage them with Windows 7 and your enterprise.

- We discussed application virtualization with RDS, RemoteApp, and App-V.
- We discussed the VDI using Hyper-V and how we could leverage a virtual desktop to deploy a large number of corporate desktops quickly to both local and remote users.

- We discussed the value of the new VECD license from Microsoft. This license offers several benefits to desktops under *subscription advantage* and is the best way to utilize this license for a diverse userba se.
- We discussed user session virtualization and the best methods to implement it. Using the folder redirection in Windows Server 2008, Group Policies can redirect the profile folders to minimize their size. We can use roaming profiles to apply user customizations to a base desktop without the need to actually make a change in the desktop configurations.
- Finally, we discussed MED-V and how we can use it to take the advantages of the Windows XP Mode and Virtual PC to the enterprise to allow legacy applications to be run on current Windows desktop operatings ystems.

Although this may seem to be a lot of information all at once, you should start seeing the benefits of virtualization on the desktop. If you are working in the IT department of a company, this may offer you a better plan to help keep your projects on track by eliminating the normal stumbling blocks to a new desktop deployment.

Windows 7 Troubleshooting and Performance Tools

INFORMATION IN THIS CHAPTER

- ActionC enter–M aintenance
- ActionC enter– Troubleshooting
- ResourceM onitor
- Event Viewer
- Troubleshooting WindowsS ervices
- ProblemS tepsR ecorder
- Summary

Hopefully, you won't run into many issues with your Windows 7 systems, but if you do, you need to know how to effectively troubleshoot them. Windows 7 provides a variety of tools to help you troubleshoot issues with your system. You can use these tools to troubleshoot network issues, performance issues, maintenance issues, and a host of other problems. In this chapter, we will go over the Action Center, Resource Monitor, Event Viewer, and the Problem Steps Recorder (PSR).

ACTION CENTER – MAINTENANCE

The Windows 7 Action Center is an enhancement over the Security Center used in Windows Vista. The previous Security Center could only be used to troubleshoot security issues on your system. The new Action Center provides the ability to solve not only security issues but also other system issues. The Action Center can help you with maintenance issues, network issues, and many other types of issues.

DOI: 10.1016/B978-1-59749-561-5.00010-3

The Action Center can be accessed through the Control Panel or through the flag icon in the system tray in the bottom right corner of your system. It is easier to open the Action Center through the system tray icon than through the Control Panel. In order to open Action Center through the Control Panel, you have to first change your Control Panel view to either the large or small icon view. This will allow you to see all the applets in the Control Panel. Action Center does not show up in Category view.

The Action Center contains a Maintenance section, which is used to manage system maintenance. The Maintenance section of the Action Center will show discovered maintenance issues on the system and offer you a suggested method for fixing them. You can either opt to perform the fix or not. You can also opt to have Action Center stop showing alerts for certain types of issues.

As seen in Figure 10.1, one option under the Maintenance section is **Check for solutions to unreported problems**. When your system runs into issues, you can report these issues to Microsoft for a potential fix. Because these issues are possibly already being investigated, the Action Center gives you

■ **FIGURE 10.1** Action Center Maintenance Section

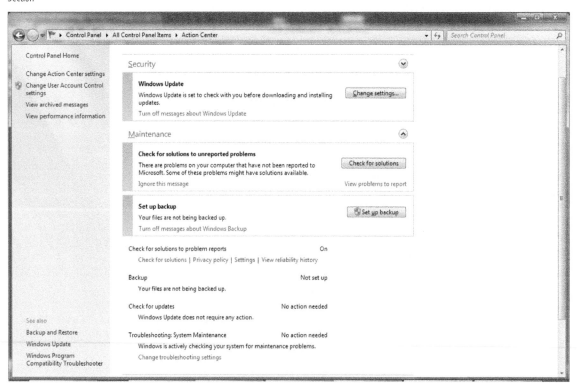

the option to search for issues that you have not yet reported to Microsoft. If Windows can figure out a solution for the issue, it will also be presented toyou .

Action Center – Maintenance Alerts

When Windows 7 finds an issue with your system, Action Center will issue an alert. If your system currently has an alert, then you will be notified through the **Action icon** in the system tray. You can then go into Action Center to find out details for the alert.

The system in Figure 10.2 appears to have a driver issue. There is a new driver update available for the system that needs to be downloaded. Having the appropriate drivers is crucial for your system to run properly. This is why the Action Center wants to ensure you have the most up-to-date drivers possible. If you do not, you will be presented with a warning and an opportunity to download and install the driver.

Within the warning section for the driver issue, there is an option for **View message details**. If you click this button, you will be taken to the Message

■ **FIGURE 10.2** Action Center – Maintenance Issue Found

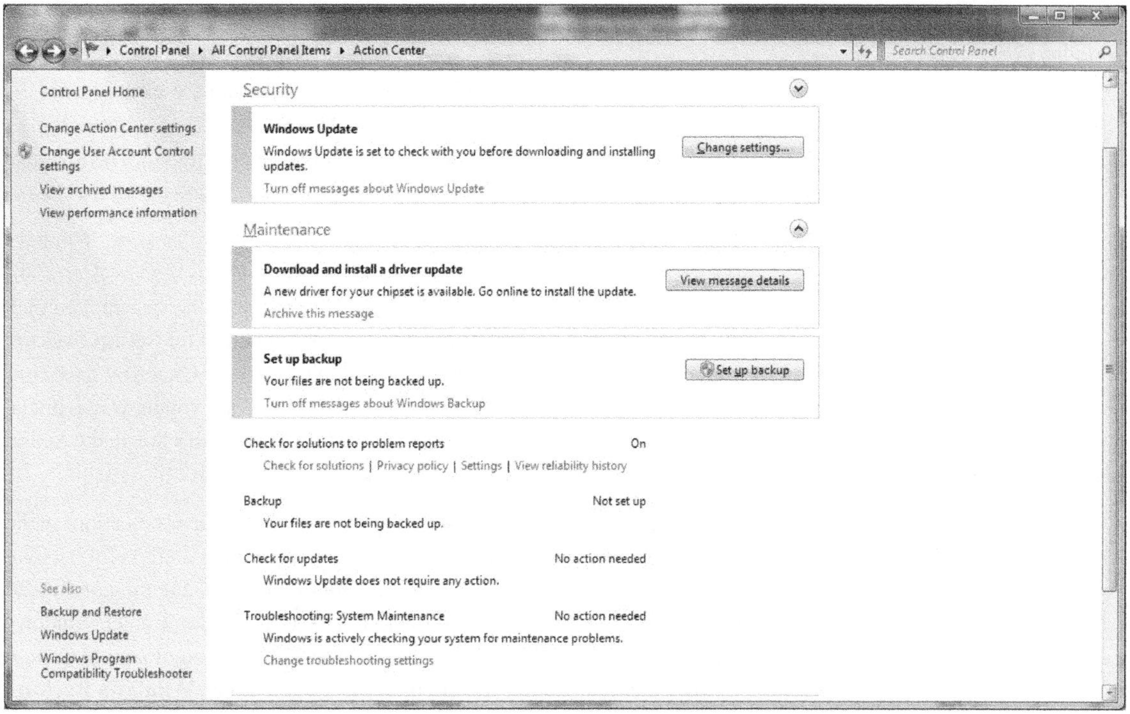

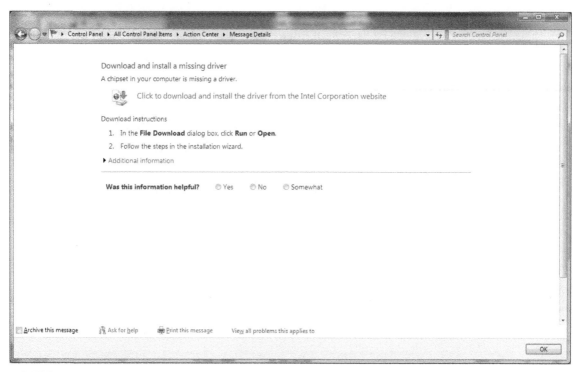

FIGURE 10.3 Message Details Window

Details window, as seen in Figure 10.3. Here, you can see exactly what the problem is and what needs to be done. We see that there is a new chipset driver that needs to be downloaded and installed for our system. The Message Details window even gives you the ability to download and install the driver.

The system also appears to have an issue with system backups. Windows Backup has not yet been configured on the system. This is seen by Alert Center as an issue because if something were to happen to the system, you may not be able to recover your data. If you click the button for **Set up backup**, you can configure your system to do Windows Backup. Once you have configured backups, the Action Center will then start giving you messages on the status of your backups. For example, if one of your backups failed, the Action Center will let you know so that you can address whatever the issue is.

In some cases, you may want to turn off Windows Backup notifications in the Alert Center. Let's say, for example, you use some other method for backing up your important data. You wouldn't want the Action Center to continue to prompt you to set up Windows Backup. Disabling Action Center Windows Backup messages is easy. In the backup message section of Action Center, simply select the option for **Turn off messages about Windows Backup**. Action Center will no longer issue alerts for Windows Backup.

Action Center – Maintenance Items

In addition to the alerts that appear in the Maintenance section of Action Center, there is a general maintenance area where you can view maintenance information about your system. The following are four standard sections that appear in this general maintenance area: **Check for solutions to problem reports**, **Backup**, **Check for updates**, and **Troubleshooting: System Maintenance**.

Check for Solutions to Problem Reports

When certain errors occur on your system, you have the ability to generate problem reports. These problem reports can be automatically sent to Microsoft for analysis. This section of Action Center allows you to find out if solutions are available for problem reports you have submitted. In this section, you have four options to choose from. The **Check for solutions** option will actually do the check for solutions to problem reports that have been submitted. Action Center will query the Microsoft site to determine if solutions have been given for issues that you have reported. When you generate and send problem reports over the Internet to Microsoft, personal information may also be sent. Microsoft uses its privacy policy to warn you about this transaction. The **Privacy policy** option is a Web link that allows you to view highlights of Microsoft's Windows 7 privacy policy that pertain to items like problem reports that send user information over the Internet. The Web page also gives you the option to view Microsoft's full privacy policy.

The **Settings** option brings up the Problem Reporting Settings window as seen in Figure 10.4. The Settings window allows you to configure how much information is sent to Microsoft in a problem report and whether solution checks are done either manually or automatically. These settings are only changed for the current user. If you want to change the settings for everyone, select the option for **Change report settings for all users**. If there are certain programs for which you do not want problem reports to be generated, you can exclude them by using the **Select programs to exclude from reporting** option. This will bring up the Advanced Problem Reporting Settings window, where you can specify programs to exclude from reporting. The Problem Reporting Settings window also includes an option for **Read the Windows Error Reporting Privacy statement online**. This option will direct you to the Microsoft Web site where you can read the Windows 7 PrivacyH ighlights.

The **View reliability history** option brings up the Reliability Monitor window, as seen in Figure 10.5. Reliability Monitor gives you an index rating that relates to your overall system reliability. This rating takes application failures, Windows failures, various warnings, and other information

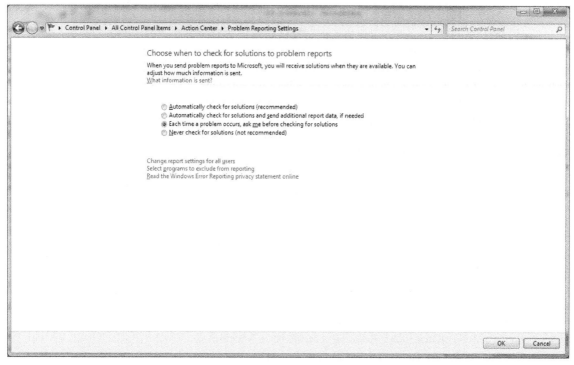

■ FIGURE 10.4 Problem Reporting Settings Window

into account. If you click the column for a particular day, you can view all the events that were generated for that day. You can then double-click a particular message to view the details for that also.

Backup

This section holds information about Windows Backup. If Windows Backup messages have been disabled in the Alert Center, this section will allow you to enable them. Once they are enabled, this section will give you status information on the last backup that took place. You can see when the last backup was run and the results of that backup session.

Check for Updates

This section gives information about Windows Update and identifies whether there is a problem with your Windows Update configuration. If there is a problem with your Windows Update configuration, Alert Center will notify you.

Troubleshooting: System Maintenance

Windows 7 will check your system for problems with your system maintenance settings. By selecting the option for **Change troubleshooting**

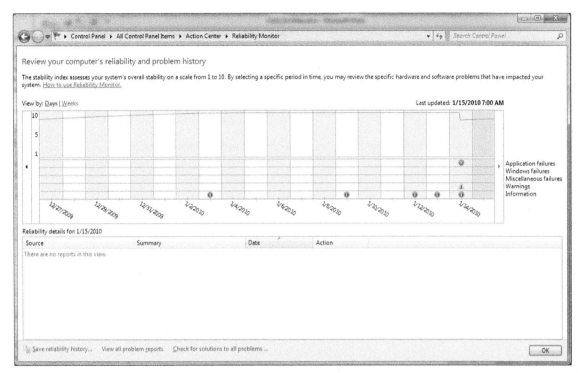

■ **FIGURE 10.5** Reliability Monitor

settings, you can use the Change Settings window, as seen in Figure 10.6, to adjust whether or not Windows will automatically check for issues, and what happens when issues are found. You can choose whether or not you want users to be able to use the Windows Online Troubleshooting service. You can also choose whether you want to allow troubleshooting to immediately begin when the troubleshooter is started.

ACTION CENTER – TROUBLESHOOTING

At the bottom of the Action Center is the **Troubleshooting** option. Selecting this option will bring up the Troubleshooting window. The Troubleshooting window will guide you through getting help in troubleshooting problems that you may be experiencing on your system.

Programs

The Programs section allows you to troubleshoot issues that you may have while running various programs on your system. Often, programs designed for earlier versions of Windows will have trouble running on Windows 7. Sometimes, you have to wait for the latest version of the program. Sometimes, you can adjust your settings to allow these programs to run properly

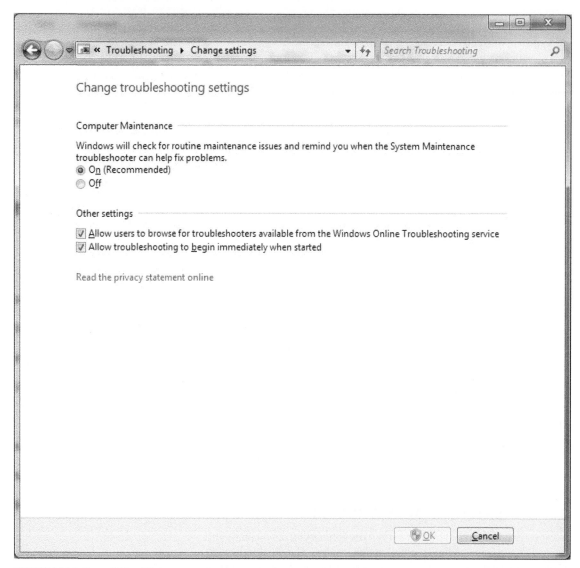

FIGURE 10.6 Change Settings Window

on Windows 7. The Programs section will help you determine if certain settings will be able to help the program perform properly. The Programs section only has one option: **Run programs made for previous versions of Windows**.

Run Programs Made for Previous Versions of Windows

Selecting this option brings up the Program Compatibility wizard, which will take you through the steps of selecting the program that causes issues and fixing whatever the problem might be.

To use the Program Compatibility wizard, do the following:

1. On the initial screen of the Program Compatibility wizard, you must decide if you want to use advanced settings or not. This advanced option allows for two things. First, it allows you to run the wizard as administrator. Second, it allows you to apply repairs automatically. Click **Next**.

2. The wizard will scan your system and attempt to detect all the programs running on the system. You are asked to select the program you are having difficulty with. If you don't see the correct program, choose **Not listed** and you will be prompted to enter the location of the program. Click **Next**.

3. You will be presented with two options:

   a. **Try recommended settings** – This option will run the programs with settings suggested by Windows.

   b. **Troubleshoot program** – This option will allow you to choose specific settings to troubleshoot specific issues with the program. These issues might deal with permissions, screen resolution, or a hostof ot hers.

4. Next, when you are prompted to start the program, do so and click **Next**.

5. If the program runs properly, you can save the settings. If it does not run properly, you can try other settings.

HardwareandS ound

This section provides options for troubleshooting issues with your system devices and your system sound. There are four options in this section: **Configure a device, Use a printer, Troubleshoot audio recording**, and **Troubleshoot audio playback**.

Configure a Device

Selecting this option will bring up the Hardware and Devices wizard. This wizard will attempt to diagnose and solve device issues on system. To use the Hardware and Devices wizard, do the following:

1. On the initial screen of the wizard, you must decide if you want to use advanced settings or not. This advanced option will allow you to automatically apply repairs. Click **Next**.

2. The wizard will attempt to determine if there are driver issues on your system. If there are issues, you will be prompted to fix the issues. Many times, this will mean downloading an updated driver. Click **Next**.

3. If all your devices are now working properly, choose **Close the trouble-shooter**. If not, you have the option to **Explore additional options**.

> **NOTE**
> If WindowsU pdatei sn otc on-figured to download and install device drivers, you will receive a warning message when running thew izard.

Use a Printer

Selecting this option will bring up the Printer wizard. This wizard will help you troubleshoot issues that might prevent your print jobs from being printed properly.

To use the Printer wizard, do the following:

1. On the initial screen of the Printer wizard, you must decide if you want to use advanced settings or not. This advanced option allows for two things. First, it allows you to run the wizard as administrator. Second, it allows you to automatically apply repairs. Click **Next**.
2. The Printer wizard will check for printers running on your system. You are then prompted to select the printer you are having trouble with. Select the printer and click **Next**.
3. The Printer wizard will attempt to detect the problem and propose a solution. By selecting **Apply this fix**, you attempt to fix the printer.
4. You are then asked to try the printer again. If the printer prints properly, choose **Close the troubleshooter**. If not, you have the option to **Explore additional options**.

Troubleshoot Audio Recording

This option will launch the Recording Audio wizard, which will help you fix issues that you are having while recording audio.

To use the Recording Audio wizard, do the following:

1. On the initial screen of the Recording Audio wizard, you must decide if you want to use advanced settings or not. This advanced option allows you to determine if you want to apply repairs automatically. Click **Next**.
2. The Recording Audio wizard will check for possible audio problems on the system. The wizard will display audio issues and potential solutions. Select the issues that you want to fix and click **Next**.
3. If one of the fixes requires manual intervention, the next screen will allow you to perform the fix. Follow the on-screen instructions and click **Next**.
4. If your audio recording now works properly, choose **Close the troubleshooter**. If not, you have the option to **Explore additional options**.

Troubleshoot Audio Playback

This option will launch the Playing Audio wizard, which will help you fix issues that you are having while playing audio.

To use the Playing Audio wizard, do the following:

1. On the initial screen of the Playing Audio wizard, you must decide if you want to use advanced settings or not. This advanced option allows you to determine if you want to apply repairs automatically. Click **Next**.
2. The Playing Audio wizard will check for possible audio problems on the system. The wizard will display audio issues and potential solutions. Select the issues that you want to fix and click **Next**.
3. If one of the fixes requires manual intervention, the next screen will allow you to perform the fix. Follow the on-screen instructions and click **Next**.
4. If your audio recording now works properly, choose **Close the troubleshooter**. If not, you have the option to **Explore additional options**.

Networka ndI nternet

The Network and Internet section will help you troubleshoot issues connecting to a network, connecting to the Internet, or sharing files. The Network and Internet section contains two options: **Connect to the Internet** and **Access shared files or folders on other computers**.

Connect to the Internet

This option will launch the Internet Connections wizard, which will help you if you are having trouble connecting to the Internet.

To use the Internet Connections wizard, do the following:

1. On the initial screen of the Internet Connections wizard, you must decide if you want to use advanced settings or not. This advanced option allows for two things. First, it allows you to run the wizard as administrator. Second, it allows you to apply repairs automatically. Click **Next**.
2. Now you have the option to choose whether to try to connect to www.microsoft.com or to some other specific Web site.
3. Windows will try to connect to the Web site. If the Web site connects properly, choose **Close the troubleshooter**. If not, you have the option to **Explore additional options**.

Access Shared Files or Folders on Other Computers

This option will launch the Shared Folders wizard, which will help you if you are having trouble connecting to a network share.

To use the Shared Folders wizard, do the following:

1. On the initial screen of the Shared Folders wizard, you must decide if you want to use advanced settings or not. This advanced option allows for two things. First, it allows you to run the wizard as administrator. Second, it allows you to apply repairs automatically. Click **Next**.
2. Now you have the option to enter the network share that you are trying to connect to. Click **Next**.
3. Windows will try to connect to the network share. If a connection cannot be made, Windows will try to determine what the problem is and offer a solution for the problem. Select the solution you want to try and click **Next**.
4. If one of the fixes requires manual intervention, the next screen will allow you to perform the fix. Follow the on-screen instructions and click **Next**.
5. If you can now properly connect to the share, select **Close the trouble-shooter**. If not, you have the option to **Explore additional options**.

Appearancea ndP ersonalization

This section allows you to configure your Windows 7 desktop personalization settings. This section contains only one option: **Display Aero desktop effect**.

Display Aero Desktop Effect

This option will launch the Aero wizard, which will allow you to configure Aero desktop options.

To use the Aero wizard, do the following:

1. On the initial screen of the Aero wizard, you must decide if you want to use advanced settings or not. This advanced option allows you to determine if you want to automatically apply repairs. Click **Next**.
2. The Aero wizard will check for possible video problems like desktop theme, color depth, and display settings. The wizard will display video issues and potential solutions. Select the issues that you want to fix and click **Next**.
3. If one of the fixes requires manual intervention, the next screen will allow you to perform the fix. Follow the on-screen instructions and click **Next**.
4. If Aero now works properly, choose **Close the troubleshooter**. If not, you have the option to **Explore additional options**.

SystemandS ecurity

This section will help you fix general system issues and security issues. The System and Security section contains four options: **Fix problems with Windows Update, Run maintenance tasks, Improve Power usage**, and **Check for performance issues**.

Fix Problems with Windows Update

This option will launch the Windows Update wizard. This wizard will help troubleshoot issues that you may have running Windows Update. To use the Windows Update wizard, do the following:

1. On the initial screen of the Windows Update wizard, you must decide if you want to use advanced settings or not. This advanced option allows for two things. First, it allows you to run the wizard as administrator. Second, it allows you to automatically apply repairs. Click **Next**.
2. The wizard will now check for Windows updates.
3. If there are issues with running Windows Update, you will be prompted to fix the issues.
4. Next, you are prompted to open Windows Update.
5. If Windows Update now works properly, choose **Close the troubleshooter**. If not, you have the option to **Explore additional options**.

Run Maintenance Tasks

This option will launch the System Maintenance wizard, which will help clean up your system by removing unused items and performing various maintenance tasks.

To use the System Maintenance wizard, do the following:

1. On the initial screen of the System Maintenance wizard, you must decide if you want to use advanced settings or not. This advanced option allows for two things. First, it allows you to run the wizard as administrator. Second, it allows you to automatically apply repairs. Click **Next**.
2. The System Maintenance wizard will check for issues like broken shortcuts, unused desktop icons, improper system time, and disk volumee rrors.
3. If errors exist, you are prompted to fix the errors.
4. If no errors are found and you are satisfied, you can choose the option to **Close the troubleshooter**. If you are not satisfied, you have the option to **Explore additional options**.

Improve Power Usage

This option will run the Power wizard, which allows you to fine tune your system's power management settings. These settings help maximize power usage and can help save battery life.

To use the Power wizard, do the following:

1. On the initial screen of the Power wizard, you must decide if you want to use advanced settings or not. This advanced option allows you to determine if you want to automatically apply repairs. Click **Next**.
2. The Power wizard will scan the system for issues. Select the issues that you want to fix and click **Next**.
3. The Power wizard will attempt to fix the issues. If manual intervention is needed, you will be notified.
4. If you are satisfied with the results and the new settings, you can choose the option to **Close the troubleshooter**. If you are not satisfied, you have the option to **Explore additional options**.

Check for Performance Issues

This option will run the Performance wizard. The Performance wizard helps you maintain or increase system performance by minimizing resource utilization.

To use the Performance wizard, do the following:

1. On the initial screen of the Performance wizard, you must decide if you want to use advanced settings or not. This advanced option allows for two things. First, it allows you to run the wizard as administrator. Second, it allows you to apply repairs automatically. Click **Next**.
2. The Performance wizard will scan the system for performance improvement suggestions. Select the issues that you want to fix and click **Next**.
3. The Performance wizard will attempt to fix the issues. If manual intervention is needed, you will be notified.
4. If you are satisfied with the results and the new settings, you can choose the option to **Close the troubleshooter**. If you are not satisfied, you have the option to **Explore additional options**.

RESOURCE MONITOR

Resource Monitor is a tool provided in Windows 7 for monitoring system resources. You can use it for troubleshooting or for just figuring out what can be done to fine tune your system and increase performance. Using

Resource Monitor is easy. It can be accessed by running **resmon.exe** from the Start menu.

Resource Monitor will show information about processes, services, and certain hardware devices. Throughout Resource Monitor you have the ability to start, stop, and restart a process. You also have the ability to suspend processes, resume processes, end processes, and end process trees.

Resource Monitor groups the information it displays in order to make it easier to understand. The following are five tabs in Resource Monitor: **Overview, CPU, Memory, Disk**, and **Network**. Each tab provides useful information for seeing what's going on with your system.

ResourceM onitorO verview Tab

The **Overview** tab of Resource Monitor, as seen in Figure 10.7, gives you a general overview of what is happening in your system. If you want more detailed information than what is given in the sections on the **Overview** tab, you have to go to the other tabs. There are four sections on the **Overview** tab: CPU, Disk, Network, and Memory.

■ **FIGURE 10.7** Resource Monitor – **Overview** Tab

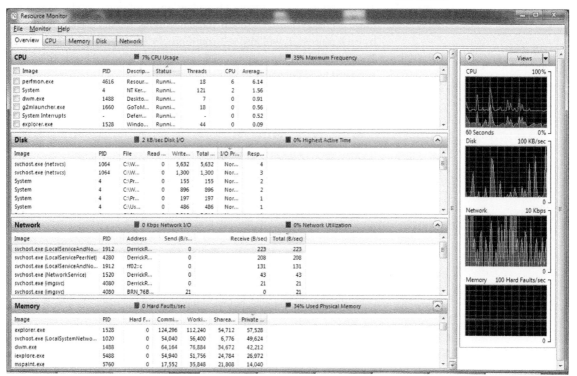

CPU

The CPU section of the **Overview** tab gives information on processes running on the system. You can find out process IDs, number of threads used, CPU consumption, and average percent of CPU consumption. This can help you determine if a process is hogging up the CPU.

Disk

The Disk section of the **Overview** tab gives information on disk activity. You can see which processes are using the disk. You can see read rates and write rates. This can help you determine if a process is causing excessive disk usage.

Network

The Network section of the **Overview** tab gives information about the network activity. It shows processes, the network address they are connected to, bytes sent, and bytes received. This can help you determine if a process is flooding the network.

Memory

The Memory section of the **Overview** gives information about memory usage on the system. It will tell you the working set and private bytes used by each process. It will also tell you if processes are generating hard faults. You can use this information to tell you if a process is leaking memory or if you need to add memory to your system.

ResourceM onitorC PU Tab

The Resource Monitor **CPU** tab, as seen in Figure 10.8, provides detailed CPU usage information. You can get CPU information services and processes running on the system. In the pane on the right, you can view total CPU usage or CPU usage per processor. It helps to know if one CPU is being pegged. This generally means there is some misbehaving service or process utilizing your resources. This is especially noticeable if there is a misbehavings ingle-threadeda pplication.

The Resource Monitor **CPU** tab has four sections: Processes, Services, Associated Handles, and Associate Modules. Each of these sections can help you in different ways. Often, you might have to use information from multiple sections to figure out what the true issue is.

Processes

The Process section of the **CPU** tab provides the same information shown in the CPU section of the **Overview** tab. It gives you a good overview of what's happening with the CPU in your system. You can see the process ID,

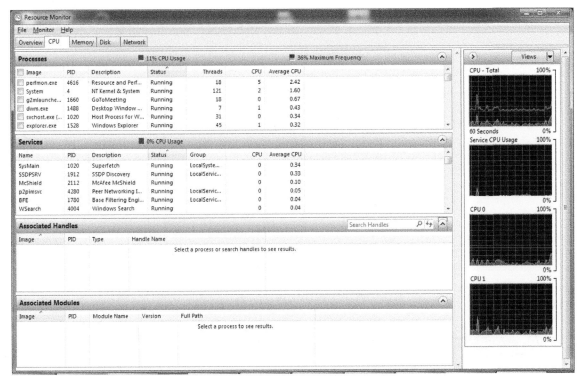

■ **FIGURE 10.8** Resource Monitor –
CPU Tab

description, status, threads, percent CPU usage, and average CPU usage for
processes running on the system.

Services

The services section of the **CPU** tab gives you information on what processing resources are being used by the services running on your system. You
can see service name, process ID, service description, service status, service
group, percent CPU usage, and average CPU usage.

Associated Handles

The Associated Handles section gives you information on what handles are
being used by various processes. The Associated Handles section is empty
until you select a process in the Process section of this tab. This section will
tell you the type of handle and the handle name for each handle used by the
selected process.

Associated Modules

The Associated Modules section gives you information on which modules are
used by a given process. Like the Associated Handles section, the Associated

Modules section is empty until you select a process in the Process section of this tab. The Associated Modules section will provide you with the module name, version, and path for the modules used by the selected process.

ResourceMoni torMem ory Tab

The Resource Monitor **Memory** tab, as seen in Figure 10.9, provides detailed memory-usage information. You can get memory information for the processes running on the system. In the pane on the right, you can view the total amount of physical memory used by the system, the commit charge for the system, and the total number of hard page faults committed per second on the system. This information can help you determine if you need to add more physical memory to the system.

The Resource Monitor **Memory** tab has two sections: Processes and Physical Memory. Each section provides different information to help you troubleshoot your memory issues. One section focuses on individual processes, the other focuses on the entire system.

■ **FIGURE 10.9** Resource
Monitor – **Memory** Tab

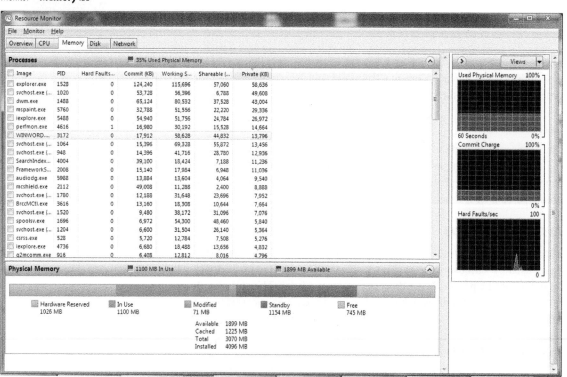

Processes

The Processes section of the **Memory** tab gives information on memory usage for each process. This tab shows the same information as the Memory section of the **Overview** tab. You can see process name, process ID, hard faults/second, committed bytes, working set, shareable bytes, and private bytes for the processes running on the system.

Physical Memory

The Physical Memory section of the **Memory** tab gives information on physical memory usage in the system. This section will show you the total amount of memory in the system, the total amount of memory available to the operating system, the amount of memory in use, and the amount of free memory. Depending on the operating system used and whether it's 32-bit or 64-bit, all of the memory in the system may not be available to the operating system.

ResourceM onitorD isk Tab

The Resource Monitor **Disk** tab, as seen in Figure 10.10, provides information on disk usage on the system. In the right pane, you can see disk

■ **FIGURE 10.10** Resource Monitor – **Disk** Tab

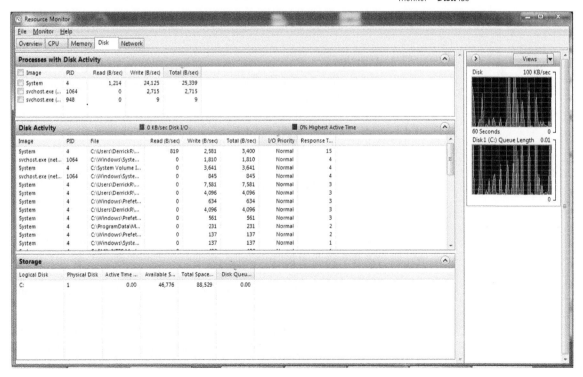

activity and disk queue length. This can help you determine if your disk is processing requests fast enough, or if you need to do something to increase disks peed.

The Resource Monitor **Disk** tab has three sections: Processes with Disk Activity, Disk Activity, and Storage. These sections provide information on individual process and overall disk usage.

Processes with Disk Activity

The Processes with Disk Activity section of the Resource **Monitor** tab gives information on disk usage by the processes running on the system. This section does not give individual disk access per process, but overall usage per process. Many times a single process can access the disk in multiple ways. This is not shown here. You can view process name, process ID, reads/second, writes/second, and total bytes/second.

Disk Activity

This Disk Activity section of the Resource Monitor **Disk** tab gives the same information as the Disk section of the **Overview** tab. This section gives information on individual disk access per process. You can see what each process is accessing on the disks. You can see process name, process ID, reads/second, writes/second, total bytes/second, I/O priority, and response time.

Storage

The Storage section of the Resource Monitor **Disk** tab gives information on overall disk usage. Information is given per logical volume. You can view which physical drive each logical drive resides on. You can also view active time, available space, total space, and disk queue length for each logical drive.

ResourceM onitorN etwork Tab

The Resource Monitor **Network** tab, as seen in Figure 10.11, gives information on network activity on the system. You can view network usage information, connection information, and port information. In the right pane, you can see total network usage, number of Transmission Control Protocol (TCP) connections, local area network (LAN) usage, and wireless network usage. This can help you figure out if a network bottleneck is occurring either on a specific network or on all networks.

The Resource Monitor **Network** tab provides detailed information on what's happening with your network connections. You can use this information to troubleshoot connection issues or port conflicts. The Resource Monitor

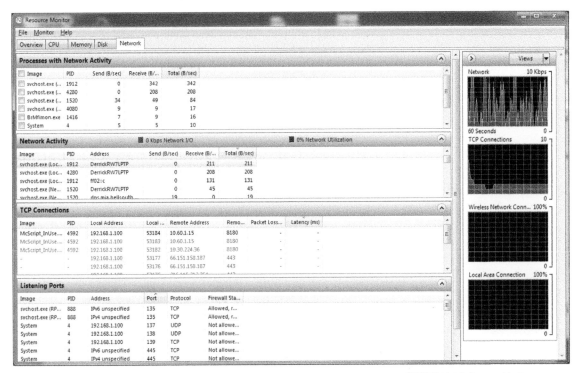

■ **FIGURE 10.11** Resource Monitor – **Network** Tab

Network tab has four sections: Processes with Network Activity, Network Activity, TCP Connections, and Listening Ports.

Processes with Network Activity

The Processes with Network Activity section of the **Network** tab gives general network activity information. You can see the processes that are running, process ID, bytes sent, bytes received, and total bytes. This can help you determine if a process is generating excess network activity.

Network Activity

The Network Activity section provides the same information that's found in the Network section of the **Overview** tab. You can see process name, process ID, remote address, sent bytes, received bytes, and total bytes. You can use this information to determine what remote systems your system is communicating with, and how much data is being sent between the two systems.

TCP Connections

The TCP Connections section of the **Network** tab shows active TCP connections. You can see what remote systems you are connected to and what

TCP ports are being used. This section shows process name, process ID, local address and port, remote address and port, packet loss, and latency. The information in this section can help troubleshoot dropped connections, which are often a result of high latency and/or packet loss.

Listening Ports

The Listening Ports section of the **Network** tab gives you information about the services and processes on your system that are waiting to service network requests. These services are listening on either a TCP or a User Datagram Protocol (UDP) port. This section shows process name, process ID, listening address, port, protocol, and firewall status.

The Listening Ports section of the **Network** tab can come in very handy. It can tell you what ports a given service is listening on. This is very useful if you are trying to figure out why a given service is not accepting requests. It can also help you resolve port conflicts. You may be trying to configure a service to start on a particular port, but you keep receiving a message about the port being in use. You can use the Listening Ports section to determine what service may be using the port you are trying to configure the new service with.

EVENT VIEWER

The Event Viewer has long been the central repository for logging in Windows systems. Windows 7 is no exception. Event Viewer allows you to get a better look at what's really going on with your system. You can see user information, application information, and system information. The amount of information that can be collected in Event Viewer can be somewhat overwhelming. This is why it's important to have a good understanding of what is logged where, and why. Having this understanding will allow you to better focus your efforts. Event Viewer can be accessed by going to **Start | All Programs | Administrative Tools | Event Viewer**. You can also access Event Viewer by adding the Event Viewer snap-in to a custom Microsoft Management Console (MMC).

OverviewandSum mary

When you open Event Viewer, you are presented with the Overview and Summary view, as seen in Figure 10.12. The Overview and Summary view gives you a summary of the events that have happened within Event Viewer.

At the top, you have the Summary of Administrative Events. This is a summary of all the events that have been logged to Event Viewer. The events

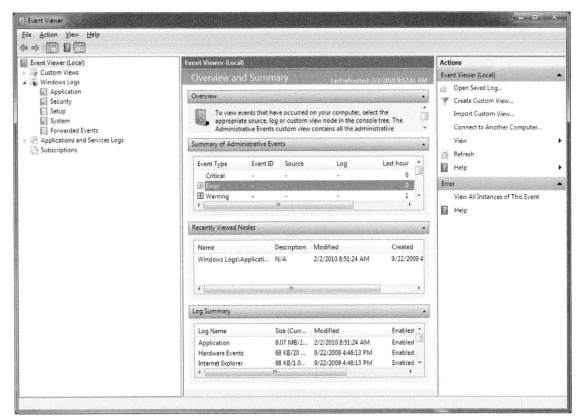

■ **FIGURE 10.12** Event Viewer Overview and Summary

are ordered by event type, then subordered by event ID, and then by source. This can help you determine what types of issues most often plague your system. The Summary of Administrative Events section also allows you to view all occurrences of a certain event. Simply right-click on the event and select **View All Instances of This Event**. You will then be presented with a summary page that has all occurrences of this event listed.

You also have the Recently Viewed Nodes section. This section will list out any default logs or custom views you have in display while in Event Viewer. If you want to return to a particular view, simply right-click on the view and select **View events in this custom view/log**. You will then be taken to that view.

Finally, you have the Log Summary section. This section gives you the properties of all the logs being tracked in Event Viewer. You can view the name of the log, the size, when it was last modified, whether the log is enabled or disabled, and the retention policy for the log.

WindowsL ogs

Windows Logs are what most people are used to seeing in a typical Event Viewer session. These logs represent logging for the basic functionalities within Windows 7. Items logged to the Windows Logs will have the following information associated with them:

- Level – This option represents the logging level of the event. It will give information, warning, error, or critical. Critical is the most serious event.
- **Keywords** – This is seen in the Security log. It denotes the type of event logged. It will either be audit success or audit failure.
- **Date and Time** – This is the date and time the event was logged.
- **Source** – This will tell you which module or subsystem reported the information.
- **Event ID** – Each different type of Event Viewer log entry has a different Event ID. This option will help you better understand the nature of the log entry.
- **Task Category** – If there is a task associated with an event log entry, it should be associated with a category. This will help you understand the nature of the entry and a possible cause.

When you open an entry in Event Viewer, you will be taken to the **General** tab of the Event Properties window, as seen in Figure 10.13. You will be able to view all the general information associated with the event. You will see Log Name, Source, Event ID, Level, User, OpCode, Logged (date and time), Task Category, Keywords, and Computer. You also have the choice to use Online Help to view more information about the entry. Event Viewer will also give you an option to copy the contents of the event so it can be pasted somewhere else, like an e-mail.

There are five logs in the Windows Logs section: Application, Security, Setup, System, and Forwarded Events.

Application Log

The Application log is where you can find information about applications that are running on your system. You can find information about Windows 7 applications, other Microsoft applications, and various third-party applications. The Application log is very useful in determining why an application is not functioning properly.

Security Log

The Security log holds auditing events. You can audit everything from system access to file access. You will view success events and failure events. The Security log is very useful in trying to determine if someone is trying to

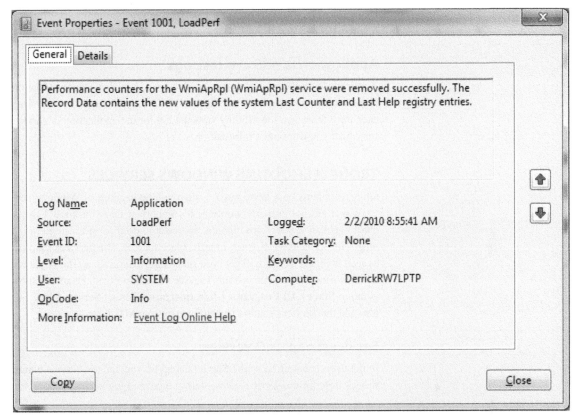

Performance counters for the WmiApRpl (WmiApRpl) service were removed successfully. The Record Data contains the new values of the system Last Counter and Last Help registry entries.

Log Name: Application
Source: LoadPerf   Logged: 2/2/2010 8:55:41 AM
Event ID: 1001   Task Category: None
Level: Information   Keywords:
User: SYSTEM   Computer: DerrickRW7LPTP
OpCode: Info
More Information: Event Log Online Help

■ **FIGURE 10.13** Event Properties –
General Tab

gain access to your system. The Security log can also help you determine if an application is trying to access something it does have rights to, or trying to perform a function it does not have rights to do. Many times, this can indicate a service that is being started with an account with insufficient permissions.

Setup Log

The Setup log is for certain setup and installation events. For example, certain Windows Update-initiated installations will be logged.

System Log

The System log will show events logged by the operating system and Windows services. The System log can be used to determine what services didn't start and possibly why they didn't start.

Forwarded Events

The Forwarded Events log will show event entries sent to the computer from other computers. This log is disabled by default. In order to receive entries in the Forwarded Events log, you must enable subscriptions and subscribe to a remote system.

Applicationsa ndS ervicesL ogs

Applications and Services logs are a collection of logs that offer information about specific services and applications. These applications and services each have their own log. Simply view the log for the application or service for which you want more information.

TROUBLESHOOTING WINDOWS SERVICES

Often, problems on a Windows 7 system will be because of Windows services that are not properly working. It's important that you know how to check whether services are running, and what to do if services are not running. The Services MMC snap-in is the place for this. The Services snap-in, as seen in Figure 10.14, will give you status information for all the Windows services running on your system. The Services snap-in can be accessed by going to **Start | All Programs | Administrative Tools | Services**. You can also add the Services snap-in to your own custom MMC console.

ServicesSnap -inO verview

In the overview section of the Services snap-in, you can see service name, service description, service status, startup type, and log-on information for

■ **FIGURE 10.14** Services MMC Snap-in

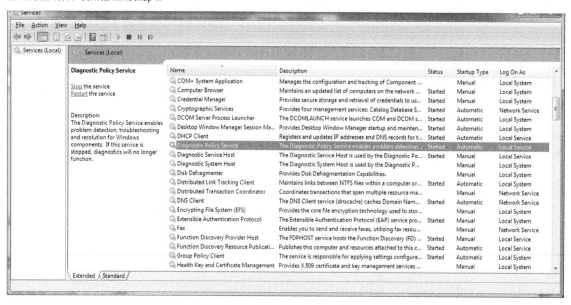

the service. If you are having trouble with a particular service, you can see right away if the service is running or not. Let's start by going over what some of these items mean.

Name and description are pretty self-explanatory. Status is the current state of the service. A service status is generally either started, starting, or stopping. A service that has a status of starting or stopping for a long period of time generally indicates that the service has hung and that there is an issue that needs to be addressed.

Startup type denotes how the service will start. There are four different startup types: *automatic(delayed start), automatic, manual*, and *disabled*. If a service has a startup type of automatic(delayed start), it will start automatically, but not right away. If a service has a startup type of automatic, it will start automatically and immediately. If a service has a startup type of manual, either the user or some program must start it. If a service has a status of disabled, it cannot be started at all.

One thing you will always want to check is whether services with a startup type of automatic are not running. This can generally signify a problem. You can then try to figure out why the service is not started. Sometimes, simply starting the service manually will work. You have to be careful here, though. Sometimes, services with a startup type of automatic are not always supposed to be running. In these cases, the service will generally either start periodically or start when there is work for it to do. When it is done doing its work, then it will automatically stop.

Log On As determines what credentials will be used to start as service. Services can be started using local user accounts, domain user accounts, or built-in system accounts. For security reasons, you should make sure that services start using the minimal rights possible. But, you have to be careful here. If the account specified in the service configuration doesn't have enough rights, then the service may either not start or start but not function properly. Another thing you have to watch for is service account passwords. When you configure a Log On As account for a service, you need to make sure that you have entered the correct password for that account. If not, the service will not start properly.

Service Tasks

Often, you will have to perform simple actions on your services while troubleshooting. For example, you may need to stop or restart a service. The Overview section of the Services snap-in provides ways for performing simple tasks on your services. If you right-click on a service, you can start, stop, pause, resume, and restart the service.

Windows 7 Services

In order to properly troubleshoot services, it's important that you have a good idea of what services belong on the system and what the services do. This could be very difficult to remember. Table 10.1 should help you with this. It includes a listing of the most common Windows 7 services.

Table 10.1 Common Windows 7 Services

Display Name	Service Name	Default	Notes
ActiveX Installer (AxInstSV)	AxInstSV	Manual	
Adaptive Brightness	SensrSvc	Manual	Disable if no ambient light sensor on machine
Application Experience	AeLookupSvc	Manual (Started)	
Application Host Helper Service	AppHostSvc	Not Installed	
Application Identity	AppIDSvc	Manual	
Application Information	Appinfo	Manual (Started)	
Application Layer Gateway Service	ALG	Manual	
Application Management	AppMgmt	Manual	
ASP.NET State Service	aspnet_state	Not Installed	
Background Intelligent Transfer Service	BITS	Manual	Used for Windows Updates
Base Filtering Engine	BFE	Automatic (Started)	
BitLocker Drive Encryption Service	BDESVC	Manual	Used for encryption
Block Level Backup Engine Service	wbengine	Manual	
Bluetooth Support Service	bthserv	Manual	Disable if no Bluetooth devices
BranchCache	PeerDistSvc	Manual	Disable if not on a network
Certificate Propagation	CertPropSvc	Manual	Disable if no smart card
Client for NFS	NfsClnt	Not Installed	
CNG Key Isolation	KeyIso	Manual	
COM+ Event System	EventSystem	Automatic (Started)	
COM+ System Application	COMSysApp	Manual (Started)	
Computer Browser	Browser	Manual	If computer is not connected to a network
Credential Manager	VaultSvc	Manual	
Cryptographic Services	CryptSvc	Automatic (Started)	
DCOM Server Process Launcher	DcomLaunch	Automatic (Started)	
Desktop Window Manager Session Manager	UxSms	Automatic (Started)	
DHCP Client	Dhcp	Automatic (Started)	Can disable if static IP
Diagnostic Policy Service	DPS	Automatic (Started)	
Diagnostic Service Host	WdiServiceHost	Manual (Started)	
Diagnostic System Host	WdiSystemHost	Manual (Started)	
Disk Defragmenter	defragsvc	Manual	

Table 10.1 Common Windows 7 Services *Continued*

Display Name	Service Name	Default	Notes
Distributed Link Tracking Client	TrkWks	Automatic (Started)	Disable if not on a network
Distributed Transaction Coordinator	MSDTC	Manual (Started)	
DNS Client	Dnscache	Automatic (Started)	Can disable if static DNS
Encrypting File System (EFS)	EFS	Manual	
Extensible Authentication Protocol	EapHost	Manual	
Fax	Fax	Manual	
Function Discovery Provider Host	fdPHost	Manual	
Function Discovery Resource Publication	FDResPub	Automatic (Started)	
Group Policy Client	gpsvc	Automatic (Started)	For corporate networks with AD
Health Key and Certificate Management	hkmsvc	Manual	
HomeGroup Listener	HomeGroupListener	Manual	For home networks
HomeGroup Provider	HomeGroupProvider	Manual	For home networks
Human Interface Device Access	hidserv	Manual	
IIS Admin Service	IISADMIN	Not Installed	
IKE and AuthIP IPsec Keying Modules	IKEEXT	Manual	
Indexing Service	CISVC	Not Installed	Slowed down Vista
Interactive Services Detection	UI0Detect	Manual	
Internet Connection Sharing (ICS)	SharedAccess	Disabled	Keep disabled unless your machine is a gateway
IP Helper	iphlpsvc	Automatic (Started)	If no IPv6 you can disable
IPsec Policy Agent	PolicyAgent	Manual	
KtmRm for Distributed Transaction Coordinator	KtmRm	Manual	
Link-Layer Topology Discovery Mapper	lltdsvc	Manual	
LPD Service	LPDSVC	Not Installed	
Media Center Extender Service	Mcx2Svc	Disabled	
Message Queuing	MSMQ	Not Installed	
Message Queuing Triggers	MSMQTriggers	Not Installed	
Microsoft .NET Framework NGEN v2.0.50727	clr_optimization_v2.0.50727	Manual	
Microsoft FTP Service	ftpsvc	Not Installed	
Microsoft iSCSI Initiator Service	MSiSCSI	Manual	Disable unless you have iSCSI
Microsoft Software Shadow Copy Provider	swprv	Manual	
Multimedia Class Scheduler	MMCSS	Automatic (Started)	
Net.Msmq Listener Adapter	NetMsmqActivator	Not Installed	
Net.Pipe Listener Adapter	NetPipeActivator	Not Installed	

Continued ...

Table 10.1 Common Windows 7 Services *Continued*

Display Name	Service Name	Default	Notes
Net.Tcp Listener Adapter	NetTcpActivator	Not Installed	
Net.Tcp Port Sharing Service	NetTcpPortSharing	Disabled	
Netlogon	Netlogon	Manual	Disable if not in a corporate network
Network Access Protection Agent	napagent	Manual	Disable if not in a corporate network
Network Connections	Netman	Manual (Started)	
Network List Service	netprofm	Manual (Started)	
Network Location Awareness	NlaSvc	Automatic (Started)	
Network Store Interface Service	nsi	Automatic (Started)	
Offline Files	CscService	Automatic (Started)	Can disable if not using offline files
Parental Controls	WPCSvc	Manual	Can disable if not using
Peer Name Resolution Protocol	PNRPsvc	Manual	
Peer Networking Grouping	p2psvc	Manual	
Peer Networking Identity Manager	p2pimsvc	Manual	
Performance Logs & Alerts	pla	Manual	
Plug and Play	PlugPlay	Automatic (Started)	
PnP-X IP Bus Enumerator	IPBusEnum	Manual	
PNRP Machine Name Publication Service	PNRPAutoReg	Manual	
Portable Device Enumerator Service	WPDBusEnum	Manual (Started)	
Power	Power	Automatic (Started)	
Print Spooler	Spooler	Automatic (Started)	Can disable if no printer
Problem Reports and Solutions Control Panel Support	wercplsupport	Manual	
Program Compatibility Assistant Service	PcaSvc	Manual	
Protected Storage	ProtectedStorage	Manual	
Quality Windows Audio Video Experience	QWAVE	Manual	
Remote Access Auto Connection Manager	RasAuto	Manual	
Remote Access Connection Manager	RasMan	Manual	
Remote Desktop Configuration	SessionEnv	Manual	
Remote Desktop Services	TermService	Manual	
Remote Desktop Services UserMode Port Redirector	UmRdpService	Manual	
Remote Procedure Call (RPC)	RpcSs	Automatic (Started)	
Remote Procedure Call (RPC) Locator	RpcLocator	Manual	
Remote Registry	RemoteRegistry	Manual	Should disable
RIP Listener	iprip	Not Installed	
Routing and Remote Access	RemoteAccess	Disabled	
RPC Endpoint Mapper	RpcEptMapper	Automatic (Started)	

Table 10.1 Common Windows 7 Services *Continued*

Display Name	Service Name	Default	Notes
SeaPort	SeaPort	Not Installed	
Secondary Logon	seclogon	Manual	Disable if only one user
Secure Socket Tunneling Protocol Service	SstpSvc	Manual	
Security Accounts Manager	SamSs	Automatic (Started)	
Security Center	wscsvc	Automatic (Delayed Start, Not Started)	
Server	LanmanServer	Automatic (Started)	
Shell Hardware Detection	ShellHWDetection	Automatic (Started)	
Simple TCP/IP Services	simptcp	Not Installed	
Smart Card	SCardSvr	Manual	Disable if no smart card
Smart Card Removal Policy	SCPolicySvc	Manual	Disable if no smart card
SNMP Service	SNMP	Not Installed	
SNMP Trap	SNMPTRAP	Manual	Disable if not using SNMP
Software Protection	sppsvc	Automatic (Delayed Start, Not Started)	
SPP Notification Service	sppuinotify	Manual	
SSDP Discovery	SSDPSRV	Manual (Started)	
Storage Service	StorSvc	Manual	Only available on Professional and Enterprise
Superfetch	SysMain	Automatic (Started)	
System Event Notification Service	SENS	Automatic (Started)	
Tablet PC Input Service	TabletInputService	Manual	Disable if not on tablet
Task Scheduler	Schedule	Automatic (Started)	
TCP/IP NetBIOS Helper	lmhosts	Automatic (Started)	
Telephony	TapiSrv	Manual	
Telnet	TlntSvr	Not Installed	
Themes	Themes	Automatic (Started)	
Thread Ordering Server	THREADORDER	Manual	
TPM Base Services	TBS	Manual	
UPnP Device Host	upnphost	Manual	
User Profile Service	ProfSvc	Automatic (Started)	
Virtual Disk	vds	Manual	
Volume Shadow Copy	VSS	Manual (Started)	Used with System Restore for HDD
Web Management Service	WMSVC	Not Installed	
WebClient	WebClient	Manual	If disabled you cannot surf the Web
Windows Audio	AudioSrv	Automatic (Started)	
Windows Audio Endpoint Builder	AudioEndpoint-Builder	Automatic (Started)	
Windows Backup	SDRSVC	Manual	Disable if you do not backup
Windows Biometric Service	WbioSrvc	Manual	Disable if no biometric device
Windows CardSpace	idsvc	Manual	

Continued ...

Table 10.1 Common Windows 7 Services *Continued*

Display Name	Service Name	Default	Notes
Windows Color System	WcsPlugInService	Manual	
Windows Connect Now – Config Registrar	wcncsvc	Manual	
Windows Defender	WinDefend	Automatic (Delayed Start, Not Started)	
Windows Driver Foundation – User-mode Driver Framework	wudfsvc	Manual	
Windows Error Reporting Service	WerSvc	Manual	Disable if you do not want Windows error reports
Windows Event Collector	Wecsvc	Manual	
Windows Event Log	EventLog	Automatic (Started)	
Windows Firewall	MpsSvc	Automatic (Started)	Disable if using third-party firewall
Windows Font Cache Service	FontCache	Manual	
Windows Image Acquisition (WIA)	stisvc	Manual	
Windows Installer	msiserver	Manual	Will not be able to install anything if disabled
Windows Live Family Safety	fsssvc	Not Installed	Additional component to parental controls
Windows Management Instrumentation	Winmgmt	Automatic (Started)	
Windows Media Center Receiver Service	ehRecvr	Manual	Disable if you do not share media via Windows Media Player
Windows Media Center Scheduler Service	ehSched	Manual	Disable if you do not share media via Windows Media Player
Windows Media Player Network Sharing Service	WMPNetworkSvc	Manual (Started)	Disable if you do not share media via Windows Media Player
Windows Modules Installer	TrustedInstaller	Manual	
Windows Presentation Foundation Font Cache 3.0.0.0	FontCache3.0.0.0	Manual	
Windows Remote Management (WS-Management)	WinRM	Manual	
Windows Search	WSearch	Automatic (Delayed Start, Started)	Disable to increase speed and if you do not search on the desktop
Windows Time	W32Time	Manual	Disable if you do not want to update the time with a server
Windows Update	wuauserv	Automatic (Delayed Start, Not Started)	Disable if you do not want Windows updates
WinHTTP Web Proxy Auto-Discovery Service	WinHttpAutoProxy Svc	Manual (Started)	
Wired AutoConfig	dot3svc	Manual	Disable if no wired LAN adapter
WLAN AutoConfig	Wlansvc	Manual	Disable if no wireless LAN adapter
WMI Performance Adapter	wmiApSrv	Manual	
Workstation	LanmanWorkstation	Automatic (Started)	Do not disable
World Wide Web Publishing Service	W3SVC	Not Installed	Install to run a Web server
WWAN AutoConfig	WwanSvc	Manual	Disable if no wireless WAN adapter

ServiceP roperties

Sometimes, it will be necessary for you to change the configuration information for your services. In order to change configuration information, you must access the properties for a service. To access the properties for a service, right-click on the desired service and select **Properties**. This will bring up the service properties window. The service properties window has four tabs: **General, Log On, Recover**, and **Dependencies**.

General

The **General** tab of the service properties window, as seen in Figure 10.15, will give you general information about the service. You can see the service name, the display name, and the description. The actual service name is helpful when searching for the service in your system registry. Services in

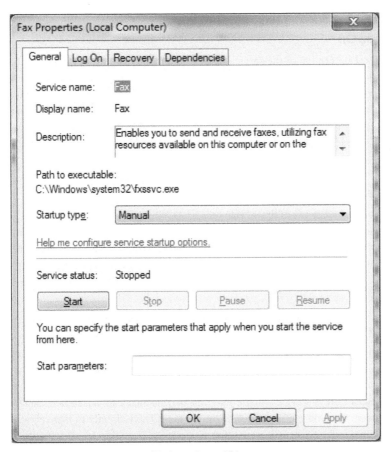

■ **FIGURE 10.15** Service Properties Window – **General** Tab

the registry are listed through the service name. Sometimes, you will have to go into the registry to manually tune a service in order to get it to properly perform.

The **General** tab also displays the path to the executable used for the service. In order to fix an issue with a service, you may need to replace the executable it uses. You can also use the executable name to find the service in Task Manager. If you are having trouble stopping the service using the Services snap-in, you can use Task Manager to terminate the executable for the service. You can also configure the startup type for the service; either automatic(delayed start), automatic, manual, or disabled.

Finally, the **General** tab allows you to view and change the status of the service. You can start, stop, pause, or resume a service from here. You can also configure option start parameters for the service. Make sure you configure these parameters correctly because bad start parameters can prevent a service from starting at all.

Log On

The **Log On** tab of the service properties window, as seen in Figure 10.16, allows you to configure account log on options for a service. You can configure a service to start with the Local System account or an account that you specify. For security reasons, you should use the Local System account sparingly. The Local System account can perform almost any function on the system. So if a service that is running using the Local System account is compromised, the entire system can be compromised.

Recovery

The **Recovery** tab of the service properties window, as seen in Figure 10.17, allows you to control the outcome if a service encounters a failure. If a service fails, you can have it automatically restart, run a program, or restart the computer. The run a program option is useful if you need to gather debugging information, or if there are several actions that need to be performed before the service can be properly restarted again.

Dependencies

The **Dependencies** tab of the service properties window, as seen in Figure 10.18, allows you to view the dependencies related to a given service. The top section will show those services on which the current service depends on. A service will not start if its dependencies are not started. Sometimes, the failure of a service to start is not related directly to that service. Sometimes, it's because one of that service's dependencies did not start.

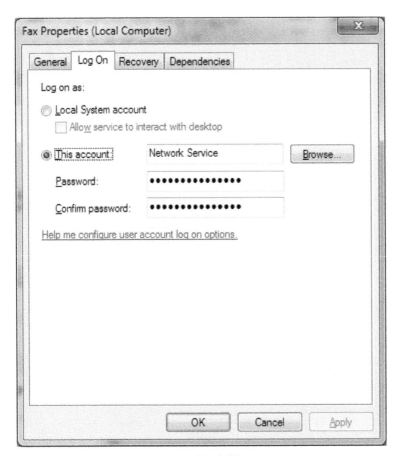

■ **FIGURE 10.16**   Service Properties Window – **Log On** Tab

If you have a service that is not starting, you need to make sure all of its dependenciesha ves tarted.

The bottom section will show what services depend on the current service. Again, if the current service does not start, then the services that depend on it will not start. This will help you see the impact of the current service failing. If you want to create or remove a service dependency, you can do this by editing the service properties in the Registry.

PROBLEM STEPS RECORDER

The Problem Steps Recorder, or PSR, is a troubleshooting tool developed by Microsoft. Sometimes, when you are having trouble with a system, it's hard to describe what's going on. This is especially true when communicating

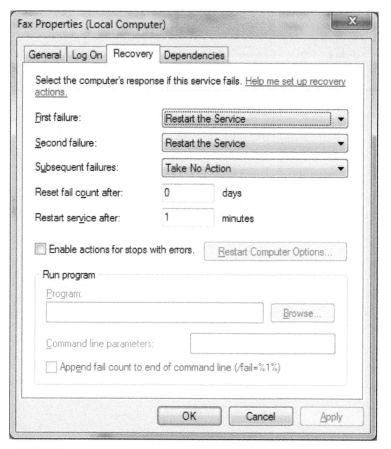

FIGURE 10.17 Service Properties Window – **Recovery** Tab

over the phone. If a support technician can't get a true understanding of the issue, then it will be difficult for them to fix the issue. The PSR attempts to solve this issue.

The PSR allows you to do a visual recording of what's happening on your system. This recording can then be sent to a technician for review. Now in addition to hearing your description of what's going on, the technician can actually see what's going on.

Accessingt hePSR

Accessing the PSR can be a bit tricky. One option is to run the command **psr.exe** from the **Run** menu. The other option is to open the Control Panel. Then in the search window, enter **problem**. Then under the **Troubleshooting** section, select **Record steps to reproduce a problem**.

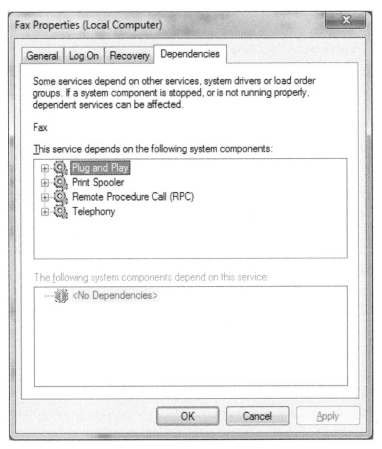

■ **FIGURE 10.18** Service Properties Window – **Dependencies** Tab

Using thePSR

The PSR is pretty straightforward and easy to use. There isn't any precon-figuration that needs to be done. There are some optional settings that can be configured, but they are not necessary in order to use the PSR efficiently. Simply launch the PSR and start recording.

Making Recordings

Making recordings with the PSR is easy. Just perform the following steps:

1. Once the PSR is open, click **Start Record**.
2. Perform the steps needed to reproduce the issue or problem.
3. Optional: If you want to record notes, use the **Add Comment** option.

4. Click **Stop Record**.
5. Now, you will be prompted to save the recording. Specify a location and file name. Click **Save**.

A zip file will be saved. This zip file will contain an MHT file, which contains the actual recording.

Running the PSR as Administrator

When running in normal mode, the PSR may have a problem recording windows that are running as administrator. If you attempt to run the PSR in normal mode and you have windows open that are running as administrator, you will receive a Problem Steps Recorder Warning message as seen in Figure10 .19.

In order to ensure you can record windows running as administrator, you have to run the PSR as administrator. In order to do this, perform the following steps:

1. Opent heP SR.
2. From the drop-down menu on the far right (as seen in Figure 10.20), select **Run as administrator**.
3. If the User Account Control window appears, select **Yes** to allow the PSR to make changes to the computer. You can now begin recording.

PSR Settings

The PSR allows you to configure settings for how and where to store recordings and captures. If you choose **Settings** from the drop-down menu

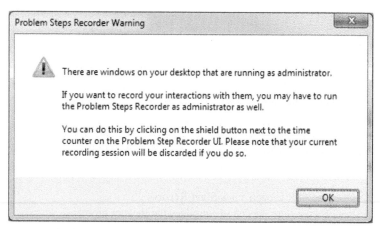

■ **FIGURE 10.19** Problem Steps Recorder Admin Warning

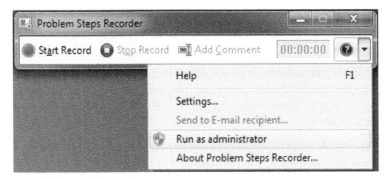

■ **FIGURE 10.20** PSR Drop-down Menu

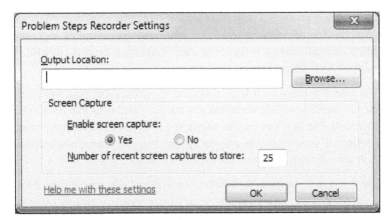

■ **FIGURE 10.21** Problem Steps Recorder Settings Window

on the far right, you will be taken to the PSR Settings window as seen in Figure 10.21. You can set the following:

- **Output Location** – If you specify an output location, your recordings will default to this location. Once this is set, at the end of your recording, you will not be prompted where to save the file.
- **Screen Capture | Enable screen capture** – This setting determines whether or not screen shots will be captured. The default option is **Yes**. Sometimes, you may want to turn off screen captures because there is sensitive information displayed on the screen. You can still record click information without the screen shots.
- **Screen Capture | Number of recent screen captures to store** – This setting controls how many screen captures will be stored. The key is that PSR store the most recent shots. If you exceed the number set here, PSR will discard older screen captures to make room for the new ones.

WARNING
When you change the settings in the PSR, they are only used until you close the PSR. When you close the PSR and reopen it, the settings will be reset to the default.

■ SUMMARY

The Action Center provides a centralized place for receiving notification about issues on your system. You can see system maintenance issues, Windows Update issues, hardware issues, and many other types of issues. Not only will the Action Center help you determine what problems your system may be experiencing, but also it will offer possible solutions for these problems.

Resource Monitor is a performance tool that can be used to monitor resource usage on your system. You can monitor CPU usage, disk usage, network usage, and memory usage. Usage is broken down in several different ways to make analysis easier for you.

Event Viewer provides a central place for logging events on your Windows 7 system. You can view System logs, Application logs, Security logs, and others. The information in these logs can be crucial in figuring out what is going on with your system.

Windows 7 is based on a large collection of services that perform different functions. Sometime these services can have problems that need to be addressed. The Services snap-in allows you to monitor and control service information for the services on your system. You can control how services will start and what happens when there is a failure.

The Problem Steps Recorder (PSR) is a useful tool that can help you overcome some of the difficulties that occur when remotely troubleshooting an issue. If you cannot decipher what the actual issue is, it's hard to figure out a solution. The PSR allows a user to record the issue so that the person troubleshooting the issue can get a visual representation of what's going on, not just a verbal one.

SubjectI ndex

Page numbers followed by f indicates a figure and t indicates a table.

Printed and bound by CPI Group (UK) Ltd, Croydon, CR0 4YY

03/10/2024

01040342-0015